OPEN IT-BASED INNOVATION: MOVING TOWARDS COOPERATIVE IT TRANSFER AND KNOWLEDGE DIFFUSION

T0138046

IFIP – The International Federation for Information Processing

IFIP was founded in 1960 under the auspices of UNESCO, following the First World Computer Congress held in Paris the previous year. An umbrella organization for societies working in information processing, IFIP's aim is two-fold: to support information processing within its member countries and to encourage technology transfer to developing nations. As its mission statement clearly states,

> IFIP's mission is to be the leading, truly international, apolitical organization which encourages and assists in the development, exploitation and application of information technology for the benefit of all people.

IFIP is a non-proftmaking organization, run almost solely by 2500 volunteers. It operates through a number of technical committees, which organize events and publications. IFIP's events range from an international congress to local seminars, but the most important are:

- The IFIP World Computer Congress, held every second year;
- Open conferences;
- Working conferences.

The flagship event is the IFIP World Computer Congress, at which both invited and contributed papers are presented. Contributed papers are rigorously refereed and the rejection rate is high.

As with the Congress, participation in the open conferences is open to all and papers may be invited or submitted. Again, submitted papers are stringently refereed.

The working conferences are structured differently. They are usually run by a working group and attendance is small and by invitation only. Their purpose is to create an atmosphere conducive to innovation and development. Refereeing is less rigorous and papers are subjected to extensive group discussion.

Publications arising from IFIP events vary. The papers presented at the IFIP World Computer Congress and at open conferences are published as conference proceedings, while the results of the working conferences are often published as collections of selected and edited papers.

Any national society whose primary activity is in information may apply to become a full member of IFIP, although full membership is restricted to one society per country. Full members are entitled to vote at the annual General Assembly. National societies preferring a less committed involvement may apply for associate or corresponding membership. Associate members enjoy the same benefits as full members, but without voting rights. Corresponding members are not represented in IFIP bodies. Affiliated membership is open to non-national societies, and individual and honorary membership schemes are also offered.

OPEN IT-BASED INNOVATION: Moving Towards Cooperative IT Transfer and Knowledge Diffusion

IFIP TC8 WG 8.6 International Working Conference
October 22–24, 2008, Madrid, Spain

Edited by

Gonzalo León
Universidad Politécnica de Madrid
Madrid, Spain

Ana M. Bernardos
Universidad Politécnica de Madrid
Madrid, Spain

José R. Casar
Universidad Politécnica de Madrid
Madrid, Spain

Karlheinz Kautz
Copenhagen Business School
Frederiksberg, Denmark

Janice I. DeGross
University of Minnesota
Minneapolis, Minnesota USA

 Springer

Open IT-Based Innovation: Moving Towards Cooperative
IT Transfer and Knowledge Diffusion
Edited by Gonzalo León, Ana M. Bernardos, José R. Casar,
Karlheinz Kautz and Janice I. DeGross

p. cm. (IFIP International Federation for Information Processing, a Springer Series in Computer Science)

ISSN: 1571-5736 / 1861-2288 (Internet)

ISBN: 978-1-4419-4681-2   eISBN: 978-0-387-87503-3

Printed on acid-free paper

Copyright © 2008 by International Federation for Information Processing.
Softcover reprint of the hardcover 1st edition 2008
All rights reserved. This work may not be translated or copied in whole or in part without the written permission of the publisher (Springer Science+Business Media, LLC, 233 Spring Street, New York, NY 10013, USA), except for brief excerpts in connection with reviews or scholarly analysis. Use in connection with any form of information storage and retrieval, electronic adaptation, computer software, or by similar or dissimilar methodology now known or hereafter developed is forbidden.

The use in this publication of trade names, trademarks, service marks and similar terms, even if they are not identified as such, is not to be taken as an expression of opinion as to whether or not they are subject to proprietary rights.

9 8 7 6 5 4 3 2 1

springer.com

Contents

Part 4:   Analysis of Cases

Part 5:   Open Innovation Experiences

Part 6:   Design Science and Cases in IT

Part 7:   Case Studies in Telecommunications

Part 8:   Case Studies in Software Businesses

Part 9:   Public Administration and Government

Part 10: On-Going Research

Part 11: Panels

Part 12: Notes from Industry Experiences

Part 13: Annex

WELCOME

On behalf of IFIP Working Group 8.6, it is a great pleasure to welcome you to Madrid and to our 2008 Working Conference on Open IT-Based Innovation: Moving Towards Cooperative IT Transfer and Knowledge Diffusion.

For almost 15 years, WG 8.6 has been exploring research and practice on the diffusion of innovations, technology adoption, and the transfer and implementation of information systems. Our understanding has blossomed as a result of our community inquiry into the domain of diffusion and we have investigated this territory in numerous ways—from theory and methods to frameworks and tools, as well as organizational contexts. If at any time, we felt that our problem space might become "old news" or our journey exhausted, this has not proved to be true. We are still challenged: the failure rate for new technologies and new systems remains high. As Gordon Davis noted recently, in the introduction to our event in Manchester in 2007, "there is still an important viable mission for WG 8.6 in exploring issues of why some innovation efforts are successful and others fail."[1] And so, there is a lot for the community of WG 8.6 to learn and also to share as we "practice what we preach."

That said, I have been struck by how many of our recent 8.6 working conferences reflect a second wave of inquiry, where diffusion theory and practice has become a lens through which to examine a host of associated topics that are germane to information systems research, such as organizational dynamics of innovation, agility and agile methods, networks and networked systems, and adaptability and competitiveness. The study of diffusion has demonstrated value in its own right—and its health is evident in its focus, at the same time that this area of study is not in danger of becoming isolated. Here, at Madrid, our dialogue and debate expands further to explore Open IT-based innovation—where the nature of the innovation *and* the process of innovating are subject to new challenges of dynamism, complexity, asymmetry, and uncertainty. Welcome to our ongoing conversation.

Linda Levine
Software Engineering Institute, Carnegie Mellon University
Chair, IFIP WG 8.6, Diffusion, Transfer and Implementation
of Information Technology

---

[1]Gordon B. Davis, "Foreword" in *Organizational Dynamics of Technology-Based Innovation: Diversifying the Research Agenda*, T. McMaster, D. Wastell, E. Ferneley, and J. I. DeGross (eds), Boston: Springer, pp. xi-xiii.

PREFACE

The 11th Working Conference of IFIP WG 8.6, Open-IT Based Innovation: Moving Towards Cooperative IT Transfer and Knowledge Diffusion, organized in Madrid in October 22–24, 2008, follows the series started in Oslo in 1995 and continues in the footprints of the past year's conference in Manchester.

This year, although the Madrid Conference addresses the usual topics covered in previous WG8.6 conferences, the emphasis is on the issue of *open innovation* and its relationships with technology transfer and diffusion in the field of information technology. This issue is deeply modifying the way that knowledge is generated, shared, transferred, diffused, and used across the world as a side effect of globalization. It affects the organizational structure, partnerships, roles assumed by stakeholders, and technology transfer and diffusion models and instruments. Industry, academia, and governments are simultaneously concerned. Although the concept applies to all industrial sectors, IT companies were early innovators.

The analysis of the contents of this book allows the identification of some trends in technology transfer and diffusion issues as a part of the innovation process. The same problem is addressed in very different ways and extrapolation is not straightforward. Even innovation terminology is not clearly shared by different subcultures in the field. This book includes the 30 papers selected by the Program Committee, some invited papers, and short descriptions of two panels. The international character of the Conference is easily perceived by browsing through the affiliations of the authors and the very different perspectives used to deal with the Conference issues. Authors coming from 14 different countries joined at the Conference by providing a nice environment to facilitate mutual learning.

The content of the papers ranges from theoretical aspects to case studies in different countries and sectors showing a rich diversity in scenarios and experiences. The papers in this volume follow the structure of the sessions of the Conference.

Two panels have been organized: "Corporate Experiences in Open Innovation" and "Open Innovation in Mobile and Convergent Communications." The first panel focuses on the way that open innovation schemes are modifying the internal structure and partnership of large IT corporations, in many cases influencing their strategic positioning. The second panel focuses on one of the hot topics in the telecom field: mobile and convergent communications and the diffusion of new services. Here, the goal is to debate the consequences on the transfer and diffusion of mobile telecom services with the participation of operators and equipment providers.

As General Chair of the Conference, I would like to thank the members of the Program Committee for their very valuable effort in evaluating the received papers.

Thirty-three experts have committed their efforts to ensure a high quality level of the Conference. Furthermore, the continuous advice received from Tom McMaster, Linda Levine, and other IFIP officers has been very useful to facilitate the success of the Conference. Our acknowledgments should be also conveyed to the authors, panelists, and panel and sessions chairpersons; their effort is collected in the book.

Nothing would have been possible without the cooperation of the Universidad Politécnica de Madrid and, especially, the School of Telecommunication Engineering and the Center for Technology Diffusion taking the responsibility for the local organization. To be more explicit: Profs. Jose Ramón Casar, Ana M. Bernardos, Roberto Prieto, Juan Meneses, Javier Portillo, and Fernando Calle, as members of the organizing committee, have been crucial in the organization process. July Muñoz, as a secretary, and a group of students acting as volunteers have also contributed to the Conference.

Finally, it is my honor to mention the entities supporting the Conference: First of all, the Spanish Ministry of Science and Innovation (formerly the Ministry of Education and Science), IBM Spain, Ericsson Spain, Telefónica I+D, and the Mayor's Office of the "Ayuntamiento de Madrid" (City Hall).

Gonzalo León
IFIP 8.6 2008 Conference General Chair

CONFERENCE CHAIRS

General Chair
Gonzalo León
Vice President for Research
Universidad Politénica de Madrid, Spain

Program Chairs
Karlheinz Kautz
Professor
Copenhagen Business School, Denmark

Juan Mulet
General Director
Fundación Cotec para la Innovación Tecnológica, Spain

Organizing Chair
José Casar
Director, Center for Technology Diffusion
Universidad Politénica de Madrid, Spain

CONFERENCE SPONSORS

Spanish Ministry for Science and Innovation
IBM
Ericsson
Madrid City Council
Telefónica I+D
Universidad Politénica de Madrid

The Organization was supported by the Centre for Technology Diffusion of the Universidad Politécnica de Madrid

PROGRAM COMMITTEE
Deborah Bunker, University of New South Wales, Australia
Michael Cavanagh, Balmoral Consulting, United Kingdom
Thomas Chesney, Nottingham University Business School, United Kingdom
Linda Dawson, Monash University, Australia
Brian Donnellan, National University of Ireland, Ireland
Yogesh K. Dwivedi, Swansea University, United Kingdom
Amany R. Elbanna, Loughborough University, United Kingdom
Elaine Ferneley, University of Salford, United Kingdom
Robert G. Fichman, Boston College, United States
Andreas Gadatsch, Bonn-Rhein-Sieg University, Germany
Helle Z. Henriksen, Copenhagen Business School, Denmark
José Jiménez, Telefónica I+D, Spain
Tor J. Larsen, Norwegian School of Management, Norway
Linda Levine, Software Engineering Institute, United States
Julio López, Ericsson, Spain
Kalle Lyytinen, Case Western Reserve University, United States
Lars Mathiassen, Georgia State University, United States
Tom McMaster, University of Salford, United Kingdom
Michael Newman, University of Manchester, United Kingdom
Nigel de Noronha, Audit Commission, United Kingdom
Jan Pries-Heje, Roskilde University, Denmark
Yacine Rezgui, University of Salford, United Kingdom
Juan C. Rincón, Siemens España, Spain
Frantz Rowe, Université de Nantes, France
Paloma Sánchez, Universidad Autónoma de Madrid, Spain
Duncan Shaw, Nottingham University Business School, United Kingdom
Pål Sørgaard, Telenor R&D, Norway
E. Burton Swanson, University of California, Los Angeles, United States
Richard Veryard, Everware-CBDI, United Kingdom
Richard Vidgen, University of Bath, United Kingdom
David Wastell, Nottingham Business School, United Kingdom
David Wilson, University of Technology, Australia
Robert Zmud, University of Oklahoma, United States

ORGANIZING COMMITTEE
- Ana M. Bernardos, Associate Manager, Center for Technology Diffusion, Universidad Politécnica de Madrid
- Roberto Prieto, Director, Office for R&D Projects, Universidad Politécnica de Madrid
- Javier Portillo, Vice Director, Research Strategy, School of Telecommunications Engineering, Universidad Politécnica de Madrid
- Juan M. Meneses, Director, IT Innovation Circle of the *Comunidad de Madrid*, Universidad Politécnica de Madrid
- Fernando Calle, Vice Director, Research Strategy, School of Telecommunications Engineering, Universidad Politécnica de Madrid

SECRETARIAT
Julia Muñoz, Universidad Politécnica de Madrid

Part 1:

Studies on Diffusion and Adoption

1 THE DIFFUSION OF RESEARCH ON THE ADOPTION AND DIFFUSION OF INFORMATION TECHNOLOGY

Yogesh K. Dwivedi
Michael D. Williams
Swansea University
Swansea, UK

Banita Lal
Nottingham Trent University
Nottingham, UK

Abstract   *The considerable level of investigation into information systems and technology acceptance and diffusion to date has witnessed the use of an extensive range of exploratory techniques examining numerous diverse systems and technologies in a myriad of different contexts. The aim of this paper is to provide a comprehensive and systematic review of the literature relating to such adoption and diffusion issues in order to establish the current "state of play" in the domain along a number of dimensions including unit of analysis, research paradigm employed, technology examined, and theoretical models and constructs. Our findings suggest that the positivist paradigm, empirical and quantitative research, the survey method, and TAM theory were used predominantly when investigating the topics of adoption and diffusion of technology. Although the adoption of broad range of technologies has been examined, our results indicate that a number of technologies have so far received relatively little investigative attention.*

Keywords   Adoption, acceptance, diffusion, information systems, IT, ICT, research context, research issues, research method, theories

Please use the following format when citing this chapter:

Dwivedi, Y. K., Williams, M. D., and Lal, B., 2008, in IFIP International Federation for Information Processing, Volume 287, Open IT-Based Innovation: Moving Towards Cooperative IT Transfer and Knowledge Diffusion, eds. León, G., Bernardos, A., Casar, J., Kautz, K., and DeGross, J. (Boston: Springer), pp. 3-22.

1   INTRODUCTION

The quest to ensure user-acceptance of information systems and technology (IS/IT) is an ongoing management challenge (Schwarz and Chin 2007), and one that has attracted the attention of the IS community to the extent that IS/IT adoption and diffusion research is considered to be among the more mature areas of exploration within the discipline (Hirschheim 2007; Venkatesh et al. 2007). This considerable level of investigation has witnessed the use of a wide range of exploratory techniques examining many different systems and technologies in countless different contexts, to the extent that even the most cursory examination of the extant literature will reveal a variety of stakeholder perspectives, technologies and contexts, units of analysis, theories, and research methods. For instance, contexts vary from the societal to the industrial, to the organizational and individual, and many theories and models—such as the technology acceptance model (TAM), diffusion of innovation (DoI) theory, theory of planned behavior (TPB), and institutional theory—have been utilized to study an assortment of adoption and diffusion related issues. Recently, researchers have begun extending their reach beyond the commonly addressed organization and user perspectives. For example, studies related specifically to the adoption of technology within the household context are beginning to emerge (Brown and Venkatesh 2005; Dwivedi et al. 2006; 2008a; Venkatesh and Brown 2001) adding yet further variability to the body of existing research in terms of contexts and units of analysis.

Reviewing and profiling the existing literature on IS/IT adoption and diffusion is likely to be of use to researchers in assisting them to identify currently under-explored themes, and to select theories and methods appropriate to their investigation, all of which are critical issues for conducting fruitful original and rigorous research. This will also help to identify existing strengths and weaknesses of pertinent research streams, promote discussion regarding critical issues in the area, and assist in the identification of alternative theoretical and methodological perspectives (Venkatesh et al. 2007).

qThere have been a number of reviews and meta-analytic articles published in the area to date. However, perhaps due to the customary inclination of researchers to make use of TAM, almost all existing studies have focused primarily upon reviewing the literature relating to technology acceptance rather providing a more comprehensive review on the broader area of adoption and diffusion. A number of these studies are discussed further in section 2. The general aim of this paper, therefore, is to provide a more comprehensive and systematic review of the literature pertaining to IS/IT adoption and diffusion research in order to ascertain the current "state of play" of the field along a number of dimensions. This overall aim is realized by means of the following objective: (1) to identify the journals publishing most articles on IS/IT adoption, acceptance, and diffusion; (2) to present the general trends on adoption and diffusion research according to the year of publication; (3) to identify countries (and hence areas of greatest activity) with the largest number of publications on IS/IT adoption, acceptance, and diffusion; (4) to identify authors active in the area of IS/IT adoption, acceptance, and diffusion; (5) to classify the publications according to three keywords, *adoption, acceptance,* and *diffusion*; (6) to identify the various *units of analysis* commonly utilized in IS/IT adoption, acceptance, and diffusion research; (7) to classify adoption and diffusion publications according to the research paradigm; (8) to classify adoption and diffusion publications on the basis of their use of primary research data (empirical and nonempirical); (9) to classify adoption and diffusion publications on the basis of the nature of the primary research data (quantitative and qualitative); (10) to classify adoption and diffusion publications according to the research methods employed; (11) to explore and identify the various technologies examined; (12) to explore the theories and theoretical constructs utilized when examining the adoption, acceptance, and diffusion of IS/IT within various contexts.

In order to realize these objectives, a systematic and comprehensive review of 883 articles appearing in 337 different peer-reviewed journals during the period 1970–2007 was conducted. The remainder of this paper is structured as follows. In section 2, we present a brief discussion of the existing literature reviewing adoption and diffusion research in the IS field. In section 3, we provide a discussion of the method we employed in our analysis of the trends of adoption and diffusion research. Our findings are presented and discussed in section 4 and, finally, section 5 presents our conclusions from this work and the limitations of our approach.

2 LITERATURE REVIEW

A number of review and meta-analysis articles have previously been published on the general theme of this paper (see Bagozzi 2007; Benbasat and Barki 2007; Choudrie and Dwivedi 2005a, 2005b; Dwivedi, Williams et al. 2008; Dwivedi, Williams, and Venkatesh 2008; Hirschheim 2007; Jeyaraj et al. 2006; King and He 2006; Legris et al. 2003; Lucas et al. 2007; Schwarz and Chin 2007; Silva 2007; Venkatesh et al. 2007). It should be noted that all but few of these studies (Choudrie and Dwivedi 2005b; Dwivedi, Williams et al. 2008; Dwivedi, Williams, and Venkatesh 2008; Jeyaraj et al. 2006) have adopted a rather narrow perspective of the area by focusing on reviewing and critiquing material that deals specifically with the issue of technology acceptance, particularly those works employing TAM or some aspect of it.

Choudrie and Dwivedi (2005b) considered the literature in general and examined the range of research methods used for studying technology adoption issues by reviewing 48 articles published in peer reviewed journals between 1985 and 2003. Despite attempting to extend the scope of such review articles, this study has two palpable limitations: first, its analysis was restricted to the research methodology employed, and second, its findings were based on a review of only 48 articles. The work of Jeyaraj et al. (2006) was based on a comparatively larger sample (99 articles), and provides a rigorous review of the predictors, linkages, and biases in IT innovation adoption research (thereby focusing on theoretical constructs), but again only gives consideration to publications appearing up until 2003.

To the best of our knowledge, there is no article that has yet provided a broad representation of the adoption, acceptance, and diffusion of IS/IT/innovation literature by systematically profiling a larger and more timely set of existing publications in terms of author, institution, country, publication year, research paradigm employed, nature of primary data, research methods, theories and theoretical constructs, and technology examined. It has been suggested by previous studies that such research is of importance in order to encourage debate about critical issues in the IS field (Hirschheim 2007) and to assist in the identification of alternative theoretical and methodological perspectives

(Venkatesh et al. 2007). It is, therefore, suggested that the material presented in this paper will form a useful and incremental contribution to the existing knowledge of IS/IT/ICT/innovation adoption and diffusion

3   RESEARCH METHODOLOGY

The research presented in this paper employed a combination of bibliometric analysis, historical analysis (Chao et al. 2007) and meta-analysis (Avison et al. 2008; Palvia and Pinjani 2007) as a means of categorizing accumulated knowledge on adoption and diffusion of IS/IT/ICT. Chao et al. (2007) employed both bibliometric analysis and historical analysis in examining technology trends and forecasts of RFID, while a meta-analysis approach was adapted by three recently published studies profiling the theoretical and methodological underpinnings of articles published in the *Information Systems Journal* (Avison et al. 2008), *Information & Management* (Palvia and Pinjani 2007), and *Journal of Electronic Commerce Research* (Dwivedi, Kiang et al. 2008). Given the overall aim of this paper, our approach employs a combination of these techniques.

For the purpose of conducting this research, we made use of the academic journals database provided by Thomson Scientific (previously known as the Institute for Scientific Information). Thomson Scientific publishes the Science Citation Index (SCI) and the Social Science Citation Index (SSCI) as two of three elements of its Web of Science® product. The reason for selecting this database is that the majority of IS journals are included either within the SCI or the SSCI. Therefore, it is possible to search for and locate a significant proportion of the published material on diffusion and adoption of IS/IT/ICT across various disciplines using the Web of Science® search facility. Moreover, restricting the search activities to a single publication database removed many of the potential problems of duplication inherent in the use of multiple data sources. The Web of Science® product provides two main search techniques: a general search and an advanced search. The search technique used within this research exercise was the general search. The main reason for employing a general search approach was simply that its easy to use characteristics facilitate the repetition of searches without any confusion, making it a straightforward process to obtain consistent results in repetitive searches provided the same search criteria are applied. This method of data collection was also adapted by a previous study on RFID (Chao et al. 2007).

In order to identify publications specific to the adoption and diffusion area, two sets of search terms were employed in this study. The first set of search criteria included three key words: DIFFUSION, ADOPTION, and ACCEPTANCE. The search was restricted to occurrences of any of these keywords appearing in the article title in order to avoid locating publications where keywords might have appeared generally within the main text. However, if one of these words appeared in the article title, it suggested that the focus of the article was adoption and diffusion in some form. A second set of search terms comprising keywords such as IT, INFORMATION TECHNOLOGY, IS, INFORMATION SYSTEM, INFORMATION SYSTEMS, ICT, INFORMATION AND COMMUNICATION TECHNOLOGY, INFORMATION AND COMMUNICATION TECHNOLOGIES, and INTERNET was also applied. In this case, the search was restricted to occurrences of any of the keywords appearing in the article topic/keywords list. Combining the two sets of search terms resulted in the extraction of 883 records providing details on publications relating to adoption, acceptance, or diffusion of IS/IT/ICT. All 883 items were then examined manually in order to cross-check and confirm the relevance of the search results.

A number of analyses were then conducted on the search output employing the various analysis tools available in the Web of Science[®]. Count and percentage data was generated for the assorted variables utilized to categorize the search output. Variables analyzed included subject category, journal in which an article appeared, year of publication, author, author's institution, and the country in which the research was conducted. A further detailed manual analysis was then conducted in order to extract various items of information that could not be obtained directly from the Web of Science[®] database. In order to do so, we examined each of the abstracts of the articles contained in the search results. Then these abstracts were individually scrutinized in order to obtain and record information such as the unit or level of analysis, the research paradigm, issues pertaining to primary data, the form of technology examined, and so on. It is important to note that due to time constraints and the amount of effort required to conduct the analysis, some of the results presented in this paper arise from the analysis of a subset of 301 of the total 883 articles available for consideration. We are continuing to analyze the remaining 582 publications; the results of the entire analysis will be reported elsewhere when available.

Data obtained from this analysis relating to the variables under examination were first recoded in SPSS v.14, and then count and percentage values generated. With the exception of variables referring to the methodological approaches, data on all the other variables were recorded without considering the prespecified categories. For the methodological variables, we adopted categories from the previous studies of Avison et al. (2008), Choudrie and Dwivedi (2005b), Dwivedi, Kiang et al. (2008), Dwivedi, Williams, and Venkatesh (2008), Galliers (1992), and Galliers and Land (1987).

4   FINDINGS

4.1   Adoption and Diffusion Studies According to Subject Category

A total of 107 Web of Science[®] subject categories have published research on adoption and diffusion of IS/IT/ICT. Table 1 illustrates the top 20 Web of Science[®] subject categories, the largest number of articles (292) appearing within the "Computer Science, Information Systems" category on adoption and diffusion of IS/IT/ICT. This is followed by the "Information Science & Library Science" category (240), and then the "Management" category (237). The lowest count (16) presented in this table is for subject category "Planning & Development." For remaining 87 categories, article count varies between 15 to 1 articles. The lowest number of articles in our study (1) appeared in the 35 different categories while 2 articles each appeared in 16 different categories preceded by 5 categories with only 3 articles each and 10 categories with 4 articles each. It is important to note at this point that these results are indicative only, and are intended to provide a representation of the main areas of study in which research articles on adoption and diffusion of information systems are likely to appear. Clearly, extending the number of keywords and altering the categories included would alter the results,

Table 1. IS/IT/ICT Adoption and Diffusion Studies According to Subject Category

Subject Category (N = 107)	Article Count (n = 883)	% of 883
Computer Science, Information Systems	292	33.07%
Information Science & Library Science	240	27.18%
Management	237	26.84%
Business	92	10.42%
Operations Research & Management Science	70	7.93%
Computer Science, Interdisciplinary Applications	65	7.36%
Engineering, Industrial	59	6.68%
Economics	46	5.21%
Medical Informatics	36	4.08%
Computer Science, Theory & Methods	35	3.96%
Telecommunications	32	3.62%
Health Care Sciences & Services	30	3.40%
Communication	29	3.28%
Computer Science, Software Engineering	25	2.83%
Computer Science, Artificial Intelligence	24	2.72%
Ergonomics	24	2.72%
Psychology, Multidisciplinary	21	2.38%
Computer Science, Cybernetics	20	2.27%
Engineering, Electrical & Electronic	16	1.81%
Planning & Development	16	1.81%

although, it is argued, not to the extent that it would substantially alter the overall profile.[1]

Table 2 presents the breakdown of our search output according to the journals in which the articles on adoption and diffusion of IS/IT/ICT appeared. A total of 337 outlets have published 883 articles on adoption and diffusion of IS/IT/ICT. Table 2 illustrates the top 20 source titles, suggesting that the largest number of articles (60) on adoption and diffusion appeared in the journal *Information & Management* and the least number of articles (1) resulting from our search activities appeared in 223 source titles. Other journals that have published a significant number of articles on adoption and diffusion include *European Journal of Information Systems* (26), *IEEE Transactions on Engineering Management* (23), *Journal of the American Medical Informatics Association* (19), *MIS Quarterly* (19), *Information Systems Research* (17), and *Journal of Computer Information Systems* (17). Our findings further reveal that of the journals publishing the highest numbers of articles on adoption and diffusion of IS/IT/innovation, only few (*European Journal of Information Systems* and *Journal of Information Technology*) are based in Europe, all the others being based in North America. This could be due to the fact that a large number of the articles in our search results were quantitative in nature, and it could well be the case that U.S.-based journals are comparatively more sympathetic to such material (Lyytinen et al. 2007; Palvia and Pinjani 2006). The list also suggests

---

[1]Due to space limitations, not all subject categories are listed here. The categories and other information relating to the development of this paper are available from the authors.

Table 2. IS/IT/ICT Adoption and Diffusion Studies According to Journal

Journal Title	Article Count (n=883)	% of 883
Information & Management	60	6.80%
European Journal of Information Systems	26	2.94%
IEEE Transactions on Engineering Management	23	2.60%
Journal of the American Medical Informatics Association	19	2.15%
MIS Quarterly	19	2.15%
Information Systems Research	17	1.93%
Journal of Computer Information Systems	17	1.93%
Decision Support Systems	16	1.81%
International Journal of Information Management	14	1.59%
Journal of Information Technology	14	1.59%
Industrial Management & Data Systems	13	1.47%
Journal of Management Information Systems	13	1.47%
Technovation	11	1.25%
Telecommunications Policy	11	1.25%
Communications of the ACM	10	1.13%
Decision Sciences	10	1.13%
International Journal of Human-Computer Studies	10	1.13%
International Journal of Medical Informatics	9	1.02%
Internet Research-Electronic Networking Applications and Policy	9	1.02%
Journal of Business Research	9	1.02%

that although the majority of journals are from the Information Systems discipline, a number of journals from other disciplines (*Journal of the American Medical Informatics Association, Telecommunication Policy, International Journal of Medical Informatics,* and *Journal of Business Research*) have also published IS/IT/ICT adoption and diffusion research. This clearly shows the cross-disciplinary nature of IS/IT adoption and diffusion research.[2]

4.3 Adoption and Diffusion Studies According to Year of Publication

Our findings (illustrated in Table 3) reveal that the number of articles published on adoption and diffusion has constantly increased from 1989 (when three papers were published in various journals) to 2007 (which has so far seen 123 papers appear). To date, the largest number of articles (142) appeared in 2006, closely followed by 2005 and 2007, each with a count of 123 articles. Prior to 1989, a low number of articles appeared in each year, with no articles at all appearing in our selected journals during some years.

---

[2]Due to space limitations, not all source titles are listed here. A complete list is available from the authors.

Table 3. Adoption and Diffusion Studies Published from 1970 through 2007

Year	Article Count (n = 883)	% of 883	Year	Article Count (n = 883)	% of 883	Year	Article Count (n = 883)	% of 883
2006	142	16.08%	1997	35	3.96%	1990	5	0.57%
2005	123	13.93%	1999	27	3.06%	1989	3	0.34%
2007	123	13.93%	1994	19	2.15%	1980	2	0.23%
2003	85	9.63%	1995	13	1.47%	1985	2	0.23%
2004	66	7.47%	1992	12	1.36%	1987	2	0.23%
2002	60	6.80%	2008	11	1.25%	1970	1	0.11%
2001	47	5.32%	1993	10	1.13%	1978	1	0.11%
1998	38	4.30%	1996	10	1.13%	1981	1	0.11%
2000	38	4.30%	1991	6	0.68%	1984	1	0.11%

While it may be argued that the increasing number of articles appearing post-1989 illustrates increasing levels of interest and research activity in the subject area, the lack of articles prior to this time may be attributed to a number of reasons, including that not all of the journals in our search list were published in each year. This point is particularly applicable to the earlier years considered.

4.4 Adoption and Diffusion Studies According to Country

Our findings (illustrated in Table 4) disclose that the research presented in the 883 publications we identified on adoption and diffusion was conducted in 52 countries. By

Table 4. IS/IT/ICT Adoption and Diffusion Studies According to Country

Country	AC (n = 883)	Country	AC (n = 883)	Country	AC (n = 883)
USA	463	India	8	South Africa	2
UK	78	New Zealand	8	Turkey	2
Peoples R China	50	Austria	6	Botswana	1
Canada	47	Brazil	6	Dominican Rep	1
Taiwan	44	Japan	6	Egypt	1
Australia	39	Sweden	6	Ethiopia	1
South Korea	33	Switzerland	6	Indonesia	1
Germany	29	Belgium	5	Malawi	1
Netherlands	26	Hong Kong	5	Mexico	1
Singapore	26	Portugal	5	Philippines	1
Spain	18	U Arab Emirates	5	Poland	1
Italy	17	Ireland	4	Slovakia	1
France	13	Saudi Arabia	4	Slovenia	1
Finland	12	Fed Rep Ger	3	Thailand	1
Denmark	11	Kenya	3	Uruguay	1
Greece	9	Malaysia	3	Vietnam	1
Israel	9	Nigeria	3		
Norway	9	Ghana	2		

far the largest amount of published activity has taken place in the United States, with a number of others countries (including the United Kingdom, China, Canada, Taiwan, Australia, South Korea, Germany, the Netherlands, and Singapore) also being the location of a substantial amount of research activity resulting in publications that appeared in our search results.

A number of countries (including Finland, France, India, Ireland, Malaysia, and the Philippines) have been the location of research resulting in a low number of publications, and, given the overall level of research activity in such countries, and indeed the supposed high-profile of ICT, this is perhaps a surprising result and indicates that there is opportunity for additional research based in such counties to take place in order to further expand the existing knowledge base.

4.5 Authors Actively Involved in Publishing Adoption and Diffusion Research

A total of 1,767 authors contributed to the 883 articles on adoption and diffusion of IS/IT/ICT. Table 5 lists the authors most actively involved in conducting and publishing adoption and diffusion related research. It appears that the most productive author in adoption and diffusion research (in terms of journal publications across the journals in our search) is Venkatesh, V with 15 articles, followed by Chau, PYK, with 10 articles. Thereafter three authors (Davis, FD; Morris, MG, and Tam, KY) contributed eight articles each, two authors (Kraemer, KL and Zhu, K) contributed seven articles each, four authors contributed six articles each and five authors contributed five articles each (see Table 5 for names). This is followed by 13 authors with 4 articles each and 45 authors contributed 3 articles each.

From the list of 1,767 authors, 132 contributed 2 articles each, while a vast majority of authors (1,561 authors) contributed to just 1 article in the set of journals comprising our search data.[3]

4.6 Adoption and Diffusion Studies According to Institution

A total of 732 institutions are represented by authors contributing to the 883 articles on adoption and diffusion of IS/IT/ICT. Table 6 identifies the institutions apparently most active in the area of adoption and diffusion research. The overall number of contributions from each university varies from 1 to 19. Clearly the National University of Singapore (with 19 publications) has contributed the largest number and can, therefore, be seen a leading center of adoption and diffusion related research. This is closely followed by the University of Maryland (with 18 publications). A number of other institutions also have been the source of a noteworthy number of publications over the years, including the Georgia State University and the Hong Kong University of Science and Technology, each with 16 publications; Florida State University, University of Cali-

---

[3]Due to space limitations, not all authors are listed here. A complete list is available from the authors.

Table 5. Authors Actively Involved in Publishing IS/IT/ICT Adoption and Diffusion Research

Author	AC	Author	AC	Author	AC
Venkatesh, V	15	Prasad, J	4	Kim, M	3
Chau, PYK	10	Ramamurthy, K	4	Lee, SM	3
Davis, FD	8	Riemenschneider, CK	4	Lewis, LF	3
Morris, MG	8	Thong, JYL	4	Lin, CA	3
Tam, KY	8	Benbasat, I	3	Lou, H	3
Kraemer, KL	7	Chang, IC	3	Lyytinen, K	3
Zhu, K	7	Cheng, TCE	3	Mbarika, VWA	3
Agarwal, R	6	Cheung, CMK	3	Molla, A	3
Hu, PJH	6	Choudrie, J	3	Nault, BR	3
Premkumar, G	6	Chukmaitov, A	3	Pervan, G	3
Teo, TSH	6	Damsgaard, J	3	Pries-Heje, J	3
Brooks, RG	5	Dexter, AS	3	Quaddus, M	3
Igbaria, M	5	Dinlersoz, EM	3	Rai, A	3
Lai, VS	5	Dwivedi, YK	3	Ravichandran, T	3
Lee, MKO	5	Farn, CK	3	Saunders, C	3
Menachemi, N	5	Forman, C	3	Shih, HP	3
Bajwa, DS	4	Foster, W	3	Straub, DW	3
Bhattacherjee, A	4	Gefen, D	3	Wang, YS	3
Brown, SA	4	Goldfarb, A	3	Watanabe, C	3
Fichman, RG	4	Hardgrave, BC	3	Wu, JH	3
Grover, V	4	Hong, SJ	3	Xu, S	3
Hwang, HG	4	Hong, WY	3	Xu, SX	3
Lee, J	4	Karahanna, E	3	Yang, H	3
Ngai, EWT	4	Kauffman, RJ	3	Yu, CS	3
Pavlou, PA	4	Kemerer, CF	3		

fornia–Irvine, and the University of Wisconsin contributed to 14 publications each. Table 6 illustrates that six universities contributed 12 articles each, followed by the University of Arizona with 11 contributions and seven universities each contributing 10 articles. A further five universities contributed nine articles each, while Harvard and the University of Pennsylvania were the source of eight articles each. These and the remaining institutions are identified in Table 6. A further 116 universities (not listed) contributed two articles each, while 488 universities were the source of just one article.[4]

The largest amount of research activity resulting in journal publications has occurred at universities in the United States, and, to an extent, at institutions based in Singapore and Hong Kong. It is interesting to note that only four European universities appear in our list (Athens University of Economics & Business, Bocconi University, Brunel University, and Free University of Amsterdam), which includes only one university from the United Kingdom. The list also includes two Australian universities (Curtin Unive-

---

[4]Due to space limitations, not all institutions producing fewer than five articles over the period under study are listed here. The complete list is available from the authors.

Table 6. Universities Facilitating IS/IT/ICT Adoption and Diffusion Research Resulting in Journal Publications

University	AC	University	AC	University	AC
Natl Univ Singapore	19	Iowa State Univ	9	Texas Tech Univ	6
Univ Maryland	18	Natl Chung Cheng Univ	9	Univ Colorado	6
Georgia State Univ	16	Univ So Calif	9	Univ Dayton	6
Hong Kong Univ Sci & Technol	16	Univ Utah	9	Univ Georgia	6
Florida State Univ	14	Harvard Univ	8	Univ Missouri	6
Univ Calif Irvine	14	Univ Penn	8	Univ New S Wales	6
Univ Wisconsin	14	Brunel Univ	7	Univ S Carolina	6
Michigan State Univ	12	Chinese Univ Hong Kong	7	Univ Western Ontario	6
Univ Arkansas	12	Curtin Univ Technol	7	Yonsei Univ	6
Univ Houston	12	George Washington Univ	7	Arizona State Univ	5
Univ Minnesota	12	Natl Sun Yat Sen Univ	7	Athens Univ Econ & Business	5
Univ N Carolina	12	Ohio State Univ	7	Bocconi Univ	5
Univ Texas	12	So Illinois Univ	7	Boston Univ	5
Univ Arizona	11	Stanford Univ	7	Duke Univ	5
Carnegie Mellon Univ	10	Syracuse Univ	7	Free Univ Amsterdam	5
City Univ Hong Kong	10	Univ Illinois	7	Louisiana State Univ	5
Hong Kong Polytech Univ	10	Univ Michigan	7	Miami Univ	5
Indiana Univ	10	Univ Virginia	7	Nyu	5
Univ British Columbia	10	Washington State Univ	7	United Arab Emirates Univ	5
Univ Hong Kong	10	Clemson Univ	6	Univ Alabama	5
Univ S Florida	10	Natl Cent Univ	6	Univ Pittsburgh	5
Drexel Univ	9	Rutgers State Univ	6		

sity of Technology and the University of New South Wales). However, the list is overall largely dominated by additional U.S.-based institutions. Our results, therefore, provide a strong indication that adoption and diffusion research resulting in journal publications takes place primarily in the United States, Singapore, and Hong Kong, with comparatively lower levels of activity (to date) taking place elsewhere.

4.7 Language of Publications

Our findings disclose that the research presented in the 883 publications we identified on adoption and diffusion was communicated in seven languages. By far the largest amount of articles were communicated in English (869), with a very few numbers of articles published in German (9), Finnish (1), French (1), Russian (1), Slovak (1), and Spanish (1).

Table 7. Use of Adoption, Acceptance, or Diffusion in Article Title

Keyword	Count (n = 301)	Percent
Adoption	178	59.1
Acceptance	81	26.9
Diffusion	42	14.0

4.8 Document Type

The findings suggest that the research presented in the 883 publications we identified on adoption and diffusion were largely research articles (806), followed by 42 review articles and 15 editorials. Very few articles were classified as a book review (7), meeting abstract (5), news item (4), letter (2), or note (2).

4.9 Adoption, Acceptance or Diffusion?

Although the findings presented thus far include the total 345 articles identified from our search activities, hereafter only 301 articles provide the basis for the basis for profiling adoption and diffusion research output. At this stage, all articles from *Communications of the ACM* and a number of articles from other outlets were necessarily eliminated due to the non-availability of abstracts for analysis. The primary reason for excluding the *Communications of the ACM* articles from the analysis is that the format and content of articles as published differ from other IS journals, and hence, it is often difficult to extract methodological and theoretical information from them. Three keywords, ADOPTION, ACCEPTANCE, and DIFFUSION, were employed to search published output for this study. Table 7 presents information on the number of occurrences of each term in our search results. It can be seen from Table 7 that the keyword ADOPTION was used by the largest number of articles (178) followed by ACCEPTANCE (81), with the term DIFFUSION being employed by the least number of items appearing in our search results (42).

4.10 Adoption and Diffusion Studies According to Unit/Level of Analysis

The results of our exploration into the most common forms of unit of analysis employed are presented in Table 8. It can be seen that the majority of articles (105) appearing in our search results examined adoption and diffusion issues at the organizational level, closely followed by studies focusing on user adoption and acceptance of IS/IT (92). Far fewer articles were found to examine adoption and diffusion in the context of Groups/ Teams (2) and the household (3).

Table 8. Unit of Analysis

Unit of Analysis	Count (n = 301)	%	Unit of Analysis	Count (n = 301)	%
Organization/Firm	105	34.9	Industry	4	1.3
User	92	30.6	Stakeholders	3	1.0
Consumer	42	14.0	Household	3	1.0
SME	26	8.6	Other	3	1.0
Subject/Theory/Tool/System	20	6.9	Group/Team	2	0.7
Country	7	2.3			

4.11 Adoption and Diffusion Studies According to Research Paradigm

The findings clearly indicates that positivism (used in 225 articles, 74.8 percent) is the dominant or most popular research paradigm among adoption and diffusion researchers, followed some way behind by the interpretive paradigm (being employed in 42 articles, 14.0 percent). We have labeled the third category "Descriptive/Conceptual/ Theoretical" (being employed in 27 articles, 9.0 percent) and it includes papers that do not neatly fit into either positivist or interpretive categories, primarily comprising articles based on literature reviews, personal view points, or studies that are highly conceptual in nature (Avison et al. 2008). For seven articles (2.3 percent), the paradigm was unclear and hence it was not apparent if they should be placed in either the positivist or interpretive category.

4.13 Research Methodology: Empirical Versus Nonempirical

A very large proportion of articles within our search results (273 articles, 90.7 percent) were empirical in nature in comparison to articles that fell within the nonempirical category (23 articles, 7.6 percent). However, for five articles (1.7 percent), it was not possible to determine if they were empirical or nonempirical in nature, due to the lack of relevant information.

4.13 Research Methodology: Quantitative Versus Qualitative

The findings suggest that the quantitative approach has dominated adoption and diffusion research within the IS discipline. A total of 195 articles (64.8 percent) employed a quantitative approach (which also includes descriptive quantitative articles) in comparison to the qualitative approach which was employed by only 68 articles (22.6 percent) and conceptual approach at third place with 26 articles (8.6 percent). Four articles (1.3 percent) employed a mix of data types, while for eight articles (2.7 percent) it was not possible to determine the primary approach employed.

Table 9. Research Methods (Categories are adapted from Avison et al. 2998; Dwivedi, Williams et al. 2008; Dwivedi, Williams, and Venkatesh 2008)

Research Method	Count (n = 301)	%	Research Method	Count (n = 301)	%
Survey	173	57.5	Laboratory experiment	3	1.0
Case Study	46	15.3	Secondary Data Analysis	3	1.0
Literature analysis/ Conceptual/Meta-analysis	29	9.6	Field experiment	2	.7
Field Study	11	3.7	Content Analysis	2	.7
Interview	7	2.3	Action research	1	.3
Mathematical model	6	2.0	Not Known	12	4.0
Multi-method	6	2.0			

4.14 Research Methods

Table 9 illustrates that although a total of 12 different research methods were recorded from our data analysis activities, the majority of studies (173) in our results employed survey methods. The other major category employed was case study, which was used in 46 articles. Other approaches identified include literature review/conceptual/ meta-analysis (29), field study (11), and interview (7). All remaining categories were employed by very few studies, with only one article employing action research.

4.15 The Technology Examined

Table 10 lists the diverse range of technologies examined in the 301 publications that formed our search results. It is clear from Table 10 that the scope is broad and, to an extent, reflects the emergence of different technologies over the period under consideration. In order to organize the technologies effectively, we have grouped them in the following broad categories: communication, electronic commerce, information systems, information technologies, Internet, mobile, and website. In Table 10, the figures in parentheses indicate the number of articles in each case, and it can be seen that the IS category has been most widely studied, followed by electronic commerce related issues. The least studied broad area to date appears to be that of mobile technology, although Table 10 reveals a range of specific technologies, applications, and contexts that appear to have received little investigative attention.

4.16 Theories/Models and Theoretical Constructs

Table 11 illustrates the diversity of theories employed in the study of adoption and diffusion concepts in relation to information systems. TAM has emerged as the most popular theory with 88 studies (29 percent) employing it, followed by DoI theory, which was used in 49 publications (16.3 percent). The third largest category was TPB, which

Table 10. Technologies Examined

Category	Technology/System
Communication (15)	Communication Standards (1); Email (9); Fax (1); Instant Messaging/ Wireless SMS (3); High Speed Data Services (1)
Electronic Applications & Technologies (74)	B2B Exchanges (1); B2B Marketplaces (1); B2B Portals (1); B2B, P2P and e-Speak (1); C2C Auction System/Online Escrow Services (1); E-banking/Internet Banking/Electronic Billing/Virtual Banking (7); E-Business/E-Business Technologies (7); E-Commerce/E-Shopping/E-Commerce Technologies (25); E-Marketplace (2); Electronic Service (1); Electronic Tax Filing (1); Electronic Trading (3); Price Comparison Shopping (1); EDI (9); E-Learning System and technology (2); E-Government/E-Gov Services/E-Voting (5); Electronic Health Records (EHRs)/Electronic Patient Record (EPR) (2); Application Service Oriented Medical Records (1); E-Sales, C-Procurement (1); Products in Electronic Markets (1); Proprietary and Open Systems (1)
Information Systems/Systems/ IS Development/ IS Management (80)	Agile Adoption Practices (1); Application Service Provision (ASP) (1); BPR (2); B2B Eprocurement System (1); Business to Business Ordering System (1); CASE (8); Client Server Systems (1); Computer-based Information Systems (1); CRM (2); Design Methodologies of Component Based Architecture (1); Document Management System (1); DSS&TPS (1); End-user Computing (1); Enterprise Application Integration (EAI) (1); Enterprise Digital Transformation (1); Enterprise Level Systems (1); Enterprise Resource Planning (ERP) (8); Expert Systems and Expert Systems in Banking Industry (5); Expert Systems Advice (1); Group Support Systems (GSS) (2); Groupware (1); Lotus Notes (1); Healthcare Information Systems and Healthcare Information Technology (HIT) (3); Information Systems (6); Sales Information Systems (1); Hedonic Information Systems (1); Securities Trading Systems (1); IOS (2); IS Development Methods (ISDMs) (1); IS Process Innovation (1); EIS (4); Knowledge (1); Office Suite Applications - Spreadsheet, Database, Word, Graphics (2); Open Systems (2); Recommendation Agent (1); Outsourcing (3); Systems (2); System Development Methodology (1); System/Technology Use (1); User Involvement (1); Volitional/Voluntary Systems (1); Software System (1); Electronic Brain Storming (1); Software Development Tool (1); Software Re-use (2); Virtual Community Service – Avatar (1); Visual Information (1); Telecommuting (2)
Information Technology/ICT/ Technology/Soft-ware (70)	Advanced Manufacturing Technology (1); Broadband and Broadband Mobile Services (7); Collaborative Information Technology (1); Data warehouse (3); DBMS & Distributed DBMS (3); Digital Library (1); Family Technology Resource Center (1); IT (17); IT in Education (1); IT Innovation (2); Mandated IT (1); IT Platform (1); ICT (3); Personal Computer (PC)/Personal Computing (6); Tablet PC (1); Radio Frequency Identification (RFID) (1); Public Grid Computing (1); Self-Service Technology (1); Commercial Software Packages (1); Windows technology (1); Smart Card-based Payment Systems/micro payment infrastructure (2); Telemedicine Technology (4); Videotex newspaper (1); Knowledge Management Technologies (1); Object-oriented Technologies/Object technology (2); Tech. Mediated Distance Education (TMDE) (1); Technological Innovations (1); Technology (2); ATM (2)

Category	Technology/System
Internet/Online (26)	Internet (11); Internet-based product customisation (1); Internet Based Learning Medium (ILM) (1); Internet Retailing (1); ISPs (1); Internet Standards - IPv6 (1); Intranet (1); ISDN-Integrated Services Digital Network (1); National Infrastructure (1); On-line Learning Systems (1); Online Consumer Behaviour (1); Online Investing (1); Online Retailing (1); Online Services (1); Online Shopping (1); Online stock trading (1)
Mobile (11)	3G Mobile Computing Device (1); Mobile (Cell) Phone Banking (1); Mobile Broadband Wireless Access Technology-Based (MBWA) games (1); Mobile Commerce (3); Mobile ICT Adoption (1); Mobile Internet (1); Multi-purpose Information Appliances-Mobile Data Services (1); Wireless Internet Service via Mobile Technology (WIMT) (2);
Website (16)	Web-based Training (WBT) (1); Web Services (1); Websites (8); Websites-Information Searching (1); Website-Women-centric (2); Intermediary Website (1); Infomediaries Websites (1); Business Homepage (1)

Table 11. Theories Used

Theories	TAM	TPB	TRA	DoI	Trust	SE	MM	PCUM	SCT
Count	88	17	8	49	7	8	2	3	2
Percent	29.2	5.6	2.7	16.3	2.3	2.7	.7	1	.7

was utilized in 17 studies, followed by TRA and SE, each contributing to eight studies. There were 47 other theories utilized in the 301 publications. In addition to these theories, 182 theoretical constructs were recorded from the various studies.[5] The large number of theories and theoretical constructs employed clearly indicates the diversity of adoption and diffusion research in the IS research.

5   SUMMARY AND CONCLUSIONS

Our intention in this paper has been to provide an overview of the current state of adoption, acceptance, and diffusion research by presenting the results of a systematic and comprehensive review of 883 articles appearing across 337 different peer-reviewed journals during the period 1970–2007. We have presented the results of our investigation along a series of dimensions including the journals most often publishing articles on IS/IT adoption, acceptance, and diffusion, authors most active in the subject area (in terms of articles published), the most commonly used units of analysis, methodological practice and use of primary data, the theories and theoretical constructs utilized, and contexts and technologies examined. Our intention in conducting our investigation is to provide a

---

[5]Due to space limitations, the theoretical constructs are not listed here. The complete list is available from the authors.

useful and usable resource for future researchers. In keeping with previous state of play studies of this nature, we posit that our findings highlight "promising lines of inquiry as well as the ones that are neglected and in need of renewed attention" (Palvia and Pinjani 2007, p. 10). Further, we argue that the findings of this study may help in directing limited and valuable research resources to fruitful lines of inquiry as well as strengthening the area of research by facilitating consideration of less used but useful alternative theoretical and methodological perspectives.

Although the three keywords, adoption, acceptance, and diffusion, are often used interchangeably by IS researchers, our results suggest that adoption is preferred over other two terms. It might be a point of further research to examine what determines the use of one of these three terms over the other. When considering research in terms of the research paradigm, the positivist approach is currently employed to a much greater extent than both the interpretive and descriptive/theoretical approaches. This suggests clear indication of adoption and diffusion researchers neglecting other paradigms, which has implications for editors, reviewers, and authors. Similarly, the utilization of empirical and quantitative techniques and survey research methods appears to have been much preferred over other available alternatives. It is clear that a rich diversity of theories and theoretical constructs exist within the extant literature, but researchers to date have overwhelmingly made use of just one theory, TAM, and its associated constructs "perceived usefulness" and "perceived ease of use." This suggests that IS/IT adoption and diffusion research is gradually moving toward overall homogeneity, which is clearly likely to weaken the field of technology adoption research. Therefore, we believe there are clear messages for authors to make greater use of the theoretical and methodological variety available to them, and for journal reviewers and editors to support the use of such alternative approaches, otherwise adoption and diffusion research itself will diffuse only within a limited domain. We anticipate this paper will prove to be a useful source of information for those readers who wish to learn more about the various facets pertaining to the existing body of published technology adoption and diffusion research in IS journals. Moreover, readers also may benefit by becoming aware of how the various research approaches and methods fit with the different theories, models, and units of analysis.

However, we fully acknowledge that our study has a number of limitations, and readers should be aware of these and indeed interpret the material presented in this paper within the context of these limitations. First, our search activities were restricted to occurrences of the three keywords in the article titles only, and we fully acknowledge that there may be numerous studies that lack all three keywords in the title, but still focus upon adoption and diffusion in the main text. For example, the works of Benbasat and Barki (2007), Choudrie and Dwivedi (2005a), and Lucas et al. (2007) focus on adoption and diffusion, but they did not appear in our search results as they lack all three keywords in the title. A further limitation is the extraction of theoretical and methodological data from limited search outputs. We limited our search to the journals indexed only in Web of Science®, but there are many well-known journals in the IS field that are not indexed in this product, and this clearly will have limited our ability to identify all relevant articles, although further research is required to determine the extent of the influence of such factors. Although we believe that this paper has analyzed the largest number of articles in comparison to other existing review articles on this theme, we believe that comprehensive research is still required in order to reduce the impact of the limitations we have identified in order to provide a greater understanding of the domain of IS/IT adoption research.

References[6]

Avison, D., Dwivedi, Y. K., Fitzgerald, G., and Powell, P. 2008. "The Beginnings of a New Era: Time to Reflect on 17 Years of the *ISJ*," *Information Systems Journal* (18:1), pp. 5-21.

Bagozzi, R. P. 2007. "The Legacy of the Technology Acceptance Model and a Proposal for a Paradigm Shift," *Journal of the Association for Information Systems* (8:4), pp. 244-254.

Benbasat, I., and Barki, H. 2007. "*Quo vadis*, TAM?," *Journal of the Association for Information Systems* (8:4), pp. 211-218

Brown, S. A., and Venkatesh, V. 2005. "Model of Adoption of Technology in Households: A Baseline Model Test and Extension Incorporating Household Life Cycle," *MIS Quarterly* (29:3), pp. 399-426. .

Choudrie J., and Dwivedi, Y. K. 2005a. "The Demographics of Broadband Residential Consumers of a British Local Community: The London Borough of Hillingdon," *Journal of Computer Information Systems* (45:4), pp. 93-101.

Choudrie, J., and Dwivedi, Y. K. 2005b. "Investigating the Research Approaches for Examining the Technology Adoption in the Household," *Journal of Research Practice* (1:1), pp. 1-12 (available at http://jrp.icaap.org/content/v1.1/choudrie.pdf).

Dwivedi Y. K., Choudrie J., and Brinkman, W. P. 2006. "Development of a Survey Instrument to Examine Consumer Adoption of Broadband," *Industrial Management and Data Systems* (106:5), pp. 700-718.

Dwivedi Y. K., Kiang, M., Williams, M. D., and Lal, B. 2008. "Profiling Research Published in the *Journal of Electronic Commerce Research*," *Journal of Electronic Commerce Research* (8:2), pp. 77-91.

Dwivedi, Y. K., Williams, M. D., Lal, B., and Schwarz, A. 2008. "Profiling Adoption, Acceptance, and Diffusion Research in the Information Systems Discipline," in *Proceedings of the 16th European Conference on Information Systems*, W. Golden, T. Acton, K. Conboy, H. van der Heijden, and V. Tuuainen, Galway, Ireland, June 9-11.

Dwivedi, Y. K., Williams, M. D., and Venkatesh, V. 2008. "Guest Editorial: A Profile of Adoption of Information & Communication Technologies (ICT) Research in the Household Context," *Information Systems Frontiers* (http://dx.doi.org/10.1007/s10796-008-9101-8).

Galliers, R. D. 1992. "Choosing Information Systems Research Approaches," in *Information Systems Research: Issues, Methods and Practical Guidelines*, R. D. Galliers (ed.), Oxford, UK: Blackwell Scientific, pp. 144-162.

Galliers, R. D., and Land, F. F. 1987. "Choosing an Appropriate Information Systems Research Methodology," *Communications of the ACM* (30:11), pp. 900-902.

Hirschheim, R. 2007. "Introduction to the Special Issue on 'Quo Vadis TAM—Issues and Reflections on Technology Acceptance Research,'" *Journal of the Association for Information Systems* (8:4), pp. 203-205.

Jeyaraj, A., Rottman, J. W., and Lacity, M. C. 2006. "A Review of the Predictors, Linkages, and Biases in IT Innovation Adoption Research," *Journal of Information Technology* (21), pp. 1-23.

King, W. R., and He, J. 2006. "A Meta-Analysis of the Technology Acceptance Model," *Information & Management* (43), pp. 740-755.

---

[6]Due to space limitations, the articles analyzed for this review are not listed here, but the articles and other information relating to the development of this paper are available from the authors.

Legris, P., Ingham, J., and Collerette, P. 2003. "Why Do People Use Information Technology? A Critical Review of the Technology Acceptance Model," *Information & Management* (40), pp. 191-204.

Lucas, H. C., Swanson, E. B., and Zmud, R. W. 2007. "Implementation, Innovation, and Related Themes Over the Years in Information Systems Research," *Journal of the Association for Information Systems* (8:4), pp. 206-210.

Lyytinen, K., Baskerville, R., Iivari, J., and Te'eni, D. 2007. "Why the Old World Cannot Publish? Overcoming Challenges in Publishing High-Impact IS Research," *European Journal of Information Systems* (16:4), pp. 317-326.

Palvia, P., and Pinjani, P. 2007. "A Profile of Information Systems Research Published in *Information & Management*," *Information & Management* (44), pp. 1-11.

Schwarz, A., and Chin, W. 2007. "Looking Forward: Toward an Understanding of the Nature and Definition of IT Acceptance," *Journal of the Association for Information Systems* (8:4), pp. 230-243.

Silva, L. 2007. "Post-Positivist Review of Technology Acceptance Model," *Journal of the Association for Information Systems* (8:4), pp. 255-266.

Venkatesh, V. 2006. "Where to Go from Here? Thoughts on Future Directions for Research on Individual-Level Technology Adoption with a Focus on Decision Making," *Decision Science* (37), pp. 497-518.

Venkatesh, V., and Brown, S. A. 2001. "A Longitudinal Investigation of Personal Computers in Homes: Adoption Determinants and Emerging Challenges," *MIS Quarterly* (25:1), pp. 71-102.

Venkatesh, V., Davis, F. D., and Morris, M. G. 2007. "Dead or Alive? The Development, Trajectory and Future of Technology Adoption Research," *Journal of the Association for Information Systems* (8), pp. 267-286.

About the Authors

Yogesh K. Dwivedi is a lecturer in Information Systems at the School of Business and Economics, Swansea University, Wales, UK. He obtained his Ph.D. from the School of Information Systems, Computing and Mathematics, Brunel University. His doctoral research has been awarded the Highly Commended Award by the European Foundation for Management and Development and Emerald Group Publishing Ltd. His current research focuses on examining diffusion of IS research and also understanding the adoption and diffusion of ICT in organizations and society. As well as having presented at leading IS conferences such as European Conference on Informatoin Systems and the Americas' Conference on Information Systems, he has co-authored several papers which have appeared (or are forthcoming) in international referred journals such as *Communications of the ACM, Information Systems Journal, Journal of Computer Information Systems, Industrial Management and Data Systems*, and *Information Systems Frontiers*. He has authored a book, *Consumer Adoption and Use of Broadband*, and co-edited the *Handbook of Research on Global Diffusion of Broadband Data Transmission*. He is a member of the Association for Information Systems and Life Member of the Global Institute of Flexible Systems Management, New Delhi. He can be reached by at ykdwivedi@gmail.com.

Michael D. Williams is a professor in the School of Business and Economics at Swansea University. He holds a B.Sc. from the Council for National Academic Awards, an M.Ed. from the University of Cambridge, and a Ph.D. from the University of Sheffield. He has implemented and evaluated information systems in domains including finance, telecommunications, manufacturing, and government, is the author of numerous refereed and invited papers, and has obtained external research funding from sources including the European Union, the Nuffield Foundation, and the Welsh Assembly Government. He currently serves as an invited member of the Project Expert

Group for a European Union funded project examining transformative use of ICT. He can be reached at m.d.williams@swansea.ac.uk.

Banita Lal is a lecturer in the Nottingham Business School, Nottingham Trent University, UK. She obtained her Ph.D. and M.Sc. in Information Systems from the School of Information Systems, Computing and Mathematics, Brunel University. Her research interests involve examining the individual and organizational adoption and usage of ICTs and technology-enabled alternative forms of working. She has published several research papers in internationally refereed journals such as *Industrial Management and Data Systems*, *Information Systems Frontiers*, *Electronic Government*, *International Journal of Mobile Communications*, and *Transforming Government: People, Process and Policy*, and has presented several papers at several international conferences. She can be reached at banita.la.@ntu.ac.uk.

2 CITATION PATTERNS IN MIS: An Analysis of Exemplar Articles

Tor J. Larsen[†]
Department of Leadership and Organizational Management
Norwegian School of Management
Oslo, Norway

Linda Levine[†]
Software Engineering Institute
Carnegie Mellon University
Pittsburgh, PA U.S.A.

Abstract   The present research examines MIS exemplar articles, analyzing their citation patterns in MIS and other scientific fields. Using **MIS Quarterly** articles of the year and peer-nominated articles, we identified 36 exemplar MIS articles. In all, 421 journals contained articles that cited the exemplars. Our five findings are: (1) the MIS exemplars cover a wide range of themes, (2) the average lifetime for an exemplar article (as expressed through the citations made to the article) is 17 years, as compared with an 11 year expected life time for scientific journal articles, (3) the dominant life-cycle pattern for an exemplar takes the form of a bell curve, (4) exemplar articles that were conceptual in nature are not cited any more frequently than articles treating contemporary issues, and (5) conceptual contributions have a longer lifetime of citation activity than contemporary exemplars. Future research will more closely examine MIS and its reference disciplines, as is revealed through extensive citation analysis of the exemplars.

Keywords   Citation analysis, bibliometrics, scientometrics, diffusion of research, exemplar articles, MIS research agenda

[†]The authors are listed in alphabetical order but have contributed equally to the article.

Please use the following format when citing this chapter:

Larsen, T. J., and Levine, L., 2008, in IFIP International Federation for Information Processing, Volume 287, Open IT-Based Innovation: Moving Towards Cooperative IT Transfer and Knowledge Diffusion, eds. León, G., Bernardos, A., Casar, J., Kautz, K., and DeGross, J. (Boston: Springer), pp. 23-38.

1   INTRODUCTION

The evolution of the discipline of Management Information Systems (MIS)[1] has been discussed by Baskerville and Myers (2002) and explored through empirical analyses of journals and citation patterns (Grover et al. 2006a, 2006b; Holsapple et al. 1994; ISWorld[2]; Mylonopoulos and Theoharakis 2001; Pfeffers and Ya 2003; Straub 2006; Vessey et al. 2002; Wade et al. 2006a, 2006b; Walstrom and Hardgrave 2001). These publications build on the notion that MIS continuously borrows ideas and findings from other fields, in the spirit of innovation and exchange (Culnan 1986; Davis 2000). As the body of knowledge has grown, MIS articles have come to cite other MIS publications more frequently, and thus the field has evolved into a more mature academic discipline (Cheon et al. 1993; Culnan and Swanson 1986; Katerattakanakul et al. 2006), creating its own body of research. In tandem, in the discipline of information science, researchers continue to examine and debate the appropriateness, value, and methods of citation analysis in its own right (Bauer and Bakkalbasi 2005; Garfield 1987; Jacso 2005; Perkel 2005).

Ongoing discussion has focused on the nature of the MIS core and subareas (Larsen and Levine 2005). Orlikowski and Baroudi (1991) argue that MIS research exhibits a single set of philosophical assumptions regarding the nature of the phenomena studied, and what constitutes valid knowledge about these phenomena. Weber (1987) claims that MIS consists of multiple areas of activity, each employing its own theories, which are to a large extent borrowed from other scientific fields. In Weber's view, there is no unified theory of MIS; he asserts that the field will not make theoretical advancements until a paradigm is developed. Orlikowski and Iacono (2001) reinforce these concerns. They question the identity of MIS and claim that scientific progress cannot be made without a unified theory of the IS/IT artifact. Further attempts have been made to define and circumscribe the IT artifact (Benbasat and Zmud 2003; Larsen 1998; Orlikowski and Iacono 2001; Whinston and Geng 2004). Some view the diversity in MIS as a problem (Benbasat and Weber 1996), while others see diversity and openness as providing fertile ground for research in subfields of MIS (Ives et al. 2004; Lyytinen and King 2004; Myers 2002; Robey 1996; Weber 2003). Additionally, MIS and its subfields are of interest to many other scientific fields (Davis 2000). This lends support to Baskerville and Myers' (2002) claim that MIS has matured into a bona fide source of reference for researchers in other scientific fields.

The present investigation is the first step in a research project concerned with the use of MIS research publications in the field of MIS and in other fields. Such empirical research addressing the use of scientific publications commonly employs citation analysis. Small (1973, 1978) observes that a citation is evidence of acceptance of meaning and

---

[1]Different labels are used to refer to the field, for example: Information Technology (IT), Information Communication Technology (ICT), Information Systems (IS), Management Information Systems (MIS), and Information Management (IM). Knowledge Management Systems (KMS) is another term that is increasingly in use. Each term has its proponents; however, the terms are often used interchangeably. For the sake of clarity and consistency, we use the term Management Information Systems.

[2]Located at http://home.aisnet.org.

is viewed as a standard symbol for ideas represented in the text. Any analysis of citations requires a dataset. Our investigation employs a set of exemplar MIS articles. Using *MIS Quarterly* "articles of the year" and peer-nominated articles, we identified 36 MIS exemplars. These are not "exemplars" in Kuhn's (1970) sense, where exemplars serve as the foundation of a paradigm. Rather, our exemplars are illustrative of important contributions in the field of MIS. This leads us to the following research question:

How are these exemplar MIS articles cited in the field of MIS and other fields?

The first phase of this research is focused on citation analysis and citation patterns of the exemplars—not on making distinctions among scientific fields. Future research will more closely examine MIS and its reference disciplines, as is revealed through more extensive citation analysis of the exemplars. The present article proceeds to cover background and propositions, method, analysis, discussion, and conclusions.

2 BACKGROUND AND PROPOSITIONS

Our research question rests on two assumptions: (1) that science can be distinctly separated into fields, each with its own recognized scientific journals; and (2) that MIS is recognized as a field. Kuhn (1970) defines a scientific field as distinct (from other sciences) when a high level of consensus about a paradigm, shared theoretical structures, and commonly applied methodological approaches can be found.

According to Ritzer (1975), a paradigm consists of four basic components: (1) a model to be emulated, (2) an image of the subject matter, (3) theories, and (4) methods and instruments. Pfeffer (1993) suggests that the maturity of paradigm development in a field is dependent upon 14 elements, including social ties, departmental issues, faculty, and publication. These elements have not been systematically investigated in MIS. However, researchers concur that a common set of agreed upon theories derived from a paradigmatic platform does not exist in MIS (Agarwal and Lucas 2005; Benbasat and Weber 1996; Monod and Boland 2007; Orlikowski and Iacono 2001; Weber 2003). For the most part, MIS is seen as a field without a dominant paradigm.

An additional qualification is in order. The concept of paradigm, as Kuhn defines it, is derived from research in the physical sciences. This perspective may not serve well in the social sciences, where pluralistic models are more appropriate as the basis for understanding and analysis (Banville and Landry 1989). Given that MIS is a social science, multiple theories and approaches compete for attention and status (Avison et al. 2001; Benbasat and Weber 1996; Davis 2000; Robey 1996; Weber 1987). Thus, researchers contend that diversity and rival interpretations are the rule in MIS (Benbasat and Zmud 2003; Ives et al. 2004; Whinston and Geng 2004).

In keeping with this view, a set of articles deemed important to the field of MIS would cover a range of themes and theories (Alavi and Carlson 1992). Indeed, Baskerville and Myers (2002) declare (Table 1, p. 4) that research contributions in MIS include five bodies of knowledge, each with concepts, theories, processes, and applications.

Proposition 1: A set of exemplar MIS articles covers a wide range of themes.

To further our investigation into these exemplar MIS articles, and the range of themes and theories that are expressed, we perform an analysis of citation patterns. In particular, we attend to these patterns over time, in order to discern the prospect of a citation life cycle of the exemplar articles:

Proposition 2a: The average *expected life time* for a journal article (as expressed through the citations made to the article), is 11 years (Kronman 2007). Since an exemplar is outstanding by definition, the average life time is expected to exceed 11 years.

Proposition 2b: The dominant life cycle pattern for an exemplar article will take the form of a bell curve, illustrating the following *shape* over time: increase in number of citations, plateau/peak, and, finally, decrease.

Proposition 2c: Within the set of exemplars, we expect that articles that reflect *conceptual* contributions (e.g., theory and research methods) will be cited more frequently than articles that treat *contemporary* or "hot" issues (e.g., specific approaches and methods in consulting, or technology platforms and environments).

Proposition 2d: Within the set of exemplars, we expect that articles that reflect conceptual contributions will have a *longer lifetime* of citation activity than exemplars that treat contemporary or hot issues.

3 METHOD

Citation analysis involves several types of study, including direct citation, co-citation analysis, and bibliographic coupling.[3] Small (1973) observes that direct citation—the citing of an earlier document by a new document—and bibliographic coupling have received considerable attention. Bibliographic coupling links source documents. However, in measuring co-citation strength, researchers measure the degree of relationship or association between papers as perceived by the population of citing authors. Furthermore, because of this dependence on the citing authors, these patterns can change over time, just as vocabulary co-occurrences can change as subject fields evolve (Small 1973,

---

[3]Citation analysis should not be confused with classification analysis. Classification studies constitute one of the major approaches to investigating patterns in research (Vessey et al. 2002, 2005). One specific instance employs meta-analysis techniques. Meta-analysis uses the common variables and relationships in empirical data to discern general and overarching patterns across different studies. Another classification approach takes a broader perspective and consists of analysis of topic or subject matter. This process involves selecting a topic and reviewing many journals and conference proceedings in order to find evidence of patterns, trends, similarities, and differences. The articles considered in a topical analysis may be either quantitative or qualitative and need not adhere to any common method (Larsen and Levine 2007).

p. 265). Small observes that many information scientists focus attention on the operation of document retrieval systems serving scientists in various fields. The scientists who are served by these systems comprise an *invisible college* (Crane 1972)—networks of scientists "in frequent communication with one another and involved with highly specialized subject matters" (Small 1980, p. 183).

Culnan and Swanson (1986) use citation analysis to measure how MIS is evolving as a standalone discipline separate from its foundation disciplines of computer science, management science, and organization behavior. Their analysis studied 271 articles across seven outlets (six journals and one conference proceedings) over the period of 1980–1984. They concluded that (1) MIS remains less established than its foundation disciplines, (2) MIS is growing and maturing in terms of output and cited references, and (3) there is no consensus as to a body of work integral to the field. Culnan (1986) examines trends in MIS research, and observes that MIS management issues have emerged as a subfield. Moreover, the traditional emphasis on technology and technical issues has been displaced by a strong organizational and managerial focus. Culnan considers the intellectual structure of MIS research and, based on co-citation analysis, she identifies five invisible colleges (or informal clusters of research activity): foundations, psychological approaches to MIS design and use, MIS management, organizational approaches to MIS design and use, and curriculum.

Citation analysis remains a popular means to investigate the nature of the discipline. For example, Katerattanakul and Hong (2003) assess the quality of *MIS Quarterly* and compare this assessment to other journals of other disciplines. They conclude that *MISQ* ranks favorably in comparison with specialty journals and respectably among general journals (of specific disciplines). More recently, Straub (2006) summarizes citation research activity and comments on its contribution to understanding the evolution of the discipline.

In creating our own citation data, we employed four steps: (1) we defined a portfolio of exemplar MIS articles, (2) we identified any articles which cited these exemplars, (3) we prepared data for keyword analysis of exemplar articles, and (4) we prepared the citation data, including the analysis of life-cycle patterns. These steps are described below in chronological order.

Step 1: Defining a Portfolio of Exemplar MIS Articles

While many reports on journal quality and ranking exist (Pfeffers and Ya 2003), we were unable to locate a definitive list of classic or seminal MIS articles. We employed two approaches for compiling our list of exemplar MIS articles: (1) award winning articles and (2) evaluation by peers. First, our sample of award winning articles was drawn from *MIS Quarterly* "articles of the year" and Society for Information Management (SIM) competition-winner articles. Some might criticize the inclusion of SIM articles; however, the ongoing debate on the relevance of MIS indicates that practitioner-oriented material is important. Similarly, *MIS Quarterly* no longer distinguishes between "practice" and "science" articles.

For the period 1993–1999, *MISQ* named eight articles of the year. For the period 1994-2000, five SIM competition articles were named. Henceforth, these are referred to as "award articles."

Table 1. Peer-Nominated Articles and the Journals in Which They Appear

# of Peer Nominated Articles	Journal Title
7	*MIS Quarterly*
6	*Management Science*
3	*Communications of the ACM*
2	*IBM Systems Journal*
2	*Information Systems Research*
1	*Accounting, Management and Information*
1	*European Journal of Information Systems*
1	*Harvard Business Review*

Note: The data for this table are based on entries 14 through 36 in Appendix A.

Second, we reflected that peers might have their personal MIS research article favorites. We identified 17 peers who were well known in the community.[4] The 17 peers were contacted by e-mail and asked to nominate their "top four" classic or influential articles in the field of MIS. After one e-mail reminder, 15 had responded. Two of the 15 respondents felt they could not nominate any articles, leaving us with 13 peers who identified 24 contributions. One of these 24 nominations was dropped, since it was a book, leaving us with 23 "peer-nominated articles" (see Appendix A for details.) None of the award articles were peer nominated. We refer to the grand total of 36 articles as "exemplar articles"—consisting of the two categories of award articles (13) and peer-nominated articles (23).

MIS Quarterly is the dominant outlet, having published 20 of the 36 exemplar articles. The 23 peer-nominated articles were published in the journals identified in Table 1.

As Table 1 shows, *MIS Quarterly* and *Management Science* have together published more than 50 percent of the peer-nominated articles. All of the journals are rated as high quality publication outlets by MIS academics (AIS World MIS Journal Rankings[5]). These journals are also predominately published in the United States.

Step 2: Locating the Journals Citing Our 36 MIS Exemplar Articles

In this activity, we looked at the 36 exemplar articles and where they were cited in other (articles in) journals. The social citation index was used for this purpose; it is the dominant, authoritative source for scientific research. In all, 421 journals were identified as having articles citing one or more of the 36 exemplar articles.

---

[4]We do not claim that our list of peers is indisputable. Some of the peers requested anonymity with regard to participation, article nominations, and comments. Therefore, peer names are not made available.

[5]Available at http://www.isworld.org/csaunders.rankings.htm (accessed March 12, 2008).

Our data are best represented in the form of a large table: with the 36 exemplar articles (columns) and the 421 journals, representing articles, that cited these exemplar articles (rows). The intersecting cell for each entry shows the number of times that X journal has cited Y exemplar article from the time of publication until the end of data collection, August 2006. The raw data are available from the authors.

Step 3: Preparing Data for Keyword Analysis of Exemplar Articles

Given Proposition 1, which asserts that "a set of exemplar MIS articles covers a wide range of themes," we performed a keyword analysis of the exemplar articles. We created a table, with 149 keywords (rows) and our 36 exemplar articles (columns). In the analysis section we report on common terminology and on the frequency of use.

Step 4: Preparing the Citation Life Cycle Data

Once the table of exemplar articles and journals citing these exemplars was complete, we attempted to "roll up" the data for citation frequency, according to time periods. We attempted an analysis based on a five year increment, as well as an analysis based on a shorter period of one year. Subsequently, we settled on a middle ground—a three year increment. The three year period allowed us sufficient detail to see the development patterns occurring over time, without excessive granularity. By necessity, in our analysis, more recent exemplars have an abbreviated history.

4   ANALYSIS

Proposition 1 postulates that the 36 exemplar MIS articles would cover a wide range of themes. Our analysis of keywords demonstrates the wide variety of topics and themes that are dealt with in the exemplar articles. A total of 149 unique keywords were identified, with minimal overlap of 1.2 occurrences. Only seven keywords occur three times. Moreover, the keywords which occur most often are generic in nature (e.g., management information systems, case study, information technology, management, and systems analysis).

Inspection of article titles (see Appendix A) and abstracts shows that each article addresses a separate issue. In fact, the diversity is so great that no obvious patterns or threads are evident. We find that Proposition 1 is strongly supported. It is possible that the field of MIS is not diverse but rather our methods for selection of exemplar MIS articles have lead us to this result. We cannot adjust for the bias but simply observe that none of the articles in our sample were nominated by more than one source (award article or peer). If some agreement on exemplar articles existed, some degree of overlap in nominations would have occurred. The lack of multiple, overlapping nominations strengthens our belief that accepting Proposition 1 is correct.

According to Kronman (2007), the average expected life time for a journal article (as expressed through the citations made to the article), is 11 years. Since an exemplar is "outstanding" by definition, our Proposition 2a asserts that the lifetime is expected to exceed 11 years. We define a citation life time as beginning with the exemplar's year of publication and ending when no further citations are being made to that exemplar. In addition, since our data collection stopped in 2006, we can only say that our articles of 11 years and younger remain active, and their future citation patterns are unknown.

The 36 exemplar articles range in age from 7 years to 30 years old. Six papers are under 11 years old. (These six articles are excluded from analysis for Proposition 2a because they are under 11 years of age *and* still active. Had they become inactive they would have been included in the analysis for Proposition 2a.) Of the 30 remaining, only one article of 23 years age became "inactive"—and was no longer being cited as of 2004. Of the same 30, the average number of years of citation activity is 16.7. Thus, the citation life time exceeds eleven years and Proposition 2a is supported.

Overall, it is important to note that the number of citations made to the 36 exemplars increases over time (the correlation between year of publication and total number of citations made is $r = -0.35$, where $p = 0.04$). The rate of citation activity over time is considered in Proposition 2b.

Our Proposition 2b is focused on the life-cycle patterns of citations in the exemplar articles. We postulate that the dominant life-cycle pattern for an exemplar article will take the form of a bell curve, illustrating the following shape over time: increase in number of citations, plateau or peak, and, finally, decrease. The shape that we predict is different from Kronman's (2007) slope of consistent decline, from year of publication until the end of citation activity.

To detect life-cycle patterns, we required a minimum 12 year period of citation activity (or four increments of three years). Our scrutiny of exemplars with shorter citation life times yielded discrete data points rather than distinctive patterns. As a result, 13 exemplars were omitted from the citation life-cycle analysis (having fewer than four increments of three years). For each of the remaining 23 exemplars, we reviewed the citation data over the 3 year increments. We examined the sequence for each to discern its development over time—and whether the citation data reflected an increase, plateau or peak, and decrease. We were looking for trends or changes of some magnitude (a minimum of 10 percent change between neighboring values). This analysis was largely quantitative; however, it was necessary to interpret permutations of change. For example, in some instances, we saw small differences in numerical value and we were reluctant to label these as an increase or decrease. Similarly, in a string of values such as 25, 14, and 25, we elected to interpret this as a plateau rather than as a decrease followed by an increase.

For the most part, we find that Proposition 2b is supported. The results of the analysis demonstrate that 18 out of the 23 exemplars follow this bell-shaped pattern. Among the five exceptions, we observed two variations. Most notably, four articles enjoyed a sustained increase in citation activity throughout their life cycles, up until 2006. Among these four is Daft and Lengel's article from 1986, which is by far the most widely cited of all the exemplars, with 712 citations over a period of 21 years. The final variation consists of one exemplar with a total of 9 citations over 23 years, represented in a long plateau pattern.

Our Proposition 2c states that within the set of 36 exemplars, we expect that articles that reflect *conceptual* contributions (e.g., theory and research methods) will be cited more frequently than articles that treat *contemporary* or hot issues (e.g., specific approaches and

Table 2. Summary of Propositions

Prop. #	Proposition Text	Test Result
P1	A set of exemplar MIS articles will cover a wide range of themes.	Supported
P2a	The average expected lifetime for a journal article (as expressed through the citations made to the article), is 11 years. Since an exemplar is outstanding by definition, the average lifetime is expected to exceed 11 years.	Supported
P2b	The dominant life cycle pattern for an exemplar article will take the form of a bell curve, illustrating the following shape over time: increase in number of citations, plateau/peak, and, finally, decrease.	Largely supported
P2c	Within the set of exemplars, we expect that articles that reflect conceptual contributions (e.g., theory and research methods) will be cited more frequently than articles that treat contemporary or "hot" issues (e.g., specific approaches and methods in consulting, or technology platforms and environments).	Not supported
P2d	Within the set of exemplars, we expect that articles that reflect conceptual contributions will have a longer lifetime of citation activity than exemplars that treat contemporary or hot issues.	Supported

methods in consulting, or technology platforms and environments). We used the title, abstract, and keywords from each exemplar to decide upon its orientation—whether conceptual or contemporary. This process of inspection resulted in a determination of 25 conceptual and 11 contemporary exemplars. The one way ANOVA test yielded an f value = 1.69, where $p = 0.20$. Consequently, Proposition 2c is not supported.

The authors formulated Proposition 2d to investigate whether exemplars that reflected conceptual contributions would have a longer lifetime of citation activity than exemplars that treated contemporary or hot issues. The result of this one way ANOVA yielded an f value = 4.93, where $p = 0.03$. The mean value for conceptual articles is 17.6 years, and the mean value for contemporary articles is 12.6 years.

The propositions and test results are summarized in Table 2.

5   DISCUSSION

The present study has met with many challenges. Our approach to the identification of exemplar MIS articles may be biased. *MIS Quarterly* may have selected its articles of the year for any number of reasons. A similar concern also applies to the peer nominations. Peers were not chosen by an expert panel; rather, they are a convenience sample. More profoundly, the present effort builds on the assumption that there exists, at least to some degree, a unified field called MIS—and that we are capable of making judgments about it based on exemplars and associated citation activity.

As we have indicated, there is a small community conducting and evaluating citation research. Starbuck (2007) investigates the citations of papers published between 1981 and 2004 in 509 journals and finds an average of 0.8 citations per paper in business and management and of 0.7 in business finance. Hence, much academic research is *not* contributing in intended ways to science (Rynes et al. 2001; Van de Ven 2007). In an attempt to measure MIS "research importance," Loebbecke et al. (2007) report on the average number of citations per article, in six journals, from 1996 to 2005. The total number of articles in their dataset is 1,178. They find that the articles in *MISQ* have the greatest number of citations; however, these are still surprisingly few over the 10 year period (MISQ = 21.8, ISR = 14.5, EJIS = 4.5, ISJ = 3.8, JSIS = 3.7 and JIT = 3.0).

Van de Ven (2007) supports the position that academics rarely cite each others' work. More generally, he extends this argument and asserts that the gulf between science and practice is widening. On the one hand, scientists fail to put their knowledge into practice, and on the other hand, managers are not taking responsibility for seeking out pertinent literature or reflecting and recording the value and utility of their own lessons for applied research. He concludes that "organizations are not learning fast enough to keep up with changing times" (p. 2).

The present study uses exemplar articles as its sample. However, we are able to compare and contrast our findings with that of others conducting citation research on publications, more broadly, in MIS and the social sciences (e.g., Culnan and Swanson 1986; Kronman 2007; Loebbecke et al. 2007; Starbuck 2007; Vessey et al. 2002, 2005). Our exemplars appear to have greater impact than is found in these other studies. The total number of citations made to the exemplars is, on average, 125.2 (1977–2006). We found that only one of our exemplars had entered an inactive period (no longer being cited). The remaining 35 exemplars are still being cited, and their lifetime extends into the future. At the outset, we knew that the exemplars were outstanding by definition—by virtue of the awards or peer nominations that they received. As a result of our analysis and comparisons, we can confirm that they are also outstanding in their impact.

We have found that citation patterns are rarely investigated as they evolve over time. In addition, the pattern over time is more complex than acknowledged. The bell shape that we found depicts a more nuanced transformation than is reflected in a simple linear decline (Kronman 2007). For example, we discovered that sometimes plateaus persist for a long period and may incorporate smaller modulations and fluctuations. Also noteworthy: several exemplars show a consistent pattern of increased citation activity, as is dramatically portrayed in the case of Daft and Lengel (1986).

We discovered that *conceptual* and *contemporary* exemplars are not significantly different with respect to the volume/frequency of citation activity. However, conceptual studies endure and have a longer lifetime of citation activity than contemporary studies. Logically, the contemporary exemplars may have a more limited and concentrated use—in light of their being focused on hot topics. In circumstances like this, the whole pattern of citation activity may be compressed—incorporating a quicker rise in the number of citations and then a faster fall. Future research is needed to further explore the distinction between conceptual and contemporary articles.

Additionally, to better understand the role that citation plays in research, it would be useful to conduct studies that combine citation and classification methods. This would help us to understand the different circumstances under which articles are cited—whether for background, to establish credibility, or as an essential element in formulating the research. We can only understand so much about citation activity by counting things.

6 CONCLUSIONS

The present research examines the role of MIS exemplar articles through the lens and method of citation analysis. The 36 exemplar articles, representing outstanding MIS research contributions, is a convenience sample. We have no explicit definition of "exemplar MIS article" characteristics. Rather, our acceptance of *MIS Quarterly* award articles and peer nominations is an example of referring judgment to other authoritative sources without control over selection procedure or evaluation criteria.

This paper represents the first phase of our research into MIS and its reference disciplines as revealed through MIS exemplars and their citation patterns. Our findings are limited to the exemplars and their citations, and we do not address the matter of referencing disciplines or subfields. This is the focus of the next phase of the research. In this initial phase, we have found that our MIS exemplars do, indeed, cover a wide range of themes. This aligns with established views: many have already addressed the matter of diversity in MIS—and its promise and pitfalls. Some hanker for a core while others view the wide range of ideas as a healthy sign of possibilities, and assert that we must innovate and allow "many flowers to bloom." However, the question remains: When is the level of diversity so extreme that dialogue becomes noise? When is openness counterproductive?

We discovered that the average lifetime for an exemplar article (as expressed through the citations made to the article) is 17 years, compared with an 11 year expected life time, in general, for journal articles. We also ascertained that the dominant life-cycle pattern for an exemplar takes the form of a bell curve, illustrating an increase in the number of citations, followed by a plateau/peak, and, finally, a decrease in the number of citations. In terms of exemplar type, we refuted the proposition that articles that were conceptual in nature would be cited more frequently than articles treating contemporary or hot issues. However, we were able to confirm that conceptual contributions have a longer lifetime of citation activity than contemporary exemplars.

In summary, citation analysis is largely objective, factual, and based on data. However, interpretation is required in framing the research questions and facts, and in analyzing and communicating the results. This method offers a single, powerful lens on the dynamics of the discipline, but it is also a partial view. We recognize that, by itself, citation research is insufficient to characterize the workings of the discipline—as it does not come to grips with the substantive content that makes up the datasets and dialogue. To date, citation analysis has been employed to a limited extent since it is difficult and cumbersome to perform. The advent of tools and electronic databases offers dramatic opportunity for conducting this type of research in the future.

Acknowledgments

The authors would like to thank Ira Monarch, Sheila Rosenthal, and Ronald Weber for their helpful suggestions and support on earlier versions of this article.

References

Agarwal, R., and Lucas, Jr., H. C. 2005. "The Information Systems Identity Crisis: Focusing on High-Visibility and High-Impact Research," *MIS Quarterly* (29:3), pp. 381-398.

Alavi, M., and Carlson, P. 1992. "A Review of MIS Research and Disciplinary Development," *Journal of Management Information Systems* (8:4), Spring, pp. 45-62.

Avison, D., Fitzgerald, G., and Powell, P. 2001. "Reflections on Information Systems Practice, Education, and Research: 10 Years of the Information Systems Journal," *Information Systems Journal* (11:1), pp. 3-22.

Banville, C., and Landry, M. 1989. "Can the Field of MIS be Disciplined?," *Communications of the ACM* (32:1), pp. 48-60.

Baskerville, R. L., and Meyers, M. D. 2002. "Information Systems as a Reference Discipline," *MIS Quarterly* (26:1), pp. 1-14.

Bauer, K., and Bakkalbasi, N. 2005. "An Examination of Citation Counts in a New Scholarly Communication Environment," *D-Lib Magazine 11* (9), September (available at http://www.dlib.org//dlib/september05/bauer/09bauer.html; accessed March 12, 2008).

Benbasat, I., and Weber, R. 1996. "Research Commentary: Rethinking 'Diversity' in Information Systems Research," *Information Systems Research* (7:4), pp. 389-399.

Benbasat, I., and Zmud, R.W. 2003. "The Identity Crisis Within the IS Discipline: Defining and Communicating the Discipline's Core Properties," *MIS Quarterly* (27:2), pp. 183-194.

Crane, D. 1972. *Invisible Colleges: Diffusion of Knowledge in Scientific Communities*, Chicago: University of Chicago Press.

Cheon, M. J., Grover, V., and Sabherwal, R. 1993. "The Evolution of Empirical Research in IS: A Study in IS Maturity," *Information & Management* (24:3), pp. 107-119.

Culnan, M. 1986. "The Intellectual Structure of Management Information Systems, 1972-1982: A Co-citation Analysis," *Management Science* (32:2), pp. 156-172.

Culnan, M. J., and Swanson, E. B. 1986. "Research in Management Information Systems, 1980-1984: Points of Work and Reference," *MIS Quarterly* (10:3), pp. 289-302.

Daft, R. L., and Lengel, R. H. 1986. "Organizational Information Requirements: Media Richness and Structural Design," *Management Science* (32:5), pp. 554-571.

Davis, G. B. 2000. "Information Systems Conceptual Foundations: Looking Backward and Forward," in *Organizational and Social Perspectives on Information Technology*, R. Baskerville, J. Stage, and J. I. DeGross (eds.), Norwell, MA: Kluwer Academic Publishers, pp. 61-82.

Garfield, E. 1987. "Citation Data is Subtle Stuff: A Primer on Evaluating a Scientist's Performance," *The Scientist* (1:19), April, pp. 229-230.

Grover, V., Ayyagari, R., Gokhale, R., Lim, J., and Coffey, J. 2006a. "A Citation Analysis of the Evolution and State of Information Systems within a Constellation of Reference Disciplines," *Journal of the Association for Information Systems* (7:5), May, pp. 270-324.

Grover, V., Ayyagari, R., Gokhale, R., Lim, J., and Coffey, J. 2006b. "About Reference Disciplines and Reference Differences: A Critique of Wade et al.," *Journal of the Association for Information Systems* (7:5), May, pp. 336-350.

Holsapple, C. W., Johnson, L. E., Manakyan, H., and Tanner, J. 1994. "Business Computing Research Journals: A Normalized Citation Analysis," *Journal of Management Information Systems* (11:1), Summer, pp. 131-140.

Ives, B., Parks, M. S., Porra, J., and Silva, L. 2004. "Phylogeny and Power in the IS Domain: A Response to Benbasat and Zmud's Call for Returning to the IT Artifact," *Journal of the Association for Information Systems* (5:3), March, pp.108-124.

Jacso, P. 2005. "Google Scholar and the Scientist," available at http://www2.hawaii.edu/~jacso/extra/gs/; accessed March 12, 2008.

Katerattanakul, P., Han, B., and Rea, A. 2006. "Is Information Systems a Reference Discipline," *Communications of the ACM* (49:5), pp. 114-118.

Katerattanakul, P., and Hong, S. 2003. "Quality and Knowledge Contribution of MISQ: A Citation Analysis," *Communications of the Association for Information Systems* (11), pp. 271-288.

Kronman. U. 2007. "Bibliometrics—What, Why, and How?," available at http://infomgt.bi.no/research/tor-is-concepts/Kronman-Ulf-Bibliometrics.pdf; accessed March 12, 2008.

Kuhn, T. S. 1970. *The Structure of Scientific Revolutions* (2nd ed.), Chicago: The University of Chicago Press.

Larsen, T. J. 1998. "Information Systems Innovation: A Framework for Research and Practice," in *Information Systems Innovation and Diffusion: Issues and Direction*, T. J. Larsen and E. McGuire (eds.), Hershey, PA: Idea Group Publishing, pp. 411-434.

Larsen, T. J., and Levine, L. 2005. "Searching for Management Information Systems: Coherence and Change in the Discipline," *Information Systems Journal* (15:4), pp. 357-381.

Larsen, T. J., and Levine, L. 2007. "The Identity, Dynamics, and Diffusion of MIS," in *Organizational Dynamics of Technology-Based Innovation: Diversifying the Research Agenda*, T. McMaster, T. Wastell, D. Ferneley, and J. I. DeGross (eds.), New York: Springer, pp. 163-177.

Loebbecke, C., Berthod, O., and Huyskens, C. 2007. "Research Importance in the Information Systems Field: A Citation Analysis," in *Proceedings of the 28th International Conference on Information Systems*, Montreal, Canada, December 9-12, pp. 1-15.

Lyytinen, K., and King, J. L. 2004. "Nothing at the Center?: Academic Legitimacy in the Information Systems Field," *Journal of the Association for Information Systems* (5:6), June, pp. 220-246.

Monod, E., and Boland, R. J. 2007. "Editorial: Special Issue on Philosophy and Epistemology: A 'Peter Pan Syndrome'?," *Information Systems Journal* (17:2), pp. 133-141.

Mylonopoulos, N. A., and Theorharakis, V. 2001. "Global Perceptions of IS Journals," *Communications of the ACM* (44:9), pp. 29-33.

Myers, M. D. 2002. "The IS Core–VIII: Defining the Core Properties of the IS Discipline: Not Yet, Not Now," *Communications of the Association for Information Systems* (12), pp. 582-587.

Orlikowski, W. J., and Baroudi, J. J. 1991. "Studying Information Technology in Organizations: Research Approaches and Assumptions," *Information Systems Research* (2:1), pp. 1-28.

Orlikowski, W. J., and Iacono, C. S. 2001. "Research Commentary: Desperately Seeking the 'IT' in IT Research—A Call to Theorizing the IT Artifact," *Information Systems Research* (12:2), June, pp. 121-134.

Perkel, J. M. 2005. "The Future of Citation Analysis," *The Scientist* (19:20), October (available at http://www.garfield.library.upenn.edu/papers/futureofcitationanalysists102405.pdf).

Pfeffer, J. 1993. "Barriers to the Advance of Organizational Science: Paradigm Development as a Dependent Variable," *Academy of Management Review* (18:4), pp. 599-620.

Pfeffers, K., and Ya, T. 2003. "Identifying and Evaluating the Universe of Outlets for Information Systems Research: Ranking the Journals," *The Journal of Information Technology Theory and Application* (5:1), pp. 63-84.

Ritzer, G. 1975. "Sociology: A Multiple Paradigm Science," *The American Sociologist* (10), August, pp. 156-167.

Robey, D. 1996. "Research Commentary: Diversity in Information Systems Research: Threat, Promise, and Responsibility," *Information Systems Research* (7:4), pp. 400-408.

Rynes, S. L., Bartunek, J. M., and Daft, R. L. 2001. "Across the Great Divide: Knowledge Creation and Transfer Between Practitioners and Academics," *Academy of Management Journal* (44:2), pp. 340-355.

Small, H. 1973. "Co-citation in the Scientific Literature: A New Measure of the Relationship Between Two Documents," *Journal of the American Society for Information Science*, July-August, 265-269.

Small, H. 1978. "Cited Documents as Concept Symbols," *Social Studies of Science* (8:3), August, pp. 327-340.

Small, H. 1980. "Co-citation Context Analysis and the Structure of Paradigms," *The Journal of Documentation* (36:3), pp. 183-196.

Starbuck, W. H. 2007. "What the Numbers Mean," available at http://pages.stern.nyu.edu/~wstarbuc/whatmean.html; accessed March 12, 2008).

Straub, D. 2006. "The Value of Scientometric Studies: An Introduction to a Debate on IS as a Reference Discipline," *Journal of the Association for Information Systems* (7:5), May, pp. 241-246.

Van de Ven, A. H. 2007. *Engaged Scholarship: A Guide for Organizational and Social Research*, Oxford, England: Oxford University Press.

Vessey, I., Ramesh, V., and Glass, R. L. 2002. "Research in Information Systems: An Empirical Study of Diversity in the Discipline and Its Journals," *Journal of Management Information Systems* (19:2), Fall, pp. 129-174.

Vessey, I., Ramesh, V., and Glass, R. L. 2005. "A Unified Classification System for Research in the Computing Disciplines," *Information & Software Technology* (47:4), pp. 245-255.

Wade, M., Biehl, M., and Kim, H. 2006a. "Information Systems is 'Not' a Reference Discipline (And What We Can Do About It)," *Journal of the Association for Information Systems* (7:5), May, pp. 247-268.

Wade, M., Biehl, M., and Kim, H. 2006b. "If the Tree of IS Knowledge Falls in a Forest, Will Anyone Hear? A Commentary on Gover et al.," *Journal of the Association for Information Systems* (7:5), May, pp. 326-334.

Walstrom, K. A., and Hardgrave, B. C. 2001. "Forums for Information Systems Scholars: III," *Information & Management* (39:2), pp. 117-124.

Weber, R. 1987. "Toward a Theory of Artifacts: A Paradigmatic Base for Information Systems Research," *Journal of Information Systems*, Spring, pp. 3-19.

Weber, R. 2003. "Editor's Comments: Still Desperately Seeking the IT Artifact," *MIS Quarterly* (27:2), pp. iii-xi.

Whinston, A. B., and Geng, X. 2004. "Operationalizing the Essential Role of the Information Technology Artifact in Information Systems Research: Gray Area, Pittfalls, and the Importance of Strategic Ambiguity," *MIS Quarterly* (28:2), pp. 149-159.

About the Authors

Tor J. Larsen holds an MA in Systems Thinking from the University of Lancaster, England (1975) and earned his Ph.D. in Management Information Systems (MIS) from the University of Minnesota (1989). He is professor in Knowledge Management and holds the position of Senior Vice President at the Norwegian School of Management. He has served as an associate editor for *MIS Quarterly*. Dr. Larsen has published widely, for example in *Information & Management*, *Journal of MIS*, and *Information Systems Journal*. He is a member of AIS and IFIP WG8.2 and WG8.6. In 2006, he was program co-chair for the WG8.6 Working Conference on the "Transfer and Diffusion of IT for Organizational Resilience." Dr. Larsen's research interests are in the areas of managers' use of information, knowledge management, innovation, diffusion, representation, and innovation outcome. He can be reached at Tor.J.Larsen@BI.NO.

Linda Levine is a senior member of the technical staff at Carnegie Mellon University's Software Engineering Institute. Her research focuses on acquisition of software intensive systems, agile software development, system interoperability, diffusion of innovations, and knowledge integration and transfer. She holds a Ph.D. in Rhetoric from Carnegie Mellon University. She is a member of the Association for Information Systems, IEEE Computer Society, National Communication Association, and cofounder and Chair of IFIP Working Group 8.6 on Diffusion, Transfer and Implementation of Information Technology. Contact her at ll@sei.cmu.edu.

APPENDIX A. LIST OF EXEMPLAR MIS ARTICLES IN OUR SAMPLE

MIS Quarterly, Article of the Year:

[1] Klein, H. K., and Myers, M. D. 1999. "A Set of Principles for Conducting and Evaluating Interpretive Field Studies in Information Systems," *MIS Quarterly* (23:1), pp. 67-94.

[2] Kumar, K., van Dissel, H.G., and Belli, P. 1998. "The Merchant of Prato – Revisited. Toward a Third Rationality of Information Systems," *MIS Quarterly* (22:2), pp. 199-226.

[3] Ngwenyama, O. K., and Lee, A. S. 1997. "Communication Richness in Electronic Mail: Critical Social Theory and the Contextuality of Meaning," *MIS Quarterly* (21:2), pp. 145-167.

[4] Hitt, L. M., and Brynfolfsson, E. 1996. "Productivity, Business Profitability, and Consumer Surplus: Three Different Measures of Information Technology Value," *MIS Quarterly* (20:2), pp. 121-142.

[5] Mukhopadhyay, T., Kekre, S., and Kalathur, S. 1995. "Business Value of Information Technology: A Study of Electronic Data Interchange," *MIS Quarterly* (19:2), pp. 137-156.

[6] Leidner, D. E., and Jarvenpaa, S. L. 1995. "The Use of Information Technology to Enhance Management School Education: A Theoretical View," *MIS Quarterly* (19:3), pp. 265-281.

[7] Hess, C. M., and Kemerer, C. F. 1994. "Computerized Loan Origination Systems: An Industry Case Study of the Electronic Markets Hypothesis," *MIS Quarterly* (18:3), pp. 251-274.

[8] Orlikowski, W. 1993. "Case Tools as Organizational Change: Investigating Incremental and Radical Changes in Systems Development," *MIS Quarterly* (17:3), pp. 309-340.

MIS Quarterly, SIM Best Article:

[9] Cooper, B. L., Watson, H. J., and Goodhue, D. L. 2000. "Data Warehousing Supports Corporate Strategy at First American Corporation," *MIS Quarterly* (24:4), pp. 547-567.

[10] Roepke, R. P. 2000. "Aligning the IT Human Resource with Business Vision: The Leadership Initiative at 3M," *MIS Quarterly* (24:2), pp. 327-343.

[11] El Sawy, O. A., Malhotra, A., Gosain, S., and Young, K. M. 1999. "IT-Intensive Value Innovation in the Electronic Economy: Insight from Marshall Industries," *MIS Quarterly* (23:3), pp. 305-334.

[12] Cross, J., Earl, M. J., and Sampler, J. L. 1997. "Transformation of the IT Function at British Petroleum," *MIS Quarterly* (21:4), pp. 401-423.

[13] Caron, J. R. 1994. "Business Reengineering at CIGNA Corporation," *MIS Quarterly* (18:3), pp. 233-250.

Peer Nominated Articles:

[14] Markus, L., and Robey, D. 1988. "Information Technology and Organizational Change: Causal Structure in Theory and Research," *Management Science* (34:5), pp. 583-598.

[15] DeLone, W., and McLean, E. 1992. "Information Systems Success: The Quest for the Dependent Variable," *Information Systems Research* (3:1), pp. 60-95.

[16] Hirschheim, R., and Klein, H. 1989. "Four Paradigms of Information Systems Development," *Communication of the ACM* (32:10), pp. 1199-1216.

[17] Hammer, M. 1990. "Reengineering Work: Don't Automate, Obliterate," *Harvard Business Review* (68:4), July-August, pp. 104-112.

[18] Henderson, J. C., and Venkatraman, N. 1993. "Strategic Alignment: Leveraging Information Technology for Transforming Organizations," *IBM Systems Journal* (32:1), pp. 4-16.

[19] Myers, M. D. 1997. "Qualitative Research in Information Systems," *MIS Quarterly* (21:2), pp. 241-242.

[20] Brancheau, J. C., and Wetherbe, J. C. 1987. "Key Issues in Information Systems Management," *MIS Quarterly* (11:1), pp.23-45.

[21] Goodhue, D., and Wybo, M. D. 1992. "The Impact of Data Integration on the Cost and Benefits of Information Systems," *MIS Quarterly* (16:3), pp. 293-311.

[22] Ives, B., and Jarvenpaa, S. L. 1991. "Applications of Global Information Technology— Key Issues for Management," *MIS Quarterly* (15:1), pp. 33-49.

[23] Malone, T. W., Yates, J., and Benjamin, R. I. 1987. "Electronic Markets and Electronic Hierarchies," *Communications of the ACM* (30:6), pp. 484-497.

[24] Lee, A. S. 1989. "A Scientific Methodology for MIS Case Studies," *MIS Quarterly* (13:1), pp. 33-50.

[25] Daft, R. L., and Lengel, R. H. 1986. "Organizational Information Requirements: Media Richness and Structural Design," *Management Science* (32:5), pp. 554-571.

[26] DeSanctis, G., and Gallupe, R. B. 1987. "A Foundation for the Study of Group Decision Support Systems," *Management Science* (33:5), pp. 589-609.

[27] Sprague, R. H. 1980. "A Framework for the Development of Decision Support Systems," *MIS Quarterly* (4:4), pp. 1-26.

[28] Dickson, G. W., Senn, J. A., and Chervany, N. L. 1977. "Research in Management Information Systems: The Minnesota Experiments," *Management Science* (23:9), pp. 913-923.

[29] Ives, B., Hamilton, S., and Davis, G. B. 1980. "A Framework for Research in Computer-Based Management Information Systems," *Management Science* (26:9), pp. 910-934.

[30] Boland, Jr., R. J. 1984. "Sense-Making of Accounting Data as a Technique of Organizational Diagnosis," *Management Science* (30:7), pp. 868-882.

[31] Hirschheim, R., Klein, H. K., and Lyytinen, K. 1996. "Exploring the Intellectual Structures of Information Systems Development: A Social Action Theoretical Analysis," *Accounting, Management and Information* (6:1/2), pp. 1-64.

[32] Orlikowski, W. J., and Baroudi, J. J. 1991. "Studying Information Technology in Organizations: Research Approaches and Assumptions," *Information Systems Research* (2:1), pp. 1-28.

[33] Avergou, C., Siemer, J., and Bjørn-Andersen, N. 1999. "The Academic Field of Information Systems in Europe," *European Journal of Information Systems* (8:2), pp. 136-153.

[34] Markus, L. 1983. "Power, Politics and MIS Implementation," *Communications of the ACM* (26:6), pp. 430-444.

[35] Bostrom, R. P., and Heinen, J. S. 1977. "MIS Problems and Failures: A Socio-Technical Perspective Part I: Causes," *MIS Quarterly* (1:3), pp. 17-32.

[36] Davis, G. 1982. "Strategies for Information Requirements Determination," *IBM Systems Journal* (21:1), pp. 4-30.

[37][6] Checkland, P. B., and Scholes, J. 1990. *Soft Systems Methodology in Action*, West Sussex, England: John Wiley & Sons, Ltd.

---

[6]The nomination is a book, hence not found in the social citation index and excluded from the analysis.

3 UNDERSTANDING THE DIFFUSION AND ADOPTION OF TELECOMMUNICATION INNOVATIONS: What We Know and What We Don't Know

Heidi Tscherning
Jan Damsgaard
Copenhagen Business School
Frederiksberg, Denmark

Abstract   *This paper provides a systematic account about what we know and what we don't know about the diffusion and adoption of telecommunication innovations. As our sample, we obtained research papers from IFIP 8.6 conferences, the International Conference on Information Systems, and the European Conference on Information Systems from the past 10 years concerning telecommunication innovation diffusion and adoption to examine what aspects of the diffusion and adoption process are accentuated or overlooked using a general view of the process. As our theoretical vehicle, we build a holistic framework that comprises the innovation, the unit of adoption, and their interaction as captured by demand pull and supply push forces. The framework also takes into account the environment that embeds the diffusion and adoption. We find that there are certain shortcomings in the existing research within the field that need to be addressed to provide a more comprehensive view of adoption and diffusion of telecommunication technologies.*

Keywords   Telecommunication, innovation, diffusion, adoption

1 INTRODUCTION

The success of the mobile phone has been unprecedented; from being almost unknown 15 years ago, most people in the developed world now own one or more mobile

Please use the following format when citing this chapter:

Tscherning, H., and Damsgaard, J., 2008, in IFIP International Federation for Information Processing, Volume 287, Open IT-Based Innovation: Moving Towards Cooperative IT Transfer and Knowledge Diffusion, eds. León, G., Bernardos, A., Casar, J., Kautz, K., and DeGross, J. (Boston: Springer), pp. 39-60.

phones. It has been embraced as the fourth technology carried by man—so in addition to the watch, the wallet, and the keys, we now also carry the mobile phone. Many people see the mobile phone as an extension of the self and in a sense we have become Cyborgs.[1]

The speed with which the mobile phone has spread has surprised most researchers. Today there are more than 3.3 billion mobile phone subscriptions in use in the world,[2] growing at the astonishing rate of 200 million phones per quarter. It is not something that is limited to the Western world, as the mobile phone spread is pandemic. By 2011, it is estimated that nearly everyone on earth will own a mobile phone.

Even though the mobile phone has claimed global victory, not all telecommunication innovations are adopted with the same pursuit. That may not in itself be surprising but it has proven quite difficult to predict which innovations will succeed and which will fail. To illustrate, some telecommunication innovations such as short message service have previously exceeded expectations in terms of speed of adoption while others, for example multimedia messaging service, have not met expectations at all. The same holds true for global system for mobile, which has been tremendously successful in many parts of the world, whereas universal mobile telecommunications system has been much less so, even though it has gained momentum more recently.

Scholars of diffusion and adoption have also focused on telecommunication innovations and many different theories have been put to the test of explaining the phenomenon with varying results (Blechar et al. 2008). There seems to be no synthesis or dominant theory that captures all relevant aspects of the telecommunication diffusion process adequately. Indeed, some may argue, there may not be one best theory that will fit all our needs for understanding different aspects of the diffusion process. We agree to that point of view and just observe that at the moment we do not have a systematic account of the experiences of using different theories. In a respond to this deficit, this paper synthesizes what we know and, by exclusion, what we do not know about the diffusion and adoption of telecommunication innovations, as we believe that contributions to the selected conferences for the past 10 years cover most important findings in this area. As an analytical tool we develop a framework based on an overall model of diffusion and adoption of innovation. All articles published in proceedings from IFIP 8.6, the European Conference on Information Systems, and the International Conference on Information Systems over the past 10 years that portray the diffusion and adoption of telecommunication innovations are analyzed using the framework to provide an overall picture of the accounts. We realize that not all of the papers on this topic have been published in these outlets, but they provide a large and broad sample of available accounts. The aim is to condense knowledge that can help scholars better navigate between theories and their explanatory power *vis-à-vis* the research question they seek to remedy.

To achieve this objective, this paper is composed as follows: It begins with an overview of telecommunication innovations, and the remarkable success of mobile

---

[1]The definition of a Cyborg is a cybernetic organism, a hybrid of machine and organism (Haraway 1991).

[2]Reuters, "Global Cellphone Penetration Reaches 50 pct," November 29, 2007, http://investing.reuters.co.uk/news/articleinvesting.aspx?type=media&storyID=nL29172095.

phones is especially noted. The subsequent sections present our research method, our model of diffusion an adoption, and a generic analytical tool for investigating diffusion and adoption literature. The investigative tool is then applied to all relevant papers from IFIP 8.6, ECIS, and ICIS from the past 10 years and an analysis is conducted. Finally, our results are condensed and final conclusions are drawn.

2 TELECOMMUNICATION INNOVATION

Since its discovery, telecommunication has changed our lives in many ways, both privately and professionally. From a diffusion and adoption point of view, the first installations suffered from a lack of critical mass. If only a few people had access to a telephone, there where few people to call and hence the benefits of adopting a telephone were limited. However, as more people adopted the telephone, the benefits of joining the adopters also increased. This phenomenon, where one additional adopter increases the utility of the other adopters, is labeled *network externalities* (conomides and Salop 1992; Shapiro and Varian 1999) or *network effects*. Once the basic universal fixed-line tele-communication infrastructure was in place, many subsequent telecommunication innova-tions shared the accomplishments and have, therefore, not had to establish critical mass by themselves (i.e., subsequent telecommunications piggy-backed on the success of the fixed-line network).

This is, for example, the case of the mobile phone, which is always connected to the omnipresent fixed-line telecommunication infrastructure. The mobile phone represents an interesting case in that it is not only a device for voice communication but it has evolved into a data communication tool and also, increasingly, into a sophisticated com-puting device that can offer many different services. As an example, many mobile phones bundle cameras, FM radio-receivers, instant messengers, music players, and internet browsers. This means that the mobile device is not a fixed, single purpose innovation but a multifaceted and open-ended device. Its adoption is, therefore, not an atomic event but something that stretches over time and is quite learning intensive; the adopter will probably never use all of the possibilities that the mobile device can offer.

From a diffusion and adoption perspective, this complicates the matter. What is really the innovation being adopted? At what point in time should we denote the inno-vation as adopted? Finally, it is worth noticing that the mobile phone has to compete with other devices or communication channels that the potential adopter already uses. So at any given time, an adopter chooses between different available alternatives to satisfy her needs (Blechar et al. 2006) and any diffusion and adoption theory that seeks to understand and predict the faith of a telecommunication innovation has to consider not only the innovation at hand but also the alternatives. It is imperative here to consider established standards and habits as captured by switching costs and lock-in effects (Shapiro and Varian 1999).

Telecommunication innovations have always been subject to regulation (Melody 1999; Petrazzeni 1995). This holds true for the right to establish infrastructure and also the right to offer telecommunication services upon such infrastructure. Even though the period from the mid 1980s until now has been characterized as a period of deregulation, it is worth noting that deregulation has only been achieved through heavy use of regulation and legislation. For example, to increase the competition in the mobile telephony market, a number of licenses have been offered. The number and terms of the licenses are regulated by some telecommunication office. This means that a diffusion and adoption theory that seeks to offer broad and relevant explanations of the telecommunication innovation has to consider the context in which the process occurs.

3   RESEARCH METHOD

To recapture, the objective of this paper is to examine what aspects of the diffusion process are accentuated or overlooked in the diffusion and adoption process as reported in scholarly work and thereby condense knowledge that can help in the navigation between theories and their explanatory power. The overall research method applied is a literature study. In order to explore the aim of the paper, we use the following elements in a holistic framework to probe and analyze the articles: type of technology, adopting unit, interaction between the innovation and adopting unit expressed as supply–push or demand–pull mechanisms, as well as the context in which the diffusion and adoption occurs. Furthermore, we also explore the underlying theory and cause and effect structure of each paper.

3.1 Data Collection

The search for articles was conducted at the AIS website to locate ECIS and ICIS papers from the past 10 years, and the key words included diffusion, adoption, innovation, telecommunication, mobile (service), UTAUT, technology acceptance, actor-network, network, institutional theory, critical mass, theory of reasoned action, and theory of planned behavior. The selection of these key words is based on the dominance they pose in diffusion and adoption research as well as the context in which this literature study is conducted. The search for IFIP 8.6 papers was conducted browsing through the last 10 years of proceedings identifying the same key words as for the ECIS and ICIS papers. Initially the combined search resulted in a total of 94 papers. However, after scanning the papers and eliminating those that were not specifically related to either a telecommunication technology or information and communication technologies in general that *could* include a telecommunication technology, we ended up with 36 papers.

Table 1. Number of Papers Investigated from the IFIP 8.6, ECIS, and ICIS Conferences, 1998–2007

	1998	1999	2000	2001	2002	2003	2004	2005	2006	2007
Conferences	0	NC	NC	0	1	1	1	0	1	2
IFIP 8.6	0			0	1	1	1	0	1	2
ECIS	0	0	0	0	4	2	4	7	3	3
ICIS	0	1	0	1	1	1	1	1	1	0

From IFIP 8.6, six papers (17 percent) were analyzed; from ECIS, we analyzed 23 papers (64 percent); from ICIS, seven papers (19 percent). No IFIP 8.6 conferences were held in the years 1999 and 2000, hence those years are marked as "NC" in the table (for an exhaustive IFIP 8.6 literature study see Henriksen and Kautz 2006).

3.2 Data Analysis

One of the authors read each paper carefully, making notes of sentences relating to the categories in our study framework. The analysis was an iterative process, and after this first categorization, the paper was reread if any category was still left empty in a search for clues to determine the right categorization.

Initially, the analysis was conducted searching for the main categories identified: type of innovation, adopting unit, interaction, and context, as well as a category for interesting observations. As the analysis progressed, it was clear that some of the categories were too broad and that is was necessary to perform a further division in some categories. It was, for example, of interest in the category "cause and effect structure" to determine how many papers investigated cause-effect or applied a process view and also whether the approach to the research was interpretive or positivistic.

Furthermore, it became clear as the analysis of an "interesting observations" category was analyzed that more categories were of interest for this analysis. An example is the "theory" categorization that seemed obvious as the papers analyzed are all papers of diffusion and adoption; however, the papers utilized both traditional diffusion and adoption theories as well as other theories.

4   MODEL OF DIFFUSION AND ADOPTION

Technology diffusion and adoption has been a key area of research in the Information Systems discipline since the influential work of (Davis 1989; Tornatzky and Klein 1982), and research has increased massively ever since.

Research has dealt with specific technologies such as the diffusion and adoption of electronic data interchange (Damsgaard and Lyytinen 1996; Lyytinen and Damsgaard 2001), Internet services (Pedersen and Ling 2003), and adoption of telecommunication services (Mahler and Rogers 1999). Researchers have also investigated such different perspectives as the level of adoption (Yoo et al. 2002), gender differences in individual technology adoption (Venkatesh et al. 2000), grouping of users into distinct profiles (Constantiou et al. 2007) and adoption of technologies in different geographical regions, for example, mobile services in German banks (Mahler and Rogers 1999) and South Korean broadband services (Yoo et al. 2002). Most papers apply one or more theoretical instrument developed for analyzing and predicting diffusion and adoption as it is recognized that technological advances and service availability do not automatically lead to widespread adoption and use (Constantiou et al. 2007). Based on previous research, a generic framework for investigation of technology diffusion and adoption is assembled. The framework is based on previous research and experience of one of the authors.

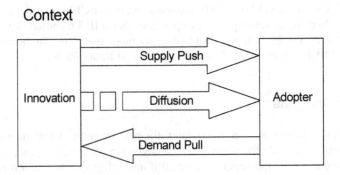

Figure 1. Holistic Framework for Investigating Technology Diffusion and Adoption (Static View)

Figure 1 shows a simple holistic framework for investigating technology diffusion and adoption of a snapshot in time. An innovation is diffused and adopted by one individual or a group of adopters as a consequence of a push from the producer or a pull from the adopters. This mechanism happens within a certain context; however, the framework shows a static view of this process and the changes that occur over a certain time period are not captured.

Often when an innovation is diffused and adopted by an adopting unit, the use of the innovation is further expanded. As the adopting unit identifies additional ways of using the innovation, or recognizes further needs in relation to the innovation, a demand pull mechanism takes place, and a transformation of the innovation transpires. This is depicted in Figure 2, which shows the process view of the holistic framework, where the innovation and the adopting unit are considered at times T0 and T1 to explore these changes.

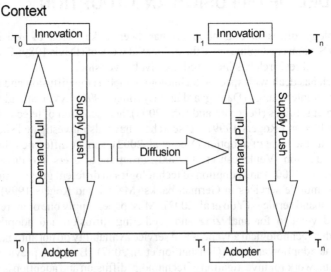

Figure 2. Holistic Framework for Investigating Technology Diffusion and Adoption (Process View)

It is, therefore, of great interest to capture the distribution of articles that take a static view and a process view on the diffusion and adoption of telecommunication innovations.

Figures 1 and 2 provide an illustration of the diffusion process of innovations. They assist in understanding the elements and mechanisms of such a process. The elements of the framework are briefly introduced next.

5   FRAMEWORK FOR ANALYZING DIFFUSION AND ADOPTION TELECOMMUNICATION LITERATURE

5.1   Type of Innovation

Telecommunication technologies have developed extensively over the past decades and the massive increase of Internet users has led to dramatic shifts in the way business is conducted.

The type of innovation investigated in this paper can be labeled a *telecommunication innovation* as the telecommunication industry is in focus. As part of the type of innovation, there are certain traits of the innovation that are interesting to investigate as they affect the diffusion and adoption process. Some technologies are integrated in the work environment and are, therefore, compulsory whereas other technologies are adopted voluntarily. According to Moore and Benbasat (1991), this issue of compulsory versus voluntary adoption of a technology is of great significance. They define the *voluntariness of use* as "the degree to which use of the innovation is perceived as being voluntary or of free will" (p. 195). One can assume that when a technology is compulsory the adoption rate is either higher as a consequence of the innovation being forced upon the adopting unit, or the opposite—the adoption rate is lower as a consequence of the adopting unit's resistance to adopting a compulsory technology. Therefore, consideration must be given to whether individuals are free to implement personal adoption or rejection decisions when examining the diffusion and adoption.

As stated above, some technologies—especially networked technologies—enjoy network externalities. It is, moreover, interesting to investigate whether the innovation only has an inherent value for the individual user (private utility) or it only has value if most people in a community of practice use it (collective utility).

5.2   Adopting Unit

Researchers have for many years acknowledged that technologies affect organizations at different levels in different ways, and sought to understand associated behavioral phenomena (Banker and Kauffman 2004). We have adopted the classification develolped by Lyytinen and Yoo (2002), who analyzed the changes in demand in services and infrastructures at the individual, team, organizational, and interorganizational[3] levels. Besides these four levels, when we found a paper studying the regional level, so we included that in our categorization.

---

[3] The interorganizational level is defined as adoption across the supply chain.

The primary focus of IS research has been done with the individual (Carlsson et al. 2006; Venkatesh et al. 2000) and the organization (e.g., Mahler and Rogers 1999; Venkatesh and Davis 2007) as the focal points, and only little research has centered on the group level. In addition, group level analysis of diffusion and adoption of technologies has, in general, considered diffusion at an aggregate level of analysis of individuals instead of acknowledging that adoption of technologies at this level maintains synergy effects and, therefore, has different adoption curves.

In our analysis, we distinguish between the following levels of analysis: individual, group/team, organizational, interorganizational, and regional levels.

5.3   Interaction Between Innovation and Adopting Unit

Technology diffusion can furthermore be understood by using two additional means of explanations: supply–push and demand–pull theories (Damsgaard and Lyytinen 1996; Zmud 1984) that display the interaction between technologies and the adopting unit.

Supply–push theories assume that the functionality of a technology enables its diffusion. The innovation is being determined before it is pushed to the users and the push forces enclose the adoption decision as a rational choice problem between a former and a new technology. The main source of information to make this decision is different communication channels (Rogers 1995), notably mass media and peer networks; however, Lyytinen and Damsgaard (2001) reported that networked technologies can also be pushed "by powerful actors (gatekeepers) such as hubs, industry associations or government" (p. 9). Moreover, through sustained innovations within technologies, supply-side organizations try to make technologies more attractive for potential clients by encouraging users to acquire technologies as a technological problem-solver.

Demand–pull theories are conversely determined by the users' rational choice (Lyytinen and Damsgaard 2001; Rogers 1995). The demand–pull theories would explain the technology diffusion by a growing demand for technological solutions created by potential clients and their needs. Users' perceived usefulness and image is improved by applying scientific or technical knowledge. This creates the demand for innovations and triggers their adoption. This could, for example, be realized in the form of new technologies. The pull perspective predicts that innovators will choose to work on topics that are perceived as problems on the demand side (Thirtle and Ruttan 1987) and accordingly increase the probability of a technology being adopted and diffused by improving its fit to the personal or business needs of the adopting unit.

Although the diffusion of a technology cannot be explained either by the supply–push or the demand–pull forces alone, it is of interest to identify the force that drives the interaction between the technology and the adopting unit when studying diffusion and adoption.

5.4   Context of Research

In addition to the supply–push and demand–pull, it is also necessary to consider the context in which the diffusion and adoption of a technology takes place. The analysis of the context is mainly a macro analysis in which the diffusion and adoption of an innovation takes place and consists of entities such as national governments, international agencies, consumers, products and services, and other entities that might have an effect or the power to change the industries within the IS field (Damsgaard and Lyytinen 2001; King et al. 1994). Our analysis provides examples of the use of context in research but will not present data in tabular form as the context is characteristic for every single study.

5.5 Theory

The underlying theory of diffusion and adoption of an innovation revolves around different diffusion theories. The perception of diffusion and adoption was initially based on five classic characteristics of innovation derived by Rogers (1995) from diffusion of innovations (DOI) literature. The exploration of diffusion and adoption of technologies in the IS field furthermore includes other theories such as the technology acceptance model (TAM) (Davis 1989), the theory of reasoned action (TRA) (Ajzen and Fishbein 1980), theory of planned behavior (Ajzen 1985), as well as extensions to the above and the unified theory of acceptance and use of technology UTAUT) (Venkatesh et al. 2000). These theories have been widely used within the IS field; however, they are reported to show significant shortcomings in their ability to capture the diffusion and adoption of telecommunication services (Blechar et al. 2006).

Diffusion of innovations theory has had considerable impact on IS and has, therefore, been a widely used instrument to explain and predict rates of IT innovation diffusion (Moore and Benbasat 1991; Rogers 1995). It derives from rational theories of organizational existence and has its roots in economics, sociology, and communication theory and has attempted to explain mainly individual adoption decisions (Lyytinen and Damsgaard 2001).

TAM is one of the most widely accepted theories to explain and predict IS acceptance and facilitate design changes before users have experience with a system (Venkatesh et al. 2000; Venkatesh et al. 2003). TAM predicts user acceptance based on two specific behavioral beliefs: perceived ease of use (PEU) and perceived usefulness (PU), which determine an individual's behavior intention (BI) to use IT and subsequently actual use (Davis 1989). Several researchers have extended its use to different settings and succeeded in demonstrating reliability and validity of the instrument (Adams et al. 1992).

The theory of reasoned action (Ajzen and Fishbein 1974, 1980) is a model for the prediction of behavioral intentions and/or behavior. The theory has been useful for identifying where and how to target strategies for changing behavior. Later, Ajzen (1985) extended the boundary condition of pure volitional control in the model to incorporate perceived behavioral control as an antecedent to behavioral intentions in the theory of planned behavior by extending the theory of reasoned action.

UTAUT is an attempt by Venkatesh et al. (2003) at unifying eight renowned models of technology acceptance, diffusion and adoption: TRA, TAM, motivational model, TPB, combined TAM-TPB, model of PC utilization, diffusion of innovations theory, and social cognitive theory. The model is validated with six longitudinal field studies in usage intention and UTAUT is regarded as a superior model to the above models individually. However, only few studies apply this theory (Anderson and Schwager 2004).

The above theories within the field of diffusion and adoption of technologies are considered during the analysis; however, some papers include other theories in their analysis or do not include theories at all. This is taken into account in the analysis, where we examine the theories employed.

5.6 Cause and Effect Structure

Causality or causation captures the directional relationship between a cause and an effect. The effect is the outcome (result) of the cause. Often in diffusion and adoption models there is an aim to identify a set of predictor variables with a certain desirable outcome (adoption). There is often a distinction between necessary and sufficient causes of adoption. For example, TAM's constructs of *perceived ease of use* and *perceived usefulness* are both necessary and sufficient conditions for the intention to adopt. This type of theory, which explains why adoption occurs, is labeled *variance theory* (Markus and Robey 1988). Process theory, on the other hand, identifies a number of necessary conditions that, through a process, explain *how* the diffusion occurs.

6   ANALYSIS AND DISCUSSION

The initial data material consisted of 94 conference contributions; however, after an initial evaluation, the material was reduced to 36 conference contributions pertaining to diffusion and adoption of a telecommunication technology.

The analysis is conducted by analyzing the conference contributions according to the six elements described above. The analysis is structured in the following way: each element is discussed in relation to the framework described above. For an overview, the discussion paragraph also contains a table showing the number of contributions within each element. The papers are referenced through a unique ID (from 1 to 36) associated with each contribution. The appendix shows a table linking each ID with a paper contribution and the elements of the framework. The analysis draws upon findings that show both findings that are representative to the articles and findings that are peculiar. The results are represented in percentages and are discussed, although the sample is relatively small, as percentages act as a visualization of the results.

6.1   Type of Innovation

All papers investigated studied a specific telecommunication technology or the more general concept of ICT. The ICT papers selected for this literature study all analyzed ICT that could irrefutably include a telecommunication technology. The majority of the papers (94 percent) deal directly with telecommunication technologies and innovations and only 6 percent of the papers concern ICT. Although several researchers have classified types of technologies, no classification has been provided within ICT or tele-communication technologies. It is, however, apparent that the majority of the papers (72 percent) analyze the diffusion and adoption of mobile devices and services such as mobile TV services (Lin and Chiasson 2007), mobile devices and services (Constantiou et al. 2005), and video streaming (Stanoevska-Slabeva and Hoegg 2005), whereas only

22 percent analyze the diffusion and adoption of broadband technologies (e.g., Choudrie and Dwivedi 2005; Damsgaard and Gao 2004). A few papers include a study of both; for example, a solution containing a combination of GPRS phone, PC, and WLAN (Breu et al. 2005) and broadband and mobile services (Middleton 2002).

Looking at the division of papers investigating the diffusion and adoption of compulsory and voluntary use of technologies, it is worth noticing that the papers contain an overweight of voluntary use (81 percent of the papers) of technologies. This is expected as these technologies are widely used in personal settings where users adopt a technology voluntarily. There is a clear correlation between voluntary use of a technology and the level of adoption analyzed (i.e., 67 percent of the papers investigating technologies adopted voluntarily were adopted at the individual level). However, at the organizational, group, and regional levels, 19 percent[4] of the papers were related to compulsory use and 14 percent[5] were related to voluntary diffusion and adoption of technologies.

There is a slight overweight of papers investigating compulsory use of technologies in organizations. Muzzi and Kautz (2004) investigated adoption of ICT through two studies and found that firms that involve high investments and a clear projection, such as ERP, videoconferences, EDI, and groupware have not been widely adopted. Most of these are technologies enforced upon employees in an organization and further research could, therefore, benefit from the investigation of compulsory use of ICT to explain this lack of adoption. As noted before, the adoption rate of a compulsory technology can be higher or lower as a consequence the adopting unit's resistance to adopting the enforced technology.

Of the papers analyzed, 17 percent are directly concerned with technologies that enjoy network externalities and 83 percent are not. However, it cannot be deduced that the technologies do not benefit from these; it is just not apparent in the papers.

Table 2. Papers Distributed on the Compulsory and Voluntary Use of Technologies

	# of papers	IFIP 8.6	# of papers	ECIS	# of papers	ICIS
Compulsory	2	4, 5	3	10, 22, 23	2	32, 36
Voluntary	4	1, 2, 3, 6	20	7, 8, 9, 11, 12, 13, 14, 15, 16, 17, 18, 19, 20, 21, 24, 25, 26, 27, 28, 29	5	30, 31, 33, 34, 35
With network effects	2	2,4,	1	11	3	30, 34, 36
Without network effects	4	1, 3, 5, 6	22	7,8, 9, 10, 12, 13, 14, 15, 16, 17, 18, 19, 20, 21, 22, 23, 24, 25, 26, 27, 28, 29	4	31, 32, 33, 35

---

[4]Compulsory use: organizational level: 14%; group level: 2.5%; regional level: 2.5%.
[5]Organizational level: 14%.

Table 3. Papers Distributed on Adopting Unit of Technologies

	# of papers	IFIP 8.6	# of papers	ECIS	# of papers	ICIS
Individual	3	1, 2, 6	17	7, 8, 9, 11, 12, 15, 16, 17, 18, 19, 20, 21, 25, 26, 27, 28, 29	5	30, 31, 33, 34, 35
Group/team	0	-	0	-	1	36
Organizational	2	3, 4	6	10, 13, 14, 22, 23, 24	1	32
Interorganizational	0	–	0	–	0	–
Regional	1	5	0	–	0	–

6.2 Adopting Unit

Approximately 69 percent of the research conducted in the past 10 years represents the individual level. This is not surprising as mobile services and technologies are often targeted to individuals and their needs. The units of adoption investigated are distributed in the papers as follows: individuals: 25 (69 percent); groups/teams 1 (3 percent); organizations: 9 (25 percent); interorganizational: 0 (0 percent); regions: 1 (3 percent). It is interesting to note that research at the interorganizational level is not represented at all.

The distribution of papers from the three investigated conferences is representative for research of the different adopting units within the IS field as such.

Diffusion and adoption of technologies in social networks have been discussed lately; however, only one paper out of 36 discusses adoption at the group level of analysis (Harrington and Ruppel 1999). They discuss practical and value compatibility and its relationship to telecommuting's adoption, diffusion, and success among IS personnel. The study is conducted in an organizational setting but the authors study group values, and, therefore, the paper has been classified as research at the group level. It should be mentioned that Sarker (2006) examined the levels of analysis issue in understanding technology adoption by groups. Sarker points out that groups should be investigated and "treated in their own right," and not as an aggregation of the individuals (pp. 1276). We concur with this point of view.

It can be argued that in the future researchers should conduct studies at the group level and within organizations. When investigating organizations, researchers should bear in mind that the internal structure of many organizations consists of working groups and teams with their own and not just a large number of individuals.

6.3 Context of Research

The context in which the research in the investigated studies takes place is of great importance to the research question posed. Most of the papers performing empirical data collection describe the context in which the study is performed with a fair amount of detail. When conducting research in the telecommunication industry, it is necessary to capture local regulations and policies for the markets investigated as these may have considerable impact in explaining the adoption and diffusion of a telecommunication innovation. Constantiou and Papazafeiropoulou (2006) explain the Danish market in detail when they investigate the provider's perspective in IP-telephony diffusion. Oh and Lee (2005) explain how alliances between mobile carriers, banks, and other related parties are formed, and analyze how technology affects competition and collaboration among them when a new convergence service is created by two, previously unrelated, industries—banks and mobile carriers—as mobile carriers had a hidden agenda to enter the financial market. This information provides a deeper understanding of the market and thereby the adoption and diffusion.

6.4 Theory

It is common for researchers to use an analytical framework in the analysis of diffusion and adoption studies. Rogers' (1995) diffusion of innovations is one of the often applied theories in numerous fields of study, but researchers have come to understand that other frameworks and theories might explain the diffusion and adoption of telecommunication technologies even better. There are still some gaps in the application of certain theoretical frameworks, and it is apparent from Table 4 that both the TRA and TPB, or even more interesting the UTAUT, are totally absent in the research conducted in this field of research the past ten years in contributions submitted to the three investigated conferences.

TAM is still the most applied theory in the field even though the application of the theory in this study seems moderate. In all, 19 percent of the papers analyze technology acceptance using this theory. TAM has been widely criticized for not being falsifiable, its questionable heuristic value, and its limited explanatory and predictive power (e.g., Szajna 1994). This could be the reason for the relatively diminished application. Researchers have attempted to explain (the lack of) diffusion and adoption of technologies using a variety of other theories relevant to the context they are investigating;

Table 4. Papers Employing the Most Applied Theories of Diffusion and Adoption

	# of papers	IFIP 8.6	# of papers	ECIS	# of papers	ICIS
DOI	2	1, 3	1	20	1	36
TAM/TRA	0	–	7	10, 13, 15, 19, 23, 25, 27	0	–
TPB	0	–	0	–	0	–
UTAUT	0	–	0	–	0	–
Other	3	4, 6, 7	10	7, 9, 12, 17, 18, 21, 22, 24, 26, 29	5	30, 31, 32, 33, 34, 35
None	2	2, 5	5	8, 11, 14, 16, 28	0	–

for example, Walden et al. (2007) apply the Braudel rule as a theoretical framework to find out why and how mobile services can make sense as a basis for viable business. They paraphrased the Braudel rule by stating that "mobile services become mobile value services when they offer the possibility to expand the limits of the possible in the structure of everyday routines" (p. 1876). They found that the mobile services investigated did not satisfy the Braudel rule.

Haghirian and Madlberger (2005) use advertising theory to analyze the consumer attitude toward advertising via mobile devices in Austria, and Cheng and Arthur (2002) propose using the trans-theoretical model of behavior change to explain the construction of a mobile internet healthcare solution for problem drinkers. Several papers choose not to apply a theoretical framework to their studies but instead conduct empirical data collection and analyze the results statistically (e.g., Abu-Samaha and Mansi 2007).

Dahlberg and Mallat (2002) use consumer perceived value (Grönroos 1997), technology acceptance model, and network externalities theory to explain managerial implications of consumer value perceptions in relation to mobile payment service development. The usage of the three theories is an attempt to impede the shortcomings of each theory individually. This implies a need for testing and evaluating more theories within the field of diffusion and adoption of telecommunication innovations to explain the observable facts.

6.5 Cause and Effect Structure

Of the papers investigated, 83 percent depict the relationship between a cause and an effect and only 17 percent take a process view and seek to explain *how* diffusion and adoption occur over time. Most research within telecommunication theory takes a static view when investigating diffusion and adoption of technologies and thereby does not take that into account when an innovation is adopted and diffused by an adopting unit, the use of the innovation is further expanded, and a transformation of the technology takes place. Wareham et al. (2002) is an example of a paper that tries to accommodate this shortcoming in research as they gather data in two stages to investigate the implications for

Table 5. Papers Depicting Cause–Effect or Process View and Research Approach

	# of papers	IFIP 8.6	# of papers	ECIS	# of papers	ICIS
Cause–effect	5	1, 2, 3, 4, 6	19	7, 8, 10, 11, 12, 13, 14, 15, 16, 17, 19, 20, 21, 23, 24, 25, 26, 27, 28	6	31, 32, 33, 34, 35, 36
Process	1	5	4	9, 18, 22, 29	1	30
Interpretive approach	5	1, 3, 4, 5, 6	9	10, 11, 13, 20, 21, 22, 24, 27, 28	4	30, 31, 32, 34
Positivistic approach	1	2	14	7, 8, 9, 12, 14, 15, 16, 17, 18, 19, 23, 25, 26, 29	3	33, 35, 36

the digital divide in wireless diffusion and mobile computing. The first sample of survey data was obtained in 1994 and contains information from 8,700 households, and the second sample was gathered in 1998 and contains over 16,000 households. Their results should be used to predict how mobile telecom diffusion may affect the digital divide as Internet access is incorporated by smartphones and wireless.

Studies taking a process view provide a dynamic and thereby more realistic view on the diffusion process, and therefore more studies should be conducted to offer further insight.

A slight majority of the studies within the field take a positivistic approach—56 percent—but the distribution of interpretive versus positivistic papers are fairly even.

7 CONCLUSION

This paper has provided a framework for analyzing what we know and what we don't know about the diffusion and adoption of telecommunication innovations and provided insight into what aspects of the diffusion and adoption process are accentuated or overlooked using a general view of the process. Three conferences have been chosen in this analysis, as the coverage at these conferences spans IS research to a wide extent. Many important contributions have been accepted in a variety of journals and we do not claim that this literature study is comprehensive; however, we believe that the elements within the diffusion and adoption framework are covered at these conferences.

Through our holistic framework, we found that most research has been conducted on the voluntary use of technologies targeting the individual. There is nearly a total absence of papers investigating the group and the interorganizational level of adoption. As social networks have gained attention in the past 10 years, this is surprising and it is therefore recommended that further research into this level of adoption be performed.

Many different theories and frameworks are used to explain the adoption and diffusion of innovations, and TAM is used frequently. It seems that researchers apply theories not only linked to adoption and diffusion to investigate further explanations to the research problem in question but also theories from other fields of study and this trend is encouraging as there is no dominant theory that captures all relevant aspects of the telecommunication diffusion process adequately. Theories that look into the network externalities from which the telecommunication technologies benefit are especially interesting when seeking explanations for diffusion and adoption.

Most studies take a cause–effect view in a snapshot in time and not a process view that could provide a dynamic and thereby more realistic view on the diffusion process and therefore more studies should be conducted to offer further insight. The distribution of interpretive versus positivistic approaches to the studies is equal and this trend should continue.

Finally, it is worth mentioning that the emerging field of neuroeconomics might complement diffusion and adoption research within information systems. Neuroeconomics seeks to develop our understanding of human behavior and, in particular, the role of emotions and emotional response (Damasio 1994; Hansen and Christensen 2007; Seo and Barett 2007). As TAM has recently been criticized for redirecting researchers' attention away from the antecedents of beliefs, not taking the IT artifact or its design into account, neglecting important outcomes of information technology (Benbasat and Barki

2007), as well as reaching maturity (Venkatesh et al. 2007), Dimoka et al. (2007) have proposed the application of neuro-science theories, methods, and tools to the field and labeled it *neuro-IS*. The field might benefit from the exploration and exploitation of cognitive neuroscience to improve and advance information systems.

This paper contributes with an overview of the existing research within diffusion and adoption of telecommunications research and provides a suggestion for areas in which further research is needed: research is needed at the group level, continual research applying different theoretical views than the widely used DOI and technology acceptance theories (e.g., theories from the field of neuroeconomics) may capture new aspects of the telecommunication diffusion process, and finally research taking a process view.

References

Abu-Samaha, A. M., and Mansi, I. 2007. "Information Technology Diffusion in the Jordanian Telecom Industry," in *Organizational Dynamics of Technology-Based Innovation: Diversifying the Research Agenda*, T. McMaster, D. Wastell, E. Ferneley, and J. I. DeGross (eds.), Boston: Springer, pp. 431-442.

Adams, D. A., Nelson, R. R., and Todd, P. A. 1992. "Perceived Usefulness, Ease of Use, and Usage of Information Technology: A Replication," *MIS Quarterly* (16:2), pp. 227-247.

Ajzen, I. 1985. "From Intentions to Actions: A Theory of Planned Behavior," in *Action-Control: From Cognition to Behavior*, J. Kuhl and J. Beckman (eds.), New York: Springer-Verlag, pp. 11-39.

Ajzen, I., and Fishbein, M. 1974. "Factors Influencing Intentions and Intention-Behavior Relation," *Human Relations* (27:1), pp. 1-15.

Ajzen, I., and Fishbein, M. 1980. *Understanding Attitudes and Predicting Social Behavior*, Englewood Cliffs, NJ: Prentice-Hall.

Anderson, J. E., and Schwager, P. H. 2004. "SME Adoption of the Wireless LAN Technology: Applying the UTAUT Model," in Proceedings of the 7th Annual Conference of the Southern Association for Information Systems, Savannah, GA, February 27-28, pp. 39-43 (http://sais.aisnet.org/2004/Anderson%20&%20Schwager.pdf).

Banderker, N., and Van Belle, J.-P. 2006. "Mobile Technology Adoption by Doctors in Public Healthcare in South Africa," in *Proceedings of the 14th European Conference on Information Systems*, J. Ljunberg and M. Andersson (eds.), Gothenburg, Sweden, June 12-14, pp. 1-13 (http://www.commerce.uct.ac.za/InformationSystems/Research&Publications/2006/ECIS06%20223%20Mobile%20Techn%20in%20Healthcare.pdf).

Banker, R. D., and Kauffman, R. J. 2004. "The Evolution of Research on Information Systems: A Fiftieth-year Survey of the Literature in Management Science," *Management Science* (50:3), pp. 281-298.

Benbasat, I., and Barki, H. 2007. Quo Vadis, Tam?," *Journal of the AIS*, (8:4), pp. 211-218.

Blechar, J., Constantiou, I. D., and Damsgaard, J. 2006. "Exploring the Influence of Reference Situations and Reference Pricing on Mobile Service User Behavior," *European Journal of Information Systems* (15:3), pp. 285-291.

Breu, K., Hemingway, C., and Ashurst, C. 2005. "The Impact of Mobile and Wireless Technology on Knowledge Workers: An Exploratory Study," in *Proceedings of the 13th European Conference on Information Systems*, Regensburg, Germany, May 26-28, pp. 1-12 (http://aisel.aisnet.org/Publications/ECIS/2005/20050098.pdf).

Carlsson, C., Carlsson, J, Hyvönen, K., Puhakainen, J., and Walden, P. 2006. "Adoption of Mobile Devices/Services—Searching for Answers with the UTAUT," in *Proceedings of the 39th Hawaii International Conference on System Sciences*, Los Alamitos, CA: IEEE Computer Society Press, pp. 132-142.

Carlsson, C., Carlsson, J., and Walden, P. 2005. "Mobile Services for the Hospitality Industry," in *Proceedings of the 13th European Conference on Information Systems*, Regensburg, Germany, May 26-28.

Cheng, E., and Arthur, D. 2002. "Constructing a Virtual Behavior Change Support System: A Mobile Internet Healthcare Solution for Problem Drinkers," in *Proceedings of the 10th European Conference on Information Systems*, Gdansk, Poland, June 6-8 (http://is2.lse.ac.uk/asp/aspecis/20020030.pdf).

Choudrie, J., and Dwivedi, Y. 2005. "Investigating Broadband Diffusion in the Household: Towards Content Validity and Pre-Test of the Survey Instrument," in *Proceedings of the 13th European Conference on Information Systems*, Regensburg, Germany, May 26-28 (http://aisel.aisnet.org/Publications/ECIS/2005/20050044.pdf)..

Choudrie, J., Papazafeiropoulou, A., and Lee, H. 2003. "Applying Stakeholder Theory to Analyze the Diffusion of Broadband in South Korea: The Importance of the Government's Role," in *Proceedings of the 11th European Conference on Information Systems*, Napoli, Italy, June 15-21 (http://is2.lse.ac.uk/asp/aspecis/20030031.pdf).

Constantiou, I. D., Damsgaard, J., and Knutsen, L. 2007. "The Four Incremental Steps toward Advanced Mobile Service Adoption," *Communications of the ACM* (50:6), pp. 51-55.

Constantiou, I. D., Damsgaard, J., and Knutsen, L. 2005. "Beware of Dane-geld: Even if Paid, M-Service Adoption Can be Slow," in *Proceedings of the 13th European Conference on Information Systems*, Regensburg, Germany, May 26-28.

Constantiou, I., and Papazafeiropoulou, A. 2006. " The Providers' Perspective in IP-Telephony Diffusion: Insights from the Danish Market," in *Proceedings of the 14th European Conference on Information Systems*, J. Ljunberg and M. Andersson (eds.), Gothenburg, Sweden, June 12-14, pp. 608-617.

Coursaris, C., Hassanein, K., Head, M., and Bontis, N. 2007. "The Impact of Distractions on the Usability and the Adoption of Mobile Devices for Wireless Data Services," in *Proceedings of the 15th European Conference on Information Systems*, St. Gallen, Switzerland, June 7-9.

Dahlberg, T., and Mallat, N. 2002. "Mobile Payment Service Development—Managerial Implications of Consumer Value Perceptions," in *Proceedings of the 10th European Conference on Information Systems*, Gdansk, Poland, June 6-8, pp. 649-657 (http://is2.lse.ac.uk/asp/aspecis/20020144.pdf)

Damasio, A. R. 1994. *Descartes' Error: Emotion, Reason, and the Human Brain*, New York: G. P. Putnam.

Damsgaard, J., and Gao, P. 2004. "Mobile Telecommunications Market Innovation: The Transformation from 2G to 3G," in *Proceedings of the 12th European Conference on Information Systems*, T. Leino, T. Saarinen, and S. Klein, Turku, Finland, June 14-16 (http://is2.lse.ac.uk/asp/aspecis/20040038.pdf).

Damsgaard, J., and Lyytinen, K. 1996. "Government Strategies to Promote the Diffusion of Electronic Data Interchange (EDI): What We Know and What We Don't Know," *Information Infrastructure and Policy* (5:3), pp. 169-191.

Damsgaard, J., and Lyytinen, K. 2001. "The Role of Intermediating Institutions in Diffusion of Electronic Data Interchange (EDI): How Industry Associations in the Grocery Sector Intervened in Hong Kong, Finland, and Denmark," *The Information Society* (17:3), pp. 195-210.

Davis, F. D. 1989. "Perceived Usefulness, Perceived Ease of Use, and User Acceptance of Information Technology," *MIS Quarterly* (13:3), pp. 319-340.

Dimoka, A., Pavlou, P. A., and Davis, F. D. 2007. "Neuro-IS: The Potential of Cognitive Neuoscience for Information Systems Research," in *Proceedings of the 28th International Conference on Information Systems*, Montreal, Canada, December 9-12 (http:// www. agsm.ucr. edu/faculty/staff/pavlou/ICIS_Dimoka_Pavlou_Davis_2007.pdf).

Dutta, A., and Roy, R. 2001. "The Mechanics of Internet Diffusion in India: Lessons for Developing Countries," in *Proceedings of the 22nd International Conference on Information Systems*, V. Storey, S. Sarkar, and J. I. DeGross (eds.), New Orleans, December 16-19, pp. 587-592.

Dwivedi, Y. K., Choudrie, J., and Weerakkody, V. 2006. "Broadband Adoption in the UK Household: Towards Reliability and Construct Validity of a Survey Instrument," in *Proceedings of the 14ᵗʰ European Conference on Information Systems*, J. Ljunberg and M. Andersson (eds.), Gothenburg, Sweden, June 12-14.

Economides, N., and Salop, S. C. 1992. "Competition and Integration among Complements, and Network Market-Structure," *Journal of Industrial Economics* (40:1), pp. 105-123.

Goh, K.-Y., Lee, C and Lee, C. 2003. "Information Technology Product Bundling in the Prescence of Complementarities, Quality Uncertainty and Network Effects: An Agent-Based Approach," in *Proceedings of the 24ᵗʰ International Conference on Information Systems*, S. T. March. A. Massey, and J. I. DeGross (eds.), Seattle, WA, December 14-17, pp. 497-510.

Grönroos, C. 1997. "Value-Driven Relational Marketing: From Products to Resources and Competences," *Journal of Marketing Management* (13:5), pp. 407-439.

Haghirian, P., and Madlberger, M. 2005. "Consumer Attitude Toward Advertising via Mobile Devices—An Empirical Investigation Among Austrian Users," in *Proceedings of the 13ᵗʰ European Conference on Information Systems*, Gdansk, Poland, June 6-8 (http://is2.lse.ac.uk/asp/aspecis/20050038.pdf).

Hampe, F., and G. Schwabe (2002). "Enhancing Mobile Commerce: Instant Music Purchasing over the Air," in *Seeking Success in E-Business: A Multidisciplinary Approach*, K. V. Andersen, S. Elliot, P. Swatman, E. Trauth, and J. Bjørn-Andersen (eds.), Norwell, MA: Kluwer Academic Publishers, pp. 107-131.

Hansen, F., and Christensen, S. R. 2007. *Emotions, Advertising and Consumer Choice*, Copenhagen: Copenhagen Business School Press.

Haraway, D. 1991. "A Cyborg Manifesto: Science, Technology, and Socialist-Feminism in the Late Twentieth Century," *Simians, Cyborgs and Women: The Reinvention of Nature*, New York: Routledge, pp. 149-181.

Harrington, S., and Ruppel, C. 1999. "Practical and Value Compatibility: Their Roles in the Adoption, Diffusion and Success of Telecommuting," in *Proceedings of the 19ᵗʰ International Conference on Information Systems*, P. De and J. I. DeGross (eds.), Charlotte, NC, December 13-15, pp. 103-112.

Henriksen, H. Z., and Kautz, K. 2006. "An Analysis of IFIP TC 8 WG 8.6 – In Search of a Common Theoretical Denominator," in *The Past and Future of Information Systems: 1976-2006 and Beyond*, IFIP World Computer Congress, TC8, Information Systems Stream, Santiago, Chile, August 21-23, pp. 143-152.

King, J. L., Gurbaxani, V., Kraemer, K. L., McFarlan, F. W., Raman, K. S., and Yap, C. S. 1994. "Institutional Factors in Information Technology Innovation," *Information Systems Research* (5:2), pp. 139-169.

Knebel, U., Leimeister, J. M., and Krcmar, H. 2007. "Personal Mobile Sports Companion: Design and Evaluation of IT-Supported Product-Service Bundles in the Sports Industry," in *Proceedings of the 15ᵗʰ European Conference on Information Systems*, St. Gallen, Switzerland, June 7-9.

Leimeister, J.-M., Daum, M., and Krcmar, H. 2002. "Mobile Virtual Healthcare Communities: An Approach to Community Engineering for Cancer Patients," in *Proceedings of the 10ᵗʰ European Conference on Information Systems*, Gdansk, Poland, June 6-8, pp. 1626-1637 (http://is2.lse.ac.uk/asp/aspecis/20050038.pdf).

Lin, S., and Chiasson, M. W. 2007. "A Dynamic Approach to Context Diffusion Research: An Actor-Network Theory Study of Mobile TV Service," in *Organizational Dynamics of Technology-Based Innovation: Diversifying the Research Agenda*, T. McMaster, D. Wastell, E. Ferneley, and J. I. DeGross (eds.), Boston: Springer, pp. 315-330.

Lyytinen, K., and Damsgaard, J. 2001. "What's Wrong with Diffusion of Innovations Theory?," in *Proceedings of the IFIP TC8/WG 8.1. Fourth Working Conference on Diffusing Software Products and Process Innovations*, M. A. Ardis and B. L. Marcolin (eds.), Deventer, The Netherlands: Kluwer B.V., pp. 173-190.

Lyytinen, K., and Yoo, Y. 2002. "Research Commentary: The Next Wave of Nomadic Computing," *Information Systems Research* (13:4), pp. 377-389.

Mahler, A., and Rogers, E. M. 1999. "The Diffusion of Interactive Communication Innovations and the Critical Mass—The Adoption of Telecommunications Services by German Banks," *Telecommunications Policy* (23), pp. 719-740.

Markus, M. L., and Robey, D. 1988. "Information Technology and Organizational Change: Causal Structure in Theory and Research," *Management Science* (34:5), pp. 583-598

McManus, P., and Standing, C. 2004. "The Value of Life Histories in Researching the Adoption and Use of M-Services," in *Proceedings of the 12th European Conference on Information Systems*, T. Leino, T. Saarinen, and S. Klein (eds.), Turku, Finland, June 14-16 (http://is2.lse.ac.uk/asp/aspecis/20040107.pdf).

Melody, W. H. 1999. "Telecom Reform: Progress and Prospects," *Telecommunications Policy* (23:1), pp. 7-34.

Middleton, C. 2002. "Exploring Consumer Demand for Networked Services: The Importance of Content, Connectivity and Killer Apps in the Diffusion of Broadband and Mobile Services," in *Proceedings of the 23rd International Conference on Information Systems*, L. Applegate, R. Galliers, and J. I. DeGross (eds.), Barcelona, Spain, December 15-18, pp. 391-399.

Moore, G. C., and Benbasat, I. 1991. "Development of an Instrument to Measure the Perceptions of Adopting an Information Technology Innovation," *Information Systems Research* (2:3), pp. 192-222.

Muzzi, C., and Kautz, K. 2004. "Information and Communication Technologies Diffusion in Industrial Districts," in *Networked Information Technologies: Diffusion and Adoption*, J. Damsgaard and H. Z. Henriksen (eds.), Norwell, MA: Kluwer Academic Publishers, pp. 19-39.

Ney, M., Schätz, B., Höck, J., and Salzmann, C. 2004. "Introducing Mobility: The mPolice Project," in *IT Innovation for Adaptability and Competitiveness*, B. Fitzgerald and E. Wynn (eds.), pp. 383-405.

Oh, S., and Lee, H. 2005. "How Technology Shapes the Actor-Network of Convergence Services: a Case of Mobile Banking," in *Proceedings of the 26th International Conference on Information Systems*, D. Avison, D. Galletta, and J. I. DeGross (eds.), Las Vegas, NV, December 11-14, pp. 483-493.

Pedersen, P., and Ling, R. 2003. "Modifying Adoption Research for Mobile Internet Service Adoption Crossdisciplinary," in *Proceedings of the 36th Hawaii International Conference on System Sciences*, Los Alamitos, CA: IEEE Computer Society Press.

Petrazzeni, B. A. 1995. *The Political Economy of Telecommunications Reform in Developing Countries: Privatization and Liberalization in Comparative Perspective*, Westport, CT: Praeger Publishers.

Rogers, E. M. 1995. *Diffusion of Innovations*, New York: Free Press.

Sarker, S. 2006. "Examining the 'Level of Analysis" Issue in Understanding Technology Adoption by Groups: Social, Behavioral, and Organizational Aspects of Information Systems," in *Proceedings of the 27th International Conference on Information Systems*, Milwaukee, WI, December 10-13, pp. 1275-1286.

Scheepers, H., and McKay, J. 2004. An Empirical Assessment of the Business Value Derived from Implementing Mobile Technology. A Case Study of Two Organizations," in *Proceedings of the 12th European Conference on Information Systems*, T. Leino, T. Saarinen, and S. Klein (eds.), Turku, Finland, June 14-16 (http://is2.lse.ac.uk/asp/aspecis/20040149.pdf).

Scheepers, H., and Scheepers, R. 2004. "The Implementation of Mobile Technology in Organizations: Expanding Individual Use Contexts," in *Proceedings of the 25th International Conference on Information Systems*, R. Agarwal, L. Kirsch, and J. I. DeGross (eds.), Washington, DC, December 12-15, pp. 171-181.

Sell, A., Patokorpi, E., Walden, P., and Anckar, B. 2004. "Adoption of Mobile Technology: An Empirical Study on Females Working in Elderly Care,"in *Proceedings of the 12th European Conference on Information Systems*, T. Leino, T. Saarinen, and S. Klein (eds.), Turku, Finland, June 14-16 (http://is2.lse.ac.uk/asp/aspecis/20040154.pdf).

Seo, M.-G., and Barett, L. F. 2007. "Being Emotional During Decision Making—Good or Bad? An Empirical Investigation," *Academy of Management Journal* (50:4), pp. 923-940.

Shapiro, C., and Varian, H. R. 1999. *Information Rules: A Strategic Guide to the Network Economy*, Boston: Harvard Business School Press.

Stanoevska-Slabeva, K., and Hoegg, R. 2005. "Towards Guidelines for Design of Mobile Services," in *Proceedings of the 13th European Conference on Information Systems*, Regensburg, Germany, May 26-28.

Szajna, B. 1994. "Software Evaluation and Choice: Predictive Evaluation of the Technology Acceptance Instrument," *MIS Quarterly* (18:3), pp. 319-324

Thirtle, C. G., and Ruttan, V. W. 1987. *The Role of Demand and Supply in the Generation and Diffusion of Technical Change*, Chur, Switzerland: Harwood Academic Publishers GmbH.

Tornatzky, L. G., and Klein, K. J. 1982. "Innovation Characteristics and Adoption-Implementation," *IEEE Transactions on Engineering Management* (EM-29:1), pp. 28-45.

Van der Heijden, H. 2003. "Measuring Attitudes Towards Mobile Information Services: An Empirical Validation of the HED/UT Scale," in *Proceedings of the 11th European Conference on Information Systems*, Napoli, Italy, June 16-21 (http://is2.lse.ac.uk/asp/aspecis/20030166.pdf).

Van der Heijden, H., Ogertschnig, M., and Van der Gaast, L. 2005. "Effects of Context Relevance and Perceived Risk on User Acceptance of Mobile Information Services," in *Proceedings of the 13th European Conference on Information Systems*, Regensburg, Germany, May 26-28.

Venkatesh, V., and Davis, F. 2007. "A Theoretical Extension of the Technology Acceptance Model: Four Longitudinal Field Studies," *Management Science* (46:2), pp. 186-204.

Venkatesh, V., Morris, M. G., and Ackerman, P. L. 2000. "A Longitudinal Field Investigation of Gender Differences in Individual Technology Adoption Decision-Making Processes," *Organizational Behavior and Human Decision Processes* (83:1), pp. 33-60.

Venkatesh, V., Morris, M. G., Davis, G. B., and Davis, F. D. 2003. "User Acceptance of Information Technology: Toward a Unified View," *MIS Quarterly* (27:3), pp. 425-478.

Wainwright, D. W., and Waring, T. S. 2006. "The Politics of ICT Diffusion: A Case Study in a UK Primary Health Care Trust," in *The Transfer and Diffusion of Information Technology for Organizational Resilience*, B. Donnellan, T. J. Larsen, L. Levine, and J. I. DeGross (eds), Boston: Springer, pp. 71-90.

Walden, P., Han, S., Carlsson, C., and Majlender, P. 2007. "The Sleeping Giant—A Longitudinal Study Surveying the Mobile Service Market in Finland," in *Proceedings of the 15th European Conference on Information Systems*, St. Gallen, Switzerland, June 7-9.

Wang, Y., and Yuan, Y. 2006. "The Role of SMS in Mobile Data Service Diffusion in China: A Longitudinal Case Study Based on Actor-Network Theory," in *Proceedings of the 27th International Conference on Information Systems*, Milwaukee, WI, December 10-13, pp. 1737-1756.

Wareham, J., Levy, A., and Cousins, K. 2002. "Wireless Diffusion and Mobile Computing: Implications for the Digital Divide," in *Proceedings of the 10th European Conference on Information Systems*, Gdansk, Poland, June 6-8.

Yoo, Y., Lyytinen, K., and Yang, H. D. 2002. "The Role of Standards in Innovation and Diffusion of Broadband Mobile Services: The Case of South Korea," *Journal of Strategic Information Systems* (14:3), pp. 323-353.

Zmud, R. W. 1984. "An Examination of Push-Pull Theory Applied to Process Innovation in Knowledge Work," *Management Science* (30:6), pp. 727-738.

About the Authors

Heidi Tscherning is a Ph.D. student at the Center for Applied ICT, Copenhagen Business School, Denmark. She holds a Master's degree in Business Administration and Economics from the Copenhagen Business School and has seven years of experience in industry working with project management on three IT projects for Danish Defence as well as IT management consulting. Her research is focused on diffusion and adoption of advanced mobile services with a special interest in social networks. Heidi Tscherning can be reached at ht.caict@cbs.dk.

Jan Damsgaard is a professor and the director of Center for Applied Information and Communication Technology at Copenhagen Business School, Denmark. He holds a Master's degree in Computer Science and Psychology and a Ph.D. in Information Systems. His research focuses on the diffusion and implementation of networked and standard-based technologies such as intranets, EDI, and mobile and wireless technologies. He has presented his work at international conferences (ICIS, ECIS, PACIS, HICSS, IFIP 8.2., 8.4, and 8.6) and in international journals *(Information Systems Journal, Journal of Strategic Information Systems, Information Society, Information Technology and People, Communications of the ACM,* and *Journal of the Association for Information Systems).* JD has worked and done research at a number of institutions, including Aalborg University, Denmark; Case Western Reserve University, USA; University of Jyväskylä, Finland; University of California at Irvine, USA; and Hong Kong University of Science and Technology, China. JD can be reached at damsgaard@cbs.dk.

Appendix

This appendix provides an overview of the papers analyzed from the IFIP 8.6, ECIS, and ICIS conference proceedings from 1998 through 2007. The table shows all elements of the framework for each conference contribution. For further information on the papers, see the References.

ID	Author(s)	Conference	Year	Compulsory/Voluntary	With/Without Network Effects	Adopting unit	Interaction	Theory	Cause Effect/Process	Methodology
1	Lin & Chiasson	IFIP 8.6	2007	V	w/o	I	Pull	DOI, other	C-E	I
2	Abu-Samaha & Mansi	IFIP 8.6	2007	V	w	I	Pull	None	C-E	P
3	Wainwright & Waring	IFIP 8.6	1998	V	w/o	O	Pull	DOI	C-E	I
4	Ney et al.	IFIP 8.6	2004	C	w	O	Pull	Other	C-E	I
5	Muzzi & Kautz	IFIP 8.6	2004	C	w/o	R	Push	None	Process	I
6	Hampe & Schwabe	IFIP 8.6	2002	V	w/o	I	Pull	Other	C-E	I
7	Coursaris et al.	ECIS	2007	V	w/o	I	Pull	Other	C-E	P
8	Knebel et al.	ECIS	2007	V	w/o	I	Pull	None	C-E	P
9	Walden et al.	ECIS	2007	V	w/o	I	Pull	Other	Process	P
10	Banderker & Van Belle	ECIS	2006	C	w/o	O	Pull	TAM	C-E	I
11	Constantiou & Papazafeiropoulou	ECIS	2006	V	w	I	Pull	None	C-E	I
12	Dwivedi et al.	ECIS	2006	V	w/o	I	Push	Other	C-E	P
13	Breu et al.	ECIS	2005	V	w/o	O	Pull	TAM	C-E	I

ID	Author(s)	Conference	Year	Compulsory/Voluntary	With/Without Network Effects	Adopting unit	Interaction	Theory	Cause Effect/Process	Methodology
14	Carlsson et al.	ECIS	2005	V	w/o	O	Pull	None	C-E	P
15	Choudrie and Dwivedi	ECIS	2005	V	w/o	I	Push	TAM, DOI	C-E	P
16	Constantiou et al.	ECIS	2005	V	w/o	I	Push	None	C-E	P
17	Haghirian & Madlberger	ECIS	2005	V	w/o	I	Push	Other	C-E	P
18	Stanoevska-Slabeva & Hoegg	ECIS	2005	V	w/o	I	Pull	Other	Process	P
19	Van der Heijden et al.	ECIS	2005	V	w/o	I	Pull	TAM	C-E	P
20	Damsgaard & Gao	ECIS	2004	V	w/o	I	Pull	DOI, other	C-E	I
21	McManus & Standing	ECIS	2004	V	w/o	I	Pull	Other	C-E	I
22	Scheepers & McKay	ECIS	2004	C	w/o	O	Pull	Other	Process	I
23	Sell et al.	ECIS	2004	C	w/o	O	Pull	TAM	C-E	P
24	Choudrie & Papazafeiropoulou	ECIS	2003	V	w/o	O	Pull	Other	C-E	I
25	Van der Heijden	ECIS	2003	V	w/o	I	Pull	TAM	C-E	P
26	Cheng & Arthur	ECIS	2002	V	w/o	I	Pull	Other	C-E	P
27	Dahlberg & Mallat	ECIS	2002	V	w/o	I	Pull	TAM, other	C-E	I
28	Leimeister et al.	ECIS	2002	V	w/o	I	Pull	None	C-E	I
29	Wareham et al.	ECIS	2002	V	w/o	I	Pull	Other	Process	P
30	Wang & Yan	ICIS	2006	V	w	I	Push	Other	Process	I
31	Oh & Lee	ICIS	2005	V	w/o	I	Push	Other	C-E	I
32	Scheepers & Scheepers	ICIS	2004	C	w/o	O	Push	Other	C-E	I
33	Goh et al.	ICIS	2003	V	w/o	I	Push	Other	C-E	P
34	Middleton	ICIS	2002	V	w	I	Pull	Other	C-E	I
35	Dutta & Roy	ICIS	2001	V	w/o	I	Push	Other	C-E	P
36	Harrington & Ruppel	ICIS	1999	C	w	G	Push	DOI	C-E	P

Part 2:

Key Aspects in Innovation

4 EXPLICIT AS ENABLER FOR UNDERSTANDING THE TACIT

Anna Börjesson Sandberg
Ericsson AB and IT University of Gothenburg
Gothenburg, Sweden

Carl Magnus Olsson
Software Engineering & Management
IT University of Gothenburg
Gothenburg, Sweden

Abstract   *Knowledge that can be expressed in words and numbers (i.e., explicit knowledge) only represents the tip of the iceberg in organizational knowledge. Explicit knowledge may be communicated in formal, systematic language, using standard notations. This paper reviews how explicit knowledge is used within software engineering, and has found that this tip is important to store organizational knowledge, discuss improvements, and communicate competences. We further discuss how the tip can be viewed as a facilitator for understanding tacit knowledge, such as context dependent actions, commitments, and involvement. To support these arguments, we have studied software engineering units within Ericsson AB during the period 2005–2007 to learn more about software engineering process descriptions and notations in practice. Findings indicate that unambiguous process descriptions are dependent on obvious software process notations and that the explicit nature of described software processes serve as a vital catalyst in initiating discussions of tacit knowledge.*

Keywords   Software engineering, explicit knowledge, tacit knowledge, software process notations, software process descriptions

Please use the following format when citing this chapter:

Sandberg, A. B., and Olsson, C. M., 2008, in IFIP International Federation for Information Processing, Volume 287, Open IT-Based Innovation: Moving Towards Cooperative IT Transfer and Knowledge Diffusion, eds. León, G., Bernardos, A., Casar, J., Kautz, K., and DeGross, J. (Boston: Springer), pp. 63-82.

1   INTRODUCTION

Dividing knowledge in the categories explicit/tacit or codified/personalized has, since the mid-1990s, been widely accepted through the seminal work of Nonaka and Takeuchi (1995) and Hansen et al. (1999). Explicit knowledge is knowledge that is transmittable in formal, systematic language, while tacit knowledge is knowledge that is rooted in actions, commitment, and involvement in a specific context. For the purposes of this paper, we are listing explicit and tacit knowledge (Nonaka and Takeuchi 1995) as comparable with codified and personalized knowledge (Hansen et al. 1999). Explicit knowledge has previously been argued as representing only the tip of the iceberg of the body of all possible knowledge (Polanyi 1966).

Three process notation techniques dominate today, focusing on activities, objects, or roles (Kueng et al. 1996). Activity oriented techniques are supported by BPMN (business process modeling language), object oriented techniques are support by UML/SPEM 2.0 (unified modeling language/software process engineering meta-model), while role oriented techniques are supported by RAD (role activity diagraming). In our study, we found that none of these have clearly established itself to be state-of-the-art, nor do they have well know, deployed, and successfully diffused tools supporting them (which in itself hinders effective management of explicit knowledge).

This study reports on three cycles of action research at a major development unit within the telecom company Ericsson AB we knew was heavily involved in this issue. Specifically addressed in this paper, we asked ourselves, how do software process descriptions affect understanding of software engineering knowledge? We argue that we cannot describe explicit knowledge in ways where it can be understood by the mass without a standard notation for process descriptions, and, without describing the explicit knowledge, we are hindered from effectively understanding and managing tacit knowledge. Through quantitative studies of process descriptions and qualitative interviews with senior engineers and managers, our research elaborates on the role played by explicit knowledge in forming an understanding of tacit aspects. As explicit knowledge, we have focused on the role software process descriptions, software process notations, and tools supporting formalization of software processes play in our study. Results indicate that the main reasons for having a described software process were storing organizational knowledge, discussing improvements, and communicating competences. The described process was identified as necessary for getting a common view of the current software engineering situation to discuss both improvements and competences for specific contexts. The explicit knowledge was thereby found to be an enabler for managing actions, commitment, and involvement between individuals for specific situations (i.e., for understanding and managing the tacit knowledge). More specifically, we have found that the explicit nature of described software processes serves as a vital catalyst in initiating discussions of tacit knowledge.

We conclude that effectively managing explicit knowledge through commonly described software processes is far more important than just managing the tip of the iceberg of all possible knowledge. Aside from our contributions to process notations, this work also draws on the established concepts of tacit and explicit knowledge—well known and with considerable use primarily within knowledge management—to illustrate that these still have a considerable role to play. In our literature study, we could find no previous linking of software process notations (or models) with these concepts.

We present the theoretical context in section 2 by discussing knowledge management and software process notations. In section 3, we then describe the action research approach taken, and present the findings of each action research cycle in section 4. Discussion and analysis of the results follow in section 5, while the paper's conclusions are summarized in section 6.

2 THEORETICAL CONTEXT

This section explains the two main theoretical parts used in this paper. First, we present basic knowledge management theories and explain how we have made use of them in our study. Second, we present existing software process notations, and research related to them, while reflecting on how the growing interest in globally distributed software development makes our study even more relevant. For both sections, we have included promising future extensions of the context.

2.1 Knowledge Management

Knowledge management is an old management tradition where skills have been passed on in generations from parents to their children within family businesses, and exchanging know-how has been vital to survival. Over time, economies have shifted from natural resources to intellectual assets and managers started in the mid-1990s, to get interested in the concept of managing knowledge. However, as early as the 1960s, Polanyi (1996, p. 4) argued "we can know more than we can tell" and he divided knowledge in two categories. *Explicit knowledge* refers to knowledge that is transmittable in formal, systematic language. Explicit knowledge is more simply explained by saying it is knowledge that can be expressed by words and numbers. This type of knowledge only represents the tip of the iceberg of all possible knowledge. *Tacit knowledge* is rooted in action, commitment, and involvement in a specific context. Nonaka and Takeuchi (1995) made these two categories well known when analyzing Japanese innovation companies, where they proposed four different modes of knowledge conversion: socialization (from tacit to tacit), externalization (from tacit to explicit), combination (from explicit to explicit), and internalization (from explicit to tacit).

The research of Hansen et al. (1999) is also well-cited in the knowledge management area. They argue a company can choose to adopt two different knowledge management strategies, and claim that companies without a knowledge management strategy sooner or later die. Hansen et al. distinguish between *codified* and *personalized knowledge*. Knowledge is, in their view, codified to support a people-to-document strategy (i.e., knowledge is extracted from the person who created it). It is made independent of that person and is reused for a variety of purposes. In contrast, personalized knowledge is knowledge handed person-to-person (i.e., typically knowledge shared in brainstorming sessions and one-on-one conversations). As Hansen et al. argue, "A company's knowledge management strategy should reflect its competitive strategy: how it creates value for customers, how that value supports an economic model, and how the company people deliver on the value and the economics (1999, p. 3).

Mathiassen et al. (2003) argue that both Nonaka and Takeuchi and Hansen et al. make no distinction between tacit and personalized knowledge, or explicit and codified knowledge. For the purposes of this study, we have knowingly elected to do the same as Nonaka and Takeuchi, and Hansen et al., as this paper represents an analysis of how explicit knowledge is understood in an organization. Adding a further level of analysis to our study prior to having established the role explicit knowledge plays in diffusing software management practices seems somewhat premature. Depending on outcomes, Mathiassen et al. could possibly be a useful next iteration in the action research conducted at the site. Somewhat differently from Nonaka and Takeuchi, as well as Hansen et al., Mathiassen et al. argue that codification of knowledge plays a crucial role both in relation to maturing professional practices and in relation to the use of information technology to support knowledge management. It is, therefore, important that people engaged in knowledge management activities appreciate the problems and opportunities related to the codification of knowledge. Mathiassen et al. distinguish between four different types of professional knowledge: situated (personalized and tacit), exemplary (personalized and explicit), community (codified and tacit), and procedural (explicit and codified).

At this time, we do not intend to argue whether or not there is a difference between codified and explicit knowledge, but we acknowledge arguments made to distinguish between them in favor of understanding and appreciating the importance of codified and explicit knowledge within software engineering.

2.2 Software Process Notations in the Context of Distributed Development

Ellmer and Merkl (1996) present strong arguments for the importance of described development processes to be successful as software organization, and describe its role as organizational memory: "A process model is an explicit representation of process knowledge and may thus serve as a means for storing and retrieving organizational knowledge about software process execution" (p. 60). Such a described software process is typically both codified and explicit. Arguments such as those of Ellmer and Merkl have been accepted increasingly in research as well as practice over the last decade. Today, however, we are seeing software development increasingly become a global activity. This move toward distributed work challenges us to revisit our established work practices, and has seen growing academic interest (see the *MIS Quarterly*'s Special Issue on Information Systems Offshoring (32:2), June 2008). Considerable work has been reported on cultural differences, communication, and distributed communities (reviewing a task-technology fit perspective—Maruping and Agarwal 2004; elaborating on political, cultural, and global aspects—Nicholson and Sahay 2001; leveraging time-zone management in distributed work—Carmel 2006). Remarkably little is to be found currently when looking at the role of formal process notations, but Sahay (2003) represents an exception to this. Considering his perspective is on global software alliances of small to medium sized companies, rather than multinational ones such as what our study examines, this paper settles for acknowledging that an interesting comparison could be made in future publications.

Looking specifically at existing process notations, Johansson (2007), as a partial input to this study, found four groups of software process notations that we recall below.

- Activity-oriented process notations supported by business process modeling language (BPMN). These notations focus on the definition of processes as a sequence of activities. Examples of activity-oriented techniques are further discussed by Owen and Raj (2005) and White (2004).
- Object-oriented process notations supported by unified modeling language/software process engineering meta-model (UML/SPEM 2.0). These notations leverage the more comprehensive modeling constructs of object-orientation to capture processes. Object-oriented process notations are further discussed by Haumer (2006), Kalnins and Vitolins (2006), and Russel et al. (1994).
- Role-oriented process notations supported by role activity diagraming (RAD). These notations describe business processes based on the specific organizational roles and responsibilities involved. These techniques are discussed by Ould (1995) and Ould and Huckvale (1995).
- Speech-act oriented process notations (not supported by any identified process notation language). The speech-act oriented notations view processes in the context of the speech-act language action paradigm. These notations are discussed by Kueng et al. (1996). Considering the speech-act oriented process notation is barely mentioned outside of Kueng et al., we will be limiting our use of it to recognizing its existence, but refrain from further research on it before we bring it into the ongoing study on which this paper reports.

When reflecting on what makes a good software process notation, we recognize that Ould and Huckvale (1995, p. 334) list a number of features that must be met to achieve high-quality process descriptions. Concepts, objects, and relationships represented in the process description should be intuitively familiar, so that people can readily understand and talk about them. The notation should be easy for readers to grasp, after a limited verbal introduction. The notation should be unambiguous (another way of saying that it should have formal syntax and semantics) so that it can be analyzed and, possibly, enacted. It should be possible for the notation to draw attention to the purposes of what people do rather than the detail of how they do it. Finally, the notation should be able to handle complexity.

We also recognize that there are different types of information from which it should be possible to retrieve a process description (Curtis et al. 1992, pp. 77). This includes what is going to be done, who is going to do it, when and where will it be done, how and why will it be done, and who is dependent on it being done. If a described process is used there are, according to Ould and Huckvale, several ways that this model can help organizations to be more effective. It may be used

- *As a focus for discussion.* If we use a good process notation that has a clear syntax and semantics together with process description guidelines, it will help the organization to ask the right questions and bring important points in focus for discussion.
- *As a mean for communicating a process to others.* In this way other people can use the process as a guide and they will save valuable time since they do not have to

develop a new process over and over again. This view is also supported by Curtis et al. (1992).

- *As a basis for analysis.* It is possible through analysis to find weaknesses in the process or to identify if a certain process does not give any value.
- *For designing a new process.* When creating different process descriptions and comparing them, it is possible to find the best solution and to use it.
- *As a baseline for continuing process improvement.* It is possible that the process models can be used to find different measures in how well the process works and in this way initiate improvements to the process. This view is also supported by Curtis et al.

Today there are three acknowledged ways to describe software processes that are supported by a process notation language. We also understand that a high quality process description needs to meet several different requirements. This is the type of process description that we define as a valuable explicit record of the organizational memory.

3   METHOD

This study has the dual goal of both understanding software process notations used in practice and contributing to the body of knowledge on the same theme. Collaborative practice research (CPR) (Mathiassen 2002) supports the realization of this dual goal, while at the same time supporting the insider/outsider perspective (Bartunek and Louis 1996) that has been a beneficial aspect of this research project. One of the two authors has been working within Ericsson with process descriptions, tools for describing processes, try-outs, learning sessions, and data collection during the period 2005–2007 and taken the insider role. The other author joined the research project in the later phases, taking the outsider role and contributing with interview design, interviews, analysis, discussions, and questioning in an unbiased way. This study has also benefitted from the assistance of a master's thesis (Johansson 2007). The data collection design and the research method used (presented below) have helped us to answer the research question: How do software process descriptions affect understanding of software engineering knowledge?

The study is based on action research (Baskerville and Wood-Harper 1996, 1998; Davison et al. 2004; Galliers 1992) with a focus on understanding the current process description situation, the awareness of the current situation, and the value of and use for a described process. Baskerville and Pries-Heje (1999) argue that the fundamental contention of action research is that a complex social process can be studied best by introducing changes into that process and observing the effects of these changes. We collected data throughout the research project in three iterative cycles as defined by Susman and Evered (1978). Each cycle includes the activities diagnosing, action planning, action taking, evaluating, and specifying learning. The activities in respective iteration are summarized in Table 1.

Table 2 summarizes the data sources used in the study. The many different data sources have facilitated triangulation (Patton 1987; Yin 1994) and analysis in an unbiased way.

Table 1. The Three Iterations Explained through Susman and Evered's (1978) Action Research Phases

Phase	Iteration 1: Process Description Situation	Iteration 2: Process Description Awareness	Iteration 3: Value of and Use for Described Processes
Diagnosing	Need to understand actual process description situation	Need to understand the level of awareness around the process description situation	Need to understand value of and use for process descriptions.
Action Planning	Planned to investigate all existing process descriptions within one major development unit	Planned to present the iteration 1 investigation for selected units and review literature for process notations standards	Planned to interview 12 senior managers and engineers. Questions defined based on learning from iteration 1 and 2.
Action Taking	Searched and found 13 different process descriptions, which were analyzed with help of 10 different attributes (see section 4.1)	Presented the iteration 1 investigation for selected units and reviewed the literature for process notation standards	Interviewed the 12 senior managers and engineers.
Evaluating	Found processes differed in most of the defined attributes	Main concerns for the current process description situation: • Lack of a tool for process modeling • No standard used when describing processes	Wanted to use the described process to store organizational knowledge, discuss improvements and communicate knowledge and competence.
Specifying Learning	Very varying process descriptions	Process descriptions do not follow any obvious standard process notation	Process descriptions (explicit knowledge) enable tacit knowledge.

Table 2. Data Sources

Data Sources	Explanation
Direct involvement	We were directly involved in investigating process description situation, deploying process situation results, and conducting interviews
Formal interviews	We executed 12 formal interviews with senior managers and engineers of 1 hour each
Literature review	We reviewed the literature to understand what standard process notations exited
Open-ended, semi-structure interviews	We had informal interviews and discussions with practitioners who were users of the process descriptions
Process descriptions	We reviewed and analyzed 13 different formal and approved processes
Process description presentations	We presented, analyzed, and discussed the process description situation with two selected units

The questions used during the formal interviews in iteration three were designed based on understanding gained from both the process description investigation in iteration one and the literature review in iteration two. The table in Appendix A presents the questions used. Extensive use of laddering (Reynolds and Gutman 1988), that is, asking a series of neutral probing questions to stimulate respondents to elaborate and explain their answers, was employed during the questioning.

4   THE CASE

In mid-2005, we started to analyze the use of different process notations for managing explicit software engineering knowledge (i.e., process descriptions used in software development). We wanted to understand what hinders effective management of explicit software engineering knowledge. The investigation was made in three main iterations. When starting iteration one, it was not obvious what iterations two and three would be, or if they would be necessary. Iterations were defined as a result of the previous iteration and a need to understand more about process notations for managing explicit software engineering knowledge. In iteration one, we wanted to understand the actual process description situation for software engineering. In iteration two, we wanted to create awareness within Ericsson about the situation and, by that, receive valuable feedback on how to proceed. The third and last iteration was designed to understand in detail the value of and use for a described process for software engineering. The three following sections describe how the iterations were executed and their results.

4.1   Iteration One: Process Description Situation

To understand the actual process description situation for software engineering, we analyzed a major development unit within Ericsson AB consisting of more than 1,500 employees, geographically distributed over five sites, in two different European countries. First, we searched the Ericsson intranet for approved formal processes for software engineering and then analyzed the different processes based on a number of attributes that would help us understand their quality (see Table 3). Thirteen different approved formal process descriptions were found in the search and formed the basis of the further analysis. It is important to note that these 13 process descriptions covered different parts of the software engineering scope (e.g., products development, software development, systems development, and project management).

The analysis revealed the following situation:

1. There was no obvious structure used for the entry pages. Processes used within the same development unit often had similar entry pages, but not always.
2. Seventy percent the analyzed processes were web-based and 30 percent were document-based. The document-based processes used Word, Frame Maker, Power Point, Excel, or Visio.
3. None of the processes followed specific notation guidelines.
4. The size of the processes varied from 70 to 3,600 links and from 22 to 230 pages.
5. The percentage of broken links varied from 1.3 to 67 percent.
6. The number of templates varied from 0 to 1,500.
7. The number of unavailable templates varied from 0 to 1,050.
8. Almost all (90 percent) of the process had an appointed and known process owner.
9. Seventy percent of the processes had recently (within 6 months) been updated and 20 percent had been updated within the past year.
10. Eighty percent of the processes had a formal revision state.

Table 3. Attributes Used to Analyze the Quality of the Approved Formal Processes

#	Process Description Attribute	Explanation
1	Entry page	The style of the entry page of the process
2	Layout	Web based or document based process description
3	Notation	Following specific process notation guidelines (either home-made or standard)
4	Size	Number of links (web based) or number of pages (document based)
5	Percent of broken links	Number of the links not working compared to number of links in web/document
6	Number of templates	Number of templates
7	Number of unavailable templates	Number of unavailable templates
8	Process owner	If there was an appointed and known owner of the process
9	Process updates	When was the process last updated
10	Approve revision	Has the process a formal revision state

The analysis of the process descriptions revealed a varying situation when it came to appearance, notation, size, and quality. We understood that no formal process notation was used to describe the explicit software engineering knowledge, but we still did not understand how much of a problem this was.

4.2   Iteration Two: Process Description Awareness

At this point, we knew that the process description situation varied and that there was no obvious process notation for managing diffusion of software engineering knowledge. To create awareness about this situation, we made a presentation explaining these facts and communicated it to selected Ericsson units working with improving software engineering and the described processes. Specifically, at the end of 2005 and during 2006, we communicated the result within the Ericsson unit globally responsible for processes, methods, and tools for research and development and within a local Ericsson unit developing a product for the data communication network.

The immediate reaction was that the lack of a tool for process modeling was the main reason for the current process description situation. This conclusion was mainly based on the fact that numerous variants for different layouts (#2, Table 3) were used and, if a tool would have been used, specific notations would be followed (#3, Table 3). The lack of quality (#4 – #7, Table 3) of the described processes was mainly understood as a result of difficult manual maintenance that could be helped by a tool for describing processes.

Both the global and the local unit started initiatives to describe their engineering processes in a tool. They elected to start using rational method composer (RMC). The communication of the process description situation ended with an awareness that helped initiate actions to improve the situation. Within the started initiatives, it very soon became clear that only a tool would not be enough to deal with the current process description situation. Process notations (#3, Table 3) and process modeling guidelines were requested to assist in describing the processes in the tool. This awareness helped manifest an initiative to understand and learn more about process notation languages, starting with researching the literature of known process notations. This was done as a part of Johansson's (2007) master's thesis, which found that there were three different process notation techniques (activity-, object-, and role-oriented) (see section 2.2).

4.3 Iteration Three: Value of and Use for Described Processes

The awareness of the current process description situation, combined with the newly acquired knowledge about the need for and lack of deployed process notations, made us interested in understanding the actual value of and use for a described process. Maybe we would find explanations for the current process situation if we understood how engineers valued a described process and what they wanted to use it for.

We interviewed 12 senior engineers (see section 3 and Appendix A). The interviews revealed both what the interviewees valued as important for a well described process and what they wanted to use it for (Johansson 2007). Figure 1 presents a diagram of what the

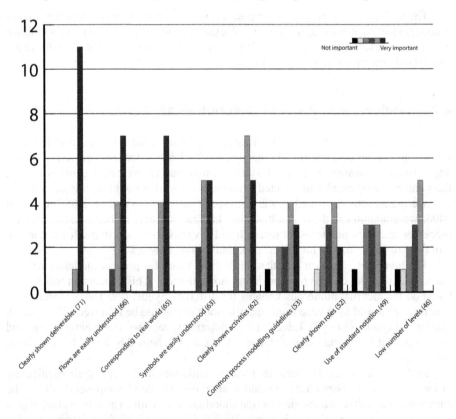

Figure 1. What Is Important for a Well Described Process?

interviewees valued as important for a described process. Number in parentheses give a summary of the score, with not important equal to one point and very important equal to six points.

Contrary to what was found in the literature, the interviewees indicated "clearly shown deliverables" as most important for a well described process. As one interviewee argued, "*that deliverables are clearly shown is very important for software process quality. It is in the interfaces between deliverables that product quality is created and the deliverables should be well defined in order to reach high quality in a software processes description.*" "Clearly shown deliverables" was followed by "easily understood process flows," "high correspondence to real world," and "easily understood symbols." "Use of standard notation" was valued as more important than not important by two thirds of the interviewees, but it was ranked in eighth place compared to other, more valued attributes. Some of the interviewees saw these standard notations as a form of restriction that might suffocate people creativity if they were too rigorous. On the other side, some of the interviewees saw it as mandatory that there should be a restriction in how to describe or model a specific software process. The attribute that ranked quite high in the literature, "clearly shown roles," was not valued as important at all by the interviewees. One interviewee said, "*Focus on roles often gives negative effect in that often when we start projects we begin with a plan of what roles we need and not what we will do. We don't have the free mind set about what roles are in software processes; instead we lock a role to a certain position and this causes more damage than benefit.*" Another interviewee said, "*It is nice that the roles are visible, but most important are activities and that their input and outputs are visible.*"

Figure 2 presents a diagram for what the interviewees valued as the important reasons for having described processes. The interviewees wanted to use the described process to "store organizational knowledge," "discuss improvements," and "communicate knowledge and competence." Several of the interviewees saw a close relation between "store organizational knowledge" and "communicate knowledge and competence." Regarding the attribute "discuss improvements," one interviewee said, "*It is first when the software process is described that we can be sure we talk about the same thing. Described software processes also play a role when initiating change [provides a given starting point] and enables comparison with actual events.*" Another interviewee, who also agreed about the importance of storing organizational knowledge, said, "*Today we are not so good at storing organizational knowledge; it is boring to read documents created by other people.*" Furthermore, "finding weaknesses and problems," "increasing product quality," and "measuring improvements" were valued as important, but with somewhat lower rank than the first three. In addition to these attributes, which are all mentioned in the literature as important attributes for a described process, the interviewees mentioned 11 other attributes.

We finalized the interviews by asking an open question to name tools used for describing processes that the interviewees had come in contact with, used, or heard. The interviewees named 14 different tools. The six most frequently named tools were Rational Method Composer (mention by 11 interviewees), Microsoft PowerPoint (mentioned by 6 interviewees), HWDP (a local variant was mention by 5 interviewees), HTML (mention by 4 interviewees), PLCM (a local variant was mention by 3 interviewees), and Microsoft Visio (mention by 3 interviewees). The interviewees had no common view about what tools to use for describing processes, but they all agreed about

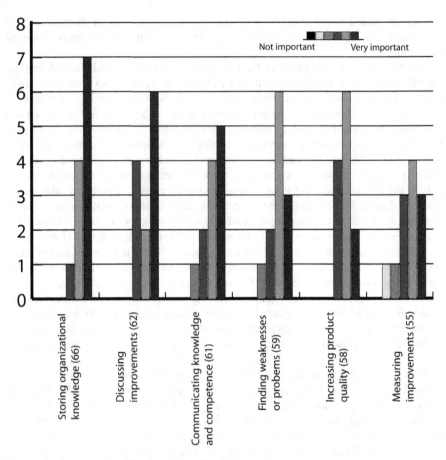

Figure 2. Reasons for Having Described Processes

the importance of having a tool for describing processes. One interviewee said, *"Today we have such advanced and complex software processes that we must use a high-quality tool to be able to control them; Microsoft PowerPoint won't do the job anymore and we cannot do it using free-hand illustrations."* Another interviewee said, *"When using Microsoft PowerPoint, [the projects need to give good reviews] in order to find gaps in the deliverables or roles,"* and continued by noting that it is also *"hard to keep the described software process models and links to the processes [updated]."*

5   ANALYSIS AND DISCUSSION

Recollecting the notions of tacit and explicit knowledge, and motivated by the growing work in globally distributed software development, we set out to answer the question, how do software process descriptions affect understanding of software engineering knowledge? We specifically looked to answer the question from the perspective of a globally active organization. In this section, we analyze and discuss our findings. First, we present the process description situation and awareness; second, we present a deeper analysis of the value of and use for described processes. We conclude the section by discussing implications for practice and research.

5.1 Lacking Obvious Standard Software Process Notation

In iteration one, we investigated a major development unit within Ericsson working with software engineering and found 13 different formal and approved process descriptions. These 13 process descriptions were analyzed through 10 different attributes as defined in Table 3. The analysis revealed that, for software engineering, there were no obvious standard software process notations to enable diffusion of knowledge. An ocular inspection of the 13 process description showed that none of the 3 identified software process notations (BPMN, SPEM, or RAD, see section 2.1) were used. Ould and Huckvale (1995) argue for the importance of unambiguous process descriptions in order for them to be useful. Also, the investigated attributes (#4 – #7, Table 3) indicated that no obvious standard software process notation was followed as there was a large difference in size, tool used, and quality.

In iteration two, we presented the result from iteration one and there was one common view on why the process descriptions varied: lack of a tool. This common understanding was likely based on the fact that numerous variants for different layout (#2, Table 3) were used and if a tool would have been used, specific notations would be followed (#3, Table 3). The lack of quality (#4 – #7, Table 3) of the described processes was mainly understood as a result of difficult manual maintenance that could be helped by a tool for describing processes. What was even more interesting for this conclusion was that no one questioned the result. In practice, this is very uncommon. It is likely that this depended on employees already having a gut feeling this was the situation, but there had been no prior attempts to visualize it. It is important to mention that several of the investigated process descriptions (the ones with good quality) were appreciated among users and provided employees with several benefits in the software engineering area.

We conclude that the investigation of the 10 attributes for the 13 process descriptions found, the reactions from employees during the process situation presentation, and the literature survey indicate that today there are no obvious standard software process notations to manage diffusion of explicit knowledge.

Unambiguous process descriptions are dependent on obvious software process notations. Established tools for describing software processes is likely an important enabler of this.

Larsen et al. (2008) study the role of modeling in achieving information systems success. One of their findings argues that the usage of UML is linked to project success. Similar to our study, we see here a close correlation between the two studies regarding the value of explicit knowledge.

This conclusion was provided further support in the third iteration of the action research, as "use of standard notation" was leaning toward needed by two thirds of the interviewees (see Figure 1). One interviewee argued that a standard notation is still needed, explaining that "*there should be mandatory restrictions on how to describe or model a specific software process.*" At the same time, another interviewee was afraid a standard notation would suffocate people creativity. Our interpretation of this is that while software process notations are needed, the current notations may not provide the obvious support that is needed in all instances. Nevertheless, the importance of having a tool for describing the process was still clearly argued: "*Today we have such advanced and complex software processes that we must use a high-quality tool to be able to control them; Microsoft PowerPoint won't do the job anymore, and we cannot do it using free-hand illustrations.*"

5.2 Explicit Knowledge Facilitates Diffusion of Tacit Knowledge

Managing knowledge can be analyzed through the two categories, explicit and tacit knowledge (Nonaka and Takeuchi 1995; Polanyi 1966). Explicit knowledge is knowledge that can be expressed with words and numbers (e.g., process descriptions), while tacit knowledge is knowledge that is rooted in actions, commitment and involvement in a specific context (e.g., when designing a software architecture or defining software requirements).

From the interviews in iteration three, we learned that for a process description to be valuable, "clearly shown deliverables," "easily understood process flows," "high correspondence to real world," and "easily understood symbols" were highly important. All of these but learly shown deliverables are also recognized by the literature to be of importance for a valuable process description (Lindland et al. 1994; Ould and Huckvale; 1995). This is somewhat remarkable, considering our study indicated that learly shown deliverables was in fact the most important driver for generating value when using described processes (see Figure 1).

> Clearly described deliverables is a key driver for making the explicit knowledge—through described software processes—useful. Clearly described deliverables thus may become an important representative to understand the tacit knowledge.

Furthermore, storing organizational knowledge, discussing improvements, and communicating competences were the main reasons for using the described process. One interviewee said, "*It is only when the software process is described that we can be sure we talk about the same thing. Described software processes also play a role when initiating change [provides a given starting point} and enables comparison with actual events,*" and thus points at the close relation between explicit and tacit knowledge and in particular how the explicit can act as a catalyst for understanding the tacit. Our interviewees confirm what Ellmer and Merkl (1996) argued, that the described process was perceived as needed to manage organizational memory. The described process (i.e., explicit knowledge) was a facilitator to initiate discussion and improvement of all kinds of software engineering activities where actions, commitments, and involvement are important ingredients (i.e., tacit knowledge).

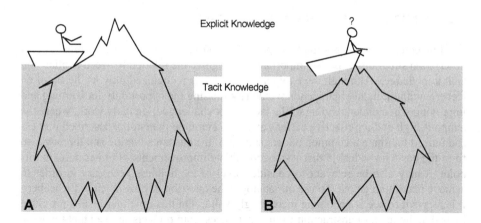

Figure 3. Explicit Knowledge Facilitates Viewing Tacit Knowledge

Explicit knowledge only represents the tip of the iceberg of the entire body of possible knowledge (Polanyi 1966). Having said this, we do not argue that it is either possible or necessary to see the complete iceberg. However, without a clear view of this tip (Figure 3a), there is a risk we might fail to see the rest of the iceberg, where challenges may need to be understood in order to be managed (Figure 3b).

Mathiassen et al. (2003) argue that codification of knowledge plays a crucial role both in relation to maturing professional practices and in relation to the use of information technology to support knowledge management. They also argue that people engaged in knowledge management activities should appreciate the problems and opportunities related to the codification of knowledge. Mathiassen et al.'s argument strengthens our view on the close relation between explicit and tacit knowledge, and our core argument that explicit knowledge is an important enabler of understanding the tacit within software engineering practice.

The explicit nature of described software processes serves as a vital catalyst in initiating discussions of tacit knowledge. These discussions enable valuable improvement suggestions to both tacit (e.g., work practices) and explicit (e.g., process descriptions) knowledge.

Nonaka and Takeuchi (1995) and Hansen et al. (1999) argue that innovation emerges from new interactions between explicit and tacit. This argument is supported by the result from our study, visualized in Figure 2, where "discussing improvements" (e.g., tacit knowledge) was valued as the second most important reason for having described processes (i.e., explicit knowledge).

We thus conclude by arguing that diffusing explicit software engineering knowledge is hindered by the lack of obvious standard notations for software processes and the tools to support them. In this way, the lack of obvious standard software process notations also hinders understanding tacit software engineering knowledge.

5.3   Implications for Practice and Research

For practice, it is important to spend time on understanding the current process description situation. It is also important to recognize the relation between explicit and tacit knowledge. Although the explicit knowledge is recognized only as the tip of an iceberg, without it, an organization would risk missing the opportunity for learning and improving when understanding of the tacit is not challenged. In daily work, where the tempo is high and unreflective actions are more common than not, a described process can indeed facilitate a common understanding of the current situation and thereby also form the basis for valuable discussions to initiate improvements. Furthermore, at this point, it may also be relevant to consider level of explicitness necessary in order to achieve maximum gains. To use our analogy, the question of how much of the iceberg it is relevant to see is becoming increasingly valid. On this note, our results provided hints that the level of abstraction from experiences from projects showed that the issue is far from obvious. On the one hand, enriching the explicit knowledge was recognized as potentially beneficial, but at the same time, several interviewees voiced concern that the process would be impossible for those not already experienced in using it, and that the overall purpose of guiding development would be defeated as any question directed toward a fully explicit process would result in so many answers—all depending on situation—that it would become almost impossible to know which experience to draw upon. Striking the right balance in what to make explicit would thus be an interesting area for further studies to see where practice may shed light on what works and why.

For research, it is important to understand that there is a lack of an obvious standard software process notation. Or at least, there is a lack of studies on deployed standard software process notations to be relied on as best practice examples. The software business would benefit from either having more focus on finding a valuable software process notation or by finding out why an already potentially valuable standard software process notation is not widely deployed. There are, of course, numerous explanations for why deployment fails, but it is likely some of them are related directly to understanding the value of a described process from a knowledge management perspective. From an agile software development perspective, it would be useful to understand more about how agile processes may be described and how they can facilitate understanding tacit knowledge.

Finally, as this study is limited to one software company (although involving many people at different sites and countries), it is possible that these findings are dependent on cultural issues related to this specific company such as process immaturity or lack of process competence. Other research in the software process improvement area (Börjesson 2006; Börjesson et al. 2007; Börjesson and Mathiassen 2004) has shown that software process awareness, attention, and focus are high in the company.

6   CONCLUSIONS

This study aimed to understand more about software process descriptions used in practice. For this paper, we specifically looked at the research question, how do software process descriptions affect understanding of software engineering knowledge? Through action research during the period 2005–2007, we investigated 13 formal and approved process descriptions in a 1,500 employee unit working with software engineering with the telecom company Ericsson AB. The investigation was followed by presentations of the investigation and interviews of 12 senior managers and engineers. The study was framed and discussed in relation to the software process notations and knowledge management literature. The study is finalized by arguing that unambiguous process descriptions are dependent on obvious software process notations, where clearly described deliverables are a key driver for making the explicit knowledge—through described software processes—useful, and that the explicit nature of described software processes serves as a vital catalyst in initiating discussions of tacit knowledge.

Acknowledgments

We appreciate the valuable comments from the anonymous reviewers for this conference. We would also like to mention our appreciation for the high quality work by our master's thesis student, Per Johansson, during the spring of 2007.

References

Bartunek, J. M., and Louis M. R. 1996. *Insider/Outsider Team Research*, Thousand Oaks, CA: Sage Publications, Inc.

Baskerville, R., and Pries-Heje, J. 1999. "Grounded Action Research: A Method for Understanding IT in Practice," *Management and Information Technology* (9), pp.1-23.

Baskerville, R. L., and Wood-Harper, A. T. 1996. "A Critical Perspective on Action Research as a Method for Information Systems Research," *Journal of Information Technology* (11), pp. 235-246.

Baskerville, R. L., and Wood-Harper, A. T. 1998. "Diversity in Information Systems Action Research Methods," *European Journal of Information Systems* (7:2), pp. 90-107.

Börjesson, A. 2006. "Improve by Improving Software Process Improvers," *International Journal of Business Information Systems* (1:3), pp. 310-338.

Börjesson, A., Baaz, A., Pries-Heje, J., and Timmerås, M. 2007. "Measuring Process Innovations and Efficiency," in *Organizational Dyanmics of Technology-Based Innovation: Diversifying the Research Agenda*, T. McMaster, D. Wastell, E. Ferneley, and J. I. DeGross (eds.), New York: Springer, pp. 181-196.

Börjesson, A., and Mathiassen, L. 2004. "Successful Process Implementation," *IEEE Software* (21:4), pp. 36-44.

Carmel, E. 2006. "Building Your Information Systems from the Other Side of the World: How Infosys Manages Time Zone Differences," *MIS Quarterly Executive* (5:1), pp. 43-53.

Curtis, B., Kellner M. I., and Over, J. 1992. "Process Modeling," *Communications of the ACM* (35:9), pp. 75-90.

Davison, R., Martinsons, M., and Kock, N. 2004. "Principles of Canonical Action Research," *Information Systems Journal* (14), pp. 65-86.

Ellmer, E., and Merkl, D. 1996. "Considerations for an Organizational Memory in Software Development," in *Proceedings of the 10th International Software Process Workshop* Ventron, France, June 17-19, pp. 60-62.

Galliers, R. D. 1992. "Choosing an Information Systems Research Approach," in *Information Systems Research: Issues, Methods, and Practical Guidelines*, R. D. Galliers (ed.), Oxford, UK: Blackwell Scientific Publications, pp. 144-162.

Hansen, N., Nohria, N., and Tierney, T. 1999. "What's Your Strategy for Managing Knowledge?," *Harvard Business Review* (77:2), pp. 106-116.

Haumer, P. 2006. "Software & Systems Process Engineering Meta-Model (SPEM 2.0)," Object Management Group, Needham, MA (http://www.omg.org/cgi-bin/doc?ad/06-11-03).

Johansson, P. 2007. "Software Process Notations: The Role and Quality of Described Processes," unpublished Master's Thesis, Chalmers University of Technology, Gothenburg, Sweden.

Kalnins, A., and Vitolins, V. 2006. "Use of UML and Model Transformations for Workflow Process Definitions," available through Cornell University Library (http://arxiv.org/abs/cs.SE/0607044).

Kueng, P., Bichler, P., Kawalek, P., and Schrefl, M. 1996. "How to Compose an Objectoriented Business Process Model," in *Method Engineering on Method Engineering: Principles of Method Construction and Tool Support: Principles of Method Construction and Tool Support*, S. Brinkkemper, K. Lyytinen, and R. J. Welke (eds.), London: Chapman & Hall Ltd., pp. 94-110.

Larsen, T. J., Niederman, F., Limayem, M., and Chan, J. 2008. "The Role of Modeling in Achieving Information Systems Success: UML to the Rescue?," *Information Systems Journal*, forthcoming.

Lindland, O., Guttorm, S., and Sölvberg, A. 1994. "Understanding Quality in Conceptual Modeling," *IEEE Software* (11:2), pp. 42-49.

Maruping, L. M., and Agarwal, R. 2004. "Managing Team Interpersonal Processes Through Technology: A Task-Technology Fit Perspective," *Journal of Applied Psychology* (89:6), pp. 975-990.

Mathiassen, L. 2002. "Collaborative Practice Research," *Information, Technology & People* (14:4), pp. 321-345.

Mathiassen, L., Robertson, M., and Swan, J. 2003. "Cracking the Code: The Dynamics of Professional Knowledge," paper presented at the European Knowledge Management Conference, San Francisco, CA.

Nicholson, B., and Sahay, S. 2001. "Some Political and Cultural Issues in the Globalization of Software Development: Case Experience from Britain and India," *Information and Organization* (11), pp. 25-43.

Nonaka, I., and Takeuchi, H. 1995. *The Knowledge Creating Company. How Japanese Companies Create the Dynamics of Innovation*, New York: University Press, Inc.

Ould, M. A. 1995. *Business Processes*, Bath, UK: John Wiley & Sons Ltd.

Ould, M., and Huckvale, T. 1995. "Process Modeling: Who, What and How—Role Activity Diagramming, in *Business Process Change: Concepts, Methods and Technologies*, W. Kettinger and V. Grover (eds.), Hershey, PA: Idea Group Publishing, pp. 330-349.

Owen, M., and Raj, J. 2005. "PMN and Business Process Management," Telelogic (http://www.telelogic.com).

Patton, M. Q. 1987. *How to Use Qualitative Methods in Evaluation*, Newbury Park, CA: Sage Publications, Inc.

Polanyi, M. 1966. *The Tacit Dimension*, New York: Anchor Day.

Reynolds, T. J., and Gutman, J. 1988. "Laddering Theory, Method, Analysis, and Interpretation," *Journal of Advertising Research*, February-March, pp. 11-31.

Russel, N., ter Hofstede, A. H., van der Aalst, W. M., and Wohed, P. 2006. "On the Suitability of UML 2.0 Activity Diagrams for Business Process Modelling," in *Proceedings of the 3rd Asia-Pacific Conference on Conceptual Modelling* (Volume 53), Hobart, Australia, pp. 95-104.

Sahay, S. 2003. "Global Software Alliances: The Challenge of 'Standardization,'" *Scandinavian Journal of Information Systems* (15), pp. 3-21.

Susman, G., and Evered, R. 1978. "An Assessment of the Scientific Merits of Action Research," *Administrative Science Quarterly* (23), pp. 582-603.

White, S. 2004. "Process and Modeling Notations and Workflow Patterns," BP Trends, March (http://bptrends.com/publicationfiles/03-04%20WP%20Notations%20and%20Workflow%20Patterns%20-%20White.pdf).
Yin, R. 1994. *Case Study Research*, Newbury Park, CA: Sage Publication, Inc.

About the Authors

Anna Börjesson Sandberg is a senior specialist in research and development working at the telecom company Ericsson AB in Gothenburg, Sweden. Both her working tasks and research are focused on software process improvement, process descriptions, change management, and change agency. Anna has been working within the software Industry since 1994. She strives to become a reflective practitioner through combining daily industry work with action research. In January 2006, she received her Ph.D. in Applied IT from the IT University of Gothenburg. Anna is a member of IEEE and ACM. Contact her at anna.sandberg@ericsson.com.

Carl Magnus Olsson is a Ph.D. student at the University of Limerick, Ireland, and works at the IT University of Gothenburg, Sweden. He has held a guest researcher position at the Operations Management and Information Systems Department of Northern Illinois University, and was a participant in the ICIS Doctoral Consortium in Seattle, 2003. Carl Magnus has previously worked professionally with software improvement for six years. His publications include conference papers at IFIP WG 8.2, IFIP WG 8.6, the European Conference on Information Systems, and the International Conference on Information Systems. Contact him at carl.olsson@ituniv.se.

Appendix A: Questions for Cycle Three

#	Questions (for # 1–17, 19: Value on a six grade scale from strongly disagree to strongly agrees to the statement)
1	"I believe described processes are important for discussing improvements." Why?
2	"I believe described processes are important for communicating knowledge and competence." Why?
3	"I believe described processes are important for storing organizational knowledge." Why?
4	"I believe described processes are important for finding weaknesses or problems." Why?
5	"I believe described processes are important for measuring improvements." Why?
6	"I believe described processes are important for increasing product quality." Why?
7	"I believe described processes are important for other reasons." Which and why?
8	"I believe it is important for high process quality that the model corresponds to 'the real world.'" Why?
9	"I believe it is important for high process quality with a low number of levels (clicks) to reach information." Why?
10	"I believe it is important for high process quality that the symbols are easily understood." Why?
11	"I believe it is important for high process quality that the flows are easily understood." Why?

12	"I believe it is important for high process quality that a standard notation is used." Why?
13	"I believe it is important for high process quality that common process modeling guidelines are used." Why?
14	"I believe it is important for high process quality that roles are clearly shown." Why?
15	"I believe it is important for high process quality that deliverables are clearly shown." Why?
16	"I believe it is important for high process quality that activities are clearly shown." Why?
17	"I believe something else is important for high process quality." What and why?
18	What tools for modeling software processes do you know of?
19	"I believe tools for modeling software processes are important." Why?

5 APPLYING USAGE MODELS TO INNOVATE INFORMATION TECHNOLOGY SOLUTIONS

Sigal Louchheim
Intel Corporation
Folsom, CA U.S.A.

Petra Langwald
Judy Ossello
Intel Corporation
Hillsboro, OR U.S.A.

Abstract   *The pro-innovation bias is frequently reflected in the deployment of new information technologies by IT departments. The implicit assumption is that IT innovations should be adopted, and if they are not, the problem lies with the target audience rather than with the innovation itself or with the diffusion methods applied.*

In this work, we have taken a usage model driven approach to identify innovative opportunities for improving collaboration within geographically dispersed teams of design engineers. Our primary goal was to establish the basis of a repeatable process using this approach in IT, driving the development of innovations that are desirable, useful, and usable to the target audience.

A usage model describes users and their goals, as well as the context and process of system use. Our process focused on creating three model components: ethnographic data, personas, and scenarios. From these components, we identified short-, mid-, and long-term opportunities for improving the collaboration experience.

Keywords   IT innovation practices, IT adoption, user-centered innovation, usage model

Please use the following format when citing this chapter:

Louchheim, S., Langwald, P., and Ossello, J., 2008, in IFIP International Federation for Information Processing, Volume 287, Open IT-Based Innovation: Moving Towards Cooperative IT Transfer and Knowledge Diffusion, eds. León, G., Bernardos, A., Casar, J., Kautz, K., and DeGross, J. (Boston: Springer), pp. 83-96.

1   INTRODUCTION

Employees at large information technology companies, such as Intel Corporation, are accustomed to deployments of newer and faster technology and products with more features. We usually justify these deployments from business or technology perspectives, such as decreasing total cost of ownership, increasing security, or enabling new business opportunities. As Rogers (2003) discusses, the agency that sponsors the innovation has a pro-innovation bias. Rogers describes the pro-innovation bias as the implication that the innovation in question is diffused and adopted by the entire target audience, quickly, without resistance and with no changes made to the innovation.

End users often do not have a voice in this process. Generally, however, users want to accomplish a goal or they desire an experience, and the technology is a tool to achieve these needs rather than an end in itself, which can create challenges in the diffusion of the information technology product. To build desirable, useful, and usable products, we need to understand who uses the products and what their needs are. This understanding constitutes the *usage perspective*. The other two perspectives that any product or service has are the technology and business perspectives. The balanced integration of all three perspectives yields the most compelling solutions as explained by Simmons (2006) and portrayed in Figure 1.

When Brown (2002, p. 107) details the learnings of Xerox PARC, he explains that

> the successful company of the future must understand how people really work and how technology can help them work more effectively....It must rethink traditional business assumptions and tap needs that customers don't even know they have yet.

He states that researching new work practices is equally important to researching new technologies and details that

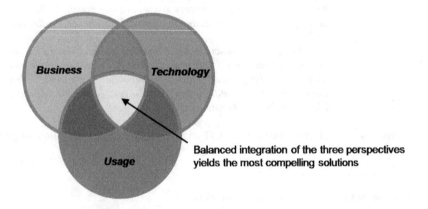

Figure 1. The Three Perspectives: Usage, Business, and Technology

this means going beyond the typical view of technology as an artifact—hardware and software—to explore its potential for creating new and more effective ways of working, what we call studying technology in use.

We address this very challenge in our work, by developing a usage model driven approach. This approach enhances the way we create and innovate by deriving the requirements from user needs and goals.

A challenge was presented to our IT department: engineering team managers know that their geographically dispersed design engineers faced difficulties collaborating, but were not sure of the best way to address the problems. We suggested a usage model driven approach to discover opportunities for improving the engineers' experience. We have not traditionally used this approach for IT solutions.

This work has two goals: to establish the basis for a repeatable usage model driven approach and apply it on a case study. Our case study is on improving the globally dispersed collaboration experience of design engineers. Hence, this work describes two results: (1) The usage model driven approach we defined. This is a repeatable process that that can be used in future innovative projects in IT and make their adoption more likely. (2) The high-impact opportunities for business units and IT to improve the collaboration experience among dispersed design engineers.

The rest of the paper is structured as follows. In section 2 we briefly describe the usage model structure, followed by an overview of the usage model driven approach we introduce in section 3. In the following four sections we describe each one of the components of the usage model driven approach: ethnographic data in section 4, personas in section 5, scenarios in section 6 and identifying innovation opportunities in section 7. In section 8 we conclude with a discussion.

2 THE USAGE MODEL

To provide a compelling user experience, we must identify who our users are and understand their goals, needs, and desires in context. This means also understanding our users' social and physical environment.

We apply a usage model driven approach to achieve this goal. This approach can be valuable during the early stages of project definition to explore the viability of an innovation. The usage information that we gather at this early stage feeds into subsequent planning and development, helping guide decisions in terms of the user experience and helping us create solutions that meet user goals. The results can also be applied in later phases of the project, all the way through the validation of the solution and the application of the diffusion channels.

2.1 Usage Model Structure

A usage model, defined by Simmons (2006), captures data about users and their goals, the context in which they use the system, and the way they use it. Usage models describe system usage in context, at a level that identifies the system's benefits to its users.

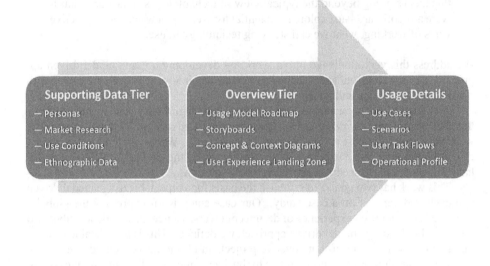

Figure 2. Usage Model Tiers and Components

The usage model driven approach consists of three steps.

- **User:** identify the innovation's (system's) users and discover their goals
- **Usage:** define how the users use the system
- **Requirements:** derive the functional and nonfunctional requirements, transforming the description from a user's perspective into a technical description of the innovation

As depicted in Figure 2, the usage model structure contains three tiers, corresponding roughly to the three steps above: supporting data, usage overview, and usage details.

As Simmons (2005) explains, the supporting data tier provides the depth and background to the other two tiers in the model. It includes quantitative data based on market research and qualitative data emerging from ethnographic studies. For a specific project or innovation, we develop selected components of the model depending on the scope and context of the project. The usage overview tier forms the introduction to the information in the other tiers, and is especially valuable to management because it summarizes findings, whereas the other two tiers provide details. The usage details tier includes the main descriptions of the system use. This information guides the design, validation, and communication of the project, as well as helps manage the scope by relating it to usage. This tier plays a key role in tracing the system's technology features and their impact on users. For example, we could understand the impact that removing a feature might have on the user experience by tracing back the requirement using the usage details. A full description of the usage model is provided by Simmons (2006).

3 OVERVIEW OF THE USAGE MODEL DRIVEN APPROACH

We had dual goals in this work: first, to define the basis of a repeatable process that we could use in future innovative projects in IT, both in their formation as well as in their successful diffusion; second, to discover high-impact opportunities for business units and IT to improve the collaboration experience among globally dispersed design engineers, which was the challenge that was presented to us.

To achieve these goals, we initiated a project aimed at taking a fundamentally user-centered approach to gain a better understanding of design engineers' dispersed collaboration needs. Through this work we developed the repeatable approach that enables us to focus on user-derived opportunities for innovation that we describe here.

We knew that there were gaps in our understanding of design engineers. To address that, we focused our efforts on developing research components that could improve our understanding, rather than imposing a solution that would be a fit for our own collaboration needs. We developed three usage model components: ethnographic data and personas in the supporting data tier and scenarios in the usage details tier, as shown in Figure 3. The personas enable us to clarify and understand who the target audience is and what the target audience's goals and contexts are, as detailed in section 5. The scenarios enable us to define how the system is used and how it will be used in terms that relate directly to the target audience's goals.

The ethnographic data we collected through real-world observations and interviews guided our development of both the personas, which describe who engineers are, and the scenarios, which describe how they act in their contexts to achieve their goals. We also had access to limited market research data that helped us frame the scope of the ethnographic data collection; we chose three or four people to observe and interview in each of the audience segments.

One way of identifying opportunities or getting user requirements is to approach the users, or the customers, and ask them to identify their needs. However, users may have difficulties in articulating their needs on demand. For example, many of the managers of globally dispersed design engineers are familiar with some of the issues contributing

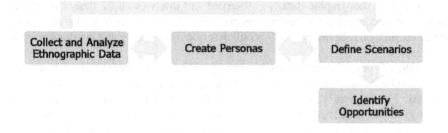

Figure 3. The Usage Model Driven Approach Overview

to poor collaboration, such as the ones imposed by technological and physical constraints. However, these managers may have difficulty in articulating how team culture and improvised temporary solutions (work-arounds) impact collaboration. As Spradley (1979) notes, our cultures provide us with the lenses through which we see, interpret, and describe the world. Users are similarly "imprisoned" in "a particular reality that is taken for granted as 'the reality'" (p. 10) and should not be expected to be able to articulate, on demand, their needs. The process usage model driven approach we introduce in this work allows us to identify the user needs—including the latent user needs—and derive from them the opportunities to improve their experience.

The following four sections describe the four components of our usage model driven approach, as well as key learning we have gained. Throughout our work, we have found that since the usage model approach is relatively new to our IT department, few people had experience with it. Gaining proficiency in usage models is important for the seamless implementation of this process. It was also important to understand the constraints that confine the process: the complexity of the proposed innovation, the resources available to perform the data collection and analysis, the time lines, etc.

4   ETHNOGRAPHIC DATA

According to Spradley (1979, p. 5), "the essential core of ethnography is this concern with the meaning of actions and events to the people we seek to understand," making ethnographic data essential in creating personas. He explains that there are three general sources for cultural inferences: what people say, how they act, and the artifacts they use. Ethnography seeks to capture an understanding of human culture that includes both the explicit and tacit knowledge with which members of the culture are familiar, without presupposing any hypotheses, or, as Spradley (1979, p. 4) says, "ethnography starts with a conscious attitude of almost complete ignorance" and that "rather than studying people, ethnography means learning from people."

4.1 Ethnographic Data Collection

To gather ethnographic data, we observed and interviewed 22 design engineers working on silicon and board design projects at four different sites in the United States, India, and Malaysia. Spradley (1979, 1980) describes observation and interview methodologies.

To identify potential participants to observe and interview, we started by identifying four major silicon and board design projects with globally dispersed teams across several locations. The projects were in different product life cycle phases such as exploration, planning, development, and deployment. Two main variables influenced our individual recruitment efforts from each team: project role and physical location. To focus on highly collaborative work responsibilities we looked for individuals who play a part in consolidating work products across several roles. These individuals do not necessarily have management authority, but may be responsible for project deliverables.

We recruited potential participants through their managers; we first contacted the managers for approval to observe and interview engineers within their organizations. The managers then solicited volunteers. We found it best to contact these participants directly to introduce the project and the methodology. Since the observations and interviews require a time commitment from the users and their management's support, it is important to contact both. The process of identifying appropriate participants and getting a commitment both from them and their managers took us approximately three weeks. Some potential participants perceive observations and interviews as intrusive. It was important to detail how the participants' privacy would be protected and clarify in advance what information and activities will be collected and observed. We note that the population sample we observed and interviewed were a self selecting sample, comprised of volunteers.

We observed participants for an average of two half-days, followed by an interview. To observe participants, members of our team unobtrusively shadowed participants during their work days as they worked at their desks, attended meetings, and performed other activities. It is important for the observations to include both the person being observed, what they say, and their activities, as well as their environment, both physical and the people with whom they interact. We took comprehensive notes throughout the process. We believe that photographs, video, and audio recordings could also help minimize the risk of losing information.

During the open-ended, semi-structured interviews, we asked participants detailed questions about their backgrounds, the processes and tools they used to do their jobs, with whom they typically collaborated, challenges they experienced in collaborating, and other areas.

4.2 Ethnographic Data Analysis

We stored all this data in a central repository, and developed our results by iteratively comparing data gathered during the observations and interviews of different participants and looking for patterns in the similarities and differences between them. Analyzing these patterns helped us to organize participants' actions and motivations in common situations into eight to ten general areas of interest, or themes. We relied on this analysis during the rest of our usage model development.

We have found that it was valuable to have two people conducting the observations and the interviews. When two people conduct the interview, one is able to focus on guiding the interview and the other on taking notes. Both in conducting interviews and in observation, when two people conduct the process, they can discuss the data and remind each other of salient points that the other might have missed or forgotten, and lead to a faster and more thorough discovery of significant patterns in the data.

It is important to allocate enough time for data analysis, creating the model components, and iterative validation of results. For every hour we spent on observations and interviews, we spent about three hours analyzing the data and writing the other usage model components.

5   PERSONAS

Cooper (2004) and Cooper and Reimann (2003) introduced personas to develop a precise description of a narrow target audience and what they wish to accomplish in context. Personas are hypothetical user archetypes of actual users. They are defined with rigor and precision, based on real data; ethnographic data is one of the primary sources of data for persona development, the other being market research. Personas are believable: they have a name, a face, personal details, and so forth. This allows people who use them to create a mental connection to the persona described, even though it does not describe a real person.

Personas are differentiated by their goals, their needs, their desires, and their contexts. They are described within their social, physical, and environmental contexts and may include workflow and skill levels as well as quotes to make the persona more credible and complete. Personas are relevant to the market, as shown through quantitative research. The personas enable decisions to be made based on user goals, and reduce the chance we design for ourselves or people just like us or that we include features in the innovation or project simply because they are appealing to us. Personas ensure that the entire project team, including the stakeholders, has a shared vision and reduce the chance we will make "convenient" assumptions about users and their lives.

Personas help focus on meeting user goals. Personas have five major characteristics: (1) they are memorable; (2) they are based on real data but are not a description of a real person, rather are a deliberate composite that only includes deliberate quirkiness; (3) they are narrowly defined; (4) they are not an average of the data, but rather highlight specific target audiences on which we are focusing; (5) they are representative, capturing key characteristics of the target audience segment.

We began the persona development process using a template that included the persona's goals, attitudes, skill levels, challenges, and frustrations as well as a detailed narrative of the persona's environment. As we established our personas, we iterated through periods of data analysis, persona writing, and reviews. During the data analysis, we examined the patterns and themes emerging from the ethnographic data, identified recurrent themes, and grouped them by similarities. This helped us identify common collaboration goals, challenges, and activities around which we built the personas. We then filled in this structure with narrative descriptions based on the ethnographic data typical of each persona. Note that we did not include suggestions on product design.

We found that it is critical for those involved in conducting observations and interviews to also take part in analyzing the data and creating personas and scenarios. Their familiarity with the details of the data brought richness to the final results. Similarly, prior experience and expertise in creating personas and scenarios clearly enhances the results.

Through this process, we identified four personas, each with a different collaboration focus based on how the individual's work connected to that of others.

One of our personas described a design engineer technical lead, whom we named Pradeep Mishra. He coordinates the work of his team on subsections of chip design, takes the lead in reviewing architectural specifications and changes, and collaborates with validation and mask design teams during the design process. This approximately 900-word persona describes his other work responsibilities and skills in detail. It also provides personal information that helps build a more complete picture, such as his age, education, the languages he speaks, and how long it takes him to commute to his work site in India. The persona describes his frustrations, such as sometimes being unable to reach team members to troubleshoot problems. Very importantly, it also describes his goals, including fast access to information and people to solve the team's issues. In section 6, a sample scenario describing Pradeep problem solving across sites is described.

Our other personas described a project manager and two engineers, each with a different collaboration focus.

Note that we developed personas around our user population, those design engineers whose dispersed collaboration experience we were challenged with improving through our proposed innovations. In our analysis we did not include those people who will be paying for the diffusion and implementation of the innovation, but will not necessarily be using it. Their needs may need to be included, and in some cases, even personas may need to be developed for them, but that will need to be done separately. Similarly, we excluded the support personnel, stakeholders, and subject matter experts and did not create personas for those classes, either.

6 SCENARIOS

A scenario is a narrative that describes how a user interacts with the innovation, which can be a product or a service, to achieve a goal or task. A scenario is a realistic depiction of that interaction, and like personas, scenarios are based on supporting data and are described in context. Scenarios can build on personas, using a persona in the central role. A scenario typically describes a single path of interaction between the persona—including potentially other protagonists—and a product or service. A single path refers to the specific chain of activities with which the persona is engaged given the options available at the time, without including "what-if" conditions that would describe additional, divergent paths that could have been taken under different conditions. Alexander and Maiden (2004) provide a comprehensive range of scenario techniques and discuss the practices in this area both from the academia and the industry perspectives.

We used the scenarios to derive opportunities and requirements and to communicate with stakeholders.

Scenarios are very effective when they present richly detailed descriptions. To develop our scenarios, we reviewed our personas and ethnographic data and identified tasks necessary for the personas to meet their collaboration goals.

For each persona, we identified two to four scenarios. To help us understand current tasks and difficulties, we created an as-is state of the scenario describing current conditions. Based on the persona's goals and needs as well as the challenges of the existing environment, we derived a to-be state describing the persona's desired state. We made to-be scenario states technology agnostic to avoid imposing design solutions at an early stage.

Scenarios covered specialized and general situations such as meetings, integrating versions of design files, tracking issues, and interpreting new specifications. We present a sample scenario below that focuses on problem solving across sites. The persona this scenario is focused on is Pradeep Mishra, a design engineer technical lead. We first present the as-is state, describing the current condition in real-time problem solving and design interaction. Then, we present the to-be state, describing in a technology-agnostic manner the state where the effect is of improved effectiveness of communication. Notice that the to-be scenario is technology agnostic, so that no technology requirements are imposed at this early stage. The gap analysis between as-is and to-be versions of scenarios enables the identification of opportunities to innovate and improve the collaboration experience.

6.1 As-Is Sample Scenario

Pradeep and his team of design engineers in India are preparing for a phone meeting with the validation engineers in Russia. Pradeep called the meeting because the teams cannot understand why validation tests are failing, despite exchanging e-mails about the problem for two days. He usually prefers e-mail and instant messaging for these discussions: phone meetings are difficult because each team's accent is almost incomprehensible to the other. However, in this case, the e-mail exchanges are too slow and the teams are not making progress.

The two teams call in to the meeting. Pradeep asks if the Russian group has the presentation file he sent earlier—he cannot share it using real-time collaboration software because of the unstable network connection between the two sites. The Russian team leader says he is projecting the presentation in their conference room. The file is large, containing text, code, and drawings; it took Pradeep two hours to put together because he tried to anticipate everything they might discuss during the meeting.

Pradeep talks through the slides. As long as he stays with the prepared material, the Russians respond with thoughtful questions that make Pradeep believe they understand what he is saying.

However, he wishes he could see if they were confused or nodding in agreement. When one Russian, Ivan, describes a logic flow, Pradeep's team shakes their heads, so Pradeep asks Ivan to repeat himself so they can understand. Frustrated, Pradeep eventually asks an engineer on his team, Anand, to draw what Ivan is describing. Pradeep's team cannot understand Anand's sketch. Pradeep finally asks Ivan if he can make a sketch and send it to him later so the team can look it over.

6.2 To-Be Sample Scenario

Pradeep's team has been corresponding with the Russian group for two days but they still cannot understand why validation tests are failing. To solve the issue quickly, Pradeep schedules a virtual meeting in which the participants can see visual cues from each site.

Pradeep discusses why his team is experiencing difficulties. He can see that Sergei, one of the Russian engineers, is looking tired, but the rest of the Russian team is looking alert. Anand, on Pradeep's team, can tell that Ivan understands the point he made, and the conversation moves quickly. Once, Ivan asks Pradeep to repeat a phrase three times. Ivan still cannot understand, so Pradeep communicates using a written message. Everybody in India can see the Russian engineers nodding when they see it. When Ivan discusses the logic flow problem, another engineer creates a visual sketch for the group. The teams agree that this is a key problem, so Pradeep assigns a team member to work with Ivan to solve it, and the meeting ends early.

7 IDENTIFYING OPPORTUNITIES FOR INNOVATION

By following the usage model driven approach we have defined, we were able to identify the goals and needs as well as the existing needs and challenges in collaboration of globally dispersed engineers. To discover high-impact opportunities for innovation that will improve the collaboration experience of geographically dispersed design engineers, we identified the gaps between the existing state and user goals. We exposed these gaps by comparing the as-is and to-be versions of the scenarios that we developed for the design engineers.

These gaps revealed the frustrations design engineers encounter in performing their tasks, the hurdles that prevent them from performing their tasks efficiently, and opportunities for improving their dispersed collaboration experience.

The usage model driven approach revealed short-, medium-, and long-term opportunities for innovation, which are differentiated and enumerated below. We validated these opportunities with user representatives including the engineers themselves, our subject matter experts, stakeholders, and our sponsors. Together, we prioritized the innovation opportunities and recommended which should be pursued first to meet the business unit's needs.

7.1 Short-Term Opportunities

Short-term opportunities are those where the problem domain and potential solutions are well understood. The innovations in this case have been developed and are ready to be tested through proof of concepts and pilots as part of the initial diffusion into the target audience. The understanding of the target audience that we have accumulated through this process will continue to play a role through this process.

The short-term opportunities that we have identified through this work include

- Seeing nonverbal cues during the dispersed collaborative interaction. This is particularly important in Asia, where even more attention is paid to nonverbal cues.
- Sharing visual artifacts, such as sketches, across sites.

7.2 Mid-Term Opportunities

Mid-term opportunities are those where the problem domain is well understood but the solution domain is not. That means that we need to explore potential solutions before selecting one for testing and then diffusion.

The mid-term opportunities we have identified through this work include

- Decreasing delays in sharing information between sites. Specific focus areas that we identified under this theme include
  - Communicating decisions and plans
  - Increasing availability and accessibility of information
  - Ensuring information shared locally is communicated globally to the team
  - Sharing sketches or large files
- Facilitating an environment that supports synchronous, asynchronous, and external collaboration.
- Finding people and managing interruptions. For example, in India we observed frequent interruptions in meetings due to participants answering phone calls.

7.3 Long-Term Opportunities

Long-term opportunities are those where we need to investigate the problem domain further to fully understand it before we can explore the solution. These opportunities were not directly stated in the data gathered through observations and interviews, but surfaced when we analyzed the data. An example for a long-term opportunity is the lack of consistent and comprehensive support of the engineering methodology within the system architecture.

8   SUMMARY AND DISCUSSION

Christensen (2005) highlights the role of innovation for sustained success of companies. Diffusion of innovation remains a significant problem that confronts IT organizations. The evolving and rapidly changing environment that IT needs to support requires a keen understanding on the part of IT practitioners of not only the technology and business perspectives, but also of the usage perspective. The repeatable process that we developed can enable other IT teams to achieve that: to satisfy—and even delight—their users by utilizing the understanding they gain of who their users are, and of their users' goals, needs, challenges, frustrations, and environments. In short, by applying the repeatable process we have described, teams can gain an understanding of the social and physical contexts of their target audience and how their target audience is going to interact with the proposed innovation, how it will be used.

The information on both the users in their context and how they will use the innovation can be used to derive requirements for an innovation that will be easier to diffuse, since it will answer the critical question of "what's in it for me" for users in terms that incentivize their adoption of the innovation. As Rogers (2003) discusses, this is a significant challenge in diffusion of innovation in general, and it is true for us in IT.

Increasing productivity remains a central challenge for IT, and as organizations become globally dispersed, the challenges of working in those environments become significant for IT.

In this work we tackled both issues. We examine how to create a repeatable process through which IT innovations could be more oriented to addressing user goals. We also address the productivity challenge by examining how to innovate and improve the globally dispersed collaboration. We found that the usage model driven approach provided an effective way to explore problems in collaboration among dispersed project teams. The approach yielded valuable results in a situation where we knew difficulties existed but were not sure of the best way to address them.

By applying this approach at an early stage, we identified short-, medium-, and long-term opportunities for improving collaboration. We also developed the basis of a repeatable process for use in IT projects.

Deploying user-centered methods within IT presents some specific challenges. Users and IT may have conflicting goals and motivations, solutions are often based on off-the-shelf solutions from vendors, and IT may prefer one-size-fits-all solutions while end users prefer solutions that solve their unique problems. We believe that our usage model driven approach addressed these challenges by helping better understand users' goals. By applying the lessons we learned during this project, we expect to improve the innovation process for future IT projects.

Employing a usage model driven approach is a change in the IT development process, which creates another innovation diffusion challenge: overcoming inherent resistance of the IT organization to change, even when the change promises to deliver benefits. It will require commitment from IT and its business unit partners to understand and address business unit needs using this approach, and is the setting for our future work.

References

Alexander, I. F., and Maiden, N. 2004. *Scenarios, Stories, Use Cases Through the Systems Development Life Cycle*, Chichester, England: John Wiley & Sons.

Brown, J. S. 2002. "Research That Reinvents the Corporation," *Harvard Business Review* (80:8), pp. 105-115.

Christensen, C. M. 2005. *The Innovator's Dilemma: When New Technologies Cause Great Firms to Fail*, Boston: Harvard Business School Press.

Cooper, A. 2004. *The Inmates Are Running the Asylum: Why High Tech Products Drive Us Crazy and How to Restore the Sanity* (2nd ed.), Indianapolis, IN: Sams Publishing.

Cooper, A., and Reimann, R. 2003. *About Face 2.0: The Essentials of Interaction Design*, Indianapolis, IN: Wiley Publishing Inc.

Rogers, E. M. 2003. *Diffusion of Innovations* (5th ed.), New York: Free Press.

Simmons, E. 2005. "The Usage Model: A Structure for Richly Describing Product Usage During Design and Development," in *Proceedings of the 13th IEEE International Conference on Requirements Engineering*, Paris, France, August 29-September 2, pp. 403-410.

Simmons, E. 2006. "The Usage Model: Describing Product Usage during Design and Development," *IEEE Software* (23:3), pp. 34-41.

Spradley, J. P. 1979. *The Ethnographic Interview*, New York: Holt, Rinehart and Winston.

Spradley, J. P. 1980. *Participant Observation*, New York: Holt, Rinehart and Winston.

About the Authors

Sigal Louchheim is an internationally recognized expert in the area of interestingness, the discovery of what is interesting (new, actionable, etc). She received her Ph.D. in Computer

Science in 2003. Sigal is focusing on creating compelling user experiences and adoption strategy and design. Sigal can be reached at sigal.louchheim@intel.com.

Over the past 16 years **Petra Langwald** has program managed complex projects and aligned activities across international teams in various disciplines: software, marketing, hardware, and IT. She has worked in technology companies in Germany, France, and the United States as a program manager and business analyst. Petra can be reached at petra.langwald@intel.com.

Judy Ossello studied the adoption and development of information technology-based solutions that solve strategic and tactical business problems at DePaul University. In addition to working for Intel, she is pursuing an MBA with Babson College to develop a greater understanding of information technology-based solutions from a managerial, financial, and organizational perspective. Judy can be reached at judy.ossello@intel.com.

6 SEEKING THE *FACE* OF INNOVATION WITH THE ETHICAL COMPASS OF EMMANUEL LÉVINAS

Gabriel J. Costello
Galway-Mayo Institute of Technology and
Centre for Innovation and Structural Change
National University of Ireland
Galway, Ireland

Brian Donnellan
Business Information Systems Group
National University of Ireland
Galway, Ireland

Abstract   *A recent biographer has described the philosophy of Emmanuel Lévinas as being permeated by one simple but profound theme: Western philosophy has at best ignored and at worst suppressed the "Other." The approach of this study involved a concept-centric examination of innovation terminology assembled from key papers in the area. The analysis presents evidence of the lack of regard in the literature for the human dimension, with the notable exception of the work of Andrew Van de Ven and his collaborators. Consequently, an ethical definition of innovation is proposed inspired by the theoretical lens of Lévinas. We argue that the work makes a practical and philosophical contribution to the emerging debate on ethics by the Information Systems community. Furthermore, we suggest that our analysis has implications for diffusion of innovations research increasingly being carried out in an open-innovation paradigm.*

Keywords   Emmanuel Lévinas, ethics, phenomenology, Claudio Ciborra, Andrew Van de Ven

Please use the following format when citing this chapter:

Costello, G. J., and Donnellan, B., 2008, in IFIP International Federation for Information Processing, Volume 287, Open IT-Based Innovation: Moving Towards Cooperative IT Transfer and Knowledge Diffusion, eds. León, G., Bernardos, A., Casar, J., Kautz, K., and DeGross, J. (Boston: Springer), pp. 97-117.

1   INTRODUCTION

Davis (1996, p. 1) has described the philosophy of Emmanuel Lévinas as being permeated by one simple but profound theme: "Western Philosophy has consistently practiced a suppression of the *Other*." The principal objective of this paper is to examine the *face* of innovation—extracted from definitions of the phenomenon in seminal papers— through the lens of the ethical philosophy of Lévinas. Furthermore, the study aims to continue the debate proposed by Claudio Ciborra that the position of information and communications technology (ICT) in organizations requires a shift from the present focus on the *scientific paradigm* to an alternative center of gravity: human existence in everyday life. Such a shift, we argue must take us to the world of philosophy (Downie 2005) and in particular to one of its first questions broadly framed by Socrates: How should I live? The study addresses the implications of Lévinas's theoretical lens for two areas: our understanding of the term *innovation* and the consequences of *open IT-based* innovation for diffusion of innovations (DOI) research. The approach consists of examining innovation terminology through a concept analysis of over 30 definitions (Webster and Watson 2002); assembled from key papers and guided by the vision of Lévinas. The analysis indicates that only the work of Van de Ven and his colleagues (Van de Ven et al. 2000) addresses the major contemporary ethical issues facing the information systems community: the human dimension and the use of resources. In addition, the paper argues that the work of Lévinas can save Ciborra's Copernican revolution from the quagmire of solipsism. The work is important in the context of the current priority being given to the debate on ethics by the Information Systems community. The paper is organized as follows. First, the development of the philosophy of Lévinas is presented in the context of his engagement with the phenomenology of Edmund Husserl and Martin Heidegger. Then the influence of phenomenology on contemporary information systems research is presented, chiefly through the work of Claudio Ciborra. Following this, a brief overview of the literature on innovation and information systems is outlined and an analysis of innovation definitions is presented in the form of a concept matrix. Resulting from this, a definition of innovation is proposed based on the Lévinasian *éthique*. Finally the implications for innovation studies are discussed and future work is proposed in the concluding section.

2   BACKGROUND

Recently, views within the information systems literature express the need for researchers to have a firm philosophical basis for their work. For example, Weber (2003) contends that there is a requirement to improve theory-building skills and in doing so researchers must "reflect deeply on and understand the ontological and epistemological assumptions" (p. v) and be true to their philosophical position. Such a philosophical program, we argue, must involve what Quinton (2005, p. 702) describes as a rationally critical and systematic thinking on the "conduct of life (ethics or the theory of value)." This section will trace the philosophical antecedents of the work of Lévinas to the phenomenological program of Edmund Husserl and then consider the influence of phenomenology on the IS debate.

2.1 The Phenomenology of Edmund Husserl

Edmund Husserl, the founding father of Phenomenology, is regarded as having start instigated one of the most important philosophical movements of the 20th century (Grossmann 2005). The system has had an immense influence in Europe in areas spanning psychology, law, values, aesthetics, and religion (Inwood 2005a). He considered that philosophy should be carried out as a rigorous science using the structured methodology of reason and his vision was that the phenomenological approach (of bracketing the natural world and a reduction to pure consciousness) could overcome and synthesize the radical disagreements of contemporary philosophy. Husserl's original studies were in the area of mathematics and his most influential teacher was the philosopher Franz Brentano. His philosophy underwent a transition from his earlier studies on the phenomenology of mathematical and logical concepts to the transcendental idealism developed in his later major work, *Ideas: General Introduction to Pure Phenomenology* (see "Introduction" in Elveton 1970). Lauer (1965) argues that with the passage of time a precise definition of *phenomenology* became more difficult but proposed that the term could be traced back to a "distinction made by Kant between *phenomenon* or appearance of reality in consciousness, and the *noumenon*, or being of reality itself" (p. 2). However, he points out that Husserl rejected what he perceived as the *dualism* of Kant. Lauer continues to explain the phenomenology of Husserl as both a method and a philosophy. Method in so far as it provides the steps that must be followed "to arrive at the pure phenomenon, wherein is revealed the very essence not only of appearances but also of that which appears" (p. 8). In the realm of philosophy "it claims to give necessary, essential knowledge of that which is" (p. 8). Thus phenomenology advocates a "return to things because a 'thing' *is* the direct object of consciousness in its purified form" (p. 9). This approach was in opposition to illusions, verbalisms, or mental constructions implied by many contemporary movements. In connection with the philosophy of the mind, Horner and Westacott (2000) explain that phenomenology attempts to describe exactly what happens when a person is conscious of something and that the approach typically is set in motion by recounting the way things truly appear to us. This is in contrast to other approaches that examine the role of brain processes in relation to consciousness or discuss the mind–brain controversy. Rather poignantly, as many of his pupils set out on very independent paths, Husserl in later years saw himself more and more as a leader without followers. Paul Ricoeur, who translated Husserl's *Ideas I* and commented extensively on him, even stated that the "the history of phenomenology is the history of Husserlian heresies" (Moran 2000, p. 3). However such remarks must be placed in the context of a tragic period in European history during which Husserl's name was dropped from the Freiberg faculty lists in 1936 coupled with his deep personal disappointment with the direction that Martin Heidegger had taken phenomenology (Moran 2000, p. 90).

2.2 Lévinas: Face-to-Face with the *Other*

Born in Lithuania, Emmanuel Lévinas is credited with introducing phenomenology to France after his studies with Husserl and Heidegger, who were major influences on his work. His considerable volume of publications over a period of 60 years made him a key catalyst in the development of French 20th century philosophy, including the emergence of the existentialism of Jean-Paul Sartre and Maurice Merleu-Ponty (Davis 1996, p. 3). His major work *Totality and Infinity* (1961) explored such themes as time death, and relations with others and increasingly his philosophy was concerned with marking out an ethical face-to-face with the Other: a concept that while "immediate and singular, is none the less transcendent" (Ainley 2005, p. 512). Lévinas gave phenomenology a radical ethical orientation variously described as his phenomenology of alterity (*alterité*) or his phenomenology of sociality that starts from the experience of "the face" (*le visage*) and emanates from the other's proximity. The colorful philosopher Alphonso Lingis (1998) has described the concept of *face* as the "central moment of all of Lévinas's phenomenology" and goes on to explain that while the theoretical structure of his work begins with an "ontological elucidation of what it mean to be existent" (p. xxix), his subsequent analysis of the intentional or transcending led him to a region "otherwise than being" (xix). This latter reference is to Lévinas' most notable later work, *Otherwise than Being, or, Beyond Essence*, which Moran sees in part as a response to criticism by Jacques Derrida. Lévinas's use of the term *face* has become the hallmark of his legacy and in his writing stands for the "real concrete presence" of another which "blossomed into a metaphor" for many aspects of the person and culture (Moran 2000, p. 347).

Bergo (2007) states that Lévinas's "phenomenological descriptions of intersubjective responsibility are built upon an analysis of living in the world" and are unique to him. However, we would argue that this is unfair to Husserl, who many years earlier in his lectures on nature and spirit had "maintained that an objective external world can only be experienced inter-subjectively (i.e., by a plurality of individual knowing subjects) who are in a position to exchange information with each other" (Posselt 2005, p. 53). Significantly, this lecture became the inspiration for Edith Stein's doctoral thesis on empathy, a topic closely related to the *Other* of Lévinas.

Now, we propose, it is worth examining the relationship of Lévinas with the two most influential phenomenologists of our time, Edmund Husserl and Martin Heidegger, drawing from a number of studies (Bergo 2007; Davis 1996; Lingis 1998; Moran 2000). In this regard we must admire Lévinas's timing: arriving in Freiburg in 1928, where he was able to attend the last lectures of Husserl on phenomenological psychology and intersubjectivity together with Heidegger's first seminars when he became Husserl's successor that same year. Lévinas was very appreciative of the amount of time afforded to him by Husserl but was clearly captivated by what Inwood (2005b) describes as the enthralling brilliance of Heidegger's lecturing style. During this period, Moran tells us that Lévinas sided with Heidegger's formulation of being-in-the-world against Husserl's transcendental idealism. His first publication was a review of Husserl's *Ideas I* where in the conclusion, he rejected "quasi-solipsistic egological reduction" (Moran 2000, p. 323) as a means to pursue authentic objectivity, and presented the first steps in his long journey of phenomenological intersubjectivity. This is an important point for one of the aims of our paper, namely to consider the implications of Ciborra's call for IS researchers to return to the human person, a topic we will return to later. Significantly, Lévinas's award winning thesis presented for his doctorate at the University of Strasburg in 1929 and published the following year was titled *The Theory of Intuition in Husserl's Phenomenology*. Both Davis and Moran describe Lévinas's reorientation from his initial use of Heidegger's phenomenology to support his critique of Husserl's subjectivism, to the point where Heidegger became the object of a "complete rebuttal" (Davis 1996, p. 21). Two factors seem to have come into play here. Firstly in the purely philosophical realm, where he is quoted by Davis (1996, p. 21) as concluding that the Heideggerian destruction of metaphysics enforces a major flaw in Western thought:

> [T]his supremacy of the Same over the Other seems to me to be entirely maintained in the philosophy of....He does not destroy, but rather he epitomizes a whole current of Western thought....The *Dasein* that Heidegger puts in the place of the soul, of consciousness, of the Ego, retains the structure of the Same.

The second important factor was his realization, when alerted by Alexander Koyré, of the influence of National Socialism on Heidegger, which according to Moran horrified Lévinas and opened his eyes to Heidegger's emphasis on *authenticity* as in fact masking a self-centered weakness that was open to exploitation by such totalitarian ideologies.

One aspect of the work of Lévinas that also needs to be addressed is literally a matter of semantics. This facet is important for our paper, which has few references from the main literature that is associated with ethics. Lévinas did not discuss issues such as laws, rules, rights, duties, and the language or logic of ethical enquiry (Davis 1996, p. 47). He had a more ambitious program; that of developing a *first philosophy* or what Derrida (quoted in Bergo 2007) called writing an "ethics of ethics." Both Moran and Davis translate this word, from the French *éthique*, as his study of "the ethical" analogous to someone studying "the political" rather than just politics. This is also the reason why we chose *compass* in the title when referring to the Lévinasian ethic rather than using, for example, *program*.

Having at this stage introduced the work of Lévinas as it emerged from the phenomenology of Husserl and tested in the ferment of Heidegger, we will now consider implications for the information systems field chiefly in relation to the *labyrinth* of Claudio Ciborra.

2.3 The Influence of Phenomenology on the Information Systems Debate

Ciborra clearly acknowledges the influence of phenomenology, especially in his later work where he proposes that a return to its origins can provide an antidote to the *Krisis* he saw unfolding in the information systems field. He specifically admits his debt to Husserl's 1934 lectures on the *Crisis of European Sciences and Transcendental Phenomenology* and the resulting analysis that the "crisis comes about due to the separation between people and science" (Ciborra 2002, p. 15). Martin Heidegger was a major influence on Ciborra, who harnessed his ideas on technology to analyze such concepts as information infrastructure. However, it must be remembered that Heidegger's phenomenology moved significantly away from many of the positions of Husserl. It is reasonable to deduce that Ciborra's development of the idea of *bricolage* was influenced by the suggestion of Heidegger in his work *Being and Time* that "our knowledge and basic way of encountering the world are obtained through the use of, and not the scientific description of, objects" (Ciborra 2000, p. 90).

This section has presented the work of Lévinas in the context of the antecedent development of phenomenology by Husserl and the subsequent influence of phenomenology on the contemporary information systems debate chiefly through the work of Claudio Ciborra.

2.4 A Note on the Research Approach

One aspect of the approach in this paper has been to follow the advice of Gian-Carlo Rota to Robert Sokolowski as he embarked on writing his book on phenomenology. Rota suggested that philosophers should follow the lead of mathematicians who are more inclined to extract and use rather than engage in complex exegesis. As a result, Sokolowski developed his book in order to offer the possibility of "philosophical thinking at a time when such thinking is seriously called into question or largely ignored"(Sokolowski 2000, p 2) . This paper is no more than a modest attempt to facilitate debate among the DOI community on an important area of philosophy. Furthermore the approach is broadly that of responding to the following questions:

- Does the philosophy of Emmanuel Lévinas affect our current understanding of *innovation* terminology?
- What are the resulting implications for the conduct of DOI research in an open IT-based paradigm?

Additionally, the writing style takes heed of Kerlin's (1997) lament concerning the introduction of the "deadly impersonal" third person to debates in philosophy and business ethics "under the influence of the social sciences" (p. 1432). Furthermore, he argues that the first person facilitates lively writing and avoids any "hesitation to state positions" (p 1432).

2.5 A Brief Engagement with the *Life-World (Lebenswelt)*[1]

The rigor versus relevance debate still resonates from 2007 European Conference on Information Systems, where precursor essays such as that of Benbasat and Zmud (1999) had not lost any of their topicality. Is not the subject of *relevance* particularly challenging as we struggle to engage with one of the most profound and influential philosophers of our time? Let us briefly provide a short incident from the *life-world* that provided one inspiration for this paper. Our research and supervision of undergraduate projects takes us to a number of MNC (multinational corporation) subsidiaries that span a wide area of industrial sectors from medical devices and software development to electro-mechanical services. During a plant tour of a subsidiary in the teeth of much local and corporate change, the manager showed notice boards where he had, with the

---

[1]Husserl, in his later work *Experience and Judgement* (1938), emphasized the importance of returning to the *life-world (Lebenswelt)*, the world of our ordinary experience (Moran 2000, p. 12)

permission of the staff, placed organization charts that contained photographs with the years of service of each person in the subsidiary. The reason, he explained, was that he wanted anyone who came to the plant, especially those deciding its future, "to see the *faces* of its people." This statement impressed very much and immediately brought to mind the philosophical perspective of Emmanuel Lévinas.

3 SEEKING THE FACE OF INNOVATION

This section will first provide a very brief flavor of some of the debates within the general management and IS literature on the subject of innovation. Following this we will examine over 30 definitions of innovation in light of our previous review of the ethical philosophy of Emmanuel Lévinas.

3.1 Innovation and Information Systems

The voluminous and eclectic innovation literature has been recently described as a fragmented corpus (Adams et al. 2006). In an important antecedent paper, Wolfe (1994) concluded that it had made little contribution to the understanding of innovative behavior in organizations and his evaluation of the results as being "inconclusive, inconsistent and characterized by low levels of explanation" (p. 405) was surely a pointed criticism of the field. Slappendel's (1996) subsequent mapping of the literature on innovation in organizations in terms of three theoretical regions—the individualist perspective, the structuralist perspective, and the interactive process perspective—is highly regarded and has been profitably applied by the IS community to the analysis of software process improvement innovations (Kautz and Nielsen 2004). Recently, there have been some noteworthy attempts to provide a more holistic appreciation of the innovation landscape such as the compilations by Fagerberg et al. (2005) and by Shavinina (2003). However, Fagerberg's (2005, p. 20) conclusion that "our understanding of how knowledge—and innovation—operates at the organizational level remains fragmentary" and "that further conceptual and applied research is needed" indicates a scarcity of progress in the intervening period. Moving closer to home, Avgerou (2002) comes to the surprising conclusion that "the term innovation is not actually widely used" (p. 141) in the information systems literature. Swanson (1994), who has been notable among the IS research community in addressing the subject, argues that the innovative deployment of information technology is "increasingly crucial to competitive survival and success" (p. 1069). In the context of this conference theme of open-innovation, Chesbrough's (2003, p. 12) description of innovation as a "difficult process" is in line with the sentiments of the above literature.

One of the main challenges of a review of innovation is the range of definitions from a wide body of literature. In their analysis of the terms *innovation* and *innovativeness* from 21 empirical studies in the new product development literature, Garcia et al. (2002, p. 110) discovered that "no less than fifteen constructs and at least 51 distinct scale items" were used, leading to a great deal of ambiguity.

3.2   Andrew Van de Van and the Minnesota Studies

The work of Andrew Van de Van has made a significant contribution to innovation scholarship since the early 1980s. We will now give a brief overview of his work and its significance should become apparent when our analyses of the data are presented in section 3.3. This pioneering work was carried out during the Minnesota Innovation Research Program (MIRP) and its publications are generally known as the Minnesota studies (Van de Ven et al. 2000). A testimony to the enduring quality and wide-regard of these seminal studies is the fact that although the book was originally published in 1989 and subsequently taken out of print, it was reprinted in the year 2000. The MIRP program was carried out by approximately 40 researchers, now scattered among faculty across the globe, who conducted longitudinal studies of 14 innovations during the 1980s. Significantly, Van de Ven and his team "returned to the library" in the 1990s as they considered that if it took 10 years to gather the data, then they "deserved at least ten years to analyze and make sense of the data" (Van de Ven et al. 2000, p. xx). As this paper is focused on analyzing *definitions* of innovations, it is worth pausing and reflecting here on his definition of the phenomenon (Van de Ven 1986, p. 591).

> Innovation is defined as the development and implementation of new ideas by people who over time engage in transactions with *others* within an institutional context.[2]

As a result, four basic factors are implicit in the definition: new ideas, people, transactions, and institutional context. We will discuss the implications of Van de Ven's work, for the theme of this paper, in the remaining sections.

3.3   Definitions of Technological Innovation: An Analysis

In the course of his work, McInerney (2004) assembled over 30 author-centric definitions of innovation from publications since 1960. These were built, like Russian dolls, from antecedent work by Rahmanseresht (1988) and Zain (1993) with Schumpeter's (1934) earlier definition being added by the authors in recognition of its significance in innovation studies.

A content analysis of the innovation definitions was then carried out through converting the author-centric definitions in the literature into a concept-centric format in order to identify the most common concepts and also ones that may require further attention (Webster and Watson 2002). Additional dimensions were also added to the concept matrix, shown in Appendix A, to facilitate the analysis. The concepts are categorized into whether they are an adjective (for example new, radical), a noun (for example product, market), or a verb (for example implementation, adoption), and numbered 16, 33, and 18 respectively. Another objective was to enable a meta-analysis of the table in order to investigate if the definitions can contribute to the development of

---

[2]We have added the italics as in the context of this paper, the use of the term *others* takes on added significance.

theory, for example whether they exhibit *parsimony* or have any *theoretical glue* (Whetten 1989). The rows provide the paper references from which the concepts were extracted and their occurrence. The sorting order from left to right was not done alphabetically in order to try to indicate chronologically when the concept appeared in the literature. The frequency of use of a particular concept in the definitions is indicated from the number of asterisks in the table columns. For example, while *product* and *process* were used by Schumpeter and many others early on, the idea of "know-how" was introduced by Freeman in 1982. No effort has been made at this stage to apply any *frugality* to an evidently *un-parsimonious* table using, for example synonyms, as it was decided just to use the raw data for this study.

The important result of this analysis, we believe, is that there are only two references to *people* (or our *Other* in this study) and one reference to *resources*, densely crowded into the table in Appendix A, but which can be further examined using the wonders of a word processing "zoom" button—or a magnifying glass! This, we believe, is extremely important as it covers the two major areas of ethics: the role of people and resources in the development and implementation of an innovation. Furthermore, the former and latter are tied together within such debates as that of justice. Surely the other significant feature is that these two definitions both emanate from the work of Andrew Van de Ven and his colleagues in the 1980s. There are many other analyses that we believe can be extracted from this table, but our basic focus here is the search for a human "element" in the innovation literature through examination of important definitions. However, even a cursory look at the cluster of the asterisks and comparing them with Schumpeter's original definition would lead to a suspicion: *la plus ça change, la plus c'est la même chose.*

4   DISUSSION

We have now worked our way through the origins of phenomenology to the ethic of Lévinas and then applied our gleanings to the world of innovation studies. Previously the ethical concept of the *Other* has been applied to the role of *innovation* in literary studies (Attridge 1999) while this work relates it to technological innovation. Based on our analysis, we will first propose a novel definition of innovation and then consider its practical implications for DOI research in the era of open IT-based innovation.

4.1   An Ethical Definition of Innovation

The table of innovation definitions in Appendix B contains an array of concepts that, for the most part, do not take into account the human aspect of the phenomenon. Therefore, we believe it is incumbent on us to attempt to stimulate some debate by offering a starting point. We have chosen to do this by taking one highly regarded definition, that of Zaltman et al. (1973), sprinkling it with the scholarship of Van de Ven, and adding Ciborra's human focus in order to propose a Lévinasian inspired definition. Those who are interested and unimpressed but would like to join this nascent open source community are invited to examine the database of definitions in the appendix—distilled from over 30 years of scholarly endeavor.

Proposition: *An innovation is a human activity resulting in an artifact, idea, practice, organization, learning, or information system—perceived to be new by the unit of adoption—that is cognizant of the Lévinasian Other. Consequently, ethical issues must be considered that affect initiating, implementing, and using the innovation together with the associated employment of resources.*

We will now discuss implications of this new conceptualization for DOI research, the open innovation paradigm and the legacy of Claudio Ciborra.

4.2   Implications for DOI Research in the Context of Open IT Innovation

The novel innovation definition described in the previous section will now be examined using the following themes from the ethical and DOI literature: *consequences* of the diffusion of innovations and *responsibility* vis-à-vis an innovation.

Rogers' (2003) *magnum opus* does not deal with the topic of ethics *per se* but the section on *consequences* specifically raises questions of a profound ethical nature, which the following quotations illustrate (p. 440):

> Instead of asking, as much past diffusion research has done—"What variables are related to innovativeness?"—future investigations need to ask, "What are the effects of adopting innovations?"

> Most past diffusion research stopped with an analysis of the decision to adopt a new idea, ignoring how this choice is to be implemented and with what consequences.

In his summary of the chapter devoted to consequences of innovation, Rogers defines two important goals of diffusion programs: raising the level of *good* in a system and fairness in the distribution of the *good*. Such concepts such as the common good and justice fall under the traditional philosophical taxonomy of the *theory of value* (or ethics). Furthermore, consequentialism is controversial ethical philosophy in its own right (Hooker 2005) and because of its importance in Rogers' innovation development process invites further reflection outside of this study.

Responsibility is an important concept in the study of moral and ethical philosophy (Klein 2005). We will now deal with the issue of *responsibility* by referring to Kerlin's (1997) joust with Peter French on the metaphysical and practical implications of the latter's work on corporate ethics. Kerlin brings French to task for treating a corporation as a "moral agent in its own right" since "we cannot reason with the organisation or shame it" and we are unable to attribute *responsibility* to an abstraction. He furthermore emphasizes that "our moral discourse is with the creators of the structures" (p. 1437).

Chesbrough's (2003) seminal publication on *open innovation* and its recent academic offspring (Chesbrough 2006) does not deal with the issue of ethics directly. However, we argue that the distributed nature of this new paradigm driven largely by advances in ICT adds additional urgency to tackling the issues of *consequences* and *responsibility* discussed above. The loosening of ties implicit in such cloudy conceptualizations as *value constellations* (Vanhaverbeke and Cloodt 2006) reinforces the dangers of Kerlin's Wizard-of-Oz syndrome where it becomes increasingly difficult to attribute responsibility to the composite innovation and its consequences. Interestingly, almost 15 years before Chesbrough's publication, the Minnesota Studies were examining network relationships using the concept of *transactions*. In its only indexed entry on ethics, it argued that the notion of trust among parties was a critical ethical element in the design of "transaction structures" (Ring and Van de Ven 2000). In this section of our paper, we have argued that the ethical concepts of *consequences* and *responsibility* have practical implications for the DOI research in the context of the open IT paradigm. We will now present the case that the Lévinasian theoretical lens has philosophical implications for research in this area and the wider IS landscape.

4.3 Implications for Ciborra's Copernican Revolution

One of Ciborra's enduring themes is his call to "go to the origins of phenomenology." According to Resca (2006), "the adoption of phenomenological philosophy represents a significant point of transition in Ciborra's work" and Ciborra (2002, p. 170) states this clearly in his chapter on *Kairos* (and *Affectio*):

> We can find shelter by going to the origins of phenomenology, the philosophical line of thought that in the last century celebrated the notion of situatedness.

Ciborra argued that the position of ICT in organizations requires a shift from the present focus on the scientific paradigm to an alternative center of gravity: human existence in everyday life. Furthermore he described this realignment in terms of a Copernican revolution in the way organizations introduce and use ICT. He writes passionately about "How to get closer to practice, then, and the real life of systems in use in a fresher way?" (2002, p. 6). He proposes a new emphasis on activities such as improvisation and bricolage as part of his concern for "human existence as a neglected factor in the implementation of complex systems and organizations" (2002, p. 8). In the final lines of his "Invitation" (2002, p. 9), he continues the grand theme of a Copernican revolution by stating "I want to contribute to a transition of the field towards an Age of the Baroque in the development and management of technology in organisation and society."

While this paper has more modest objectives, we argue that our approach of engaging with the issue of ethics in information systems continues the broad aim of Ciborra's legacy and the current IS debate on ethics. However, one problem we believe is embedded in Ciborra's revolution: the danger of a return to *solipsism* a "view that only oneself exists" (Squires 2005, p. 883). The counteraction of this embedded tendency became the whole *raison d'être* of the lifework of Lévinas. The message, we argue, from Emmanuel Lévinas is that there is "someone else out there" and innovators and the information systems community must recognize their *face* and engage with it. However, one question remains that makes us uneasy: Is the Lévinasian *Other* overly sentimental, presenting us with an untenable perfection? No, we believe Lévinas himself answers this in his poetic style:

Autonomy, the philosophy which aims to ensure the freedom, or the identity, of beings, presupposes that freedom itself is sure of its right, is justified without recourse to anything further, is complacent in itself, like Narcissus. When, in the philosophical life that realizes this freedom, there arises a term foreign to the philosophical life, other—the land that supports us and disappoints our efforts, the sky that elevates us and ignores us, the forces of nature that aid us and kill us, things that encumber us or serve us, men who love us or enslave us—it becomes an obstacle; it has to be surmounted and integrated into this life (1998b, p. 49).

4.4 Suggestion for Future Work and Limitations of the Study

We have endeavored to firmly root the paper within the general theme of the ethics of *innovation*. Consequently, we believe that there are a number of areas that require exploring in order to address the practical and philosophical implications for DOI research in an open-innovation era. In the area of practice, section 4.2 argued that research into the concept of *consequences* has been called for by Rogers and this is salient to the ethical debate. Also, the important question of who assumes *responsibility* for a technical innovation fashioned in the new open-world requires further debate.

In the area of philosophy, Lévinas's assessment of Heidegger can provide a basis for further stimulating debates given the latter's current influence on our field and on philosophical debates in general. We also propose that engaging with Lévinas with his ethical emphasis on the "face of the human other" furthers the exploration of the work of Husserl and has particular resonance with the examination of *empathy* by his pupil Edith Stein (1989). The importance of empathy in research has been stressed by Susman and Evered (1978), while Leonard (1998) has proposed the importance of *empathic* design. Additionally, McNerney's (2001) thesis described Lévinas's influence on the development of Karol Wojtyla's philosophy of *participation*—a major theme of Kelly's (2005) award-winning paper that we believe invites deeper study.

Furthermore we suggest that our analysis can provide the groundwork for a rediscovery and a philosophical revaluation of the contribution of Andrew Van de Ven to innovation studies.

This paper is limited by the lack of assessment of the broader ethical literature vis-à-vis the information systems discipline. The analysis of the innovation definitions, while parsing the significant words, did sacrifice some rich *meanings*, for example those embedded in Nonaka (1990). Also, future work is required to further refine the matrix analysis, rationalize the constructs, expand the range of definitions, and extract those with an information systems focus to assist the field.

5   CONCLUSIONS

It is now almost 10 years since Larsen, in his assessment of IS innovation and diffusion research, declared that the "human actor as the basis unit for investigation has simply not gotten the level of attention it needs" (1998, p. 414). The aim of this paper has been to address this perennial issue by exploring the human aspects of innovation studies through the ethical lens of Emmanuel Lévinas and in particular his phenomenology of the *Other*. The approach involved the examination of over 30 definitions of innovation that were organized into a concept matrix from key papers in the area. The analysis concluded that the human person (the *Other* of innovation) has been ignored in the scholarly terminology with the notable exception of the work of Andrew Van de Ven, a finding that supports the hypothesis that the thesis of Lévinas holds in the reference frame of innovation studies. As a result, an ethical definition of innovation was proposed in order to invite further reflection by the IS community on an ancient philosophical question: How do we live? Added to this is a very modern philosophical question prompted by Angle and Van de Ven (1989): How do we ethically use our resources in the activity of innovation? In the discussion section, the paper argued that ethical questions are implicit in Rogers' work and the advent of the open IT paradigm adds urgency to furthering debate on these topics. We then placed our work in the context of the call by Claudio Ciborra that the position of ICT in organizations requires a shift from the present focus on the scientific paradigm to an alternative center of gravity: human existence in everyday life. However, the paper contended that the work of Lévinas can save Ciborra's Copernican revolution from a return to the predicament of solipsism which continues, wittingly or unwittingly, the suppression of the *Other*. Future work was suggested for a more comprehensive analysis of the innovation concept matrix and also to examine the implications of Lévinas's *éthique*—together with the work of other philosophers of his *genre*—for the development of information systems research. Finally, we suggest that our analysis can provide the groundwork for a rediscovery and a philosophical revaluation of the contribution of Andrew Van de Ven to innovation studies. Above all, we must agree with Larsen (1998, p. 411) that these are still "exciting research questions that need our attention."

Acknowledgments

The authors are grateful to the anonymous reviewers for their very helpful comments on an earlier version of this paper.

References

Adams, R., Bessant, J., and Phelps, R. 2006. "Innovation Management Measurement: A Review," *International Journal of Management Reviews* (8:1), pp. 21-47.

Ainley, A. 2005. "Lévinas, Emmanuel," in *The Oxford Companion to Philosophy*, T. Honderich (ed.), Oxford, UK: Oxford University Press, pp. 512-513.

Angle, H. L., and Van de Ven, A. H. 1989. "Suggestions for Managing the Innovation Journey," in *Research on the Management of Innovation: The Minnesota Studies*, A. H. Van d Ven, H. L. Angle, and M. S. Poole (eds.), New York: Harper and Row, pp. 590-607.

Attridge, D. 1999. "Innovation, Literature, Ethics: Relating to the Other," *Publications of the Modern Language Association* (114:1), Special Topic: Ethics and Literary Study (January 1999), pp. 20-31.

Avgerou, C. 2002. "New Socio-Technical Perspectives of IS Innovation in Organizations," in *ICT Innovation: Economic and Organizational Perspectives*, C. Avgerou and R. Larovere (eds.), Cheltenham, UK: Edward Elgar, pp. 141-161.

Becker, S. W., and Whisler, T. L. 1967. "The Innovative Organization: A Selective View of Current Theory and Research" *The Journal of Business* (40:4), pp. 462-469.

Benbasat, I., and Zmud, R. W. 1999. "Empirical Research in Information Systems: The Practice of Relevance," *MIS Quarterly* (23:1), pp. 3-16.

Bergo, B. 2007. "Emmanuel Lévinas," in *The Stanford Encyclopedia of Philosophy* E. N. Zalta (ed.) (http://plato.stanford.edu/archives/spr2007/entries/levinas/).

Burgelman, R. A., Maidique, M. A., and Wheelwright., S. C. 1996. *Strategic Management of Technology and Ennovation* (2nd ed.), Chicago: Irwin.

Chesbrough, H. W. 2003. *"Open Innovation: The New Imperative for Creating and Profiting from Technology,* Boston: Harvard Business School.

Chesbrough, H. W. 2006. "Open Innovation: A New Paradigm for Understanding Industrial Innovation," in *Open Innovation: Researching a New Paradigm*, H. Chesbrough, W. Vanhaverbeke, and J. West (eds.), Oxford, UK: Oxford University Press, 1-24.

Ciborra, C. 2000. "A Critical Review of the Literature on the Management of the Corporate Information Infrastructure," in *From Control to Drift: The Dynamics of Corporate Information Infrastructures*, C. U. Ciborra (ed.), Oxford, UK: Oxford University Press, pp. 15-40.

Ciborra, C. 2002. *The Labyrinths of Information: Challenging the Wisdom of Systems,* Oxford, UK: Oxford University Press.

Davies, M. 1988. *The Management of Technological Innovation in Small and Medium Sized Firms in Cyprus*, unpublished Ph.D. thesis, Department of Management Studies, Brunel University.

Davis, C. 1996. *Lévinas: An Introduction*, Cambridge, UK: Polity Press.

Derrida, J. 1980. "Violence and Metaphysics," in *Writing and Difference* (trans. A. Bass), Chicago: University of Illinois Press, pp. 79-153.

Downie, R. S. 2005. "Ethics and Morality," in *The Oxford Companion to Philosophy*, T. Honderich (ed.), Oxford, UK: Oxford University Press, p. 271.

Downs Jr., G. W., and Mohr, L. B. 1976. "Conceptual Issues in the Study of Innovation," *Administrative Science Quarterly* (21:4), pp. 700-714.

Drucker, P. 1985. *Innovation and Entrepreneurship: Practice and Principles*, London: Heinemann.

DTI. 1994. "Innovation Definition," Department of Trade and Industry, London, UK.

Elam, M. 1993. *Innovation as the Craft of Combination: Perspectives on Technology and Economy in the Spirit of Schumpeter*, Ph.D. Thesis, Linköping Studies in Arts and Science No. 95.

Elveton, R. O. (ed./trans.). 1970. *The Phenomenology of Husserl: Selected Critical Readings*, Chicago: Quadrangle Books.

Evan, W. M., and Black, G. 1967. "Innovation in Business Organizations: Some Factors Associated with Success or Failure of Staff Proposals," *The Journal of Business* (40:4), pp. 519-530.

Fagerberg, J. 2005. "Innovation: A Guide to the Literature," in *The Oxford Handbook of Innovation*, J. Fagerberg, D. Mowery, and R. R. Nelson (eds.), Oxford, UK: Oxford University Press, pp. 1-26.

Fagerberg, J., Mowery, D., and Nelson, R. R. (eds.). 2005. *The Oxford Handbook of Innovation*, Oxford, UK: Oxford University Press.

Freeman, C. 1982. *The Economics of Industrial Innovation* (2nd ed.), London: Frances Pinter.

Garcia, R., and Calantone, R. 2002. "A Critical Look at Technological Innovation Typology and Innovativeness Terminology: A Literature Review," *Journal of Product Innovation Management* (19:2), pp. 110-132.

Gardiner, P., and Rothwell, R. 1985. "Tough Customers: Good Designs," *Design Studies* (6:1), pp. 7-17.

Grossmann, R. 2005. "Phenomenology," in *The Oxford Companion to Philosophy*, T. Honderich (ed.), Oxford, UK: Oxford University Press, pp. 695-697.

Hooker, B. 2005. "Consequentialism," in *The Oxford Companion to Philosophy*, T. Honderich (ed.), Oxford, UK: Oxford University Press, pp. 162-165.

Horner, C., and Westacott, E. 2000. *Thinking through Philosophy: An Introduction*, Cambridge, UK: Cambridge University Press.

Hyvärinen, L. 1990. "Innovativeness and its Indicators in Small- and Medium-Sized Industrial Enterprises," *International Small Business Journal* (9:1), pp. 64-79.

Inwood, M. J. 2005a. "Husserl, Edmund," in *The Oxford Companion to Philosophy*, T. Honderich (ed.), Oxford, UK: Oxford University Press, pp. 408-410

Inwood, M. J. 2005b. "Heidegger, Martin," in *The Oxford Companion to Philosophy*, T. Honderich (ed.), Oxford, UK: Oxford University Press, pp. 371-375.

Kautz, K., and Nielsen, P. A. 2004. "Understanding the Implementation of Software Process Improvement Innovations in Software Organisations," *Information Systems Journal* (14:1), pp. 3-22

Kelly, S. 2005. "New Frontiers in the Theorization of ICT-Mediated Interaction: Exploring the Implications of a Situated Learning Epistemology," in *Proceedings of the 26th International Conference on Information Systems*, D. Avison, D. Galletta, and J. I. DeGross (eds.), Las Vegas, NV, December 11-14, pp. 495-505.

Kerlin, M. J. 1997. "Peter French, Corporate Ethics and the Wizard of Oz," *Journal of Business Ethics* (16), pp. 1431-1438.

Kimberly, J. R. 1981. "Managerial Innovation," in *Handbook of Organizational Design*, P. C. Nystrom and W. H. Starbuck, New York: Oxford University Press, pp. 84-104.

Klein, M. 2005. "Responsibility," in *The Oxford Companion to Philosophy*, T. Honderich (ed.), Oxford, UK: Oxford University Press, p. 816.

Knight, K. E. 1967. "A Descriptive Model of the Intra-Firm Innovation Process," *The Journal of Business* (40:4), pp. 478-496.

Larsen, T. J. 1998. "Information Systems Innovation: A Framework for Research and Practice," in *Information Systems Innovation and Diffusion: Issues and Directions*, T. J. Larsen and G. McGuire (eds.), Hershey, PA: Idea Group Publishing, pp. 411-434.

Lauer, Q. 1965. *Phenomenology: Its Genesis and Prospect*, New York: Harper & Row.

Leonard, D. 1998. *Wellsprings of Knowledge: Building and Sustaining the Sources of Innovation*, Boston: Harvard Business School Press.

Lévinas, E. 1998a. *Otherwise than Being, or, Beyond Essence*, Pittsburgh, PA: Duquesne University Press.

Lévinas, E. 1998b. "Philosophy and the Idea of Infinity," *Collected Philosophical Papers* (trans. A. Lingis), Pittsburgh, PA: Duquesne University Press, Chapter 4, pp. 47-59.

Lingis, A. (trans.). 1998. "Translators's Introduction," in *Collected Philosophical Papers*, E. Lévinas, Pittsburgh, PA: Duquesne University Press, pp. vii-xxxi.

McInerney, D. P. A. 2004. *Innovative Regions: A Comparative Analysis of the Innovative Activities of Indigenous and Non-indigenous Small and Medium Sized Enterprises (SMEs) in the Shannon and Dublin Regions of Ireland*, unpublished Ph.D. thesis, University of Limerick, Ireland.

McNerney, J. 2001. *Footbridge Towards the Other: A Philosophical Investigation into the Notion of the Human Person in the Writings of Karol Wojtyla with Special Reference to the Paradigm of the Neighbour*, unpublished M.Litt. thesis, Department of Philosophy, University College Dublin, Ireland.

Mohr, L. B. 1969. "Determinants of Innovation in Organizations," *The American Political Science Review* (63:1), pp. 111-126.

Moran, D. 2000. *Introduction to Phenomenology*, New York: Routledge.

Nelson, R. R., and Winter, S. G. 1977. "In Search of Useful Theory of Innovation," *Research Policy* (22:2), pp. 36-76.

Nonaka, I. 1990. "Redundant, Overlapping Organization: A Japanese Approach to Managing the Innovation Process," *California Management Review* (32:3), pp. 27-38.

Nystrom, H. 1990. *Technological and Market Innovation: Strategies for Product and Company Development*, Chichester, UK: Wiley.

Porter, M. 1990. *The Competitive Advantage of Nations*, New York: Free Press.

Posselt, T. R. 2005. *Edith Stein: The Life of a Philosopher and Carmelite*, Washington, DC: ICS Publications.

Quinton, A. 2005. "Philosophy," in *The Oxford Companion to Philosophy*, T. Honderich (ed.), Oxford, UK: Oxford University Press, pp. 702-706.

Rahmanseresht, H. 1988. *Towards a Revised Model of Innovation in Organisations*, unpublished Ph.D. thesis, University of Hull.

Resca, A. 2006. "Knowledge: Climbing the Learning Ladder to a 'Phenomenological' View," *Journal of Information Technology* (21:3), pp. 203-210.

Rickards, T. 1985. *Stimulating Innovation: A Systems Approach*, London: Pinter.

Ring, P. S., and Van de Ven, A. H. 2000. "Formal and Informal Dimensions of Transactions," in *Research on the Management of Innovation: The Minnesota Studies*, A. H. Van d Ven, H. L. Angle, and M. S. Poole (eds.), New York: Oxford University Press, pp. 637-662.

Roberts, E. B. 1988. "Managing Invention and Innovation," *Research-Technology Management*, (31), pp. 11-29.

Rogers, E. M. 2003. *Diffusion of Innovations* (5th ed.), New York: Free Press.

Rogers, E. M., and Shoemaker, F. F. 1971. *Communication of Innovations: A Cross-Cultural Approach*, New York: The Free Press.

Rowe, L. A., and Boise, W. B. 1974. "Organizational Innovation: Current Research and Evolving Concepts,: *Public Administration Review* (34:4), pp. 284-293.

Schumpeter, J. A. 1934. *The Theory of Economic Ddevelopment: An Inquiry into Profits, Capital, Credit, Interest, and the Business Cycle*, Boston: Harvard University Press.

Shavinina, L. V. (ed.). 2003. *The International Handbook on Innovation*, Oxford, UK: Pergamon Press.

Shepard, H. A. 1967. "Innovation-Resisting and Innovation-Producing Organizations," *The Journal of Business* (40:4), pp. 470-477.

Slappendel, C. 1996. "Perspectives on Innovation in Organizations," *Organization Studies* (17:1), pp. 107-129.

Sokolowski, R. 2000. *Introduction to Phenomenology*, New York: Cambridge University Press.

Squires, R. 2005. "Solipsism," in *The Oxford Companion to Philosophy*, T. Honderich (ed.), Oxford, UK: Oxford University Press, p. 883.

Stein, E. 1989. *On the Problem of Empathy* (trans. W. Stein) (3rd rev. ed.), Washington, DC: ICS Publications.

Susman, G. I., and Evered, R. D. 1978. "An Assessment of the Scientific Merits of Action Research," *Administrative Science Quarterly* (23:4), pp. 582-603

Swanson, E. B. 1994. "nformation Systems Innovation among Organizations," *Management Science* (49:9), pp. 1069-1092.

Swanson, E. B., and Ramiller, N. C. 1997. "The Organizing Vision in Information Systems," *Organization Science* (8:5), pp. 458-474

Swanson, E. B., and Ramiller, N. C. 2004. "Innovating Mindfully with Information Technology," *MIS Quarterly* (28:4), pp. 553-583

Thompson, V. A. 1965. "Bureaucracy and Innovation," *Administrative Science Quarterly* (10:1), Special Issue on Professionals in Organizations, pp. 1-20.

Van de Ven, A. H. 1986. "Central Problems in the Management of Innovation," *Management Science* (32:2), pp. 590-607.

Van de Ven, A. H., Angle, H. L., and Poole, M. S. (eds.). 2000. *Research on the Management of Innovation: The Minnesota Studies*, New York: Oxford University Press.

Vanhaverbeke, W., and Cloodt, M. 2006. "Open Innovation in Value Networks," in *Open Innovation: Researching a New Paradigm*, H. Chesbrough, W. Vanhaverbeke, and J. West (eds.), Oxford, UK: University Press, pp. 258-284.

Vrakking, W. J. 1990. "The Innovative Organization," *Long Range Planning* (23:2), pp. 94-102.

Weber, R. 2003. "Editor's Comments: Theoretically Speaking," *MIS Quarterly* (27:3), pp. iii-xii.

Webster, J., and Watson, R. T. 2002. "Analyzing the Past to Prepare for the Future: Writing a Literature Review," *MIS Quarterly* (26:2), pp. xiii-xxiii.

Whetten, D. A. 1989. "What Constitutes a Theoretical Contribution?," *Academy of Management Review* (14:4), pp. 490-495.

Wilson, J. 1966. "Innovation in Organizations: Notes toward a Theory," in *Approaches to Organizational Design*, J. Thompson (ed.), Pittsburgh, PA: University of Pittsburgh Press, pp. 193-218.

Wolfe, R. A. 1994. "Organizational Innovation: Review, Critique and Suggested Research Directions," *Journal of Management Studies* (31:3), pp. 405-431.

Yin, R., Heald, K., and Vogel, M. 1977. *Tinkering with the System: Technological Innovations in State and Local Services* Toronto: Lexington Books.

Zain, M. 1993. *A Field Study of Adoption and Implementations of Innovations by Manufacturing Firms in Malaysia*, unpublished Ph.D. thesis, Manchester Business School.

Zaltman, G., Duncan, R., and Holbek, J. 1973. *Innovations and Organizations*, New York: Wiley

About the Authors

Gabriel J. Costello is a lecturer at the Galway-Mayo Institute of Technology, Ireland. He is currently undertaking a Ph.D. in MIS at the Centre for Innovation and Structural Change (CISC), National University of Ireland, Galway. The research is investigating the area of *information systems and innovation* with an emphasis on its challenges for practice, theory, and philosophy. Prior to this he worked for 20 years in the telecommunications industry. Gabriel can be contacted at gabrielj.costello@gmit.ie.

Brian Donnellan is a lecturer and researcher in the Cairnes Postgraduate School of Business and Public Policy in the National University of Ireland, Galway (NUIG). His research interests lie primarily in the area of innovation systems, a broad area that encompasses knowledge management, new product development, and technology management. Prior to joining the NUIG faculty, he spent 20 years working in the ICT industry. Dr. Donnellan is currently associated with the Centre for Innovation and Structural Change (CISC), an interdisciplinary research center in NUIG investigating the innovation processes and policies that are fundamental to the development of a knowledge-based economy. Dr. Donnellan is responsible for the interorganizational systems research stream in CISC. The goals of this research stream are to investigate the salient operational features of inter-firm networks and collaborative relationships, including those with a regional dimension, to determine the extent to which interorganizational systems provide a platform for value-added partnerships, and to devise feedback loops between research and teaching so that course materials and delivery are informed by best practice in the area. He can be contacted at brian.donnellan@nuigalway.ie.

Appendix A. A Concept Matrix of Innovation Definitions (Developed from McInerney 2004)

Concept categories across columns:

CONCEPT: Adjective — 1 New, 2 Novel, 3 New to org., 4 Early Use, 5 Postmarket, 6 First, 7 Symbolization, 8 Departure, 9 Radical, 10 Incremental, 11 Alternative, 12 Technical, 13 Competitive Advantage, 14 Combination, 15 Successful, 16 Worthwhile

CONCEPT: Noun — 1 Product, 2 Process, 3 Supply, 4 Market, 5 Organization, 6 Idea, 7 Service, 8 Trade, 9 Procedure, 10 Practice, 11 Invention, 12 Discovery, 13 Object, 14 Program, 15 Artefact, 16 System, 17 Technique, 18 Information, 19 Equipment, 20 Commercial Activity, 21 Entrepreneurial Tool, 22 Know-how, 23 Business, 24 Outcome, 25 Industry, 26 Budgeting System, 27 Technology, 28 Way of doing things, 29 Enterprise, 30 Materials, 31 Method, 32 Delivery system, 33 Production System

CONCEPT: Verb — 1 Generation, 2 Acceptance, 3 Implementation, 4 Change, 5 Adoption, 6 Introduction, 7 Evolve, 8 Design, 9 Manufacture, 10 Management, 11 Commercialization, 12 Learning, 13 Development, 14 Realize, 15 Exploit, 16 Interaction, 17 Creation, 18 Making thing happen

OTHER — Resources, PEOPLE

Publication Year	Author(s)
1934	Schumpeter
1965	Thompson
1967	Wilson
1967	Becker & Whisler
1967	Knight
1967	Evan and Black
1971	Rogers & Shoemaker
1973	Rowe & Boweic
1973	Zaltman et al.
1977	Nelson & Winter
1977	Yin et al.
1979	Downs & Mohr
1981	Kimberly
1982	Freeman
1985	Rickards
1985	Gardiner & Rothwell
1985	Drucker
1986	Van de Ven
1988	Rahmanseresht
1988	Davies
1988	Roberts
1989	Angle & Van de Ven
1990	Nonaka
1990	Nystrom
1990	Vrakking
1990	Porter
1990	Hyvarinen
1992	Elam
1993	Zain
1994	DTI
1996	Burgleman et al.

Appendix B. Definitions of Innovation

Definitions taken mainly from the work of (McInerney 2004) which was developed from antecedent studies by Rahmanseresht (1988) and Zain (1993).

Innovation Definition	Author
New products, new methods of production, new sources of supply, the exploitation of new markets and new ways to organize business	Schumpeter (1934)
Generation, acceptance, and implementation of new ideas, processes, products and services.	Thompson (1965)
An innovation or more precisely a major innovation is a fundamental change in a "significant number" of tasks.	Wilson (1966)
The first or early use of an idea by one of a set of organizations with similar goals.	Becker & Whistler (1967)
An innovation is the adoption of a change which is new to an organization and to the relevant environment.	Knight (1967)
The implementation of new procedures or ideas s whether a product of invention or discovery, will be referred to as "innovation."	Evan & Black (1967)
When an organization learns to something it did .not do before and it proceeds to do it in a sustained way a process of innovation has occurred	Shepard (1967)
The successful introduction into an applied situation of means or cods that are new to the situation	Mohr (1969)
An innovation is an idea, practice, or object perceived as new by an individual. It matters little, as far as human behaviour is concerned whether or not an idea is objectively new as measured by the lapse. of time since its first uses or discovery....if the idea seems new and different to the individual, it is innovation	Rogers & Shoemaker (1971)
The successful utilization of processes, programs, or products which arc new to an organization and which are introduced as a result of decisions within that organization.	Rowe & Boise (1974)
New idea, practice, or material artefact perceived to be new by the relevant adopting unit.	Zaltman et al. (1973)
Innovation is defined as the earliness or extent of use by a given organization of a given new idea, where new means only now to the adopting agent, and not necessarily to the world in general.	Downs & Mohr (1976)
A portmanteau to cover the wide range of variegated processes by which man's technologies evolve over time.	Nelson & Winter (1977)
Innovation includes any discrete idea, practice or material artefact that is introduced for the first time...and is seemingly discontinuous with past practice. The term technological innovation moreover, refers to those innovations that consist of (1) an artefact or material (2) a computer system or (3) an analytic idea or practice that lends itself to quantitative symbolization.	Yin et al. (1977)

Innovation Definition	Author
A managerial innovation is any program product or technique which represents a significant departure from the state of the art of management at the time it first appears and which affects the nature, location, quality or quantity of information that is available in the decision making progress	Kimberly (1981)
Industrial innovation includes the technical design, manufacturing, management, and commercial activities invoked in the marketing of a new (or improved) process or equipment.	Freeman (1982)
Commercialization of invention.	Rickards (1985)
Innovation does not necessarily imply the commercialization of only a major advance in the technological state of the art (radical innovation) but it includes also the utilization of even small-scale changes in technological know-how (incremental innovation).	Gardiner & Rothwell (1985)
Innovation is the specific tool of entrepreneurs, the means by which they exploit change as an opportunity for a different business or service. It is capable of being presented as a discipline, capable of being learned, capable of being practiced.	Drucker (1985)
The process of development and implementation of new ideas by people who over time engage in transactions with others within an institutional context.	Van de Ven (1986)
The process whereby an adoption unit chooses a significant alternative that is perceived as superior to and/or different from some current practice or outcome and attempts to realize it so that a deficiency in the practice or outcome can be corrected or so that either/or both can be improved.	Rahmanseresht (1988)
Innovation includes the opening up of markets, the conquest of new sources of supply of materials, new forms of organization of an industry, including the creation or breaking up of monopoly positions as well as process and product innovations.	Davies (1988)
The generation of an idea while innovation incorporates both invention and exploitation.	Roberts (1988)
A purposeful, concentrated effort to develop and implement a novel idea that is of substantial technical, organizational and market uncertainty that entails a collective effort of considerable duration and that requires greater resources than are held by the people undertaking the effort.	Angle & Van de Van (1989)
Innovation is a product of the interaction between necessity and chance, order or disorder, continuity and discontinuity.	Nonaka (1990)
Any renewal designed and realized, that strengthens organization's competitiveness.	Vrakking (1990)
Companies achieve competitive advantage through acts of innovation. They approach innovation in its broadest sense, including both new technologies and new ways of doing things.	Porter (1990)
The creation of the future—the process of bringing new ideas (products, processes, know-how, budgeting systems, management techniques, etc.) into use.	Nystrom (1990)

Innovation Definition	Author
Innovativeness is a combination of technological, enterprise and market and other environmental dimensions by which means that a small and medium sized industrial enterprise develops and adopts new ideas, also other than technical ones, for industrial use or for markets earlier than other corresponding enterprises.	Hyvärinen (1990)
The combining of materials in a novel fashion to produce other things or the same things by a different method.	Elam (1993)
The process of matching organizational and environmental means and needs.	Zain (1993)
Successful exploitation of new ideas.	DTI (1994)
The "combined activities leading to new marketable products and services and/or new production and delivery systems."	Burgelman et al. (1996)

Part 3:

Cross-Organizational and Cultural Issues

7   EFFECTS OF CULTURAL ORIENTATION ON ATTITUDE TOWARD ANONYMITY IN E-COLLABORATION

Yingqin Zhong
Na Liu
John Lim
Department of Information Systems
National University of Singapore
Singapore

Abstract   *The important role of attitude in the acceptance and diffusion of technology has been widely acknowledged. Greater research efforts have been called for examining the relationships between cultural variables and attitude toward technology. In this regard, this study investigates the impact of cultural orientation (focusing on an individual's degree of collectivism) on attitude toward e-collaboration technology. A theoretical model is proposed and subsequently tested using a questionnaire survey involving 236 data points. Self-reliance, competitive success, and group work orientation are found as significant indicators reflecting an individual's degree of collectivism, which in turn influences willingness to participate, evaluation of collaborative effort, and preference for anonymity feature. Subsequently, the three variables are found to affect perceptions about decision quality, enjoyment, uncertainty, and pressure in e-collaboration.*

Keywords   Attitude, cultural orientation, degree of collectivism, anonymity, e-collaboration

1   INTRODUCTION

In the current business environment, the massive shift toward a global digital economy has manifested the prominence of e-collaboration technology in supporting

Please use the following format when citing this chapter:

Zhong, Y., Liu, N., and Lim, J., 2008, in IFIP International Federation for Information Processing, Volume 287, Open IT-Based Innovation: Moving Towards Cooperative IT Transfer and Knowledge Diffusion, eds. León, G., Bernardos, A., Casar, J., Kautz, K., and DeGross, J. (Boston: Springer), pp. 121-138.

distributed virtual teams. Computer-mediated communications (CMC) tools can increase participation, create greater equality of influence, and reduce domination, production blocking, and cognitive interference. Carrying out group brainstorming tasks in computer-mediated environments has been considered more productive than face-to-face settings in academic institutions, training establishments, governments, and international organizations (Riegelsberger et al. 2005). In decision-making tasks, CMC tools facilitate users in analyzing alternatives, negotiating, and building consensus among group members. These tools are found effective in reducing production blocking, free riding, sucker effect, and evaluation apprehension. They are also found to be positively related to group cohesion and member satisfaction (Reinig and Shin 2002). Many studies have been conducted to investigate the adoption and diffusion of global e-collaboration (e.g., Lefebvre et al. 2006; Munkvold 2005). While many of these studies have pointed out the importance of organizational factors (such as top management support and firm characteristics) in the adoption and diffusion of e-collaboration systems, few have looked at this issue from the individual user's perspective (Lefebvre et al. 2006).

Diffusion is "the process by which an innovation is communicated through certain channels over time among the members of a social system" (Rogers 1995, p. 5). IT diffusion refers to the spread of information technology (Eder and Igbaria 2001). Concerning individual users' progression in forming the attitude toward technology, Rogers' (1995) work highlights the important role that attitude plays in predicting technology acceptance; this has been widely accepted (Albirini 2006). Attitude is defined as "a psychological tendency that is expressed by evaluating a particular entity with some degree of favor or disfavor" (Eagly and Chaiken 1993, p. 1). In other words, attitude reflects some sense of "goodness" or "badness" toward a particular entity perceived by an individual. This paper studies the impact of attitude toward e-collaboration as well as attitude toward collaboration outcomes, with an aim to contribute to the understanding in acceptance and diffusion issues of e-collaboration.

However, the perceived advantage of collaborative technology and the subsequent attitude toward e-collaboration can vary significantly among individual adopters of different cultural backgrounds. Culture plays an imperative role in explaining the differences of patterns exhibited in IT usage (Srite and Karahanna 2006). Prior research has indeed emphasized the influences of culture on technology acceptance and diffusion, as some technology features do embed certain cultural assumptions in their design (Zhang et al. 2007). One of these features is anonymity, which has been commonly used in communication. Promoting equality, openness, and directness in communication, unidentified communications enabled by anonymity features may favor individualists at the expense of collectivist users. Diffusion research has noted that an individual's acceptance of technology is culturally constructed, suggesting the importance of understanding cultural influences in the diffusion of collaborative technology (Anderson 1991). Arising from the trend of globalization, the design of collaborative systems should not only consider technology features but also the intellectual models of users who are implicitly carriers of specific cultural orientations (Zhang et al. 2007).

Culture is fundamentally conceptualized as shared symbols, norms, and values of behaviors in a social collectivity, such as country (Hofstede 1991; Hui and Triandis 1986; Triandis 1995). In particular, cultural orientation reflects an individual's basic beliefs, preferences, or tendencies (Alavi and McCormick 2004); it has a direct impact on technology usage and social behaviors in computer-mediated collaborations (Ji et al. 2004).

Cultural orientation affects self-concept, verbal and nonverbal expressions, and inter-personal relationships in communications. The interference of CMC tools on communication process connotes the cultural influences; in other words, an individual's cultural orientation contributes to the way in which one accepts and approaches collaborative technologies. For example, studies based on the technology acceptance model (TAM) have reported varying results in terms of predictive power across different cultural contexts including North American, European, Arabic, and Asian countries (Hu et al. 1999; Rose and Straub 1998; Straub et al. 1997). In accordance, greater research efforts are needed in investigating the relationships between cultural variables and IT adoption determinants (Leidner and Kayworth 2006; Srite and Karahanna 2006).

A problem in prior IS research is that theoretical propositions proposed about specific national cultures do not address the underlying mechanisms that make these cultures different (Zhang et al. 2007). In this regard, Earley (1993) and Wagner (1995) suggest that the concept of *degree of collectivism* may explain the difference in individual behaviors. The individualism-collectivism dimension has been described as the single major cultural dimension in social behaviors, and recognized to have a direct impact on how people use technologies (Niles 1998). This dimension, capturing the relative importance people accord to personal interests and to shared pursuits, has been studied at both individual and national levels. Particularly, it has been widely accepted as an index to use in explaining individual differences even within a single country (Alavi and McCornick 2004; Wagner 1995; Workman 2001). Previous research suggests that the degree of collectivism can affect people's intention to participate in unidentified communications, with greater degree of collectivism stimulating more active participation (Watson et al. 1993). For example, in identified communications, individualists tend to contribute more arguments to the discussion in attempting to make their mark on the final decision. In contrast, collectivists would mask their positions to avoid conflicts or delay the process of consensus building, even if they think their arguments are valid. This study will contribute to this line of research by exploring the impact of people's cultural orientation—in terms of degree of collectivism—on their attitude toward e-collaboration, which is an important indicator pertaining to technology acceptance and diffusion.

The remainder of this paper is organized as follows. Section 2 proposes a research model and provides theoretical supports for the hypotheses development. We test this model empirically through a survey study, which is described in section 3. Next, the data analysis is presented. Finally, findings are discussed and implications are drawn.

2 RESEARCH MODEL AND HYPOTHESES DEVELOPMENT

The theory of reasoned action (TRA) (Ajzen and Fishbein 1980) has long been recognized as an imperative framework in attitude studies as well as IT adoption research. TRA suggests that, in order to predict a specific behavior, it is necessary not only to measure general attitude about performing the behavior, but also the attitude concerning the expected results by performing the behavior (Lutz 1981). Building upon TRA to provide a further investigation of attitude toward behavior, Eagly and Chaiken (1993) propose the composite attitude–behavior model, which highlights that attitude concerning the expected results—attitude toward target—is affected by attitude toward performing the behavior. Triandis (1995) suggests that an individual's attitude toward performing certain behaviors is heavily influenced by his/her degree of collectivism; these behaviors are embedded in a person's orientation so that he/she generally acts in the same way. Therefore, it is posited that degree of collectivism affects attitude toward performing the behavior, which in turn affects attitude concerning the expected results.

Based on Triandis' work and Eagly and Chaiken's composite attitude–behavior model, we propose a research model as depicted in Figure 1. The related constructs are defined in Table 1. In this model, users' attitude toward e-collaboration is reflected in three constructs including willingness to participate, evaluation of collaborative effort, and preference for anonymity feature. Users' attitude concerning collaboration outcomes is in the form of decision quality, uncertainty, enjoyment, and pressure.

Earley (1993) and Wagner (1995) propose that an individual's collective orientation may be multidimensional and more complex than a simple preference. The cultural dimension individualism-collectivism has been defined as cultural syndromes (Triandis 1995). That is, individualism and collectivism are differentiated by several defining attributes. In line with Anakwe et al. (1999) and Wagner, we investigate degree of collectivism (DC) in terms of four facets including self-reliance, competitive success, group work orientation, and group-goal summation.

2.1 Degree of Collectivism

Individualism and collectivism have been widely used at the individual level to conceptualize individual's collective orientations (Alavi and McCornick 2004; Wagner 1995; Workman 2001). In general, when working in groups, individualists prevail in group tasks over relationships and group members are expected to be frank and candid (Wagner 1995). On the other hand, collectivists tend to prioritize group interests over individual recognition and rewards; the focus is on group harmony rather than on confrontation. Collectivists consider relationships are more important than the task. A spec-

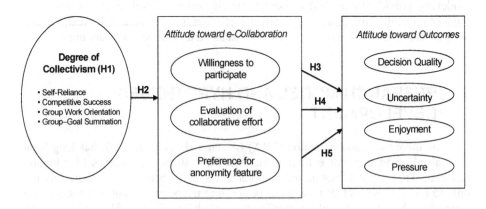

Figure 1. Research Model

Table 1. Defining the Variables in the Research Model

Variable	Definition
Degree of collectivism (Anakwe et al. 1999; Wagner 1995)	The degree of an individual's cultural orientation reflecting the collectivist's characteristics. A spectrum can be formed with individualism and collectivism as the two ends.
Self-reliance (Alavi and McCormick 2004)	Defining self as an autonomous entity independent of groups.
Competitive success (Triandis 1995)	The tendency to define status and success as a function of specific accomplishments in competition.
Group work orientation (Kim et al. 1994)	The tendency to be driven by social norms, duties, and obligations.
Group–goal summation (Triandis 1995)	The tendency to subordinate personal goals to group goals.
Willingness to participate (Wagner 1995)	The willingness to contribute to the accomplishment of group goals in collaborative processes.
Evaluation of collaborative efforts (Spence 1985)	Perception of the potential difficulties involved in the collaboration process.
Preference for anonymity feature (Klein and Dologite 2000)	Preferred degree of anonymity supported in the communication.
Decision quality (Ocker and Yaverbaum 2001)	The efficacy in making effective decisions.
Uncertainty (Downey and Slocum 1975)	The probability of failure in the task due to the lack of information about behaviors of other members.
Enjoyment (Ryan and Deci 2000)	Joy expected to gain from the collaboration.
Pressure (Ryan and Deci 2000)	Anticipating pressure faced in the collaboration.

trum can be formed with individualism and collectivism as the two ends, and along this spectrum, points are representing different degree of collectivism (Triandis and Gelfand 1998; Wagner 1995).

First, among individualists, the self is defined to be independent of other members in a group task—*self-reliance*; the self-reliance factor has been the key idea of many studies investigating degree of collectivism as an individual characteristic (Alavi and McCormick 2004). A second defining attribute of the individualist, *competitive success*, refers to the emphasis on high self-esteem in the form of winning a competition (Triandis 1995). Third, collectivists tend to be more group oriented, which implies an emphasis on relationship even when they are disadvantaged (Kim et al. 1994). Finally, collectivists are concerned more with the group goals than their personal pursuits. They place top priority in doing what is "right" for the group. On the other hand, when conflict exists, individualists will attempt to reach personal goals prior to the group interests (Triandis 1995). Aligning with existing literature, we expect that

H1a.   *Self-reliance is negatively related to degree of collectivism.*
H1b.   *Competitive success is negatively related to degree of collectivism.*

H1c.   Group orientation is positively related to degree of collectivism.
H1d.   Group-goal summation is positively related to degree of collectivism.

2.2 Attitude toward Participating in E-Collaboration

Group members' voluntarily contribution is essential in group tasks (Wagner 1995). For individualists whose self-definitions arouse interest in the pursuit of personal gains, collaboration is proved attractive only if working with others leads to the attainment of personal benefits that cannot be obtained by working alone. In other instances, individualists are likely to avoid collaboration even when they are working in a group task. In contrast, cooperation is valued by collectivists whose self-definitions favor the pursuit of group interests (Triandis 1995). Research suggests that differences in people's degree of collectivism are likely to affect their collaboration in groups, with greater collectivism stimulating greater willingness and tendency to participate in group work (Zhang et al. 2007).

H2a.   Degree of collectivism is positively related to user's willingness to
*   participate.*

Moreover, given the same task, individualists tend to perceive more efforts are required in collaboration as compared to collectivists. In attending to group performance and well-being, collectivists are likely to seek and contribute to cooperative endeavors that benefit their groups, irrespective of the immediate personal implications of these endeavors (Spence 1985; Wagner 1995).

H2b.   Degree of collectivism is negatively related to user's evaluation of
*   collaboration efforts toward a given task.*

Previous studies have reported contradictory effects with the introduction of anonymity in a group process. On one hand, anonymity decreases conformance pressure on the participants in a group setting (Nunamaker et al. 1991; Valacich et al. 1992). On the other hand, studies have suggested that the absence of gender and other status cues eliminates biased devaluation of contributors (Klein and Dologite 2000; Flannagin et al. 2002). In such instances, it is possible for some individualists to reason that they will not receive credit for their notable contributions. Collectivists' self-esteem is not derived from calling attention to their own abilities or contributions; instead, their prime interest is to promote group interests (Wink 1997). Thus, they tend to perceive unidentified communication as an effective mechanism to avoid confrontation and maintain harmony. In contrast, individualists tend to expect that their contributions could arouse attention and gain personal influence in the group decision (Goncale and Staw 2006). Consequently, they tend to prefer identified communication media.

H2c.   Degree of collectivism is positively related to user's preference for
*   anonymous features for a given task.*

2.3 Attitude toward Collaboration Outcomes

Decision quality (George et al. 1990) is measured as a component of collaboration outcome. Decision quality perceived by the participants is an important indicator to reflect collaboration effectiveness and their efficacy in group potency (Ocker and Yaverbaum 2001). Additionally, past research has found that group task performance in terms of uncertainty should improve when task requirements are matched to a fitting technology (Alavi et al. 1995). Uncertainty is regarded as the lack of information needed to make a decision about a future event (Downey and Slocum 1975), and the probability of loss (Peter and Ryan 1976; Taylor 1974). People participating in an e-collaboration task would perceive uncertainty as the probability of failure in group tasks due to the lack of information about the behaviors of other members. Studies have shown that perceived uncertainty may deter people from participating and actively contributing in a group task (Ryan and Deci 2000).

Intrinsic motivation refers to the incentive about the inherent satisfaction from an activity rather than the actual reward or outcomes (Ryan and Deci 2000). When being intrinsically motivated, a person tends to act for the fun or challenge entailed rather than the external rewards (Ryan and Deci 2000). Intrinsic motivation in the context of e-collaboration refers to positive factors in the form of enjoyment (Kim et al. 2006). Moreover, Ryan and Deci (2000) regard pressure perceived by participants as an important inhibitor for participation in the virtual environment.

To enable effective collaboration, group members must first be willing to share information and then have an opportunity to contribute (Zhang et al. 2007). Depending on how they view themselves relative to other group members, people with high willingness to participate in a group work tend to have more self-initiated efforts contributing to the completion of group tasks even under adverse condition (Augustinova et al. 2005). Hence, willingness to participate is negatively related to uncertainty perceived by users. Also, self-enhancement is a basic need of people to see themselves in a positive light in relation to others; therefore, people with higher willingness to participate tend to have higher intrinsic motivation in joining the e-collaboration tasks and they would perceive the collaboration with more enjoyment and less pressure (Pratt 1998).

H3a.   *User's willingness to participate is positively related to perceived decision quality.*

H3b.   *User's willingness to participate is negatively related to perceived uncertainty in communication.*

H3c.   *User's willingness to participate is positively related to enjoyment in communication.*

H3d.   *User's willingness to participate is negatively related to pressure in communication.*

Tasks requiring a high level of collaboration among members tend to involve conflicts among group members. Research has shown that in an e-collaboration context, members experience fewer hassles and perform better for tasks requiring loose interdependency among members as compared to tasks requiring tight interdependency (Lam 1997). Therefore, people who perceive a task as requiring great collaboration efforts tend to expect a higher level of uncertainty, and consequently worse performance. Similarly, they expect less enjoyment and more pressure in tasks demanding greater efforts to resolve conflicts in collaboration.

H4a. *User's evaluation of collaboration efforts is negatively related to perceived decision quality.*

H4b. *User's evaluation of collaboration efforts is positively related to perceived task uncertainty in communication.*

H4c. *User's evaluation of collaboration efforts is negatively related to perceived enjoyment in communication.*

H4d. *User's evaluation of collaboration efforts is positively related to perceived pressure in communication.*

Anonymity in e-collaboration may decrease evaluation apprehension (the fear of negative evaluation from other members), increase member participation (Alavi et al. 1995, Chester and Gwynne 1998), and enhance the amount of information generated by the team (Alavi 1994). Higher level of anonymity in collaboration tends to be associated with better decision quality and less uncertainty perceived by members. Moreover, anonymity provides members with equal opportunities to express their ideas by reducing the cues of social status among members. Research has shown that the reduction of social cues in CMC can lead to less fear of disapproval from others, and subsequently encourage greater participation (Dubrovsky et al. 1991; Siegel et al. 1986).

H5a. *User's preference for anonymity feature is positively related to perceived decision quality.*

H5b. *User's preference for anonymity feature is negatively related to perceived uncertainty in communication.*

H5c. *User's preference for anonymity feature is positively related to perceived enjoyment in communication.*

H5d. *User's preference for anonymity feature is negatively related to perceived pressure in communication.*

3   RESEARCH METHOD

A questionnaire survey was conducted for this study. Data were collected from undergraduate students of a large university and module credit was given as incentive. We chose usage of the university collaborative learning system as the target behavior to ensure familiarity and well-formed beliefs from the respondents. Only responses from those who had prior experience in both identified and unidentified communications were included in the analysis, which yielded 236 data points. These respondents came from different countries to ensure sufficient variance in the degree of collectivism; 67 percent of the respondents were male; the age of respondents ranged from 19 to 31, with a mean of 23 (S.D. = 1.845). All research variables were measured using multi-item scales, which were derived from previously published studies (see Table 2).

Table 2. Measurement Model

Constructs	Item Loading	Composite Reliability	Cronbach's Alpha	Variance Extracted
Social Reliance (SR)		.906	.794	.829
(Anakwe et al. 1990; Wagner 1995)				
SR1	.804			
SR2	.810			
Competitive Success (CS)		.804	.630	.584
(Anakwe et al. 1990; Wagner 1995)				
CS1	.487			
CS2	.640			
CS3	.774			
Group Work Orientation (GWO)		.864	.858	.622
(Anakwe et al. 1990; Wagner 1995)				
GWO1	.628			
GWO2	.692			
GWO3	.638			
GWO4	.593			
Group–Goal Summation (GGS)		.831	.843	.516
(Anakwe et al. 1990; Wagner 1995)				
GGS1	.637			
GGS2	.773			
GGS3	.752			
GGS4	.712			
GGS5	.626			
Willingness to Participate (WP)		.870	.776	.691
(Kim and Song 2004)				
WP1	.668			
WP2	.686			
WP3	.750			
Evaluation of Collaboration Effort		.940	.870	.886
(ECE) (Lu and Argle 1991)				
ECE1	.736			
ECE2	.628			
Preference for Anonymity Feature		.921	.897	.660
(AF) (Kim and Song 2004)				
AF1	.686			
AF2	.714			
AF3	.826			
AF4	.840			
AF5	.783			
AF6	.894			
Decision Quality (DQ)		.864	.765	.679
(Paul et al. 2005)				
DQ1	.441			
DQ2	.550			
DQ3	.246			

Constructs	Item Loading	Composite Reliability	Cronbach's Alpha	Variance Extracted
Uncertainty (UNC)		.767	.610	.457
(Son et al. 2006)				
UNC1	.445			
UNC2	.631			
UNC3	.713			
UNC4	.479			
Enjoyment (ENJ)		.896	.682	.600
(Ryan and Deci 2000)				
ENJ1	.739			
ENJ2	.857			
ENJ3	.762			
ENJ4	.461			
ENJ5	.828			
ENJ6	.716			
Pressure (PRE)		.610	.603	.277
(Ryan and Deci 2000)				
PRE1	.625			
PRE2	.655			
PRE3	.332			
PRE4	.472			
PRE5	.660			

4   DATA ANALYSES

Partial least squares (PLS), as a structural equation modeling (SEM) technique, was used to assess both the research model and the psychometric prosperities of the scales. SEM analysis was chosen over regression analysis in order to analyze the direct and indirect paths in a single analysis (Barclay et al. 1995; Gefen et al. 2000). Moreover, PLS has been widely used in information systems research to analyze research models consisting of both formative and reflective constructs (Wasko and Faraj 2005). PLS was chosen over LISREL due to the exploratory nature of the research (Barclay et al. 1995; Gefen et al. 2000).

In this study, we treated degree of collectivism as a formative variable, with self-reliance, competitive success, group work orientation, and group-goal summation as subordinate constructs (Chin 1998; Diamantopoulos and Winklhofer 2001). Other variables were modeled as reflective. For the second-order variable, we created the superordinate second-order construct using factor scores for the first-order constructs (Chin et al. 2003; Wold 1989).

4.1   Measurement Model

PLS accessed the measurement scales by examining the convergent validity (Cook and Campbell 1979) and discriminant validity (Campbell and Fiske 1959). In PLS, the convergent validity of measurement scales was determined via three tests: item relia-

Table 3. Discriminant Validity of Constructs

Construct	SR	CS	GWO	GGS	WP	ECE	AF	DQ	UNC	ENJ	PRE
SR	.910										
CS	-.330	.764									
GWO	-.283	.405	.788								
GGS	-.300	.249	.550	.718							
WP	-.269	.180	.451	.422	.831						
ECE	.161	-.202	-.457	-.355	-.455	.942					
AF	-.198	.222	.040	.055	.003	-.130	812				
DQ	-.101	.331	.532	.320	.309	-.339	.177	.824			
UNC	-.236	.208	.316	.333	.251	-.376	.259	.194	.676		
INT	-.110	.175	.446	.217	.346	-.337	.062	.335	.108	.774	
PRE	-.106	.277	.170	.288	.144	-.348	.442	.172	.287	.352	.526

bility, the composite reliability of constructs, and the average variance extracted by constructs. The test results are reported in Table 2. Given that most constructs had reliability scores above 0.7 and all items had reliability scores above 0.5, we deemed the measurement items possessed adequate reliability, although some Cronbach's alphas were reported marginally below 0.7 (Chin 1998). Composite reliabilities of most constructs exceed Nunnally's (1978) criterion of 0.7 except for pressure. The average variances extracted were all about 50 percent except for pressure and uncertainty. These results indicated that the convergent validity of the measurement model was fair.

To ensure the discriminant validity, the squared correlations between constructs should be less than the average variance extracted for a construct. Table 3 reported the results of discriminant validity, which was checked by comparing the diagonal to the non-diagonal elements; all items fulfilled the requirements except for the construct pressure. Because of the lack of strong theoretical reasons to remove the construct, pressure remained in the structural model.

4.2 Structural Model

The path coefficients and explained variances for the model using a bootstrapping procedure are shown in Figure 2. Each hypothesis corresponded to a path in the structural model. Hypotheses were tested at the 5 percent significance level. The results reveal that self-reliance (t = -7.9213, p < 0.001), competitive success (t = 5.0988, p < 0.001), and group work orientation (t = 13.9695, p < 0.001) were found to be significant indicators for degree of collectivism, but group-goal summation was not (t = 1.4416, p = 0.151). Degree of collectivism significantly affected willingness to participate (t = 6.5921, p < 0.01), evaluation of collaboration effort (t = -2.8966, p < 0.01), and preference of anonymity feature (t = 2.0746, p < 0.05). Willingness to participate was found to have significant impact on perceived decision quality (t = 3.2128, p < 0.01) and enjoyment (t = 2.3111, p < 0.05), but not on uncertainty (t = 1.7555, p = 0.08) or pressure (t = 0.1059, p = 0.916). Evaluation of collaboration effort was proven as a significant predictor for decision quality (t = -2.3374, p < 0.05), uncertainty (t = 2.9905, p < 0.01), and enjoyment (t = -2.5768, p < 0.05), but not for pressure (t = -0.8947, p = 0.372). The

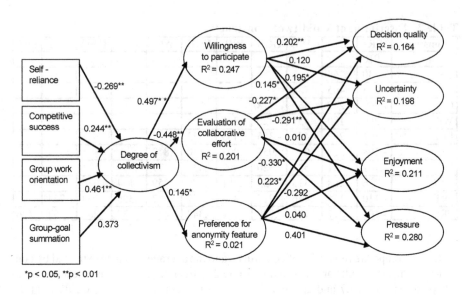

*p < 0.05, **p < 0.01

Figure 2. PLS Results

preference for anonymity feature was revealed to influence perceived decision quality significantly (t = 2.0994, p < 0.05); however, it had no significant impact on uncertainty, enjoyment, or pressure. The results of hypotheses testing were summarized in Table 4.

Table 4. Results of Hypotheses Testing

Hypothesis (Path)	Path Coefficient (b)	*t*-Value	Hypothesis Supported?
H1a. SR → DC (+)	-0.269	-7.9213	Yes
H1b. CS → DC (+)	0.244	5.0988	Yes
H1.c. GWO → DC (+)	0.461	13.9695	Yes
H1d. GGS → DC (+)	0.373	1.4416	No
H2a. DC → WP (+)	0.497	6.5912	Yes
H2b. DC → ECE (-)	0.488	-2.8966	Yes
H2c. DC → AF (+)	0.145	2.0746	Yes
H3a. WP → DQ (+)	0.202	3.2128	Yes
H3b. WP → UNC (-)	0.120	1.7555	No
H3c. WP → ENJ (+)	0.195	2.3111	Yes
H4a. ECE → DQ (+)	-0.227	-2.3374	No
H4b. ECE → UNC (-)	-0.291	-2.777	Yes
H4c. ECE → ENJ (+)	-0.330	-2.5768	No
H4d. ECE → PRE (-)	-0.292	-0.8947	No
H5a. AF → DQ (+)	0.145	2.0994	Yes
H5b. AF → UNC (-)	0.2234	2.9905	No
H5c. AF → ENJ (+)	0.040	0.3231	No
H5d. AF → PRE (-)	0.401	1.0944	No

5   DISCUSSION AND IMPLICATIONS

In general, the empirical results are encouraging and provide support for most of the hypotheses. Prior research on individualism–collectivism has found that growing up in a particular country shapes a person's perceptions, which can be used to predict behaviors across a wide variety of situations (Brockner 2003). However, previous research by and large did not explicitly conceptualize and operationalize the multi-dimensionality of the individualism–collectivism concept in investigating its complex impact on IT acceptance. The current study has further provided a deeper understanding, revealing that self-reliance, competitive success, and group work orientation are significant predictors for degree of collectivism. This study also suggests that group-goal summation is not in line with the other factors in reflecting degree of collectivism. Arguably, it is because there was no group task assigned to the participants in this study; they might not have thought of the possible conflicts between personal goals and group goals. Future studies should look into the influence of this factor in circumstances when personal pursuits and group task do not align.

The results of this study suggest that users' degree of collectivism plays an important role in their attitude toward e-collaboration. Degree of collectivism has been found to be a significant predictor for participants' willingness to participate, evaluation of collaboration effort, and preference of anonymity feature. Participants' willingness to participate is shown to have significant impact on their perceived decision quality and enjoyment gained from the e-collaboration. Participants' evaluation of collaboration effort is proven to be an important predictor for perceived decision quality, uncertainty, and enjoyment. Participants' preference for anonymity feature is shown to have significant impact on their perceived decision quality and uncertainty. Moreover, in this study, the participants do not perceive pressure as an inhibitor which would negatively affect the collaboration; we posit that pressure may be associated with other contextual factors other than perception.

Prior to discussing the implications of our work, some limitations of the study must be acknowledged. Although recent research has found that students essentially have the same values and beliefs as workers, future studies need to examine the findings across a wider range of individuals in different environments and with different collaborative systems (Strite and Karahanna 2006). Different methodologies are also needed to triangulate results and capture actual usage of technology.

Implications can be drawn from the current study for practitioners to design and promote e-collaboration tools. This study advocates that people of varying degree of collectivism perceive e-collaboration differently. As attitude is a dominant factor in predicting acceptance and subsequent usage of a technology, collaborative systems should include functions that facilitate the appropriate level of social support to users with varying degree of collectivism so as to increase their incentive and intention to use the system. For example, users should be allowed to adjust the degree of anonymity in communication to their level of comfort.

In terms of theoretical contributions, the current study adds new insights into the understanding of attitude studies in IT adoption research. More importantly, this study offers detailed characteristics of cultural orientation in predicting user acceptance. To keep our theoretical model succinct and relevant, this study has focused on the cultural dimension of individualism–collectivism and the anonymity feature. However, it should be noted that other dimensions of culture may not necessarily follow the same pattern in affecting users' attitude toward e-collaboration, as they can and do display as separate theoretical constructs (El-Shinnawy and Vinze 1997). Accounting for all factors in one study is unwieldy; future research should look into other cultural dimensions and other technological aspects.

6   CONCLUSIONS

To understand how attitude toward technology is affected by an individual's cultural orientation, this study investigates the influence of degree of collectivism on evaluations about e-collaboration. Attitude toward e-collaboration is studied in terms of two set of attributes, namely attitude toward participating in e-collaboration and attitude toward outcomes; the links between the two sets of attributes have also been investigated. A theoretical model is proposed and subsequently tested in a questionnaire survey involving 236 data points. Self-reliance, competitive success, and group work orientation are found to be significant indicators concerning a person's degree of collectivism. Degree of collectivism influences willingness to participate, evaluation of collaborative effort, and preference for anonymity feature in e-collaboration. These three variables subsequently affect perceptions about decision quality, enjoyment, uncertainty, and pressure in the collaboration.

References

Ajzen, I., and Fishbein, M. 1980. *Understanding Attitudes and Predicting Social Behavior*, Englewood Cliffs, NJ: Prentice-Hall.

Alavi, M. 1994. "Computer-Mediated Collaborative Learning: An Empirical Evaluation," *MIS Quarterly* (18:2), pp. 159-174.

Alavi, M., Wheeler, B. C., and Valacich J. S. 1995. "Using IT to Reengineer Business Education: An Exploratory Investigation of Collaborative Telelearning," *MIS Quarterly* (19:3), pp. 293-312.

Alavi, S. B., and McCormick, J. 2004 "Theoretical and Measurement Issues for Studies of Collective Orientation in Team Contexts," *Small Group Research* (35:2), pp. 111-127.

Albirini, A. 2006. "Teachers' Attitudes toward Information and Communication Technologies: The Case of Syrian EFL Teachers," *Computers & Education* (47), pp. 373-398.

Anakwe, U. P., Kessler, E. H., and Christensen, E. W. 1999. "Distance Learning and Cultural Diversity: Potential Users' Perspective," *The International Journal of Organizational Analysis* (7:3), pp. 224-243.

Anderson, J. L. 1991. "The Receptor Culture and the Consultant's Visit," *Notes on Translation* (5:4), pp. 23-30.

Augustinova, M., Oberlé, D., and Stasser, G. L. 2005. "Differential Access to Information and Anticipated Group Interaction: Impact on Individual Reasoning," *Journal of Personality and Social Psychology* (88:4), pp. 619-631.

Barclay D. C., Higgins, C., and Thompson, R. 1995. "The Partial Least Squares Approach to Causal Modeling: Personal Computer Adoption and Use as an Illustration," *Technology Studies* (2:2), pp. 285-308.

Brockner, J. 2003. "Unpacking Country Effects: On the Need to Operationalize the Psychological Determinants of Cross-National Differences," *Research in Organizational Behavior* (25), pp. 333-367.

Campbell, D. T., and Fiske, D. W. 1959. "Convergent and Discriminant Validation by the Multitrait-Multimethod Matrix," *Psychological Bulletin* (56:1), pp. 81-105.

Chester, A., and Gwynne, G. 1998. "Online Teaching: Encouraging Collaboration through Anonymity," *Journal of Computer-Mediated Communication* (4:2) (http://jcmc.indiana.edu/vol4/issue2/chester.html; accessed on March 14, 2008).

Chin, W. W. 1998. "Issues and Opinions on Structural Equation Modeling," *MIS Quarterly* (22:1), pp. 7-16.

Chin, W. W., Marcolin, B. L., and Newsted, P. R. 2003. "A Partial Least Squares Latent Variable Modeling Approach for Measuring Interaction Effects: Results from a Monte Carlo Simulation Study and an Electronic-Mail Emotion/Adoption Study," *Information Systems Research* (14:2), pp. 189-217.

Cook M., and Campbell, D. T. 1979. *Quasi-Experimentation: Design and Analysis Issues for Fields Settings*, Boston: Houghton Mifflin.

Diamantopoulos, A., and Winklhofer, H. M. 2001. "Index Construction with Formative Indicators: An Alternative to Scale Development," *Journal of Marketing Research* (38:2), pp. 269-277.

Downey, H. K., and Slocum, J. W. 1975. "Uncertainty: Measures, Research, and Sources of Variation," *Academy of Management Journal* (18:3), pp. 562-578.

Dubrovsky, V. J., Kiesler, S., and Sethna, B. N. 1995. "The Equalization Phenomenon: Status Effects in Computer-Mediated and Face-to-Face Decision-Making Groups," *Human Computer Interaction* (6), pp. 119-146.

Eagly, A. H., and Chaiken, S. 1993. *The Psychology of Attitude*, Fort Worth, TX: Harcourt Brace Jovanovich Publishers.

Earley, P. C. 1993. "East Meets West Mideast: Further Explorations of Collectivistic and Individualist Work Groups," *Academy of Management Journal* (36), pp. 319-348.

Eder, L. B., and Igbaria, M. 2001. "Determinants of Intranet Diffusion and Infusion," *Omega – The International Journal of Management Science* (29), pp. 233-242.

El-Shinnawy, M., and Viaze, A. 1997. "Technology, Culture and Persuasiveness: A Study of Choice Shifts in Group Settings," *International Journal of Human Computer Studies* (47), pp. 473-496.

Flanagin, A. J., Tiyaamornwong, V., O'Connor, J., and Seibold, D. R. 2002. "Computer-Mediated Group Work: The Interaction of Member Sex and Anonymity," *Communication Research* (29:1), pp. 66-93.

Gefen, D., Straub, D., and Boudreau, M. C. 2000. "Structural Equation Modeling Techniques and Regression: Guidelines for Research Practices," *Communications of the AIS* (7:7), pp. 1-78.

George, J. F., Easton, G. K., Nunamaker Jr., J. F., and Northcraft, G. B. 1990. "A Study of Collaborative Group Work with and Without Computer-based Support," *Information Systems Research* (1:4), pp. 394-415.

Goncale, J. A., and Staw, B. M. 2006. "Individualism–Collectivism and Group Creativity," *Organizational Behavior and Human Decision Processes* (100), pp. 96-109.

Hofstede, G. 1991. *Cultures and Organizations: Software of the Mind*, London: McGraw-Hill.

Hu, P. J., Chau, P. Y. K., Sheng, O. R. L., and Tam, K. Y. 1999. "Examining the Technology Acceptnace Model Using Physical Acceptance of Telemedicine Technology," *Journal of Management Information Systems* (16:2), pp. 91-112.

Hui, C. H., and Triandis, H. C. 1986. "Individualism and Collectivism: A Study of Cross-Cultural Researchers," *Journal of Cross-Cultural Psychology* (17), pp. 225-248.

Ji, L. J., Zhang, Z., and Nisbett, R. E. 2004. "Is it Culture or Is it Language? Examination of Language Effects in Cross-Cultural Research on Categorization," *Journal of Personality and Social Psychology* (87:1), pp. 57-65.

Kim, M. S., Sharkey, W. F., and Singelis, T. M. 1994. "Relationship between Individuals' Self-Construals and Perceived Importance of Interactive Constraints," *International Journal of Intercultural Relationships* (18), pp. 117-140.

Kim, Y. H., Hamilton, R., Zheng, J., and Baylor, A. L. 2006. "Scaffolding Learner Motivation through a Virtual Peer," in *Proceedings of the 7th International Conference on Learning Sciences*, S. A. Barab, K. E. Hay, and D. T. Hickey (eds.), Bloomington, IN, June 27-July 1, pp. 335-341.

Kim, Y. J., and Song, J. 2004. "Unveiling User Characteristics in Virtual Communities and the Impact on E-Commerce," in *Proceedings of the 25th International Conference on Information Systems*, R. Agarwal, L. Kirsch, and J. I. DeGross (eds.), Washington, DC, December 12-15, pp. 207-220.

Klein, E. E., and Dologite, D. G. 2000. "The Role of Computer Support Tools and Gender Composition in Innovative Information System Idea Generation by Small Groups," *Computers in Human Behavior* (16), pp. 111-139.

Lam, S. K. 1997. "The Effects of Group Decision Support Systems and Task Structures on Group Communication and Decision Quality," *Journal of Management Information Systems* (13:4), pp. 193-215.

Lefebvre, L. A., Lefebvre, G., Hen, L., and Mendgen, R. 2006. "Cross-Border E-Collaboration for New Product Development in the Automotive Industry," in *Proceedings of the 39th Annual Hawaii International Conference on System Sciences*, Los Alamitos, CA: IEEE Computer Society Press, pp. 8-18.

Leidner D. E., and Kayworth, T. 2006. "*Review*: A Review of Culture in Information Systems Research: Toward a Theory of Information Technology Culture Conflict," *MIS Quarterly* (30:2), pp. 357-399.

Lu, L., and Argyle, M. 1991. "Happiness and Cooperation," *Personality and Individual Differences* (12), pp. 1019-1030.

Lutz, R. J. 1981. "The Role of Attitude Theory in Marketing," in *Perspectives in Consumer Behavior* (3rd ed.), H. H. Kassarjian and T. S. Robertson (eds.), Englewood Cliffs, NJ: Prentice Hall, pp. 233-250.

Munkvold, B. E. 2005. "Experiences from Global E-Collaboration: Contextual Influences on Technology Adoption and Use," *IEEE Transactions on Professional Communication* (48:1), pp. 78-86.

Niles, F. S. 1998. "Individualism–Collectivism Revisited," *Cross-Cultural Research* (32), pp. 315-341.

Nunamaker, J. F., Dennis, A. R., Valacich, J. S., Vogel, D. R., and George, J. F. 1991. "Electronic Meeting Systems to Support Group Work," *Communications of the ACM* (34:7), pp. 41-60.

Nunnally, J. C. 1978. *Psychometric Theory* (2nd ed.), New York: McGraw-Hill.

Ocker, R. J., and Yaverbaum, G. J. 2001. "Collaborative Learning Environments : Exploring Student Attitudes and Satisfaction in Face-to-face and Asynchronous Computer Conference Settings," *Journal of Interactive Learning Research* (12:4), pp. 427-448.

Paul, S., Samarah, I. M., Seetharaman, P., and Mykytyn Jr., P. P. 2005. "An Empirical Investigation of Collaborative Conflict Management Style in Group Support System-Based Global Virtual Teams," *Journal of Management Information System* (21:3), pp. 185-222.

Peter, J. P., and Ryan, M. J. 1976. "Investigation of Perceived Risk at Brand Level," *Journal of Marketing Research* (13:2), pp. 184-188.

Pratt, M. C. 1998. "To Be or Not to Be? Central Questions in Organizational Identification," in *Identity in Organizations: Building Theory through Conversations*, D. A. Whetten and P. C. Godfrey (eds.), Thousand Oaks, CA: Sage Publications, pp. 171-207.

Reinig, B. A., and Shin, B. 2002. "The Dynamic Effects of Group Support Systems on Group Meetings," *Journal of Management Information Systems* (19:2), pp. 303-325.

Riegelsberger, J., Sasse, M. A., and McCarthy, J. D. 2005. "The Mechanics of Trust: A Framework for Research and Design," *International Journal of Human-Computer Studies* (62:3), pp. 381-422.

Rindfleisch, A., and Heide, J. B. 1997. "Transaction Cost Analysis: Past, Present, and Future Applications," *Journal of Marketing* (61:4), pp. 30-54.

Rogers, E. M. 1995. *Diffusion of Innovations* (4th ed.), New York: The Free Press.

Rose, G., and Straub, D. 1998. "Predicting General IT Use: Applying TAM to the Arabic World," *Journal of Global Information Management* (6:3), pp. 39-46.

Ryan, R. M., and Deci, E. L. 2000. "Intrinsic and Extrinsic Motivations: Classic Definitions and New Directions," *Contemporary Educational Psychology* (25), pp. 54-67.

Siegel, J., Dubrovsky, V. J., Kiesler, S., and McGuire, T. W. 1986. "Group Processes in Computer-Mediated Communication," *Organizational Behavior and Human Decision Processes* (3), pp. 157-187.

Son, J. Y., Kim, S. S., and Riggins, F. J. 2006. "Consumer Adoption of Net-Enabled Infomediaries: Theoretical Explanations and an Empirical Test," *Journal of the Association for Information System* (7:7), pp. 473-508.

Spence, J. T. 1985. "Achievement American Style: The Rewards and Cost of Individualism," *American Psychology* (40), pp. 1285-1295.

Srite, M., and Karahanna, E. 2006. "The Role of Espoused National Cultural Values in Technology Acceptance," *MIS Quarterly* (30:3), pp. 679-704.

Straub, D. W., Keil, M., and Brenner, W. 1997. "Testing the Technology Acceptance Model Across Cultures: A Three Country Study," *Information and Mangement* (33), pp. 1-11.

Taylor, J. W. 1974. "Role of Risk in Consumer Behavior," *Journal of Marketing* (38:2), pp. 54-60.

Trandis, H. C. 1995. *Individualism and Collectivism*, Boulder, CO: Westview Press Inc.

Triandis, H. C., and Gelfand, M. J. 1998. "Converging Measurement of Horizontal and Vertical Individualism and Collectivism," *Journal of Personality and Social Psychology* (74), pp. 118-128.

Valacich, J. S., Jessup, L. M. Dennis A. R., and Nunamaker, J. F. 1992. "A Conceptual Framework for Anonymity in Electronic Meetings," *Group Decision and Negotiation* (1:3), pp. 219-241.

Wagner III, J. A. 1995. "Studies of Individualism–Collectivism: Effects on Cooperation in Groups," *Academy of Management Journal* (38), pp. 152-172.

Wasko, M. M., and Faraj, S. 2005. "Why Should I Share? Examining Social Capital and Knowledge Contribution in Electronic Networks or Practice," *MIS Quarterly* (29:1), pp. 35-57.

Watson, W. E., Kumar, K., and Michelson, L. K. 1993. "Cultural Diversity's Impact on Interaction Process and Performance: Comparing Homogeneous and Diverse Ttask Groups," *Academy of Management Journal* (36), pp. 590-602.

Wink, P. 1997. "Beyond Ethnic Differences: Contextualizing the Influence of Ethnicity on Individualism and Collectivism," *Journal of Social Issues* (53), pp. 329-349.

Wold, H. 1989. "Introduction to the Second Generation of Multivarate Analysis," in *Theoretical Empiricism* H. Wold ed.), New York: Oragon House, pp. 7-11.

Workman, M. 2001. "Collectivism, Individualism and Cohesion in a Team-Based Occupation," *Journal of Vocational Behavior* (58), pp. 82-97.

Zhang, D., Lowry, P. B., Zhou, L., and Fu, X. 2007. "The Impact of Individualism–Collectivism, Social Presence, and Group Diversity on Group Decision Making under Majority Influence," *Journal of Management Information Systems* (23:4), pp. 53-80.

About the Authors

Yingqin Zhong is currently a doctoral candidate in the Department of Information Systems at the National University of Singapore. She holds a B.Sc. (Honors) degree in Computing and a M.Sc. degree in Information Systems from the National University of Singapore. Her research interests center around the cultural issues in e-collaboration, focusing on the adoption and usage of collaborative learning technology. She has recently coordinated a data collection effort that involves institutions in China. Her papers have been published in *Information Resources Management Journal* and *International Journal of Web-Based Learning and Teaching Technologies*. Yingqin can be reached by e-mail at zhongyin@comp.nus.edu.sg.

Liu Na is a Ph.D. candidate in the Department of Information Systems at the School of Computing, National University of Singapore. She received her B.Sc.(Honors) in Information Systems from NUS in 2006. Her research interest focuses on IT and education, particularly from the human–computer interaction perspective. Her work has been presented at the Pacific Asia Conference on Information Systems. Liu can be reached by e-mail at liuna@comp.nus.edu.sg.

John Lim is an associate professor in the School of Computing at the National University of Singapore. Concurrently, he heads the Information Systems Research Lab. Dr. Lim graduated with First Class Honors in Electrical Engineering and a M.Sc. in MIS from the National University of Singapore, and a Ph.D. from the University of British Columbia. His current research interests include e-commerce, collaborative technology, negotiation support, IT and education, and IS implementation. He has published in MIS and related journals including *Journal of Management Information Systems, Journal of Global Information Management, Decision Support Systems, International Journal of Human Computer Studies, Organizational Behavior and Human Decision Processes, Behavior and Information Technology, International Journal of Web-based Learning and Teaching Technologies, Journal of Database Management,* and *Small Group Research.* He can be reached by e-mail at jlim@nus.edu.sg.

8 EXPLORING THE INFLUENCE OF COLLECTIVENESS ON VALUE CREATION ADOPTION IN AN INFORMATION TECHNOLOGY ORGANIZATION

Chalee Vorakulpipat
Yacine Rezgui
Research Institute for the Built and Human Environment
University of Salford
Salford, UK

Abstract   The objective of this empirical study is to explore the influence of socio-cultural factors, with a focus on collectiveness, on knowledge-value creation practices in a Thai information technology organization. The research adopts an interpretive stance and employs a case study approach involving multiple data collection methods. The paper is based on one author's personal expertise and close involvement in the selected case study organization. Using a grounded theory research approach, the study indicates that while collectiveness is overall perceived as a positive Thai cultural feature, it critically influences (1) the social network ties and relationship between employees within and across teams, (2) the resulting level of trust, and (3) the ability to share and create knowledge effectively in the organizational socio-cultural environment. The study is limited to a Thai organization, but can be generalized to other organizations that exhibit similar characteristics. This empirical study provides a foundation to further the research and the validation of the summary of themes that emerged from this empirical study.

Keywords   Value creation, collectiveness, knowledge management, interpretive case study, grounded theory, Thailand

Please use the following format when citing this chapter:

Vorakulpipat, C., and Rezgui, Y., 2008, in IFIP International Federation for Information Processing, Volume 287, Open IT-Based Innovation: Moving Towards Cooperative IT Transfer and Knowledge Diffusion, eds. León, G., Bernardos, A., Casar, J., Kautz, K., and DeGross, J. (Boston: Springer), pp. 139-157.

1   INTRODUCTION

A knowledge-based perspective of the organization has emerged in the strategic management literature (Alavi and Leidner 2001; Nonaka and Takeuchi 1995). Organizational knowledge is recognized as a key resource and a variety of perspectives suggest that the ability to marshal and deploy knowledge dispersed across the organization is an important source of organizational advantage (Teece 1998; Tsai and Ghoshal 1998). Furthermore, it is widely acknowledged that one of the key sustainable advantages that a firm can have comes from what it collectively knows, how efficiently it uses what it knows, and how readily it acquires and uses new knowledge (Davenport and Prusak 1998). Traditional organizations are beginning to comprehend that knowledge and its interorganizational management, as well as individual and organizational capability building, are becoming crucial factors for gaining and sustaining competitive advantages (Preiss et al. 1996). The gaining popularity of knowledge management (KM) has been reinforced by the quest for innovation and value creation. The positive relationship between knowledge management and value creation has been discussed extensively in the literature (Chase 1997; Despres and Chauvel 1999; Gebert et al. 2003; Liebowitz and Suen 2000). Davenport et al. (1998) argue that value creation takes place and is facilitated by (1) creating knowledge repositories, (2) improving knowledge access, (3) enhancing cultural support for knowledge use, and (4) managing knowledge as an asset (Davenport et al. 1998). In this context, KM is perceived as a framework for designing an organization's goals, structures, and processes so that the organization can use what it knows to learn and create value for its customers and community (Choo 1999).

The scope and definition of KM has evolved over the years. At present, it is perceived that there are three generations of KM (Vorakulpipat and Rezgui 2008). The first generation takes into account knowledge sharing or "supply-side KM," focusing on IT-driven KM (Koenig 2002; McElroy 1999). The second generation emphasizes knowledge creation or "demand-side KM" (McElroy 1999). The third generation tends to focus on value creation (Rezgui 2007; Vorakulpipat and Rezgui 2006a, 2007, 2008). Value creation is grounded in the appropriate combination of human networks, social capital, intellectual capital, and technology assets, facilitated by a culture of change. Value here is not understood in monetary terms, but rather as subjectively perceived desirable outcomes (such as willingness to share and create knowledge, social cohesion, collaboration, etc.). Therefore, value creation in this paper is defined as any process of creating knowledge value, as subjectively perceived by users, out of existing knowledge practices across an organization.

Value creation or knowledge-value creation has become an important ingredient to sustain competitiveness in developing countries (Wagner et al. 2003). Very few articles, unfortunately, have reported value creation implementations and strategies in developing countries. The latter includes China (Burrows et al. 2005), Malaysia (Wei et al. 2006), India (Chatzkel 2004), and sub-Saharan Africa (Okunoye 2002). These studies have identified several distinctive features, including varying levels of expertise to adapt and adopt technologies, distinctive socio-cultural features, and lack of availability of human and financial resources to nurture value creation practices (Okunoye 2002). A call has been made for further research to explore value creation practices in different organizational and cultural (regional, national, and international) contexts in developing economies.

Although technology plays an important role in the successful implementation of KM initiatives (Koenig 2002), a number of distinctive socio-cultural features such as collectiveness have an equally important role and influence (Chaidaroon 2004), in particular in the cultural context of developing countries. Collectiveness here may relate to collectivist culture and social relationship. People in a collectivist culture are "supposed to look after the interest of their ingroup and to have no other opinions and beliefs than the opinions and beliefs in their ingroup. ...The collectivist society is tightly integrated" (Hofstede 1983, p. 79).

Thailand is an example of a developing country where a number of distinctive cultural features have been identified, including collectiveness (Chaidaroon 2004). It therefore represents an interesting case to conduct a study on the influence of collectiveness on knowledge value creation practices within an organizational context. While value creation practices in Thailand have been reported later than in other countries in the region, several private and public organizations, in particular information technology or "high-tech" organizations, have already initiated ambitious KM programs and initiatives (Vorakulpipat and Rezgui 2006b). There is an interesting trend in the region to promote a competitive economy through technology and knowledge infused practices at a societal level. For example, the Ninth Malaysian Plan (2006-2010) has as one of its objectives to raise the capacity for knowledge and innovation, whereas the Ministry of Research and Technology (MRT) of Indonesia has identified information and communication technology (ICT) as a priority field to add value to its industries.

The aim of this paper is to explore the influence of collectiveness on value creation practices in a selected Thai IT organization. As such, the core research question is, how does collectiveness (as a distinctive characteristic) influence, and how is influenced by, knowledge-value creation practices in an organizational context? The paper makes two main contributions. First, drawing on the rich data of a Thai IT organization, it generates a grounded understanding of the influence of collectiveness on value creation. The grounded theory allows the identification of patterns in data; by analyzing these patterns, researchers can derive theory that is empirically valid (Glaser and Strauss 1967; Martin and Turner 1986). This is because "the theory-building process is so intimately tied with evidence that it is very likely that the resultant theory will be consistent with empirical observation" (Eisenhardt 1989, p. 547). While it is likely believed that building theory from a limited number of cases is susceptible to researchers' preconceptions (Orlikowski 1993), Glaser and Strauss (1967) argue that the number of cases is not so crucial, and a single case can indicate a general conceptual category or property. The iterative comparison within the site, methods, evidence, and literature leads to unfreezing thinking and the potential to generate theory with less researcher bias than theory built from incremental studies (Eisenhardt 1989). Second, the paper proposes a summary of themes developed from the grounded analysis of gathered primary data evidence from the case study, using social capital and related literature.

The key audience for the paper is the KM and interpretive information systems research communities, with a particular focus on KM/IS adoption in developing countries. The authors wish to contribute to the interpretive case study literature, and that dealing with KM/IS adoption. Practitioners may find it useful to take into account the findings reported in this paper to implement and adopt value creation in their organization, while researchers may want to further research across different industries or international settings.

The paper is organized into six sections. Following this introduction, the paper presents related literature, and then the research methodology employed in this study, which involves a case study approach. The research results are then given, followed by the discussion. Finally, the conclusions are drawn.

2   RELATED RESEARCH

It has been highlighted that technology adaptations in developed countries occur continuously in response to misalignments, gradually leading to a successful alignment (Leonard-Barton 1988).   This is in contrast to developing countries, which tend to rapidly adopt technology created by developed countries, often in an *ad hoc* way (Archibugi and Pietrobelli 2003). Developed countries concentrate more than 84 percent of the world's scientific and technological production (National Science Foundation 2002). Developing countries have only marginally increased their participation in this, which emphasizes the scientific and technological gaps that exist with the developed world. Also, in several of the information technology installations that were created and adapted for organizations in developing countries, local (regional and national) factors were not taken into account. This has resulted in outcomes that do not fit the needs of the direct beneficiaries in the developing nations (Cyamukungu 1996).

While the above is applicable to KM, the crucial issue might not relate only to technology but also include other factors, such as cultural-based resistance. "Technology, designed and produced in developed countries, is likely culturally-biased in favor of industrialized socio-cultural systems, technology transferred to developing countries meets cultural resistance" (Straub et al. 2001, p. 6). Moreover, it is reported that there is a significant gap in the understanding and maturity of KM between Asian developing companies and those in developed countries. This can be explained by the fact that American and European companies have had KM strategies and initiatives in place for over a decade, while Asian developing companies are still attempting to understand and apply the concept of KM (Yao et al. 2007).

In terms of culture, Chaidaroon (2004) indicates that collectiveness is a characteristic that distinguishes Thai culture and communication styles from the Western (developed countries) counterparts.   Hofstede (1983) argues that developing or poor countries such as Thailand exhibit a strong sense of collectivism while developed or wealthy countries tend to be more individualist.   Komin (1990) reports that Thai people placed more emphasis on social relationships (collectivist culture) as opposed to task achievements. Thai people generally believe that their work will be accomplished smoothly if their good relationship is maintained. Based on this evidence drawn from the literature, conducting an exploratory study in Thailand is beneficial to further research and understand the role and impact of collectiveness on value creation in different developing countries and cultural contexts.

In general, research on human and organizational aspects related to KM has focused on understanding the socialization and organizational dimension of KM (Becerra-Fernandez and Sabherwal 2001; Gold et al. 2001).   The concept of social capital has recently been adopted within the discipline (Adler and Kwon 2002; Cohen and Prusak 2001; Huysman and Wulf 2006; Lesser 2000; Nahapiet and Ghoshal 1998), emphasizing the role of trust and social cohesion within the organization (Vorakulpipat and Rezgui 2006a). Clearly, the higher the level of social capital, the more communities are stimulated to connect and share knowledge (Huysman and Wulf 2006).

3   RESEARCH APPROACH

The research aims at investigating the role of socio-cultural factors in the context of knowledge-value creation in a Thai IT organization. The authors thus needed to gain an in-depth understanding of value creation practices in the selected case study. Empirical studies that collect such data can be broadly classified as *interpretive case studies* (Walsham 1995). This type of approach has been selected since it aims to understand human thoughts and action in social and organizational contexts and to produce deep insights into IS phenomena (Klein and Myers 1999). However, there are significant differences of methodology and theory under the broad interpretive case studies. The remainder of this section is devoted to describing the specific approach adopted in the research and the reasons for the choices.

The research methodology is based on grounded theory (Glaser and Strauss 1967). This is motivated by the facts that (1) grounded theory "is an inductive, theory discovery methodology that allows the researcher to develop a theoretical account of the general features of a topic while simultaneously grounding the account in empirical observations or data" (Martin and Turner 1986, p. 141), (2) grounded theory facilitates "the generation of theories of process, sequence and change pertaining to organizations, positions and social interaction" (Glaser and Strauss 1967, p. 114), and (3) there are few guidelines for analyzing qualitative data (Miles and Huberman 1994) and it has been argued that grounded theory approaches are particularly well suited to dealing with the type of qualitative data gathered from interpretive field studies (Martin and Turner 1986; Oates 2005).

Site selection was guided by a technique of theoretical sampling (Strauss and Corbin 1998, p. 201): "data gathering driven by concepts derived from the evolving theory and based on the concept of making comparisons." BETA (the name of the organization has been disguised), a Thai IT research service organization that conducts research in information technology, was selected as a case study for the investigation as the authors believe that BETA exhibits a KM-rich environment to address the research question. Also, the site selection depends on easy access to the case study. It is worth noting that one of the authors is not only employed by BETA in an IT department but had a close involvement and critical role in BETA in IS and KM implementation involving a diverse group of managers and employees for over a decade. Indeed, the researcher has, over the years, acquired substantial personal knowledge of the organization's culture and work environment. Therefore, the organization welcomed the author to conduct this in-depth case study, and was willing to provide information openly and support this research. Also, because of his involvement and role in the organization, the researcher aimed to analyze the collected data in an interpretive way based on his own experience.

BETA was founded over 20 years ago. It employs more than 600 people, a majority of whom are highly educated and work in research and development production departments. For over a decade, BETA has acted as a research supplier to Thai industry.

Following the increasing demand for R&D, BETA has transformed itself from a supply-driven to a demand-driven organization. This demand-focused strategy has helped BETA address and meet the needs of Thai organizations more effectively. In the late 1990s, management initiated a large KM program. In the first stage, a collaborative system was deployed and adopted to help staff collaborate more effectively while promoting knowledge-friendly practices. Also, physical and virtual social spaces have been provided for sharing knowledge. Later, management deployed a knowledge repository system to encourage staff to codify tacit knowledge and experience into a reusable form. A number of incentives have been introduced, including monetary rewards and recognition to motivate people to share and create knowledge. While KM initiatives have been underpinned by IT, it was found that the organization was not successful in achieving the objectives of those initiatives and the overall results were less than desired. It may be perceived that a socio-culture feature like collectiveness in place has critically influenced the achievement of KM initiatives. For example, people preferred sharing tacit knowledge in social events to sharing and/or storing codified knowledge in the knowledge repository system provided. This results in the need for research on the influence of collectiveness in BETA.

In BETA, data were collected through a variety of methods: semi-structured interview, observation, and documentation. An interview guide was developed to collect critical qualitative data from all four "core" production (R&D) departments. The interview guide was designed to fit with the organization based on the researcher's experience. The questions involved a number of areas (i.e., organization nature, teamwork and organization environment, information technology adoption, knowledge sharing and creation, and organizational change).

Before interviewing, the selected interviewees were encouraged to explain their knowledge background including their level of previous education, work experience, KM experience, etc. In this stage, the researcher was able to set the direction of the interview and select the questions to be asked. During the interview, selected questions in a number of areas were asked to capture their perception of value creation adoption.

Twelve top managers and key people from the production departments were subjectively selected as interviewees as they were perceived to have permission to provide critical (or sensitive) data and constructive comments. Tape recording was used for nine interviewees, while the others requested not to be recorded during the interview.

Besides collecting sensitive data from manager and key person perspectives, additional data from employees were captured in the mode of direct observation (Yin 2003) during the entire study. The researcher was provided an opportunity to observe the employees' working styles, environments, and reactions. Moreover, as the researcher has been positioned in BETA for over a decade, he had a great chance to discuss informally some underlying issues with his colleagues and other employees. In addition, documentation about the organization was examined.

The data triangulation technique was chosen to analyze data collected from multiple sources (Yin 2003) since "it is particularly beneficial in theory generation as it provides multiple perspectives on an issue, supplies more information on emerging concepts, allows for cross-checking, and yields stronger substantiation of constructs" (Orlikowski 1993, p. 312). In this research, there were multiple realities that were interpreted by different viewpoints. Therefore, a broad variety of these have been made in the field study. The BETA case was supposed to illustrate differing viewpoints among employees, managers, and the researcher. As an interpretive stance was adopted, the findings of this study would comprise the researcher's own interpretations and those of others (respondents: employees and managers) who were involved in the study. However, as only the researcher had control in the study, the work is ultimately presented from the researcher's perspective, a typical criticism of interpretive studies. Moreover, since the interpretive study may require sensitivity to possible biases and systematic distortions in the narratives collected from the participants (Klein and Myers 1999), the researcher might not take the informants' views at face value.

Finally, the process of data collection, coding, and analysis is iterative (Glaser and Strauss 1967). This iterative process only finishes when it becomes clear that further data no longer triggers new modifications to the data categories and emerging theory, that is, the research has reached "theoretical saturation" (Strauss and Corbin 1998). Eisenhardt (1989) notes that overlapping data analysis with data collection can allow researchers to take advantage of flexible data collection and make adjustments freely during the data collection process. In the research, this process of data collection, coding, and analysis was taken to validate that the researcher had captured the perspectives of the informants on the topic. Pattern coding techniques of qualitative analysis (Miles and Huberman 1994) were used to summarize segments of the data from interview transcripts and observation notes, and then to determine categories or pattern codes.

4   RESEARCH RESULTS

A number of categories or pattern codes emerged from the data analysis using pattern coding techniques of qualitative analysis. These are information and communication technology (ICT), team working, structure and culture, and knowledge sharing. The pattern coding here is processed iteratively. These categories are discussed below.

4.1   Information and Communication Technology

Analysis of the interview transcripts suggests that ICTs help address personal barriers as employees feel more at ease when communicating via electronic means as opposed to face-to-face in social or work contexts. Moreover, e-mail plays an important role and seems to be preferred to telephone and face-to-face interactions, in particular when these involve interactions between employees and their senior staff.

The interviewees highlight that communication beyond time and space supported by technology (Internet, intranet, extranet) improves work performance as employees can work and learn "any time/any where." Intranets and extranets are highly valued as they promote flexible working, including access to document repositories and knowledge, while minimizing physical social interactions between employees. However, it is observed that this can have the adverse effect of hindering social cohesion bewteen employees, which is essential to develop trust and sustained relationships. The research reveals that this can also result in a number of social disadvantages, including

*   lack of social-oriented communication that is essential to develop trust among employees

- high task orientation that results in effectiveness without efficiency
- inappropriate time management between social life and work

These disadvantages are also caused by the attempt to replace traditional communication (such as the face-to-face method) with virtual methods underpinned by technology. It is very difficult to change an organization's culture. It is suggested that this failure can be solved by adapting the (ICT) strategy to the (Thai) culture instead of the (Thai) culture to the (ICT) strategy. That is, technology should be adopted as a tool to enhance the overall organizational processes while retaining the current human networks and social-oriented communications. For example, the primary purpose in adopting an e-mail system is to reduce delivery time and prevent delays or document loss in transfer (such as for sending files and announcements), rather than to replace a formal meeting or face-to-face interaction. It is observed that staff should not be forced to use virtual communication supported by technology if social-oriented communication is needed.

4.2 Team Working

Gathered data suggest that tasks and R&D in BETA are achieved through teams formed by the management, and this emerges as the preferred mode of working across the organization. Hence, strong social relationships among employees are critical to promote effective working. It has been reported that bureaucratic (hierarchical) organizational structure is perceived to inhibit positive social relationships among employees, in particular when teams involve members at various levels of the organizational structure. The interviewees have reported that a number of socio-emotional factors, including shyness (not speaking up) and seniority, inhibit teamwork effectiveness as employees usually believe that they should act in a receiver role in their team and should not elaborate and argue their own ideas against those of older or senior staff. Some respondents suggest that a more participative culture should underpin teamwork to gradually overcome the overall bureaucratic environment that characterizes work at BETA. Promoting appropriate teamwork environment and atmosphere help staff reduce their shyness and fears by encouraging them to contribute effectively through constructive comments to managers or team leaders. One interviewee states that shyness may make employees miss an opportunity to sustain ties with others:

> *When we've got some guests wanting to visit our offices, our colleagues tend to be shy and nervous to meet them. The problem is that they try to avoid discussing with them and present our work to them. I recognize that this is a Thai behavior, but it would be better if they could get to socialize and know others. Keeping up ties with significant people who visit us is always good.*

4.3 Structure and Culture

It is observed that the dominant bureaucratic (hierarchical) organizational structure within BETA may inhibit effective communication and employees' participation and contribution, also leading to personal barriers. This is reflected in existing working procedures (e.g., reporting layers) and may generate conflicting corporate cultures. Although the hierarchical structure and culture in place is perceived to help increase trust and respect for senior staff, it inhibits self-development as this amplifies employees' personal barriers. One respondent confirmed this:

> *The ideas are always finalized by only senior members. Young members usually keep quiet, as they tend to be concerned about, and fear, the negative impact of criticizing ideas expressed by older members.*

Nevertheless, the respondents perceive that this bureaucratic structure is widely accepted in Thai organizations, and it is a non-changeable organizational feature. Despite this, they feel that promoting participation within a hierarchical organization can improve a sense of collectiveness and help remove personal barriers.

4.4 Knowledge Sharing

The respondents perceive that sharing knowledge by informal or traditional face-to-face interaction is preferred to virtual means supported by technology (such as a web-based discussion forum or a knowledge repository system) despite acknowledged personal barriers. It has been reported that collective knowledge sharing in informal (facet-to-face) contexts, such as discussion forums and coffee breaks, is highly valued as this method can break personal barriers between employees and management by (1) establishing stronger relationships to develop trust among them, and (2) practicing and improving their presentation skills to gain confidence. One interviewee clearly explains that gaining confidence to remove personal barriers should be addressed before sharing knowledge in a team.

> *Firstly our objective is not knowledge sharing. We just want to practice their [employees'] presentation skills to reduce shyness and gain self-confidence. I'm quite sure they have good knowledge of their work, but this has always been difficult to share with others. They need to practice how to speak confidently in public and make the audiences understand them.*

On the other hand, virtual contexts also have been also developed to break personal barriers, as participants do not need to identify themselves and thus express their facial emotion. While this method seems promising, some interviewees believe that it is too informal beause facial emotions cannot be expressed through this channel, as it is very important in formal interactions to avoid misunderstanding during communication. One manager gives an example about a preference for face-to-face interaction and mistrust of virtual communication:

> *I prefer to meet my colleagues in person. Even when I send them an e-mail, I must go to see them suddenly to confirm receipt of my e-mail—"Have you received my e-mail?"—then I continue to talk with them physically.*

Also, the evidence shows an example about the failure of the virtual method, gathered from the observation:

> *One of help desk staff received a complaint e-mail from our executive. He spent several hours thinking about the reply message that would satisfy the executive. He then asked his colleagues to help him reply. Finally, an e-mail was sent at the end of the day. That is, he and his colleagues spent the whole day just to answer one e-mail. However, the executive replied angrily to the e-mail because of the unsatisfactory answer and, especially, the late reply.*

Another example of the failure of the virtual method and the success of the traditional method, gathered from observation, is a case of an interaction between an employee and a manager through a help desk system (a web board for end-users to report technical errors and for help desk staff to respond to the incidents):

> *One senior manager reported a technical error in a help desk system. Once one of the help desk staff received the report, he answered immediately by typing the results in the system. Later, the manager raised a new question because the answer was still unclear. The help desk staff member answered again. However, the manager was not satisfied with the answers and asked again. The conversation through the system continued for several days. The manager became upset, and the help desk staff member was worried because it wasted time. Then I [the participant] asked the help desk staff, "Why don't you go to see her in person and talk?" The help desk staff member was surprised with the overlooked, easy and promising solution. The help desk staff member was happy for a while, and then became unhappy suddenly. The help desk staff member said, "But our boss doesn't like this old-fashioned method....It is a non-IT solution."*

5   DISCUSSION

As grounded theory facilitates "the generation of theories of process, sequence and change pertaining to organizations, positions and social interaction" (Glaser and Strauss 1967, p. 114), it is essential to base the discussion on existing relevant theories. This discussion will be based on social capital theory. Nahapiet and Ghoshal (1998) suggest that social capital should be considered in terms of three dimensions. First, the structural dimension refers to opportunity to connect with each other. Second, the relational dimension refers to the character of the connection between individuals and motivation to share knowledge. This is best characterized through trust, norms, obligation, and respect. Third, the cognitive dimension refers to ability to cognitively connect with each other in order to understand what the other is referring to when communicating and sharing knowledge. The discussion of collectiveness elaborates on how collectiveness is (1) supporting employees to work in teams, (2) impacting on trust between them, and (3) promoting value creation. Thus, this section will involve the three dimensions of structural opportunity, relational motivation, and cognitive ability.

5.1 Structural Dimension

The structure dimension of social capital focuses mainly on the density of networks and on bridging structural holes (Burt 1992; Wasserman and Faust 1994). Studying social networks would reveal how collectiveness is supporting team formation in BETA.

The results show that BETA clearly supports employees' opportunity to work in a team rather than to work individually. However, it is observed that a team is generally formed by management; individuals are not allowed to form a team freely. Since a team is established by people who are not involved in it (management), the team members may not have close relationships with one another, especially those who are from different departments and sometimes other organizations. That is, collectivist or participatory culture is needed in a team to help create network ties.

Therefore, the organization's knowledge values must be created through the network of relationships possessed by people in collectivist cultures. As also reported in Thanasankit and Corbitt (2000), Thai society constructs its reality as group or social interests rather than individual interests. Strong social relationships and collectiveness are perceived as a critical factor to create more opportunities for team members to participate in problem solving and decision making, and offer a range of different skills, abilities, knowledge, and experience to ensure that creative ideas are supported. Also, as highlighted in Nahapiet and Ghoshal, social capital is defined as the sum of the actual and potential resources embedded within, and derived from, the social network controlled by an individual or social unit; social capital also plays an important role as an aid to adaptive efficiency and to creativity and learning. It facilitates cooperative behavior, thereby encouraging the development of new forms of association and innovative organization (Fukuyama 1995; Jacobs 1965; Putnam 1993).

As outlined in Rezgui (2007), a knowledge-based organization needs all of its employees to share a culture that promotes the virtues of knowledge acquisition and sharing, requiring a number of essential attributes. These attributes are perceived to help create an opportunity for knowledge sharing and creation in BETA, including

- A culture that recognizes tacit knowledge and social networks, resulting in the promotion of open dialogue between staff, allowing them to develop social links and share understandings. BETA has valued sharing tacit knowledge in informal contexts, such as discussion forums and coffee breaks. This method is perceived to (1) break down barriers between employees and management, (2) establish stronger relationships among them, (3) allow employees to reduce personal barriers and gain confidence, and (4) practice and improve their presentation skills.
- The support of communities of practice where members continuously increase their understandings of their collective tasks. The results show that BETA has provided physical and virtual spaces to support communities of practice such as web-based discussion forum, resulting in efficiency in obtaining both tacit and explicit knowledge, and good connections between employees.

5.2 Relational Dimension

The relational dimension here is based on socially attributed characteristics of the connection between individuals, such as trust. Its aim is to discuss how collectiveness is impacting on trust between people. The results show that team collaboration through face-to-face communication such as formal training creates stronger social relationships and promotes trust, while these are difficult to establish in virtual contexts due to the lack of emotional expressions. Therefore, team members in BETA are aware of the greater societal acceptance of face-to-face rather than virtual interaction. Based on Thai culture, virtual communication such as e-mail may form bridges between people (e.g., across different sections or locations) but it does not create bonds (such as the case of the help desk staff member and the manager). Indirect communication strategies sometimes create a communication gap and misunderstanding during interactions, which is seen as a very well liked culture but not so well trusted, respected, or admired, even when compared with other Asian cultures from the Westerner's perspective (Hendon 2001).

As such, the research acknowledges the pivotal and strategic role that human networks play in developing trust in the particular context of the collective characteristic of Thai culture, as reported in Chaidaroon (2004). This has resulted in increased awareness, knowledge quality, and business intelligence, which have in turn triggered a value-added dimension that did not exist prior to initiating the change processes. Human networks are facilitated and nurtured by providing informal forums that can be assimilated into communities of practice. These are complemented with virtual spaces to share knowledge (including sensitive information) protected by a role access control system. The collective characteristic of Thai society is exemplified by the dimension given to team working. However, it has been shown that human networks can only be effective if the social conditions that underpin collaboration are met (including trust). This emphasizes the role that social capital plays in creating organizational value underpinned by strong human networks. A participatory culture helps develop trust, respect, and understanding for others at different levels in BETA.

Clearly, a culture of confidence and trust in which people are willing to communicate is perceived to initiate value creation. The results confirm the employees' perception that sharing knowledge through face-to-face interactions creates stronger social relationships and promotes trust, while these are difficult to establish in virtual contexts, as the expression of emotions is difficult. There are concerns about mistrust and confidentiality in the authentication and authorization features of the virtual environments, as also reported in Rezgui (2007).

5.3 Cognitive Dimension

The cognitive dimension here refers to the ability of human actors to cognitively connect with each other to share and create knowledge in both physical and virtual contexts. The discussion, therefore, will correspond to analysis of how collectiveness is promoting value creation. The evidence shows that formal and informal communication, through physical human collaborations such as formal training and meetings, is perceived to be effective in promoting value creation including knowledge sharing and creation.

Also, most employees in BETA express a preference for sharing tacit knowledge and experience through face-to-face interaction. They prefer learning via exchanging their experiences within social contexts to individual learning from documentation. However, management perceives that tacit knowledge gathered from people collaboration should be converted into explicit knowledge in order to store in a shared database, thus a knowledge repository system has been deployed in BETA. The knowledge repository system is used to store best practices and failures in the form of documentation, created during collaboration such as informal forums and training. The system also provides great value for the organization, in particular in the context of staff loss. This strategy encourages the learning of lessons from failure as well as success.

In terms of socio-technical perspectives, BETA shows concern about the lack of social-oriented communication and social events caused by the tendency to completely rely on computer technology, which results in people feeling that they are "stuck" in front of their computers. This perception leads to KM fallacies or traps that directly influence the perceived functionality of IT applications for the support of KM initiatives (Huysman and de Wit 2002). As reported in Huysman and Wulf (2006), these KM fallacies relate to the tendency of organizations to concentrate too much on the IT role supporting value creation practices, especially knowledge sharing, resulting in the "IT trap." It is important to recognize that IT is not independent from the social environment, as it is not the technology itself, but the way people use it that determines the role of IT in supporting value creation practices (Huysman and Wulf 2006). Therefore, the organization's success with the use of IT will not depend on IT skills, but the appropriate social context that can benefit from electronic communication technology (Zack and McKenny 2000). It is suggested that information systems aimed at value creation need to maintain the integrity of the social communities in which knowledge is embedded (Boland and Tenkasi 1995) in order to avoid the IT trap. This requires the use of socially embedded technologies or collaborative system, influenced by the belief structures (perceived ease-of-use and perceived usefulness) of TAM (Davis 1989). In the case study, collaboration through virtual communication is highly valued overall, and the functionality of options such as the discussion forum has been described as important in nurturing knowledge sharing within a social context, as confirmed in related literature (Ellis et al. 1991; Poltrock and Grudin 1995). Clearly, in BETA, this socio-technical perspective can be perceived as a vital tool in bridging the gap between the social context and the use of IT, and also promoting value creation. Social and technical aspects must be blended successfully to produce social capital.

5.4 Initial Theory Generation

The analysis of the case study for this research reveals how collectiveness influences value creation in a Thai organization. While, the discussion portrays collectiveness as essential, it has drawn a number of interesting findings. For example,

- IT is perceived to help gain confidence and break personal barriers, but it may not help develop trust and sustained social relationship among people, and may not be suitable in a bureaucratic organizational structure. Instead, promoting participation can improve a sense of collectiveness and help remove personal barriers.

- Virtual communication may form bridges between people but it does not create bonds.
- The use of IT can have the adverse effect of hindering social cohesion between employees and developing trust and sustained relationships.
- Overall, a socio-technical perspective should not be overlooked in collectivist culture. This helps bridge the gap between the social context and the use of IT and promotes value creation.

However, the discussion also opens up areas where collectiveness is very much subject to interpretation. The fact that it is perceived as difficult to change an organizational culture in Thailand does not necessarily equate with negativity. Some perceptions are accepted as a key and non-changeable feature of Thai culture. People in the organization prefer to preserve their culture (e.g., bureaucratic structure) regardless of the impact on value creation.

Using the concept of social capital, the study characterizes Thai people's experience with value creation. A summary of themes including variables of the influence of collectiveness on value creation practices (Table 1) conceptualizes the thinking presented in this study in the general form, using three perspectives (technology, organization, and people) divided into six attributes (technology, organizational structure, change process, human network, social capital, and knowledge sharing and creation ability), analyzed from the generated pattern codes and related discussion.

First, the variable in the technology perspective refers to the level of influence of adopted technology in promoting a sense of collectiveness. Second, the variables in the organization perspective (organizational structure and change process attributes) refer to the level of the role of organizational issues, including organizational structure and change, in addressing collectiveness. Finally, the variables in the people perspective (human network, social capital, and knowledge sharing and creation ability attributes) refer to the level of the role of social networking, social capital, knowledge sharing and

Table 1. Summary of Themes Including Variables of the Influence of Collectiveness on Value Creation Practices

Perspectives	Attributes	Collectiveness
Technology	Technology	Technology influence in promoting a sense of collectiveness
Organization	Organizational structure	Perceived role of organizational structure in nurturing collectiveness across individuals and teams
	Change Process	Perceived role of collectiveness in the adoption of organizational change
People	Human Network	Perceived role of human network in nurturing collectiveness
	Social Capital	Perceived role of social capital in enhancing a sense of collectiveness
	Knowledge Sharing and Creation Ability	Perceived influence of knowledge sharing and creation in addressing collectiveness

creation, and KM motivation in nurturing, enhancing, and addressing collectiveness. Each variable in the summary of themes helps researchers determine the level of value creation influence in each attribute and perspective. Practitioners may find it useful to take into account the levels measured by researchers to implement and adopt value creation in their organization. The recommended future research is detailed in the next section.

6 CONCLUSION

The research has investigated the influence of collectiveness on knowledge-value creation practices in BETA, a Thai organization. It demonstrates that an exploratory study on KM within a specific organization is far from being objective as the multiple realities associated with KM practices play out in various ways, resulting in the need for an interpretive case study to conduct the research. The use of the grounded theory approach has helped generate a set of insights, concepts, and interactions that address the critical organizational KM elements—elements from the cases in developing countries largely overlooked in the KM literature.

The summary of themes generated from the empirical findings suggests that collectiveness, a distinctive characteristic of Thai culture, critically influences, and is influenced by, a number of KM attributes in terms of technology, organization, and the people perspective. The research demonstrates how collectiveness influences, and is influenced by, the value creation adoption that people in BETA have experienced. The study is limited to a Thai organization, leading to the recommendations for further research. Validation of the theory, and extension or simplification of the variables, is suggested.

Further investigation in other Thai organizations is highly recommended to validate and test the summary of themes, and then attempt to generalize it to Thailand. Further studies in Thailand may take into account the following issues:

- **Validation**: The need for the validation of the theory developed in this research is essential to determine the level of value creation influence on variables in each attribute and perspective. The levels can be measured by survey questionnaire using a scale. Each variable is assumed to develop a number of questions. For example, a variable "Technology influence in promoting a sense of collectiveness" may involve many questions in relation to intention to use, perceived usefulness, voluntariness, client satisfaction, etc. Moreover, this further research aims to test whether the selected organization will represent the same culture as BETA, influencing or influenced by the value creation practices, and whether the collectiveness feature is representative of the whole country.
- **Extension or Simplification**: During an investigation, the variables in the theory could be extended or simplified if the researcher thinks they are subjectively fit for the case, depending on many factors such as duration of field study, organizational culture, the researcher's experience, appropriation, etc. For example, three perspectives (technology, organization, and people) and six attributes (technology, organi-

zational structure, change process, human network, social capital, and knowledge sharing and creation ability) could be subjectively extended, where appropriate.

Besides collectiveness, further studies on different distinctive characteristics are important. Other distinctive cultural aspects such as shyness, seniority, power distance, conscientiousness, and masculinity/femininity appear in Thailand and some developing countries. It would be interesting to further the research on the influence of these aspects on value creation practices. In addition, further studies within the context of developing countries are highly recommended to manifest the status of value creation practices in these countries, to test the extent to which there is a positive or negative trend toward value creation awareness, and to investigate the need for the theory developed in this research. However, the extent to which richness of data can be captured about value creation practices within an unfamiliar organization by case study method remains unclear. Further studies may be conducted by using alternative research methodologies such as action research and ethnography.

References

Adler, P., and Kwon, S. W. 2002. "Social Capital: Prospects for a New Concept," *Academy of Management Review* (27:1), pp. 17-40.

Alavi, M., and Leidner, D. 2001. "Review: Knowledge Management and Knowledge Management Systems: Conceptual Foundations and Research Issues." *MIS Quarterly* (25:1), pp. 107-36.

Archibugi, D., and Pietrobelli, C. 2003. "The Globalization of Technology and its Implications for Developing Countries Windows of Opportunity or Further Burden?," *Technological Forecasting & Social Change* (70), pp. 861-83.

Becerra-Fernandez, I., and Sabherwal, R. 2001. "Organizational Knowledge Management: A Contingency Perspective," *Journal of Management Information Systems* (18:1), pp. 23-55.

Boland, R., and Tenkasi, R. 1995. "Perspective Making and Perspective Taking in Communities of Knowing," *Organization Science* (6:4), pp. 350-72.

Burrows, G. R., Drummond, D. L., and Martinsons, M. G. 2005. "Knowledge Management in China," *Communications of the ACM* (48:4), pp. 73-6.

Burt, R. S. 1992. *Structural Holes: The Social Structure of Competition*, Cambridge, MA: Harvard University Press.

Chaidaroon, S. S. 2004. "Effective Communication Management for Thai People in the Global Era," in *Proceedings of International Conference on Revisiting Globalization & Communication in the 2000s*, Bangkok, Thailand, August 5-6.

Chase, R. L. 1997. "Knowledge Management Benchmarks," *Journal of Knowledge Management* (1:1), pp. 83-92.

Chatzkel, J. 2004. "Establishing a Global KM Initiative: The Wipro Story," *Journal of Knowledge Management* (8:2), pp. 6-18.

Choo, C. W. 1999. "The Art of Scanning the Environment," *Bulletin of the American Society for Information Science* (25:3), pp. 13-19.

Cohen, D., and Prusak, L. 2001. *In Good Company: How Social Capital Makes Organizations Work*, Boston: Harvard Business School Press.

Cyamukungu, M. 1996. "Development Strategies for an African Computer Network," *Information Technology for Development* (7), pp. 91-4.

Davenport, T. H., DeLong, D. W., and Beers, M. C. 1998. "Successful Knowledge Management Projects," *Sloan Management Review* (39:2), pp. 43-57.

Davenport, T., and Prusak, L. 1998. *Working Knowledge: How Organizations Manage What They Know*, Boston: Harvard Business School Press.

Davis, F. D. 1989. "Perceived Usefulness, Perceived Ease of Use, and User Acceptance of Information Technology," *MIS Quarterly* (13:3), pp. 319-40.

Despres, C., and Chauvel, D. 1999. "Knowledge Management(s)," *Journal of Knowledge Management* (3:2), pp. 110-23.

Eisenhardt, K. M. 1989. "Building Theories from Case Study Research," *Academy of Management Review* (14:4), pp. 532-50.

Ellis, C. A., Gibbs, S. J., and Rein, G. L. 1991. "Groupware: Some Issues and Experiences," *Communications of the ACM* (34:11), pp. 38-58.

Fukuyama, F. 1995. *Trust: Social Virtues and the Creation of Prosperity*, London: Hamish Hamilton.

Gebert, H., Geib, M., Kolbe, L., and Brenner, W. 2003. "Knowledge-Enabled Customer Relationship Management: Integrating Customer Relationship Management and Knowledge Management Concepts," *Journal of Knowledge Management* (7:5), pp. 107-123.

Glaser, B., and Strauss, A. 1967. *The Discovery of Grounded Theory*, Chicago: Aldine Publishing Company.

Gold, A. H., Malhotra, A., and Segars, A. H. 2001. "Knowledge Management: An Organizational Capabilities Perspective," *Journal of Management Information Systems* (18:1), pp. 185-214.

Hendon, D. W. 2001. "How to Negotiate with Thai Executives," *Asia Pacific Journal of Marketing and Logistics* (13:3), pp. 41-62.

Hofstede, G. 1983. "The Cultural Relativity of Organizational Practices and Theories," *Journal of International Business Studies* (14:2), pp. 75-89.

Huysman, M., and de Wit, D. 2002. *Knowledge Sharing in Practice*, Dordrecht, The Netherlands: Kluwer Academic Publishers.

Huysman, M., and Wulf, V. 2006. "IT to Support Knowledge Sharing in Communities, Towards a Social Capital Analysis," *Journal of Information Technology* (21), pp. 40-51.

Jacobs, J. 1965. *The Death and Life of Great American Cities*, London: Penguin Books.

Kaplan, B., and Duchon, D. 1988. "Combining Qualitative and Quantitative Methods in Information Systems Research: A Case Study," *MIS Quarterly* (12:4), pp. 571-586.

Klein, H., and Myers, M. 1999. "A Set of Principles for Conducting and Evaluating Interpretive Field Studies in Information Systems," *MIS Quarterly* (23:1), pp. 67-94.

Koenig, M. E. D. 2002. "The Third Stage of KM Emerges," *KMWorld* (11:3), pp. 20-1.

Komin, S. 1990. "Culture and Work Related Values in Thai Organization," *International Journal of Psychology* (25), pp. 681-704.

Leonard-Barton, D. 1988. "Implementation as Mutual Adaptation of Technology and Organization," *Research Policy* (17), pp. 251-67.

Lesser, E. L. 2000. *Knowledge and Social Capital: Foundations and Applications*, Boston: Butterworth Heinemann.

Liebowitz, J., and Suen, C. Y. 2000. "Developing Knowledge Management Metrics for Measuring Intellectual Capital," *Journal of Intellectual Capital* (1:1), pp. 54-67.

Martin, P. Y., and Turner, B. A. 1986. "Grounded Theory and Organizational Research," *The Journal of Appled Behavioral Science* (22:2), pp. 141-157.

McElroy, M. W. 1999. "The Second Generation of Knowledge Management," *Knowledge Management*, October, pp. 86-88.

Miles, M. B., and Huberman, A. M. 1994. *Qualitative Data Analysis*, Thousand Oaks, CA: Sage Publications.

Nahapiet, J., and Ghoshal, S. 1998. "Social Capital, Intellectual Capital, and the Organizational Advantage," *Academy of Management Review* (23:2), pp. 242-266.

National Science Foundation. 2002. "Science and Engineering Indicators," National Science Board, Washington, DC.

Nonaka, I., and Takeuchi, H. 1995. *The Knowledge-Creating Company: How Japanese Companies Create the Dynamics of Innovation,* New York: Oxford University Press.

Oates, B. J. 2005. *Researching Information Systems and Computing,* Oxford, UK: Sage Publications.

Okunoye, A. 2002. "Towards a Framework for Sustainable Knowledge Management in Organisations in Developing Countries," in *Proceedings of The IFIP World Computer Congress Canada,* K. Brunnstein and J. Berleur (eds.), Montreal, Canada, August 25-30, pp. 225-237.

Orlikowski, W. J. 1993. "CASE Tools as Organizational Change: Investigating Incremental and Radical Changes in Systems Development," *MIS Quarterly* (17:3), pp. 309-340.

Poltrock, S., and Grudin, J. 1995. "Groupware and Workflow: A Survey of Systems and Behavioral Issues," in *Proceedings of CHI'95, ACM Conference on Human Factors in Computing Systems,* I. Katz, R. Mack, and L. Marks (eds.), Denver, Colorado, May 7-11, pp. 355-356.

Preiss, K., Goldman, S. L., and Nagel, R. N. 1996. *Cooperate to Compete: Building Agile Business Relationships,* New York: Van Nostrand Reinhold.

Putnam, R. D. 1993. "The Prosperous Community: Social Capital and Public Life," *American Prospect* (13), pp. 35-42.

Rezgui, Y. 2007. "Knowledge Systems and Value Creation: An Action Research Investigation," *Industrial Management & Data Systems* (107:2), pp. 166-82.

Straub, D., Loch, K., and Hill, C. 2001. "Transfer of Information Technology to Developing Countries: A Test of Cultural Influence Modelling in the Arab World," *Journal of Global Information Management* (9:4), pp. 6-28.

Strauss, A., and Corbin, J. 1998. *Basics of Qualitative Research,* London: Sage Publications.

Teece, D. 1998. "Capturing Value from Knowledge Assets: The New Economy, Markets for Know-How, and Intangible Assets," *California Management Review* (40:3), pp. 55-79.

Thanasankit, T., and Corbitt, B. 2000. "Cultural Context and its Impact on Requirements Elicitation in Thailand," *The Electronic Journal on Information Systems in Developing Countries* (1:2), pp. 1-19.

Tsai, W., and Ghoshal, S. 1998. "Social Capital and Value Creation: The Role of Intrafirm Networks," *Academy of Management Journal* (41:4), pp. 464-476.

Vorakulpipat, C., and Rezgui, Y. 2006a. "From Knowledge Sharing to Value Creation: Three Generations of Knowledge Management," in *Proceedings of the 2006 IEEE International Engineering Management Conference,* M. T. de Costa Dória (ed.), Salvador, Brazil, September 17-20, pp. 214-220..

Vorakulpipat, C., and Rezgui, Y. 2006b. "A Review of Thai Knowledge Management Practices: An Empirical Study," in *Proceedings of the 2006 IEEE International Engineering Management Conference,* M. T. de Costa Dória (ed.), Salvador, Brazil, September 17-20, pp. 209-213.

Vorakulpipat, C., and Rezgui, Y. 2007. "Value Creation: The Next Generation of Knowledge Management," in *Proceedings of the 2007 Information Resources Management Association International Conference,* M. Khosrow-Pour, Vancouver, Canada, May 19-23, pp. 416-419.

Vorakulpipat, C., and Rezgui, Y. 2008. "An Evolutionary and Interpretive Perspective to Knowledge Management " *Journal of Knowledge Management* (12:3), pp 17-34.

Wagner, C., Cheung, K., Lee, F., and Ip, R. 2003. "Enhancing E-Government in Developing Countries: Managing Knowledge through Virtual Communities." *Electronic Journal on Information Systems in Developing Countries* (14:4), pp. 1-20.

Walsham, G. 1995. "Interpretive Case Studies in IS Research: Nature and Method," *European Journal of Information Systems* (4:2), pp. 74-81.

Wasserman, S., and Faust, K. 1994. *Social Network Analysis: Methods and Applications,* Cambridge, UK: Cambridge University Press.

Wei, C. C., Choy, C. S., and Yeow, P. H. P. 2006. "KM Implementation in Malaysian Telecommunication Industry: An Empirical Analysis," *Industrial Management & Data Systems* (106:8), pp. 1112-1132.

Yao, L. J., Kam, T. H. Y., and Chan, S. H. 2007. "Knowledge Sharing in Asian Public Administration Sector: The Case of Hong Kong," *Journal of Enterprise Information Management* (20:1), pp 51-69.

Yin, R. K. 2003. *Case Study Research Design and Methods* (3rd ed.), Thousand Oaks, CA: Sage Publications.

Zack, M. H., and McKenny, J. L. 2000. "Social Context and Interaction in Ongoing Computer-Supported Management Groups" in *Knowledge, Groupware and the Internet*, D. E. Smith (ed.), Boston: Butterworth-Heinemann.

About the Authors

Chalee Vorakulpipat is a Ph.D. student in the Research Institute for Built and Human Environment (BuHu) at the University of Salford. He has worked as a research assistant in the National Electronics and Computer Technology Center of Thailand. He has been involved in several projects in information systems development. His research interests include information systems, knowledge management, social and organizational studies, and software development. He can be contacted at c.vorakulpipatt11@salford.ac.uk.

Yacine Rezgui is the (founding) Director of the Informatics Research Institute at the University of Salford, and a Professor of Applied Informatics. He worked for several years in industry as an architect and as a project manager on information technology research and development projects. For the past 15 years, he has led and been involved in over 15 national and European multidisciplinary research projects. He conducts research in areas related to software engineering (including service-oriented architectures), information and knowledge management, and virtual enterprises. He has over 100 refereed publications in these areas, appearing in international journals such as *Interacting with Computers, Information Sciences,* and *Knowledge Engineering Review*. He is a member of the British Computer Society. He can be contacted at y.rezgui@salford.ac.uk.

9 INTERORGANIZATIONAL SYSTEMS ADOPTION: A Socio-Technical Perspective

Deborah Bunker
University of New South Wales
Sydney, Australia

Karlheinz Kautz
Copenhagen Business School
Frederiksburg, Denmark

Clayton Pyne
University of New South Wales
Sydney, Australia

Abstract   *This paper discusses a case study of an electronic data interchange (EDI) interorganizational system (IOS) adoption project between two organizations (ProvideCo and BuildCo) highlighting that IOS adoption is not only technological in nature and orientation but that organizational factors also play their part. As a result of the case analysis and key findings, an interorganizational collaboration model (Barratt 2004) is amended to explain and highlight the effect of organizational factors on IOS adoption. The amended model includes the relationship of technology (IOS) adoption to cross-functional collaborative activities and risk, power, opportunism, and trust.*

Keywords   Interorganizational systems, collaboration, information systems adoption

1   INTRODUCTION

Interorganizational systems (IOS) exist to support and implement cooperation and strategic alliances between two or more organizations. Interorganizational collaboration in the adoption of an IOS is driven by sharing investment costs, spreading IOS risks, and

Please use the following format when citing this chapter:

Bunker, D., Kautz, K., and Pyne, C., 2008, in IFIP International Federation for Information Processing, Volume 287, Open IT-Based Innovation: Moving Towards Cooperative IT Transfer and Knowledge Diffusion, eds. León, G., Bernardos, A., Casar, J., Kautz, K., and DeGross, J. (Boston: Springer), pp. 159-175.

accessing each organization's resources (Kumar and van Dissel 1996). The benefits espoused by companies collaborating in IOS adoption, however, are believed to inadvertently (and somewhat ironically) cause conflict between the collaborating organizations. IOS have proved difficult to implement and there has been a failure to understand with whom to collaborate and the timing of such a collaboration (Barratt 2004). Some researchers even go so far as to say that integrated supply chain benefits cannot be achieved by all firms (Sakaguchi et al. 2002). This study provides an explanation of the relationship and impact of an IOS electronic data interchange (EDI) adoption and the collaborative culture of the organizations that adopt it. An organization's collaborative culture is shown to have a significant impact on the success of IOS adoption. As the benefits of interorganizational collaboration can only be realised if the collaboration is sustained over time, it is important that the inhibitors to interorganizational collaboration are understood, so risks can be anticipated and identified early in order to guard against the possibility of conflict and adverse impact on IOS adoption.

The links between EDI, IOS, and business success are evident throughout the literature. Positive financial performance and effective supply chain arrangements are closely linked (D'Avanzo et al. 2003). Reducing cost has typically been a preeminent driver of IOS adoption and the formation of value chain relationships, but enhancing revenue is also of prime importance (D'Avanzo et al. 2003). With this renewed strategic focus on value chain relationships, there exists a significant research gap in understanding the impact that the underlying IOS adoption has on the collaborative culture that drives the success of interorganizational collaborations. Cox (1999) believes that there are serious intellectual flaws in some of the lean thinking literature, in the equity, trust, and openness views of collaboration. Cox argues that understanding strategic and operational supply chain management is dependent on understanding the existing power structures. If they do not, Cox argues, then both practitioners and academics will recommend strategies and operational practices that are inappropriate for the supply chains in which they operate.

The central argument of this paper highlights that IOS adoption is not just technological in nature and orientation, but that cultural elements of an organization also play their part. In the remainder of the paper, we assess the current state of the literature, present the modified Barratt (2004) framework, our research method, and our case organizations as well as the EDI IOS under study. We then describe and discuss our findings, further modify the Barratt framework, and finish with some conclusions.

2   LITERATURE REVIEW

This paper focuses on the effects of technology adoption on the cultural, coordination, and mediating factors of interorganizational collaboration, which are thought to be driven by (and drive) IOS adoption success. The background literature, therefore, is dealt with through these themes. The concept of collaborative culture is first explained, followed by the concepts of interdependency and coordination and the potential inhibiting elements of trust (distrust), power, and opportunism on IOS adoption. IOS (technology) adoption is then looked at as a strategic element for interorganizational collaborators to consider.

2.1 Collaborative Culture

Collaborative culture drives the coordinating activities of joint planning and decision making, joint performance metrics and process alignment, and is the basis for collaborative success (Kumar and van Dissel 1996; Wigand and Benjamin 1995). Two key elements repeat themselves in the literature as the defining qualities of collaboration: information exchange and communication and trust, and mutuality and communication.

Akin to the supply chain, value chains require high **degrees of information exchange** in order to maximize coordination: process alignment, joint decision making, and joint performance metrics (Mason-Jones and Towill 1997). Without sufficient information sharing such coordination would be unattainable. IOS have a role in this information sharing as they are the vehicle for facilitating the interorganizational activities. Information sharing is about sharing knowledge and learning for collaborative activities such as joint planning, forecasting, and process alignment. Zeng and Pathak (2003) define *information integration* as exchanges of information and knowledge via collaborative information sharing, planning, forecasting and replenishment. Information sharing assists partners to align to share learning, rather than just knowledge appropriation (Spekman et al. 1998). Adoption of IOS create virtual value chains, where supply is no longer based on inventory, but on information (Barratt 2004; Scott 2000). There is also a need to develop broad interfaces between organizations potentially to overcome the lack of internal coordination (Barratt and Green 2001). Information sharing is facilitated by open communication and broad contact lines at organizational boundaries so as to prevent the collaboration from dissipating when certain resources withdraw from the arrangement. Information sharing and communication, therefore, together comprise an integral element of the collaborative culture required of a value chain participant in the IOS adoption process.

A minimum level of interfirm trust is indispensable for any strategic alliance to be formed and to function (Das and Teng 1998); **some trust is required to initiate interorganizational collaboration** (Webb 1991). Communication and proactive information exchange are both tactics to boost trust among partners (Das and Teng 1998). The building of trust requires a willingness to communicate over a range of issues (Webb 1991). Making mutual adaptations, and recognizing mutual benefits (Scott 2000), according to the partnership is an effective way to develop trust (Das and Teng 1998). Mutuality in this study is taken from Scott's (2000) definition of mutual trust: the expectation shared by participants that they will meet their commitments to one another. With mutual trust, partners will reciprocate openness and sharing of information and knowledge over time. Communication then helps to further enhance trust because it enhances interaction between partners (Leifer and Mills 1996). This demonstrates the cyclical nature of trust; that is, reciprocated trust is the basis for cooperation (Axelrod 1984; Creed and Miles 1996; McAllister 1995). A common implicit perspective from shared information and experiences and joint knowledge creation, reciprocity in a partnership, and trading personnel with the partner build effective trust (Scott 2000). The concepts of trust, mutuality, and communication are inextricably linked and collectively drive the collaborative culture of organizations in the adoption of an IOS.

2.2 Interorganizational Collaboration

Interdependence creates risks that must be managed through increased coordination between firms to capture the potential productivity improvements enabled by new interorganizational relationships (Clark and Lee 2000). Interdependencies are inherent in the coordinating activities of process alignment, joint decision making and value chain, or joint performance metrics. Interorganizational collaboration can be viewed as a set of processes crossing organizational boundaries that create interdependencies, which need to be coordinated to achieve the goals of the two organizations. The interdependencies created by an interorganizational relationship constrain how the organizations can achieve the goal of the collaboration. This is known as the coordination problem and has been covered extensively by Thompson (1967) and Galbraith (1977), who explored how dependencies may be structured to maximize organizational performance.

Coordination is managing activity dependencies (Kim 2001) and is represented as process alignment, joint decision making and value chain, or joint performance metrics. Coordination often manifests itself with respect to an IOS adoption in the form of formal mechanisms that assist in the coordination of interdependent activities (Thompson 1967). Coordination, as a subset of collaboration, is more challenging than that within a single firm as it requires joint implementation of policy and process changes between independent firms (Clark and Lee 2000). Since the adoption of the IOS requires not only supply chain transformation but also organizational process change,

> managing relationships among the dependent elements' [coordination] is indispensable for higher performance and lower coordination costs that are hallmarks of successful IOS adoptions....[Furthermore,] increased interdependence without increased coordination represents an unacceptable increase in risk for both partners involved in the interorganizational relationship, but expanded coordination provides important benefits in addition to enabling firms to deal with increasing levels of dependence (Clark and Lee 2000, p. 91).

Increased interdependence without the corresponding coordination becomes a barrier to the adoption of the IOS.

2.3 Mediating Factors

Literature across the fields of psychology, economics, sociology, and organizational sciences **focus on trust** in the context of both intra- and interorganizational collaboration (Huxham and Vangen 2003). Trust is a means of coping with uncertainty (Butler and Gill 1995). Trust as a concept is important in this study as trust mitigates opportunistic behavior (Huxham and Vangen 2003). **Opportunism** can be a significant barrier to effective IOS adoption, as it can cause suboptimal outcomes for supply chain members as they individually pursue their own optimal outcomes (Katz et al. 2003). Opportunistic behaviors manifest themselves differently, depending on the type of IOS being adopted (Clark et al. 2001).

EDI data sharing, as an example of IOS adoption, brings with it a minimal **increase in risk** as EDI service providers shirk their responsibilities for information receipt and delivery (Clark et al. 2001). The possibility of a renegotiation of rates by the providers of EDI systems also exists. If we consider the connectivity of extended EDI, it may be used to send invoices and where firms are willing to share data (Clark et al. 2001). It is the extended use of EDI that is open to data poaching by suppliers as data volumes increase (Clark et al. 2001). These levels of connectivity, and the potential risks associated with them, are of primary focus as organizations adopt their EDI IOS.

As trust is seen to be the eliminator of the **fear of opportunism**, the negating of power differences, and thus interagency and mistrust, is also a key concept within this study (Huxham and Vangen 2003). This sees the concept of power emerge as key to understanding the factors inhibiting interorganizational collaboration and stimulating interorganizational conflict. Moreover, value chain innovation means nothing if a participant cannot leverage their power over the critical resources in the chain and appropriate the majority of value for themselves (Cox 1999). This perspective in the literature states that it is natural for a company to act opportunistically. As IOS adoption is closely related to the elements of trust and opportunism, it is also intimately related to the power relations evident within and between organizations.

Huxham and Vangen (2003) make the **link between power and trust** and postulate that collaborative achievements erode trust, as collaborative achievements are manifestations of power, which are barriers to building trust. Eden and Huxham (2001) and Cox (1999) claim that organizations naturally try and impose control as control is manifested through attempting to influence an organization's collaborative partnerships. Cox also argues that organizations seek to create a hierarchy of structural dominance: a situation in which there is a dominant player within a supply chain, who is able to own and control the key resources that appropriate value.

Kumar and van Dissel (1996) propose that factors that are barriers to, or facilitators of, IOS have different enablers and technologies that must be investigated by IOS researchers. A second related aim of the Kumar and van Dissel study was to instigate research on trading partner conflict cause and resolution in an e-environment.

2.4 Strategic Elements

Sharing of computing technology allows for more flexibility and closer organizational integration (Holland 1995). IOS adoption facilitates interorganizational activity, whether it is a continuous replenishment program for a supermarket, vendor managed inventory, or an out-sourced billing process. IOS adoption also facilitates cross functional activities (joint planning/decision making). While this is the lean "enabling" view of technology, literature consistently implies that IOS are inextricably linked to the collaborative culture of the organizations adopting them, which in turn drives the effectiveness of coordinating activities. IOS adoption has an impact on the cultural elements, which effectively drive the collaborative culture of the organization and ultimately the success of the relationship between the adopting parties.

IOS are envisaged by an organization to harness the advantages of making the transition from interorganizational competition to interorganizational cooperation (Kumar and van Dissel 1996). Despite the economic, operational, and strategic advantages, organizations are still grappling with the concept that IOS are difficult to implement (Barratt 2004). Kumar and van Dissel liken IOS to any human endeavor, where cooperation between organizations can sometimes become conflict. While much of the literature has concerned itself with traditional economic, technical, and socio-political risks, few researchers have examined a link between the IOS adoption and the interorganizational collaborative process.

3   RESEARCH FRAMEWORK

For the purposes of combining various elements of the literature and for its relevance to the topic and substance of the research, we adapted Barratt's (2004) model of inter-organizational collaboration (see Figure 1). This model defines interorganizational collaboration elements and brings clarity to how the IOS adoption may affect and be affected by interorganizational collaboration. We have also drawn on the interorganiza-tional conflict literature (power, trust and opportunism) and incorporated this into the model as elements of power; trust (distrust) and opportunism are the drivers of inter-organizational conflict. We thought it pertinent, therefore, to reflect on how these ele-ments might impact the IOS adoption and the interorganizational collaboration. Barratt's model has thus been modified to include of the relationship (arrowed) of *technology (IOS) adoption* to *collaborative culture* through *power, risk, and opportunism*.

Barratt argues that organizations rely too much on technology to build IOS rather than focusing on the needs of their partners and the development of trustworthy rela-tionships. Interorganizational collaboration has been stifled recently due to the impact that the technology is having on the collaborative culture of the organization. The modified Barratt research model assumes that the collaborative culture largely drives the success of the adoption, and it is therefore vital to understand the socio-technical link between the IOS adoption and the organizational culture of the collaborating organizations.

This study seeks to utilize this model as a starting point to understand the relation-ship of an IOS adoption to

(1) Cultural elements of an interorganizational collaboration (shared culture, information exchange and communication, win–win approach, and mutuality)
(2) Coordination elements of an interorganizational collaboration (cross functional activities, joint decision making/planning, joint value chain metrics, process alignment)
(3) Mediating factors within an interorganizational collaboration (power, risk, oppor-tunism and trust and commitment)

4   THE RESEARCH METHOD

A case study approach was used to examine the recent adoption of an EDI IOS, based on the mature standards of EDI, to facilitate invoicing for BuildCo. BuildCo out-sourced this business process to ProvideCo, and it is the interorganizational collaboration

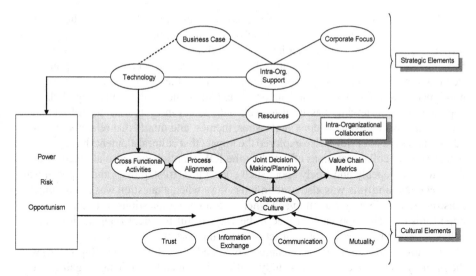

Figure 1. The Research Model for the Study: Interorganizational Collaboration
(Modification of Figure 5, "The 'Cultural' Elements of Supply Chain Collaboration" in Mark Barratt, "Understanding the Meaning of Collaboration in the Supply Chain," *Supply Chain Management: An International Journal* (9:1), 2004, p. 36. Republished with permission from Emerald Group Publishing.)

required for the adoption of this IOS between BuildCo and ProvideCo that concerns this study. The data analysis in this study includes an assessment of the cultural and coordination elements and mediating factors of the organization and how these contribute to the effectiveness of the interorganizational collaboration and the subsequent IOS adoption.

The research approach was "bricoleur-like," where a variety of sources were drawn upon pragmatically. This approach specifies that researchers use an assortment of techniques in an inventive manner to accomplish the research aims (Neuman 2003). The field method used accommodated multiple research techniques to gain knowledge (Schatzman and Anselm 1973).

Semi-structured in-depth one-on-one interviews with one key informant in BuildCo and one key informant in SupplyCo served as an effective way to extract the underlying feelings and emotions toward the interorganizational collaboration. A decision was made to sacrifice the breadth offered by possible multiple informants within ProvideCo and BuildCo for the depth and richness offered by an extensive interview with one key informant from each organization, who were both in a direct relationship with one another throughout the IOS adoption process.

The two informants functioned as IT managers for the EDI IOS adoption project, and were both the key contact for the project for their respective organization. They also operated as IT consultants directly involved with the system adoption through their work in developing and implementing the system and the new processes required between the value chain participants. Further to this, both respondents had knowledge of the wider interorganizational relationships between ProvideCo and BuildCo.

These detailed interviews were particularly relevant for understanding the collaborative process between ProvideCo and BuildCo, allowing the researchers to probe the difficulties, problems, and conflict involved. At times the interviews were directive, to focus on certain concepts the literature had revealed and to probe vague responses or fleeting references and utterances of the interviewees. Other stages of the interview were nondirective, allowing the respondent to fully explain issues as they felt compelled. This approach to interviewing was used to seek out special insights into the collaborative process, always focusing on emergent issues, themes, and motifs that related to the IOS adoption. These interviews also explored the impact that cultural elements have on interorganizational collaboration as effected by the IOS adoption, and also allowed respondents to speak openly and freely about such concepts as trust, power, and opportunism.

Scenario analysis was also used in interviews when a question was too politically sensitive to ask directly (mainly used when encountering questions of trust, power, or opportunism). This approach proved to be very useful for identifying socio-political behaviors and the potential for conflict between the parties.

Documentary analysis (of documents obtained from BuildCo and SupplyCo) was the primary source of data for this study and was informed by the insights gained from the two interviewees. The documents allowed the researchers to fully understand the technological architecture of the EDI IOS being adopted before interviewing the key informants, thus allowing for socio-political issues to be knowledgeably probed in the interviews. The documents also complemented interviews by allowing claims made by the respondents to be compared to the meanings in the documents. In this way, documentary artifacts offered a means of triangulating the data by offering another perspective on the EDI IOS adoption. Artefacts included functional specifications from BuildCo, ProvideCo, and third party value chain participants, e-mail correspondence, meeting minutes, the complete set of ProvideCo testing documentation, and the complete set of documents directly used by ProvideCo in its collaboration with the BuildCo Timber division. Documentation also allowed for the effective understanding of the EDI architecture and implementation between ProvideCo and BuildCo and their interorganizational collaboration over time.

This data was indexed, classified, and summarized (Neuman 2003), with the primary aim of reducing the data to a perceived factual base (Jick 1979). The data analysis utilized a thematic approach where interviews, scenarios, and documents were coded around the themes elaborated within the literature and the modified Barratt (2004) model.

The case study was conducted over six months and required frequent consultations with BuildCo and ProvideCo, where a researcher was often on site full time for some weeks. This case is more innovative than most in the IOS adoption literature as it seeks out both sides of IOS adoption and interorganizational collaboration, simultaneously seeking to understand collaboration as a holistic subject comprising of many interrelationships through culture alignment and technology use (Klein and Myers 1999). The literature claims that there has been much conflict in IOS adoption in practice and that the relevance of recent literature has been limited due to the fact that academics are not truly becoming immersed in the collaborative processes of adoption, and are therefore not realizing the power structures and struggles for value appropriation. This approach also allowed for the link between the technology adoption and elements within the Barratt model to be fully explored.

5   CASE BACKGROUND

This section includes background about ProvideCo and BuildCo, indicating where the informants were positioned within their respective organizations, as well as background information on the EDI IOS adoption.

5.1   ProvideCo

ProvideCo claims to be Australia's leading provider of quality information and image management services, helping leading businesses and major governing bodies to communicate effectively with their customers. It has 900 employees in branches in Sydney, Melbourne, Brisbane, Adelaide, Canberra, and Perth who provide services including consultancy in services integration, solutions development, and process reengineering; data formatting and management; document design and creation; document collation and distribution; response capture and conversion management; image storage and retrieval in billing, Internet billing, database management, ballots, elections, public floats, privatization, demutualization, and the digitization, storage, and retrieval of essential business information. Their clients include telecos, government agencies, financial services organizations, and media companies.

Their group IT structure (departments) consists of NSW Consulting Team, Victorian Consulting Team, Research and Development (R&D), and National IT. The NSW Consulting Team manager has direct reporting responsibility to the Group IT/R&D manager, who reports to the board and managing director. There is a participative management style evident in ProvideCo, where cross-functional teams are often assembled from across Group IT/R&D due to the skill sets and expertise required by the project.

The informant, CC, is an IT consultant within the NSW Consulting Team (Group IT/R&D). CC works directly with the personnel within the organization as required without restriction from management. Consultants within the NSW consulting team meet with the NSW Consulting Team manager on an *ad hoc* basis as required. Depending on demand and market conditions, each IT consultant may have sole responsibility for as many as 10 projects simultaneously.

5.2   BuildCo

BuildCo describes itself as a large building and construction materials company headquartered in Australia, with leading local and international market positions. It employs 13,000 people at many sites in Australia, the United States, and Asia. Its organizational divisions include Australian Construction Materials; Cement, Clay & Concrete Products; Plasterboard; Timber; and BuildCo USA. BuildCo has around A\$4 billion sales per annum and its products and services include construction materials; cement, clay and concrete products; plasterboard; timber; and BuildCo (USA), which are the direct product outputs from its divisional structure. BuildCo's clients include construction companies, retail outlets, and subcontractors.

BuildCo has been a longstanding institution in Australia, a large respected company that is closely intertwined with the evolution of the Australian building and construction industry since the 1940s. It has a long and successful history of mergers and acquisitions, which steadily built the business in a diversity of industries until February 2000, when a de-merger resulted in the listing of BuildCo separately from another spin-off company. The Timber Division of BuildCo is a national business employing around 600 people in hardwood, plywood, and softwood operations predominantly on the east coast of Australia, which manufactures and distributes a broad range of products for domestic and export markets. The group IT structure (departments) comprise of decentralized IT units in each part of the business.

Informant MB is an IT consultant within the Timber Division. As can be seen from the description of BuildCo's history and the businesses within the business unit, IT is not a core competency of BuildCo. IT within BuildCo is seen as a facilitator that provides opportunity to streamline business processes and improve the efficiency of non-core functions within the company. MB confirmed this in the case, saying the "next move [for Timber] is to push all transactions through ProvideCo." The lack of IT expertise of BuildCo Timber is another dominant factor within the case. When asked whether there is any coordination of IT across the business units, MB responded, "Each business system manager from each division meets on a bi-monthly basis." Despite these meetings, there is no evidence in the case that these meetings are having any positive impact on the collaboration with ProvideCo, as BuildCo was always uncoordinated in their approach to the project from an aggregate perspective.

5.3 The IOS Collaboration: EDI Adoption

Clark et al. (2001) state that as an example of IOS collaboration EDI increased from 10% in 1990 to 30% in the late 1990s. The implementation of an EDI IOS serves, therefore, as a valid and applicable example to relate such socio-political elements as shared culture, power and opportunism in an IOS adoption. Our focus in this paper is on the interorganizational collaboration that takes place between ProvideCo and the BuildCo Timber Division. This necessarily crosses organizational boundaries in the analysis of such issues as trust and opportunistic behavior, as the collaboration between BuildCo and ProvideCo is mediated by the relationships held between them. The case background of these companies, outlined above, serves to provide for the wider context of understanding of their collaboration in the IOS adoption and its use.

EDI is an evolving technology, which has been impacted (by varying degrees in different industries) by the rapid growth of the Internet. In recent years, there has been a divergence from traditional EDI, where transmission is facilitated by private/value-added networks, to the standardized TCP/IP protocol offered by Internet EDI (Kumar and Crook 1999).

Throughout the case interviews, the respondents constantly discussed the segregation of the BuildCo business into autonomous product divisions as a point of conflict between ProvideCo and BuildCo. The collaboration between ProvideCo and BuildCo was at times stifled due to the lack of coordination between the BuildCo's business units. This was because the BuildCo Timber Division, which is the division of focus here, was not the only business unit within BuildCo implementing the EDI IOS project. The identical requirement was placed on other BuildCo divisions by their head office. The project was being delivered by ProvideCo to the Cement Division, which occurred after delivery to the Timber Division. At the same time Timber was being developed, requirements gathering and analysis was also being performed for the Plasterboard Division of BuildCo.

Frustrations and annoyances arose between ProvideCo and BuildCo as ProvideCo was having to communicate the identical requirements to multiple business units within BuildCo as each BuildCo division had completely separate IT systems. This caused ProvideCo to be constantly repeating requirements that were identical across the different units. BuildCo was not interested in coordinating among the divisions in order to simplify the implementation. The BuildCo Timber business manager explains that "synergies within one division cannot be abstracted across BuildCo, which adds to the complexity of implementation. ProvideCo did not understand this issue, but by the same token BuildCo was not upfront in explaining the complexity of its divisions." This was a significant source of frustration for ProvideCo. The segregated structure of the BuildCo business units and their absolute independence of each other led to opportunistic behavior and other conflicts that damaged the relationship. Although the structure of the BuildCo business is contextual to the Timber Division of focus, its impact on the collaboration is critical to understanding the nature of the collaboration in this case study.

The Timber & Hardware Exchange (T&HE) is a business-to-business eCommerce system that provides business document exchange using the Internet and is a service offered by a third party (Pacific Commerce) through an exchange software program and infrastructure. The T&HE is responsible for validating the hardware industry working group standards for the transmission of EDI in the Edifact format, as well as for transmission of the data once received from ProvideCo (i.e., an industry supplier/wholesaler or service provider) to the receiver CustomerCo (an industry customer). The T&HE is the primary point of validation in the process before the data is forwarded from BuildCo through ProvideCo to the CompanyCo head office for payment (see Figure 2). The T&HE is the IOS being adopted by ProvideCo and BuildCo and the focus of their inter-organizational collaboration.

6   CASE STUDY FINDINGS

A number of key findings relating to the research questions became evident as the story of the IOS adoption and the associated interorganizational collaboration between BuildCo and ProvideCo emerged from the interview, scenario, and documentary data.

Research Question 1: What is the relationship of IOS adoption to cultural elements of an interorganizational collaboration (shared culture, information exchange and communication, win–win approach, and mutuality)?

Collaboration in each phase of the IOS adoption process differs significantly. Effective collaboration at different phases within IOS adoption seemed to require different cultural elements in different proportions. Early project collaboration required more of a shared culture and win-win approach in order to overcome the major obstacles of "*conflicting requirements*" and negate the need to "*fly by the seat of our pants*" (BuildCo Timber). Hence, conflicting requirements were constantly mentioned when respondents

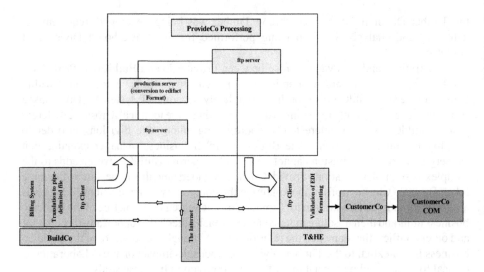

Figure 2. T&HE Process Flows

referred to the difficulty of the early project phase collaboration. The only way this was overcome was by "*making the effort to get together (face to face) and include other parties to iron out requirements.*" This revealed that, in the early stages of collaboration in IOS adoption such as requirements gathering and analysis and design, the collaborative elements required for success are very different from those needed for development, testing, implementation, and production. In the early project phases, the parties had to adopt a win–win approach through proactive behavior and share a culture to overcome conflicting requirements. This further substantiates the link in the model between the collaborative culture and coordination by sharing a mutual win–win perspective on understanding conflicting and slipping requirements. BuildCo and ProvideCo were both exhibiting a collaborative culture to achieve a higher level of coordination. Such inter-action resulted in a degree of trust developing between the stakeholders: "*We can trust ProvideCo in dealing with the other party transparently and then filtering back requirements and responses [of other stakeholders] to BuildCo.*" This contrasts directly with what made the collaboration successful through the development, implementation, and production stages of the project. Information exchange and communication was the predominant cultural element that contributed to the success of these phases of the project. During implementation, communication was occurring at least three or four times per week between both IT consultants MB and CC, although in production, daily operational issues were handled by other people at ProvideCo. BuildCo confirmed this high degree of interlock between the companies throughout the development, implemen-tation, testing and production phases confirming that there is "*daily e-mail commu-nication to a number of people other than CC.*" Although unintended, the insight that interorganizational collaboration may be markedly different over different phases of the IOS adoption is an interesting one.

Collaboration over the IOS adoption differed greatly from each cultural perspective. From the perspective of the two respondents, and also as evident in the supporting documentation, a win–win approach and shared culture was vital for strategic imperatives like project initiation and early stage project analysis and design, whereas information exchange and communication were more related to overcoming daily production issues in the live project environment. With respect to the cultural elements explored in this study, it can be said that operational collaboration and strategic collaboration are distinct, as posited by Cox (1999). For these two organizations, it was very different to collaborate over issues such as missing fields in pipe-delimited files than over which projects should be given the "green-light" for development in a value chain.

Research Question 2: What is the relationship of IOS adoption to coordination elements of an interorganizational collaboration (cross functional activities, joint decision making/planning, joint value chain metrics, process alignment)?

IT planning must be fully integrated with business planning (intra-organizational coordination) to maximiz interorganizational coordination. This IOS adoption project plays a more reactive and facilitating role in BuildCo. Strategically, BuildCo and ProvideCo were conducting business planning, but this did not include the divisional BuildCo IT managers. The disjointedness between strategic business planning and IT planning posed many problems for the interorganizational collaboration. ProvideCo quite often found itself dealing with contradicting imperatives from different BuildCo business units while trying to satisfy the strategic planning it had conducted with BuildCo at a strategic level. The business units had no participation in, or knowledge of, this level of planning. BuildCo would impose strategic level plans on the IT managers. Both organizations were heavily coupled with respect to operational planning and decision making. The levels of planning occurring in the case and the lack of clarity around some coordination issues further supports the notion that fully integrated IT and business planning are essential for IOS adoption.

Joint performance metrics are useful as a tool to mitigate risk and maximize coordination. The lack of clarity around the issue of joint performance metrics in this value chain has led to this key finding. The complexity around joint metrics indicated a convoluted approach by BuildCo, where the Timber Division was not using all of the available information that it actually had at its disposal for monitoring performance effectively. The lack of clarity around performance metrics detracted from the coordination attainable between the value chain parties. Joint value chain metrics, utilized fully, may help identify problems more expediently, allowing for better solutions to be reached in a shorter time frame. This also cultivates a more competitive value chain with decreased overall throughput times leading to more efficient business processes. Therefore, joint decision making, joint planning, and joint value chain metrics are all vital to effective collaboration. These elements allow organizations to coordinate more effectively both at an operational level and at a strategic level.

Research Question 3: What is the relationship of IOS adoption to mediating factors within an interorganizational collaboration (power, risk, opportunism and trust, and commitment)?

Risk perception may inhibit collaborative behavior (power, trust, distrust, and opportunism). The IOS adoption does bring a direct level of risk with it. Risk is aggregated in the model as potential harm to culture through the elements of power, opportunism, and distrust. The level of risk, therefore, is reflected by the possibility that power, opportunism, and distrust will impact cultural elements in a negative fashion, ultimately leading to loose binding behavior caused by a lack of a collaborative culture. The risk of this occurring, to some extent, directly comes from the technology adopted for the interorganizational collaboration (or the perceived "riskiness" of the technology).

Risk is related to technology adoption. In the case, this is evidenced by the fact that BuildCo assumed the majority of risk for the end-to-end process, as a point of failure would prevent them from billing CustomerCo. Here, the risk of not billing relates to the process flows created by the sequentially dependent nature of the EDI technology. Clark et al. (2001) posit that these new processes (increased data sharing through technology) and new policies (operational integration) arising from the implementation cause a very large increase in risk. This is consistent with issues express by informants in this study.

Trust, power, and opportunism are affected by and come from collaboration. Elements like shared culture, win–win approach, and mutuality are important for strategic collaboration. ProvideCo and BuildCo lacked strength in trust, power, and opportunism, but were very adept at information exchange and communication. This aligned with ProvideCo and BuildCo collaborating inefficiently at a strategic level, but effectively at an operational level. These elements (shared culture, win–win approach, mutuality, information exchange, and communication), collectively constitute the collaborative culture of an organization, and are embedded to a greater or lesser degree within the organization's culture independent of the current collaboration. Conversely, the concepts of power, opportunism, and trust can come from experience of the current collaboration (e.g., the issue of BuildCo's corporate structure and its direct effect on ProvideCo's relationship with them).

Trust, power, and opportunism are affected by and come from cross functional activities. Trust can be grouped with the concepts of power and opportunism as they are all affected by and come from the current interorganizational collaboration between the companies. For example, mediation of the cross-functional activities (cultural elements) are affected by the fact that sensitive information was obtained by the BuildCo Plasterboard Division on the Timber EDI IOS adoption. This decreased the trust ProvideCo had in BuildCo, making them increasingly wary of BuildCo. This lack of trust, therefore, mediated the cultural elements, which saw a marked decrease in the win–win approach, level of shared culture and volume of information exchange that ProvideCo would adopt in future dealings with the Plasterboard Division. In this instance, the lack of trust had a negative impact on the shared culture, the win–win stance of the players, and also decreased the amount of information exchange and communication. Furthermore, the opportunistic behavior shown by Plasterboard also affected the overall interorganizational relationships and power balances and was reflected in the idiosyncratic trust ProvideCo had in BuildCo, namely the trust CC had in MB. Beyond this personal relationship, there was a significant level of distrust and lack of confidence between the companies.

7   CONCLUSION

As a result of the case study findings, the Barratt model has been amended to indicate that cultural elements are intrinsic to interorganizational collaboration while mediating/inhibiting elements are indirectly impacted by the technology adoption and from the repeated interorganizational collaboration (through cross functional activities) Risk has also been indirectly related to IOS adoption. As can be seen in the modified model (see Figure 3), the cross functional activities, through repeated interaction, directly give rise to the concepts of power, opportunism, trust, and, therefore, risk. Collaborative cultural elements have been shown by the case study to be antecedent to any interorganizational collaboration and dependent on such intra-organizational factors as internal business structure, management vision, and the beliefs promoted throughout the organization. ProvideCo's mantra of flexibility and fitting the customer's requirements at all costs are examples of how the elements of a collaborative culture grow organically from within an organization and precede interorganizational collaboration. In aiming to conduct business flexibly, ProvideCo exhibited an inherent need to attain a shared culture, exchange information frequently, and communicate effectively. BuildCo's data also highlights examples of the impact of a deficient internal business structure on interorganizational collaboration. The BuildCo structure had a negative impact on the cultural elements of both organizations, which revealed the mediating/inhibiting factors of trust, risk, power, and opportunism. This study has allowed for a more comprehensive view of interorganizational collaboration to be reached from modifying an existing model (Barratt 2004).

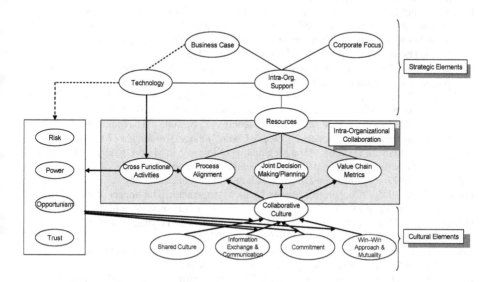

Figure 3. The Amended Research Model: ProvideCo and BuildCo (modification of Figure 5, "The 'Cultural' Elements of Supply Chain Collaboration" in Mark Barratt, "Understanding the Meaning of Collaboration in the Supply Chain," *Supply Chain Management: An International Journal* (9:1), 2004, p. 36)

The amended model (see Figure 3) also indicates that dealing with the concepts of trust, power, and opportunism, which come from cross-functional activities, is of vital importance to the effectiveness of an organization's collaborative culture and the interorganizational collaboration flowing from it. It is with the acknowledgment and development of such concepts as power, opportunism, and trust (distrust) that managers will fully harness the potential of their IOS adoption and interorganizational or value chain relationships.

References

Axelrod, R. 1984. *The Evolution of Cooperation*, New York: Basic Books.

Barratt, M. 2004. "Understanding the Meaning of Collaboration in the Supply Chain," *Supply Chain Management: An International Journal* (9:1), pp. 30-42.

Barratt, M. A., and Green, M. 2001. "The Cultural Shift: The Need for a Collaborative Culture," in *Proceedings of the 2001 Supply Chain Knowledge Conference*, Cranfield School of Management, November.

Butler, R., and Gill, J. 1995. "Learning and Knowledge in Joint Ventures: The Importance of Trust," paper presentation, British Academy of Management Annual Conference, Sheffield.

Clark, T. H., Croson, D. C., and Schiano, W. T. 2001. "A Hierarchical Model of Supply-Chain Integration: Information Sharing and Operational Independence in the US Grocery Channel," *Information Technology and Management* (2), pp. 261-288.

Clark, T. H., and Lee, H.G. 2000. "Performance, Interdependence and Coordination in Business-to-Business Electronic Commerce and Supply Chain Management," *Information Technology and Management* (1), pp. 85-105.

Creed, W., and Miles, R. 1996. "Trust in Organizations: A Conceptual Framework Linking Organizational Forms, Managerial Philosophies, and the Opportunity Costs of Control," in *Trust in Organizations: Frontiers of Theory and Research*, R. M. Kramer and T. R. Tyler (eds.), Thousand Oaks, CA: Sage Publications, pp. 16-38.

Cox, A. 1999. "Power, Value and Supply Chain Management," *Supply Chain Management: An International Journal* (4:4), pp. 167-175.

Das, T., and Teng, B. 1998. "Between Trust and Control: Developing Confidence in Partner Cooperation in Alliances," *Academy of Management Review* (23:3), pp. 491-512.

D'Avanzo, R. D., Lewinski, H. V., and Van Wassenhove, L. N. 2003. "The Link Between Supply Chain and Financial Performance," *Supply Chain Management Review* (7:6), pp. 40-47.

Eden, C., and Huxham, C. 2001. "The Megotiation of Purpose in Multi-Organizational Collaborative Groups," *Journal of Management Studies* (38:3), pp. 373-391.

Galbraith, J. 1977. *Organization Design*, Reading, MA: Addison-Wesley.

Holland, C. P. 1995. "Cooperative Supply Chain Management: The Impact of Interorganizational Information Systems," *Journal of Strategic Information Systems* (4:2), pp. 117-133.

Huxham, C., and Vangen, S. 2000. "Ambiguity, Complexity and Dynamics in the Membership of Collaboration," *Human Relations* (53:6), pp. 771-806.

Jick, T. D. 1979. "Mixing Qualitative and Quantitative Methods: Triangulation in Accumulation," *Administrative Science Quarterly* (24), pp. 602-611.

Katz, J. P., Pagell, M. D., and Bloodgood, J. M. 2003. "Strategies of Supply Communities," *Supply Chain Management: An International Journal* (8:4), pp. 291-302.

Kim, H. W. 2001. "Modeling Inter- and Intra-Organizational Coordination in Electronic Commerce Deployments," *Information Technology and Management* (2), pp. 335-354.

Klein, H. K., and Myers, M. D. 1999. "A Set of Principles for Conducting and Evaluating Interpretive Field Studies in Information Systems," *MIS Quarterly* (23:1), pp. 67-88.

Kumar, R. L., and Crook, C. W. 1999. "A Multi-Disciplinary Framework for the Management of Interorganizational Systems," *The DATA BASE for Advances in Information Systems* (30:1), pp. 22-37.

Kumar, K., and van Dissel, H. G. 1996. 'Sustainable Collaboration: Managing Conflict and Co-operation in Interorganizational Systems," *MIS Quarterly* (20:3), pp. 279-300.

Leifer, R., and Mills, P. 1996. "An Information Processing Approach for Deciding upon Control Strategies and Reducing Control Loss in Emerging Organizations," *Journal of Management* (22), pp. 113-137.

Mason-Jones, R., and Towill, D. R. 1997. "Information Enrichment: Designing the Supply Chain for Competitive Advantage," *Supply Chain Management* (2:4), pp. 137-148.

McAllister, D. 1995. "Affect- and Cognition-Based Trust as Foundations for Interpersonal Cooperation in Organizations," *Academy of Management Journal* (38:1), pp. 24-59.

Neuman, W. L. 2003. *Social Research Methods Qualitative and Quantitative Approaches* (5ᵗʰ ed.), Boston: Allyn and Bacon.

Sakugachi, T., Nicovich, S. G., and Dibrell, C. C. 2002. "Development of an Integrated Supply Chain Model," in *Proceedings of the 8ᵗʰ Americas Conference on Information Systems*, R. Ramsower and J. Windsor (eds.), Dallas, TX, August 9-11, pp. 2350-2351.

Schatzman, L., and Anselm, L. 1973. *Field Research: Strategies for a Natural Sociology*, Englewood Cliffs, NJ: Prentice-Hall.

Scott, J. E. 2000. "Facilitating Interorganizational Learning with Information Technology," *Journal of Management Information Systems* (17:2), pp. 81-113.

Spekman, R. E., Spear, J., and Kamauff, J. 2002. "Supply Chain Competency: Learning as a Key Component," *Supply Chain Management: An International Journal* (7:2), pp. 41-55.

Thompson, J. D. 1967. *Organizations in Action*, New York: McGraw-Hill.

Webb, A. 1991. "Coordination: A Problem in Public Sector Management," *Policy and Politics* (19:4), pp. 229-241.

Wigand, R. T., and Benjamin, R. I. 1995. "Electronic Commerce: Effects on Electronic Markets," *Journal of Computer-Mediated Communication* (1:3) (http://jcmc.indiana.edu/vol1/issue3/wigand.html)

Zeng, A. Z., and Pathak, B. K. 2003. "Achieving Information Integration in Supply Chain Management through B2B E-Hubs: Concepts and Analyses," *Industrial Management and Data Systems* (103:9), pp. 657-665.

About the Authors

Deborah Bunker is a senior lecturer at the School of Information Systems, Technology & Management at the University of New South Wales. She holds a Ph.D. in Information Systems Management. Her research interests are in IS philosophy, IS management, IS adoption and diffusion, and e-Commerce/e-Business. She has published widely in these areas. Deborah is a founding member and the Vice-Chair of IFIP TC 8 WG 8.6 on the adoption and diffusion of IT. She can be reached at d.bunker@unsw.edu.au.

Karlheinz Kautz is a professor in Systems Development and Software Engineering at the Department for Informatics at Copenhagen Business School. He holds a Ph.D. in systems development. His research interests are in the diffusion and adoption of information technology innovations, evolutionary systems development, and system development methodologies for advanced application areas, the organizational impact of IT, knowledge management, and software quality and process improvement. He has widely published in these areas. Karl is a founding member and is past Chairman of the IFIP TC 8 WG 8.6 on the adoption and diffusion of IT. He can be reached at Karl.Kautz@cbs.dk.

Clayton Pyne has been a student for the degree of Business Information Technology (Honours) at the University of New South Wales and has been a researcher for the project, which builds the basis for the research described here.

Part 4:

Analysis of Cases

10 TECHNOLOGICAL FRAME INCONGRUENCE, DIFFUSION, AND NONCOMPLIANCE

Polly Sobreperez
Salford Business School
University of Salford
Salford, UK

Abstract   *The technological frames of reference strand of social shaping of technology theory is used to overlay the issues arising from a case study looking at noncompliance with information systems. A recent review of the theory suggests that although frame content is often addressed, frame structure, the process of framing, and the characteristics and outcomes of frames are largely overlooked. This paper attempts to address this shortfall by applying the indicators identified by case study research to the frames of different groups and using them to highlight differing perceptions and attitudes. In this way, the author suggests that issues surrounding noncompliance should not be dismissed as resistance but instead should be further studied by managers and developers, leading to accommodation of differing views. Further examination of frame incongruence reveals dependence on inefficient or ineffective organizational situations and thus these indicators can be useful in future studies to identify and address procedural, acceptance and cultural issues leading to acts of noncompliance.*

Keywords   Social shaping, technological frames, resistance, workaround

1 INTRODUCTION

This paper builds on work published in 2005/2006 that identified categories of non-compliance with information systems (Ferneley et al. 2005; Ferneley and Sobreperez 2006). This work identified antecedent conditions underpinning various types of non-

Please use the following format when citing this chapter:

Sobreperez, P., 2008, in IFIP International Federation for Information Processing, Volume 287, Open IT-Based Innovation: Moving Towards Cooperative IT Transfer and Knowledge Diffusion, eds. León, G., Bernardos, A., Casar, J., Kautz, K., and DeGross, J. (Boston: Springer), pp. 179-196.

compliant behaviors concluding that certain behaviors, perceived as resistance, occur for more positive and supportive reasons and that managers should not dismiss all non-compliance as resistance, but should look more closely at reasons for such behaviors.

In an attempt to understand why these occurrences of noncompliance continue to occur in organizations, we now tie in the technological frames of reference aspect of social shaping of technology (Bijker 1995;Orlikowski and Gash 1994) and apply this theory to data, not previously published, arising from the same case study to identify differing groups and their standpoints. A recent review of technological frames theory suggests that most applications fail to investigate the process of framing, the cultural and institutional foundations of frames, and the characteristics and consequences of frame structure (Davidson 2006). We attempt to address this issue by applying, in a single case study, the notion of technological frame incongruence across identified relevant social groups, and use indicators for noncompliance to construct contrasting technological frames. This action outlines clearly that groups of employees who interact with information have widely disparate views of the nature and purpose of the information they use, and that this can stifle congruence or commensuration of attitudes to information systems.

The issue of frame commensurability (Khoo 2001) is addressed and we believe this study clearly highlights the differing attitudes of groups across a commensurate framework structure. In addition, the application of technological frames helps to identify areas where management, supervisors, and developers take different standpoints and dismiss or minimize noncompliant behaviors and their subsequent negative impact on data integrity, accuracy of reporting, and organizational culture. Ibe organizational ideal is seeking technological frame congruence (Orlikowski and Gash 1994) and the comparison of stances across different dimensions helps to identify the differing attitudes, beliefs and viewpoints of the relevant social groups. In this way areas in which these differing standpoints have contributed to conditions that are precursors for noncompliant behavior are highlighted. This action may assist in categorizing, across other contexts, those behaviors that are harmless, hindering, or, vitally, essential to the completion of tasks, processes, or roles within an organization (Davis and Hufnagel 2007; Ferneley and Sobreperez 2006). Finally, the author identifies possible tools and techniques that may be useful in organizations to highlight frame incongruence and thus signal where adjustments should be made to perceptions, opinions, and mind-sets.

2   THEORETICAL AND RESEARCH BACKGROUND

Effective diffusion of innovation is considered essential to the adoption of information systems (Baskerville and Pries-Heje 1997) and any resistance or noncompliance is usually considered harmful, undesirable, and deviant, to be managed or minimized as a standard human reaction to change (Franz and Robey 1984; Lyytinen and Hirschheim 1987). In contrast, several researchers have noted that resistance can be seen as a positive force and should be studied more closely rather than dismissed as recalcitrance or reaction to fear of change (Hirschheim and Newman 1988; Levine 1997; Markus 1983; Mumford et al. 1978).

If we accept that technologies are prefigured by existing forms of work organization, at least in part, then the diffusion of technical change must be designed, developed, and implemented with particular objectives concerning work transformation. The study of the implementation of technology has been seen as an important site for innovation. In this view, Fleck (1988) coins the term *innofusion* to describe "learning by struggling" and lends weight to the view of the user, who manages, through trial and exploration, to identify needs and requirements and to attempt to have these incorporated in future versions and configurations. In this way, technological development is a spiraling rather than linear process, as innovation takes place not only at design, but also at implementation and this feeds into future changes. This implies the abandonment of the notion of technology as *equipment* only and acknowledges influences on the adoption, diffusion, configuration, and usage of technologies.

This ties in well with studies of noncompliance or *resistance* as it is often these acts of struggling, trial, and exploration that are seen as resistant by those who are distanced from the user/technology interface (Lapointe and Rivard 2005; Marakas and Hornik 1996; Martinko et al. 1996). In addition, other groups interacting with systems or with information produced may have different views and perceptions. The concept of technological frames has emerged, capturing the interactions among members of a relevant social group (Orlikowski and Gash 1994). The term *frames* refers to the concept of frames of reference, borrowed from cognitive psychology, and defined by Gioia (1986, p. 56) as "a built-up repertoire of tacit knowledge that is used to impose structure upon and impart meaning to otherwise ambiguous social and situational information to facilitate understanding."

These frames include assumptions, knowledge and expectations expressed through language, visual images, metaphors, and stories. Frames are constructed as interactions around an artefact or process, and comprise shared elements such as tacit knowledge, objectives, organizational constraints, shared methods, procedures, and problems. In this way the relationships between relevant social group members are captured but made fluid and open to change where the elements change. Frames are flexible in structure and content and have variable dimensions that shift in relevance and content over time and according to changing context. According to Orlikowski and Gash (1994), frames typically operate in the background and can be helpful in that they reduce uncertainty of conditions, structure organizational experience, and allow common interpretations of ambiguity; they can also have constraining effects in that they reinforce established and possibly negative assumptions and knowledge, inhibit creative problem solving and distort information to fit existing cognitive structures. Orlikowski and Gash use framework dimensions across three domains common to most organizations to contrast their case study frames. These are *nature of technology, technology strategy (including motivation and criteria of success)*, and *technology in use (including priorities and resources, training, ease-of use, and security and quality policies)*.

There has been widespread application of technological frames theory to explain individual case-based phenomenon (Davidson and Pai 2004; Iivari and Abrahamsson 2002; Khoo 2001; Lin and Cornford 2000; Lin and Silva 2005; McGovern and Hicks 2004), but there is need for tools to help build a cumulative base of empirical findings or of cross-case comparisons (Chiasson and Davidson 2005). Davidson (2006) suggests that more emphasis on the process of framing, the cultural and institutional foundations of frames, and the characteristics and consequences of frame structure will add to this body of study and assist in cross-case comparisons.

Orlikowski and Gash suggest an ideal of frame congruence, where frames of relevant social groups related in structure and content are aligned. Congruence of technological frames implies similar expectations around the role of technology in business processes and incongruence implies important differences in expectations or assumptions around key technological aspects. The existence of incongruent technological frames suggests that differences in the view of division of labor, autonomy of employees, and status and position of individuals are consciously or implicitly built into information systems by systems planners and designers (Hirschheim and Klein 1989). In addition, Khoo (2001) suggests that the appropriateness or commensurability of frame structure is addressed. Where frames are incommensurate, the concepts in one frame cannot be addressed in other frames as there are no common meanings given to structural headings.

This paper attempts to add to the study of frame structure; in particular, the characteristics and consequences of frame structure are augmented under the *technology in use* heading by the application of three further subheadings. These are taken from the findings of the earlier study into noncompliance and are used to create a useful frame structure which clearly highlights the notion of frame incongruence as a starting point for looking at areas where the differing attitudes of groups of people have serious consequences on acceptance, progress, and confidence in organizational information systems.

3 RESEARCH APPROACH: CASE STUDY

The case study described took place in 2004–2005 and a detailed description is found in Ferneley and Sobreperez (2006). To enable the reader to contextualize the research without recourse to the previous paper, a brief outline follows. The case study setting was a UK County Fire and Rescue Service and the original research objective was to identify, classify, and understand noncompliance with information systems. The case study setting was selected because it was a highly operationally controlled environment, with clear preset routines, procedures, and practices. The culture was historically quasi-militaristic in that rank uniforms are worn, military language is used, national flags are flown, and superior ranks are deferred to in conduct, speech, and dress. In all, these elements have created an environment where it might be supposed there would be an emphasis on conformity and little opportunity for deviation. The County Fire and Rescue Service is concerned with managing fire and rescue incidents with minimal damage to people and property and the information context was the recording and reporting of these incidents. As incidents are reported to the Fire Service, a centralized control office records details including location, reporting details, personnel and equipment dispatched immediately and subsequently, routes taken, dispatch and arrival times, and a log of all communications with the deployed teams.

A detailed electronic report (FDR1) is completed after the incident using an on-line form with semi-structured questions and any level of officer can be assigned the responsibility of completing the report. Structured attributes include cause of fire, location within the address, degree and speed of fire spread, number of casualties, other emergency services involved, specific equipment used, and arrival and departure times. In addition, there are free format responses for incident handling strategies and evaluation. Reports are summarized by a centralized office that then presents the abstracted results to management for use in planning allocation of future human and physical resources. In addition, the summarized data is reported to the Office of the Deputy Prime Minister (ODPM) where it is compared with data from other regions. The national data is then published and national funding and policy decisions are made based on the data.

Data collection included participant observation based on watching and listening, individual and group semi-structured interviewing, and document analysis. Interviews typically began with generic questions allowing users to express their opinions on the use of technology before moving to more specific questioning. Semi-structured interviews of between 40 minutes and 1.5 hours were conducted with 3 senior managers and 8 middle managers chosen for their wealth of experience and the diverse range of roles that they occupied. In addition 3 data analysis personnel were interviewed representing staff responsible for collating and distributing the data under analysis. Within fire stations, 24 taped group semi-structured interviews of between 1.5 and 3 hours were conducted with groups of between 8 and 15 fire officers who worked together as a team or "watch." Group interviews revealed situations where information systems were unable to record the actuality of events and various work-arounds had been implemented. In addition, individuals were questioned as they were observed entering data, and were questioned closely on their reasons for responding in particular ways.

Key personnel outside the operational fire service also were interviewed including two interviews at the County Statistics Office and two at the Office of the Deputy Prime Minister (ODPM) in Watford. This was in order to follow through on the statistics produced by the consolidation of fire incident records by region and determine how distortions were handled. A total of four interviews took place at these locations with statisticians, data entry clerks, and technicians dealing with data from regional counties. The data was analyzed using inductive coding and grounded theory principles of categorizing and clustering data. The aim was to allow a conceptual framework to emerge during the course of study as the data was gathered. This detailed process is described in Ferneley and Sobreperez and underpins the original intention to identify different types of noncompliance.

In the case study, relevant social groups were identified as the firefighters themselves involved in a particular incident, the station officers using the information systems, developers, installers and maintainers of information systems, senior staff involved in debriefing, local statisticians involved in recording, compiling, and presenting information for the county, national staff consolidating, synthesizing, and presenting national information, and politicians and policy makers involved in designing, funding, and managing a national fire and rescue service.

4 DATA ANALYSIS

In their seminal paper on technological frames, Orlikowski and Gash (1994) identify three domains which characterize case work and context. These cover the technology, why it was introduced, and how it was used: *nature of technology*, which refers to understanding of capabilities and functionality; *technology strategy*, which refers to understanding of motivation and vision behind adoption; *technology in use*, which covers understanding of day-to-day use and associated conditions and consequences.

The context of this paper focuses on the technology in use domain as the initial case study purpose was to investigate reasons for non compliance with information systems by end users. Orlikowski and Gash subdivide this domain into *priorities and resources, training, ease of use,* and *policies for security and quality.*

In searching for explanations for noncompliance with information systems, the notion of frame congruence or commensurability provides a useful tool for identifying areas where different groups of users have differing beliefs and attitudes to workplace situations and where conflicts occur leading to systems usage, which is different from that expected by developers and managers. The case study data highlighted three sub-divisions of technology in use in which perceptions of and attitudes about technology in use differed greatly. The quotes in this section have been deliberately selected from the wealth of data collected in the case study and have not been previously published. Instead, the data has been revisited and quotes that reveal or expose the attitudes of differing groups of stakeholders were chosen for their appropriateness, succinctness and clarity.

4.1 Proceduralization

Proceduralization includes situations where systems enforce procedures contrary to effective working practices. For example, enforcing step by step chronological proce-dures where concurrent steps or different ordering is more efficient, either occasionally or regularly. Where procedures are enforced, employees tend to work around these, using activities such as incorrect job sequencing, retrospective data entry, and preemptive processing.

For example, one firefighter noted,

We have to complete the FDR1 before we have had chance to have a debriefing.

In other words, the whole picture of the incident is not synthesized but the FDR1 must be completed within a certain time frame which local statisticians see as a positive constraint.

The FDR1 must be completed while the incident is fresh in their minds.

In addition, local statisticians considered that the online FDR1 form gave ample opportunities for freedom of expression,

Allowing free text requires a level of interpretation which may require further investigation.

At the same time, they considered the form to balance free-from and closed questions well to improve standardization:

Standardization removes ambiguities.

Whereas firefighters felt constrained by the form, commenting,

The form doesn't let you describe what really happened, it's just making the fire fit the form.

The report I saw was not the fire I went to.

We sometimes request equipment we "may" need and then justify it later by describing the incident as though we needed the kit.

There were also differences between the firefighters and their senior officers in this issue. A senior officer was certain that firefighters were very careful over recording details:

Information is used in court for insurance, to refuse housing and occasionally to remove children from families. Fire officers are very careful how they enter data.

These examples show clearly that different groups of information users take different stances over proceduralization. Senior officers and statisticians believe that proceduralization is in line with and useful to the data collection process. Firefighters believe the system to be obstructive and do not consider information gathering to be important. They see their "real" work as fire fighting, rescuing, and protecting and lives and property, and information gathering as bureaucratic paper shuffling.

4.2 Acceptance

The issue of acceptance includes behaviors such as nonuse of system in favor of manual or earlier systems, and avoidance of system usage. This incorporates situations where users do not identify themselves to the system, time spent recording accurately is seen as a waste and is avoided, and personal attribution is avoided by misuse of user names.

Differing attitudes to these is encapsulated by remarks by the firefighters:

Once it's logged in it's logged in for the day, I have never seen anyone log out and back in under their own password.

Clearly this is not the perception of local statisticians, who note

Firefighters are trained to use computers to record incidents and recording is done accurately and immediately after the incident. The form is very precise and there is no room for ambiguity.

Every individual has their own login details and this drives funding and training programs.

National statisticians at the ODPM were fervent supporters of the recording systems, commenting

The system has been in use since phased implementation began in 1994 and works well to capture the data required by government.

Before 1998, local statistics offices brigades coded their own data and there were many anomalies and ambiguities and much data was unusable.

County fire brigades are accredited after 18 months of external measurements and are then allowed to perform their own internal quality checks.

The intention is that brigades provide routine FDR1 information as electronic data only, there are no paper forms.

In contrast, however, local statisticians were not so enthusiastic about the system and commented

At the end of the training we gave up and went back to manual systems.

They were, however, under the impression that their work was vital and important and were proud of their accreditation status.

Only accredited county brigades send their information directly.

Sending information to the ODPM is the most important work we do.

However national statisticians noted that some of their carefully collated work was unused.

Not everything collected is used; political considerations have changed at every level since the FDR1 was designed.

These quotes point out the different attitudes of groups to the acceptance of the system. Local statisticians considered it more important than did the firefighters, but national statisticians had an overview and awareness of future plans that was in contrast to local implementation, even pointing out that some of the carefully collected and compiled information is not used.

4.3 Culture and Control

Culture and control covers organizational culture and management supervision and control. Widespread deception, setting and ignoring of inappropriate targets, and falsifying of deliberate inaccuracies were observed and described. These behaviors are underpinned by a culture of collective noncompliance and a perception of systems that do not properly support the work done in terms of holistic overview, and opportunity to exercise professional judgement. This includes situations where systems do not allow collaborative recording, or where recording is overlooked in favor of contingent action in emergency situations.

Firefighters' comments include

We record time of arrival early so as to meet targets.

If we say cause of fire is "arson" we have to liaise with the police; better to say "unknown."

There is active discouragement of IT use among the lads.

We cannot record what really happened if it is against guidelines or policy.

We work as a team, as a unit, it doesn't matter how incidents are recorded or who does it.

Senior Fire Officers loftily assured

We are encouraging greater use of information systems to support record keeping and to instigate knowledge sharing and knowledge management across the service.

4.4 Summary

Among firefighters, the recording of incidents using the computerized form was seen as "paperwork," bureaucratic and irrelevant to the work of firefighting. There was no feeling of ownership or possession of data and little interest in accuracy. Firefighters with the task of entering the data saw it as an imposition from regional and central statistics offices and not owned by the firefighters themselves. Regional and national statisticians saw the compilation, consolidation, and presentation of statistics as intrinsic and central to not only their own personal and individual work but to the work of the regional and national fire service in general, feeding into policy and procedure. The collection of management data for the purposes of monitoring and control is misunderstood, viewed with suspicion and deprioritized by a workforce frustrated by software applications that appear to obstruct what they perceive as their "proper work."

Staff at both the regional and national statistics office believed the database collecting information about individual incidents was malleable, flexible, and customizable, that they could manipulate it in many ways to produce their required information. However, the users, who did not use the same interface, thought it inflexible, over-standardized, clumsy and awkward to use, and even obstructive in its capacity to support true incident reporting.

The local statistics office workers clearly believe the system is tight and that firefighters are adequately trained. The perception is that the system is well utilized within the region and that accurate data is forwarded to appropriate government departments. This perspective was evident where visits to the local statistics office of the county force and the Office of the Deputy Prime Minister revealed quite different attitudes to the information systems and to issues such as acceptance, approval, confidence, and trust.

It is interesting to note that all senior officers have been firefighters at some time in their career, so have some awareness of the local and individual use of the system. They have an overview of the use of individual statistics rather than the collation of information seen by statisticians and display a management view of knowledge management across the service. The firefighters perceive that the recording system and the organizational circumstances force inaccuracies.

Local offices are very concerned with their own provision and were proud of their accreditation status. They had some criticisms of the system but had found ways to work around some elements through recourse to manual systems. The National Statistics Office had a nationwide overview and awareness of future plans not available to local offices. At the time of the interview, only three county brigades were accredited but a lofty intention was communicated. Interestingly, the National Statistics Office revealed that not all of the carefully compiled information was used, although local offices were not aware of this. From the case study, it is believed that there is a high degree of commensurability and that the members of relevant social groups are aware of and addressing the same areas. For example, in the case study, firefighters and managers share frames about incidents, but managers share frames concerning statistics with local and national statisticians.

The existence of incongruent technological frames can clearly be seen in the context of the case study, where views of the division of labor, autonomy of employees, and status and position of individuals are consciously or implicitly built into information systems by systems planners and designers (Hirschheim and Klein 1989).

5   DISCUSSION

Diffusion and innovation has been underdeveloped and has become stagnant across the case study organization. The Fire Service and other emergency services do not make use of collaborative, mobile, or workflow technologies that may be suitable in this specialized area. The entire information system is still following technology models from the 1980s—for example, the practice, undertaken by all regional offices, of posting a floppy disk in a padded envelope to the ODPM was referred to as electronic data interchange.

Rogers' (1995) theory of diffusion includes four main elements: innovation, communication, time and social systems. The innovation itself, more suitable technologies, has many advantages that are observable and trialable but there is little knowledge of the advantages of these within the Fire Service. The data from the case study revealed that social systems and communications were such that firefighters who generated information, and the only people who could verify or refute any implications drawn, had little interest in accuracy of detail or presentation. They felt, in particular, that information was owned by regional and national statisticians and was used for purposes outside their knowledge, understanding, and control. Firefighters and station officers had awareness of the implications of target benchmarks and performance indicators, but felt that data was twisted and manipulated at various stages to meet unachievable targets, and to provide regional and national policy makers with information they wanted to see. Senior personnel were not interested in innovation and senior information systems personnel were concerned only with centralized data collection and not in supporting firefighters at the scene of incidents.

Social shaping theory suggests that a process of action and interaction involving communication and collaboration between groups form and shape technology (Porac et al. 1989; Van Maanen and Schein 1979). The different levels and areas of expertise in many overlapping fields, and the different objectives, priorities, and concerns of these groups, suggest that there is considerable potential for poor communication, discord, and conflict. For example, from the case research, there is conflict between the political expediency of recording short arrival times to fire incidents by firefighters, and the accuracy of recording required by statisticians.

The particular issue of innovation within organizations also includes issues of structure including the degree of centralization, organizational complexity, level of formality, interconnections between departments and resources, and size.

Rogers suggests that a high degree of centralization and a high degree of formality are negatively correlated with innovation and that high levels of interconnections, high levels of complexity, and large size of organizations are positively correlated with innovation. Clearly, and as outlined earlier, there is a high degree of centralization and formality within the Fire Service

Rogers also adds a stratum of leadership and posits that the attitude toward change held by leaders will influence innovation along with system openness and interactions with those in the same industry using innovative technologies. All senior firefighters, including those in management, will have been junior firefighters earlier in their careers and thus perceive that they know and understand the systems used. Any innovations will be outside of their knowledge and they may wish to ensure knowledge and power relations by keeping things as they are. In addition, although there are similarities with other emergency services, the Fire and Rescue Service is unique in the nature of its business and is unlikely to come across other information systems that meet requirements, although international collaboration in these matters might be a useful starting place.

Rogers suggests that organizational size and complexity are positively correlated with innovation due to the possibility of access to higher knowledge and expertise. However, others have highlighted the complexity of interactions between groups as a probable cause of even further problems where complex human action, not necessarily understood in depth by developers and technical specialists, is to be supported using information systems. (Fincham et al. 1995) This is particularly true in the Fire Service where firefighters, both individually and as a group, bring a large amount of tacit experience and knowledge to any situation. Each incident is extremely idiosyncratic and must be dealt with so dynamically that there can be no "right answer" to the way it is handled. Approaches are and must be contingent on the location and severity of the incident; the speed of occurrences, events, and responses; the skills and expertise of those present; and the response of the control center and senior officers present or not. As each incident is unique, it becomes difficult to apply rules and guidelines and superficially similar incidents may be dealt with entirely differently in response to a variety of factors too complex and problematic to identify. In view of this, it becomes increasingly challenging to create information systems to match and support workforce action or to manage knowledge across an organization involved in highly complex individualistic, distinctive incidents that need to be grouped and consolidated in a variety of ways to be presented to policy makers and managers.

Rogers also draws attention to types of innovation decisions and identifies three types: optional, collective, and authority. The description of the quasi-militaristic culture in the research approach section informs us that Fire Service decisions are likely to be authority based.

The characteristics and consequences of framing (Davidson 2006) are addressed in this paper through the selection of three indicators developed from the case study data. These may be reconciled with the technology in use structural elements of Orlikowski and Gash (1994), but are less quality, security, and policy oriented and more aligned to the issue of noncompliance. These may prove useful as a way of cutting across organizational boundaries to find common perceptions in information systems usage and to reach accommodation of parallel but differing requirements rather than compliance with an imposed system.

Within the Fire Service, firefighters and local and national statisticians never met each other and had little direct interaction. Use of the three indicators underpinning noncompliant behavior were contextually relevant to all social groups and were recognized and acknowledged as areas of concern. Use of these conditions takes a step closer to acknowledgment of these issues and forms a framework for identifying and addressing the differing attitudes and perceptions and noting where noncompliance is harmless, hindering, or essential (Ferneley and Sobreperez 2006). This distinction is important in determining which behaviors to study further and identify as critique. "The seeds of innovation grow out of resistance and defensive patterns that suppress resistance, suppress innovation" (Levine 1997, p. 167).

This paper brings the notion of incongruent or incommensurate technological frames of reference into the study of resistance and its underlying motivations. From the perspective of the firefighter, systems hindered working practices; from a management perspective, any noncompliant behavior had negative ramifications as data integrity was destroyed and workplace routines and regulations were regularly flouted. Again, viewed through a different technological frame, noncompliance may be regarded as a positive force and may also highlight a dynamic organizational culture and willingness to innovate and improvise (Petrides et al. 2004). Noncompliance with a system that does not properly match and support work practice may lead to development of new and better systems that improve this aspect. This can only be true if systems specifiers and information users are aware of system shortcomings and are willing to appraise, assess, and review systems in the light of knowledge about the motivations for noncompliance.

The cultural and institutional foundations of differing frames (Davidson 2006) can be distinguished by the differing educational backgrounds, career paths, workplace, and data usage of the relevant social groups, which are very clear in this case study and which may account for incompatible attitudes to data collection and utilization. Understandings, interpretations, and expectations of information systems are framed and reframed through the exercise of power (Lin and Silva 2005) and the case study shows that in the context of data collection and usage, operational firefighters are in the least powerful position. Similarly, there are power issues between local and national statisticians in that local statisticians must feed data through for consolidation and comparison with other regional services and clearly would not wish this to reflect badly on their local service. In this way, then, power is exercised through the enforced denial of actual events, which may be contrary to guidelines by firefighters, and the acceptance of information known to be inaccurate by statisticians and senior firefighters.

The framing and reframing process facilitates frame congruence. Lin and Silva's (2005) study details the process by rephrasing and renaming issues, artefacts, and purposes so that common ground is carefully reconstructed. The Fire Service case study is built upon commonly accepted terminology within the organization and stakeholders refer to these elements using common language and understanding. The characteristics and consequences of frame structure may be addressed by the acceptance of these conditions as recognizable by relevant social groups.

The three indicators are brought together from this case study but are also found in other empirical studies. Enforced and inappropriate proceduralization is notably found in a study of the print industry (Bowers et al. 1995), where a new system required printshop workers to take tasks in job number order when more appropriate groupings would use same paper size or type to avoid paper loading time overhead.

The acceptance issue is found not only in this case study but across other studies such as Timmons' (2003) study of nursing, which found that much electronic record keeping was simply not done. In addition, and in common with this case study, on many occasions users did not identify themselves for fear of attribution of errors and inaccuracies.

Culture and control issues are recorded in other case studies, in particular, studies call centers where the perception is that workforces are closely monitored (Bain and Taylor 2000; Callaghan and Thompson 2001; Lankshear et al. 2001; Sewell and Wilkinson 1992). It may be that all workplaces ignore this type of behavior up to a point to allow some breathing space, but within this case study there was a definite management attitude of "as long as we get our data..." and the reflection of actuality was not considered important or perhaps too difficult to confront.

In all cases, managers and developers have specified a system that is counter-efficient and continue to insist it be utilized by a workforce that has been perfunctorily consulted because it meets management's requirements but does not adequately match and support the actual work undertaken. This seems particularly true in situations where the system does not support or allow collective recording, or where the recording is ignored in favor of emergency actions such as firefighting or nursing. Emergency actions that contravene policy or guidelines are routinely undertaken but not recorded and such actions are found across other case studies such as work-arounds in a medical context (Kobayashi et al. 2005) or nursing (Timmons 2003).

Due to the shortcomings of the imposed system, and the unequal power relations between the designer/manager and end user, it is the end user who must typically work around the system to try and get the job done. This is in line with the notion of frame incongruence and Davidson's (2006) view that the shift toward congruence must be made by those lower in the power relation stakes.

Where incongruence is shown, the implication is that one or several relevant social groups will need to shift or modify their frames of reference in order to resolve incongruence. Davidson concludes that this change is likely to be required by the user or operator and not by the designer, consultant, manager, executive champion, or financer of the project. This view highlights power relations and it becomes difficult to see how interpretive processes are separate from political influences. The very idea of communicating and cooperating with users undermines the status, power, and privilege of managers, developers, and those who "know best" how to organize work activity. The groups involved in information technology often have different priorities and goals and this creates the potential for conflict and controversy (Dunlop and Kling 1991).

Walsh (1995) has also suggested that studies of structure would be more useful than studies of content, as effective frame structure may differ during early planning, requirements definition, implementation, and operation of a new IT application. Clearly, frames of reference may also change with the changing organizational circumstances such as diversification of products, markets, or distribution channels, or changes in organizational structure such as mergers and acquisitions, which may bring aboard enormous and quickly moving changes to hardware, software, communications, and data sets that must be quickly accommodated and for which existing software was not written or specified.

Orlikowski and Gash provide limited guidance on the question of frame structure and include only categories or domains of knowledge, highlighting frame incongruence as differing frame content. If the frame structure is included, then frame incongruence becomes a process of development among diverse stakeholders changing as a project moves through different stages of diffusion and may facilitate the change process, lightening the interpretive burden and revealing patterns of association that clarify positions. In this way, frame incongruence may not always be problematic but may provide signposts to areas for further investigation.

The first step in identifying differing viewpoints is to gather data and an interesting technique from the case study has been the use of focus groups to extract deeper, richer, and group centered meaning from accounts of incidents. Participants shared experiences and reflected on incidents, often gaining additional knowledge of cause and effect, or reasons why certain actions were taken. Significantly, some details only emerged when those in attendance were given the opportunity to discuss the incident as a group. Individual interviews would not have given this opportunity and observation would not have revealed attitudes and beliefs. Thus, the full picture of the incident only came into being as a result of the focus group activity. As stories were generated collaboratively, they progressed, frequently over the course of a single focus group session, from fragmented and fractional elements, to a complete story where reasons for actions and decisions, not clear at the time of the incident, fell into place. Participants were able to complete their partial view of the incident and the background to particular behaviors, evaluations, and judgements became clear, forming a more complete view in the minds of participants. The implications for future research might allow this technique to be used in other scenarios where group collaboration is vital for completion of a dynamic, real-life incident or project. Examples include an operating theater, a marketing presentation, a sales convention, any type of performance event including artistic or sporting events. A five-step model is outlined by Leonard and Swap (1999) to facilitate group activity and lead to the clash of ideas, or "creative abrasion," innovation opportunities, generation of novel options, convergence on a solution, and creation of a creative ecology. These tools open channels of communication and groups are made aware of differing viewpoints, thus a foundation for congruence is made possible.

6   CONCLUSION

Information from different groups across a single case study has been examined and reveals differences in attitudes and perceptions about information systems. The technological frames construct is used to contrast thoughts, opinions, and mind-sets of different groups toward noncompliance with information systems. Three indicators are employed to provide structure for the frames of reference and these were identified within the case study as precursors for noncompliant behavior. The emergence and understanding of these precursors were understood and widely discussed throughout the organization and thus commensurability was ensured. The overlaying of technological frames theory and the application of case study findings points out very clearly the differing attitudes, perceptions, and expectations of the diverse groups, both to systems usage and to any noncompliant behavior.

The use of these dimensions in the structure of the frames led to a more meaningful comparison than more general structures such as how technology is used. This approach is useful in bringing issues to light and raising awareness of those concerned with implementation of the contradictions between the beliefs of organizational members and actual system functionality. The characteristics and consequences of the selection of frame structure components highlight concerns in that noncompliant behavior becomes a result of indicators within the control of managers, supervisors, and developers. The differing technological frame views of relevant groups indicate issues that are within the control of managers and developers and that could be addressed in future planning and implementation. In this way nonoperational groups take responsibility for cultural attitudes, control of data entry, proceduralization, and systems acceptance.

We suggest that issues surrounding noncompliance should not be dismissed as resistance but should be addressed by managers and developers and become a skeleton or framework for understanding problems and developing organizationally aligned solutions. The contribution of this study, then, is to point out that case study findings can interlock and intersect across theoretical areas and the use of the technological frames of reference provides a useful way to clearly demonstrate the existence of relevant social groups and the congruence or otherwise of their technological frames, thereby clearly highlighting areas of concern.

The framework used by Orlikowski and Gash (1994) is augmented by three further subdivisions of proceduralization, acceptance, and culture and control, which serve to focus more clearly on issues of noncompliance and seek understanding and accommodation of viewpoints rather than dismissal of issues important to users and to successful implementation of information systems across an organization.

References

Bain, P., and Taylor, P. 2000. "Entrapped by the 'Electronic Panopticon'? Worker Resistance in the Call Center," *New Technology Work and Employment* (15:1), pp. 2-18.

Baskerville, R., and Pries-Heje, J. 1997. "IT Diffusion and Innovation Models: The Conceptual Domains," in *Facilitating Technology Transfer Through Partnership: Learning from Practice and Research*, T. McMaster, E. Mumford, E. B. Swanson, B. Warboys, and D. Wastell (eds.), London: Chapman & Hall, pp. 28-38.

Bijker, W. E. 1995. *Of Bicycles, Bakelites, and Bulbs: Toward a Theory of Sociotechnical Change*, Cambridge, MA: The MIT Press.

Bowers, J., Button, G., and Sharrock, W. 1995. "Workflow from Within and Without: Technology and Co-operative Work on the Print Industry Shopfloor," in *Proceedings of the*

European Conference on Computer Supported Cooperative Work, H. Marmolin, Y. Sundblad, and K. Schmidt (eds.), Dordrecht, The Netherlands: Kluwer Academic Publishers, pp. 51-66.

Callaghan, G., and Thompson, P. 2001. "Edwards Revisited: Technical Control and Call Centers," *Economic and Industrial Democracy* (22:1), pp. 13-37.

Chiasson, M., and Davidson, E. 2005. "Taking Industry Seriously in Information Systems Research," *MIS Quarterly* (29:4), pp. 599-606.

Davidson, E. 2006. "A Technological Frames Perspective on Information Technology and Organizational Change," *Journal of Applied Behavioral Science* (42:1), pp. 23-39.

Davidson, E., and Pai, D. 2004. "Making sense of Technology Frames: Promise, Progress and Potential," *Information Systems Research: Relevant Theory and Informed Practice,* B. Kaplan, D. Truex, D. Wastell, T. Wood Harper and J. I. DeGross. Boston: Kluwer Academic Publishers, pp. 473-491.

Davis, C., and Hufnagel, E. 2007. "Through the Eyes of Experts: A Socio-Cognitive Perspective on the Automation of Fingerprint Work," *MIS Quarterly* (31:4), pp. 681-703.

Dunlop, C., and Kling, R. 1991. *Computerization and Controversy: Value Conflicts and Social Choices*, Boston: Academic Press.

Ferneley, E., and Sobreperez, P. 2006. "Resist, Comply or Workaround: An Examination of Different Facets of User Engagement with Information Systems," *European Journal of Information Systems* (15:4), pp. 345-356.

Ferneley, E., Sobreperez, P., and Wilson, F. A. 2005. "Tricks or Trompe L'Oeil? An Examination of Workplace Resistance in an Information Rich Managerial Environment," in *Proceedings of the 13ᵗʰ European Conference on Information Systems*, D. Bartmann, F. Rajola, J. Kallinikos, D. Avison, R. Winter, P. Ein_Dor, J. Becker, F. Bodendorf, and C. Weinhardt (eds.), Regensberg, Germany, pp. 484-494 (http://is2.lse.ac.uk/asp/aspecis/20050041.pdf).

Fincham, R., Fleck, J., Procter, R., Scarborough, H., Tierney, M., and Williams, R. 1995. *Expertise and Innovation: Information Strategies in the Financial Services Sector*, Oxford, UK: Oxford University Press.

Fleck, J. 1988. "Innofusion or Diffusation? The Nature of Technological Development in Robotics," Edinburgh PICT Working Paper No 4, Edinburgh University.

Franz, C. R., and Robey, D. 1984. "An Investigation of User-Led Systems Design: Rational and Political Perspectives," *Communications of the ACM* (27:12), pp. 1202-1209.

Gioia, D. A. 1986. "Symbols, Scripts and Sensemaking: Creating Meaning in the Organizational Experience," *The Thinking Organization: Dynamics of Organizational Social Cognition*, H. P. Sims, Jr., D. A. Gioia, and Associates (eds.), San Francisco: Jossey-Bass: 49-74.

Hirschheim, R., and Klein, H. K. 1989. "Four Paradigms of Information Systems Development," *Communications of the ACM* (32:10), pp. 1199-1216.

Hirschheim, R. A., and Newman, M. 1988. "Information Systems and User Resistance: Theory and Practice," *Computer Journal* (31:5), pp. 398-408.

Iivari, N., and Abrahamsson, P. 2002. "The Interaction Between Organizational Subcultures and User-Centered Design: A Case Study of an Implementation Effort," in *Proceedings of the 35ᵗʰ Annual Hawaii International Conference on Systems Science*, Los Alamitos, CA: IEEE Computer Society Press.

Khoo, M. 2001. "Community Design of DLESE's Collections Review Policy: A Technological Frames Analysis," in *Proceedings of the First ACM/IEEE-CS Joint Conference on Digital Libraries*, Roanoke, VA, pp. 157-164.

Kobayashi, M., Fussell, S., Xiao, Y., and Seagull, J. 2005. "Work Coordination, Workflow and Workarounds in a Medical Context," in *Proceedings of the Conference on Human Factors in Computing Systems*, Portland, OR, pp. 1561-1564.

Lankshear, G., Cook, P., Mason, D., Coates, S., and Graham, B. 2001. "Call Center Employees' Responses to Electronic Monitoring: Some Research Findings," *Work, Employment and Society* (15:3), pp. 595-605.

Lapointe, L., and Rivard, S. 2005. "A Multilevel Model of Resistance to Information Technology Implementation," *MIS Quarterly* (29:3), pp. 461-491.

Leonard, D. A., and Swap, W. C. 1999. *When Sparks Fly: Igniting Creativity in Groups,* Boston: Harvard Business School Press.

Levine, L. 1997. "An Ecology of Resistance," *Facilitating Technology Transfer through Partnership: Learning from Practice and Research.* T. McMaster, E. Mumford, E. B. Swanson, B. Warboys, and D. Wastell, London: Chapman & Hall, pp. 163-174.

Lin, A., and Cornford, T. 2000. "Framing Implementation Management," in *Proceedings of the 21st International Conference on Information Systems*, W. J. Orlikowski, S. Ang, P. Weill, H. C. Krcmar, and J. I. DeGross (eds.), Brisbane, Australia, pp. 197-205.

Lin, A., and Silva, L. 2005. "The Social and Political Construction of Technological Frames," *European Journal of Information Systems* (14:1), pp. 49-59.

Lyytinen, K., and Hirschheim, R. 1987. "Information Systems Failures: A Survey and Classification of the Empirical Literature," *Oxford Surveys in Information Technology*, Volume 4, P. Zorkoczy (ed.), New York: Oxford University Press, pp. 257-309.

Marakas, G. M., and Hornik, S. 1996. "Passive Resistance Misuse: Overt Support and Covert Recalcitrance in IS Implementation," *European Journal of Information Systems* (5:3), pp. 208-220.

Markus, M. L. 1983. "Power, Politics, and MIS Implementation," *Communications of the ACM* (26:6), pp. 430-444.

Martinko, M. J., Henry, J. W.,and Zmud, R. W. 1996. "An Attributional Explanation of Individual Resistance to the Introduction of Information Technologies in the Workplace," *Behavior & Information Technology* (15:5), pp. 313-330.

McGovern, T., and Hicks, C. 2004. "How Political Processes Shaped the IT Adoption by a Small Make-to-Order Company: A Case Study in the Insulated Wire and Cable Industry," *Information and Management* (42:1), pp. 243-257.

Mumford, E., Land, F., and Hawgood, J. 1978. "A Participative Approach to Planning and Designing Computer Systems and Procedures to Assist This," Impact of Science on Society (28:3), pp. 235-253.

Orlikowski, W. J., and Gash, D. C. 1994. "Technological Frames: Making Sense of Information Technology in Organizations," *ACM Transactions on Information Systems* (12:2), pp. 669-702.

Petrides, L. A., McClelland, S. I., and Nodine, T. R. 2004. "Costs and Benefits of the Workaround: Inventive Solution or Costly Alternative," *International Journal of Educational Management* (18:2), pp. 100-108.

Porac, J. F., Thomas, H., and Baden Fuller, C. 1989. "Competitive Groups as Cognitive Communities: The Case of Scottish Knitwear Manufacturers," *Journal of Management Studies* (26:4), pp. 397-416.

Rogers, E. M. 1995. *Diffusion of Innovation* (4th ed.), New York: Free Press.

Sewell, G., and Wilkinson, B. 1992. "'Someone to Watch over Me': Surveillance, Discipline and the Just-in-Time Labor Process," *Sociology* (26:2), pp. 271-289.

Timmons, S. 2003. "A Failed Panopticon: Surveillance of Nursing Practice via New Technology," *New Technology Work and Employment* (18:2), pp. 143-153.

Van Maanen, J., and Schein, E. 1979. "Towards a Theory of Organizational Socialization," *Research in Organizational Behavior* (1), B. M. Staw (ed.), Greenwich, CT: JAI Press, pp. 209-264.

Walsh, J. P. 1995. "Managerial and Organizational Cognition: Notes from a Trip Down Memory Lane," *Organization Science* (6:3), pp. 280-321.

About the Author

Polly Sobreperez was born in York and currently lives in Manchester with her husband. She has worked in the IT industry, then as an IT trainer, as a college lecturer, and as a university lecturer. She has taught many aspects of information technology and is particularly interested in databases, teaching and learning technology, and resistance to information systems. Polly can be reached at p.sobreperez@salford.ac.uk.

11 XENIA: A Metaphor for Sense-Making and Acting in Information Systems Innovation

Allen Higgins
Warwick Business School
University of Warwick
Coventry, UK

Simeon Vidolov
Frank Frößler
Doreen Mullaney
School of Business
University College Dublin
Belfield, Ireland

Abstract   *This paper draws on Ciborra's insightful concept of xenia (i.e., hospitality) to analyze how successful infrastructural service innovation was managed at the local operations of an international financial services firm. The xenia concept problematizes the information system development (ISD) orthodoxy and points to issues and aspects that are often overlooked or considered irrelevant in structured methodologies. In interpreting the findings of the empirical study— in which a highly successful (but radical) big bang transition from one technology platform to another takes place over a single weekend—we suggest that IS implementation and development is an emergent process in which technology and users are continually redefined. This process resembles an emotional "meeting" between host and guest who, over time, develop mutual familiarity and acceptance. Further, we argue that the metaphor of xenia opens space for reconsidering conventional but socially sterile approaches to IS innovation; xenia offers a radically different way for understanding and acting upon ISD. Our analysis highlights the intrinsic socio-technical inter-play underlying IS development and implementation, and raises questions*

Please use the following format when citing this chapter:

Higgins, A., Vidolov, S., Frößler, F., and Mullaney, D., 2008, in IFIP International Federation for Information Processing, Volume 287, Open IT-Based Innovation: Moving Towards Cooperative IT Transfer and Knowledge Diffusion, eds. León, G., Bernardos, A., Casar, J., Kautz, K., and DeGross, J. (Boston: Springer), pp. 197-209.

about the importance of local cultures of "hospitality" and ways they may be cultivated and nurtured in order to alleviate the meeting between technology and organizations.

Keywords   Xenia, guest host relations, systems implementation, organization metaphor, hospitality

1   INTRODUCTION

Over the years, a rich body of literature on information systems development and implementation has generated interesting insights into the role of the developers, users, and technology during the implementation process. However, in this paper, we argue that previous work has often neglected the messiness of IS implementation and the resulting emotional implications for both users and developers. More specifically, emphasizing methods and processes, practitioners and scholars alike overlook the mundane and everyday experience of development and use, thereby missing important features of interest. Our concern is, therefore, to understand how users and developers make sense of new information systems and embed them in their daily work routines.

Traditional models of IS implementation carry with them the assumption that designers, engineers, and users are able to implement requirements directly into technological objects. That is, the material object is understood as perfectly malleable during the developmental process as stakeholders try to shape their intentions into the artefact. For example, informed by the rational social management approach, Lewin's (1952) change model, consisting of a suite of unfreezing, changing, and freezing, has strongly influenced stage-based approaches. These approaches propose to subdivide implementation processes into sequential stages, with each stage having generic, inherent characteristics (see Cooper and Zmud 1990; Kwon and Zmud 1987). In order to achieve the intended outcome, the specific issues of each stage need to be addressed sufficiently. Munkvold (1999), for example, developed a holistic stage model for implementation processes within distributed organizations by mapping the various challenges in the different stages. However, stage-based approaches have been criticized for relying on a rational–economic interpretation of organizational processes and for assuming that the world functions in the form of objective cause–effect relationships with universally applicable rules (Fitzgerald 1996; Walsham 1993). Thus, the stage-based approach is criticized for being too rigid, mainly focusing on explicit economic, physical, or information processing features, and for limiting the social context in which technology is developed according to chosen formal and easily managed relationships (Ciborra 2002, 2004). Furthermore the development and implementation process is presented conventionally as a rational–technological process, but in practice structured methodologies are used as a kind of social defense, where graphics, structures, and diagrams impart complex IS implementation work with the outward appearance of manageability (Wastell 1996).

Disavowing overly rational approaches to IS development and implementation, we align our analysis to an alternative literature that takes the role of technology as well as of the human agents seriously. Drawing upon Ciborra's concept of *xenia* (hospitality relations) allows us to theorize how users, developers, and the technological artefact evoke emotional responses as they relate to and make sense of each other during the implementation process. We develop the argument that a culture of hospitality needs to be cultivated and nurtured before, during, and after the actual IS implementation. The carefully managed relationship between the host (users) and the guest (technology) can reduce the level of anxiety among potential users and, therefore, increase the acceptance of technology introduction. We develop this argument by referring to a large IS implementation project within an international financial service organization.

In the following section, we describe the concept of xenia and emphasize its usefulness for understanding the socio-technical dynamics of ISD processes. In sections 3 and 4, we proceed by presenting an insightful in-depth, interpretive field study of IS development and implementation at the local operations of an international financial services organization. In section 5, we illustrate and develop the notion of xenia with reference to the case study. Finally, in section 6, we attempt to summarize the key conclusions of the paper.

2 XENIA

Ciborra highlights the fluidity of social organization and the situated contingencies of ISD initiatives. In so doing, he advocates loosening our grip on the methodological frame to open up other ways of thinking and conceptualizing system development. More specifically, he offers metaphors that can help us make sense of the software developer process and sensitize us to the socio-technical dynamics in ISD (Ciborra 1998, 2002). The concept of *xenia*, or hospitality, is used as a grounding metaphor to explore and interpret the complexities of how we might go about designing, developing, and implementing technologies for organizations or social groups. The idea of host–guest relations opens possibilities for a "new constellation of issues, words, and understanding, referring in particular to existential dimensions, such as life world, identity, and commitment" (Ciborra 2002, p. 104). The notion of hospitality points to the extra effort involved in coping, accepting, and embedding new technologies into work practices. This kind of activity cannot be represented geometrically: "it is made of absorbed coping, care, being there amidst ambiguity, intimacy, sporting hospitality as well as tamed hostility towards what the new and unknown is unveiling" (Ciborra 1998, p. 14).

Xenia encourages turning a critical eye to the process of acceptance and embeddedness of technology in the flow of everyday practice. We can be more attentive to how technologies are invited in and coped with, welcomed (or not), to accommodate and be accommodated, until becoming folded into our taken-for-granted beliefs about technologies. The ambiguous and interchangeable roles of host and guest reveal the dynamic dance between work practices and technology; the way things go is not determined by properties of people, workplaces, or even the technology (Grint and Woolgar 1997). The ISD process becomes an ongoing performance, a process of alignment, adjustment, and subtle transformations of technology and work practices. This vision also challenges a belief that the material side of IT artefacts can be givens, stable or fixed entities (Orlikowski and Iacono 2000), and calls attention instead to the practices in which they are implied, assembled, transformed, and held stable. This is a vision of technology as an "unpredictable and ambiguous guest" that encounters the *host* (i.e., us, the organization) where both become engaged in forms of "reciprocal cultivation by enriching and sharing" their cultures and practices (Ciborra 2002, pp. 115-116).

Ciborra's xenia emphasizes alternate interpretations of innovation, ideas of *introduction* or *bringing in*. Xenia, hospitality, shifts our concerns about technology and users together, introducing each other, changing and accommodating each other's potential. The drifting and shifting of technology, its changing service or affordance through developers' frequent tinkering and improvisations—intrinsic to system development and system use—are manifestations of the encounter between the guest and the host and their continuous learning about each other; the adjustment of their identities and cultures. Structured models and methodologies, and their assumptions about stable and predictable technology, do not capture the uncertainty of this sometimes emotional meeting and continuous strife (and striving) for symmetrical acceptance, for respect.

3   RESEARCH DESIGN

This case study considers the occasion of infrastructural service innovation within State Bank (SB), a newly acquired subsidiary of International European Bank (IEB), an international banking firm.[1] The goal of the study was to describe events, attitudes, and actions surrounding a project to integrate the national organization's IS infrastructure with its parent firm. The research was designed to analyze the experience of (successful) radical infrastructural service innovation in the local operations of IEB. In terms of conventional ISD theories, successful outcomes usually lend themselves to seemingly obvious appeals to *success factor determinants*; for example, that systems generally work as designed (technologically determined), or deciding between introducing a system in a big bang or in stages depends on specific factors (social idiosyncrasy). We consider, however, that rich, thickly descriptive case studies of IS successes are important sources of information of the practice (not just factors) of successful projects and so we present a rich case study with the goal of *informing* the practice of developers, users, customers. etc.

The field study phase for this case study consisted of 15 semi-structured interviews with 11 key informants who were identified in a snowball approach (Miles and Huberman 1994). Interviews commenced 6 months after the national innovation project had concluded.[2] Interviews were carried out within the firm's premises—at the international group headquarters, the national head office, and national branch offices. Interviewees include the VP for technology, VP for treasury, capital/regional manager, regional head of human resources, head of training, and line staff involved in the development, configuration, and use of relevant subsystems.

Interviews are the principle form of data gathering employed by this study. Questions were put to interviewees in a semi-structured manner and ranged over the field of analysis suggested by our reading of the hospitality metaphor. Interview data was validated first by being transcribed and presented to interviewees for separate review, and second by cross comparison with other interviews and against secondary documentary data. Furthermore the researchers read and reviewed all notes, transcripts, and secondary

---

[1]State Bank (SB) and International European Bank (IEB) are pseudonyms.

[2]It is relevant to note that IEB subsequently commenced a very similar acquisition, assimilation, and integration exercise with another firm the year after its integration of SB.

documentary evidence (press releases, corporate documentation, etc.) to carry out joint analysis and reflection. The process of analysis involved repeated discussions among the researchers to debrief, analyze, and interpret the field data as the case study was being written up.

The research was designed as an interpretive case study. The case method is closely associated with interpretive information systems research and is suggested for settings where existing theoretical models are inoperable, contradictory, or only weakly informative. Walsham (1993) recommends interpretive research methods where research attempts to produce "an understanding of the *context* of the information system, and the *process* whereby the information system influences and is influenced by its context" (pp. 4-5). The approach accepts that researchers obtain only indirect access to actors' interpretations of their lived work, histories, and contexts. This knowledge is subjective and co-constructed through the researcher's interaction with those actors. The researcher's role is one of sense-making and framing a narrative from interviewees' experiences and historical events; to present events, context, and processes in rich detail.

The following section presents a narrative composite of interviewees' accounts of the origination, introduction, and implementation of the radically new IS infrastructure within SB. This account is based on interviews carried out with members of the organization (identified by pseudonyms) some months after the "big bang."

4 IEB: A CASE STUDY OF SERVICE INNOVATION

The financial industry's modes of organization and business models are widely held to be malleable and engineered. They avail of advances in technology, competitive environments, and regulatory change, responding to changing opportunities in global markets as new offerings and potentials are realized (e.g., outsourcing, self managed bank accounts, real-time financial transactions). On-going restructuring of the financial industry, its modes of organization and business models, has taken place in response to new entrants, new markets, and the further evolution of the global financial industry. These changes have been facilitated, if not driven, by IS and ICT (information and communications technology) innovations.

In the early 2000s, IEB acquired a national banking firm, State Bank (SB). This acquisition led to a period of dramatic change for the national operations of the now integrated firm. The organizational structure within IEB is a classic hierarchy, with IEB group management having ultimate responsibility for organizational strategy. A subsidiary like the national operation of SB, with its own operational hierarchy, reports into the group function. At the national branch/subsidiary level, the structure devolves into individual functions or departments such as human resources, marketing, business, and local branches; however IEB group headquarters is the nexus of the whole organization with responsibility for key functions like business development, IT, and finance.

IEB's seemingly smooth integration of newly acquired subsidiaries has been a defining characteristic of its continuing success as a leading financial services company both in Europe and abroad. The acquisition of SB initiated a substantial technology investment into SB's operations by IEB. The project to align the two organizations' IS infrastructures began in earnest once the acquisition was completed. IEB's approach to integration required the complete replacement of SB's existing infrastructure and the adoption of new technology and work practices by the national workforce. However, rather than conforming to conventional wisdom for deploying large scale IS implementations[3] IEB employed a big-bang roll-out approach to the project. The big bang event happened over a single long weekend one year after the acquisition. At this point they also shut down and decommissioned all previously used systems; these were removed *permanently* from operation over the same weekend.

While the process of development and configuration of the new IS infrastructure commenced immediately after the acquisition, it was paralleled with a period of preparing for the anticipated change. This parallel work consisted of systemic and systematic planning and development impacting all levels of the organization. While the financial industry is global, it must adapt to local (i.e., national) regulations, arrangements, and behavior. Anticipating this need for local knowledge, staff in SB had conducted extensive research of the domestic market and details of this research were fed back into the development and adaptation plans for IEB's centralized system. Throughout the organization and at multiple levels, staff referred to the need to customize IEB's standard services to the local market. This customization or configuration was identified as a major factor in the claimed success of the overall project.

> *The group business development unit takes any issues from a local level and formulates an appropriate strategy. The local groups are important because they are close to the market and will get feedback directly from this market.*
> (Joe, Business Development Manager)

Within the overall change program, as many as 60 to 70 individual projects were ongoing at any one time. This system of implementation was very structured and was adapted from previous similar ventures by IEB.

> *The system was in operation in IEB and they have introduced it to other firms and subsidiaries previous to our takeover, so they were aware of the issues and processes before they began. It was easy to see this wasn't the first time they had done this type of integration.* (Sean, Senior Cash Manager)

The project team supporting the development and implementation of the new IS and services initiative was organized along different lines than IEB's overall organizational structure (i.e., as a network as opposed to a hierarchy). In the project team, functions and individuals were fluid and transferable, originating from a variety of locations within the organization. While a single overarching project manager was responsible for ensuring the whole project was delivered in a timely manner, the overall project consisted of 60 or 70 subprojects addressing different organizational levels and functions. Expert guides familiar with the system from IEB's other international branches were drafted in and

---

[3]Conventional deployment policies range over phased introductions (introducing greater functionality in stages) through staged roll-out (switching or upgrading sites separately). Big bang IS transitions are rarely recommended, particularly where a firm's entire operational and production capacity is actualized through software and IS.

placed in positions where they could move within the national operation as and when required. A customer task force was also set up to deal specifically with customer issues and was responsible for supporting the transition to the new system.

Because there were members of the implementation team over from [head office], all staff were given adequate opportunity to become familiar with the system. It was essentially a hand-holding exercise in many cases. (Sean, Senior Cash Manager)

It was good because we recognized that not everybody had all the answers and we knew that we had to deal with different people for different things. We had people called "super-users" and "champions" who were an expert in a particular area. (Mary, Branch Manager)

To ensure a culture of fear or indifference did not develop, IEB put in place a *learning infrastructure* that both enabled and encouraged staff to learn and become familiar with the new system and its functions. Personal laptops and Internet access were given to staff for use at home, enabling staff access to IEB's new systems and complete their training programs either at work or at home. On completion of training program stages, staff were given financial incentives; with laptops to keep and fully paid-up home broadband, the staff had an additional impetus to learn and explore the new systems on their own time. Supplementary material was also put in place to assist both staff and customers throughout the transition process. This material included IT support data, the website, pamphlets, training courses, and seminars.

Some internal issues and conflicts arose during this period of preparation as the centralized IS was configured and adapted to the requirements of the local market.

When we were launching the system, IT originally drafted the training manual. However, I had to re-write the entire document to translate it to English or to "user-friendliness"! (Sarah, HR Manager)

Meanwhile, staff from a variety of departments and professional roles (e.g., the trade union, HR, IT, communications, legal) took on significant tasks in customizing, generating, and developing facets of the local system.

One year after the acquisition, IEB's new system went operational nation-wide over a single weekend. The new system completely superseded the technology, processes, and practices previously in use.

Essentially, it was a big bang concept. ...Obviously as well, if there are requests from customers to changes or further products from the system, these will be communicated to the group and developed at that level. Our requests to the development team are driven by customers and markets. We are continually trying to evolve. (Sean, Senior Cash Manager)

On Monday, staff (and customers) were faced with new technology and systems and had to entirely change their working practices—practices that were a necessary component of the successful delivery of IEB's services and products.

There is no comparison with this system to our previous system. This system was introduced over a long weekend and essentially what happened was we left the building on the Thursday evening and when we came back there was an entirely new system in operation—no similarities. This system provided new thinking for cash management. Although this was a serious change for us internally, it was also a serious change for our customers also. They were also moving to an entirely new system. Although, they were able to immediately see the benefits and these were made very clear to them. (Sean, Senior Cash Manager)

Overall it was a real mind set change for both customers and staff. (Mary, Branch Manager)

While all interviewees referred to the roll-out or big bang event, they generally considered it to be unremarkable. The change-over to the new systems seemed to be obvious and inevitable from the employee's point of view. And while the underlying technology of the IS was also very important and necessary, its presence and shape seemed both *obvious* and *given* as far as they were concerned. The biggest challenge referred to was in the *mind set change* and the *new thinking* demanded of customers and employees to use it effectively.

Positively for IEB, the changeover appeared to be a success; there were few apparent adverse effects and all involved claimed that the transition process was smooth and problem free. In assessing the impact of the new system, benefits and new prospects conferred on the organization were cited.

It is hoped to give more information, and empowerment to management and staff...greater access to information and more efficient methods of performance management and reporting...more efficient for the HR department. Because it is a centralized system and there is one structured form for all, this will lead to greater transparency across the organization...greater flexibility for management and staff. (Sarah, HR Manager)

Contrasting the previous system to IEB's new system, the difference and improvement conveyed by interviewees was palpable. They claimed the new technology has led to benefits and efficiencies, both internally and externally.

The system enables greater transparency, with customers seeing the same information on their screen as the business managers internally within the bank. (Sean, Senior Cash Manager)

The main thing is that everything is much more immediate...everything is now done in real time....The system is far superior to what we had....Another substantial benefit is the fact that we now have e-mail. With the old system, we only had internal e-mail, which was rarely used; we had no electronic access to the outside world. (Mary, Branch Manager)

Previously, the organization had a primarily paper-based system, coupled with an online system with limited functionality. In the new regime, staff operated a completely online system, managing real-time events and constructing new capabilities, services, and products for customers as a result.

> *There is no hiding with this system...from a customer's point of view they can customize their [service]....Essentially, it is a self-service for customers.* (Joe, Business Development Manager)

The services provided with this new system were claimed to be unrivaled within the local market. Interviewees claimed the switch-over has facilitated the introduction of new financial product offerings for customers. The customers experience of IEB's systems is functionally equivalent to that of its employees; the IS constitutes a common infrastructure shared by all. Since its introduction, SB has benefitted from continued market success, with customer numbers increasing at a higher rate than competitors, increased efficiencies for staff, and prestigious award recognition for its innovations.

5 DISCUSSION

IEB's big bang event happened over a long weekend one year after the acquisition, at the same time all previously used systems were shut down and decommissioned, gone forever. But how did IEB achieve this seemingly simple outcome? Were employees simply *made* to adopt the new technology? Was it a matter of a new infrastructure being technologically superior to an outmoded one? Was user adaptation simply an individual cognitive exercise—where *use* was somehow appropriated *through use*? What can we learn from IEB's approach to handling the high risk strategy for a step transformation of its entire IS/IT infrastructure?

It is evident that the local operations of IEB underwent a radical transformation in the period subsequent to the acquisition. These transformations were associated with the swift transition from one suite of IS/IT infrastructural services to another. But a big bang approach to deployment or implementation of an IS project is conventionally regarded as bad practice (Beck 2000; Yardley 2002) and so IEB presents us with an unusual case. Their experience was successful, with minimal disruption to customer services, employee performance, corporate operations, and interbank operation. The outcome of this case is contraindicated in terms of conventional ISD theories and lends itself to trite or obvious appeals to success factors. Conventional analyses may offer nice histories, but they are often poor indicators for practice. When the case is interpreted through the lens of *xenia*, however, we are presented with a rich palette of descriptive possibilities and understanding that illuminates and informs both what happened *and* informs how actors might engage in future. We suggest that employing the lens of xenia to analyze what happened reveals interesting aspects that may otherwise be ignored or considered irrelevant to the origination, development, and management of infrastructural innovation. The following highlights insightful episodes before, during, and after the meeting of the host and the guest.

As described by Ciborra, a meeting between users and technology—between host and guest—can be traumatic, especially if the host's identity is threatened. The "hostility and anxiety" (Ciborra 2002, p. 109) caused by the potential meeting with the foreign visitor (new technology) was addressed in IEB by crafting a learning infrastructure. This learning infrastructure appeared to cultivate a culture of solidarity and encourage acceptance, that is, "to extend their (staff) internal network of solidarity to include the outsider" (Ciborra 2002, p. 112) in order to stimulate positive expectations and feelings toward the guest and mitigate conflicts and frictions during the meeting itself. Different materials and resources, such as IT support data, pamphlets, and websites, were put in place to enable the staff to learn and become familiar with the new guest (i.e., the system and its functions). Incentives were also offered to encourage the host to learn more about the guest and therefore be prepared for their future meeting and cohabitation. Developing familiarity and knowledge of the Other (technology), through different learning programs, incentives, and resources, was initiated from the beginning of the project. These activities of "managing boundaries between what or who is known, and what and who is unknown" (Ciborra, 2002, p. 110) were part of the overall agenda of IEB to create and sustain hospitality and friendliness in order to enable the staff to be receptive and adopting toward the new technology as a guest.

IEB, apparently, knew that despite careful planning and design, new technology "appears to the user suddenly as an ambivalent, threatening stranger" " (Ciborra 2002, p. 115). Developers in this particular case can be understood as *mediators*, mediating between the technology as a guest and the users and clients as hosts. As argued by Ciborra, "if the project goals, and plans, do not make sense to those called on to implement them, only perfunctory or distracted compliance will follow. This can lead to many unexpected consequences for both successful and failed innovations" (2002, p. 108). In order to overcome such potential problems, IEB put efforts into developing hospitality that would alleviate the meeting between the host and the guest. The perceptions and attitudes, associated with the previous guest, and the related institutionalized ways of acting and perceiving work practices had to be changed and new hospitable and friendly attitudes toward a new guest would have to be nurtured. Efforts in this direction were put in place in the local offices immediately upon acquisition by IEB.

IEB brought in experts who were already familiar with the system from its other international branches in order to increase workers' familiarity with the new technology and inculcate a proper habitus of the organization (Bourdieu 1977). These experts were boundary spanners (Levina and Vaast 2005) who were supposed to bridge the knowledge (cultural) gap between the host and the guest. They were familiar with the guest, his habits and ways of action, and although their own knowledge of the system/guest was situated and bound to their own contexts, they were still able to cross the socio-technical boundaries and facilitate a process of developing familiarity and hospitality where "hospitality is about crossing a boundary and reaching out to the Other, stranger" (Ciborra 2002, p. 112). The boundary spanners were also important in sustaining the host's confidence and trust and reducing his (organizational) anxiety at a future meeting with the ambiguous stranger. The presence of experts that had already dealt with the guest improved the emotional atmosphere in the host's house.

The meeting, moment of truth, or catastrophe point Ciborra 2002, p. 112) took place all of a sudden, over a weekend, and climactically brought the host and the guest together. Faced with the guest (new system) at their table, staff and customers adjusted to a new way of working, a new practice and identity. These processes were shaped through hospitable exchanges, gifts (computers to keep), and commitments in the process of serving the guest. The guest also passed through preparation for the meeting. The developers, by familiarizing with the objectives of the system and structures of the organization, "endowed (it) with affordances...that trigger a network of commitments by the host" (Ciborra 2002, p. 114). Despite the developers' attempts to accommodate the host, the situated nature of the meeting with these affordances can become either constraints or enablers for the host. In contrast with the straightforward command and control typical for structured methodologies, the developers—being here the puppeteers of the meeting—created an open-ended process in which the host showed hospitality and "serves the guest" but the guest will also begin to "align the host to certain needs and constraints" (Ciborra 2002, p. 114). Ciborra argues for acceptance of the guest's intrinsic ambiguity and mystery, he encourages its acceptance as a practical way of coping with technology: "To be sure, an effective host must be able to exercise various forms of care depending upon the unpredictable circumstances in the unfolding of hospitality" (Ciborra 2002, p. 115).

The aftermath of the project showed that the skillful crafting and cultivating of hospitality that served the guest, reciprocally resulted in well accepted affordances, enablers, concessions, privileges, and freedoms for the host and its identity. The process of change and adjustment always involves conflicts and friction. The interviews with staff showed that the new system drew and compelled them to use completely new ways of working but interviewees also appreciated the new system and its affordances. In Ciborra's terms, the project was successful because the host was prepared and met the guest with trust and friendliness, coupled with "releasement of control" so that he remained the "master of the house" (2002, p. 114). In other words, the potentially hostile and ambiguous stranger had demands and requests, which were fulfilled by the host, but the guest was prepared and bought gifts that encouraged the hospitality and facilitated the initial meeting and acceptance by the host. In this case, IEB overcame the challenges of a high risk infrastructural cut-over through the practices of cultivating or nurturing hospitality, for example, by encouraging friendliness between the guest and the host, to enable the seeming inevitability of a successful result..

6 CONCLUSIONS: XENIA, A METAPHOR FOR PRACTICE

This paper aims to show how subtle and slow *reciprocal cultivation* (Ciborra 2002, p. 116) is carried out through the sharing and enriching of cultures and practices. It also reveals the messy and heterogeneous nature of the socio-technical hosting relationship and coexistence and points to aspects of technological innovation that are ignored or considered irrelevant in the structured methodologies. The emotional meeting between the fluid technology and its hosts was alleviated by a preparation that involved the creation of cultural tolerance to the Other, stimulating gradual familiarity and under-standing. The meeting itself involved unexpected turns and mutual reshaping of socio-technical identities, which resulted in an amalgamated coexistence through the dynamic repertoire of practices.

The metaphor of xenia (or hospitality) shifts our conceptions to a concern for tech-nology and users together, introducing each other, changing and accommodating each to the other's potentials. The user (host) is here but the developer as well; the developer is both inside and outside the tent of hospitality. The developer becomes a double or triple agent, an interloper in the technological, the broker in the middle who introduces the stranger; a puppeteer behind the stranger (guest, technology) who reconfigures it on the fly. The performance is dynamic, the technology is fluid, the user may approve or be offended but the performance goes on as the guest and host explore each others' stances to find a fit. This approach implies changed technology, but also changed users; it opens the possibility of larger narratives, accounts that spotlight emotions, identities, power, interests, and action implicit in the sociality of introduction.

Acknowledgments

We would like to thank the reviewers for their insightful feedback and the members of SB and IEB for their encouragement and cooperation in allowing access to their organization. The research was supported in part by a University College Dublin School of Business research seed funding grant for Globally Distributed Services in UCD's Centre for Innovation, Technology and Organization (CITO).

References

Beck, K. 2000. *Extreme Programming Explained: Embrace Change*, Reading, MA: Addison-Wesley.
Bourdieu, P. 1977. *Outline of a Theory of Practice*, Cambridge, UK: Cambridge University Press.
Ciborra, C. U. 1998. "Crisis and Foundations: An Inquiry into the Nature and Limits of Models and Methods in the Information Systems Discipline," *Journal of Strategic Information Systems* (7), pp. 5-16.
Ciborra, C. U. 2002. *The Labyrinths of Information: Challenging the Wisdom of Systems*, Oxford, UK: Oxford University Press.
Ciborra, C. U. 2004. "Encountering Information Systems as a Phenomenon," in *The Social Study of Information and Communication Technology: Innovation, Actors, and Contexts*, C. Avgerou, C. Ciborra, and F. Land (eds.), Oxford, UK: Oxford University Press.
Cooper, R. B., and Zmud, R. W. 1990. "Information Technology Implementation Research: A Technological Diffusion Approach," *Management Science* (36), pp. 123-139.
Fitzgerald, B. 1996. "Formalized Systems Development Methodologies: A Critical Perspective," *Information Systems Journal* (6), pp. 3-23.
Grint, K., and Woolgar, S. 1997. *The Machine at Work: Technology, Work and Organization*, Cambridge, UK: Polity Press.
Kwon, T. H., and Zmud, R. W. 1987. "Unifying the Fragmented Models of Information Systems Implementation," in *Critical Issues in Information Systems Research*, R. J. Boland and R. A. Hirschheim (eds.), Chichester, UK: John Wiley & Sons.
Levina, N., and Vaast, E. 2005. "The Emergence of Boundary Spanning Competence in Practice: Implications for Implementation and Use of Information Systems," *MIS Quarterly* (29:2), pp. 335-363.
Lewin, K. 1952. "Group Decision and Social Change," in *Readings in Social Psychology* (3rd ed.), E. E. Maccoby, T. M. Newcomb, and E. L. Hartley (eds.), London: Methuen & Co.
Miles, M. B., and Huberman, A. M. 1994. *Qualitative Data Analysis: An Expanded Sourcebook*, Thousand Oaks, CA: Sage Publications.

Munkvold, B. E. 1999. "Challenges of IT Implementation for Supporting Collaboration in Distributed Organizations," *European Journal of Information Systems* (8), pp. 260-272.

Orlikowski, W. J., and Iacono, C. S. 2000. "The Truth Is Not out There: An Enacted View of the 'Digital Economy,'" in *Understanding the Digital Economy*, E. Brynjolfsson and B. Kahin (eds.), Boston: MIT Press.

Walsham, G. 1993. *Interpreting Information Systems in Organizations,* Chichester, UK: John Wiley & Sons.

Wastell, D. G. 1996. "The Fetish of Technique: Methodology as a Social Defense," *Information Systems Journal* (6), pp. 25-40.

Yardley, D. 2002. *Successful IT POroject Delivery: Learning the Lessons of Project Failure,* Edinburgh, UK: Addison-Wesley.

About the Authors

Allen Higgins is a Ph.D. candidate at the University of Warwick under the supervision of Joe Nandhakumar. His studies are focused on the intersubjectivity of software development work, accessed ethnographically, seeking to describe aspects related to how programmers and users understand and access the objects they create, processes of creating and maintaining the ensembles of actors composing processes of innovation. Allen can be reached by e-mail at a.c.higgins@warwick.ac.uk.

Simeon Vidolov is a Ph.D. candidate with the Centre of Innovation, Technology & Organization (CITO) at University College Dublin. His research interests lie in the area of distributed forms of working and organizing. More specifically, he is currently examining the roles and interlinkages between corporeality and materiality in geographically distributed software projects. Simeon can be reached by e-mail at simeon.vidolov@ucd.ie.

Frank Frößler received his Ph.D. in 2008 from University College Dublin, and is a research assistant with the Management Information Systems Group in the the Centre for Innovation, Technology, and Organization (CITO) at University College Dublin. His research interest concerns the extent to which new technologies enable and constrain innovative forms of organizing work. Currently, he is focusing on the implications of Skype and Sametime in software development projects. Frank can be reached by e-mail at frank.froessler@ucd.ie.

Doreen Mullaney is a graduate of the Michael Smurfit School of Business, University College Dublin and currently works in the international financial services sector. Her interests focus on organizational learning and knowledge management.

12 WHO HAS THE POWER OVER SPACES OF INNOVATION? The Role of Technology in ICT-Triggered Change Processes

Anneli Linde
Henrik C. J. Linderoth
Umeå School of Business
Umeå University
Umeå, Sweden

Abstract   *ICT-triggered change processes are known to be unpredictable and tech-nologies are not used the way designers or managers intend because of actor groups' innovation when ICT is deployed. The examination of sources of inno-vation in ICT-triggered change processes has had a socio-cognitive bias toward learning and the way actors make sense of ICT. This paper addresses the role of technology for actors in spaces of innovation. The aim of the paper is to analyze how features of ICT shape spaces for innovation in ICT-triggered change processes. To achieve this, two longitudinal case studies of the deployment of two ICT systems are analyzed. By analyzing features as programs of action inscribed in an ICT, we conclude that programs of action can be grouped along the dimensions "use/not use," "what to do," and "how to do." These dimensions will shape actor groups' spaces of innovation and their potential influence on deployment of ICT. Furthermore, we address how inscribed programs of action shape the need for temporal alliances between actor groups during the deployment of an ICT system.*

Keywords   Organizational change, ICT, programs of action, inscriptions, actor network theory

Please use the following format when citing this chapter:

Linde, A., and Linderoth, H. C. J., 2008, in IFIP International Federation for Information Processing, Volume 287, Open IT-Based Innovation: Moving Towards Cooperative IT Transfer and Knowledge Diffusion, eds. León, G., Bernardos, A., Casar, J., Kautz, K., and DeGross, J. (Boston: Springer), pp. 211-226.

1   INTRODUCTION

During the past few decades, information and communication technologies (ICTs) have been used as a means to change organizational work processes and structures. However, reaching an organizational transformation by implementing ICTs is known to be problematic and the technologies are not used as designers or managers intend. The slippage between designers' and managers' intentions and users' actual deployment of technology can be seen as a process of drifting. That is, the original goals and aims with a new IT system drift away from its original intention regardless of who defines the intention (Ciborra 1996). Technology drift may be a consequence of adaptations to circumstances in the context where the ICT is implemented, such as when technology projects are allowed to drift to suit different actors' needs (Holmström and Stadler 2001) or when disputes among actors involved need to be settled (Elbanna 2007). Drift can also occur when actor groups reinterpret the aim of implementing an ICT and thereby take control over the further deployment (Hanseth and Braa 1998). Drift can be regarded as a process of knowledge development and learning (Rosenberg 1982). However, in the management literature, drift of ICT-triggered change processes does not appear to be desirable. Processes are assumed to occur top-down in a controlled manner (Ciborra 2000), with the aim of at integrating all information into a system in order to reduce fragmentation and increase efficiency (Monteiro 2003). However, in practice, few ICT-triggered change initiatives are implemented in a controlled top-down mode. ICT-triggered changes also emerge from the bottom-up as a result of actors' appropriation over time of a new technology into their work practices (Orlikowski 1996). Whether implementation initiatives emerge top-down or bottom-up, new technologies never fit perfectly in an organization, implying that local adaptations are needed. This need for adaptations can also be seen as an occasion for innovation where deployment of a new ICT can trigger organizational innovation and product development (Boland et al. 2007). However, the examination of sources of innovation in ICT-triggered change processes can have a socio-cognitive bias toward learning and the way actors make sense of ICT. Research has paid limited attention to the role of ICT itself in these change processes (Monteiro and Hanseth 1995; Orlikowski and Yates 2006) and has not addressed the role technology plays in innovation with respect to change processes. Is there any relations between the characteristics of an ICT and different actor groups' possibilities to innovate in the change process? This question is legitimate to ask because technology designers delegate roles and competencies to human and nonhuman entities that comprise a socio-technical network that is supposed to implement the change (Akrich 1992; Latour 1992). Hence, the delegation of roles and competencies, we claim, will shape the space for innovation in the network.

Accordingly, the aim of the paper is to analyze how features of ICT shape actor groups' options to innovate in ICT-triggered change processes. To achieve this aim, two longitudinal case studies of the deployment of two ICT systems are analyzed. In selecting our cases, we tried to identify cases where the features of the implemented ICT are dissimilar in order to create an enhanced understanding of how features of an ICT shape actor groups' spaces for innovation in a change process.

2 THEORETICAL POINT OF DEPARTURE

In research on ICT-triggered changes processes, limited attention has been paid to the role ICT itself. Monteiro and Hanseth (1995) and Orlikowski and Iaccono (2001) both state that researchers need to be more specific about technological artefacts when analyzing the introduction of an ICT system into an organization and not take the technology for granted. They claim that this approach will shed light on critical impacts, or failure of impacts on different organizational levels. Taking the technology into consideration also raises the challenge of articulating the technology's characteristics (Orlikowski and Yates 2006) without reifying them through a form of contingent determinism (Bridgman and Wilmot 2006) and without reducing them to the social (Berg 1997). One path to move away from the determinist account is to recognize the under-standing that members of a social group come to have of particular technological artefacts, expressed as technological frames (Orlikowski and Gash 1994). These include an actor group's shared understanding of the following:

- the technology's opportunities and function
- the motive or vision behind the adoption decisions and the technology's eventual value for the organization
- how the technology will be used day-to-day and possible or actual pre-conditions and consequences connected with technology use

The analysis of technological frames can help highlight how actor groups make sense of ICT or special aspects of ICT, unveiling actor groups' conceptions of the spaces of innovation. However, when analyzing technological frames, Davidson (2006) argues that context for examining technological frames needs to be expanded to the organiza-tional fields to include cultural assumptions and institutional logics, reinforcing tech-nological frames. Further, technology frames are continuously constructed and refined in practice through inferences of actors' past experiences as well as obtaining new knowledge emerging from actors' interactions with technology (Linderoth and Pellegrino 2005). How can we approach technology and its features in order to increase the understanding of actors' spaces for innovation?

We argue that a way of approaching technology features is to use the concept of inscriptions (Akrich 1992) as an analytical tool. Inscriptions refer to programs of actions inscribed in technological artefacts that originate from technology designers' assumptions about the potential user and the context for use. Technology designers' inscribed programs delegate roles and competencies to the components of a socio-technical network, including human and nonhuman entities of the system (Akrich 1992; Latour 1992). When a program of action is inscribed into a piece of technology, the technology could become an actor imposing its inscribed programs of action on its user (Monteiro 2000, p. 77). Thus, the mode in which ICT-triggered change processes unfold depends on programs of action inscribed in an ICT system and how actors, in the setting that would be transformed, act upon the inscribed programs of action.

How can we understand the inscribed programs of actions in practice? Let us consider a Web-based system for booking airline tickets. In this system, a wide array of assumptions about me as a user and the programs of actions that I have to perform if I should get my ticket are inscribed. It is assumed that I have a computer, I can use it, I would be able to read and understand the language on the Web pages, I can navigate the Internet, and I have a valid credit card. Furthermore, I have to go through a number of procedures to book my flight, selecting a flight, typing my name, e-mail address, credit card number, accept the terms of conditions, etc. The programs of actions are inscribed and I have to follow these restrictions if I want a ticket. But I have some degree of freedom concerning when and where I want to travel, which carrier I prefer (if I book via an Internet-based travel agent), which class of travel I would like (as long as my intentions are to take a flight between places with airports of decent size). Compare these programs of actions with inscribed programs of action in a paper clip. Briefly, the designer has assumed that I want to fold a paper pile of a certain thickness and that my hands and fingers are of certain size and strength. But the designer cannot inscribe any programs of action that govern me to use the clip in an intended way. On the contrary, it is just my fantasy that delimits my appropriation of the paper clip. If a power perspective is applied to these two cases, in the former case, technology designers together with the actors selling the airline tickets control via the system my actions when I want to order an airline ticket. In the latter case, I as a user have the power over how I use the paper clip and my spaces for innovation are rather large. In the former case, my spaces of innovation as a user are limited because programs of actions are strengthened by inscribing them into the system (Hanseth and Monteiro 1997). Hence programs of actions inscribed in technological artefacts can give me as a user a varying flexibility, or spaces of innovation, with regard to the actions I perform. But a crucial issue when it comes to ICT-triggered changes and the spaces of innovation in the process is if I use the ICT at all: Do I perform any action at all by means of the ICT, a precondition for the change process to unfold?

How are users imposed to use the ICT in order to achieve some kind of change? How are inscribed programs of action strengthened to trigger a change process with intended or unintended outcomes? By drawing on Hanseth and Montiero's (1997) analytical point of view, three ways of strengthening inscribed programs of action can be identified. First, programs of action can be linked to large and complex actor networks in the surroundings. For example, programs of actions inscribed in laws are strengthened by police, courts, and prisons to impose the desired behavior on me as a citizen. Second, a program action can be aligned with a surrounding actor network. For example, the program of action inscribed on signs in hotel bathrooms encourages me to reuse the towels (and save money for the hotel owner), aligning the company and guest with the growing consciousness of environmental issues. Third, a program of action can be strong in itself. However, from this perspective, we claim that programs of action are not *per se* strong. They are strengthened by removing alternative ways of action. For example, Ryan Air wants us as passengers to book the airline tickets via their Webpage. This program of action is strengthened by removing or complicating alternative programs of action. Have you, for example, seen a Ryan Air ticket office downtown? Furthermore, on the front Webpage, no contact information is given. That is a few clicks away. If I want to book my tickets via telephone, I am charged 30 cents per minute if I do not live in Ireland.

To conclude, programs of action inscribed in an ICT will have an impact on activities performed by means of the ICT. In this sense, more or less space for innovation is delegated to the user. Actions are performed as a matter of the options the user is directed to take or as a matter of not using the ICT.

3   DATA COLLECTION AND CASE DESCRIPTIONS

Features of an ICT, in this paper, are regarded as programs of actions inscribed in an ICT and will have consequences for actor groups' spaces of innovation in an ICT-triggered change process. Accordingly, we tried to choose cases where the programs of action inscribed differ with regard to variations in the inscribed actions to perform by means of the ICT and variations in how inscribed actions are performed. Thus, on the surface, the cases appear quite dissimilar; however, they were chosen to demonstrate general situations when ICT is interpreted by actors creating networks of users conducting organizational changes.

The empirical base is from two ICT implementation projects aimed at organizational change. Both projects have been studied as longitudinal case studies over several years. The first case concerns the implementation of a project management model at Swedish customs, and the second concerns the implementation of telemedicine (video conferencing) systems in a Swedish health care organization.

3.1   The Project Management Model Project

One of the consequences of today's "projectified" society (Lundin and Söderholm 1995) is a trend toward a standardization of project activities by means of formalized, generic project management models, PMMs (Gunnarson et al. 2000). The rationale behind this development seems to be a quest for a common conceptual platform and work methods for all projects. One of today's well-known, commercially available, IT-based PMMs, PROPS, was originally developed by the telecom company Ericsson and applied in Ericsson subsidiaries worldwide. The model is comprehensive, covering the single-project perspective as well as the organization's business interests, including leadership and organizational long-term strategies. This is a multiproject perspective. PROPS is not only intended as a guide for the project manager, it is also a monitoring and control tool for managers at different levels in the organization (Räisänen and Linde 2004). PROPS describes what to do and when to do it, but not how to do it. This means that the model has to be adapted to new settings such as documents, tools, and best practice. These should be tailored for the needs of specific organizations.

The goal of the management change project studied was the redesign and implementation of PROPS at the Swedish Customs Authority. The case study focused on top management, the team in charge of the implementation, project managers using the model, the model (the ICT), and some major local settings. In all, 31 semi-structured interviews, as well as numerous informal discussions and mail conversations with top-management, members of the project office, project managers, and members of the project group have been carried out during 1999–2002, with follow-ups in 2004, 2006, 2007, and early 2008. Project-specific documentation and the PMM were analyzed. In addition, on-site observations at the project office, four local offices, and project group meetings were carried out in 19 visits to the organization.

In 1999, a decision was made to "projectify" the Swedish Customs Authority (i.e., to create an effective multiproject organization). To fulfil this goal, a project group—consisting of representatives from head-office, local offices, and the IT department—was formed. The project manager was a top manager from the development department. The vision of this group was that the PROPS model would function as the intermediary through which the organization would govern all of its projects, support its project managers, and increase knowledge about handling project portfolios. As one of the initiators put it, PROPS would "bring order to their project organization." Thus the initial goal of the project was to implement PROPS within the organization.

In the early stage of the project, during the planning stage, the goal and task shifted focus from a straightforward implementation of the model and change of the organization to a redesign of the PMM. The new vision resulted in wide-ranging changes to the model enacted through multiple negotiations and realignments of spokespersons for and against it. To gain support for the PMM project and increase project management knowledge, specific PROPS courses were offered to relevant actors at all levels of the organization.

To help change the organization and to facilitate the implementation phase in the project, a new organizational unit, the project office, was created. As advocated by the PMM, their task was, in the long term, to function as a support unit for the projects in the organization and, in the short term, to support the transformation process in effective multiproject management. Members of the project office became an essential part of the implementation and organizational change.

Despite painstaking efforts to prepare for organizational change and to adapt the model to its new context, the actual implementation of the PMM generated many problems and caused enormous delays. At the beginning of 2002, a tentative model was finally launched on the intranet. However, a major part of the user test of the model and the implementation of organizational change was still incomplete. In 2004, the new multiproject management approach could finally be described as implemented, even though there were still ongoing activities related to adaptation and change. During the following years, there was a slow stabilization of use. From time to time, at least parts of the inherent ideas in the PMM were questioned and not everything went smoothly. However, the PMM project is seen and described as a success by the organization and the PMM perceived as a natural part of the ICT. Hence all major development projects and IT projects at the Swedish Customs Authority are now using the PMM. The project manager is an official and most wanted role, and all together the effect on the organization of the implementation of this model is substantial and can be found at all levels in the organization.

3.2 The Telemedicine Project

Telemedicine consists of IT applications supporting health-care services via electronic transmission of information or expertise in order to improve the effectiveness of resource utilization and allocation (Bashshur 1995). Generally, telemedicine is based on different video conferencing systems to which optical medical equipment can be connected to transmit live or still pictures. The general interest in telemedicine technology increased slowly in the early 1990s. In the mid-1990s, a boom could be witnessed regarding the number of telemedicine projects in the Swedish health care sector.

The methods used for studying the project were semi-structured interviews and participant observation between 1994 and 1999. A total of 63 interviews with medical specialists, general practitioners, hospital managers, and politicians were conducted.

From 1994 through 1999, on-site observations were conducted at 18 meetings of the project group. Ten of the observations were done before the installation of the systems. After the first study, informal contacts have been kept with informants in the actual settings. Seven follow-up interviews have been conducted with representatives for the project settings studied between 1996 and 1998, with two managers at a central support function, and representatives from clinics that started using telemedicine after 2000. Additionally, document studies have been conducted and a database containing 1,650 telemedicine consultations that took place between June 2003 and January 2006 has been analyzed.

The country studied was an early adopter of telemedicine. In 1994, concrete general goals were identified for the coming telemedicine projects. The general goals are as follows: to increase value for patients through access to medical specialists irrespective of location; to support the development of competence in the organization; to decrease the costs of the county council; and to investigate the long-term effects telemedicine may have on the structure of health care in the county. A project group, consisting of physicians and personnel from the department of medical technology, looked for adequate equipment and planned for the introduction of the technology to determine the physical location and the need for education. In August of 1996, the telemedicine equipment was purchased and installed.

During the pre-study phase, two projects crystallized: general telemedicine (GTE) and telepathology (PAT). In both projects, the technical platform was a video-conferencing system that could be connected to medical equipment. The GTE project addressed communication between general practitioners at health centers and specialists at the county or university hospitals. The specialties involved were dermatology, ortho-paedics, and otolaryngology. Most specialists were located at the university hospital; the orthopaedists were located both at the university and county hospitals. By connecting optical equipment to the video conferencing system, it was possible for general practitioners to examine, the ear or the skin of a patient and transmit pictures, live or still, to the specialists. The specialists could then advise the general practitioners about further treatment of the patient and whether the patient should be hospitalized.

The PAT project concerned communication between medical specialists, allowing gynaecologists and surgeons at a county hospital to communicate with pathologists and cytologists at the university hospital. In this case, there were two major applications. The first application was the remote examination of frozen sections and of cytological sections. The pathologists and cytologists at the university hospital could manoeuver a microscope placed at the county hospital. The microscope, connected to a video system, was used to examine the sections. The standard question from county hospital physicians was whether a section was malignant. The second application was to gain further infor-mation concerning the section samples sent from the county hospital using an expert consultation. When additional information was required, the pathologist at the university hospital could mobilize appropriate specialists and set up a videoconference.

Although telemedicine did not boom in terms of frequency of use during the first three years (1996–1998), the project was perceived as beneficial and the county manage-ment continued to fund further development. The technology had a spokesperson at the top management level, the research and development manager, who had a positive attitude toward new technologies and projects. Accordingly, today there are approxi-mately 100 telemedicine units installed at health centers, hospitals, and administrative units. Furthermore, in 1999, a telemedicine center was established at the university hospital. The center should promote telemedicine use and be a support function for departments introducing the technology. However, the two people responsible for the center stated that it is hard to implement applications into ordinary routines. Often the projects ran very well, but when results were implemented in daily operations, it was much harder. They were still waiting for a breakthrough that would generate clear engagement from top management and department managers. However, in 2006, the manager for the telemedicine center stated that the county used telemedicine more than any other county in Sweden.

4   WHERE ARE THE SPACES FOR INNOVATION?

Earlier, we claimed that programs of action inscribed in an ICT bring more or less flexibility to the organization in which the ICT is deployed. In this section, we will analyze the spaces for innovation in the two cases studied by examining how the ICT was interpreted, how the organizations were changed, and if spaces for innovation were closed or maintained in order to achieve sustainable changes.

4.1   Interpreting Spaces for Innovation

The support for the idea to implement the PMM as a tool for an effective multi-project organization was strong in the organization and the ideas inscribed in the PMM of how such an organization would be constructed and organized were well described by the initial designers of the PMM. The designers of the PMM tried to create an ICT solution with limited space for innovation and one of their goals with this product was to create a standard for managing multiproject organizations (Räisänen and Linde 2004). However, when it comes to the implementing organization, the knowledge amongst users as well as management of the final effect of the PMM was notably unclear at the beginning of the implementation, as was the knowledge of the range of adaptations and development to be done before the model could be an effective tool in the organization. Hence there was an initial planned approach to the implementation with a group from different parts of the organization, a redesigner group, engaged to make changes in the PMM and then implement it. Notable is that there was no detailed plan from manage-ment on how this implementation actually should be carried out. However, the redesigner group had to interpret the PMM as a whole, the text inscribed, and the context. Even if the intended result of that process was to create a PMM that reflected management ideas of how to do things, the process ended with only slight modifications when compared to the original model. It became clear that in order to fully understand the PMM and its complexity, and further to decide what changes to make both in the PMM as well as in the organization, the process needed to be divided into several steps and more potential future users had to be engaged. The power of the interpretation of the model had to be handed over to the new actor groups in the organization, the users.

In the telemedicine case there was, as in the PMM case, at the outset a consensus among actor groups concerning the overall goals. However, there were not many clear ideas of what should be done in order to achieve a change and what arrangements were needed to accomplish a sustainable change. The uncertainty of what should be done can be seen as a consequence of the technology designers' delegation of a rather large space of innovation to the adopting organization (i.e., to identify and decide on an appropriate uses of the technology). Furthermore, it was delegated to the adopting organization to identify how to make use compulsory if indeed a change was wanted. Nevertheless, ideas soon took shape when the clinics of dermatology, otolaryngology, orthopaedics, surgery pathology, and cytology, together with two remote health centers, were included in the first stages of the project. Consequently, there were two central ideas. First, health centers should have the opportunity to consult medical specialists to discuss the further treatment of a patient, for example, whether the patient should be sent to the hospital a few hundred kilometers away. Second, medical specialist (surgeons) at a county hospital should have the option to receive urgent answers on frozen tissues from pathologist or cytologists, in order to make decisions on how to proceed with surgery. Still, it was unclear what should be done in order to come closer to the goals expressed.

The insight that that technology designers had delegated to user to innovate applications for the technology was rather clear among the actor groups involved. In interviews, hospital managers clearly expressed that it was the physicians' responsibility to find out how the technology would be used. This activity would, furthermore, be a part of physicians' ordinary development duties. In this sense, no further spaces for innovation were created. Physicians in the project group were well aware of the fact that they had precedence of interpretations regarding the innovation of telemedicine applications. This belief was so deeply rooted that three smaller teams were created in the GTE project, before the equipment was installed, in order to find out in which situations technology could be used in the different medical specialties. Rather soon, however, an insight developed of the necessity to test and experiment with the technology in order to find appropriate applications and how to organize activities. In the PAT project, the project manager had a clear idea of two applications and he had even developed a flowchart of how activities would be organized.

4.2 Changing the Organization by Innovation, Restriction, or Alignment

When looking into the further change process when the PMM was diffused and used throughout the organization, it was clear that the designers and the management in the organization had succeeded in the way that the space for interpretation concerning "what to do" was limited, or even accepted to a degree of irreversibility. However, how to carry out specific work procedures that were stipulated in the PMM, changing the organization, etc. (i.e., how to do activities) was still to be innovated and decided by management and users during the implementation and practical use. Several actors and actor groups felt that they had the responsibility and legitimacy to interpret the PMM and decide not only how to use the model and for what, but also to identify work procedures in detail. During the first years, the presence of spokespeople in local contexts had a significant influence on the frequency of use of the PMM and change in behavior and work structures. Networks representing different interpretations of the new model could be found in different projects, departments, and groups crossing organizational boundaries, all struggling to make their ideas of multiproject organizing the common view. Most of these networks were represented by enthusiastic actors, holding high positions in the organizational hierarchy. Their power positions provided them with the legitimacy needed to interpret "how to do," and the space to experiment with and develop the technology, as well as to prescribe routines that supported inscriptions in the PMM. Furthermore, they also could grant similar privileges to their colleagues, which helped to strengthen the ideas inscribed in the PMM. The major actor groups with clear precedence of the interpretation of the PMM were the redesign group, key people at the project office, the top manager in the IT department, and some successful project managers.

However, the space for interpretations and innovation had to be reduced if the intended control of the project organization was to be reached. The project management office was established at the start of the implementation by the management of the organization. The project office was responsible for the official ideas of how to use the model and how and what to change. The project office was the main tool for management to control and restrain the interpretation of the PMM and, through negotiation processes with those different actors and actor groups discussed above, reach a consensus. Another essential part of the process for the development and stabilization of new work procedures was the establishment of a group of professional project managers. Those project managers became and still are the main carrier of the ideas inscribed in the PMM, tightly connect to the project management office and, by that, also related to the management of the organization.

If the possibilities for a broad range of interpretations and use of the implemented PMM on an overall level were quite restricted in the PMM case and the focus was on how to carry out activities, it was very much the opposite in the telemedicine case.

Spaces for innovation, regarding the appropriation of telemedicine, were considered to be rather large by physicians. For example, the project manager stated that "*it is only your imagination that puts the limits.*" A physician stated that "*you always have to take into consideration when you can do a consultation in order to test the limits.*" Accordingly, the project in some settings was characterized by testing what could be done with the telemedicine technology. These activities continued after the first project was finished, but the entire time they were dependent upon the will of single individuals. However, after the first project finished, the county management gradually increased the spaces for innovation by continuously investing in new equipment and upgrading existing equipment. Furthermore, the county management maintained spaces for innovation on the county level by the foundation of the TeleMedLab in 1999. This department proactively works for the dissemination of telemedicine use in the county by testing new equipment, supporting clinics in testing and implementing the technology, and maintaining and upgrading existing equipment.

In the PAT project, the idea of how to organize the use of telemedicine was relatively clear, which can be seen as consequence of the clearly defined applications. This, in many ways, was an opposite situation compared to the PMM case. However, in the GTE project, and for some years after the project, the issue of how to organize the use of telemedicine shifted back and forth. In the early stages of the project, opinions shifted between planned and urgent/*ad hoc* consultations. At the outset, planned consultations were considered as the best way of organizing consultations, probably due to the fact that other activities was organized in this mode. But after a year and visits at a few demonstrations of the equipment, the project group decided that most consultations should be *ad hoc*, mainly because patients and general practitioners would gain immediate benefits. The consultations between general practitioners and dermatologists, however, needed to be planned beforehand, due to the dermatologists not having their own equipment.

Ad hoc consultations could be a way of improving health care services for patients in rural areas, as well as general practitioners for getting immediate feedback on their opinions, but not taken into considerations was that *ad hoc* use would require spaces for innovation for the actor groups concerned in order to change work procedures to fit this way of working. The need to change routines became obvious when general practitioners complained about the time that they needed to spend on "chasing" medical specialists at the university hospital, or when medical specialists had difficulties because they were called away from the activities with which they were occupied when a request from an *ad hoc* consultation emerged. Furthermore, a general practitioner claimed that *ad hoc* use would have required changed views on roles and relationships between primary care and hospital care. Suddenly primary care could put demands on hospital care, making it a service provider to primary care. Even if this interpretation not was verbalized among medical specialists, telemedicine is gradually being reinterpreted as something that medical specialists use for offering services to other hospitals. When the use between June 2003 and January 2006 is studied, 72 percent of the 1,650 consultations conducted were initiated from a hospital and 60 percent of that is with other hospitals. Only 10 percent of the consultations are initiated from a health center dealing with clinical issues. In this way, the need for organizational innovations and rethinking of roles and relationships among actor groups is decreased. Deployment of the technology can now follow prevailing routines that just have to be modified to the new medium

4.3 Closing, Maintaining, or Ignoring Spaces for Innovation

By following the deployment of telemedicine over 14 years, we see that use can fade away as suddenly as it emerged. Among the eight settings involved at the outset, telemedicine is today actively used in three settings, all at hospitals, and the heavy users are clinical or laboratory departments. The exploration of the quite large space for innovation given to users and management was, at the outset, mostly reinforced by the idea of *ad hoc* use. But the need for organizational innovations made the telemedicine drift toward planned use that can be seen as an adaptation to existing routines (see Holmström and Stadler 2001). Accordingly, how the technology is used today has been standardized, but what the technology is used for is more diversified. The use varies considerably from setting to setting and the challenge for actor groups involved is to maintain a sustainable change triggered by the use of telemedicine. However, the county management has tried to keep the spaces for innovation open by investing in equipment and in the TeleMedLab. In this sense, no unified use is strived for.

In the PMM case, the situation is to some degree much opposite. The ideas inscribed in the PMM and the change to a multiproject organization seems to be well established even if far from everything inscribed in the PMM is used or used as intended, and much more than intended is handed over to actor groups like the project managers to decide.

Hence the ideas of projects as a work-form and project managers as an established professional role are totally accepted and integrated in the management of the organization. Rules and regulations have been added and adapted over the years by top management to enforce the ideas represented in the PMM and, in addition, courses related to ideas promoted in the PMM have been given to the employees, all examples of action taken by management to keep control. However, the implemented change is no longer directly dependent on the actual ICT, the PMM; it is integrated in the work culture and by that it probably would be hard and complicated to take away even if some of the changes fade and the PMM is no longer used. In that sense, this is a successful implementation that could be described as a translation that reached a point of stabilization.

5   CONCLUDING DISCUSSION

The aim of the paper has been to analyze how features of an ICT shape actor groups' options and possibilities to innovate in ICT-triggered change processes. We have described two ICT implementation processes in which programs of actions inscribed in the ICT were interpreted, changed, and put into use by actor groups. We have argued that ICT systems contain programs of action that either could give considerable spaces for innovation when the technology is deployed, or that are rather restricting. Based on the analysis, we have identified three dimensions of inscribed programs of action to be sorted out. These dimensions could also be considered different levels in an interpretation process of an ICT. The first dimension concerns actors' interpretations if they have a choice to use the ICT. For the second dimension, if actors' choose to, or must, use the ICT, what alternatives for usage exit, or could exist? The third dimensions concerns how detailed, or limited, the system is in how activities should be conducted. Based on our findings and elaborating on ideas presented by Akrich (1992), Hanseth and Monteiro (1997), and Linderoth (2000), the three dimensions are labeled

- Use/not use: To what extent does a program of action give flexibility in choice of acceptance of usage or rejection of usage of that specific program of action?
- What to do: To what extent does the program of action allow flexibility of usage alternatives?
- How to do: To what extent does the program of action allow flexibility in how activities will be conducted?

The first dimension, use/not use, is the key to understanding the change process and the key for management in the organization to control, in order to generate any action at all. This flexibility is connected to the entire ICT system, as well as to single programs of action. In both of the cases we studied, actors had at the outset significant flexibility in the choice of using the system or not. In the PMM case, however, flexibility in the dimension use/not use diminished, on an overall level, when the implementation proceeded. Management was rather successful in strengthening the use dimension through regulations, connecting the PMM to trends in society and connecting the use of the PMM to powerful role models, which made rejection of the PMM and resistance to change nearly impossible. In the telemedicine case, programs of action also gave management an opportunity to delimit the choices of use/not use. However, this opportunity was not given attention nor understood. This implied that the precedence of interpretation of whether the technology would be used or not was handed over to actors in local settings where the technology was deployed.

In the second and third dimension, what to do and how to do, there are some basic differences between the cases, with regard to how inscribed programs of action shaped actor groups' spaces of innovation. The PMM model prescribed rather detailed what to do in order to create and manage an efficient multiproject organization, while in the telemedicine case, what to do was based on some generic interpretations in the organizational field, implying that innovating what to do is a prerequisite for a change process to proceed. This means that, in the first case, designers successfully and consciously have allowed room for interpretation and delimited the space for innovation, while in the latter case there were no such aspirations from the designers.

However, in the third dimension, the situation was the opposite. In the PMM case, the designers have delegated to management and users innovation on how to use the model. However, space for innovation is also inscribed in the model, because the user and management have to innovate in order to able to use the model and achieve the desired change. On the other hand, in the telemedicine case, the technology designers had clear ideas on how to use the technology: actors in two, or more, sites are mutually present and solving whatever issues they want and it can be beneficial to transmit live or still pictures in order to ease the solving of issues.

Furthermore, against the previous discussion, it is of great importance to emphasize that the idea of a classification of the programs of actions that are inscribed in the technology should not be misinterpreted as some kind technology determinism. Instead, we have showed that an ICT consists of a mixture of inscribed programs of actions that both allow considerable space for innovation, as well as notable limited space for innovation and flexibility. Hence, these programs of action are not fixed but need to be put into relation to the interpreter and the context. This implies that the ICT, in order to be manageable and an implementation and change able to forecast the ICT, has to be analyzed in its context and situation. Considerable action must be taken by management in the organization in order to balance the space of innovation to the possibilities to control and forecast.

5.1 Who Controls Spaces of Innovation?

As discussed, the programs of action have implications for different actor groups' possibilities to exercise power on the ICT-triggered change process and the space for innovation. In the cases studied, actor groups' possibilities to exercise power over the process shifted back and forth between designers, managers, and users over time and with regard to what dimension of programs of action are in focus (see Figure 1).

The shifting power is also a consequence of the spaces of interpretation given to, or taken by, different actors groups. A generic ICT gives users and management large spaces of interpretation, implying that use can be very disparate and leading to varying transformation of organizational units. On the other hand, if spaces for interpretation are limited, the organizational transformation can be unified, but the actors can refuse to use

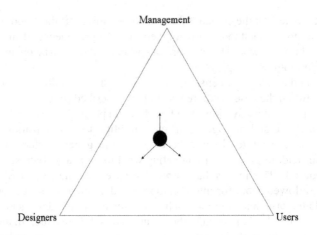

Figure 1. Shifting Power over ICT-Mediated Change Processes

the ICT due to the limited spaces for interpretation. However, in order to make the change process proceed and reach some kind of unified transformation of an organization, alliances are needed among actor groups from time to time. For example, management and users need to accept how ICT should be used, management needs to keep user spaces for innovation, for example, by investing in more equipment or funding support functions (see Linderoth 2007).

   To conclude, trying to delimit the space for innovation also delimits the development potential in the organization and it could also increase resistance to change while the power of the interpretations obviously is not in the hands of the user. On the other hand, a high grade of flexibility could result in such disparate use of the ICT that the overall aim of the implementation and change is jeopardized or that the matter of changing behavior and work procedures and any use of the ICT could be ignored without consequences. From a development and an innovation perspective, this is a dilemma.

References

Akrich, M. 1992. "The De-Scription of Technical Objects," in *Shaping Technology/Building Society*, W. E. Bijker and J. Law (eds.), Cambridge, MA: MIT Press, pp. 205-224.

Bashshur, R. L. 1995. "On the Definition and Evaluation of Telemedicine," *Telemedicine Journal* (2:1), pp. 19-30.

Berg, M. 1997. "Of Forms, Containers, and the Electronic Medical Record: Some Tools for a Sociology of the Formal," *Science, Technology, and Human Values* (22:4), pp. 403-423.

Boland Jr., R. J., Lyytinen, K., and Yoo, Y. 2007. "Wakes of Innovation in Project Networks: The Case of Digital 3-D Representations in Architecture, Engineering, and Construction," *Organization Science* (18),pp. 631-647.

Bridgman, T., and Willmott, H. 2006. "Institutions and Technology—Frames for Understanding Organizational Change: The Case of a Major ICT Outsourcing Contract," *The Journal of Applied Behavioral Science* (42:1), pp. 110-126.

Ciborra, C. U. 1996. "Introduction: What Does Groupware Mean for the Organizations Hosting It?," in *Groupware and Teamwork*, C. U. Ciborra (ed.), Chichester, UK: . John Wiley & Sons, pp. 1-19.

Davidson, E. 2006. "A Technological Frame Perspective on Information Technology and Organizational Change," *The Journal of Applied Behavioral Science* (42:1), pp. 23-39.

Elbanna, A. R. 2008. "Strategic Systems Implementation: Diffusion Through Drift," *Journal of Information Technology* (123:2), pp. 89-96.

Gunnarsson, S., Linde, A., and Loid, D. 2000. "Is Standardization Applicable to Project Managers of Multi-Project Companies?," in *Paradoxes of Project Collaboration in the Global Economy: Interdependence, Complexity and Ambiguity*, in *Proceedings of the IRNOP IV Conference: Paradoxes of Project Collaboration in the Global Economy: Interdependence, Comlexity and Ambiguity*, The International Research Network on Organizing by Projects, Sydney, Australia, January 9-12, pp. 136-146.

Hanseth, O., and Braa, K. 1998. "Technology as a Traitor: Emergent SAP Infrastructure in a Global Organization," in *Proceedings of the 19th International Conference on Information Systems*, R. Hirschheim, M. Newman, and J. I. DeGross (eds.), Helsinki, December, pp. 188-197.

Hanseth, O., and Monteiro, E. 1997. "Inscribing Behavior in Information Infrastructure Standards.," *Accounting, Management & Information Technology* (7:4), pp. 183-211.

Holmström, J., and Stadler, F. 2001. "Drifting Technologies and Multi-Purpose Networks: The Case of the Swedish Cashcard," *Information and Organization* (11:3), pp. 187-206.

Latour, B. 1992. "Where Are the Missing Masses? The Sociology of a Few Mundane Artifacts," in *Shaping Technology/Building Society*, W. E. Bijker and J. Law (eds.), Cambridge, MA: MIT Press, pp. 225-258.

Linderoth, H. C. J. 2000. *Från vision till integration - Infusion av telemedicin, en översättnings-process*, unpublished Ph.D. thesos, Umeå School of Business, Umeå University.

Linderoth, H. C. J. 2007. "Make Technology Invisible, or Keep it Visible: The Role of Technology in Intra-Organizational Transfer and Integration of Project Outcomes," in *Organizational Dynamics of Technology Based Innovation: Diversifying the Research Agenda*. T. McMaster, D. Wastell, E. Ferneley, and J. I. DeGross (eds.), Boston: Springer, pp. 267-283.

Linderoth, H. C. J., and Pellegrino, G. 2005. "Frames and Inscriptions—Tracing a Way to Understand IT-Dependent Change Projects," *International Journal of Project Management* (23:5), pp. 415-420.

Lundin, R. A., and Söderholm, A. 1995. "A Theory of the Temporary Organization," *Scandinavian Journal of Management* (11:4), pp. 437-455.

Monteiro, E. 2000. "Actor-Network Theory," in *from Control to Drift: The Dynamics of Corporate Information Infrastructure*, C. U. Ciborra (ed.), Oxford, UK: Oxford University Press, pp. 71-83.

Monteiro, E., and Hanseth O. 1995. "Social Shaping of Information Infrastructure: On Being Specific about Technology," in *Information Technology and Changes in Organizational Work*, W. J. Orlikowski, G. Walsham, M. R. Jones, and J. I. DeGross (eds.), London: . Chapman & Hall, pp. 325-343.

Orlikowski, W. J. "Improvising Organizational Transformation Over Time: A Situated Chagne Perspective," *Information Systems Research* (7:1), pp. 63-92.

Orlikowski, W. J., and Iacono, S. 2001. "Research Commentary: Desperately Seeking the 'IT' in IT Research – A Call to Theorizing the IT Artifact," *Information Systems Research* (12:2), pp. 121-134.

Orlikowski, W. J., and Gash, D. 1994. "Technological Frames: Making Sense of Information Technology in Organizations," *ACM Transactions on Information Systems* (12:2), pp. 174-207.

Orlikowski, W. J., and Yates, J. 2006. "ICT and Organizational Change – A Commentary," *The Journal of Applied Behavioral Science* (42:1), pp. 127-134.

Räisänen, C., and Linde, A. 2004. "Technologizing Discourse to Standardize Projects in Multi-Project Organizations: Hegemony by Consensus?," *Organization* (11), pp. 101-122.

Rosenberg, N. 2000. *Inside the Black Box.: Technology and Economics*, Cambridge, UK: Cambridge University Press.

About the Authors

Anneli Linde is based at Umeå School of Business, Umeå University, in Sweden. Her research focuses on the development, implementation, and use of IT-based management systems in multiproject organizations and she has several publications in this area. Anneli is currently completing her Ph.D. based on comprehensive case studies on ICT-mediated change processes. Anneli has extensive experience teaching management and leadership and obtained a position as lecturer at Umeå University. In addition, she currently holds a grant for researching the construction sector, focusing on the relation between ICT and sustainability and environmental issues. She can be reached by e-mail at anneli.lindeusbe.umu.se.

Henrik Linderoth, Ph.D., holds a position as assistant professor at Umeå School of Business, Umeå University. His research interest is primarily focused on ICT-triggered change processes and consequences of projects as a form for organizing activities in an organization. Henrik has done studies of ICT use in the health care sector and is currently studying ICT use in the building and construction sector. He can be reached by e-mail at henrik.linderoth@usbe.umu.se.

Part 5:

Open Innovation Experiences

13 DECIDING ON OPEN INNOVATION: An Exploration of How Firms Create and Capture Value with Open Source Software

Lorraine Morgan
University of Limerick
Limerick, Ireland

Patrick Finnegan
University College Cork
Cork, Ireland

Abstract   *Open innovation is a paradigm that proposes that firms can and should use external as well as internal innovations/ideas. A popular example of open innovation has been open source software (OSS). The key issues facing organizational decision makers considering OSS strategies is, how does the firm create value for the customer while simultaneously extracting value for itself? However, the adoption of OSS as part of an open innovation strategy is a recent phenomenon and many unanswered questions remain. Taking the viewpoint of seven IS/IT decision makers in European firms, this paper reveals how decision makers considered aspects of value creation, capture, and networking in making decisions on adopting open source software. The findings reveal that while decision makers look to open innovation for value creation and capture, there is still a desire to remain self reliant, resulting in collaborative design (of external innovations) rather than collaborative decision making with value network partners in relation to how such innovations would help create and capture value within firms.*

Keywords   Open innovation, open source software, value creation, value capture, value network

Please use the following format when citing this chapter:

Morgan, L., and Finnegan, P., 2008, in IFIP International Federation for Information Processing, Volume 287, Open IT-Based Innovation: Moving Towards Cooperative IT Transfer and Knowledge Diffusion, eds. León, G., Bernardos, A., Casar, J., Kautz, K., and DeGross, J. (Boston: Springer), pp. 229-246.

1   INTRODUCTION AND RESEARCH MOTIVATION

For most of the 20th century, innovation happened inside the business and companies rarely looked outside for new ideas or inventions (Tapscott and Williams 2005). According to Chesbrough (2004), a paradigm shift is taking place in how companies commercialize knowledge; characterized as a move from closed innovation to open innovation. Closed innovation is a view that successful innovation needs control and that firms need to be strongly self-reliant because of uncertainty with quality, availability, and capability of others' ideas. Chesbrough (2004) proposes that with the open innovation paradigm, firms can and should use external as well as internal ideas and that internal ideas can be taken to market through external channels, outside a firm's current business, to generate value. According to Chesbrough (2006), ideal businesses resist the "not invented here" and "not sold here" syndromes in favor of open innovation. They search outside their own companies for the best ideas, seeking input from other companies, including competitors, as well as from customers, suppliers, and vendors. Most importantly, new products are not the only tangible manifestation of open innovation. Services and process transformation are equally important facets, whether it is to create enhanced customer support or to support internal business efficiencies (British Telecom 2006). Gassman and Enkel (2004) identify three core open innovation processes: (1) the outside-in process, where a company's innovativeness can increase through the integration of suppliers, customers, and external knowledge sourcing, (2) the inside-out process, where companies can earn profits by bringing ideas to market and transferring ideas to the outside environment, and (3) the coupled process where companies can combine the outside-in and inside-out processes by working in alliance with complimentary partners where give and take is vital for success. Gassman and Enkel found that while companies choose one primary process, they often integrate some elements of the other.

A popular example of open innovation is open source software, as exemplified by the Linux operating system and Apache server. A formal definition of OSS, published by the Open Source Initiative, establishes that software can be called open source if it and its source code can be freely modified and redistributed (see http://www.opensource.org). This phenomenon involves thousands of programmers contributing to large and small scale projects where the central organizing principle is that the software remains free of most constraints on copying and use common to proprietary materials (Benkler 2002). As Gassman and Enkel state, "this principal drives the evolutionary development and improvement of the software" (p. 2). Furthermore, companies interested in an OSS approach can decide on any of the three underlying open innovation processes mentioned above. For example, in the past, companies such as HP and Sun have used an outside-in process by donating research and development to the Mozilla open source project while exploiting the pooled R&D and knowledge of all contributors (i.e., academics, user organizations, individual hobbyists, etc.) to facilitate the sale of related products. The result was that these firms maximized the returns of their innovation by concentrating on their own needs and then incorporating the shared browser technology into their own integrated systems (West and Gallagher 2006). Other companies like IBM have often used an inside-out approach as part of its OSS initiative that represented spinouts in the 1990s and, more recently, donated software patents to the OSS community (West and Gallagher 2006). In addition, the aforementioned companies have also integrated elements of the coupled process by successfully cooperating with universities, research institutes, etc. in both exploiting and sharing information and knowledge.

According to Agerfalk et al. (2005), the open source movement has pragmatically shifted the center of gravity toward a more business-friendly and hybrid concept, and, in commercial settings, OSS is rapidly transforming into a viable alternative to proprietary software. Indeed this accommodation with the commercial mainstream may be a harbinger of an end to the current dominance of a proprietary, closed source software model (Fitzgerald 2006). However, despite research carried by West and Gallagher (2006) and by West (2007), the use of OSS as part of an open innovation strategy is such a recent phenomenon that many unanswered questions still persist. Furthermore, existing research is based on the experiences of U.S. firms. The shifting of focus from ownership to the concept of openness requires a reconsideration of the processes that underlie value creation and value capture, and thus necessitate consideration of the issue at the level of a business model (Chesbrough and Appleyard 2007), although the consideration of such issues using value chain analysis (Porter 1985), transaction cost economics (Williamson 1981), and the resource-based view of the firm (Barney 1991) may also prove useful. However, such approaches are based on ownership and control as the key levers in achieving strategic success. Consequently, all focus largely within the firm, or within the value chain in which the firm is embedded, and by doing so take no notice of the potential value of external resources that are not owned by the firm in question (Chesbrough and Appleyard 2007).

Chesbrough (2003) asserts that firms need a business model to profit from innovation as a successful business model may offer more value to the customer or completely replace the old way of doing things (see Magretta 2002). According to Osterwalder and Pigneur (2002, p. 2) a business model can be defined as

> a description of the value a company offers to one or several segments of customers and the architecture of the firm and its network of partners for creating, marketing and delivering this value and relationship capital, in order to generate profitable and sustainable revenue streams.

For Osterwalder and Pigneur, a business model is "the missing link between strategy and business processes" (p. 3). West and Gallagher propose that the combination of shared production and low cost of OSS has resulted in firms reconsidering their proprietary business models and that the fundamental question for a firm's business model is, how does the firm create value for the customer while simultaneously extracting some of the value for itself? However, it has been found that the use of open source by firms generally begins in ways that does not disrupt their fundamental business model, or comes at a time when their existing business model is so threatened that they are forced to make radical changes (West and Gallagher 2006). In general, the comprehension of issues surrounding OSS business models appear inadequate. As Feller et al. (2006) found, much of the research in the area of OSS to date has instead focused on socio-cultural and software engineering issues. While researchers such as Hecker (2000), Koenig (2004), Krishnamurthy (2005), and Onetti and Capobianco (2005) have undertaken much research to refine and elaborate OSS business models, revenue generation has been the main focus for most of this research, neglecting other aspects of the business model such as the value component.

Prior research has identified three key elements of a business model: value creation, value capture, and a value network (Chesbrough 2006; Chesbrough and Rosenbloom 2002; Morris et al. 2005; Teece 18761 Shafer et al. 2005; West 2007). Open innovation explicitly incorporates the business model as the source of both value creation and value capture. However, Chesbrough (2006) argues that while open source shares the focus on value creation throughout the value chain, its proponents usually deny or downplay the importance of value capture. Value creation can be defined as a universal element of recent conceptions of a business model and entails identifying relevant customer segments, the value proposition for each, and how that business model will provide that value (West 2007). Value capture explains how a firm captures value from its value creation. Some of the key steps are to define a revenue model, ensuring the cost structure is consistent with the customer's perceived value and the portion that will be captured, and that firms establish durable external relationships with customers and third parties (West 2007). However, OSS has a lower formal appropriability than proprietary software because the source code is available for reuse and modification by competitors, complementors, and customers. It has been suggested that for firms utilizing OSS, "the business model depends on selling complementary goods or services to capture value, or leveraging tacit knowledge or other intangible sources of advantage over rivals" (West 2007, p. 179). In order to understand value creation and value capture in the context of OSS, Helander and Laine (2006) argue that value needs to be defined in nonmonetary as well as monetary terms. Open innovation also both enables and builds on interorganizational collaboration, often referred to as a value network (West and Gallagher 2006) or ecosystem (Adner 2006). Dahlander (2004) proposes that in addition to inter-organizational relations, it is relations with users and developers that constitute the OSS community that are important for the firm.

With the exception of West and Gallagher (2006) and West (2007), academic research on value creation, value capture, and value networks in OS strategies appears to be rather sparse. Furthermore, literature articulating the central characteristics of OSS that enable or hinder value creation and value capture is quite limited. This paper attempts to address this gap by first investigating the circumstances that motivate European firms to embrace an open innovation strategy such as OSS. Second, it will identify the characteristics of OSS that enable or impede a firm's business model to create and capture value. The role of the value network in creating and capturing value will also be explored. The paper is organized as follows. It begins by discussing the research objective and research method. The findings are then presented. The paper concludes that there are many characteristics that have the potential to achieve value creation, value capture, and a value network. However, there also exist many characteristics that have the potential to impede value creation and value capture. In addition, OSS offers a major example of how open innovation can change a business since collaborating as part of a value network appears to be a crucial source of both value creation and value capture.

2   RESEARCH OBJECTIVE AND METHOD

The objective of this study is to (1) examine the circumstances that motivate decision makers in commercial firms to embrace an OSS strategy and (2) identify the characteristics of OSS that enable or hinder value creation, value capture, and a value network. Due to the relatively novel phenomena being examined and the scarcity of empirical work in the area, the study was categorized as exploratory. In such circumstances, Marshall and Rossman (1989) suggest that either a case study or field study research methodology can be used. The researchers decided that a field study would be appropriate as it would facilitate the collection of rich data from a larger number of organizations and would form the basis for more focused research at a later stage. A stratified sample was used to give diversity in the sample (see Patton 1990). Data collection was carried out using semi-structured interviewing in seven companies (see Table 1). Each interview lasted between 45 minutes and 2 hours. Content analysis was undertaken using coding techniques proposed by Strauss and Corbin (1990). This approach recognizes that social phenomena are complex, and seeks to develop theory systematically in an intimate relationship with the data. This form of analysis facilitates the development of substantive theory without prior hypotheses (Baskerville and Pries-Heje 2001) and can be utilized in the absence of, or in conjunction with, existing theory. In the initial phase, *open coding* was used to determine the main ideas in each transcript. These ideas were then grouped by significant headings to reveal categories and subcategories. The next step involved *axial coding*, which is the process of relating categories to their subcategories. As a list of codes began to emerge, the analysis moved to a higher or more abstract level, looking for a relationship between the codes. Once a relationship had been determined, the focus returned to the data to question the validity of these relationships.

Table 1. Companies Studied

Name	Business	Extent of OSS Adoption	Respondent
Eircom Group PLC, Ireland	Telecommunications	Some use of OS products in technical support, e.g., JBoss application server, MySQL, but quite limited adoption	Technical Architecture Manager
Nokia Research Centre, Finland	Mobile Communications	Extensive use in telecommunications infrastructure and embedded applications	Head of Software Technology
Phillips Medical Systems, Netherlands	Supplier of medical equipment and devices	Limited; involved in some OS projects; hope to increase level of adoption	International Project Leader
Sony Computer Entertainment Europe, UK	Manufacturers and distributors of entertainment systems	Extensive use in servers, consumer products, etc.; increasing levels of adoption	Technical Specialist
St. Galler Tagblatt AG, Switzerland	Media	Extensive, entire SAP software environment	Chief Information Officer
Supertramp, UK	Manufacturing	Extensive (100% open source)	Technical Director
Vodafone, Spain	Mobile Communications	None; collaborating with others to create Linux platform for mobiles	R&D Engineer Head of R&D

3   FINDINGS

3.1   What Circumstances Motivate Decision Makers in Commercial Organizations to Embrace an OSS Strategy?

The study revealed that the circumstances that motivated decision makers to embrace or to consider embracing an OSS strategy varied. In the case of Supertramp, the technical director explained that prior to OSS adoption, booming sales meant their proprietary-based IT systems were becoming overloaded and customer service was suffering as a result. He pointed out that "the company's problem was that its market share was growing and the business was growing so rapidly...the systems that we were using just were not going to scale and the scalability was what was required." Microsoft, at the time, were bringing out a volume licensing program, which meant that the company was starting to feel the push to this upgrade path. As the technical director further explained, "We were looking really at quite a significant budget, something in the region of about £15,000. This was quite an expense but we were also struggling with scalability and reliability issues and they were probably contracting more value from the business than just facing the licensing costs." This finding tends to support those of West and Gallagher (2006) who proposed that the use of OSS by firms comes at a time when their existing business model is so threatened that they are forced then to make radical changes. This was one of the things that drove the decision to adopt OSS in the company because they knew they "could go from 10 to 40 users without any more licensing costs, proprietary software costs and that the system would more than likely deliver it" (Technical Manager, Supertramp). Similar to Supertramp's case, the CIO at St. Galler Tagblatt explained that the company was attracted to the enormous cost saving potential of OSS. Previous to OSS adoption, the company found the cost of software licensing and major hardware and software upgrades quite challenging. As part of an IT strategy in 2003, the company decided to migrate the existing SAP software environment and third-party system maintenance applications to Linux while implementing MaxDB as a cost-effective alternative to their previous database system. As the CIO in the company explained, "in this strategy we declared that we wanted to use Linux whenever possible and Windows when we had to. And we wanted the cheaper Unix but with the stability of Unix. And so SAP is running out of Linux since 2004 without any problems."

For SCEE, the technical specialist explained that open source software was not at the core of their business plan or activities (which revolve around developing and releasing Playstations and Playstation games, and the sale of software). Rather, the use of OSS in products arose out of consumer demand for the product (thousands of requests from open-source programmers who believed that this product could make a significant contribution). This finding is in line with Chesbrough's (2006) suggestion that one business model that makes good business sense is to be very open with technologies that are not inputs to the core activities of the firm but still are complementary. For SCEE, it can be said that customer perceptions were the value drivers for this company, thus one of their reasons for deciding to embrace OSS. As this technical specialist revealed, "They wanted this product, they wanted to be able to have Linux running on the machine and to be able to run OSS." However, it can also be suggested that the use of OSS by this firm began in such a way that it would not interfere with their core business model, thus supporting findings from West and Gallagher. This technical specialist further explained that the Linux kit was not really made as a significant revenue source for the firm, but rather "it was made with a sort of business plan that we would break even on it. What it would do is give people a chance to get familiar with our platform from a development point of view so that people who go into the industry to make PS2 software do a better job because they have had the chance, with little cost to themselves, to get familiar with our hardware. So it was more of an intellectual game than a financial one."

According to the head of Software and Technology at Nokia Research Centre, there are two major efforts where the company has embraced OSS. One concerns the tele-communications infrastructure and products where Linux is used as one of the primary platforms and the other is Linux embedded applications. The head of Software and Technology in this company pointed out that one of the main reasons for embracing OSS was top management's desire to learn more about the software (i.e., where it could be used and how). Another reason was that the company favored components that were developed by active communities and used by many. The project leader at Philips Medical Systems also revealed that while the company has limited adoption of OSS at present, it is inevitable that they will have OSS in their products in a few years because he viewed this as the only way to get all of the software that the company needs. He further explained that pulling open source tools in the imaging systems environment would be useful because the company could use them to provide code for more platforms, reducing the risk of lock-in. Presently there are some bottom-up initiatives underway and the company is currently looking at the business values and problems of introducing OSS. For Vodafone, the R&D engineer explained that while they have not yet adopted OSS, they are interested in it and see it as a new way of collaboration that will allow them to do more things from a technological point of view (e.g., develop a new operating system for mobile phones). The R&D department in this company has already begun projects in open source and they have established contact with members of the open source community.

In contrast to the above, the technical architecture manager at Eircom explained that there was no formal policy in the company around OSS adoption and that it "crept in by osmosis." This manager felt that OSS was not a viable business approach per se and viewed it only as a development model. As he explained, "It's not a question of OS versus proprietary. We want to introduce better quality software to meet our needs. We wouldn't really discriminate on the development model used and that's all OSS is in our books, a development model that produces generally very high quality software." He further explained that "you can stand over a proprietary solution, by and large, because you can see how well the company is funded and how much they're spending on R&D and where they are bringing the product to and why, what's driving them, and you can see their profitability and so on. And you can understand that that's a natural business model that we're all aware of. You can't see that in a lot of open source products, so you don't know where it's going to end up."

3.2 Value Creation

The study found that there were many characteristics of OSS that facilitated value creation for the companies. For Supertramp, the business processes were the value drivers and, thus, the focus on creating value was to improve the efficiencies of those business processes. Implementing OSS greatly enhanced the efficiency of their business processes, which in turn dramatically improved productivity and customer service. The lower costs associated with OSS were seen as very beneficial in this case. The technical director in the company explained that one of the advantages of implementing OSS was the ability "to utilize the flexibility of OSS and make it match the business process. And the low cost of it has meant that we could spend more of our budget on analyzing the business model in the first place." He further added that if the company had continued using proprietary systems, this would have resulted in more hardware and software upgrades, causing their investment in staff and staff capability to be significantly less than it is today. Similarly, the CIO at St. Galler Tagblatt also revealed that the total cost of ownership for the company is dramatically lower than that of their previous proprietary Unix environment and calculated savings of €340,000 a year as a result of moving to Linux.

According to West (2007) customers expect a richer whole product solution (e.g. , integration, customization, and support). One mechanism for creating some value is the use of complementary assets (see Teece 1986). The technical specialist at SCEE pointed out that the lower costs associated with OSS facilitated the creation of an infrastructure that encourages participation and collaboration between the company and their customers. The company provides support websites (all running on OS based software) that give support to their customers for PS2, PSP, and PS3. As the technical specialist explained, "The whole support infrastructure that we have for developers working on games for those machines is based around our support infrastructure, our websites, our newsgroups, instant messaging services, and those are all running on OS based software." She further explained that the Linux for PS3 provides an option for third-party system software to be installed on the PS3 system instead of the system provided by SCEE, thus leveraging its value creation to customers. The head of Software and Technology at Nokia Research Centre also pointed out that the company finds it beneficial to use OSS in some of their consumer products because, in addition to saving time and money, it allows the company to shape their products according to market needs. The use of OSS in their product creates value to the customers as it offers them upgraded software, enhanced features, and improved performance. For some of its products, Nokia releases the code to the open source community, enabling both knowledge sharing and collaboration, in addition to creating value that is seen as beneficial to the community. In this way, the company not only counts on third-party developers adopting them widely, but also innovating on the core technology. In addition, the head of Software and Technology at Nokia Research Centre considered the low cost of OSS extremely valuable as it allowed the company to share expenses with other companies with whom they had made joint ventures, thus enabling more value creation in the company.

The quality, reliability, security, and performance of OSS were also perceived by all of the companies as particularly important characteristics in facilitating value creation. For example, respondents pointed out that the quality of developers, the enhanced quality from peer reviews, and the quality of OSS tools and software were superb, hence enabling their respective companies to create more value. In terms of the quality of OSS packages, the technical specialist at SCEE explained that they had many examples where they were able to pick up something that was an already established and proven tool and a serious contender with other licensed software alternatives in the market. This in turn gave the company the ability to get an entire platform of functionality together by using software that had "been reviewed and used in anger by other people" (Technical Specialist, SCEE). Similarly, the technical director at Supertramp found the quality of support, available knowledge, and willingness of the open source community quite remarkable and pointed out that he did not see that level of support availability from proprietary companies. However, while the technical architecture of Eircom viewed quality as one of the benefits of OSS, he also stated that this could only be applied to top-tier, mature, open source products like Linux, Apache, and MySQL. Similarly, the head of Software and Technology at the Nokia Research Centre agreed that some open source products like Linux have established themselves over the years but many are not as mature.

With regard to the reliability of OSS, the technical manager at Supertramp explained that "when they brought their enterprise resource planning system server down, which was running RedHat Linux, for a hardware upgrade, it had 1,011 days of time on it as it never had to be rebooted." Also in relation to the stability and security of OSS, it was found that in comparison to proprietary packages, there was no need to install anti-virus software on everything as there was no need for it. As the head of Software and Technology at Nokia Research Centre explained, "In terms of security, there are advantages because there are less viruses and worms and whatnot around compared to Windows." The technical specialist at SCEE also pointed out that "we know people are able to see how the software works, what the back end is like and really we are quite big subscribers to not going for security through obscurity but security through proper methods." In terms of performance, the technical director for Supertramp explained that by switching from Windows to Samba, the performance capacity over the networks for file sharing greatly improved. He also found that their Linux server could handle 25 or 26 clients in comparison to 14 or 15 on Windows. Similarly, the CIO of St. Galler Tagblatt discovered that by implementing OSS, the batch jobs in their SAP environment were three to nine times faster than with Unix.

However, it became apparent that there are many characteristics of OSS that have the potential to impede value creation. For example, it was found that one of the biggest obstacles to value creation was the lack of ownership issue. One likes to know that if there is a problem, they can pick up the phone and this problem can be analyzed and fixed. For example, the project leader at Philips Medical systems revealed that "if our developers cannot find the source of the problem, then it may take longer than they expected. The history of OSS tells differently but formally there is no one to go to…who is responsible for what is less clear in an open source environment." However, contrary to this, the technical director at Supertramp believed that "that's a complete façade because if you look at any end user license agreement, the first thing that they do in an license agreement, proprietary or open source, is waive all responsibility and warranty. So I think that that's just the marketing spiel that we see in breeding fear, uncertainty and doubt." The majority of the companies considered the lack of user support to be a real impediment to creating value. Some of the companies have teams of talented technicians that can cover the support risk internally. However, this is not always an option for many of the smaller organizations or very large organizations that have problems finding the right staff and competencies required to carry out this support. The technical manager at Eircom explained that, to solve the support problem, "We aligned ourselves with a third party support supplier.…In other words, we have shouldered the risk on to them. What that gives us though, in fairness, is expert support services from a competent supplier who is active in the open source community and familiar with those individual products and is in fact working with them on a daily basis in the context of their own product development."

Other issues with the potential to hinder value creation included compatibility issues and poor documentation. For example, the technical specialist at SCEE mentioned that compatibility of OSS with current tasks of developers was a concern as they sometimes were uncomfortable and unhappy with having to use OS based operating systems packages. The technical architecture manager at Eircom also pointed out that there are often issues with the compatibility of OSS products with the current technology in the company. He pointed out that the company was like a brass clock and explained, "It has to run smoothly and it has to run in a predictable fashion. When you open up the brass clock, everything inside it must be compatible…they must all be of an industrial strength. Also for a clock to be efficient, it needs to have the right number of parts in it….So when you look at the likes of open source, because you can acquire for free or very close to it…select a product and then download it and install it and so on. The issue that arises in here, for example, is that we end up with a lot of moving parts. More than we need and overlapping parts, competing parts, not the place to be." In terms of poor documentation, the IT specialist at SCEE explained that, "If you try and find a software package to access database or templating layer or whatever you are looking for, you'll find a myriad of solutions that will claim to meet your needs and some of them will have died in development some time ago."

3.3 Value Capture

Various attributes of OSS also enabled the companies to capture value in different ways. For example, the technical manager in Supertramp explained that by migrating to OSS, in addition to dramatic cost savings, the company "didn't have any data corruption and all of a sudden we had all of our data in one place, both financial and customer relationship management. It really transformed…the business process." Because the migration to OSS was so successful, the company decided to create a spinout company (i.e., the process of reaching external markets through external business ventures, with the explicit intention of providing reliable and effective IT solutions to other businesses). According to West (2007), firms have opportunities to release more value from their technologies by situating them outside the firm, but at the same time maintaining corporate involvement. Focusing on an inside-out process by transferring ideas outside the company's boundaries had clear advantages for Supertramp in terms of both value creation and value capture as they were able to leverage their experience with OSS to meet a new customer requirement, thus opening up a whole new revenue stream. OSS had already proven itself in the company and many of its staff members were experienced technically with the software, thus reducing the risk of failure in this new venture.

For SCEE, the value capture in utilizing OSS was "the fact that we can do some of the research using existing OSS tools, create some of the products based on OSS systems, and run out support sites using OSS is an extra saving that we would lose otherwise" (Technical Specialist, SCEE). By using OSS, the company could better afford an in-house team of website developers who were able to create the custom development that the company needed to increase the value of their services to developers. Therefore, the quality of the product was better and produced in less time and with fewer resources than it would otherwise need. For this company, using OSS had a direct effect on their ability to acquire and retain a new customer segment, in addition to managing ongoing relationships with them. This technical manager also explained that the company captures superior technical knowledge and pointed out that "we have been able to find staff to bring on to the team who have had experience in some of the packages that we are using, which is a great benefit." She further explained that the open platform created by the company for its PS3 product may lead to some interesting opportunities as well as aiding the technical development of people who join their industry in the future. For Nokia, the head of Software and Technology explained that the company captures value as the use of OSS in their products saves time and increases the profits of sale through money saved on software components. Working as part of a community also provides the company with access to code and engineers outside of their own development team. It is evident that both SCEE and Nokia captured value by focusing on an outside-in process where external knowledge gained from customers and the OSS community was integrated in their product development.

The escape from vendor lock-in was also seen as an important trait of OSS that enables value capture. The head of R&D at Vodafone explained that this would be one of the reasons for embracing an open innovation strategy like OSS because, he pointed out, "Every time we use a piece of software from another company, for every time that software is used, we have to pay them a certain amount of money. That's killing our margin." The technical director at Supertramp was also pleased with the sense of control in being able to change things as and when they wanted to without being forced to do so. As he explained, "One of the problems that you come across with a proprietary infrastructure is that your proprietary vendors tend to be putting their software and their systems on a release cycle and they tend to want to push you into continuing with updates and moving forward on a treadmill that suits them as the supplier." The flexibility allowed by OS licences was viewed as quite significant in capturing value for the majority of the companies because it had a dramatic impact on reducing capital expenditure, in particular for the companies that had adopted OSS. The fact that OSS encourages innovation was also viewed as advantageous in capturing value as access to the source code produces more ideas and creates opportunities for more innovation and creativity. As the technical director of Supertramp explained, "It's very straightforward to be innovative when you have access to all the code...the ability to be able to think about what can be done in the business system...now I can actually go deep into the core of my systems and I can make the systems do that because I can write into it. And that means we do innovate." Again, all of the companies found the flexibility of use associated with OSS extremely beneficial in terms of value capture, facilitating changes and customization, allowing for mixing and matching of components used, facilitating experimentation, and permitting freedom of choice in new server hardware.

However, there were also some characteristics of OSS that were viewed as impediments to value capture. For example, three of the companies mentioned that the idea of giving away the source code might be perceived by others in their respective companies as a hurdle to capturing value. As the head of R&D at Vodafone pointed out, "You know if we were to share—it's one asset for killing an idea....Somebody will have that great idea what that new thing is...that somebody could be inside Vodafone. Basically we should protect that and we cannot give that away." According to the project leader at

Philips Medical Systems, there are still many people in the company nervous about this issue but added that there are certain parts that can be given away without any problem. Difficulties in finding the right staff and developing the competencies to work with OSS were also seen as potential obstacles to capturing value. For example, the head of Software and Technology at Nokia revealed that the company finds it difficult to locate top quality staff and competencies to work with OSS, particularly where the company is attempting to embed OSS into their products and technologies. He added that, for application development, there is no problem finding staff, but for the type of work that the Nokia Research Centre is carrying out, the staff need to be well versed in OSS. Likewise, the head of R&D at Vodafone explained that the ability to create and develop new competencies requires a different way of thinking because OSS will be new to them. Another impediment to capturing value was the lack of roadmaps associated with an OSS product and its life cycle. For example, the technical infrastructure manager at Eircom believed that it was difficult to see any strategic direction for the vast majority of the products that are available in OSS. He also added that most OSS products were built to either displace an existing product or to solve a particular problem and, therefore, most of them had no strategic intent. This, he pointed out, could cause problems because as a team moves on to greater and more challenging technical projects, the product itself may not move one iota from where it currently is.

3.4 Value Network

The majority of the companies have established quite successful value networks, enabling both value creation and value capture. These networks have been extremely beneficial in terms of the high levels of knowledge and know-how being communicated and the open, transparent process in which the interaction takes place. Further, companies like Nokia Research Centre, SCEE, and Supertramp have integrated elements of the coupling process (i.e., combination of an outside-in and inside-out process), which has been a key success factor for them. For example, the head of Software and Technology at Nokia acknowledged the value in creating OSS in collaboration with others. As he explained, "We and other companies have done quite a lot in trying to make joint ventures or joint exercises around open source....we made a joint effort to enhance Linux with some features that are important for the telecom infrastructure." The company also works with communities to enhance components and develop them further. One such example is the Eclipse Foundation, an open source community whose membership includes IBM, Hewlett Packard, and Intel. This consortium is focused on creating an ecosystem that enhances, promotes, and cultivates an extensible development platform with complementary products, services, and capabilities. Nokia plans to use the Eclipse tools platform widely in its tools portfolio and is comfortable cooperating with some of their competitors to further develop and drive adoption of this shared technology.

SCEE has built up quite a significant customer base of its Linux for Playstation products and in this way benefits from extensive suggestions and feedback, which increases the value of their product. As the technical specialist explained, "We get lots of feature requests that come in and a lot of quite significant add-ons that they want us to provide." This technical specialist also explained that they had successfully collaborated with another company to produce their Linux for PS3 product. The Technical

Manager at Supertramp also outlined how its spinout company has collaborated with other companies to deliver state of the art technology systems. Similarly, Philips Medical Systems described how they have a number of collaborative projects with other firms and academic institutions. Presently, the company is one of 19 partners, including Nokia and Siemens, in the Eureka ITEA programs, which deals with OSS in a distributed development setting and is looking at business processes as well as technical processes. The R&D engineer at Vodafone also felt that "OSS is a new way of collaboration between people." The company has successfully collaborated with the Spanish government, who has funded them in their effort to develop a Linux mobile platform with other companies that include Motorola and Samsung.

4 CONCLUSION

We have examined the factors that affected the decision to adopt OSS as part of an open innovation strategy in seven European firms (see Table 2). This examination used a business model framework as it represents the architectural/logical design that connects a firm's strategy with its operational activities. Consequently, we consider it a useful lens to examine how decision makers reconcile strategic directions on open innovation with the operational aspects of adopting a particular open innovation strategy such as OSS. Consistent with findings from West and Gallagher (2006), it was obvious from the study that the use of open source by several of the firms began in a way that would not disrupt their core business model, as was the case with Sony Computer Entertainment Europe, or came at a time when their existing business model was under threat, forcing radical changes, as with Supertramp. However, it was apparent that the decision to embrace open source software proved very beneficial for the companies in which it has been implemented.

Table 2. Circumstances that Motivated Firms to Embrace an OSS Strategy

Factor	Description
Low Cost	Attracted by cost saving potential of OSS in relation to licensing and hardware/software upgrades
Scalability/Quality	Embraced OSS because of scalability and reliability issues with proprietary based IT systems
Staff Development	Could invest more resources in staff training and development
Consumer Demand	Customers wanted OSS products running on their machines
Desire of Top Management	Top management wanted to learn more about software (i.e., where it could be used and how)
OSS Components	Preference for components developed by active communities
Reduced Risk of Lock-in	Could use open source tools to provide code for more platforms, thus reducing the risk of lock-in
New way of collaboration	OSS is viewed as a new way of collaboration with other companies, OSS community, government, etc.

Additionally, it was found that there are many characteristics of OSS that enable firms' business models to create and capture value. For example, some defining characteristics that help achieve value creation include low cost, quality, and performance, while attributes such as escape from vendor lock-in, encouraging innovation, and flexibility of use enable companies to capture value. It was also found that firms adopt or take interest in open innovation strategies like OSS in order to facilitate and enhance their capacity to create and capture value to the customer (see Table 3). For example, Supertramp utilized the software to improve their business processes, thus creating value in the form of improved customer support. This finding also contributes to previous studies on OSS in the context of open innovation that generally tend to be predisposed toward product innovations and ignore innovations to improve processes or business efficiencies.

For several of the companies, OSS was also a way of entering markets and acquiring new customers. Incorporating OSS into their products created value to the customers who believed the software could make a distinctive contribution. The value creation included delivering enhanced products and improved performance, in addition to providing complementary assets to customers (e.g., support infrastructure). Deciding on an outside-in process has proved successful for companies like SCEE and Nokia Research

Table 3. How Companies Create and Capture Value

	For Company	For Customer
Value Creation	• Enhanced efficiency of business processes leading to improved quality and productivity • Reduced susceptibility to viruses, etc. • Ability to acquire new customer segments/meet customer requirements • Allows more investment in staff development/training • Lower TCO • Enables knowledge sharing/collaboration with communities, customers, etc. • Facilitates joint ventures with other companies	• Improved customer service/satisfaction • Enhanced software, upgraded features and improved performance • Provision of complementary services (e.g., support infrastructure, third-party system • Increased participation/collaboration with company
Value Capture	• Creation of spin-out company • Captures superior technical knowledge • Saves time, reduces capital expenditure and increases profits • Access to code and engineers creates more opportunities for innovation/creativity • Escape from vendor lock-in • Flexibility of use permits freedom of choice, customization, experimentation etc.	
Value Network	• Cooperation/collaboration with communities (e.g., Eclipse) • Joint ventures with companies • Collaboration with customers, government, academic institutions and other companies	

Table 4. Impediments to Value Creation and Value Capture

Impediments to Value Creation	Description	Impediments to Value Capture	Description
Lack of ownership	Inability to hold someone responsible or accountable for problems	Finding staff/ competencies	Often difficult to find top quality staff and develop competencies to work with OSS
Lack of support	No safety net as there is no support or company to back it up. Companies may need to seek out available skills and services which can be difficult and costly	Lack of road-maps with OSS products	Makes it difficult for companies to see any strategic direction with OSS
Poor documentation	Documentation outdated or may have died in development	Access to the source code	Some discomfort with releasing source code for products
Compatibility Issues	Compatibility problems with current technology, skills and tasks		

Centre in terms of value capture. As well as saving time and money, nonmonetary gains such as the technical knowledge captured were s viewed as extremely beneficial for these companies. In addition, companies like Supertramp that choose an inside-out process as part of their open innovation strategy captured value through the creation of a spinout company. It was also quite obvious in the study that OSS is a compelling example of how companies can manage a value network to create and combine internal and external innovations. In this case, many of the companies have integrated elements of a coupled process. For example, companies like Nokia Research Centre and SCEE acknowledged the value in collaborating with other companies and OSS communities and felt there were many opportunities to be gained from a value network in terms of value creation and capture. Working as part of a value network enabled several of the companies to capture value in the form of competencies and tacit knowledge that in turn created superior value for the customer. However, impediments, such as those summarized in Table 4, have the potential to hinder both value creation and capture.

In conclusion, it is evident that the decision to embrace an open innovation strategy such as OSS is most highly influenced by the potential to create and capture value within the firm. It is also apparent that the issue of external collaboration with value network members is critical to creating and capturing value with an open innovation strategy. Nevertheless, it appears that value network collaboration centers on collaborative design rather than collaborative decision making on open innovation initiatives. This suggests that while firms seek to embrace open innovation strategies, they remain strongly influenced by the desire to remain self reliant, a characteristic of the closed innovation paradigm. Finally, this study has contributed to understanding decision making on the adoption of open innovation strategies by (1) examining the circumstances that motivate decision makers to embrace an OSS strategy, (2) investigating the characteristics of OSS that enable or hinder value creation, value capture, and a value network, (3) revealing the various ways in which value is both created and captured, and (4) highlighting the importance of collaborating as part of a value network. However, the findings reported here are based on a small sample of firms so it remains to be seen how they would replicate over a more wide-ranging sample in other European countries. In addition, the study did not take into consideration variables such as organizational size, structure, and culture. Therefore, the area would benefit from further research.

Acknowledgments

This work is supported by LERO – the Irish Software Engineering Research Center, the European Commission through the FP6 project OPAALS (project no. 034824), and the Irish Research Council for the Humanities and Social Sciences (IRCHSS).

References

Adner, R. 2006. "Match Your Innovation Strategy to Your Innovation Ecosystem," *Harvard Business Review* (84:4), pp. 98-107.
Agerfalk, P. J., Deverell, A., Fitzgerald, B., and Morgan, L. 2005. "Assessing the Role of Open Source Software in the European Secondary Software Sector: A Voice from Industry," *Proceedings of the First International Conference on Open Source Systems*, Genova, Italy, July 11-15, pp. 82-87.
Barney, J. B. 1991. "Firm Resources and Sustained Competitive Advantage," *Journal of Management* (17), pp. 99-120.
Baskerville, R., and Pres-Heje, J. 2001. "Racing the E-Bomb: How the Internet is Redefining Information Systems Development Methodology," in *Realigning Research and Practice in Information Systems Development: The Social and Organizational Perspective*, N. L. Russo, B. Fitzgerald, and J. I. DeGross (eds.), Boston: Kluwer Academic Publishers, pp. 49-68.
Benkler, Y. 2002. "Coase's Penguin, or, Linux and *The Nature of the Firm*," *Yale Law Journal* (112:3), pp. 369-446.
British Telecom. 2006. "Embracing Open Innovation: A New Approach to Creating Sustainable Value," White Paper (available from www.btglobalservices.com).
Chesbrough, H. 2003. *Open Innovation: The New Imperative for Creating and Profiting from Technology*, Boston: Harvard Business School Press.
Chesbrough, H. 2004. "Managing Open Innovation," *Research & Technology Management* (47:1), pp. 23-26.
Chesbrough, H. 2006. *Open Business Models: How to Thrive in the New Innovation Landscape*, Boston: Harvard Business School Press.
Chesbrough, H., and Appleyard, M. 2007. "Open Innovation and Strategy," *California Management Review* (50:1), pp. 57-76.
Chesbrough, H., and Rosenbloom, R. S. 2002. "The Role of the Business Model in Capturing Value from Innovation: Evidence from Xerox Corporation's Technology Spin-Off Companies," *Industrial and Corporate Change* (11:3), pp. 529-555.
Chesbrough, H., Vanhaverbeke, W., and West, J. 2006. *Open Innovation: Researching a New Paradigm*, New York: Oxford University Press.
Dahlander, L. 2004. "Appropriating Returns from Open Innovation Processes: A Multiple Case Study of Small Firms in Open Source Software," unpublished paper, Chalmers University of Technology, Gothenburg, Sweden (http://opensource.mit.edu/papers/ dahlander.pdf).

Feller, J., Finnegan, P., Kelly, D., and MacNamara, M. "Developing Open Source Software: A Community-Based Analysis of Research," in *Social Inclusion: Societal and Organizational Implications for Information Systems*, E. M. Trauth, D. Howcroft, T. Butler, B. Fitzgerald, and J. I. DeGross (eds.), Boston: Springer, pp. 261-278.

Fitzgerald, B. "The Transformation of Open Source Software," *MIS Quarterly* (30:3), pp. 587-598.

Gassman, O., and Enkel, E. 2004. "Towards a Theory of Open Innovation: Three Core Process Archetypes," in *Proceedings of the R&D Management Conference*, Lisbon, Portugal, July 6-9 (http://www.alexandria.unisg.ch/Publikationen/274).

Hecker, F. 2000. "Setting Up Shop: The Business of Open Source Software," unpublished paper (online at http://www.hecker.org/writings/setting-up-shop.html).

Helander, N., and Martin-Vahvanen, H. 2006. "Multidisciplinary Views to Open Source Research," eBRC Research Reports 33, Tampere University of Technology and University of Tampere (available from http://www.ebrc.info).

Koenig, J. 2006. "Seven Open Source Business Strategies for Competitive Advantage," *IT Manager's Journal*, March 14 (http://www.riseforth.com/pdfs/Seven-Open-Source-Business-Strategies-JCK.pdf).

Krishnamurthy, S. 2005. "An Analysis of Open Source Business Models," in *Perspectives on Free and Open Source Software*, in J., Feller, B., Fitzgerald, S. Hissam, and K. Lakhani (eds.), Cambridge, MA: MIT Press, pp. 279-296.

Marshall, C., and Rossman, G. 1989. *Designing Qualitative Research*, Newbury Park, CA: Sage Publications.

Magretta, J. 2002. "Why Business Models Matter," *Harvard Business Review* (80:5), pp. 86-92.

Morris, M., Schindehutte, M., and Allen, J. 2005. "The Entrepreneur's Business Model: Toward a Unified Perspective," *Journal of Business Research* (58:6), pp. 726-735.

Onetti, A., and Capobianco, F. 2005. "Open Source and Business Model Innovation. The Funambol Case," in *Proceedings of the First International Conference on Open Source Systems*, Genova, Italy, July 11-15, pp. 224-227.

Osterwalder A., and Pigneur 2002. Y. "An e-Business Model Ontology for Modeling e-Business," in *Proceedings of the 15th Bled Electronic Commerce Conference*, Bled, Slovenia, June 17-19 (http://www.hec.unil.ch/yp/Pub/02-Bled.pdf).

Patton, M. Q. 1990. *Qualitative Evaluation and Research Methods*, Newbury Park, CA: Sage Publications.

Porter, M. E. 1985. *Competitive Advantage*, New York: The Free Press.

Shafer, S. M., Smith, J. H., and Linder, J. C. 2005. "The Power of Business Models," *Business Horizons* (48), pp. 199-207.

Strauss, A., and Corbin, J. 1990. *Basics of Qualitative Research: Grounded Theory Procedures and Techniques*, Newbury Park, CA: Sage Publications.

Tapscott, D., and Williams, A. 2005. "Realizing the Power of Innovation Webs," *Optimizemag.com*, December (http://www.cioindex.com/nm/articlefiles/2776-Optimize_InnovationWebs.pdf).

Teece, D. J. 1986. "Profiting from Technological Innovation: Implications for Integration, Collaboration, Licensing and Public Policy," *Research Policy* (15:6), pp. 285-305.

Williamson, O. E. 1981. "The Modern Corporation: Origins, Evolution, Attributes," *Journal of Economic Literature* (19:4), pp. 1537-1568.

West, J. 2007. "Value Capture and Value Networks in Open Source Vendor Strategies," in *Proceedings of the 40th Annual Hawaii International Conference on System Sciences*, Los Alamitos, CA: IEEE Computer Society Press.

West, J., and Gallagher, S. 2006. "Challenges of Open Innovation: The Paradox of Firm Investment in Open-Source Software," *R&D Management* (36:3), pp. 319-331.

About the Authors

Lorraine Morgan is a project manager at the University of Limerick, Ireland, where she has worked on several research projects on open source software. She is currently pursuing a Ph.D. in Management Information Systems at University College Cork, Ireland. Her research interests include open source software business models, open innovation, and open source software adoption. Lorraine can be reached at lorraine.morgan@ul.ie.

Patrick Finnegan holds a Ph.D. from the University of Warwick, England, and is currently a Statutory Lecturer in Management Information Systems at University College Cork, Ireland. His research interests include electronic business and IS strategy. He research appears in various journals and conference proceedings including *Information Systems Research, The Information Systems Journal, The Journal of Information Technology, The International Journal of Electronic Commerce, Information Technology & People, Database, Electronic Markets,* The European Conference on Information Systems, and the International Conference on Information Systems. Patrick can be reached at P.Finnegan@ucc.ie.

14   KNOWLEDGE DIFFUSION IN ERP DEVELOPMENT: The Case of Open Source ERP Downloads

Björn Johansson
Center for Applied ICT
Copenhagen Business School
Frederiksberg, Denmark

Abstract   *This paper reports on an investigation of challenges in enterprise resource planning systems (ERPs) development. The investigation, conducted as interviews with executives at a major ERP software vendor, identified six challenges when developing future ERPs. The challenges are then related to a question of knowledge sharing in ERP development. The question is, can downloads of open source ERPs be seen as a knowledge sharing activity with the potential to decrease the gap between ERP developers and users of ERPs? From identified challenges and by discussing reasons for the high attention and the high numbers of download of open source ERPs, the article presents some conclusions that could act as input for future research. The paper aims at building a foundation for the basic question: In what way could knowledge sharing in ERP development be improved? The main conclusion is that challenges for future development of ERPs addressed by proprietary ERP software vendors could be one reason for the high attention among developers of open source ERPs.*

Keywords   Enterprise resource planning systems, ERP, knowledge sharing, open source ERP, systems development

1   INTRODUCTION

In the past decade, we have seen an explosive of interest in enterprise resource planning systems (ERPs) as well as in free and open source software (FOSS) systems.

Please use the following format when citing this chapter:

Johansson, B., 2008, in IFIP International Federation for Information Processing, Volume 287, Open IT-Based Innovation: Moving Towards Cooperative IT Transfer and Knowledge Diffusion, eds. León, G., Bernardos, A., Casar, J., Kautz, K., and DeGross, J. (Boston: Springer), pp. 247-259.

The paper presents some of the challenges in ERP development and relates these challenges to open source ERPs attention. This is interesting at least for two reasons. First, the open source development model has changed during the past few years and the question is, how do the "new" open source development models influence future development of ERPs? Second, software vendors of proprietary ERPs face some challenges, which they need to take care of if they are to be able to stay in business in the future. The question arises of whether or not open source can serve as a useful input for figuring out how to manage future challenges. However, the basic question discussed in the paper is, can downloads of open source ERPs be seen as a knowledge sharing activity in ERP development? The paper will discuss this issue by comparing it to the reasons an individual software developer works in an open source development project and relate that to the challenges an ERP software vendor suggests future ERP developers will face.

The rest of the paper is organized in the following way: Section 2 introduces the subject by defining enterprise resource planning systems (ERPs). Section 3 then describes challenges identified and the research method used to identify them. Section 4 discusses open source ERPs and describes its status using data about open source ERP downloads. The penultimate section discusses reasons developers could have for downloading open source ERPs by relating these to the identified challenges. The final section of the paper offers suggestions for future research related to the discussion about knowledge sharing in ERP development.

2   ENTERPRISE RESOURCE PLANNING SYSTEMS

Enterprise resource planning systems have received a lot of attention in the past few years and have generated a number of reviews (e.g., Botta-Genoulaz et al. 2005; Esteves and Pastor 2001; Esteves and Bohorquez 2007; Shehab et al. 2004). ERPs are often defined as standardized packaged software designed with the aim of integrating the entire value chain in an organization (Lengnick-Hall et al. 2004; Rolland and Prakash 2000). Wier et al. (2007) argue that ERPs aim to integrate business processes and information and communications technologies into a synchronized suite of procedures, applications, and metrics that transcend the boundaries of the firm. Kumar and Van Hillegersberg (2000) say ERPs originated in the manufacturing industry, where the first generation of ERPs was introduced. Development of first-generation ERPs was an inside-out process, going from standard inventory control packages, to material requirements planning, material resources planning, and then further on expanding it to a software package aiming at supporting the entire organization (second-generation ERPs). According to Møller (2005), this evolved software package, labeled ERP II, could be described as the next generation enterprise systems. This evolution has increased the complexity both of ERP usage and development. The complexity comes from the fact that ERPs are systems meant to perform both interorganizational as well as intra-organizational integration, as well as integrating all business processes into a one-suite package (Koch 2001). ERPs, as well as the way organizations use them, have changed significantly. These changes also influence the way ERPs are developed and sold. The ERP market is prone to change, impacting not only the stakeholders in the ERP value-chain (Ifinedo and Nahar 2007; Somers and Nelson 2004), but also how these stakeholders gain competitive advantage. An organization no longer receives competitive advantage by just implementing an ERP (Karimi et al. 2007; Kocakulah et al. 2006), one reason being that ERPs focus on best practices. However, from the vendors' perspective, finding the "right" requirements and implementing these could be seen as input to competitive advantage. Downloads of open source ERPs could be an activity in which developers participate in order to increase their own knowledge about ERP development and thereby gain competitive advantage.

When reviewing the existing literature on ERPs, a major part of the research was found to be on implementation, and the main problem presented was the misfit between ERP functionality and business requirements. Soh et al. (2000) describe this as a common problem when adopting software package. The problem of "misfit" means that there is a gap between the functionality offered by the package and the functionality required by the adopting organization, a definite knowledge gap caused by the weak knowledge sharing in ERP development projects. Can open source ERPs solve this problem? The next section describes challenges identified from interviews with executives in a software vendor organization, building the base for our later discussion on the ways open source ERP development projects could be seen as a knowledge sharing activity.

3   CHALLENGES IN ERP DEVELOPMENT

This section reports briefly on an interview study done with eight executives of an ERP software vendor organization. The interviews were conducted at the vendor's offices. The interviewees have different roles, focusing on the different ERP products in the vendor's portfolio. The eight interviews lasted between 1.5 and 2 hours. The respondents were asked to describe what they see as potential problems when developing future ERPs. Follow-up questions were asked but no specific questions were prepared beforehand. The participating researchers' notes were collected and these notes acted were used to generate a summary of potential problems. The summary was analyzed for patterns, with the patterns identifying a number of problems raised by the respondents during the interviews. The analysis, which could be described as a content analysis (Krippendorff 2004), was done by asking the following questions: What problem (or problems) is the respondents talking about? At what problem was the solution described by the respondent aimed? These questions were asked because the respondents in their descriptions often referred to problems or solutions not yet completed. The analysis also asked: What could we learn from the problem described as well as from the solution? The objective of the interviews was to identify challenges in the development of future ERPs. Six areas describing challenges in ERP development were identified.

3.1   Challenge Area 1: Requirements Gathering

One of the major concerns when developing future ERPs is the time from feature identification to implementation. This challenge indicates that there is a need for an improved process for requirements management. This process should deal with the entire chain from identification of new requirements by the end-users to presenting them to the developers so they can be implemented shortly after identification. This has a clear connection to scalability and flexibility of the ERP system. Based on this, the basic problem is that it takes too long from identification of a new feature to its implementation. Another problem is whether the implemented requirements are the "correct" requirements. A summary of this challenge area is that there are deficiencies in the process for requirements management in ERP development.

3.2 Challenge Area 2: ERP Implementation

Another issue in the development of ERPs is the trade-off between a standard product and a customizable product. This is closely related to questions regarding implementation and the need for an improved process for implementation. There is also a need to clarify the relation between customization and the costs for maintenance of ERPs that are highly customized. In other words, there is a need for describing how customization should be done, if it is done, so that new upgrades can be implemented without the work needing to be redone. The challenge of improving the process of implementation is closely related to the challenge of improving requirements gathering. In both cases, time is crucial and a basic problem is that it takes too long. There are several reasons implementation takes too long, including that the system is too complex to implement, and that the people doing the implementation lack project management expertise. A possible solution is to develop software that is easier to implement, solving both the time problem and the lack of project management expertise. A summary of this challenge area is that there are deficiencies in the ERP implementation process.

3.3 Challenge Area 3: Customization Versus Configuration

Related to the implementation challenge is the question of customization versus configuration. Worth mentioning here is that there are different definitions of these terms, implying different approaches to dealing with the problems. There is a need for a clearer view on customization and configuration and their relation to upgrades and new versions. To some extent, this area was addressed above. However, that discussion dealt with customization and configuration mainly from the perspective of time. Here, the basic problem is lack of knowledge on how these system changes should be done. There is also a question about the basic architecture and how that allows for customization and configuration, which directly relats to adjusting the ERP to the business processes in the adopting organization. Also, how does customization versus configuration influence future costs of ERPs usage? However, a fundamental question—whether the organization should adjust the ERP according to its business processes or the organization should adjust its business processes to the ERP—remains. A summary of this challenge area is that it is unclear how customization and configuration relate to upgrades.

3.4 Challenge Area 4: ERP Architecture

A challenge for future ERPs is emphasizing a software architecture that supports scalability and flexibility. Scalability and flexibility need to be supported in future ERPs because there is a need to provide support for new business models and new demands from end-users without disturbing the ongoing business. Better support for scalability and flexibility would improve the organization's ability to integrate different systems, both internally and external partners. This indicates that interoperability is an important feature for future ERPs. That the basic problem with existing ERPs is that they act too much as closed boxes; there is a need for improvement of the architecture so that it better supports interoperability. Low interoperability indicates that it is hard to connect other systems with the ERP. The answer to this problem could be to develop the future ERPs more as autonomous entities. If doing so, it is important that the relations between the different autonomous entities are clearly defined. A summary of this challenge area is that the architecture of existing ERPs is inadequate, resulting in a weak support of scalability and flexibility.

3.5 Challenge Area 5: ERP and Support of Business Processes

Existing ERPs try to focus on business processes, but they do not explicitly describe the business processes supported. There is insufficient representation of business processes in existing ERPs. Future ERPs should more clearly be built on a business process notation. The basic problem stemming from the current deficiency is that ERPs are not easily adjustable to changes in business processes. The ability to quickly adjust business processes to new demands will increase in importance in the future. The difficulty of adjusting ERPs to changes in business processes currently is that ERPs are too much a "black box," making it hard to know what to change and how to change it. A summary of this challenge area is that there are insufficient representations of organizational business processes in existing ERPs.

3.6 Challenge Area 6: Variations in ERP Requirements

The huge variation among customers, industries, and countries is something that future ERPs need to consider. This variation will influence development both in terms of what requirement the ERP needs to fulfil and what business processes it has to support. The basic problem is the need for ERP flexibility to support the variety of business processes. This is, to a great extent, a problem of *all* standardized software. However, a basic question is, why it is more difficult to manage the variation within ERPs than within, for instance, a word processing package? One possible answer to that question is the range of processes in which the ERP needs to be involved in an organization. In a software application such as MS Word, the information directly used in another software application is specified. In an ERP, the information needs to be able to be transferred between different software applications without human involvement, one reason why ERPs are hard to manage. A summary of this challenge area is that the huge variations in customer requirements that exist when developing future ERPs will increase the complexity of development.

4   OPEN SOURCE SOFTWARE

The origin of open source software development can, according to Hars and Qu (2002), be traced back to the 1950s and 1960s, with macros and utilities freely exchanged in user forums. When Richard Stallman founded the Free Software Foundation (FSF), providing the conceptual foundation for open source software, it really took-off. Open source has matured and become industry-strength in many areas, such as operating systems, application servers, and security tools (Bruce et al. 2006). When it comes to applications, however, open source is not a mature area. Business applications such as customer relationship management, enterprise resource planning, content management, and business intelligence are exceptions from this. Bruce et al. (2006) describe this as the third wave of open source adoption, the first wave being the adoption of open source as operating systems and the second wave being the adoption of open source as infrastructure systems such as middleware, browsers, and databases.

Riehle (2007) states that there are two different types of open source software—community open source and commercial open source—with community open source being software developed by a community and commercial open source software being developed and owned by a for-profit entity. The major difference between them is who decides the future direction of the software. In the community case, individual developers, often in the form of a broad community of volunteers, decides on which contributions will be accepted in the source code base. The community also decides where the software is heading. In the commercial case, a company decides what will be accepted into the software code base, maintains the copyright, and decides what to implement next. There are market-entry barriers to commercial open source. In the community open source situation, no market-entry barriers exist and, therefore, given the right license, anyone can set up a company and start selling software. Riehle states that if someone starts a company delivering open source software, they do not sell the software as such; rather, they sell its provision, maintenance, and support.

Riehle describes costs as one reason why organizations adopt open source. However, he states that the cost perspective is mainly a reason for solution providers. The customer pays for the software he or she uses from a market perspective, the fee is based on the market demand. If the solution provider can produce the software cheaper by using open source, they can increase their profit or decrease the cost for delivered services to each costumer, resulting in solution providers gaining the most from open source software with increased profits through direct cost savings and the ability to reach more customers through improved pricing flexibility. Economides and Katsamakas (2006) stipulate that open source, despite the fact that it can be used for free, has costs related to usage, including learning, installing, and maintaining, which can be higher than for proprietary software.

Costs could be one motivation for why software vendors use open source. What, then, are the motivations for individuals to contribute in open source? Hars and Qu (2002) discuss potential motivations for why individuals participate in open source projects. They state that individuals' motivations can be categorized into two broad areas: internal factors and external rewards. These two categories relate to three factors: social motivations, collective motivations, and reward motivations. Proponents of open source emphasize that open source programmers are not motivated by monetary incentives. Instead, participants are said to be motivated by personal hobbies and preferences or by the rewarding sense from increasing the welfare of others (Hars and Qu 2002). Regarding information support, according to the research of Lakhani and von Hippel (2003), people respond to questions because they expect reciprocity, they "help the cause" (i.e., like the idea of open source software), they expect to gain reputation or enhance their career prospects, they consider answering questions to be intrinsically rewarding, and for some, it is part of their job (if they work in a company that sells a commercial version of the software along with documentation and support).

Although it seems that there are many benefits accruing from usage of open source software, there are indications that not too many companies adopt open source. Goode (2005) conducted research on a sample of 500 of Australia's top companies to determine why their managers rejected open source software. According to his findings, the main reasons are that managers perceive no relevance in its offerings, are concerned about unreliable or transient support sources, and the lack of available resources, or perceive no need for open source technology in their businesses. The smallest companies noted that they did not have time to implement it; they were already using commercial closed source software. This suggests that at least some respondents see the adoption of and migration to open source software as a significant undertaking, with a long and steep learning curve.

Last but not least, there is a question of measurement of an open source software package's market value. When software has no price, no purchase contracts, and no buyers and sellers, it may be difficult to estimate its impact. Thain et al. (2006) addressed this problem and came up with three suggestions: plan for measurement far in advance, use multiple techniques to collect data, and give the users stake in the measurement. This advice is meant mainly for project teams developing open source software and is not easily utilized by researchers. Another approach to estimation of the interest of open source ERP systems is presented next.

There is no doubt that there is a great interest in open source. However, the question remains if this translates to open source ERPs and, if so, why this interest exists. In order to get some kind of answer to these questions, an investigation of the distribution channel SourceForge was made. SourceForge is a distribution channel of open source projects and it is described as "the world's largest Open Source software development web site. SourceForge.net provides free hosting to Open Source software development projects with a centralized resource for managing projects, issues, communications, and code" (www.SourceForge.net). In order to get a grasp of the status of open source ERPs, a search on SourceForge was conducted at the beginning of September 2007 and repeated in November 2007 and January 2008, as shown in Table 1. The search showed that there were 336 open source ERP projects registered on September 13, 2007. On November 27, there were 356 open source projects registered. This means that in 10 weeks there had been an increase of 20 new open source ERP projects. An interesting finding is that the new projects are generally connected to existing projects, meaning they focus on developing ERPs for specific industries. Another way of showing the interest in open source ERPs is to look into downloads of the software as such. However, it is important to remember that downloads do not say anything about actual adoption and usage. It can be assumed, however, that a high number of downloads indicates an interest in open source ERPs. To examine this, downloads of six different open source ERPs were investigated. These open source ERPs were chosen based on the recommendation of a consultant working in the open source ERP sector. Table 1 shows the statistics about downloads from these six open source ERPs projects.

Table 1. Downloads of Six Open Source ERPs

Downloads/ Open Source ERPs	Start of the Project	September 13, 2007	November 27, 2007	Downloads During 10 Weeks	January 23, 2008	Downloads During 8 Weeks
Compiere	2001-06-08	1,267,160	1,296,098	+28,938	1,320,192	+24,094
OpenBravo	2006-03-09	300,716	401,262	+100,546	470,941	+69,679
OpenTaps	2005-08-10	284,429	311,964	+27,535	327,651	+15,687
Facturalux	2006-09-01	231,031	235,897	+4,866	238,753	+2,856
WebERP	2003-01-07	138,064	149,010	+10,946	156,537	+7,527
TinyERP	2005-03-25	6,953	21,116	+14,163	28,729	+7,613

Table 1 implies that open source ERPs have existed for several years. It also shows that the interest seems to have increased, since there have been an extensive number of downloads lately. As mentioned earlier, downloading an ERP does not equal ERP adoption.

An interesting question arises: What are the reasons for the increasing amount of downloads of these specific open source ERPs? Another interesting observation is that OpenBravo has been ranked as number one when it comes to overall downloads at SourceForge for quite some time. It could be interesting to see how OpenBravo relates to the challenges identified by software vendors of proprietary ERPs.

5   DISCUSSION

A major challenge (challenge area 1) identified in ERP development is how finding the correct requirement as well as the time from identification to implementation. This can be compared with discrepancies between the software and organizational practices described by Chiasson and Green (2007), as well as a combination of functionality that is "too far" or "too close." Software can be too far from the specific needs of the organization, thus requiring extensive configuration and development. Software functionality can also be too close, with irrelevant or inappropriate functionality that cannot be modified. Sia and Soh (2007) perceive a software–organization misalignment in two dimensions: institutional theory (imposed or voluntary) and ontological theory (deep structure or surface structure). The majority of imposed–deep misalignments are implemented. Imposed–surface and voluntary–deep misalignments are more often resolved via organizational adaptation and voluntary–surface misalignments are almost always resolved via organizational adaptation. Open source ERP developers may not experience the problem with discrepancies to the same extent as proprietary ERP developers. One reason could be that open source development takes place closer to the using organization, which also could be one reason for downloading of open source ERPs from other developers, as the implemented requirements in open source ERPs may be closer to the specific needs of the using organization.

Boulanger (2005) asks how a disparate loose-knit group of developers can produce for free software that has comparable quality with proprietary software. He describes the feedback loop as one difference between development of proprietary software and open source software that make it possible. The most common approach in a proprietary software development process is the waterfall model, with the development more or less following a clear structure and using a set of five well-defined phases. Boulanger presents the following five phases as a generic structure for proprietary software projects: the requirements phase, the system and software design phase, the implementation and unit testing phase, the integration and system testing phase, and the support and maintenance phase. He says that this structure is an iterative process, but that open source development phases are more intertwined in each other. Suggesting that open source development is more intertwined means that downloading open source ERPs could be to gain inspiration for what requirements to implement in another ERP. The more intertwined development process may decrease the time from identifying a specific requirement to its implementation, since the feedback is more direct.

The implementation challenge (challenge area 2), which basically is how to deal with the implementation process as such, is of interest when analyzing open source ERP downloads. It could be that downloads are made from the perspective of gaining knowledge about how to deal with the implementation. The basic idea in open source is that the end-user of the specific ERP should be able to download and implement the system by him/herself. This means that proprietary developers may download ERPs because they are searching for knowledge about solutions on architectural questions as well as how different architectures influence the implementation process.

Deciding on deploying a specific system includes questions such as usability, compatibility, features, support costs, and software quality and reliability. Boulanger argue that FOSS-developed systems are a viable alternative to proprietary systems when taking software quality and reliability into consideration. The question, then, is do developers download open source ERPs in order to gain insight into dealing with the challenge of customization versus configuration (challenge area 3)? MacCormack et al. (2006) propose that open source and proprietary code differ in modularity, that open source is more modular than proprietary software, suggesting that open source development demands a higher level of modularity. They also state that if this were not the case, the huge number of developers in an open source project would result in software with a high level of problems. The number of developers involved in an open source ERP project, however, is questionable. When looking at the number of developers on different open source ERP projects, there are not so many involved; proprietary ERP projects probably have more developers involved. However, despite the attraction that modularity holds for ERP developers, it could be one reason for downloading open source ERPs. The modularity makes it possible to download and use the knowledge of a specific solution for solving a specific need.

Bonaccorsi and Rossi (2003) explain the peculiarity of the open source movement using recent developments in the theories of collective action, of coordination in the absence of a central authority and of the diffusion of technologies in the presence of network externality. This has made it possible to throw light not only on how the phenomenon arises and finds a vast economic application, but also on the mechanisms that underlie its massive diffusion. However, many questions remain; for example, more in-depth analysis of coordination mechanisms is needed, with particular reference to the precise functioning of open source projects, in order to understand the roles of both project leaders and the minor figures who do the less prominent work. This problem was studied by Crowston et al. (2007), who provided empirical evidence about how FOSS development teams self-organize their work, specifically how tasks are assigned to project team members. "Self-assignment" was the most common mechanism across the three FOSS projects investigated. This could be connected to downloading of open source ERP solutions by developers of other open source ERP solutions. The increase of new open source ERP projects may be a result of self-assignment, and downloads could be seen as knowledge sharing between developers of different open source ERPs.

Von Krogh and Spaeth (2007) state that there has been a huge interest in open source over the past decade. They describe open source as having two distinct features. The first, and what is most probably connected to open source, is software equipped with a license that provides rights to existing and future users to use, inspect, modify, and distribute modified and unmodified software to others. The second feature is the change in the development practice of open source. According to von Krogh and Spaeth, years of development have resulted in a new practice of innovation associated with open source software. The new practice displays a very distinct development process, which means that open source projects often are initiated by a project leader or project entrepreneur. Volunteers then join the project depending on their knowledge. The result of it is that open source projects highlight a change in the nature of how software is developed. Von Krogh and Spaeth argue that the pure top-down, planned software development project has changed into an evolutionary development involving many volunteers.

The question of architecture (challenge area 4) is something that garners a great deal of attention in ERP projects. ERPs need have to have a high level of scalability and flexibility. One way to achieve this is to change the basic architecture in the direction of software-oriented architecture or event-based architecture. Open source ERP projects are the place for developers to test these kinds of solutions, implying that it is also a source of inspiration for other developers in the search of a final solution.

Providing the system with the ability to deal with a huge variation of stakeholders' requirements is a challenge (challenge area 6) with relevance not only for ERPs, but for all software packages. However, it is probably more problematic when developing ERPs since these types of systems also need to take the variations in business processes (challenge area 5) into consideration. Proponents of open source projects often say that the benefit is the closeness to the end-user. If that is the case, it suggests that the interest among developers in open source ERPs is as a source of knowledge on how to develop for a variety of requirements and business processes.

6   CONCLUDING REMARKS AND FUTURE RESEARCH

The interest in ERP development seems to be increasing at the moment. This development is of special interest when it involves closing the gap between delivered functionality and desired functionality. There is also a huge interest in downloading open source ERPs. However, there are indications that downloads not are made by using organizations when it comes to open source ERPs. This interest in downloads could be the result of dissatisfaction with proprietary ERPs, or it could be the result of maturity in the open source phenomenon. However, the most mature open source ERPs do not show the highest number of downloads. One interpretation of this could be that downloads are made from curiosity. Another is that it is a way of increasing knowledge of ERP development, indicating that the downloads are made by developers who may redirect an existing project into a new project or use the knowledge gained by investigating the functionality of the ERP downloaded.

ERPs are complex business applications and their complexity has increased as the software has matured. This complexity, to a large extent, influences development, since the software aims at supporting the entire organization's business processes, requiring that the ERP have a high level of functionality. For developers, knowledge sharing, or making sure that one has the correct knowledge, is important, providing another reason for downloading open source ERPs, at least as long as the downloaded ERP has new knowledge to share. This could explain why OpenBravo is downloaded more often than Compiere, as shown in Table 1. The most innovative open source ERPs are most downloaded, suggesting that ERP developers are searching for new, innovative solutions and using the right to inspect the software to do so.

When looking at the challenges identified by the executives at the software vendor, one must agree with the proponents of open source, who state that these challenges are in focus when developing open source ERPs, indicating that downloads of open source ERPs are of interest to developers of proprietary ERPs. This implies, then, that it would be of interest to compare in depth the development process of open source ERPs with the development of proprietary ERPs.

Riehle (2007) describes the cost perspective as a major reason why software developers adopt open source. However, this can be questioned, and it can be suggested that adoption in the form of downloading of open source is a knowledge sharing activity and a way for developers to get closer to the end-user, thereby closing the gap between delivered functionality and desired functionality. However, the main conclusion from the discussion in the paper is that there seem to be several factors involved in why downloads of open source ERPs are made and it would be interesting to further investigate knowledge sharing as a reason for the attention given open source ERPs. The challenges presented for development of proprietary ERPs could act as an interesting framework for suitable questions to ask in a future investigation about knowledge sharing and knowledge diffusion among ERP developers.

References

Bonaccorsi, A., and Rossi, C. 2003. "Why Open Source Software Can Succeed," *Research Policy* (32:7), pp. 1243-1258.

Botta-Genoulaz, V., Millet, P. A., and Grabot, B. 2005. "A Survey on the Recent Research Literature on ERP Systems," *Computers in Industry* (56:6), pp. 510-522.

Boulanger, A. 2005. "Open-Source Versus Proprietary Software: Is One Nore Reliable and Secure than the Other?," *IBM Systems Journal* (44:2), pp. 239-248.

Bruce, G., Robson, P., and Spaven, R. 2006. "OSS Opportunities in Open Source Software— CRM and OSS Standards," *BT Technology Journal* (24:1), pp. 127-140.

Chiasson, M. W., and Green, L. W. 2007. "Questioning the IT Artefact: User Practices That Can, Could, and Cannot Be Supported in Packaged-Software Designs," *European Journal of Information Systems* (16:5), pp. 542-554.

Crowston, K., Li, Q., Wei, K., Eseryel, U. Y., and Howison, J. 2007. "Self-Organization of Teams for Free/Libre Open Source Software Development," *Information and Software Technology* (49:6), pp. 564-575.

Economides, N., and Katsamakas, E. 2006. "Two-Sided Competition of Proprietary vs. Open Source Technology Platforms and the Implications for the Software Industry," *Management Science* (52:7), pp. 1057-1071.

Esteves, J., and Bohorquez, V. 2007. "An Updated ERP Systems Annotated Bibliography: 2001–2005," *Communications of the AIS* (19), pp. 386-446.

Esteves, J., and Pastor, J. 2001. "Enterprise Resource Planning Systems Research: An Annotated Bibliography," *Communications of the AIS* (7:8), pp. 1-51.

Goode, S. 2005. "Something for Nothing: Management Rejection of Open Source Software in Australia's Top Firms," *Information & Management* (42:5), pp. 669-681.

Hars, A., and Qu, S. 2002. "Working for Free? Motivations for Participating in Open-Source Projects," *International Journal of Electronic Commerce* (6:3), pp. 25.

Ifinedo, P., and Nahar, N. 2007. "ERP Systems Success: An Empirical Analysis of How Two Organizational Stakeholder Groups Prioritize and Evaluate Relevant Measures," *Enterprise Information Systems* (1:1), pp. 25-48.

Karimi, J., Somers, T. M., and Bhattacherjee, A. 2007. "The Impact of ERP Implementation on Business Process Outcomes: A Factor-Based Study," *Journal of Management Information Systems* (24:1), pp. 101-134.

Kocakulah, M. C., Embry, J. S., and Albin, M. 2006. "Enterprise Resource Planning (ERP): Managing the Paradigm Shift for Success," *International Journal of Information and Operations Management Education* (1:2), pp. 125-139.

Koch, C. 2001. *ERP-systemer—erfaringer, ressourcer, forandringer,* Copenhagen, Denmark: Ingeniøren-bøger.

Krippendorff, K. 2004. *Content Analysis: An Introduction to its Methodology,* Thousand Oaks, CA: Sage Publications.

Kumar, K., and Van Hillegersberg, J. 2000. "ERP Experiences and Evolution," *Communications of the ACM* (43:4), pp. 22-26.

Lakhani, K. R., and von Hippel, E. 2003. "How Open Source Software Works: 'Free' User-to-User Assistance," *Research Policy* (32:6), pp. 923-943.

Lengnick-Hall, C. A., Lengnick-Hall, M. L., and Abdinnour-Helm, S. 2004. "The Role of Social and Intellectual Capital in Achieving Competitive Advantage through Enterprise Resource Planning (ERP) Systems," *Journal of Engineering and Technology Management* (21:4), pp. 307-330.

MacCormack, A., Rusnak, J., and Baldwin, C. Y. 2006. "Exploring the Structure of Complex Software Designs: An Empirical Study of Open Source and Proprietary Code," *Management Science* (52:7), pp. 1015-1030.

Møller, C. 2005. "ERP II: A Conceptual Framework for Next-Generation Enterprise Systems?," *Journal of Enterprise Information Management* (18:4), pp. 483-497.

Riehle, D. 2007. "The Economic Motivation of Open Source: Stakeholders Perspectives," *IEEE Computer* (40:4), 25-32.

Rolland, C., and Prakash, N. 2000. "Bridging the Gap Between Organizational Needs and ERP Functionality," *Requirements Engineering* (5:3), pp. 180-193.

Shehab, E. M., Sharp, M. W., Supramaniam, L., and Spedding, T. A. 2004. "Enterprise Resource Planning: An Integrative Review," *Business Process Management Journal* (10:4), pp. 359-386.

Sia, S. K., and Soh, C. 2007. "An Assessment of Package–Organization Misalignment: Institutional and Ontological Structures," *European Journal of Information Systems* (16:5), pp. 568.

Soh, C., Kien, S. S., and Tay-Yap, J. 2000. "Cultural Fits and Misfits: Is ERP a Universal Solution?," *Communications of the ACM* (43:4), pp. 47-51.

Somers, T. M., and Nelson, K. G. 2004. "A Taxonomy of Players and Activities Across the ERP Project Life Cycle," *Information & Management* (41:3), pp. 257-278.

Thain, D., Tannenbaum, T., and Livny, M. 2006. "How to Measure a Large Open-Source Distributed System," *Concurrency and Computation: Practice and Experience* (18:15), pp. 1989-2019.

von Krogh, G., and Spaeth, S. 2007. "The Open Source Software Phenomenon: Characteristics that Promote Research," *Journal of Strategic Information Systems* (165:3), pp. 236-253.

Wier, B., Hunton, J., and HassabElnaby, H. R. 2007. "Enterprise Resource Planning Systems and Non-financial Performance Incentives: The Joint Impact on Corporate Performance," *International Journal of Accounting Information Systems* (8:3), pp. 165-190.

About the Author

Björn Johansson holds a Ph.D. in Information Systems Development from the Faculty of Arts and Sciences at Linköping University. He is currently working on the 3gERP project at the Center for Applied ICT at Copenhagen Business School (http://www.3gERP.org). He is a member of the IFIP Working Group 8.6 (Diffusion, Adoption and Implementation of Information and Communication Technologies), IFIP Working Group 8.9 (Enterprise Information Systems) (alternate member), and the research networks: Knowledge in Organizations (KiO)and VITS Work Practice Development, IT Usage, Coordination and Cooperation. He can be reached by e-mail at bj.caict@cbs.dk.

15 TOWARD A USER DRIVEN INNOVATION FOR DISTRIBUTED SOFTWARE TEAMS

Liaquat Hossain
David Zhou
The University of Sydney
Sydney, Australia

Abstract   *The software industry has emerged to include some of the most revolutionized distributed work groups; however, not all such groups achieve their set goals and some even fail miserably. The distributed nature of open source software project teams provides an intriguing context for the study of distributed coordination. OSS team structures have traditionally been geographically dispersed and, therefore, the coordination of post-release activities such as testing are made difficult due to the fact that the only means of communication is via electronic forms, such as e-mail or message boards and forums. Nevertheless, large scale, complex, and innovative software packages have been the fruits of labor for some OSS teams set in such coordination-unfriendly environments, while others end in flames. Why are some distributed work groups more effective than others? In our current communication-enriched environment, best practices for coordination are adopted by all software projects yet some still fall by the wayside. Does the team structure have bearing on the success of the project? How does the communication between the team and external parties affect the project's ultimate success or failure? In this study, we seek to answer these questions by applying existing theories from social networks and their analytical methods in the coordination of defect management activities found in OSS projects. We propose the social network based theoretical model for exploring distributed coordination structures and apply that for the case of the OSS defect management process for exploring the structural properties, which induce the greatest coordination performance. The outcome suggests that there is correlation between certain network measures such as density, centrality, and betweenness and coordination performance measures of defect management systems such as quality and timeliness.*

Please use the following format when citing this chapter:

Hossain, L., and Zhou, D., 2008, in IFIP International Federation for Information Processing, Volume 287, Open IT-Based Innovation: Moving Towards Cooperative IT Transfer and Knowledge Diffusion, eds. León, G., Bernardos, A., Casar, J., Kautz, K., and DeGross, J. (Boston: Springer), pp. 261-270.

Keywords   Open innovation, distributed teams, coordination, defect management process,
                    software

1   INTRODUCTION

The open source approach to software development involves a group of loosely knit volunteers that collaborate over a public medium of communication, most popularly the Internet, to create software (de Souza et al. 2005). The source code is open to public access and it is this readily available nature that advocates of open source software claim results in faster and more responsive development cycles, thus producing more robust and secure software. These inherent characteristic have some interesting connotations for OSS project teams and how the software is tested. What is phenomenal about OSS projects is that their participants tend to form a community that is "bounded by their shared interest in using/developing the system" (Ye and Kishida 2003, p. 422).

In this study, the particular coordination activities in which we are interested are related to bug reporting, fixing, and knowledge sharing post-release of the OSS. Existing literature has looked into coordination of OSS projects; however, the general focus has been coordination between developers during the pre-release phase of the project. Minimal attempts have been make to include the OSS project community's involvement. The evolution of any OSS project originates from the input or identification of defects from the OSS project's community, therefore, it seems fitting to include them in the analysis of the network structure. Due to the distributed nature of OSS project teams and communities, the participants often are geographically scattered at arbitrary locations where the only means of coordinating tasks is via message boards, open forums, or e-mail. We explore questions such as: Does the degree of centrality, betweenness, and density of the network have any bearing on the number of defects fixed per software promotion? Does the degree of centrality, betweenness, and density of the network have any bearing on the number of defects reported at different severity levels? Does the degree of centrality, betweenness, and density of the network have any bearing on the average number of days for a defect to be fixed for each project team? Does the degree of centrality, betweenness, and density of the network have any bearing on the average number of days for responses by developers on defects?

2   DEFECT MANAGEMENT PROCESS AS A COORDINATED SYSTEM

Distributed software test teams are a recent trend that has emerged due to quality and ease of communication across vast physical locations and the boundless efforts of all corporations to reduce costs associated with software development. As a result, entire projects are now divided so that teams in charge of different phases of the project can be located oceans apart. The relevance of coordination theory comes to the forefront when we analyze distributed software testing because, apart from the multiple levels of communication from the tester to steering committee that must be coordinated, the actors must contend with the physical distance between each team. By the using dependencies of coordination theory, we can deduce theoretical models that would help achieve the goal of software testing more effectively.

In order to provide some context on the coordinated system to which we are applying measures of coordination, it is only appropriate to outline the defect management process that distributed OSS teams must go through to ensure only legitimate and valid defects are accepted to be fixed. The defect management process is considered a coordinated system because it involves actors (developers and authors of the defect) performing interdependent tasks (raising and fixing defects) to achieve a common goal (advancing the OSS).

How do we know what is the most effective application of each coordination model? To answer this question, we need to apply our understanding of coordination components universal to all coordinated systems and whether the different methods of applying these components affect the results of existing metrics used to measure the effectiveness of software integration testing. Before we elaborate on the measures of OSS testing and how these relate to coordination, we need to step back and justify the validity of such metrics with regard to measuring coordination. We have previously established that OSS testing can be categorized as a coordinated system. This system comprises actors that perform interdependent tasks to achieve goals, the ultimate goal being to produce software to the community in a timely fashion, error free, and satisfying the requirements specified. In order to achieve these goals, the actors, working together and liaising with community members, must manage the components of coordination such as resource allocation, producer/consumer relationships, simultaneity constraints, and task dependencies. The measures of effectiveness include quality and timeliness, all of which are aligned with the ultimate goal of testing OSS projects.

Quality measures have a direct correlation with the producer/consumer relationship component of coordination theory. The core development team (producer) releases the software to the OSS community (consumer), then active or passive users log defect reports when they arrive at an incorrect or unexpected behavior from the system. The cause of the defect invariably relates to the producer/consumer relationship, particularly the prerequisite constraints, transfer, and usability aspects. To ensure that the software produced has a low quality of code metrics value and defect density metric value we must coordinate activities so that prerequisite constraints such as environment connectivity are correct. We must also ensure vital knowledge of the system is transferred from the development team to the test teams. The last element of usability will naturally fall into place once the previous elements are managed accurately.

The quality of code metric captures the relation between the number of weighted defects and the size of the product release.

$$\frac{W_F}{NCSPT}$$

Where W_F is number of weighted defect found post release software release. The weight of each defect is dependent on the severity. *NCSPT* is the number of *commit statements per time period.* In this metric, the lower the number is, the fewer defects or less serious defects found, thus the higher the quality of the code. Traditionally quality of code is measured using per thousand lines of code; however, this method of measure created efficiencies such as "bloaty" (Mockus et al. 2002). With proprietary software, the common practice to minimize the effects of bloaty code was to only counting every thousand lines of new code. Also, the incremental delivery model of software development means that, with each release, only sections of new code are built on existing baseline code from the previous release. By only taking the new lines of code into consideration, a more accurate depiction of the quality of the code emerges. In the spirit of avoiding bloaty code to affect the accuracy of the measure of quality, this paper used NCSPT because OSS projects are tracked according to commit statements, which are logged and tracked on the OSS project website. Each commit statement indicates patches and fixes to the software, thus the proportionality between number of total defects raised and number of commit statement indicates if the quality of the code is high or low. Naturally, a high number indicates that many defects have arisen for each commit statement, which is a clear sign of poor quality of code.

The defect density metric shows the relation between numbers of weighted defects per severity level and the total number of defects detected post-release.

$$\frac{W_{PSL}}{W_F} * 100$$

Where W_{PSL} is number of weighted defects per severity level found during the post-release period of the OSS and W_F represents the total number of weighted defects found. Using this metric, we find that the higher the number, the higher the ratio of defects detected before release and the higher the effectiveness of the test. The motivating factor behind this measure is that we can arrive at a comparison based on number of defects of a certain severity level as a proportion of overall defect numbers. Naturally, projects with high quality will have fewer defects within the high range of defect severity. The successful result of the following timeliness metric can be associated the management of simultaneity constraints and task dependencies. Imagine a typical software testing phase, with absolute certainty there are dependencies on which activities can be performed first, in parallel, and last. It is up to those in the position to coordinate the activities to ensure that those tasks categorized as high priority because many other tasks depend on their success are run first. Those that can be run in parallel are organized in such a way, and those with many dependencies on other activities are run last.

Although coordination theory is a very powerful method of analyzing areas of improvement for OSS testing, there still exist limitations and questions that must be answered. For example, what effect does personal characteristics or properties of actors have on the outcome of the testing? Would group structure affect which activities can be performed? In a distributed network of groups that must perform tasks that are inter-dependent, what type of links induce the best overall outcome for the software integration testing phases? A social network based approach will help complete this picture and offer a more rounded model when combined with our coordination model for improving the outcomes of software integration testing. Density, as described earlier, is a measure of the number of connections formed within a network as a proportion of total possible connections between all nodes of a network. Studies into density have been conducted; Crowston and Howison (2006) found a negative correlation between the project size and density of the network. From their empirical work, it would seem that the connections for certain key participants remain the same while the project grows in size, thus making the network less dense. From a coordination perspective, research has been done by Dinh-Trong and Bieman (2004) into comparing the defect density and general performance measures between different projects and seeing if indeed OSS produces better quality software. Therefore, it would be of interest to find the correlation, if any, between the network variable density and key performance indicators of OSS projects. In this paper, we test the following two assumptions:

H1: Quality of code measure is influenced by degree centrality, node betweenness, and density of the OSS team.

H2: Defect density measure is influenced by degree centrality, node betweenness, and density of the OSS team (high–medium–low severity)

3   DATA SOURCE

Data was collected via the monthly data-dump SF.net provided to the Department of Computer Science and Engineering, University of Notre Dame, for the sole purpose of supporting academic and scholarly research on the free/open source software phenomenon. We were granted access to the university's specialist wiki-supported website dedicated to the study of free/libre/open source software projects. This site provided the SF.net entity relationship diagrams, database schema definition, and SQL query functionalities required to extract the necessary data specified in the previous section. The SQL query tool was a web-based program that allowed for simple SQL queries and timed out when more complex queries were required to be executed. Therefore, the list of projects used for analysis was chosen from the 100 projects with the most active participation according to monthly download rate, forum activity, and pages view. From this list of 100 projects, only thpse with more than 7 developers and 200 bug reports were included. We felt that 7 developers provided a robust enough network for our studies and 200 bug reports represented enough instances of group interaction between the actors of the network. According to these criteria of selection, a group of 45 projects were identified to be appropriate for use in our analysis of the social network of an OSS team.

After the short list of projects to be included in the analysis was established, we went about extracting the necessary data from appropriate tables and fields according the ER-diagram and schema definitions provided by the University of Notre Dame. SQL queries were executed to extract the necessary data and the results of each query were saved as a text file with colons used as separators for each field. Each text file contains all closed status bug reports for one of the 45 projects that fit the selection criteria. The type of refinement needed for coordination measures of timeliness included conversion of the time-stamped fields such as artifact.open_date, artifact.close_date, and artifact_message. adddate, because SF.net uses UNIX formatted time-stamps for date fields. Unix time describes time as the number of seconds elapsed since midnight UTC of January 1, 1970, therefore, the following formula was applied in Excel to convert the time-stamp into a more meaningful manner.

$$\frac{UNIXtime + (365 * 70 + 19) * 86400}{86400} - 0.41667$$

Once the time format had been changed, we used existing Excel functions to calculate the duration for each fix was closed according the artifact.open_date and artifact.close_ date. Summing the total of the durations and dividing by the total number of bugs, we then have a coordination measure of time-to-fix-bugs metric for each project. A similar approach was used to calculate the time-to-respond metric, but the artifact_message. adddate was subtracted from the artifact.open_date with the average time similarly calculated by totaling the duration of each response and dividing by the total number of artifact_message.

For the measures of quality, defect density required aggregation of the different categories of the aftifact.priority field. Currently, SF.net's tracker system uses a 9-level priority system to categorize the severity of each bug, with 9 being the most severe and 1 being the least. This system presents ambiguity, when used in our analysis of the defect density, when defining the difference between a priority 5 bug and priority 4 or 6 bug. Thus to clarify the severity of the bugs raised for each project, we have concluded that due to the number of bugs found in each of the nine priority levels, one to three priority bugs are deemed "low severity," four to six priority bugs are referred to as "moderate severity," and seven to nine priority bugs are classified as "high priority." For the final measure of quality of code, total number of bugs raised and commit statements executed for each project were extracted from the project summary page.

4   RESULTS AND DISCUSSION

Using the multiple regression model of analysis, we arrived at a set of results that we can use to interpret the relationship between dependent variables of coordination and independent variables of social network characteristics. This section reports on the findings from this analysis. We analyze the regression output of the social network independent variables (centrality, betweenness, and density) regressed on both measures of quality of coordination respectively. From our analysis of the relationship between the quality of code measure and degree centrality, betweenness, and density, Excel processed the following regression model and output (Table 1):

$$Y = 2.593+11.361*Centrality+9.136*Betweenness-3.862*Density$$

We can only accept the hypothesis if for an F-test we obtain an F-statistic greater than 2.61 (critical value for F at 3, with 41 degrees of freedom) and, in addition, a significance-F value that is less than 0.05, which is the predetermined level of signi-ficance. In terms of the significance of the independent variables, each t-statistic needs be greater than 1.6829 or less than -1.6829 (critical value for a two-tailed t-test at 41 degrees of freedom) with p-values less than 0.05. If these conditions are met, then we can conclude that there is sufficient evidence of a relationship between quality of code and centrality, betweenness, and density. Interpreting the output, we accepted the hypothesis because the F value of 16.428 is greater than the critical value of 2.61 for a

Table 1. Quality of Code Output

Regression Statistics					
Multiple R	0.788236				
R Square	0.62131599				
A R Square	0.59909888				
Standard Error	13.5134966				
Observation	45				

	Df	SS	MS	F	Significance F
Regression	3	8999.8732	2999.958	16.42781	0.0062626
Residual	41	7487.19761	182.6146		
Total	44	7735.61699			

	Coefficients	Standard Error	t Statistic	P-value
Centrality	11.3614902	6.25387107	1.816713	9.36E-16
Betweenness	15.1359258	6.39409508	2.367172	2.323E-12
Density	0.86176736	0.35632672	2.41848	0.000032

5 percent level of significance. Furthermore, we concluded that each independent variable has strong significance to the model with respective p-values all being greater than 1.6829, which is the critical value for a t-distribution test at a 5 percent level of significance. Therefore, each of the β_i's contribute to the model. The moderate adjusted R-squared suggests that the model as a whole has average explanatory power and around 60 percent of the variations in observed values for quality of code can be explained by the variations of values of centrality, betweenness, and density. From the strong p-values of the independent variables, we can conclude the following:

1. For each percentage increase of centrality, on average it will increase the quality of code measure by 11.361 units, holding all other variables constant.
2. For each percentage increase of betweenness, on average it will increase the quality of code measure by 15.136 units, holding all other variables constant.
3. For each percentage increase of density, on average it will decrease the quality of code measure by 3.862 units, holding all other variables constant.

What these conclusions illustrate is that while centrality and betweenness of the network have a positive correlation with quality performance of OSS teams, interestingly, density has a negative correlation. This result suggests that increasing the level of centrality and betweenness of an OSS team will increase the number of bugs fixed per commit statement. However, increasing the communication links between actors will actually decrease this measure of quality in the coordination of defect management activities. For the measure of defect density, three separate regression analyses were conducted according to the three levels of defect that were classified for each OSS project. This is to take into the account of the mitigating factor of defect severity levels. As also previously discussed, when a defect is recognized as valid, it is assigned a severity or priority level, which is an indication of the effect this defect has on the project. Naturally, higher severity defects demand more attention because they affect the behavior of the software to a greater extent. For this reason, we decided to conduct separate regression analyses on the three levels of defect severity to see what relationships exist between that and centrality, betweenness, and density. The regression analysis produced the following model and output (Table 2):

$$Y = 2.593+11.361*Centrality+9.136*Betweenness-3.862*Density$$

Here, we can only accept the hypothesis if for an F-test we obtain an F-statistic greater than 2.61 (critical value for F at 3, with 41 degrees of freedom), and, in addition, the significance-F value is less than 0.05, which is the predetermined level of significance. In terms of the significances of the independent variables, each t-statistic needs be greater than 1.6829 or less than -1.6829 (critical value for a two-tailed t-test at 41 degrees of freedom) and p-values less than 0.05. If these conditions are met, then we can conclude that there is sufficient evidence of a relationship between quality of code and centrality, betweenness, and density. Interpreting the output, we can only tentatively accept H2(a) because the F value of 4.310 is greater than the critical value of 2.61 for a 5 percent level of significance. However, each independent variable shows poor insignificance to the model with their respective p-values all being greater than -1.6829 and less than 1.6829, which are the critical values for t-distribution test at 5 percent level of significance. Therefore, none of the β_i's contribute to the model. Furthermore, the low adjusted R-squared suggests that the model as a whole has poor explanatory power and only around 30 percent of the variations in observed values for defect density for high severity defects can be explained by the variations of values of centrality, betweenness, and density.

These results suggest that we need to do further analysis into the model and the decision was taken to include an interaction term into the model. The adjusted model included the introduction of centrality*density and betweenness*density. These two inter-

Table 2. High Severity Defect Output

Regression Statistics					
Multiple R	0.4828337				
R Square	0.2331284				
A R Square	0.1998723				
Standard Error	0.0008997				
Observation	45				

	Df	SS	MS	F	Significance F
Regression	3	0.22459875	0.07486624	3.82518	0.01665228
Residual	41	0.80244947	0.01957193		
Total	44	1.02704823			

	Coefficients	Standard Error	t Statistic	P-value	
Centrality	-0.077590007	0.08544898	-0.9080273	0.176248	
Betweenness	-0.096314342	0.08690062	-1.1083269	0.322982	
Density	-0.008513927	0.0758123	-0.1123030	0.017061	

action terms were chosen because networks with high degrees of density tend to have lower degrees of centrality and betweenness, due to the increase in connections between actors, thus reducing the centralization measure of individual actors. Intuitively this assumption can be made because as the ties among actors increase there is less need for actors to communicate through other actors; instead, they are more likely to contact the source of the knowledge, consequently reducing the need for central or between actors.

5 CONCLUSIONS

This study suggests that there is a correlation between social network characteristics and strong and poor performing projects in an OSS environment. The projects that were analyzed using our theoretical model all fit the criteria of more than 7 developers and more than 200 defect reports. The conditions we set on the data have helped to validate the strength of the results because such criteria provide a robust network of interaction between actors and facilitate varying sizes of networks. Analysis of the data displayed a normal distribution, which fit our proposed parameterized regression analysis. We believe that we have made a significant contribution into the study of distributed work groups, social network analysis, and coordination. Studies by Madey et al. (2002) have investigated the social network phenomenon, the power-law relationship in OSS development teams, and suggested looking into degrees of separation of the connection which we have analyzed through density and centrality.

References

Crowston, K., and Howison, J. 2006. "Hierarchy and Centralization in Free and Open Source Software Team Communication," *Knowledge, Techology and Policy* (81:4), pp. 65-85.

De Souza, C., Froehlich, J., and Dourish, P. 2005. "Seeking the Source: Software Source Code as a Social and Technical Artifact," in *Proceedings of the 2005 International ACM SIGGROUP Conference on Supporting Group Work*, Sanibel Island, FL, November 6-9, pp. 197-206.

Dinh-Trong, T., and Bieman, J. M. 2004. "Open Source Software Development: A Case Study of FreeBSD," in *10th IEEE International Symposium on Software Metrics*, Los Alamitos, CA: IEEE Computer Society, pp. 96-104.

Madey, G., Freeh, V., and Tynan, R. 2002. "The Open Source Software Development Phenomenon: An Analysis Based on Social Network Theory," in *Proceedings of the Eighth Americas Conference on Information Systems*, R. Ramsower and J. Windsor (eds.), Dallas, TX, August 8-11, pp. 1806-1813.

Mockus, A., Fielding, R. T., and Herbsleb, J. 2002. "Two Case Studies of Open Source Software Development: Apache and Mozilla," *ACM Transactions on Software Engineering and Methodology* (11:3), pp. 309-346.

Ye, Y., and Kishida, K. 2003. "Towards an Understanding of the Motivation Open Source Software Developers," in *Proceedings of the 25th International Conference on Software Engineering*, Portland, OR, May 3-10, pp. 419-429.

About the Authors

Liaquat Hossain's work aims to explore the effects of different types of social network structures and patterns of information technology use on coordination in a dynamic and complex environment. The primary focus of Liaquat's research is in the area of network analysis of organizational and social systems. He approaches this using social networks theory and analytical methods and applies theories and methods from sociology and social anthropology to study coordination problems in a dynamic, complex, and distributed environment. He further applies network-based theories and methods to explore the phenomenon of globally distributed work groups (referred to as outsourcing in business management literature) and its management challenges. Overall, he is interested in exploring (modeling and empirical investigation) the effects of different types of social network structures on coordination and organizational performance from a theoretical and applied perspective. In his research, he uses methods and analytical techniques from mathematical sociology (i.e., social networks analysis), social anthropology (i.e., interview and field studies), and computer science (i.e., information visualization, graph theoretic approaches, and data mining techniques such as clustering) to explore coordination problems in a dynamic, distributed and complex setting. Liaquat can be reached by e-mail at lhossain@it.usyd.edu.au.

Davis Zhao received his Bachelor of Engineering in Electrical and Information Engineering specializing in Software Engineering from the University of Sydney in 2008. He is currently working as a consultant at Accenture Australia.

Part 6:

Design Science and Cases in IT

16 HOMEWARD BOUND: Ecological Design of Domestic Information Systems

David G. Wastell
Nottingham University Business School
Nottingham, UK

Juergen S. Sauer
Department of Psychology
University of Friebourg
Friebourg, Switzerland

Claudia Schmeink
Institute of Psychology
Darmstadt University of Technology
Darmstadt, Germany

Abstract   *Information technology artefacts are steadily permeating everyday life, just as they have colonized the business domain. Although research in our field has largely addressed the workplace, researchers are beginning to take an interest in the home environment too. Here, we address the domestic realm, focusing on the design of complex, interactive information systems. As such, our work sits in the design science version rather than behavioral science paradigm of IS research. We argue that the home is in many ways a more challenging environment for the designer than the workplace, making good design of critical importance. Regrettably, the opposite would appear to be the norm. Two experiments are reported, both concerned with the design of the user interface for domestic heating systems. Of note is our use of a medium-fidelity laboratory simulation or "microworld" in this work. Two main substantive findings resulted. First, that ecologically designed feedback, embodying a strong mapping between task goals and system status, produced superior task performance. Second, that predictive decision aids provided clear benefits over other forms of user support, such as advisory systems. General implica-*

Please use the following format when citing this chapter:

Wastell, D., Sauer, J., and Schmeink, C., 2008, in IFIP International Federation for Information Processing, Volume 287, Open IT-Based Innovation: Moving Towards Cooperative IT Transfer and Knowledge Diffusion, eds. León, G., Bernardos, A., Casar, J., Kautz, K., and DeGross, J. (Boston: Springer), pp. 273-290.

tions for the design of domestic information systems are discussed, followed by reflections on the nature of design work in IS, and on the design science project itself. It is concluded that the microworld approach has considerable potential for developing IS design theory. The methodological challenges of design research are highlighted, especially the presence of additional validity threats posed by the need to construct artefacts in order to evaluate theory. It is argued that design theory is necessarily complex, modal, and uncertain, and that design science (like design itself) should be prosecuted in an open, heuristic spirit, drawing more on the proven methods of "good design" (e.g., prototyping, user participation) in terms of its own praxis.

Keywords   Design science, cognitive ergonomics, ecological design, domestic heating system, feedback, operator performance, goal setting theory

1   INTRODUCTION

The same technology that simplifies life by providing more functions in each device, also complicates life by making the device harder to learn, harder to use. The paradox of technology should never be used as an excuse for poor design... the principles of good design can make complexity manageable (D. A. Norman, *The Design of Everyday Things* 1998, p. 31).

This paper is about the design and adoption of information systems artefacts in the home. Although information and communications technologies pervade more and more of contemporary life, research in the IS field (including that of IFIP WG8.6) remains pre-occupied with the workplace (Brown and Venkatesh 2005; Venkatesh and Brown 2001). In neighboring disciplines, such as human–computer interaction and cognitive engineering, there is a smattering of design research addressing ICT in the domestic sphere. In our discipline, the few studies addressing the home environment typically concern themselves with contextual factors influencing technology adoption (e.g., Brown and Venkatesh 2005; Vijayasarathy 2004). While the importance of design factors (ease of use, usefulness, etc.) is acknowledged, such "adoption studies" intrinsically take the artefact as the object of passive study, not something to be actively and directly shaped. Beliefs and attitudes toward technology, and how these bear on intentions "to use or not to use," form the quintessential field of interest. Design is an element in this nexus, but only one component in a welter of other causal and contextual variables (social norms, demographics, and so on). The typical theoretical framing of these factor studies draws either directly on the diffusionism of Rogers (1995), or on derivative positions such as the ubiquitous technology acceptance model (Davis et al 1989).

The classic adoption study fall squarely within what Hevner et al. (2004) call the *behavioral science* approach to IS research, in contrast to the *design science* paradigm. The same broad dichotomy reappears in Gregor's (2006) typology of IS theory, which contrasts theory for *explanation and prediction* with theory for *design and action*. In both cases, what would seem to underlie the distinction is the degree to which the design of an artefact is a matter of immediate concern to the researcher, or whether the relationship to technology is passive and deferred. Although enjoying a well-established tradition with a lineage reaching back over many years (e.g., March and Smith 1995; Markus et al. 2002; Walls et al. 1992), IS design research remains a minority genre. This is as true for the deliberations of IFIP WG8.6 as it is for the field in general. Given the self-evident importance of design quality in decisions to adopt or reject technical innovations, this seems somewhat paradoxical. By reporting an example of design science in this paper, we hope to redress the balance and strengthen the presence of such research within our repertoire. By emphasizing the importance of design, we make common cause with cognitive ergonomists (notably Norman 1998 and Vicente 2003) who have inveighed against the proliferation of technical devices in modern society that are increasingly complex, opaque, and frustrating to use.

1.1 Designing for the Home

The design of information systems for the effective management of domestic central heating systems (CHS) provides our substantive focus. We shall describe and discuss two contiguous cycles of a design project funded by the German Research Council on ecological design. The overall goal of our research program is to explore the potential for energy savings through improving the design of domestic artefacts. CHS has by far the largest environmental impact of all technologies in the home and is, therefore, a priority concern. Its management is mediated by an information system, typically in the form of a paper-based periodic energy bill that provides crude information regarding energy consumption and costs. The potential for computerizing this information system, for exploring different modes of information presentation and decision support, is of obvious relevance, in terms not only of domestic economics but the broader ecological agenda.[1]

Designing for the home poses some unique challenges compared to the design of work-based systems (Sauer et al. 2007). This brings us to the second sense of "bound" in the paper's title: the group of users is characterized by a high level of heterogeneity, without the possibility of selection according to technical competence; moreover, no formal training can be given, and users in effect set their own goals and tasks, with no performance supervision, standards, or systematic feedback. In general, these contextual differences demonstrate the great importance of careful design since the potential for influencing behavior is much more limited in the home than in a work context. In our investigation, we shall focus on the range of options for displaying information and

---

[1]As one of the most complex systems within the home, CHS is of intrinsic interest. It shares problematic features with industrial process control systems (albeit in a simplified form): that is, a slow process with multiple interacting contingencies (Wickens and Hollands 2000). In particular, the lagged response and long time constants of the CHS make it difficult to manage in an optimal way. The need to improve IS design for CHS management was underscored in a preliminary survey by the authors, comprising in-depth interviews with users in their homes. This confirmed that current interfaces give generally poor feedback, providing little support for making energy-efficiency gains or understanding causal connections between system operation and costs incurred. There is also some encouraging field-based evidence that good IS design can be effective. Van Houwelingen and Van Raaij (1989) showed that goal-setting in conjunction with feedback (a novel "energy cost indicator") produced a significant reduction in energy consumption.

aiding decision-making in order to achieve the optimal balance between comfort levels and energy expenditure.

1.2   Display Design and User Support

Following Kroemer et al. (2001), we distinguish four main display categories: status displays (indicating the current system state), historical displays (information about past trends), predictive displays (projected information on future trends), and instructional displays (providing operational guidance). Research on the relative merits of different forms of display is extensive and widely scattered, clustering under various disciplinary headings: HCI, cognitive ergonomics, cognitive engineering, etc. We have not the space here to provide more than a very cursory overview of some relevant themes. As a general comment, it must be said that design absolutes are hard to find amongst the plethora of sometimes inconsistent or contradictory findings in this diverse literature.

Regarding status displays, some such feedback is essential for the operation of any device, but the choice of information to display is problematic especially where there are multiple interacting variables (Bennett et al. 2005). It might be thought that portraying historical trends is always advantageous, and such displays are indeed in widespread use. Yet the little empirical research that has been done has thrown up some negative findings (Bennett et al. 2005; Spenkelink 1990). A less equivocal picture emerges for predictive displays, with benefits reported in many domains ranging from medicine to aviation (Wickens et al 2000). Such tools are especially useful for managing lagged nonlinear systems where the anticipation of future evolution is inherently complex (Wickens et al. 2000).

Instructional displays provide qualitative feedback guiding operator action. Expert systems provide a much-hyped example of the genre. Although such systems have the potential to aid decision making in constrained, highly structured settings (Wickens and Hollands 2000), there is often considerable resistance to their use in professional domains. Medicine is one such area, where clear evidence in terms of improved decision outcomes is notably lacking (Sintchenko and Coeira 2003). This resistance recalls the disinclination noted in our field to the use of decision support systems such as executive information systems (Elam and Leidner 1995; Hung 2003). Unless perfect reliability of the decision aid can be assumed, there is evidence that simple status displays may actually be preferable to instructional displays (Sarter and Schroeder 2001), which can give misleading advice.

1.3   Research Aims and Overview

Two design experiments are reported here. In the first, the potential benefits of historical displays are evaluated, together with enhanced "ecological" feedback. The second experiment assessed the relative advantages of predictive and instructional displays. The findings of the two studies will be presented and discussed, before moving on to a more general set of reflections on the design science program, motivated by recent debate over its nature and agenda (Chatterjee and Hevner 2006; Hevner et al. 2005). As an instance of design science in action, the work offers the opportunity to reflect critically on the practice of design, and indeed design science itself. There is specific interest in the investigative approach used here, which has some innovative aspects.[2] It involves an experimental methodology incorporating a dynamic, computer-based laboratory simulation. Such "microworlds" are invaluable for investigating complex, often inaccessible, settings where direct observation of key phenomena is problematic (Brehmer and Dörner 1993); their obvious potential in IS design research has been stressed by Wastell (1997). Designing for the home is methodologically challenging. While a clear understanding of user requirements is essential, the designer is not in the advantaged position of his organizational counterpart who can directly co-opt users into the design process. Alternative, less immediate methods of accruing design knowledge must be sought. The microworld is an attempt to insert the real world into the "arc of design" at a formative stage, and it will be of interest to observe how effective this method is.

2   RESEARCH METHODOLOGY

2.1   Experiments as Heuristic Devices: Introductory Reflections

Whereas experimental research is normally associated with the rigorous version of positivism, the present work was carried out in a more heuristic spirit. While empirical evaluation is an indispensable part of design science, the strong form of directional hypothesis testing would seems at odds with the inventive, creative spirit of design (Boland and Collopy 2004). It would also seem to represent an unrealistically optimistic view of the certainties of knowledge in the realm of the artificial, a world of contingent truths rather than necessary laws (as we glimpsed in the preceding section). Given the scientific uncertainties of the terrain, strong *a priori* hypotheses were eschewed. Beyond the broad expectation that more user support will, in general, lead to better performance, we ventured forward with an open pragmatic mind to appraise empirically which design concepts work and which do not, to attempt to understand some of the underlying contingencies and to abduct some tempered generalizations.

2.2   The CHESS Microworld

As noted, the experimental work was carried out using a PC-based simulation of a generic CHS, dubbed CHESS (Central HEating System Simulation). The design of CHESS itself is of methodological relevance in relation to our general design science concerns. The version for experiment 1 was largely fashioned by the experimenters themselves (i.e., with no user involvement!) supplemented by expert feedback from

---

[2]Design theory falls into two broad categories (Venable 2006; Walls et al 1992): knowledge about the design of products and about the design process itself, corresponding to the two senses of design as noun and verb. Both categories are relevant here; we are interested in the design of complex information systems and also the methodology of design.

engineering colleagues with interests in "green design." Version 2 did involve an element of user participation, in that subjects from experiment 1 were debriefed about their experience[3] and their comments led to several useful improvements in system usability. As with any microworld, verisimilitude was only carried as far as the pragmatics of the experiment required: time-scales were greatly accelerated, energy units were arbitrary, system dynamics were highly simplified, and, of course, the psychological mimicking of comfort levels could only be mediated in the crudest of ways. Within these limitations, CHESS was designed to provide a realistic user experience, in terms of the abstract nature of the operator's task, the visual appearance of the interface, and the underlying dynamic properties of the heating system (heat losses, lags, etc.). The aim was to produce a generic model that was convincing enough to generate meaningful user engagement and glean some relevant design knowledge regarding tool support and task performance.

CHESS can be configured to represent a range of types of accommodation and heating arrangements. Specific temperature and weather profiles can also be created by the experimenter and stored prior to experimental sessions. CHESS also creates a results file in which all key performance parameters (energy consumption, comfort levels, etc.) are logged for each "day" the simulation runs. All settings made and sources of information sampled by the operator are also recorded in the results file.

A small "one person" apartment with three rooms was used for both experiments. The operator's main task was to define a heating profile for each of the rooms (i.e., sitting room, bedroom, and kitchen) according to a target temperature profile. There is a "set up" screen for each room, and the heating profile can be typed in via a dialogue box specifying the start, end, and thermostatic temperature level for one or more "heating blocks"; alternatively, the mouse may be used, drawing the block directly on a temperature by time-of-day graphic. Once the user is satisfied with the room settings s/he has made, the main simulation screen is selected (Figure 1). Clicking the "run simulation" button, fast-forwards the simulation for a complete day before pausing again; this takes around 30 seconds unless the operator decides to interrupt and intervene. Half-hourly status information on temperatures, cumulative energy use and comfort levels are provided on this screen, as well as a graphic showing diurnal trends for individual rooms.

Satisfactory comfort was defined as the attainment of a room temperature within 1 degree of the target. If the room temperature falls more than 1degree below target but within 3 degrees, "mild discomfort" is indicated. A more severe discrepancy is signaled by the "serious discomfort" indicator. Figure 1 shows the situation for one participant at 23:54, when the day is nearly at a close. Only the bedroom has a target value. Clearly the heating has been switched off slightly prematurely, reflected in the disparity between target and actual temperatures marked by the appearance of the "mild discomfort" warning.

---

[3]Interestingly, their comments related largely to usability issues and no radical proposals were made; their feedback led to a number of minor enhancements in version 2 (e.g., the provision of press-button controls for editing heating blocks). Further discussion of general issues in relation to microworld methodology may be found in Sauer et al. (2000), and a longitudinal review of one such application (CAMS) in the context of industrial process control may be found in Wastell et al. (2003)

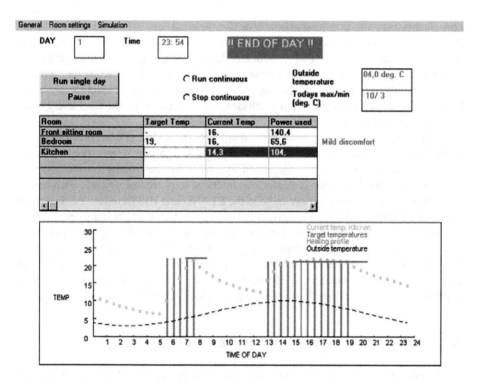

Figure 1. The Main Simulation Display Is Shown at the End of a Simulated Day. The graphic at the bottom of the display shows the outside and room temperatures (dashed and dotted curves) superimposed on the heating profile (vertical bars) and the target temperatures (horizontal lines).

A number of sources of management information were potentially available in both experiments at any point, depending on the experimental condition: a weather forecast provided a prediction of daily peak and low temperatures over the next four days. There was also a monthly report summarizing daily energy consumption and comfort levels for the house as a whole. Detailed daily reports were also potentially available, showing the hourly temperature profile for each room (akin to Figure 1) for any previous day, together with a summary of energy consumption and comfort.

3   EXPERIMENT 1

The first experiment compared the following three levels of operator support. The standard mode (STAND) was intended to represent the normal situation in most households; cumulative information only was provided in the form of an overall indication of total energy used at the current point (equivalent to reading the gas or electricity meter).

Participants were also informed of how effective they had been in heating the house (i.e., the average comfort level achieved thus far); this information was provided in aggregate form on the monthly report (i.e., without any daily breakdown). In the historical mode (HIST), participants were given full access to detailed historical information for each day, via the monthly and daily report screens. They were able to inspect the temperature and heating profiles for any room on any selected day, together with the total energy and comfort achieved for that day.

In the ecological (ECOL) mode, participants were provided with enhanced feedback in the form of a "waste estimator," which used a crude algorithm to estimate how much energy had been unnecessarily consumed by switching the heating on too soon, or switching it off too late. This indicator was intended to overcome obvious weaknesses in the basic status information available in the STAND and HIST modes. Although the two relevant status variables were presented (energy and comfort), it is not readily clear how they trade off against one another, nor how they are impacted by operator behavior. The waste indicator provides a simple example of feedback that is ecological (Rasmussen et al. 1994) in the sense that it enables the operator "to directly perceive the state of affairs in the environment...the deep structure of the work domain" and provides some guidance for adaptive action (i.e., reviewing switching on/off times).

3.1 Participants, Design, and Procedure

In all, 45 participants (30.0 percent female) were recruited from the Darmstadt University student population. They were aged 19 to 38 years (mean = 24.3 yrs) and received a payment of €25 for their participation. A one-factorial between-subjects experimental design was employed, with operator support as the primary independent variable, varied at three levels, as above. The experiment took place in a laboratory setting, and participants were tested in groups of three or four working on individual PCs, separated by screens. The testing session comprised two main phases. In the first, they were introduced to the CHESS software and initial training was given. In the second "treatment" phase, participants completed two task scenarios in their assigned feedback condition, each scenario involving the operation of the heating system for a whole month. Sessions on average lasted around 3 hours. Reflecting the home context, participants were not assigned specific goals; they were instructed to "do their best" to achieve the comfort levels prescribed by the set target temperatures while minimizing energy consumption.

User performance was measured on three dimensions: energy consumption, comfort (as defined above), and energy efficiency. Energy consumption was measured as the amount of energy (expressed as the average cost per day) consumed during task completion. The energy waste index was used to assess efficiency, although it was only fed back to participants in the ECOL condition. Patterns of information sampling and intervention were also assessed throughout. The frequency of inspection of the monthly and daily reports, the room settings, and the weather forecast were measured. System control activity was assessed by measuring the frequency of changes to the heating profiles.

Table 1. Effects of Feedback Level on Key Performance Indicators (Experiment 1)

Feedback Mode	Energy Cost per Day	Comfort (Max 100%)	Estimated Waste
Ecological (ECOL)	5.4	93.8	5.3
Historical (HIST)	5.7	92.6	13.4
Standard (STAN)	5.6	88.5	12.8
F ratio	11.8	26.7	53.2

3.2 Results

Given the multiplicity of dependent variables (nine in all, including the five measures of user interaction), a two factor MANOVA was carried out as the first step in the
formal statistical analysis, with operator support (feedback mode) and day-of-the-month
as the two independent variables. Only the second treatment month was analyzed, as
participants were at their most experienced and proficient at this point.

Wilks lambda was significant for both *support* (F = 16.9, p < 0.000) and *day* (F =
27.7, p < 0.000). Table 1 shows the impact of operator support, in terms of group
average performance levels across the month. Univariate F ratios were significant for all
parameters. Tukey *post hoc* tests indicated that participants achieved significantly higher
levels of comfort in both the HIST and ECOL conditions, and that their energy use and
waste levels were significantly reduced in the ECOL condition. All other differences
were not significant. It is apparent that while the HIST group achieved significantly
higher comfort levels than the standard group, they used more energy to realize this.
Their waste index was also the same as the standard group. Participants in the ECOL
condition, on the other hand, achieved improved comfort, but with no significant increase
in energy use; in fact, a small reduction was noted. Their waste index was less than half
the other two groups!

Table 2 summarizes patterns of user interaction with the simulation. First we note
that there is a low level of interaction with the system overall, generally less than one
interaction per day per option. Looking at the monthly trend, it was found that most
interaction occurred at the outset of the month, as would be expected, thereafter rapidly
falling away and achieving steady state at around day 6. Room screens, for instance,
were accessed 2.7 times on average on day 1 (to set/adjust heating profiles); by day 8,
this had dropped off to less than once per day (0.7). Tukey HSD *post hoc* tests revealed

**Table 2. Information Sampling and System Intervention as a Function of Feedback,
Experiment 1** (All F ratios are based on df = 2:1,318 (pooled error term))

Feedback Mode	STAN	HIST	ECOL	F ratio
Sampling of monthly report (No./day)	0.28	0.25	0.40	11.6
Sampling of historical daily reports	N/A	0.16	0.26	12.5
Accessing room screens (No./day)	0.90	0.74	1.31	14.8
Changes to profile settings (No./day)	0.82	0.60	1.07	14.9
Sampling of weather forecast	0.87	0.55	1.31	23.5

two themes. First, that for all forms of interaction, user activity was at its most prolific in the ECOL condition. Second, that for temperature forecasts and changes to heating profiles, there was consistently higher interaction in the STAND than the HIST condition, whereas for monthly reports and room screens, there were no differences between these two feedback conditions.

4   EXPERIMENT 2

The second experiment differed from the first in two substantive respects. First, in the provision of more sophisticated support tools: a predictive display and an instructional adviser, both optional features. The second difference was the posing of a more demanding heating management task, including an external temperature profile that fluctuated significantly more markedly.

Three levels of operator support were provided. The first condition (HIST2) was a direct replication of the HIST condition of experiment one. The other two conditions involved additional support tools for setting room heating profiles. The first of these (PRED) provided a predictive display showing the estimated temperature profile for that room, given the weather forecast and the heating blocks defined by the operator. Building on the results of experiment 1, an indicator of energy efficiency was also provided. This gave a comparison of the predicted performance against the optimal that could be achieved for a given set of target and forecast external temperatures.[4] In the third condition (INST), an instructional display was also available, providing explicit feedback on efficiency and comfort, as well as advice on how to improve performance (e.g., to switch on sooner and/or to set lower target temperatures).

4.1 Participants, Design, and Procedure

Forty-five new participants (48.0 percent female) took part in the study, again from the Darmstadt University student population. Their ages ranged from 19 to 47 years (mean = 23.7 yrs). They were paid €15 each for their participation, and general procedures were the same as experiment 1. Sessions lasted approximately 2 hours. After a brief overview of the experiment, participants were introduced to the CHESS software, and received practical instruction in its use. They then completed one test session involving the operation of the heating system for 30 days, which took approximately 60 minutes. This involved a complex sequence of daily scenarios modeled on typical lifestyle motifs: a normal working day, an extended working day, a weekend day including a late party, a day at home. Each scenario had a specific heating profile to be implemented.

---

[4]This assessment was more sophisticated than the waste estimator of experiment 1, and involved the use of a simple "hill-climbing" heuristic that progressively adjusted the set heating profile until the optimal level of efficiency was obtained.

4.2 Results

Again, MANOVA was performed with experimental condition (three groups) and day-of-the-month as the independent variables. This found that both factors were significant, yielding a Wilks lambda of 34.5 (p < 0.000) for the main effect of user support. Table 3 shows that whereas the participants with access to the predictive display were able to cope adequately with the more exacting challenge of this experiment, the performance of participants with only historical information was significantly impaired in terms of their ability to attain satisfactory comfort levels. Univariate F tests were significant for all three parameters in Table 3, with Tukey HSD *post hoc* comparisons indicating that the participants in the HIST2 mode, although more parsimonious in their energy use, were less effective in attaining comfort levels and showed a generally lower level of energy efficiency. No differences in performance were found between the PRED and INST groups for any parameter.

Table 4 summarizes patterns of operator interaction. The need for more intensive monitoring and intervention is borne out by these figures, which are notably elevated compared to their counterparts in experiment 1 (they show similar intensity to the levels evidenced at the outset of the month in the earlier experiment). The general pattern across conditions is striking. There are two main themes. A more active profile of interaction is consistently seen for the HIST2 condition; this is especially remarkable for the temperature forecast and the historical reports, which are hardly accessed at all in the PRED and INST conditions. The second theme is the very similar profile of interaction for the two conditions where the predictive display is available (PRED and INST). Tukey *post hoc* tests revealed this general pattern to be statistically valid for all parameters except the monthly reports, which were sampled more often in the PRED condition.

Table 3. Energy Consumption, Comfort, and Energy Efficiency Levels for the Second Experiment (Note that energy efficiency is simply comfort divided by daily energy cost)

User Support Mode	Daily Energy Cost	Comfort	Energy-Efficiency
History (HIST2)	6.0	74.4	12.4
Predictive (PRED)	6.3	90.3	14.3
Instructional (INST)	6.3	91.6	14.5
F ratio	13.8	86.5	97.6

Table 4. Information Sampling and System Intervention for Experiment 2 (All F ratios are based on df = 2:1,318 (pooled error term))

	HIST2	PRED	INST	F ratio
Sampling of monthly report (no./day)	0.34	0.45	0.13	43.2
Sampling of historical daily reports	2.8	0.7	0.3	57.7
Accessing room screens (no./day)	4.6	3.3	3.1	15.1
Changes to profile settings (no./day)	3.3	2.6	2.8	28.4
Sampling of weather forecast (no./day)	1.8	0.3	0.1	117.2

Regarding the use of the advanced support tools, there was striking evidence of a strong preference for the predictive display. This was accessed on average 10.3 times per day by participants in the INST condition, and 11.5 times per day in the PRED group (this difference was not significant, $t = 0.18$). In contrast, the energy adviser was rather scantily consulted, with the average rate of use being less than once per experimental day (mean $= 0.81$).

To triangulate these behavioral measures, participants were asked to rate their subjective opinions of the various information displays on a seven point scale, running from 1 (low utility) to 7 (very useful). The HIST2 group gave a significantly higher assessment of the value of the historical display (6.1) than either of the two other groups (4.2 and 3.7 on average for PRED and INST respectively, $F = 4.9$, $p < 0.01$). This group also gave a notably higher rating (4.3) to the weather forecast than subjects in either of the other conditions, who gave an average rating of 2.5 ($F = 12.3$, $p < .001$). Both groups with access to the predictive display rated it very highly (6.3 and 6.4 on average), markedly higher than the general evaluation of the instructional display (5.2 on average).

5   DISCUSSION

In contrast to the mainstream "behavioral" approach to research on the adoption of IT/IS, the present work takes a more active tack. The aim is to influence directly the take-up of technology by improving its design, centering attention on the delivery of relevant functionality embodied in a supportive user interface. We have also set foot in an application domain that is relatively neglected in our discipline, building on the meager discourse addressing the home environment. We noted that the home is, in many ways, a more challenging environment for the designer than the workplace, where supervision and training can help to optimize the utilization of IT. Without such support, it becomes of paramount importance that technology is well-designed if it is to be used effectively. But as others have lamented, all too often this is not the case; bad design would seem to be the norm for everyday objects (Norman 1998). Our discussion will be organized under two broad headings, following the twin aims prefigured in the "Introduction." In this penultimate section, we will reflect directly on the specific knowledge furnished regarding IS design for the home. In the final section, we will stand back and reflect more generally on design work and design science, based on our practical experiences reported here.

Our main substantive findings can be expressed in the following two generalizations. First, that historical displays, while replete with detailed management information, do not in themselves assist users to manage the heating system more effectively, whereas the provision of feedback directly indicating energy efficiency strongly motivated more interaction, which in turn enhanced performance. Secondly, that decision aids in the form of predictive displays are well-liked by users, extensively used, and engender enhanced outcomes, whereas instructional support was relatively disregarded.

Concerning the first finding, it is notable that the HIST group in experiment 1 actually intervened less often than the standard group, despite the radical improvement in their management information. By contrast, the addition of a single database field (the waste index) in the ECOL condition evoked a gestalt change in operator behavior: all information sources were sampled more frequently, including the weather forecast (strongly indicative of a more proactive orientation). Increased levels of system intervention were also observed. These changes in engagement directly translated into more energy-efficient system management, with comfort levels and energy consumption being jointly optimized. How can this dramatic transformation be explained?

For an explanation, we first return to the concept of ecological information systems design (EISD) briefly alluded to above (Rasmussen et al. 1994). The essence of EISD is the imperative to support human judgment in the management of complex problems through the clear representation of task objectives together with an information system ("measuring functions" in Rasmussen et al.'s terminology), enabling the *direct perception* of critical environmental variables and relationships. Although the *a priori* motivation for the waste indicator had been merely to provide additional feedback, it was realized retrospectively that its real potency lay elsewhere, in that it provided an implicit performance goal. The powerful influence of goals over performance is well known. Goal-setting theory (Locke and Latham 2002) argues that specific performance goals are the primary regulators of task performance, and that the mere provision of feedback will have limited potency (McCalley and Midden 2002). A clear mapping between goals and performance feedback is thus vital; its all-too-common lack is memorably described by Norman (1998) as the "gulf of evaluation."

Setting specific external goals is, however, unrealistic for the domestic environment; goals are voluntary and self-imposed in this context. Although not designed as a goal-setting mechanism (and no explicit waste goals were set), the waste indicator nonetheless carried a potent implicit goal in its moral labeling (all waste is bad and the target should, therefore, be to reduce it to zero). Not only does it set a goal but it directly conveys performance feedback against that goal, combining information from two oppositional parameters (comfort and cost) into a single unequivocal index. No mental computation is required to gauge performance; the error signal is directly given. Combining goal and feedback, it thus provides a simple example of ecological design that neatly bridges the gulf of evaluation. We thus regard the superior performance of the ECOL group as a direct reflection of the efficacy of sound ecological information system design. It is important to reemphasize, however, that the success of the waste-indicator was largely serendipitous; its teleological properties were only appreciated *ex post facto*.

Looking back at the first experiment, we can read the pattern of results as a general commentary on the contingencies of design and the limitations of design agency (Richardson 1993). Designers sometimes get it right, but sometimes they do not. Both forms of enhanced feedback were expected to enhance system management, but only one afforded genuine benefit. The same generic pattern comes through in the second study: one aid worked whereas another failed to deliver the expected gains.

The benefits we found for predictive displays[5] are consistent with the broad swathe of research that demonstrates the clear advantages of such displays in managing systems

---

[5]The poorer performance of the HIST2 group did not reflect any general lack of motivation. Indeed, this group interacted more intensively with the system, making more use of the information resources available to them, rating these resources more highly. The enhanced performance of the other two groups can thus be attributed to the superior technical tools at their disposal.

that are complex, lagged, and dynamic (Wickens et al. 2000). Regarding the benefits of instructional support, the research literature is markedly less certain, as we noted in the "Introduction." Users in our simulated home environment were apparently just as disinclined to utilize such advisory systems as are professional users in real work settings (Sintchenko and Coeira 2003). Although consistent with literature that is equivocal on the benefits of prescriptive aids, definitive conclusions should be drawn carefully. The failure could, of course, simply reflect a poorly designed implementation rather than a fundamental flaw in the concept of instructional support. Nonetheless, we may safely infer that the design of such support is more challenging than of predictive aids, and that there is a greater range of contingencies to be addressed. We may conclude that designers of complex artefacts for the home, and indeed for other environments that involve the management of dynamic processes, should, in the first instance, devote their efforts to the provision of effective predictive displays, and exercise caution in investing their design labor on forms of support that involve advice and guidance.

6   CODA: REFLECTIONS ON DESIGN AND DESIGN SCIENCE

As well as an experiment *for* design, the CHESS studies constitute an experiment on the process of designing itself. Let us begin these final reflections by considering the insights into design work (and its potential dysfunctions) revealed by the studies before considering more strategic implications for design science. First, we note that design is not a top-down, linear process moving deductively from a body of *a priori* knowledge (Boland and Collopy 2004; Weick 1990). Its open, emergent character is clearly manifest in the first experiment, where the full properties of an important design feature (the waste indicator) only came to light adventitiously, and the relevance of a significant body of "kernel theory"[6] was only fully recognized once the experimental work had been completed (i.e., goal-setting theory).

The tendency in design work to incorporate novel features that please the intellectual curiosity of the designer, rather than the pragmatic needs of users, has been dubbed "creeping featurism" (Norman 1998). This phenomenon is present in both experiments,

---

[6]The role of kernel theories in design science is highlighted by Walls et al. (1992). Kernel theories are theories emanating from the natural and social sciences that fundamentally bear on design processes and products. Goal-setting theory would seem an important kernel theory for the design of complex interactive systems, its core proposition being that specific challenging goals, broadly speaking, engender superior task performance in comparison to vague goals (such as "do-your-best") or personality attributes (e.g., achievement motivation). Important nuances should, however, be noted; for example, for complex problems, where learning and exploration are critical, setting "learning goals" (rather than performance goals) is generally more effective. Although goal-setting is inherently problematic in the domestic environment, it is not intractable and further design ideas could have been developed following the general direction suggested by the present results. It is possible, for instance, to envisage setting explicit *relative goals*, for example, setting a target for an efficiency improvement relative to past performance in similar conditions, in the manner of van Houwelingen and van Raaij (1989).

and would seem to be an endemic feature of design. Significant effort was devoted in the first experiment to the development of the historical database, which provided no real benefit for decision making (not unlike many real-life MIS!), and, in the second experiment, the expert system was relatively underutilized. We have noted that there was little user involvement in our design process. The salutary thought occurs that had we consulted our users more, it is possible that such redundant features would have been abandoned, or perhaps refined to be more useful.

An important subset of design theory concerns the efficacy and aptness of design methods and tools, and the performance of the microworld was of obvious interest. The general value of such microworlds in the context of IS research has been argued by Wastell (1997). By inserting something of the complexity of the real world into the controllable space of the laboratory, it is possible to engineer and explore realistic and important scenarios that would be difficult to examine *in vivo*. It also becomes feasible to evaluate formally the influence of a range of environmental, task, and design variables. Although artificial, the medium fidelity realism of the microworld manifestly has the dramaturgical power to engage users and to elicit realistic behavior. Certainly our users took their work seriously; this is evident from the pattern of their interaction with the system and their task performance. Of course, the simulation is not the real thing, and external validity is inevitably problematic, as for any laboratory experiment. Such limitations are certainly recognized here. Nonetheless, we believe (albeit with due circumspection) that some valid and useful design knowledge has been generated by the microworld, and that the trends seen here have a degree of generalizability. The fact that outcomes ran against some of our broad expectations in itself provides a cogent argument for the use of such empirical methods. Design science differs from other realms of science (March and Smith 1995; Walls et al. 1992) in that its knowledge-base must be judged against utilitarian criteria as well as predictive and explanatory validity. This utility test (Venable 2006) has been passed; we have confirmed the heuristic potential of microworld methodology for generating realistic behavioral data, testing ideas, and developing design theory.

Design science differs from everyday design work in its aspiration to produce *theory*, not to build specific working systems. The artefacts constructed here are simply the means to this loftier end, vehicles for testing ideas and hypotheses in the endeavor to construct a body of generalizable knowledge regarding the design of a certain class of artefact. Methodologically, we would certainly affirm design science to be challenging. The experimental psychologist deals with one primary source of validity threats in her theory-building labors, those arising from the quality of the experimental design. She has the luxury of working with highly simplified experimental models (decocting real-world phenomena into some putative canonical form) and the theoretical knowledge sought is relatively simple and well-circumscribed. In contrast, empirical realism is vital in design science, enabling knowledge to generalize across a wide range of contexts of use, tempered by relevant singularities. We should, therefore, expect to see the accumulation of a relatively unstable body of contingent knowledge punctuated by exceptions and caveats (rather than necessary, timeless truths), resisting easy codification. The design researcher must always be alert for emergent phenomena and unintended consequences, dexterously ready to switch direction, to change approach, to explore different theoretical perspectives. In this disorderly world, induction and abduction represent more relevant modes of reasoning than strict deduction, as design researchers try to make sense of the complex and inconsistent findings furnished by even relatively simple experiments such as the present ones.

Doing design science necessarily involves design work, regarding both the design of the "experimentation" (field or laboratory) and of the artefact itself. Like design, we have argued that it is best prosecuted heuristically and opportunistically, but perhaps this argument should be pushed further. There is much that reflects the *habitus* of conventional behavioral science in the present work. The experimenters were very much in charge, and the empirics had a largely linear trajectory with little adaptation to user feedback. Critical elements of good design practice were lacking, in particular prototyping and user participation. We will end on the chastening thought that, had we worked more collaboratively and iteratively with our users (using prototypes, for instance, to explore design ideas), we may well have produced not only a better artefact but more robust theory as well. Reflecting this, users in our future work will be more fully engaged as partners and coproducers of design knowledge, rather than passive guinea pigs!

Acknowledgments

We gratefully acknowledge the financial support of the German Research Foundation (DGF) for carrying out this work (Research Grant: SFB392/TFB55).

References

Bennett, K. B., Payne, M., and Walyers, B. 2005. "An Evaluation of a 'Time Tunnel' Display Format for the Presentation of Temporal Information," *Human Factors* (47:2), pp. 342-359.

Boland, R., and Collopy, F. 2004. *Managing as Designing*, Stanford, CA: Stanford University Press.

Brehmer B., and Dörner, D. 1993. "Experiments with Computer-Simulated Microworlds: Escaping Both the Narrow Straits of the Laboratory and the Deep Blue Sea of the Field Study," *Computers in Human Behavior* (9:2/3), pp. 171-184.

Brown, S. A, and Venkatesh, V. 2005. "Model of Adoption of Technology in Households: A Baseline Model Test and Extension Incorporating Household Lifecycle," *MIS Quarterly* (29:3), pp. 399-426.

Chatterjee, S., and Hevner, A. 2006. "Program Co-Chairs Message," First International Conference on Design Science Research in Information Systems and Technology, Claremont Graduate University, February 24-25 (http://ncl.cgu.edu/designconference/Cochairmsg.htm).

Davis, F. D., Bagozzi, R. P., and Warshaw, P. R. 1989. "User Acceptance of Technology: A Comparison of Two Theoretical Models," *Management Science* (35:8), pp. 982-1003.

Elam, J. J., and Leidner, D. G. 1995. "EIS Adoption, Use, and Impact: The Executive Perspective," *Decision Support Systems* (14:21), pp. 89-103.

Gregor, S.. 2006. "The Nature of Theory in Information Systems," *MIS Quarterly* (30:3), pp. 611-642.

Hevner, A. R., March, S. T., Park, J., and Ram, S. 2004. "Design Science in Information Systems Research," *MIS Quarterly* (28:1), pp. 75-105.

Hung, S. 2003. "Expert vs. Novice Use of Executive Support Systems: An Empirical Study," *Information and Management* (40:3), pp. 177-189.

Kroemer, K., Kroemer, H., and Kroemer-Elbert, K. 2001. *Ergonomics: How to Design for Ease and Efficiency*, Upper Saddle River, NJ: Prentice-Hall.

Locke, E. A., and Latham, G. P. 2002. "Building a Practically Useful Theory of Goal Setting and Task Motivation: A 35 Year Odyssey," *American Psychologist* (57:9), pp. 705-717.

March, S. T., and Smith, G. 1995. "Design and Natural Science Research on Information Technology," *Decision Support Systems* (15:4), pp. 251-266.

Markus, L.. Majchrzak, A., and Gasser, L. 2002. "A Design Theory for Systems That Support Emergent Knowledge Processes," *MIS Quarterly* (26:3), pp. 179-212.

McCalley, L. T., and Midden, C. J. H. 2002. "Energy Conservation Through Product Integrated Feedback: The Roles of Goal-Setting and Social Orientation," *Journal of Economic Psychology* (22:5), pp. 589-603.

Norman, D. A. 1988. *The Design of Everyday Things*, London: MIT Press.

Rasmussen, J., Pejtersen, A. M., and Goodstein, L. P. 1994. *Cognitive Systems Engineering*, New York: Wiley.

Richardson, A. 1993. "The Death of the Designer," *Design Issues* (9:2), pp. 34-43.

Rogers, E. M. 1995. *Diffusion of Innovations*, New York: The Free Press.

Sarter, N. B., and Schroeder, B. 2001. "Supporting Decision-Making and Action Selection Under Time Pressure and Uncertainty: The Case of In-Flight Icing," *Human Factors* (43:4), pp. 573-583.

Sauer, J., Wastell, D., and Hockey, G. R. J. 2000. "Using Micro-Worlds to Simulate Highly-Automated Work Environments: The Case of the Cabin Air Management System," *Computers in Human Behavior* (165:1), pp. 45-58.

Sauer, J., Schmeink, C., Wastell, D. 2007. "Feedback Quality and Environmentally Friendly Use of Domestic Central Heating Systems," *Ergonomics* (50:6), pp. 795-813.

Sintchenko, V., and Coeira, E. 2003. "Which Clinical Decisions Benefit from Automation: A Task Complexity Approach," *International Journal of Medical Informatics* (70:3), pp. 309-316.

Spenkelink, G. P. J. 1990. "Aiding the Operator's Anticipatory Behavior: The Design of Process State Information," *Applied Ergonomics* (21:3), pp. 199-206.

Van Houwelingen, J., and Van Raaij, W. 1989. "The Effect of Goal-Setting and Daily Electronic Feedback on In-Home Energy Use," *Journal of Consumer Research* (16:1), pp. 98-105.

Venable, J. R. 2006. "The Role of Theory and Theorizing in Design Science Research," in *Proceedings of the First International Conference on Design Science Research in Information Systems and Technology*, S. Chatterjee and A. Hevner (eds.), Claremount Graduate University, February 24-25 (http://ncl.cgu.edu/designconference/DESRIST%202006%20Proceedings/2A_1.pdf).

Venkatesh, V., and Brown, S. 2001. "A Longitudinal Investigation of Personal Computers in Homes: Adoption Determinants and Emerging Challenges," *MIS Quarterly* (25:1), pp. 71-102.

Vicente, K. 2003. *The Human Factor*, New York: Routledge.

Vijayasarathy, L. R. 2004. "Predicting Consumer Intentions to Use On-Line Shopping: The Case for an Augmented Technology Acceptance Model," *Information and Management* (41:6), pp. 747-762.

Walls, J. G., Widmeyer, G. R., and El Sawy, O. A. 1992. "Building an Information Systems Design Theory for Vigilant EIS,". *Information Systems Research* (3:1), pp. 36-59.

Wastell, D. G. 1997. "Human-Machine Dynamics in Complex Information Systems: The "Microworld" Paradigm as a Heuristic Tool for Developing Theory and Exploring Design Issues," *Information Systems Journal* (6:4), pp. 245-260

Wastell D. G., Sauer, J. S., and Hockey, G. R. J. 2993, "Using Micro-Worlds in Research on Distributed Cognition in Complex Dynamic Worlds: A Ten Year Retrospective on the Cabin Air Management System," in *Cognitive Science Approaches to Process Control,* G. van der Veer and J. F. Hoorn (eds.), Le Chesnay, France: EACE, pp. 145-150.

Weick, C. 1990. "Organizational Redesign as Improvisation," in *Organizational Change and Redesign*, G. Huber and W. Glick (eds.), New York: Oxford University Press, pp. 346-382.

Wickens, C. D., Gordon, S., and Lui, Y. 2000. *Introduction to Human Factors Engineering*, Upper Saddle River, NJ: Pearson-Prentice Hall.
Wickens, C. D., and Hollands, J. G. 2000. *Engineering Psychology and Human Performance*, Upper Saddle River, NJ: Prentice Hall.

About the Authors

David Wastell is a professor of Information Systems at Nottingham University Business School. He began his research career as a psycho-physiologist before moving into information systems. His research interests are in public sector reform, innovation and design, management epistemology, and cognitive ergonomics. He has co-organized two previous IFIP WG8.6 conferences (1997 and 2007) and was research co-chair for the IFIP WG8.2 conference in Manchester in 2004. David may be contacted at dave_wastell@hotmail.com or david.wastell@nottingham. ac.uk.

Juergen Sauer is Professor of Cognitive Ergonomics at the University of Freibourg in Switzerland, a position he took up following his previous appointment at the Darmstadt University of Technology (Germany), where the present work was conducted. His interests are in the human factors design of complex systems and the ecological design of domestic artefacts. Juergen may be contacted at juergen.sauer@unifr.ch.

Claudia Schmeink works as a research assistant at the Institute of Psychology, Darmstadt University of Technology, Germany. She has a background in educational psychology and counseling. Claudia may be contacted at schmeink@psychologie.tu-darmstadt.de.

17 THE ROLE OF COMPETENCIES AND INTERESTS IN DEVELOPING COMPLEX INFORMATION TECHNOLOGY ARTEFACTS: The Case of a Metering System

Diego Ponte
Alessandro Rossi
Marco Zamarian
Università degli Studi di Trento
Trento, Italy

Abstract   *This paper contributes to the ongoing debate on the relationship between artefacts and organizational structuration by describing the dynamics surrounding the collaborative development of information technology artefacts. The research addresses a clear gap in the literature, as cooperation in artefact design has rarely been analyzed. To explore this issue, we analyze as a case study the various attempts, undertaken by a consortium of various economic actors, at developing an electronic metering system. The main results emerging from the field study are (1) the relevance of each actor's interests as the main rationale for explaining the technical features of the artefact, (2) the role of negotiation and consensus in determining the final shape of the artefact in term of its features, and (3) the bundling/unbundling of features within the physical object as the cooperative effort rises/falls.*

Keywords   Artefacts, interests, ambiguity, competencies

1   INTRODUCTION

In the last few decades information technology artefacts have been attracting the attention of organizational scholars. The reasons behind this attention are twofold. First, the role and importance of IT artefacts (thereafter simply called artefacts) in the current

Please use the following format when citing this chapter:

Ponte, D., Rossi, A., and Zamarian, M., 2008, in IFIP International Federation for Information Processing, Volume 287, Open IT-Based Innovation: Moving Towards Cooperative IT Transfer and Knowledge Diffusion, eds. León, G., Bernardos, A., Casar, J., Kautz, K., and DeGross, J. (Boston: Springer), pp. 291-308.

economy is growing fast. Second, the introduction of artefacts within an organization often implies the modification of current patterns of action and routines. Such an introduction usually influences the layout of a firm and might be in contrast with the current way of doing things (Orlikowski 2000).

The increasing pace of technology evolution in recent years has made IT artefacts very complex objects: they embed multiple technologies and might pursue numerous complex tasks without human intervention. The reverse side of this complexity is that firms find it too much of a challenge to possess and manage all of the necessary knowledge that is needed to design and produce such artefacts. Thus, it is becoming more and more common for firms to rely on formal and informal agreements with heterogeneous partners to cooperate and to mutually complete the respective capabilities and competencies. As a consequence, conventional models, methods, and tools used to support artefact design and implementation are becoming obsolete.

From this latter point, we feel that current research is in need of a deeper understanding of the processes underlining artefact development within a network of actors (firms, research institutes, and the public sector). In fact, while it is well known that within an organization the development of new products and artefacts is a complex and tough task, this task grows in complexity when considering several nonhomogenous actors: the knowledge, language, competencies, and identities at stake might be very different and even inconsistent. Furthermore, as artefacts have been considered as reifications of the firm's competencies and knowledge, the development of an artefact by a network of firms poses the question of how different firms with different competencies will cooperate and negotiate the creation of a common framework to develop the artefact.

The paper describes and discusses the evolution of the design of a specific artefact: an electronic metering system. This artefact has been the topic of research within a consortium of firms operating in the green building/renewable energy business. The results of the analysis show that the conceptualization and evolution of the artefact was mainly driven by the interests of the actors at hand rather than by pure technical problems and concerns. First, the case study shows that the vision of the artefact's features and goals evolves as the actors working on it change over time. Second, this evolution is dependent only on the firms' interests in preserving their competencies and capabilities. A major corollary of this study is that while the technology allows the conceptualization of several possible configurations of the artefact's functionalities, the final configuration is chosen in a way that is consistent with the interests and competencies of the actors at hand. These findings make it possible to shed new light on the social processes that characterize the negotiation process around an artefact.

2   IT ARTEFACTS: BETWEEN DESIGN AND USE

IT artefacts have been defined as objects that embed sets of rules for goal-oriented action (Norman 1991, 1993). This definition allows us to identify some specific characteristics of artefacts. First, they are usually considered goal-oriented tools: they are designed to solve problems and help achieve some particular tasks and actions (Hutchins 1995). As such, artefacts often help lower the cognitive complexity of a particular activity: thus they are considered to be *crystallized solutions* for recurrent problems.

Second, as they embed already developed routines and solutions to current problems, artefacts tend to structure and shape organizational behavior. Although artefacts might be customized by users, a kind of behavior which has been called *instrumentation* (Rabardel 2003), their purpose in curbing the complexity of a particular task implies that such customization can be fulfilled only partially. In particular, users can rarely change the artefact's core.

Third, as artefacts embed solutions to some particular problems, they are considered objects that reify the knowledge and the competencies of the individuals designing and using them (Hutchins 1995). Furthermore, artefacts become part of the tools that are significant from an organizational perspective because they incorporate rules for negotiating between differing, and at times conflicting, points of view (Masino and Zamarian 2003).

In the current literature on artefacts, design and use are usually treated as different phases with different actors (experts versus users), inputs (the problem versus the artefact), outputs (the artefact versus the accomplishment of a particular task), and purposes.

Historically, analysis of artefacts began by looking at their diffusion within an environment; the design phase was barely taken into consideration (Arthur 1989; David 1986). In the last few decades, this situation has rapidly changed (Dosi 1992). Currently, scholars tend not to separate the evolution of an artefact into rigid phases: design and use are not detached (Dosi 2000; Gherardi and Nicolini 1999). This change of focus in the analysis is linked to the growing recognition that designing an artefact should be considered as a shared activity among a set of interacting actors (designer and users) (Béguin 2003; Béguin and Rabardel 2000; Bødker 1996).

Recently, this latter consideration has been put forward as a step toward recognizing that the design phase might be a phase where different heterogeneous actors and organizations interact. This might happen in situations where actors must cope with new and complex technologies, unclear problems, and innovative solutions (Albinsson et al. 2007).

Focusing on how different organizations try to collaborate to develop an artefact opens up the opportunity for new research. In fact, while it is well known that within an organization the development of new products and artefacts is a complex and tough task (Bechky 2003; Carlile 2002), this task grows in complexity when considering the interaction of several heterogeneous actors. In this latter case it is well known that knowledge, language, competencies, values and identities of the interacting actors might be idiosyncratic (Gherardi and Nicolini 1999; Woolgar 1991). Unfortunately current research has barely addressed such developments (Beck 2002). Scholars have focused on analyzing either the interaction between design and use of artefacts within individual organizations or the processes of interaction between several kinds of actors within each of the two processes (Chesbrough 2003; Perry and Sanderson 1998). Other studies have suggested the adoption of best practices, which unfortunately are not always carefully operationalized (Docherty 2006). Furthermore, other studies focus on sector-level analyses, which do not offer a rich understanding of the micro-factors influencing design and implementation (Laursen and Salter 2006).

We try to address some of these concerns by analyzing the dynamics surrounding the attempts at creating an innovative, complex artefact: an electronic metering system, developed within a private/public consortium operating in the green building/renewable energy business. This case study is relevant for at least three reasons. First, the artefact was a complex object made of heterogeneous parts (software and hardware) that implied the use of different technologies (wired communication, wireless communication) owned by different actors, representing various companies and research institutions. Second, the team of designers was made up of several heterogeneous actors (firms, research institutes, and the public sector). This team evolved over time, so consequently the goal of the artefact evolved over time. Third, the artefact did not have a commonly agreed upon and well-understood goal. In fact, more than just a set of core services (management of power consumption flows), the metering system was intended to cover a set of disparate peripheral services such as the management of gas and water consumption as well as domotics and communication services.

3   THE CASE STUDY

The context of our case study is a consortium of firms operating in the green building/renewable energy industries. The consortium, located in a highly developed region of an EU country, was born out of the voluntary initiative of private corporations and various other stakeholders with the goal of facilitating and fostering the innovation and collaboration activities of local firms working in various environmentally sustainable industries.

We focused on the *network workgroup* initiative, which is a workgroup aimed at designing and developing innovations in the business of local communication infrastructure. The main task of the workgroup, at the time, was that of designing an artefact that took care of the management of incoming/outgoing data fluxes of a building (gas, power, water, etc.).

In order to clarify the relationship between the different actors, in the next paragraph we characterize the institutional framework within which these companies operate; then we outline the main events accounting for the evolution of the artefact.

The Consortium. In March 2005, Local Government, in agreement with various economic institutions (such as the local Development Agency and the Chamber of Commerce) and various local research centers and universities, signed an agreement aimed at developing a regional "Pole of Excellence" in the green building/renewable energy business. As a result, Local Government supported the creation of a public–private Consortium, comprising over 300 private corporations as well as the most important public institutions. The official aim of the Consortium is that of supporting collaboration and innovation between its various stakeholders both at the local and global level. The Consortium began its activities in 2006. In particular, the Consortium focused on topics such as the construction of green buildings (energy efficient buildings), on high efficiency heating systems, on intelligent systems for the management of water, power, and communications flows, and on systems for the production of renewable power.

In each of these areas, the Consortium organized a series of initiatives to facilitate collaboration, the transfer of knowledge, and innovation among its stakeholders. Four of them were particularly important:

- Set up and management of technical workgroups. These workgroups aim at facing and solving specific problems and topics that are related to the green building/ renewable energy sectors. It is to be noted that each workgroup's activities are managed by a facilitator, a Consortium-selected manager who takes care of all of the practical and strategic issues of the workgroup.

- Training initiatives, aimed at raising competencies and professional roles around specific technical standards or new regulations.
- Management of public relations at the aggregate level (brand management, participation in international fairs and seminars, etc.).
- Special services dedicated to the support of innovation and the creation of new services and products.

The network workgroup belongs to the first of these activities. The next paragraph describes the evolution of the network workgroup.

The Network Workgroup. As mentioned earlier, one of the tasks of the Consortium was that of establishing several technical workgroups. The network workgroup was mentioned in the official documents of the Consortium soon after its start-up in 2005. The goal of the workgroup revolved around the idea of supplying the local area with a fully coordinated communication network that would allow "objects" (buildings, infrastructures, etc.) to "communicate with each other" with the aim of improving efficiency in the consumption of resources (power, water, gas, etc.) and of streamlining various other services, such as domotics, social assistance, etc. Out of the 300 individual members of the Consortium, 29 have taken part in the network workgroup.

Figure 1 sketches a graphical representation of the main actors involved in the debate on the innovative artefact and distinguishes between actors directly participating in the workgroup activities and those influencing the workgroup activities even if not directly involved in its activities.[1] Circles identify single agents while octagons identify members representing several actors (e.g., consortiums). The size of each circle and octagon identifies the bargaining power of each actor (either directly involved in the workgroup or not). The assessment of bargaining power is described in the methodology section. In short, the most powerful actors among those participating in the workgroup were the economic branches of the local government (LocalEnergy and LocalNet). LocalEnergy manages the local power network while LocalNet manages the public communication infrastructure.

Among the private participants, the most influential were the local consortiums of firms working in heating systems maintenance (HSMA Group), in the telecommunication sector (Com Group), and in the production and distribution of power (Power Group). Other less important actors involved in the workgroup were Houseit (a multinational in the home appliances business), X-Info (a local mid-size informatics firm) and a set of spin-off companies: TeleExp (a research center in telecommunication technologies), MicroElec (a microelectronic firm), and CareSolution (a remote health care service firm).

The figure also shows the external actors, who, although not directly involved in the workgroup, influenced and shaped the evolution of its activities. The external actors influencing the workgroup were NationalEnergy (the largest energy supplier of the country), Infomatic (a worldwide IT solutions provider), Local Government, and two political branches of Local Government (Social Affairs and Innovation Affairs offices).

---

[1]For reasons of privacy, the real names of the firms involved in the case study have been changed.

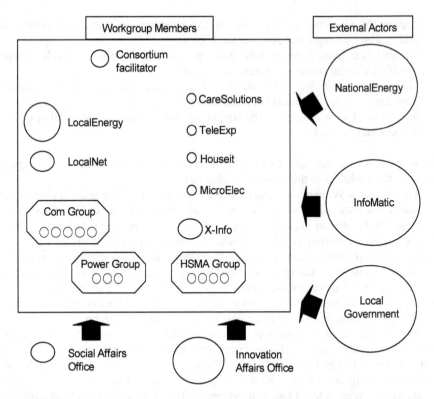

NOTES: The circles identify single actors. The size of the circle identifies the power of each actor. The octagons identify multiple actors (e.g., consortia of firms that work in the same sector). The number of circles within each octagon approximates the number of members of each consortium.
Power Group: firms working within the energy sector (supply of energy, maintenance).
Com Group: firms working within the telecommunication sector.
HSMA Group: firms working within the heating systems maintenance sector.

Figure 1. Participants of the Network Workgroup and External Actors Influencing the Innovation Debate

3.1 Methodology

The complexity of the case required the adoption of a qualitative methodology (Denzin and Lincoln 1994). In particular, the data collection was divided into two main phases. The first phase aimed at understanding the economic–institutional context in which the case study took place. This phase, performed during the first part of the 2007, was grounded on second-hand materials such as newspaper articles, official and technical papers, and institutional materials.

The second part of the data collection focused on the actual activities performed by the workgroup. The goal of this part was that of gathering data about the evolution of the artefact and the elements influencing such evolution. This part of the research was based on:

- A series of interviews with key actors of both the workgroup and the Consortium. We used structured interviews, as we wanted to focus on a specific experience (Silverman 2001): we wanted to confine the discussion to several aspects surrounding the artefact, the workgroup dynamics, and the actors involved.
- Participant observation of the activities of the workgroup (Atkinson, and Hammersley 1994; Merton et al. 1990). One of the researchers actively took part in the meetings of the workgroup. In particular, the researcher took part in several meetings that were concerned with the workgroup. This participation made it possible to track the dynamics among the different (and changing) actors.
- Document analysis. We acquired several internal documents such as agendas and minutes of meetings, as well as institutional material distributed by the Consortium.

Table 1 summarizes interviews and official meetings attended. The output of this phase was a report of the artefact's evolution and the actors involved over the period from a historical perspective.

The analysis of the data was split into two main phases. The first phase aimed at assessing the bargaining power of each actor. We also sought to establish the reasons (the interests) that motivate each actor to participate in the workgroup. The assessment of bargaining power was determined via a two-step procedure. First, we analyzed the business, market, and regulatory characteristics of each involved actor. For instance, we assumed NationalEnergy to have a high bargaining power as it controls over 80 percent of the national power distribution market. We also considered Local Government and LocalEnergy to have a high bargaining power (although less than that of NationalEnergy) as they govern and control the local power distribution market. We then considered the other actors as having less bargaining power, as they do not hold dominant positions. During the second step we adjusted this first assessment by means of the *post hoc* interviews and by taking part in the workgroup activities.

Table 1. Review of the Material Used During the Analysis

Meetings Attended	
29/05/07	Network Workgroup meeting
04/06/07	Consortium plenary meeting
05/10/07	IDDC (Innovation in Development and Design of Constructions) Committee preliminary meeting
08/10/07	Network Workgroup meeting
08/11/07	Network Workgroup meeting
Interviews	
10/05/07	Former facilitator of the workgroup
11/07/07	Current president of the Consortium
01/10/07	Current facilitator of the workgroup
24/05/07	CEO of the Consortium

The second phase of the data analysis aimed at triangulating all available data in order to establish whether the negotiation dynamics and the evolution of the artefact were driven by the interests of the actors involved. The inputs of this phase were the economic–institutional report, the historical report, and the bargaining power report as previously introduced. We were thus able to see whether the evolution of the artefact's interpretation was subject both to the indirect bargaining power indicator and to the more direct dynamics of the workgroup meetings. In the next section we briefly review the main events of the case study and discuss the findings of our analysis.

3.2 Time Line of the Main Events

This section describes the history and the evolution of the dynamics surrounding the conceptualization of the artefact under discussion during our analysis. The time line starts with a description of a prior, similar project carried out by NationalEnergy. It goes on to detail the three different stages of the evolution of the metering system (Figure 2).

3.2.1 Before 2006: The Origins

The artefact under analysis has roots in an innovation project started by National Energy, a leading power supply company. In the final years the past century, National

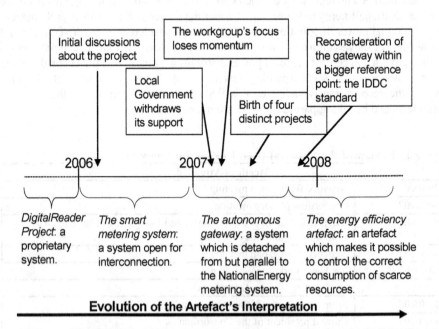

Figure 2. Review of the Case Study Time Line and Description of the Interpretive Frameworks Used to Describe the Artefact

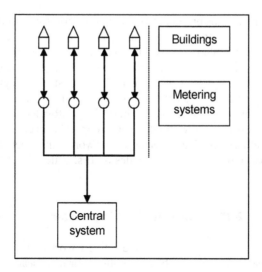

Figure 3. Outline of the DigitalReader Architecture

Energy started a project aimed at introducing the first worldwide digital metering system (hereafter called DigitalReader) as a replacement for the old electro-mechanical metering system. The research activities concerning the DigitalReader, being quite challenging, took almost 10 years from the first conceptualization to its installation. The Digital Reader (see Figure 3) was designed as a metering system able to:

- Manage data coming from both the central system and from the buildings: the system not only collected data about power usage, but also about water consumption and communication exchanges from other sources.
- Make automatic decisions and actions aimed at improving the efficiency of resources consumption. This task should have been performed—and this is the main innovation—without the direct intervention of the central system.

Due to these features the metering system was labeled "smart" (thereafter referred to as smart DigitalReader).

NationalEnergy interacted with two main high technology partners for both the design and industrialization phases of the artefact. The first partner, Chiplon, was an innovative firm engaged in the production of smart chips. Chiplon supplied National Energy with a high-tech chip that is the reason behind the improved capabilities of the smart metering system. The second partner was a multinational firm based in Europe that was responsible for the production of the metering system. The rest of the project team consisted of internal personnel.

Starting in 2001, NationalEnergy began to install the metering system. While the original device was recognized as a worldwide innovation, NationalEnergy decided to install a dumbed-down version of that system that was lacking the innovative capabilities of the smart one (automatic decisions, no need of a centralized system). The dumbed-down DigitalReader was thus presented as a digital metering system lacking the feature of interacting with the buildings. NationalEnergy also put a stop to the collaboration with Chiplon claiming that Chiplon was working on a concurrent project with other companies. Today the DigitalReader project is over, as far as its development is concerned. The dumbed-down DigitalReader has been installed in most of the country: in fact, more than 80 percent of the country's territory is covered by this system.

As previously mentioned, the evolution of the DigitalReader project is important as it sheds light on what happened within the workgroup. The electronic metering system was in fact not installed in the local area as the network—managed by LocalEnergy, a firm owned by Local Government—still relies on first generation, electro-mechanical devices.

3.2.2 2006–Spring 2007: The New Metering System

Starting in 2006, the workgroup began to actively work at the idea of an electronic metering system. Several actors (public institutions, firms, research institutes) participated in the activities of the workgroup. In 2006, during a conference organized by the Consortium, the facilitator of the workgroup launched the idea of introducing in the local area a metering system similar to the one previously discarded by NationalEnergy (the smart DigitalReader). The aim was to develop a real information gateway able to communicate both with the devices within the building and with a central system that belonged to the multi-utility company. In contrast with the solution implemented by NationalEnergy (the dumbed-down DigitalReader), which used a proprietary protocol, this gateway was intended to operate under an open communication protocol. Thus, it was open to interaction with other systems.

At this stage, several actors supported the system. This is due to the fact that the electronic metering system would have allowed several peripheral services. The workgroup identified four different types of features, each supported by different sets of actors:

- Remote maintenance of home appliances. This feature was sponsored by Houseit, a home appliance multinational.
- Remote management services. This project, led by the heating systems maintenance association (thereafter HSMA group), includes several subgoals:
  - The first set of services was intended to manage the remote-reading of water and gas consumption
  - The second set of services was intended to support security services.
  - The third set of services aimed at developing a web-based interface of the aforementioned services.
- Remote health care. This subproject, led by the spin-off company CareSolutions, was intended to function as a remote channel to provide services to the elderly and individuals who were not self-sufficient. This project was also supported by the local government social affairs committee.
- Domotics. This subproject was promoted by MicroElec, a microelectronics firm, and was intended to offer in-house services such as the remote management of the internal temperature and humidity, as well as fire prevention services.

In 2007, the initiative was presented to a local software firm, which was partly owned by InfoMatic. InfoMatic was not a participant either in the Consortium or in the workgroup, but became aware of the local project. It is worth noting that there is a business relationship between InfoMatic and NationalEnergy. InfoMatic was in fact supplying NationalEnergy with the software of the dumbed-down DigitalReader system. After this news, InfoMatic started lobbying in the local area with the aim of derailing the project. InfoMatic also informed NationalEnergy about the project.

3.2.3 Spring 2007: The Short Life of the Gateway

Thanks to the lobbying activities of InfoMatic, the project to introduce a smart metering system experienced a sudden halt. Once InfoMatic (and thus NationalEnergy) showed its opposition to the project, the local power supply company, LocalEnergy, withdrew its support. Indeed, a clarification meeting with the local government (owner of LocalEnergy), made it clear that they were opposed to the project as well, claiming that the rest of the country was using the dumbed-down DigitalReader artefact and that they were looking for a robust and reliable system rather than an innovative one.

Once the support of the local government and LocalEnergy was withdrawn from the project, the workgroup experienced a chaotic period. At that time, the goal of the workgroup became unclear. In fact, without the support of these actors the system could not be introduced in the local area. At first, some of the participants sought to go further with the project, calling it a *gateway*. The CEO of LocalNet and the manager of TeleExp were thinking about an information gateway, autonomous and separate from the NationalEnergy metering system. This parallel system would use an open communication protocol. The promoters pushed this idea on the grounds that the local government had put a lot of effort into developing a communication infrastructure throughout the whole territory (indeed LocalNet was in charge of implementing and managing this infrastructure). Their idea was that, if a local multi-utility was willing to support the project, perhaps the project could gather the necessary support from other actors. Unfortunately, this idea did not achieve any momentum. In fact, during the spring of 2007, the activities of the workgroup once again came close to a halt. Nonetheless, the relative ambiguity of the workgroup goals, and the confusion during spring 2007, lead to the start of four independent subprojects during the summer.

3.2.4 The Birth of Four Subprojects

The chaotic phase of the workgroup saw the birth of four different research proposals. As the group had lost some of its members, the facilitator of the workgroup and the managers of the Consortium were noticeably surprised at the growing number of proposals submitted concerning the artefact. These projects were promoted by different actors, none of whom was aware of the other projects.

The collaboration with LabTech and MultiPower. LocalNet and TeleExp, having failed to attract the necessary support from the workgroup, constituted the first autonomous subproject, aimed at producing a working metering device. This group was interested more in a simple object that could work promptly than in a comprehensive communication and data management project. The goal was that of discovering the real costs and practical functionalities of such an artefact.

This project was supported by a micro-electronics company, LabTech, a producer of components for the communication sector. The participants also wanted to assess the sustainability of such a project by means of field tests. The opportunity for performing a test was supplied by a multi-utility, MultiPower. This company supplies water and gas power in a nearby extensive metropolitan area. MultiPower was involved as they were already working on a very similar project.

The three minor projects. In parallel to the aforementioned project, three separate sets of firms presented three proposals to the managers of the Consortium. The peculiarity of these proposals is that they were autonomously prepared by each coalition, bypassing the role of the Consortium managers. These proposals were focused on different types of business opportunities and show a clear lineage with the projects presented in the first stage of the workgroup. The three projects were Remote Management Services (sponsored by the HSMA group), Remote HealthCare Services (led by CareSolutions), and Domotics (sponsored by the microelectronic firm MicroElec).

The outcome of these projects is at present unclear, since they are still in progress. In effect, they seem to suffer from serious lack of leadership, since they are managed neither by the facilitator of the workgroup nor by other managers of the Consortium. Nonetheless, it seems that the scope of these latter projects is exploratory in nature rather than pertaining to a tangible new business initiative.

3.2.5 Recent Developments of the Workgroup: The IDDC Standard

Since October 2007, the workgroup has shown renewed commitment to a common goal. This impulse is the result of external input. In this period, the Consortium presented its new strategic agenda for the next 10 years. This document sets out the agenda for fostering the development of green and sustainable businesses within the local area. Moreover, it sets the new guidelines to achieve such a goal. As an example, the Consortium decided to adopt, in agreement with the local government, the IDDC (Innovation in Development and Design of Constructions)[2] green-building standard as a reference point for the construction of new buildings in the local area. Here the Consortium decided to apply for the possibility to become the national reference-point of the IDDC certification.

In this context, the metering system has been proposed anew as an essential tool to efficiently manage the flux of data coming in and out of the buildings. While this is the purpose, it is not possible to describe the evolution of the situation as it is still evolving.

4   ANALYSIS

In this section, we discuss the behavior and choices of the different actors in an attempt to describe the rationale for their decisions about the artefact.

---

[2]The IDDC standard is an international protocol that includes a set of principles for the design and production of green buildings.

4.1   Until 2006: The DigitalReader Project

The behavior of NationalEnergy, although not the focus of this paper, deserves some attention. In fact, while its smart DigitalReader project was considered a worldwide innovation, NationalEnergy decided not to install it in favor of a clearly inferior device (the dumbed-down version of the original project). NationalEnergy also stopped the collaboration with Chiplon claiming that Chiplon was working on a competing device with other partners. From our point of view, the reason behind this decision might be found in the fact that Chiplon asked NationalEnergy to adopt an open communication protocol for its metering system while NationalEnergy wanted to use (and eventually adopted) a proprietary protocol. These inconsistent views about an important aspect of the metering system might be the real cause of the end of the cooperation. On the one hand, Chiplon wanted an open protocol so to have an interoperable device, while NationalEnergy wanted a proprietary device so as to avoid any possible interaction with other systems. And the position of NationalEnergy was irremovable. As a matter of fact, this behavior resulted in the deterioration of the relationship with Chiplon and with the decision to install the dumbed-down version of the DigitalReader.

4.2   2006–2007: The Smart Metering System

As already mentioned, the project of a smart metering system came to a stop due to the lobbying activities of InfoMatic. We need to underline here that the resistance was not technical in nature. The local area was still using the old electro-mechanical metering device while the installation of the new system had been planned already (about 400,000 pieces). This was a compulsory task as a recent directive of the National Power Regulation Authority urged the power supply firms to introduce an electronic metering system. For obvious reasons, the natural candidate to be installed in the local area was the dumbed-down DigitalReader (which had already gained a market share of over 80 percent).

The features of the metering system that was developed locally, as a second candidate, would have been clearly in contrast with the dumbed-down DigitalReader (which, again, had been developed by NationalEnergy in cooperation with InfoMatic, who provided the software): these characteristics might be summarized by the openness of the system protocol. The NationalEnergy/InfoMatic artefact was based on a closed communication protocol while the project of the workgroup would have adopted an open protocol, as it was in the best interest of the independent third party service providers.

The strong lobbying activities of InfoMatic convinced the local government, and thus the local power supplier (LocalEnergy) to give up their support of the project. Local Government justified its behavior by arguing that the workgroup proposal was too innovative and hazardous from an economic point of view. Indeed, Local Government and the local power supplier (LocalEnergy) were seeking a robust and longstanding artefact while the other participants of the workgroup liked the possibility of working on the innovative aspects of the artefact.

4.3 2007: The Gateway and the Birth of Several Subprojects

This phase seems to be the most intriguing as, once the support of the main local actor—Local Government—vanished, the workgroup faced serious problems. This is due to several reasons:

- There was no main actor with enough strength to dominate the negotiating workgroup.
- The withdrawal of LocalEnergy from the project resulted in the disappearance of an important test market for the device.
- The interests of the remaining actors were pulling in different directions.
- As a consequence, there was no clear understanding of what to do.

The combination of these factors lead the different coalitions belonging to the workgroup to work toward devices that incorporated only those feature that enabled their personal business opportunities. Obviously the easier way to achieve this goal was that of an unbundling of the characteristics of the original artefact. The problem for each of the coalitions, then, became attracting the interest and commitment of a utility network manager (the prospective adopter for the artefact, which in the previous phase was represented by LocalEnergy). So, while the general framework of the system was clear—producing an artefact able to gather, manage and send information in and out of a building—the four projects were modeled around specific core business and partnerships.

4.4 End of 2007: The IDDC Standard

The more recent activity of the workgroup (fall 2007) shows that the managers of the Consortium were trying to understand whether participants were keen on continuing the collaboration. Past history showed that, without a common goal and a leading actor, the workgroup dispersed and became purposeless. The IDDC standard provided the facilitator of the workgroup with a new opportunity to commit to a clear agenda. This standard was chosen as the new green-building policy of Local Government.

From the political point of view, the Consortium was attracted by the possibility to become the national reference point for the standard. The network workgroup is actively working on the possibility of introducing an electronic metering system as a necessary control system of buildings' consumption fluxes within the standardization protocol.

5   DISCUSSION

The environment in which the analysis was performed is the network workgroup, a place where actors of different backgrounds sought to collaborate toward a common goal: developing a smart electronic metering system.

The analysis showed that the workgroup underwent several contrasting events. The interpretation, characteristics, and features of the artefact evolved with the change of the involved and noninvolved actors. The main actors in the first period—NationalEnergy, InfoMatic, and Local Government—were the most influential actors in the workgroup. The withdrawal of their support from the initial project signed its immediate death warrant. The remaining actors did not have enough (economic and political) strength to put forward the project from a global point of view.

At the time that the leading actors left the group, the vision of what the artefact should do changed. Originally the metering system was conceived as a worldwide innovation similar to the one developed by NationalEnergy. Unfortunately the lobbying activities of InfoMatic, and thus NationalEnergy, who were not members of the workgroup, caused Local Government (and its operative branches) to block the project. After this halt, different alliances of firms submitted several independent subprojects. Although there is little information about these projects, it seems that only one of them saw the in-field experimental phase. This experimentation was only interested in analyzing the "pure" technical aspects of the artefact while the introduction into the market was a secondary aspect.

Finally, the workgroup gained renewed momentum thanks to the IDDC standard, which gave a new framework to make sense of and gather consensus on the artefact. Unfortunately at this stage it is not possible to further the discussion as these latter events are still under analysis. To summarize, it is possible to outline several important aspects that the case study does show.

Political rather than technical aspects lead the design phase. The findings of this study allow us to state that the dynamics surrounding the conceptualization of the metering system (and its following evolution) were driven by political aspects rather than by technical concerns. In fact, it seems that in each phase the technical aspects of the artefact were selected *ad hoc* on the basis of the interests (the political aspect) of the actors at hand. This evidence is further highlighted by the birth of the four different subprojects. Each of these projects was driven by the interest of the coalition/firm supporting it. The case study further shows that the plan of the workgroup was shaped by the intervention of external firms (i.e., firms that were not directly involved in the project). The lobbying activities of InfoMatic clearly show that the network workgroup was threatening its own interests.

Goal ambiguity of an artefact. The evidence also shows that the technological opportunity to attach several features to an artefact allows the involved actors to think of several plausible artefacts with different purposes. The artefact has been intended, alternatively, as (1) a traditional metering system, (2) an independent getaway for heterogeneous information flows, (3) a device (no matter whether smart or dumb) capable of supporting services provided by independent sources, and eventually (4) a device to optimize resource consumption. Each of these different interpretations of the artefact was supported by a different mix of actors. This latter consideration allows us also to state that the economic viability of a project is evaluated by the different actors on the basis of its ability to foster their specific interests and competencies. The case of the HSMA group gives us plenty of insight. Their interest in the project was based on its ability to remotely managing heating systems, thus dramatically curbing the maintenance costs.

Loss of leadership leads to unbundling. When the local government withdrew its support from the project, the network workgroup faced a chaotic period that resulted in several unrelated projects. The evidence shows that a leading actor, with its ideas and, moreover, with its bargaining power, might have an important aggregating function. In fact, until the leading actor (the local government) was involved in the project, the other less strategic and less powerful actors followed the main idea (the smart metering system) while trying to add to the artefact the "appropriate" features (i.e., the features in which they were interested). When the leading actor withdrew its support, the artefact was unbundled in several specialized projects, as none of the remaining actors possessed the necessary strength to maintain the cohesion of the group.

Artefacts and standardization. The case study shows that the conception of different devices with different purposes (the goal ambiguity), might become dangerous when particular conditions are met. In this situation, it is clear that the metering system was subject to the usual standardization dynamics: being basically a communication device, the artefact is subject to network effects and thus it can become the center of standardization wars (Cusumano et al. 1991; Dosi 2000; Stango 2004).

6   CONCLUSIONS

The analysis presented in this paper describes the dynamics surrounding the development of an artefact. The particularity of the case study is that the artefact has been developed within a network of heterogeneous actors. This is perhaps one of the main relevant aspects of this work as the mainstream literature barely analyzes such a collective way of designing artefacts. The findings of this analysis allowed the distillation of some important contributions to the current literature. We showed that the actors involved in the design of the artefact are more concerned with the political aspects of the artefact rather than with the technical problems to solve. Furthermore, we showed that without commitment or a common goal, the development of the artefact is a short-lived process as the goal-ambiguity, while it might be a useful tool to generate ideas at the earlier stages, subsequently causes confusion and impedes action.

This study suffers from some limitations. First, it is partial, as the dynamics surrounding the artefact are still in progress: the firms, the public sector, and the research institutes are still working on the artefact. As such, the process under study has not reached completion. It is, therefore, difficult to make clear cut comments about the results of the behavior of the different actors. Second, we aim at replicating this research, as replication is a required step to make in order to improve the quality and consistency of the findings (Yin 1994). One of the possible extensions regards the involvement of one of the other Consortium workgroups, which exist alongside the one analyzed in this paper.

Acknowledgments

The authors wish to thank Roberta Cuel, the Consortium CEO, and two anonymous referees for helpful comments on a previous draft. Financial support from MIUR (under the PRIN05 program) is gratefully acknowledged. The usual disclaimer applies.

References

Albinsson, L., Lind, M., and Forsgren, O. 2007. "Co-Design: An Approach to Border Crossing, Network Innovation," in *Expanding the Knowledge Economy: Issues, Applications, Case Studies*, P. Cunningham and M. Cunningham (eds.), Amsterdam: IOS Press, pp. 977-983.

Arthur, W. B. 1989. "Competing Technologies, Increasing Returns, and Lock-In by Historical Events," *The Economic Journal* (99), pp. 116-131.

Atkinson, P., and Hammersley, M. 1994. "Ethnography and Participant Observation," in *Handbook of Qualitative Research*, N. Denzin and Y. Lincoln, (eds.), Thousand Oaks, CA: Sage Publications, pp. 249-261.

Beck, E. 2002. "P for Political—Participation is Not Enough," *Scandinavian Journal of Information Systems* (14), pp. 77-92.

Bechky, B. A. 2003. "Sharing Meaning Across Occupational Communities: The Transformation of Understanding on a Production Floor," *Organization Science* (14), pp. 312-330.

Béguin, P. 2003. "Design as a Mutual Learning Process Between Users and Designers," *Interacting with Computers* (15:5), pp. 709-730.

Béguin, P., and Rabardel, P. 2000. "Designing for Instrument-Mediated Activity," *Scandinavian Journal of Information Systems* (12), pp. 173-191.

Bødker, S. 1996. "Creating Conditions for Participation: Conflicts and Resources in Systems Design," *Human Computer Interaction* (11:3), pp. 215-236.

Carlile, P. R. 2002. "A Pragmatic View of Knowledge and Boundaries: Boundary Objects in New Product Development," *Organization Science* (13), pp. 442-455.

Chesbrough, H. 2003. *Open Innovation: The New Imperative for Creating and Profiting from Technology*, Boston: Harvard Business School Press.

Cusumano, M. A., Mylonadis, Y., and Rosenbloom, R. S. 1991. "Strategic Maneuvering and Mass-Market Dynamics: The Triumph of VHS over Beta," *Business History Review* (66), pp. 51-94.

David, P. A. 1986. "Understanding the Economics of QWERTY: The Necessity of History," in *Economic History and the Modern Economist*, W. N. Parker (ed.), Oxford, UK: Blackwell, pp. 332-337.

Denzin, N. K., and Lincoln, Y. S. 1994. *Handbook of Qualitative Research*, Thousand Oaks, CA: Sage Publications.

Docherty, M. 2006. "Primer on 'Open Innovation': Principles and Practice. The Next 'Big Thing' in Innovation," PDMA Visions (30:2), pp. 13-17 (available at http://www.venture2.net/clientuploads/Visions_April06_Docherty.pdf).

Dosi, G. 1992. "Research on Innovation Diffusion: An Assessment," in *Innovation Diffusion and Social Behaviors*, A. Grubler and N. Nakicenovic (eds.), Heidelberg: Springer Verlag.

Dosi, G. 2000. *Innovation, Organization and Economic Dynamics. Selected Essays*, Cheltenham, UK: Edward Elgar.

Gherardi, S., and Nicolini, D. 1999. "La circolazione delle innovazioni come processo di traslazione," *Studi Organizzativi* (2), pp. 195-218.

Hutchins, E. 1995. *Cognition in the Wild*, Cambridge, MA: The MIT Press.

Laursen, K., and Salter, A. 2006. "Open for Innovation: The Role of Openness in Explaining Innovation Performance Among U.K. Manufacturing Firms," *Strategic Management Journal* (27), pp. 131-150.

Masino, G., and Zamarian, M. 2003. "Information Technology Artefacts as Structuring Devices in Organizations: Design, Appropriation and Use Issues," *Interacting with Computers* (15:5), pp. 693-707.

Merton, R. K., Fiske, M., and Kendall, P. L. 1990. *The Focused Interview: A Manual of Problems and Procedures* (2nd ed.), New York: Free Press.

Norman, D. A. 1991. "Cognitive Artefacts," in *Designing Interaction: Psychology at the Human–Computer Interface*, J. M. Carroll (ed.), Cambridge, UK: Cambridge University Press, pp. 17-38.

Norman, D. A. 1993. *Things that Make us Smart*, Reading, MA: Addison Wesley.

Orlikowski, W. J. 2000. "Using Technology and Constituting Structures: A Practice Lens for Studying Technology in Organizations," *Organization Science* (11:4), pp. 404-428.

Perry, M., and Sanderson, D. 1998. "Coordinating Joint Design Work: The Role of Communication and Artefacts," *Design Studies* (19), pp. 273-328.

Rabardel, P. 2003. "Editorial: From Artefact to Instrument," *Interacting with Computers* (15:5), pp. 641-645.

Silverman, D. 2001. *Interpreting Qualitative Data: Methods for Analysing Talk, Text and Interaction*, Thousand Oaks, CA: Sage Publications.

Stango, V. 2004. "The Economics of Standards Wars," *Review of Network Economics* (3), pp. 1-19.

Woolgar, S. 1991. "Configuring the User, The Case of Usability Trials," in *A Sociology of Monsters. Essays on Power Technology and Domination*, J. Law (ed.), London: Routledge, pp. 58-100.

Yin, R. K. 1994. *Case Study Research: Design and Methods* (2nd ed.), Newbury Park, CA: Sage Publications.

About the Authors

Diego Ponte (Ph.D., Cognitive Science and Education, University of Trento) is a research assistant at the Faculty of Economics, University of Trento. In his dissertation he analyzed the socio-economic aspects that influence and shape organizational renewal. His research interests also include organizational decision making, organizational conflict, knowledge management, information systems, innovation. Diego can be reached at diego.ponte@unitn.it.

Alessandro Rossi (Ph.D., Organization and Management, University of Udine) is an assistant professor of Business Economics and Management at the Faculties of Economics and Engineering, University of Trento. His current research interests are related to how organizations design and produce complex artefacts, with particular reference to knowledge intensive industries and to the open source/open content paradigm of production. Alessandro can be reached at alessandro. rossi@unitn.it.

Marco Zamarian (Ph.D., Organization and Management, University of Bologna) is an associate professor of Organization Theory and Behavior and Human Resource Management at the Faculty of Economics, University of Trento. His current research interests include organizational learning, knowledge creation and replication in geographically distributed contexts, the impact of IT artefacts on organizational knowledge, industrial clusters, and the evaluation of the effects of public subsidies to the private sector, in particular for technology acquisition and R&D activities. Marco can be reached at marco.zamarian@unitn.it.

18 THE VEHICLE ECOSYSTEM

Jonas Kuschel
IT University of Göteborg
Göteborg, Sweden

Abstract   *Ubiquitous computing in the vehicle industry has primarily focused on sensor data serving different ubiquitous on-board services (e.g., crash detection, anti-lock brake systems, or air conditioning). These services mainly address vehicle drivers while driving. However, in view of the role of vehicles in today's society, it goes without saying that vehicles relate to more than just the driver or occupants; they are part of a larger ecosystem, including traffic participants, authorities, customers and the like. To serve the ecosystem with ubiquitous services based on vehicle sensor data, there is a need for an open information infrastructure that enables service development close to the customer. This paper presents results from a research project on designing such an infrastructure at a major European vehicle manufacturer. Our empirical data shows how the vehicle manufacturer's conceptualization of services disagrees with the needs of vehicle stakeholders in a more comprehensive vehicle ecosystem. In light of this, we discuss the effect on information infrastructure design and introduce the distinction between information infrastructure as product feature and service facilitator. In a more general way, we highlight the importance of information infrastructure to contextualize the vehicle as part of a larger ecosystem and thus support open innovation.*

Keywords   Information infrastructure, services, ecosystem, open innovation

1   INTRODUCTION

Vehicles are probably one of the most mature ubiquitous computing environments. An increasing number of sensors and microcomputers control, measure, and operate various vehicle components. The sensor data facilitates ubiquitous services, such as air bag inflation or injection control, which we take for granted when driving. However,

Please use the following format when citing this chapter:

Kuschel, J., 2008, in IFIP International Federation for Information Processing, Volume 287, Open IT-Based Innovation: Moving Towards Cooperative IT Transfer and Knowledge Diffusion, eds. León, G., Bernardos, A., Casar, J., Kautz, K., and DeGross, J. (Boston: Springer), pp. 309-322.

most vehicle services are limited to the vehicle per se, even though there is a demand for making use of vehicle sensor data remotely. Remote vehicle diagnostics is one of the more prominent service directions in which the vehicle industry is heading, but has yet not succeeded in achieving. In this paper, our aim is to gain insights about the conceptualization and design of open information infrastructure to enable vehicle service innovations across the vehicle ecosystem.

The motivation to conduct research on remote vehicle services is constituted by the central role vehicles play in modern economies, since they carry assets, are part of wide-spanning workflows, affect the environment, or account for a company's assets. The role of a vehicle could thus be described as a node in a large interconnected ecosystem with various interfaces and interdependencies to various stakeholders and processes. These interdependencies would benefit from ubiquitous data describing the status of the vehicle, its load, or even its context to enhance existing processes or drive the innovation of novel services. However, there is as yet a lack of infrastructures and standards that support data exchange among the parts of the ecosystem (see Andersson 2006).

Our research thus aims to understand challenges in developing open information infrastructures that support service innovation and development among the ecosystem's stakeholders. In doing this, we have conducted a case study in collaboration with a major European vehicle manufacturer, where we participated in a research and development group working on infrastructure development for remote vehicle services. We spent a period of four months full-time work as project members to study a phenomenon through intervention. In doing this, we influenced the project work by introducing infrastructural thinking as described by Kuschel and Dahlbom (2007). The project had been initiated by the vehicle manufacturer since current remote vehicle services are provided by three different systems, each covering different brands or geographical markets. To achieve a homogenous solution, communication hardware on the vehicle is about to be consolidated, but the non-vehicle (off board) systems are still redundant. This makes the development of remote vehicle services costly, time extensive, and inflexible.

Information infrastructure theory outlines four major challenges in developing infrastructures: heterogeneity, evolution, control, and standardization (Nielsen 2006). Our aim here is to add to the understanding of heterogeneity, especially regarding organizations that change their business operations from products to services. Based on empirical observations, we show how the conceptualization of services affects the understanding and thus the design of information infrastructure. We argue that a product focus, such as services supporting products (Mathieu 2001), results in an understanding of information infrastructure that only mirrors vehicle features and functionalities. By applying a user perspective instead, vehicles turn out to be actors in a larger ecosystem where the information infrastructure acts as integration facilitator. We conclude that this constitutes the very condition for open innovation and thus heterogeneity.

The paper is organized as follows. In section 2, we outline our theoretical framework by presenting the theory of open information infrastructure. This is followed, in section 3, by a presentation of the research setting and method applied. The empirical findings are reported in section 4, and then discussed in section 5. Finally, in section 6, we see how the conceptualization of service relates to information infrastructure development and open innovation of services.

2   OPEN INFORMATION INFRASTRUCTURE

The advance of ubiquitous computing technology is about to change information technology services. As sensor and computing technology moves into the fabrics of everyday life, it is possible to gather personal customer information wherever the customer is located. This information may account for the basis of a service customization (e.g., changing vehicle services from being static and autonomous to ubiquitous and personal). As Fano and Gershman (2002) argue, ubiquitous services and business are about moving the location of business to the customer's location to provide services at the point of need rather than consuming services at the point of offer. This perspective complements Dourish's (2001) theory of embodied interaction: technologies participate in the world they represent. Information infrastructure is described as an important facilitator for such future nomadic and ubiquitous computing environments, where social and technical elements are combined (Lyytinen and Yoo 2002). Here we make use of the concept of open or universal information infrastructure, which Hanseth and Lyytinen (2004) describe as generally open to all possible users, even across different business sectors.

Nielsen (2006) outlines four analytical core concepts and challenges for building information infrastructures. These are heterogeneity, evolution, control, and standardization. Even though heterogeneity has been described by Nielsen as a major challenge in the literature, it also serves as the very condition for infrastructures to secure their growth. Due to the high level of heterogeneity, information infrastructures are described as evolving, influenced by their dependency path and the networks with which they are connected (Hanseth 2000). Nielsen describes this as interplay between evolution and construction. Ciborra et al. (2000), on the other hand, argue the development of information infrastructures to be out of control and drifting.

Information infrastructures require standardizations, socio-technical agreements about the properties of the infrastructure interface toward other infrastructures or systems (Hanseth and Monteiro 1997). This could be either the standardization of railway track widths to enable travel between two different railway networks or the standardization of TCP/IP to allow communication between various applications through, for example, the Internet. Since standardization is a mutual agreement between different representatives, negotiations may be tedious. Dahlbom (2000) describes infrastructures and standards as a relic of the material world, whereas information technology is immaterial and in essence a gateway technology making universal standardization less important. Hanseth et al. (1996) describe this phenomenon as the tension between standardization and flexibility in information infrastructure.

The role of information infrastructures and standards in the transportation industry has been described by Andersson (2007), who discusses the mobile-stationary divide as a challenge to integrate mobile vehicle systems and stationary management or transportation systems. Such integration will provide contextual data, such as driver tracking, which may imply social issues as a trade-off to efficiency and flexibility earnings. To address the technological challenges of the mobile-stationary divide in the transportation industry, a mobile-stationary interface standard has been implemented by a group[1]

---

[1]MSI Group (Mobile Stationary Interface Group). For further information, go to http://www.msigroup.se).

representing various stakeholders. However, Andersson (2007) describes the implementation as a problematic negotiation due to vehicle producers' proprietary standpoints,
underlying their ambition to keep contextual data for future services. Hence, the MSI
standard exemplifies the vehicle industries' reluctance to openness such as in open
information infrastructures.

Banavar et al. (2005) describe modern businesses as increasingly responsive to their
environment or "context ecosystem." They argue that since the context ecosystem comprises various context data providers, there is a need for a middleware to handle contextual data across different stakeholders of the ecosystem. Kuschel and Dahlbom (2007)
support a similar approach within the vehicle industry, outlining open information
infrastructure as a key condition for mobile services.

Bruno Latour's (1996) insights from the development of the French autonomous
train system, *Aramis*, may provide a good understanding of what we here refer to as *open
information*. The goal of the *Aramis* project was to create a public transportation system
where the subway's efficiency was supposed to be combined with the flexibility of automobiles. This was achieved by not physically linking parts of the train set, but inter-
connecting them virtually by a computer driven model controlling the wagons. In this
way, a number of wagons were able to travel the same track until reaching a junction,
where each wagon easily could choose a different track without physically decoupling
them. Wagons were designed as small units with only six seats and all passengers were
required to be seated. The idea was to design an efficient and flexible transportation
system for the Paris region and similar projects were ongoing in other locations (for
instance, Lyon). However, *Aramis* did not succeed even though the project lasted for 20
years and large amounts of money were spent. Latour analyses the failure of *Aramis* by
pointing out the autonomy of technology in the project. An electric engine driving each
wheel was considered as the most promising invention. However, the engine was only
applicable to *Aramis* itself. Further, field trials on the applicability of *Aramis* showed
that it was practically and economically not feasible to operate wagons with only six
seated passengers, even though technical field trials showed very good results. This
exemplifies how technology development in large projects faces a risk of running into
developing autonomous technologies that, in the end, are not applicable to the proposed
settings. Furthermore, the *Aramis* project and Latour's work provide insights on the
network of subjects and objects (i.e., the nonexistence of complete autonomous objects
as assumed by the *Aramis* project). In applying these thoughts to open information
infrastructure, we here refer to *openness* as the condition for the network of objects and
subjects to evolve.

3   RESEARCH CONTEXT AND METHOD

This paper is based on a case study at a major European vehicle manufacturer. The
project was initiated by the vehicle manufacturer to investigate the design of a future
information infrastructure for remote vehicle services, such as remote vehicle diagnosis.
We joined the project as participating researchers. Lyytinen and Yoo (2002, p. 386)
point to the local and personal characteristics of nomadic and ubiquitous computing,
which requires an "examination of phenomena as it unfolds." They consider various

anthropological methods to be promising in future IS research on nomadic and ubiquitous computing. Thus we combined ethnographic research (see Hughes et al. 1994; Schultze 2000) with participatory action research (Lau 1997), which provides us with observations through intervention.

In the first part of our work, we conducted an ethnographic field study at six different repair service workshops in five European countries. This study aimed to gather insights on the demand of remote vehicle services at dealerships, which are considered to play a major role in the retail and provisioning of future remote vehicle services. Furthermore, the study provided us with an understanding of existing systems. We spent one working day at each organization, observing day-to-day work practices, asking complementary questions and interviewing workshop managers, salesmen, chief diagnosticians, and service coordinators.

Our ethnographic work was followed up by a collaborative research project involving three employees from the vehicle manufacturer and one researcher. The researcher worked on a daily basis together with one of the employees and every month group meetings were held. However, discussions and ideas were exchanged frequently in shorter meetings or joint coffee breaks. All project members were situated in the same open office space. At the end of the project, a larger workshop, including product developers, was held. Our work has been documented by continuous annotations and joint internal presentations. However, the methodological focus was to intervene in the project work rather than to observe the project members' work. Therefore, our empirical work includes as well a retrospective analysis.

The objective of our research was to contribute to the project with knowledge on open information infrastructure since the concept of open information infrastructure is described as a condition to boost the development of remote vehicle services (Kuschel and Dahlbom 2007). There are currently three concurrent systems within the company that are operated by different brands or regional markets. The variety of systems is a result of acquisitions and autonomous decisions by some geographic market. However, there is ongoing work to consolidate different systems and the decision has already been made to share the same vehicle hardware across the three systems (see Figure 1, on-board vehicle platform). Nevertheless, off-board system implementations are not affected yet.

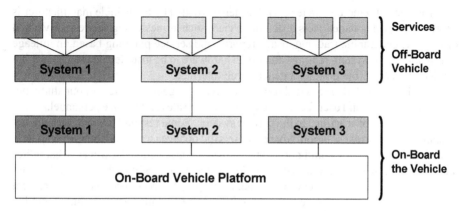

Figure 1. Overview of Current System and Service Structure

The systems differ in their market penetration, technological level, and internal support. One system has gained market success quickly, the second is considered to be technically superior, and the third has support from higher management and long-term market experience. The current systems are so-called fleet management systems that facilitate communication, control, and scheduling of a truck fleet. They make use of vehicle information such as mileage, fuel consumption, average speed, stand-still time, gear shifts, drive time, and geographical position. Two of the systems also provide some vehicle diagnostic data as input to a repair process. All data is currently incorporated in end customer services, which makes it difficult to provide the data to other vehicle stakeholders. Thus, vehicle manufacturers face a situation of not being able to address the increasing demand for remote vehicle services, since changes to the current solutions are costly and complex. To address the bottleneck situation constituted by systems that are not designed for additional application areas, this infrastructure pre-study project was initiated by the vehicle manufacturer. We mainly focused on one of the three systems.

4   FINDINGS

In what follows we report our empirical results, which reflect the four-month project work in collaboration with a European vehicle manufacturer. The results are partly structured by the main research activities (i.e., the initial fieldwork, which is reported in the first two sections, and the collaborative research project reported in the remaining sections). Our work shows the need to embrace heterogeneity by identifying the current lack thereof. Furthermore, we describe possibilities for integrating vehicle information into existing processes, which may span the stakeholders of a larger vehicle ecosystem. Finally, we identify the current system complexity and the organizational resistance challenging such integration.

4.1   Embracing Heterogeneity

The current remote vehicle service system provided by the vehicle manufacturer is a web-based portal that collects different services such as messaging between driver and dispatcher, geographic tracking, usage reports, and service planning based on mileage information. The system requires additional hardware to be installed on the vehicle, but services are accessible through a generic web interface.

We did not include the actual use of the fleet management system in our study, but discussed the sales and user feedback experienced by sales and service personnel. There was a broad span of reactions to the current system. Some respondents did see a market potential in the current solution, whereas others did not even try to sell the system to their customers because they could not identify any sales arguments. However, what unites all of the interviewees included in this study is their concern that the system does not embrace change quickly enough. Customers demand additional services, but the current system cannot comply; however, competitive solutions manage to address market demands quickly.

It seems to me that we are always a step behind. The system is technically good, despite the current problems with the new version. (Belgian sales manager)

The system is meant for transporters, but our customers are contractors and therefore it is difficult to compete against other systems. (British sales manager)

Another sales person outlined the need for local customizations or even specific services for some customers.

In the garbage collection business we have customers that invoice local authorities based on the actual mileage they have driven for collecting the garbage. Both parties are interested in receiving this data to feed their invoice and control systems. (Danish workshop manager)

Even though there is a demand for remote vehicle services, repair workshops cannot provide local implementations, since all services are managed on a global solution level. Pushing local demands to a global service is considered meaningless, resulting in successful third party providers that make use of their market knowledge and a faster speed to market process.

4.2 Integration

By observing day-to-day work at different repair workshops, we were able to study ordinary work processes to understand the current role and the future potential of remote vehicle services. We here present our empirical data, that shows the need to integrate remote vehicle services into existing processes, work procedures, and interaction patterns. In particular, we provide data on how remote vehicle services could support processes other than fleet management, which is the focus of the current systems.

I most often read out the fault codes before I delegate the job to a mechanic. I just print out the codes like this [shows a print out of error codes registered by the vehicle control system] and attach it at the back of the work order. (Chief mechanic at a Belgian workshop)

This example shows how remote vehicle information (e.g., diagnostic error codes) constitute beneficial input to the repair work description. Currently the chief mechanic connects each truck to a diagnostic computer and prints the information. In other workshops, mechanics conduct this procedure themselves during each repair. However, by integrating the remote diagnostic information into the work planning system, workshop scheduling and service preparation would be enhanced without requiring additional activities such as described in the example. The following excerpt exemplifies another lack of process integration:

We have to ask each customer about the current mileage when they arrive for service. This information we enter into a central system and then our financial service company uses the information to adjust service and leasing contracts. If the mileage differs from previous estimations, this sometimes causes trouble. Customers call us and are angry about being invoiced without expecting it. We then have to explain that they have exceeded their forecasted mileage. (Belgian workshop owner and manager)

In this case, continuous updates of mileage information would enhance the invoice process and save unwanted surprises to the customer. The financial service company would in turn benefit through adjusted cash flows. Furthermore, this example shows how small portions of remote vehicle information could improve larger existing processes and services. For instance, the same mileage information can also be used as input to the maintenance planning system that schedules service intervals.

With the new digital tachograph, drivers have to use a USB memory stick to collect the data for reporting. This is fairly complicated and should be much easier with new technology. (Swedish service manager)

This example shows how future remote vehicle services span a broader spectrum than remote vehicle diagnostics. Tachograph information describes the driver's working hours and is used by authorities, as well as for calculating the driver's salary, fleet planning, and such activities. In summary, these examples show how remote vehicle services could enhance existing services and processes. However, the empirical data also reveals the need to integrate remote vehicle services into day-to-day work practices and interaction patterns (i.e., to integrate into existing systems and work procedures), rather than providing additional ones. The following excerpts exemplify this problem:

The haulage company next door has provided us with their login credentials to the web portal. We then can login and check where the trucks are located and see if the truck will manage to arrive on time for service. We do this only for one customer, it's our boss' brother who owns the company, you know. It would be impossible to keep track of all passwords for our customers. (Belgian service coordinator)

We use [the system] on a daily basis and install it in all new units. However, it would be nice if we could use the information elsewhere. Now our customers call us and ask where the milk is. We then have to go into the system and check the vehicle's position. I mean that's a good service to our customers, but right now its tricky for us to arrange. (Fleet manager, British dairy company)

These examples show the importance of appropriate interaction possibilities as an essential part of remote vehicle services. The technical availability of vehicle information, per se, is not good enough and therefore information access has to be adequate to different work procedures.

4.3 Ecosystem

The collaborative research project on infrastructure development started with a disagreement on what the focus of our work should be. From an industry perspective, there was a demand for a gap analysis between the three concurrent systems to contribute to the design of a new infrastructure.

> *It has to be said that I had a different understanding of the project the first day. My view was very pragmatic; I mean, let's make a gap analysis between the existing systems as input to the new infrastructure. In the aftermath, I am very happy that we chose another approach where we focused on understanding the concept of infrastructure first.* (Project sponsor responding to an evaluation committee)

This retrospective comment on the project by the project sponsor confirms the importance of conceptualizing the role of information infrastructure. As the following excerpt reveals, there was a lack of understanding of what distinguishes systems from infra-structures:

> PM1:   *Yes this should be included in the future portal, I agree.*
> PM2:   *I think we should be aware to distinguish between portal and infrastructure.*
> PM1:   *Ok, call it infrastructure instead I thought it's the same.*
> PM2:   *No, the idea is to facilitate for example the current portal by an underlying infrastructure. It is the infrastructure we currently lack.*

We started off by establishing a joint understanding on two central concepts: service and infrastructure. As follows, we outline the discussion and negotiation on what constitutes information infrastructure and services in this specific context. By studying and analyzing previous documentation related to remote vehicle services, we found that the vehicle most often is outlined as centric and autonomous, neglecting the real world contextual setting. However, considering the role of modern vehicles in today's society, it is obvious that vehicles are part of a larger ecosystem including various stakeholders. We introduced this perspective as a foundation for conceptualizing the information infrastructure and the notion of service. By using this perspective, project members started to understand the information infrastructure as serving the ecosystem by offering integration services for the vehicle. Thus the notion of service changed from end customer services to infrastructural services, which in turn facilitate services making use of remote vehicle information in various settings. By this, we switched focus from the product as autonomous entity to the product as actor in a larger ecosystem.

4.4 Complexity

As part of our joint project work, we conducted a workshop with product develop-ment personnel to inform our design and to disseminate our results. The main problem pointed to by the workshop participants is the current lack of services and foremost difficulties in adding new services to the existing system (i.e., the web portal).

We currently cannot leverage new services that the market is asking for.

The lack of velocity in bringing new services to the market might be explained by the development cost related to the current system. A project manager stated resignedly,

There is nothing to get under... €² to make changes to the current system.

Such high development costs to implement new services indicates that the system is not designed to embrace change in any way. The system was initially designed for a defined purpose: an end user application. Furthermore, the defined purpose was reflected throughout the system and thus new requirements affect all parts of the system. This is a known problem, as the following excerpt and the previous one show.

The information has been designed for an end product, which makes it difficult to design new services with different requirements.

Workshop participants agreed upon the need to change the current situation. However, organizational issues rather than the system as such were pointed to as the cause of difficult situation. The following excerpts outline organizational structures as hampering the development of new services:

There are far too many stakeholders involved, which makes interfaces and roles unclear. The brands should focus more on which services to provide and less on technical solutions.

A lot of internal issues make it complex to create services.

We here witness both organizational and technical complexity. From an organizational perspective, it remains unclear what part of the organization is entitled to develop services. Technically, the current infrastructural systems are not flexible enough to embrace a change in service demand.

4.5 Resistance

Despite the problems pointed out, the current system and its service offerings were defended by some workshop participants. The complexity of selling services for an organization that is used to sell products is put forward as argument.

We do have the services but nobody is selling them.

---

²Due to a nondisclosure agreement, we cannot detail the figure.

It's different to sell services than trucks.

One workshop participant extends the problem by pointing to the design of the current service offerings to be more like products than services.

We package too many services into one service package. We sell products like the current system rather than services such as navigation. It is difficult to make customizations.

The second objective of the workshop was to introduce the concept of open or general information infrastructure (Hanseth and Lyytinen 2004), that is, to enable a general audience to develop remote vehicle services based on a shared information infrastructure. The open information infrastructure concept presented incorporates both vehicle hardware and external software implementations. The infrastructure embodies vehicle communication as a core service upon which various infrastructural service layers can be implemented to offer appropriate interfaces to different stakeholder services. In this way, the infrastructure is supposed to better support the current bottleneck of service development and thus move the focus onto user-oriented services rather than current product features. However, when presenting the concept of information infrastructure as opposed to a system, the workshop participants did not fully agree. Since infra-structuralization implies increased openness, voices were being raised about the importance of ssafety.

You should be aware that these are objects of up to 60 tons that could kill people. We of course have a responsibility in this case.

Not only safety issues were put forward as arguments against an open information infra-structure, the majority of workshop participants adopted a defensive attitude in preference to the current system. This defensive attitude contradicts their initial criticism of the current system. Thus, the extent to which resistance to an open information infrastructure refers to fundamental arguments rather than uncertainty about openness is questionable.

5 DISCUSSION

Based on our empirical data, we identify different aspects that currently challenge information infrastructure and remote vehicle service development at a European vehicle manufacturer. These are embracing heterogeneity, integration as core service, under-standing the vehicle as part of an ecosystem, and resistance to openness, which manifests in technical and organizational complexity. We here discuss how they relate to each other and constitute a general challenge to information infrastructure development.

The current approach to remote vehicle services reveals some fundamental similarities to the development of the French train system *Aramis* (Latour 1996). Both projects are based on an understanding of autonomous technology that lacks contextual integration, we argue. This is also a general problem of ubiquitous computing, as Dourish (2001) highlights in his thoughts on embodied interaction. Ubiquitous computing tends to primarily focus on the physical embodiment of technology—on minimization of computing power and extending sensor capacity—rather than embodying the use of technology in everyday life. In this paper, we highlight the role of information infrastructure to facilitate the embodiment of ubiquitous computing technology within its ecosystem.

Current remote vehicle services are designed as product features extending some selected vehicle properties. However, by studying service repair work as a future application area, we reveal a demand to embrace heterogeneity, constituted by a demand for local customizations. Furthermore, we show that these services have to be integrated into day-to-day work and processes to add user value. Thus, remote vehicle services are evolving and span heterogeneous technologies and organizations. Such socio-technical challenges in ubiquitous computing environments are best addressed by information infrastructures (Lyytinen and Yoo 2002). Even though we agree on the role of information infrastructure to leverage remote vehicle services, we here aim to stress the challenge of conceptualizing the underlying understanding of service and information infrastructure. In doing so, we distinguish between services as product features or representations and services that evolve by means of the heterogeneous network of which they are part. The latter extends the understanding of information infrastructures, from interfacing product features to instead enabling integration with the ecosystem.

However, our project reveals a resistance to such open innovation across the vehicle ecosystem. As we show, the resistance is manifested in both technical and organizational complexity. The development of new services is restricted by high development cost due to inflexibility in the current infrastructure design. The organizational complexity can be described by undefined roles and a lack of separating service development from information infrastructure development. The fleet management system in focus was developed and operated by a former spin off company, funded by different industrial investors. The company was acquired by the vehicle manufacturer to act as wholly owned but independent subsidiary. As a result of the company's independence and their strategy to also provide services to other vehicle manufacturers, they offer packaged end-customer services. Customizations are very limited and the service packages are considered of-the-shelf services. There has been a protracted discussion whether the subsidiary company should be incorporated into the vehicle manufacturer's business unit for global IT operations. This discussion culminated during our project work and resulted in finally integrating the company into the business unit for IT operations. The strongest argument for the incorporation was to add local presence through the business unit's global operations, which is considered necessary to develop new services. This strategic decision supports the argument of separating service development from the core information infrastructure.

Remote vehicle services are traditionally understood as separate service offerings complementary to the vehicle. GM's OnStar and Daimler Chrysler's FleetBoard are other examples of vehicle manufacturers organizing their remote vehicle service offerings in subsidiaries. However, our field work reveals a demand for remote vehicle services as support to existing processes and work practices, which the current service offerings do not address. Thus, the incorporation of the subsidiary is a first step to better reach out within the organization and to understand how remote vehicle services span the organization as opposed to the current understanding of services as autonomous product features. Nevertheless, the demand for an openness across the ecosystem's various stakeholders remains in order to foster open innovation of services, which in turn provides the economic foundation for an information infrastructure in the vehicle industry (Kuschel and Dahlbom 2007).

6 CONCLUSION

Even though remote vehicle services such as remote vehicle diagnostics are considered to account for a major part of vehicle manufacturers' future revenues, manufacturers are still struggling to develop appropriate services. In this paper, we report on the results of developing an information infrastructure at a European vehicle manufacturer to facilitate service development. Our study shows a disagreement between customers' demand for integrating vehicle information into the boundary spanning ecosystem of vehicle operations and the manufacturers' understanding of information infrastructure as an extension of product features. We thus contribute to information infrastructure theory by showing how the conceptualization of service affects the understanding and design of information infrastructure. We distinguish between information infrastructures exposing products as autonomous objects and infrastructures embodying the product within its ecosystem by strengthening the interplay between, as Latour (1996) puts it, subject and object. Finally, we argue that understanding this interplay constitutes the very condition for open innovation in the vehicle industry.

References

Andersson, M. 2006. "Ubiqutious Transport Systems: Negotiating Context Through a Mobile-stationary Interface," in *Proceedings of the 14th European Conference on Information Systems*, J. Ljunberg and M. Andersson (eds.), Gothenburg, Sweden, pp. 2194-2205.

Andersson, M. 2007. *Heterogeneous IT Innovation—Developing Industrial Architectural Knowledge*, unpublished Ph.D. thesis, Department of Applied IT, University of Gothenburg, Sweden.

Banavar, G., Black, J., Cáceres, R., Ebling, M., Stern, E., and Kannry, J. 2005. "Deriving Long-Term Value from Context-Aware Computing," *Information Systems Management* (22:4), pp. 32-42.

Ciborra, C., Braa, K., Cordella, A., Dahlbom, B., Failla, A., Hanseth, O., Hepsø, V., Ljungberg, J., Monteiro, E., and Simon, K. A. (eds.). 2000. *From Control to Drift: The Dynamics of Corporate Information Infrastructures*, Oxford, England: Oxford University Press.

Dahlbom, B. 2000. "Postface: From Infrastructure to Networking," in *From Control to Drift: The Dynamics of Corporate Information Infrastructures*, C. Ciborra, K. Braa, A. Cordella, B. Dahlbom, A. Failla, O. Hanseth, V. Hepsø, J. Ljungberg, E. Monteiro, and K. A. Simon (eds.), Oxford, England: Oxford University Press, pp. 212-226.

Dourish, P. 2001. *Where the Action Is: The Foundations of Embodied Interaction*, Cambridge, MA: MIT Press.

Fano, A., and Gershman, A. 2002. "The Future of Business Services in the Age of Ubiquitous Computing," *Communications of the ACM* (45:12), pp. 83-87.

Hanseth, O. 2000. "The Economics of Standards," in *From Control to Drift: The Dynamics of Corporate Information Infrastructures*, C. Ciborra, K. Braa, A. Cordella, B. Dahlbom, A. Failla, O. Hanseth, V. Hepsø, J. Ljungberg, E. Monteiro, and K. A. Simon (eds.), Oxford, England: Oxford University Press, pp. 56-70.

Hanseth, O., and Lyytinen, K. 2004. "Theorizing about the Design of Information Infrastructures: Design Kernel Theories and Principles, *Sprouts: Working Papers on Information, Environments Systems and Organizations* (4:4) Article 12 (http://sprouts.case.edu/040412.cfm).

Hanseth, O., and Monteiro, E. 1997. "Inscribing Behavior in Information Infrastructure Standards," *Accounting, Management and Information Technology* (7:4), pp. 183-211.

Hanseth, O., Monteiro, E., and Hatling, M. 1996. "Developing Information Infrastructure: The Tension between Standardization and Flexibility," *Science, Technology & Human Values* (21:4), pp. 407-426.

Hughes, J., King, V., Rodden, T., and Andersen, H. 1994. "Moving Out from the Control Room: Ethnography in System Design," in *Proceedings of the 1994 ACM Conference on Computer Supported Cooperative Work*, Chapel Hill, NC, pp. 429-439.

Kuschel, J., and Dahlbom, B. 2007. "Mobile Services for Vehicles," in *Proceedings of the 15th European Conference on Information Systems*, H. Österle, J. Schelp, and R. Winter (eds.), University of St. Gallen, St. Gallen, Switzerland, pp. 1863-1874.

Latour, B. 1996. *Aramis or the Love of Technology*, Cambridge, MA: Harvard University Press.

Lau, F. 1997. "A Review on the Use of Action Research in Information Systems Studies," in Information Systems and Qualitative Research , A. S. Lee, J. Liebenau, and J. I. DeGross (eds.), London: Chapman & Hall, pp. 31-68.

Lyytinen, K., and Yoo, Y. 2002. "Research Commentary: The Next Wave of Nomadic Computing," *Information Systems Research,* (13:4), pp. 377-388.

Mathieu, V. 2001. "Product Services: From a Service Supporting the Product to a Service Supporting the Client," *Journal of Business & Industrial Marketing* (16:1), pp. 39-61.

Nielsen, P. 2006. *A Conceptual Framework of Information Infrastructure Building: A Case Study of the Development of a Content Service Platform for Mobile Phones in Norway*, unpublished Ph.D. thesis, Department of Informatics, University of Oslo, Norway.

Schultze, U. 2000. "A Confessional Account of an Ethnography about Knowledge Work," *MIS Quarterly* (24:1), pp. 3-41.

About the Author

Jonas Kuschel is a Ph.D. student at IT University of Göteborg, Sweden. His research deals with developing future services in the vehicle industry, with a particular focus on the interdependencies between user-oriented services and information infrastructures. He can be reached at jonas.kuschel@ituniv.se.

Part 7

Case Studies in Telecommunications

19 EXAMINING FACTORS INFLUENCING THE BEHAVIORAL INTENTION TO ADOPT BROADBAND IN MALAYSIA

Yogesh K. Dwivedi
Swansea University
Swansea, UK

Mohamad H. Selamat
Muhammad S. Abd Wahab
Mohd A. Mat Samsudin
Universiti Utara Malaysia
Sintok, Malaysia

Banita Lal
Nottingham Trent University
Nottingham, UK

Abstract   *The aim of this study was to examine the factors affecting the adoption of broadband Internet in a developing country context by focusing upon Malaysia. The data relating to these factors was collected using a survey approach. The findings of this paper suggest that perceived usefulness, perceived ease of use, and social influence are significant factors for explaining the behavioral intention to adopt broadband Internet by Malaysian accountants. The paper proceeds to outline the research limitations, theoretical contributions, and implications for practice.*

Keywords   Adoption, accountant, behavioral intention, broadband, consumers, factors, Malaysia

Please use the following format when citing this chapter:

Dwivedi, Y. K., Selamat, M. H., Abd Wahab, M. S., Mat Samsudin, M. A., and Lal, B., 2008, in IFIP International Federation for Information Processing, Volume 287, Open IT-Based Innovation: Moving Towards Cooperative IT Transfer and Knowledge Diffusion, eds. León, G., Bernardos, A., Casar, J., Kautz, K., and DeGross, J. (Boston: Springer), pp. 325-342

1   INTRODUCTION

Although broadband diffusion is considered to be an important policy issue in many countries, few studies have been conducted with the goal of understanding this critical technology management issue within the context of developing countries. The reason for this lack of broadband adoption studies from the developing country perspective could be attributed to the late rollout of broadband services, slow infrastructure development, low tele-density, and slow rate of adoption. Since developing countries such as Malaysia are currently lagging in terms of broadband adoption—the current level of adoption is approximately 11 percent (Keong 2007) compared to developed countries, where adoption rates typically exceed 50 percent—it is important to undertake research that may help to explain why this is the case, and where an understanding of the determining factors may help to accelerate the process of consumer adoption in developing nations.

The deployment and adoption of broadband is still in its infancy in Malaysia. A recently published broadband market report highlighted the problem of slow broadband adoption among the general Malaysian population and the possible barriers inhibiting its widespread diffusion. The report stated that

> Malaysia has been heavily promoting itself as an Information Technology hub in the Asia region. On the back of the Multimedia Super Corridor project, high-tech companies have been at least establishing a presence in Malaysia. But the wider community has not really been embracing technology. There has been surprisingly little interest in broadband Internet, the national broadband penetration being only slightly over 3% at the end of 2006.[1]

The problem of slow broadband adoption has been taken seriously by the Malaysian government as they are continuously revising their policy and changing the target growth according to the adoption rate. Recent news from ZDNetAsia (Keong 2007) further highlights the slow growth of broadband in Malaysia and its consequences.

> The slow uptake of broadband services has led the Malaysian government to revise its earlier optimistic penetration targets, prompting industry observers to call for market reform.

> The government had previously set a target of 75 percent adoption rate by 2010, but only 11.7 percent of Malaysia's 5.5 million households currently have broadband access, up from 7 percent in 2005.

> This disappointing state of affairs recently prompted a Cabinet Committee chaired by Deputy Prime Minister Najib Tun Razak to revise the target down to 50 percent by 2010.

Given the situation of Malaysia in terms of the current adoption rate, it was thought that understanding the effect of the potential factors upon consumers' broadband adoption

---

[1]Budde.Com, "Malaysia – Broadband Market," http://www.budde.com/au/buddereports/2112/Default.aspx; accessed January 2, 2008.

and usage may help to encourage further diffusion and management of high-speed Internet. Therefore, the aim of this study was *to understand the factors affecting the adoption of broadband Internet in the Malaysian context.*

Having introduced the topic of interest, section 2 provides a brief review of relevant literature followed by a brief discussion on the theoretical basis for examining the adoption of broadband in section 3. Section 4 then provides a brief discussion of the research methods utilized for data collection. The findings are presented in section 5, with a discussion of these findings in section 6. Finally the conclusions, including the limitations and contributions of this research, are provided in section 7.

2 LITERATURE REVIEW

The adoption literature discussed henceforth provides a consideration of both macro and micro factors that drive the success or slow uptake of broadband within the context of the leading countries in terms of broadband penetration. In an initial study of broadband deployment in South Korea, Lee et al. (2003) identified three major factors comprising public sector actions, private sector actions, and the socio-cultural environment factors that explained the high rate of broadband adoption in the country. Further research suggested that six success factors are responsible for driving the high penetration rate of broadband by South Korean residential consumers (Choudrie and Lee 2004). These six key factors consist of the government's vision, strategy and commitment, facilities-based competition, pricing, the PC bang phenomenon, culture and geography, and demographics.

Among the initial studies conducted in order to understand the adoption of broadband at the individual level, the work by Oh et al. (2003) is of high relevance. That study examined the individual-level factors affecting the adoption of broadband in South Korea by combining factors taken from Rogers' (1995) diffusion theory and the technology acceptance model. The findings of that study suggest that congruent experiences and opportunities in adopting a new technology affect user attitudes through the three extended technology acceptance model constructs, namely perceived usefulness, perceived skills, and perceived resources.

Stanton's (2004) study emphasized the need to conduct an inquiry that addresses the access question and the demographics that would be useful to observe any changes in the likelihood of socio-economic groups when adopting broadband. Following on from Stanton's study, demographics of broadband consumers in the United Kingdom were examined at both the local level (Choudrie and Dwivedi 2005a) and the national level (Choudrie and Dwivedi 2006a; Dwivedi and Lal 2007). These studies highlighted the role of demographic variables such as age, income, education, and occupation in influencing broadband adoption by consumers. Further exploratory studies examined attitudinal (i.e., relative advantage, utilitarian outcomes, and hedonic outcomes) and control (skills, knowledge, facilitating conditions resources) variables to understand the behavior of broadband adopters and non-adopters. These studies suggested that both attitudinal and control variables are important for understanding broadband adoption behavior (Choudrie and Dwivedi 2006b). Building upon previous studies, a confirmatory study was also conducted that developed and validated a reliable survey instrument for measuring the perception of consumers regarding the adoption of broadband in the UK (Dwivedi 2007; Dwivedi et al. 2006).

Recently, a few follow-up studies on broadband adoption were undertaken to investigate influential factors in developing economies such as Bangladesh, India, Saudi Arabia, and Pakistan. The study on broadband adoption in Bangladesh concluded that attitude, primary influence, secondary influence, and facilitating conditions resources are important factors for explaining consumers' behavioral intentions to adopt broadband (Dwivedi, Khan, and Papazafeiropoulou 2007). The key findings of the study in Saudi Arabia were that the factors with the main influence on attitude toward adoption of broadband were usefulness, service quality, age, usage, type of connection, and type of accommodation (Dwivedi and Weerakkody 2007). Khoumbati et al. (2007) examined the factors affecting consumers' adoption of broadband in Pakistan, concluding that primary influence, facilitating conditions resources, cost, and perceived ease of use are significant factors for explaining consumers' behavioral intentions to adopt broadband in Pakistan. Finally, a study on broadband adoption within the Indian context found that the relative advantage, hedonic outcomes, and cost are significant factors for explaining consumers' behavioral intentions to adopt broadband in India (Dwivedi, Williams et al. 2007).

From the above discussion, it can be observed that the factors affecting the individual level of broadband adoption in different countries vary. This argument was further supported by a panel discussion (held at the IFIP 8.6 Working Conference in 2007) on the global diffusion of broadband. Panel members from different countries argued and agreed that the context and factors that affect broadband adoption at both the micro and macro level are diverse and, therefore, the findings from one study cannot be applied directly to study broadband adoption issues in other countries. Hence, empirical studies should be conducted to examine the influential factors in countries with slow rates of broadband adoption (Williams et al. 2007). Since the broadband adoption rate in Malaysia is unexpectedly slow, this has provided us with impetus to undertake this exploratory study in order to understand the perceptions of consumers regarding broadband adoption and its usefulness in Malaysia. A worthwhile contribution would be to understand the reasons for consumer adoption and non-adoption of subscription-based technologies such as broadband from a developing country perspective. The next section briefly discusses the theoretical basis for examining the factors of consumer adoption and non-adoption of broadband in Malaysia.

3   THEORETICAL BASIS

There are several theories such as the technology acceptance model (TAM), theory of planned behavior (TBP), theory of reasoned action (TRA), and diffusion of innovations (DoI) available to study technology adoption and diffusion related issues. This study adapted TAM as a theoretical lens. The reason for selecting TAM over other theories is simply that the TAM constructs have been more widely and successfully employed and validated to study information technology adoption than other theories. Also, previous studies on broadband adoption have found constructs such as perceived usefulness and ease of use significant in explaining the adoption of broadband. A further reason for selecting TAM is to have a comparison of the predictive power of this study with other available studies on technology adoption. However, one major limitation of

TAM is that it does not provide constructs to measure social influence (Dwivedi 2007; Hsu and Lu 2004; Lu et al. 2005; Taylor and Todd 1995; Venkatesh and Brown 2001), which previous studies on broadband have suggested to be an important factor for investigation, especially in the developing countries in Asia (Dwivedi, Khan, and Papazafeiropoulou 2007; Khoumbati et al. 2007). Keeping this in mind, the social influence construct was integrated with the TAM model. In brief, in this study it was postulated that **behavioral intentions (BI)** to adopt broadband are determined by the following three constructs: (1) **perceived usefulness (PU)**; (2) **perceived ease of use (PEOU)**; and (3) **social influence (SI)** (see Figure 1).

For the purpose of this research, these four constructs are defined as follows. BI is defined as a consumer's intention to subscribe (or intention to continue the current subscription) and make use of broadband Internet in the future (Brown and Venkatesh 2005; Dwivedi 2005, 2007; Venkatesh and Brown 2001). PU is the extent to which broadband Internet usage enhances the effectiveness of household activities such as undertaking office work at home, children's homework, information or product search and purchase, and home business (Brown and Venkatesh 2005; Dwivedi 2005; Venkatesh and Brown 2001). SI is defined as the perceived influence of friends and family upon the individual to subscribe to and use (or not to subscribe and use) broadband Internet services (Brown and Venkatesh 2005; Dwivedi 2005; Venkatesh and Brown 2001). Finally, PEOU is the degree to which using the personal computer (PC) and Internet is free from effort and easy for consumers (Venkatesh and Brown 2001). Consistent with the TAM model, we propose the following hypotheses:

H1: *Perceived usefulness will have a positive influence on behavioral intentions to adopt broadband.*

H2: *Perceived ease of use will have a positive influence on the behavioral intentions to adopt broadband.*

H3: *Perceived ease of use will have a positive influence on the perceived usefulness of broadband.*

As we have integrated the social influence construct with the TAM model, consistent with previous studies (Dwivedi 2007; Hsu and Lu 2004; Lu et al. 2005; Taylor and Todd 1995; Venkatesh and Brown 2001), we propose both direct and indirect effects of SI on BI.

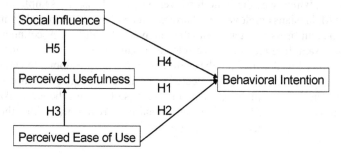

Figure 1. Modified TAM for Examining Broadband Adoption in Malaysia (Adapted from Davis 1989)

H4: *Social influence will have a positive influence on perceived behavioral intentions to adopt broadband.*

H5: *Social influence will have a positive influence on the perceived usefulness of broadband.*

4   RESEARCH METHODOLOGY

The survey method was utilized for this study (Choudrie and Dwivedi 2005b). A self-administered questionnaire comprised the primary survey instrument for data collection, since it addresses the issue of reliability of information by reducing and eliminating differences in the way that the questions are asked and how they are presented (Fowler 2002). Furthermore, questionnaires facilitate the collection of data within a short period of time from the majority of respondents, which was a significant issue for this research (Fowler 2002). Keeping this in mind, multiple and closed questions were mainly included in the questionnaire. The literature review provided an initial understanding of broadband adoption and the basis for the development of a draft questionnaire. The eventual final questionnaire consisted of a total of 13 questions. All 13 questions were close-ended, multiple, Likert scale type in nature. One was a Likert scale type question that consisted of 18 subquestions or items that included 10 items for perceived usefulness, 3 items for perceived ease of use, 3 items for social influence, and 2 items for behavioral intention. All 18 Likert scale type questions/items were adapted from Dwivedi et al. (2006) and Choudrie and Dwivedi (2006b) and demographic categories were adapted from Choudrie and Dwivedi (2006a). Although the adapted questions were rigorously validated in source studies, we conducted both a reliability test and factor analysis to confirm whether the adapted measures were internally consistent with and conformed to the rule of construct validity. The findings on these are presented in sections 5.2 and 5.3.

Since a reliable sample frame that represents the entire Malaysian population is not readily available or affordable for researchers, we focused our investigation on a particular segment of the Malaysian population: people who are employed as a Chartered Accountant. A further reason for such selection was that individuals in such a profession were more likely to have broadband at home or in their office due to professional and business needs, which was the issue for investigation. Thus, the sample of this study consisted of Malaysians employed as Chartered Accountants. The population consisted of Malaysian audit firms registered with the Malaysian Institute of Accountants.[2] Using the systematic sampling technique, we selected a sample of 302 accountancy firms by considering every fourth firm from the sample frame. The questionnaire was sent to the Chartered Accountant of each of the selected audit firms. The questionnaire was administered either as an e-mail attachment or via postal service between August and November 2007. A total of 124 usable questionnaires were returned within the specified time, resulting in a 41 percent response rate.

---

[2]According to the *Malaysian Institute of Accountants Members Directory* (Kuala Lumpur: Malaysian Institute of Accountants, 2007), there are 1,373 audit firms in Malaysia.

The initial stage of data analysis involved checking the responses and providing a unique identification number to each response. Using SPSS (version 14), the research generated the descriptive statistics (i.e., frequencies, percentage, and tables) and reliability tests, factor analysis, and regression analysis were conducted to analyze and present the research findings.

5   FINDINGS

5.1   Demographic and Internet Access Profile of Survey Respondents

Table 1 presents the demographic and Internet access profiles of the survey respondents. Of the 124 responses received, 54 percent were in the 25 to 34 year-old age group, which formed the largest response category. The 35 to 44 year-old age group was the next largest (23.4 percent). In terms of gender, more male than female respondents (m = 58.1 percent, f = 41.9 percent) participated in the survey. All respondents possessed educational qualifications, with 36.3 percent having an undergraduate degree and 4.8 percent educated to master/postgraduate level, and 8.9 percent of respondents reporting other educational qualifications. Responses for household annual income varied between 7.3 percent for the RM60,000 to RM69,000 category and 26.6 percent for the above RM70,000 category. Of the 124 respondents, only 60.5 percent represented the adopters of Internet at home and the remaining 39.5 percent were non-adopters. Of the 60.5 percent Internet adopters, 25.3 percent possessed a narrowband connection and 74.7 percent stated that they had a broadband connection at home.

5.2   Reliability Test: Test of Internal Consistency

Cronbach's coefficient alpha values were estimated to examine the internal consistency of the measure (Table 2). Cronbach's α varied between 0.80 for the behavioral intention construct and 0.95 for two constructs (i.e., perceived usefulness and social influence). The remaining construct—perceived ease of use—possessed a reliability value of 0.94. Hinton et al. (2004) have suggested four cut-off points for reliability, including excellent reliability (0.90 and above), high reliability (0.70–0.90), moderate reliability (0.50–0.70), and low reliability (0.50 and below). The aforementioned values suggest that of the four constructs, three possess excellent reliability and the remaining one illustrates high reliability. None of the constructs demonstrated moderate or low reliability (Table 2). The high Cronbach's α values for all constructs imply that they are internally consistent. That means all items of each construct measured the same content universe (i.e., construct). For example, all items of BI measured the same content universe of behavioral intention. Similarly, all items of perceived usefulness measured the content universe of the perceived usefulness construct. In brief, the higher the Cronbach's α value of a construct, the higher the reliability is of measuring the same construct.

Table 1. Demographic Information of the Survey Respondents

	Freq.	%		Freq.	%
Age			**Gender**		
25-34 Years	67	54.0	Male	72	58.1
35-44 Years	29	23.4	Female	52	41.9
45-54 Years	21	16.9	Total	124	100.0
55-64 Years	3	2.4	**Home Internet Access**		
65-74 Years	4	3.2	Yes	75	60.5
Total	124	100.0	No	49	39.5
Income			Total	124	100.0
RM20,000-RM29,000	20	16.1	**Type of Internet Access**		
RM30,000-RM39,000	12	9.7	Dial-up Metered	18	14.5
RM40,000-RM49,000	24	19.4	Dial-up Un-metered	1	.8
RM50,000-RM59,000	26	21.0	Broadband with Dsl/adsl	31	25.0
RM60,000-RM69,000	9	7.3	Broadband with Cable Modem	12	9.7
Above RM70,000	33	26.6	Wireless	13	10.5
Total	124	100.0	N/A	49	39.5
Education			Total	124	100.0
Degree	107	86.3	**Narrowband vs. Broadband**		
Master	6	4.8	Narrowband	19	25.3
Others	11	8.9	Broadband & Wireless	56	74.7
Total	124	100.0	Total	75	100.0
Alternative Internet Access Places			**Duration of Internet Connection at Home**		
Work Place	87	70.2	Less 12 Month	9	7.3
Public Access Points	9	7.3	12-24 Month	4	3.2
Local Library	2	1.6	25-36 Month	9	7.3
Internet Café	26	21.0	Above 36 Month	53	42.7
Total	124	100.0	Total	75	100.0

Table 2. Reliability of Measurements (N = 124)

Constructs	Number of Items	Cronbach's Alpha
BI: Behavioral Intentions	2	0.80
PU: Perceived Usefulness	9	0.95
PEOU: Perceived Ease of Use	3	0.94
SI: Social Influence	3	0.95

5.3 Factor Analysis: Test for Construct Validity

In order to assess construct validity (convergent and discriminant validity), factor analysis was conducted utilizing principal component analysis (PCA) with varimax as an extraction method and Kaiser normalization as a rotation method. The results of the PCA are illustrated in Table 3.

Table 3. Total Variance Explained, Eigenvalues and Rotated Component Matrix
(Extraction Method: Principal Components Analysis; Rotation Method: Varimax with Kaiser Normalization)

Items	Component		
	1	**2**	**3**
PU1	.851		
PU3	.789		
PU6	.753		
PU5	.750		
PU4	.730		
PU9	.698		
PU7	.686		
PU8	.666		
PU2	.644		
SI2		.861	
SI1		.827	
SI3		.818	
PEOU3			.909
PEOU2			.896
PEOU1			.805
Eigenvalues	**9.327**	**1.570**	**1.105**
% of Variance	**62.142**	**10.465**	**7.368**

The rotated component matrix presented in Table 3 shows the factor loadings for all three independent constructs. All items loaded above 0.40, which is the minimum recommended value in IS research (Straub et al. 2004), while cross loading of the items except PU10 was below 0.40. PU10 was cross loaded on the SI component with factor loading value .52 which is unacceptable (Straub et al. 2004); therefore, this item was excluded from the study. The remaining nine items of the perceived usefulness construct loaded on the first component. Therefore, the first component represents the underlying construct of perceived usefulness. All three items related to the social influence construct loaded on the second component. Finally, the three items related to the perceived ease of use construct all loaded on the third component (Table 3). The results suggest that the items loaded on each factor as expected. The factor analysis results satisfied the criteria of construct validity, including both the discriminant validity (loading of at least 0.40, no cross-loading of items above 0.40 except PU10, which we excluded from further analysis) and convergent validity (eigenvalues of 1, loading of at least 0.40, items that load on posited constructs) (Straub et al. 2004, p. 410). This confirms the construct validity (both discriminant validity and convergent validity) of the instrument measures used for data collection and, correspondingly, the validity of the resulting data and findings. According to a general rule of thumb, only factors with eigenvalues greater than 1 should be considered important for analysis purposes (Hinton et al. 2004; Straub et al. 2004). The results presented in Table 3 illustrate that all three constructs possess eigenvalues greater than 1. Table 4 also summarizes the total variance for the extracted

Table 4. Descriptive Statistics

	N	Mean	Std. Deviation
BI	124	5.8387	1.24049
BI1	124	5.6935	1.46047
BI2	124	5.9839	1.24929
PU	124	5.5063	1.15151
PU1	124	5.9274	1.20415
PU2	124	5.8629	1.16406
PU3	124	5.7177	1.31632
PU4	124	5.8468	1.25617
PU5	124	5.1290	1.58226
PU6	124	5.3710	1.49507
PU7	124	5.6452	1.25713
PU8	124	4.9194	1.59061
PU9	124	5.1371	1.42757
PEOU	124	5.6371	1.18635
PEOU1	124	5.7016	1.31273
PEOU2	124	5.6210	1.25971
PEOU3	124	5.5887	1.19628
SI	124	4.9677	1.39584
SI1	124	4.9919	1.46224
SI2	124	4.9758	1.51128
SI3	124	4.9355	1.43556
Valid N	124		

components. The combination of constructs accounted for a total of 80.02 percent variance in data. The largest variance (62.18 percent) was explained by the perceived usefulness construct, while the smallest amount of variation (7.36 percent) was accounted for perceived ease of use construct (Table 4).

5.4 Descriptive Statistics

Table 4 presents the means and standard deviations of the items related to all four constructs included in the study to measure the perceptions to adopt broadband. The means and standard deviations of aggregated measures for all four constructs are also illustrated in Table 4. The means and standard deviations of aggregated measures for both the BI items are also illustrated. The respondents showed strong agreement for both items of the behavioral intentions (BI1 and BI2), as the mean score varied between 5.69 (SD = 1.46) and 5.98 (SD = 1.25), with an average score of 5.84 (SD = 1.24).

A strong agreement was made for the perceived usefulness with the average score of aggregate measure (M = 5.51, SD = 1.15) where item PU1 scored the maximum (M = 5.93, SD = 1.2) and item PU8 the minimum (M = 4.92, SD = 1.59). The respondents also agreed strongly for all of the items of the perceived ease of use construct, where item

PEOU1 scored the maximum (M = 5.70, SD = 1.31) and item PEOU3 the minimum (M = 5.59, SD = 1.19), with the average score of aggregate measure (M = 5.64, SD = 1.19). Finally, a moderately strong agreement was also made for the social influence construct with the average score of aggregate measure (M = 4.97, SD = 1.39) where item SI1 scored the maximum (M = 4.99, SD = 1.46) and item SI3 the minimum (M = 4.94, SD = 1.44).

5.5 Regression Analysis: Influence of Independent Variables on Behavioral Intentions (BI) to Adopt Broadband

Regression analysis was performed with behavioral intentions as the dependent variable and a total of three variables—perceived usefulness, social influence, and perceived ease of use—as the predictor variables. A total of 124 cases were analyzed. From the analysis, a significant model emerged (F (3, 124) = 36.130, $p <$ .001). The adjusted R^2 was 0.461 (see Table 5).

All three predictor variables included in the analysis were found to be significant (see Table 6). These include SI (β = .285, p = .004), PU (β = .26, p = .011), and PEOU (β = .246, p = .005). The size of β suggests that the social influence construct has the largest impact in the explanation of variations of BI. This is followed by the perceived usefulness and then perceived ease of use (see Table 6).

Table 5. Model Summary

Model	R	R^2	Adjusted R^2	Std. Error of the Estimate
1*	.689(a)	.475	.461	.91034
2**	.754(a)	.569	.562	.76222

*Predictors: (Constant), PU, PEOU, SI; Dependent: BI
** Predictors: (Constant), PEOU, SI; Dependent: PU

Table 6. Regression Analysis: Coefficients (Dependent Variable: Behavioral Intentions)

	Unstandardized Coefficients		Standardized Coefficients		
	B	Std. Error	Beta	t	Sig.
Predictors: (Constant), PU, PEOU, SI; Dependent: BI					
(Constant)	1.583	.446		3.551	.001
SI	.254	.087	.285	2.907	.004
PU	.280	.109	.260	2.579	.011
PEOU	.258	.090	.246	2.871	.005
Predictors: (Constant), PEOU, SI; Dependent: PU					
(Constant)	1.676	.341		4.919	.000
SI	.456	.060	.553	7.576	.000
PEOU	.278	.071	.286	3.921	.000

In order to determine the indirect effect of social influence and perceived ease of use on BI via PU, a further analysis was performed. In this case, perceived usefulness was considered as the dependent variable and both social influence and perceived ease of use as the predictor variables. A total of 124 cases were analyzed. From the analysis, a significant model emerged (F (2, 124) = 79.86, $p < .001$). The adjusted R^2 was 0.562 (See Table 5). Both predictor variables included in the second analysis were found to be significant (Table 6). These include SI ($\beta = .553$, $p < .001$), and PEOU ($\beta = .286$, $p < .001$). The size of β suggests that the social influence construct has the largest impact in explaining the variations of PU. This is followed by the perceived ease of use (see Table 6).

6   DISCUSSION

The internal consistency of measures was assessed utilizing a reliability test (i.e., Cronbach's α). For an exploratory study, reliability should be equal to or above 0.60 (Straub et al. 2004). Reliability for the Cronbach's α value of various constructs in this research varied between 0.80 and 0.95 and none of the constructs possessed reliability below the recommended level of 0.60 (see Table 2). This suggests that the measures employed demonstrated an appropriate level of internal consistency. Findings from the factor analysis presented in Table 3 also confirm the construct validity (both discriminant validity and convergent validity) of the instrument measures used for data collection and, respectively, the validity of the resulting data and findings.

Figure 2 illustrates that a total of five research hypotheses were tested to examine if the independent variables significantly explained the dependent variables. All five research hypotheses were supported by the data, which suggests that all independent variables significantly explained the dependent variables (BI and PU). Previous studies suggested the significant role of factors such as perceived usefulness, perceived ease of use, and social influence in influencing consumers' behavioral intentions to adopt technologies such as the PC (Brown and Venkatesh 2005) and broadband in a developed

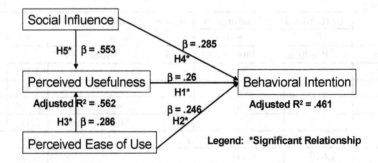

Figure 2. Factors influencing broadband adoption in Malaysia (Adapted from Davis 1989)

country (Dwivedi 2007; Dwivedi at al. 2006). In line with these findings, the results of this study suggest that these factors are also significant in terms of influencing consumers' behavioral intentions to adopt broadband in Malaysia. We also found that social influence and perceived ease of use indirectly have a significant influence on the behavioral intention via perceived usefulness.

It is possible to compare the predictability of the broadband adoption constructs to guiding models such as the technology acceptance model, theory of planned behavior, and decomposed theory of planned behavior. It can also be compared to recently published work on broadband adoption in developing countries such as Bangladesh, India, and Pakistan. This is because dependent constructs such as behavioral intention and the structure of the broadband adoption model are similar to TAM, TPB, and DTPB and previous studies on broadband adoption. Table 7 illustrates the comparison of previous studies for the adjusted R^2 obtained for the behavioral construct. The comparison clearly demonstrates that the broadband adoption model of this study performed as well as the previous studies. Adjusted R^2 for behavioral intention varied between 0.20 (Gefen and Straub 2000) to 0.57 (Taylor and Todd 1995); the adjusted R^2 for this study was found to be 0.46, which suggests the appropriate level of explained variance. This means that the independent variables considered in this study are important for understanding consumers' behavioral intentions to adopt broadband in Malaysia.

6.1 Implications

The analysis of the empirical data derived from the survey of broadband consumers revealed many lessons that will be helpful to Internet service providers (ISPs) or broadband service providers and policy makers seeking to encourage consumer adoption of

Table 7. Comparison of Behavioral Intention in Terms of Adjusted R^2

Study	Theory	Adjusted R^2 for BI
Taylor and Todd (1995)	DTP	0.57
Taylor and Todd (1995)	TPB	0.57
Taylor and Todd (1995)	TAM	0.52
Karahanna et al. (1999)	TRA + TAM	0.38
Agarwal and Karahanna (2000)	TAM & Cognitive Absorption	0.50
Gefen and Straub (2000)	TAM	0.20
Brown et al. (2002)	TAM	0.52
Koufaris (2002)	TAM + Flow Theory	0.54
Dwivedi (2005)	TPB + DTPB + MATH	0.43
Dwivedi, Khan, and Papaazfeiropoulou (2007)	TPB + DTPB + MATH	0.50
Dwivedi at al. (2007)	TPB + DTPB + MATH	0.49
Khoumbati et al. (2007)	TPB + DTPB + MATH	0.37
Current Study	**TAM**	**0.46**
Recommended level (Straub et al. 2004)	–	**0.40 or above**

broadband in Malaysia. By utilizing experience and findings gained from this research, and from studies on the developed world, Malaysian policy makers should emphasize tackling the issues of content and last-mile access, providing skills to citizens and encouraging people through social networks in order to encourage the growth and diffusion of broadband in Malaysia.

Perceived usefulness was found to be significant in explaining BI to adopt broadband, which means that consumers/citizens with strong perceptions on the usefulness of broadband are more likely to adopt the technology. This has three implications: (1) both government and ISPs should put their efforts into integration of content and applications that are compatible to *Malaysian* culture and useful in citizens' daily lives; (2) citizens and consumers should be made aware of any existing or emerging useful services, content, and applications for the wider audience either through media or via social networks, discussed below; and (3) the government should slowly switch all government services to an electronic platform and citizens should be informed that, after a certain period, government services will no longer be available via the traditional means. Thus, citizens need to be equipped with the necessary skills and faculties to access services electronically. This will certainly affect those who cannot afford the service; however, such issues can be effectively tackled by providing individuals with access to the Internet via kiosks or any other form of public access points.

The social influence construct was found to be significant in explaining consumers' BI to adopt broadband. This can be considered to have important implications for policy makers. For instance, all schools and colleges should be equipped with broadband and children should be encouraged to use the computer and Internet for educational purposes. In such situations, children may exert a positive influence on parents to subscribe to broadband. Such a strategy was successfully utilized in South Korea (Choudrie and Lee 2004). Since social influence is an important factor, ISPs should encourage existing consumers to influence their family and relatives who still do not have a broadband subscription. For this, ISPs should motivate existing consumers by offering cash back or gift vouchers on successful referral of new customers. As social influence was also found to be significant for explaining perceived usefulness, consumers/citizens are more likely to perceive broadband as more useful for various purposes if their friends or relatives have broadband and if they are well aware of the associated benefits. So, in all situations, the Malaysian government and ISPs should target social networks and social capital mechanisms for encouraging non-adopters to adopt broadband.

As illustrated in Table 6, perceived ease of use is also an important factor that influences behavioral intentions to adopt broadband, which brings mainly policy-related issues. This suggests that there is a need to equip citizens with the skills to use computers and the Internet. When it comes to the government's role in equipping citizens, it is important to take a segmented approach to identifying and providing relevant skill-oriented courses to those citizens who do not have regular opportunities to learn and use the computer, Internet, and other related emerging technologies and applications such as e-government and e-commerce. Such strategies are not yet applied in Malaysia and require fast implementation if Malaysia aims to join the list of countries leading broadband deployment and adoption.

7   CONCLUSIONS

This study examined the factors affecting the adoption and usage of broadband Internet in Malaysia. The following main conclusions are drawn from this research and are based on the underlying research assumption made in section 3. A total of three constructs (see Figures 1 and 2) were expected to be correlated to the BI of consumers when adopting Internet in Malaysia. All three constructs, namely social influence, perceived usefulness, and perceived ease of use, significantly correlated to the BI of consumers. In terms of the size of the effect of these three constructs that contributed significantly to the behavioral intentions, the social influence construct has the largest impact in the explanation of variations of BI.

As broadband technologies enable a range of communication and Internet services, studying individuals from Malaysia adds one more perspective for understanding the adoption of broadband in developing countries. Thus, this research presents one of the initial efforts in understanding the broadband adoption behavior of consumers outside the context of developed countries. The findings are specifically useful for ISPs and policy makers of Malaysia, as specified above. Factors that are reported as being significant are important and require attention in order to encourage the further adoption and usage of Internet in the country. Additionally, the cost of using the traditional telephone network is very high, so broadband Internet can be used as a replacement for offering communication services such as instant messaging or Internet protocol telephony.

This study has its limitations, such as the generalization of these findings to the whole of Malaysia and the inability to supplement the questionnaire data with interviews or adopt a longitudinal approach to data collection. However, due to time and resource constraints, such limitations could not be overcome. For instance, future research of a similar nature may entail a longer data collection period, which will subsequently eliminate any variables that may have produced anomalies in the result.

References

Agarwal, R., and Karahanna, E. 2000. "Time Flies When You're Having Fun: Cognitive Absorption and Beliefs About Information Technology Usage," *MIS Quarterly* (24:4), pp. 665-694.

Brown, S. A., Massey, A. P., Montoya-Weiss, M. M., and Burkman, J. R. 2002. "Do I Really Have To? User Acceptance of Mandated Technology," *European Journal of Information Systems* (11:4), pp. 267-282.

Brown, S. A., and Venkatesh, V. 2005. "Model of Adoption of Technology in Households: A Baseline Model Test and Extension Incorporating Household Life Cycle," *MIS Quarterly* (29:3), pp. 399-426.

Choudrie J., and Dwivedi Y. K. 2005a. "The Demographics of Broadband Residential Consumers of a British Local Community: The London Borough of Hillingdon," *Journal of Computer Information Systems* (45:4), pp. 93-101.

Choudrie, J., and Dwivedi, Y. K. 2005b. "Investigating the Research Approaches for Examining the Technology Adoption in the Household," *Journal of Research Practice* (1:1), pp. 1-12, (available at http://jrp.icaap.org/content/v1.1/choudrie.pdf).

Choudrie, J., and Dwivedi, Y. K. 2006a. "A Comparative Study to Examine the Socio-Economic Characteristics of Broadband Adopters and Non-adopters," *Electronic Government* (3:3), pp. 272-288.

Choudrie, J., and Dwivedi, Y. K. 2006b. "Investigating Factors Influencing Adoption of Broadband in the Household," *Journal of Computer Information Systems* (46:4), pp. 25-34.

Choudrie, J., and Lee, H. 2004. "Broadband Development in South Korea: Institutional and Cultural Factors," *European Journal of Information Systems* (13:2), pp. 103-114.

Davis, F. D. 1989. "Perceived Usefulness, Perceived Ease of Use, and User Acceptance of Information Technology," *MIS Quarterly* (13:3), pp. 319-340.

Dwivedi, Y. K. 2005. *Investigating Adoption, Usage and Impact of Broadband: UK Households*, unpublished PhD thesis, Brunel University.

Dwivedi Y. K. 2007. *Consumer Adoption and Usage of Broadband*, Hershey, PA: IRM Press-IGI Global.

Dwivedi Y. K., Choudrie J., and Brinkman, W. P. 2006. "Development of a Survey Instrument to Examine Consumer Adoption of Broadband," *Industrial Management and Data Systems* (106:5), pp. 700-718.

Dwivedi Y. K., and Lal, B. 2007. "Examining the Socio-Economic Determinants of Broadband Adoption in the United Kingdom," *Industrial Management and Data Systems* (107:5), pp. 654-671.

Dwivedi, Y. K., Khan, N., and Papazafeiropoulou, A. 2007. "Consumer Adoption and Usage of Broadband in Bangladesh," *Electronic Government* (4:3), pp. 299-313.

Dwivedi, Y. K., Williams, M. D., Lal, B., Weerakkody, V., and Bhatt, S. 2007. "Understanding Factors Affecting Consumer Adoption of Broadband in India: A Pilot Study," paper presented at the 5th International Conference on E-Governance, Hyderabad, India, December 28-30.

Dwivedi, Y. K., and Weerakkody, V. 2007. "Examining the Factors Affecting the Adoption of Broadband in the Kingdom of Saudi Arabia," *Electronic Government* (4:1), pp. 43-58.

Fowler, Jr., F. J. 2002. *Survey Research Methods*, London: Sage Publications Inc.

Gefen, D., and Straub, D. W. 2000. "The Relative Importance of Perceived Ease of Use in IS Adoption: A Study of E-Commerce Adoption," *Journal of the Association for Information Systems* (1:8), pp. 1-30.

Hinton, P. R., Brownlow, C., McMurray, I., and Cozens, B. 2004. *SPSS Explained*, East Sussex, England: Routledge Inc.

Hsu, C. L., and Lu, H. P. 2004. "Why Do People Play On-Line Games? An Extended TAM with Social Influences and Flow Experience," *Information and Management* (41:7), pp. 853-868.

Keong, L. M. 2007. "Malaysia Lowers Broadband Target," ZDNetAsia, September 11 (http://www.zdnetasia.com/smb/news/0,39043754,62032069,00.htm; accessed January 2, 2008).

Karahanna, E., Straub, D. W., and Chervany, N. L. 1999. "Information Technology Adoption Across Time: A Cross-Sectional Comparison of Pre-adoption and Post-adoption Beliefs," *MIS Quarterly* (23:2), pp. 183-213.

Khoumbati, K., Dwivedi, Y. K., Lal, B., and Chen, H. 2007. "Broadband Adoption in Pakistan," *Electronic Government* (4:4), pp. 451-465.

Koufaris, M. 2002. "Applying the Technology Acceptance Model and Flow Theory to Online Consumer Behavior," *Information Systems Research* (13:2), pp. 205-223.

Lee, H., O'Keefe, B., and Yun, K. 2003. "The Growth of Broadband and Electronic Commerce in South Korea: Contributing Factors," *The Information Society* (19), pp. 81-93.

Lu, J., Yao, J. E., and Yu, C. S. 2005. "Personal Innovativeness, Social Influences and Adoption of Wireless Internet Services via Mobile Technology," *Journal of Strategic Information Systems* (14:3), pp. (3), 245-268.

Oh, S., Ahn, J., and Kim, B. 2003. "Adoption of Broadband Internet in Korea: The Role of Experience in Building Attitude," *Journal of Information Technology* (18:4), pp. 267-280.

Rogers, E. M. 1995. *Diffusion of Innovations*, New York: The Free Press.York.

Stanton, L. J. 2004. "Factors Influencing the Adoption of Residential Broadband Connections to Internet," in *Proceedings of the 37th Hawaii International Conference on System Sciences*, Los Alamitos, CA: IEEE Computer Society Press.

Straub, D. W., Boudreau, M-C, and Gefen, D. 2004. "Validation Guidelines for IS Positivist Research," *Communications of the Association for Information Systems* (13), pp. 380-427.

Taylor, S., and Todd, P. A. 1995. "Understanding Information Technology Usage: A Test of Competing Models," *Information Systems Research* (6:1), pp. 44-176.

Venkatesh, V., and Brown, S. A. 2001. "A Longitudinal Investigation of Personal Computers in Homes: Adoption Determinants and Emerging Challenges," *MIS Quarterly* (25:1), pp. 71-102.

Williams, M. D., Dwivedi, Y, K., Middleton, C., Wilson, D., Falch, M., Schultz, A., Weerakkody, V., Papazafeiropoulou, A., Ramdani, B., and Gholami, R. 2007. "Global Diffusion of Broadband: Current State and Future Directions for Investigations," in *Organizational Dynamics of Technology-Based Innovation: Diversifying the Research Agenda*, T. McMaster, D. Wastell, E. Ferneley, and J. I. DeGross (eds.), Boston: Springer, pp. 529-532.

About the Authors

Yogesh K. Dwivedi is a lecturer in Information Systems at the School of Business and Economics, Swansea University, Wales, UK. He obtained his Ph.D. from the School of Information Systems, Computing and Mathematics, Brunel University. His doctoral research has been awarded the Highly Commended Award by the European Foundation for Management and Development and Emerald Group Publishing Ltd. His current research focuses on examining diffusion of IS research and also understanding the adoption and diffusion of ICT in organizations and society. As well as having presented at leading IS conferences such as European Conference on Informatoin Systems and the Americas' Conference on Information Systems, he has co-authored several papers which have appeared (or are forthcoming) in international referred journals such as *Communications of the ACM, Information Systems Journal, Journal of Computer Information Systems, Industrial Management and Data Systems*, and *Information Systems Frontiers*. He has authored a book, *Consumer Adoption and Use of Broadband*, and co-edited the *Handbook of Research on Global Diffusion of Broadband Data Transmission*. He is a member of the Association for Information Systems and Life Member of the Global Institute of Flexible Systems Management, New Delhi. He can be reached by at ykdwivedi@gmail.com.

Mohamad Hisyam Selamat is a lecturer in the College of Business, Universiti Utara Malaysia. He obtained his Ph.D. from Brunel University, an M.Sc. in Accountancy from the University of East Anglia, and an undergraduate degree in Accounting from Universiti Utara Malaysia. His current research encompasses the social aspects of information systems, broadband adoption and usage, e-government, information management, knowledge management, and organizational learning. He has written for peer reviewed journals such as the *Learning Organization and Journal of Knowledge Management* and has more than 30 papers in academic journals and international conferences on these topics. He can be reached at hisyam1349@uum.edu.my.

Muhammad Syahir Abd. Wahab is a lecturer in the College of Business, Universiti Utara Malaysia. He obtained an undergraduate degree in Accounting and an MBA in Professional Accounting from Universiti Utara Malaysia. His current research encompasses the social aspects of information systems, broadband adoption and usage, e-government, information management, knowledge management, and organizational learning. He has four papers in academic journals and international conferences on these topics. He can be rached at syahir@uum.edu.my.

Mohd. Amir Mat Samsudin is a lecturer in the College of Business, Universiti Utara Malaysia. He obtained his M.Sc. in Information Technology (Management) from Universiti Teknologi Malaysia and an undergraduate degree in Accounting from Universiti Utara Malaysia. His current research encompasses the social aspects of information systems, broadband adoption and usage, e-government, information management, knowledge management, and organizational learning. He has four papers in academic journals and international conferences on these topics. He can be reached at amir@uum.edu.my.

Banita Lal is a lecturer in the Nottingham Business School, Nottingham Trent University, UK. She obtained her Ph.D. and M.Sc. in Information Systems from the School of Information Systems, Computing and Mathematics, Brunel University. Her research interests involve examining the individual and organizational adoption and usage of ICTs and technology-enabled alternative forms of working. She has published several research papers in internationally refereed journals such as *Industrial Management and Data Systems*, *Information Systems Frontiers*, *Electronic Government*, *International Journal of Mobile Communications*, and *Transforming Government: People, Process and Policy*, and has presented several papers at several international conferences. She can be reached at banita.la.@ntu.ac.uk.

20 STANDARDIZATION AS AN ARENA FOR OPEN INNOVATION

Endre Grøtnes
Department of Informatics
University of Oslo
Oslo, Norway

Abstract   *This paper argues that anticipatory standardization can be viewed as an arena for open innovation and shows this through two cases from mobile telecommunication standardization. One case is the Android initiative by Google and the Open Handset Alliance, while the second case is the general standardization work of the Open Mobile Alliance. The paper shows how anticipatory standardization intentionally uses inbound and outbound streams of research and intellectual property to create new innovations. This is at the heart of the open innovation model. The standardization activities use both pooling of R&D and the distribution of freely available toolkits to create products and architectures that can be utilized by the participants and third parties to leverage their innovation. The paper shows that the technology being standardized needs to have a systemic nature to be part of an open innovation process.*

Keywords   Open innovation, standardization, telecommunication, Open Mobile Alliance, Android

1   INTRODUCTION

There have been different views on the relationship between standardization and innovation. As David and Greenstein (1990, p. 12) summarized,

> ...early standardization of products may encourage innovation in complementary technology and organizations, and it may promote subsequent incremental innovation designed to perfect the original technology....On the other hand *de*

Please use the following format when citing this chapter:

Grøtnes, E., 2008, in IFIP International Federation for Information Processing, Volume 287, Open IT-Based Innovation: Moving Towards Cooperative IT Transfer and Knowledge Diffusion, eds. León, G., Bernardos, A., Casar, J., Kautz, K., and DeGross, J. (Boston: Springer), pp. 343-359.

facto standardization may prematurely close off basic exploration of technological opportunities in a wide area...discouraging further investment in non-
incremental innovation.

Since then, the standardization process has changed. Standardization has gone from a
process where the market or an organization chose between different existing products
in hindsight (reactive or *ex post* standardization) to a process where companies pool their
resources to create new products and services (anticipatory or *ex ante* standardization).
Participation in standardization has become an extension of the firm's internal research
and development process, and is in many cases a vital part of a product development
cycle (Weiss and Sirbu 1990) and innovation in the firm.

Anticipatory standards define future capabilities for information and comunications
technologies in contrast to recording and stabilizing existing practices or capabilities *de
facto* (Lyytinen et al. 2008). Anticipatory standardization is a collaborative effort to
create technologies or services that do not yet exist. The participants bring with them
their knowledge, R&D capabilities, and intellectual property. Together they create specifications for new technologies, services, procedures, systems, or architectures. These
specifications become available for all participants, who can use them to create new
innovations. The specifications themselves are also innovations. The standardization
process is no longer a choice between existing technologies, but an innovation process
where new technologies, services, procedures, systems, or architectures are created from
the different parts that each participant brings into the process.

One area where standardization has been essential for innovation is the mobile
telecommunication industry (Tilson and Lyytinen 2006). Here, common development
and sharing of R&D capabilities and intellectual property has happened on a large scale
(Bekkers et al. 2002). The mobile telecommunication industry is a multi-sided market
where actors have to cooperate to get new products into the market (Armstrong 2006).
The sector has gone from a national to a regional to a global market, and in this setting
no actor is so dominant that they can set a standard or introduce a new technology unilaterally (Steinbock 2005). Introduction of new mobile services needs some coordination
and cooperation. This cooperative effort of creating and bringing new mobile services
to the market is taking place within standardization organizations, so the innovation is
also taking place within the standardization organizations. The argument brought
forward in this paper is that anticipatory standardization in mobile communication is an
open innovation process, and that the systemic nature of the technology being standardized makes it suitable for an open innovation process.

This paper will look at anticipatory standardization and the innovation process and
compare two standardization initiatives that aim to create new mobile services. The two
initiatives are the Android project from Google and the Open Handset Alliance, and the
work of the Open Mobile Alliance. The paper will give insights into the question: *How
can anticipatory standardization act as an arena for (open) innovation within the mobile
telecommunication industry?* The paper will mainly add to the research on interorganizational relationships in open innovation (Maula et al. 2006; Simard and West 2006;
Vanhaverbeke 2006; Vanhaverbeke and Cloodt 2006) and expand the literature on innovation and the work of international standardization organizations in the mobile sector
(Cargill 1989; Funk and Methe 2001; Hawkins 1999; Schmidt and Werle 1998; Tilson
and Lyytinen 2006).

The rest of the paper is structured as follows: In the next section, the open inno-vation model is introduced. Section 3 presents the Android standardization initiative and the work of the Open Mobile Alliance. It also presents the research methods used and a comparison between the two standardization activities. Section 4 discusses the findings in the two cases and section 5 draws some conclusions.

2 OPEN INNOVATION

Open innovation is a new way of thinking of innovation for firms, where they explicitly cooperate with others to create new innovations (Chesbrough 2003). Open innovation indicates a shift in how innovation processes are perceived and conducted by firms and how products are brought to market. There has been a shift from a closed to an open model. In the closed model, R&D was conducted within the boundaries of the firm and the firm was the one that exploited the innovations and brought them to market. The knowledge to innovate resided in the firm. In contrast to closed innovation, the open innovation model generally believes that knowledge is widely distributed and can be found outside the firm. Open innovation is a paradigm (model) that assumes that firms can and should use external as well as internal ideas, and internal and external paths to market, as they look to advance their technology (Chesbrough 2006).

Open innovation is about creating new inbound as well as outbound flows of knowledge to leverage the firm's innovation capabilities. In this process, firms should look for new sources of knowledge and new markets and outlets for their existing product and intellectual property rights, and collaborate with others, including customers, rivals, academics, and firms in unrelated industries in the process. Open innovation can be thought of as systematically encouraging and exploring a wide range of internal and external sources for innovation opportunities, consciously integrating that exploration with the firm's capabilities and resources, and broadly exploiting those opportunities through multiple channels (West and Gallagher 2006).

In open innovation, there is an inbound flow of external knowledge and intellectual property into the research and development process of the firm and also an outbound flow of knowledge and intellectual property so others can benefit from the discoveries of the firm. A novelty in the open innovation model is the explicit use off both inbound and outbound streams of knowledge. In the closed model, innovations that firms did not exploit themselves often just "sat on the shelf," unused (Chesbrough 2003). There were no explicit outbound flows of intellectual property; the only way to market was through the firm. The attractiveness of open innovation as a business strategy is the way it leads to exploiting the benefits from inbound ideas from outside the firm and exporting intel-lectual property (IP) that thus far has been unused (Dodgson et al. 2006). IP is a key factor for the outbound and inbound flow of technology. Without some form of protec-tion and a way to sell their technology, firms would not have a way of appropriating value from their inventions and there would be no case for open innovation (West 2006).

Two approaches for exploiting internal R&D through external channels are (1) spinouts or licensing of products to others and (2) pooling of R&D with others. Both are instances of open innovation (West and Gallagher 2006). The pooling of R&D is what happens in anticipatory standardization, where the participants brings their IP, technology, and knowledge into the process and for the most part agree to make the technology available on reasonable and nondiscriminatory terms. The nondiscriminatory part is essential since all participants then can use the contributed technology.

One can view open innovation as a kind of collaborative R&D process, where firms cooperate to develop new technologies. The aim is to combine external and internal ideas into systems and architectures. One central point for open innovation is the role of the business model. Open innovation is based on business models that create overall value for all participants. Each firm must find some way to claim (internalize/capture) some portion of that overall value. It is no longer just about getting the innovation to market first but also about building the best business model to exploit the innovation. It could be that licensing the new technology is just as smart as producing the product yourself. Here lies a part of innovation that has often been overlooked but is in focus in open innovation: finding the best path to market for the product outside of the firm's boundaries and control. In open innovation, the firm intentionally loses a little of the control over the innovation process (van de Vrande et al. 2006; West and Gallagher 2006).

Open innovation can at first sight be quite similar to open source but the two are not the same. Open source is one way of doing open innovation (von Hippel and von Krogh 2006). Both are about sharing of ideas and collaborating to develop new products, but open innovation explicitly incorporates the business model and the creation and capture of value. For open source, open standards, and open innovation, the *open* part refers to collaboration by firms in producing some shared output (West 2007). Open innovation is not open in the same way as the two others. Open innovation brings a note of realism to the discussion of open standards (and open source) by putting the capture of value onto the center stage.

One goal of open innovation is to create new value for the participating firms through the innovation process. This is quite similar to the notion of "value networks" (Christensen and Rosenbloom 1995), where firms find partners both horizontally and vertically in networks instead of only cooperating with firms within the vertical value chain (Hess and Coe 2006; Li and Whalley 2002; Teece 1986), or "innovation networks" (Dittrich and Duysters 2007), where firms develop strategic alliances with other firms to leverage their R&D. Interorganizational relations, cooperation, and networking are an important dimension of open innovation (Vanhaverbeke 2006). With both inbound and outbound flows of technology and knowledge, there must be some sort of cooperation and networking between firms in open innovation. Simard and West (2006) have developed a taxonomy of network ties that enable open innovation. They have made a distinction between formal and informal ties and deep and wide ties. Deep ties enable a firm to capitalize on its existing knowledge while wide ties enable a firm to exploit new technologies and markets.

According to von Hippel (1988), the sources of innovation differ greatly. He assumes that the innovators are distributed among different functional sources. He categorizes these sources according to what benefit they get from a given product, process, or service. The categories he ends up with are (1) users, (2) manufacturers, and (3) suppliers. These are all sources of innovation. He also shows that the sources of innovation vary from industry to industry. Firms can take on different functional roles in different settings; sometimes they can be manufactures and other times users or suppliers. In his research, von Hippel focuses on two modes of innovation: the cooperation in R&D by rival firms through informal trade of technical know-how and the concept of lead users. *Lead users* are users that face needs that are general in the market, but face them earlier than others, and they are positioned to benefit significantly by obtaining a solution to those needs. Von Hippel's models are an antecedent to the inbound flow of innovations part in the open innovation model.

The open innovation paradigm has received input from different research streams or perspectives (Gassmann 2006). Some of them are globalization of innovation, outsourcing of R&D, early supplier integration, user innovation, and external commercialization of technology. Delving into open innovation raises a number of issues: the type of industries and organizations suited for open innovation (Chesbrough and Crowther 2006), the interorganizational context of open innovation (Vanhaverbeke 2006), how users can contribute to open innovation (Piller and Walcher 2006; Prugl and Schreier 2006), how open innovation should be managed (van de Vrande et al. 2006), the use of technology in promoting open innovation (Dodgson et al. 2006), and the similarities and differences between open source and open innovation (von Hippel and von Krogh 2006; West and Gallagher 2006). This paper focuses on the work of new types of organizations and interorganizational networks that utilize some form of open innovation to create new technologies and services.

The open innovation model can be conceptualized as having inbound streams of knowledge, IP, and innovation generated externally and outbound streams of knowledge and intellectual property that are generated internally (see Figure 1). Binding it all together are business models that show how firms can innovate and generate overall value. For the individual firm, it is essential to find some way to capture value from the overall value generation. In open innovation, firms often build systems or architectures where the different parts interlink but can be developed independently. They can then compete on providing the best components too the overall architecture or they can provide enhancements to the architecture. This can be viewed as an indication that open innovation might benefit from and thrive in an environment where the technology to be developed has a systemic character.

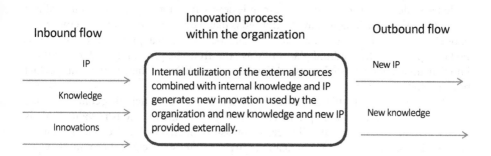

Figure 1. The Open Innovation Process

3   CASE DESCRIPTIONS

In this section, the two cases are presented and some key features of their process compared. Both are from the development of mobile services in the mobile telecommunication industry. The first case is the Android project, focusing on the development of mobile applications, the second case is the work of the Open Mobile Alliance, creating general standards for new mobile services like MMS, push-to-talk over Cellular and mobile IM.

3.1   Research Methods

The research is based on a mixed method approach (Creswell 2003). The data and the observations were interpreted based on the author's previous knowledge and experience using an interpretivist approach (Schwandt 1994). The Open Mobile Alliance (OMA) case is based on participatory observation in the period October 2006 through December 2007. More than 20 interviews with different participants and studies of the OMA members' archives were conducted. The Android project is newer and the data collection is based on archive studies, some e-mail correspondence with Google, and interviews with some of the actors that participated in both OMA and the Android project.

The two cases were chosen because they are part of the highly dynamic mobile domain and show in different ways how open innovation takes place within different standardization initiatives.

3.2   The Android Project

In November 2007, Google launched the Android platform publicly with backing by the Open Handset Alliance.

The Android platform is a complete mobile phone software stack including an operating system, middleware, and key applications. The Android platform will be made available as open source software and will be licensed under the Apache v2 license. Android has been complemented with a software development kit that makes it possible for third-party developers to develop applications for the Android platform. Android is designed so developers can access core mobile device functionality through standardized APIs. One distinguishing feature of Android is that it does not differentiate between the phone's basic and third-party applications. The idea is that all applications can be modified or replaced. The Android platform was built from the ground up and many of the initial members of the Open Handset Alliance have contributed some of their intellectual property to the project.

The Open Handset Alliance had, at the launch, 34 members including companies like Google, Intel, Motorola, and Sprint. The majority of the mobile industry value chain is represent in the Open Handset Alliance. It consists of operators, handset manufacturers, semiconductor manufacturers, application providers, and some content providers. Content providers from the music and film industry are not present. The members in the Open Handset Alliance say they have joined forces to accelerate innovation in mobile telecommunication.

At the launch, the chairman of Google said, "A fresh approach to fostering innovation in the mobile industry will help shape a new computing environment that will change the way people access and share information in the future" (OHA 2007)

Android is an architecture or a platform upon which other applications can be built (see Figure 2). It is an operating system for advanced mobile phones and competes with other operating system initiatives like Symbian and Windows mobile that can be licensed by handset manufacturers. It also competes with closed offerings like the iPhone from Apple and Blackberry from RIM.

Android depends on third-party applications developers to create applications that make it stand out from the other operating systems/platforms. To help in the development of new applications, Android has an accompanying software development kit that developers can use to develop applications for Android. To attract developers, Google has launched the Android developer challenge, which will award developers of applications on the Android platform $10 million in prizes for the best applications. The idea behind the challenge is to inspire developers to create new and innovative applications for the mobile phone.

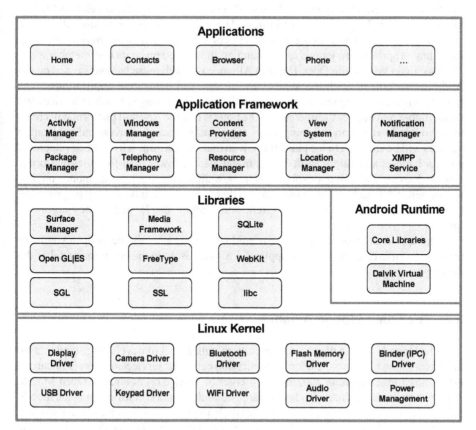

Figure 2. The Android Architecture (as presented by the Android Project; http://code.google.com/android/what-is-android.html)

The use of a toolkit for development of enhancement to a product can be viewed as part of an open innovation strategy and has been used in game development (Prugl and Schreier 2006) and to customize and personalize product offerings (Piller and Walcher 2006).

Applications for Android are developed in Java and run on *Dalvik*, a custom-made virtual machine that runs on the handset. Third-party developers have access to the same APIs as the original developers of Android. The development kit gives developers access to the same set of libraries as were used for the development of the core components.

Android relies on Linux version 2.6 for core system services such as security, memory management, process management, network stack, and driver model. The kernel also acts as an abstraction layer between the hardware and the rest of the software stack. Android is not the only mobile operating system or development platform based on Linux. Examples of other Linux-based platforms are LiMo from the LiMo Foundation and Qtopia from Trolltech.

As seen in the architecture, the Android platform provides a set of application frameworks that can be used to develop applications. Android is designed for easy reuse of components. Any developer can alter or replace any application. This gives Android a systemic character. The Apache v2 license also makes it possible for developers to close the source and make proprietary offerings. According to the alliance, this will make it possible for operators and handset manufacturers to differentiate their product offerings by adding proprietary functions or by changing the entire appearance of the phone.

One main goal of the Open Handset Alliance is to sell more handsets based on the Android platform through the availability of new and innovative applications. The thought is that appealing new applications will drive up the usage of mobile services and create higher revenue for the operators. The hope is that the Android platform will create higher overall value than the competitors so operators, manufacturers, and application vendors will be attracted to the platform. Given that the platform is free, the development cost for handset and chip manufacturers might also be lower than for other platforms. Google does not and will not explicitly state how they are going to make money on this, but the general thought in the marketplace is that Google will make money by providing advertisements to the mobile users (Helft and Markov 2007), just as they do on the Internet.

The applications developed for Android can be made available as open source or they can be offered as proprietary applications. This is up to the business model of the developer.

3.3   The Open Mobile Alliance

The Open Mobile Alliance is a consortium with a goal of developing standards for third generation (3G) mobile telecommunication networks service enablers (standards). OMA was formed in June 2002 by the merger of WAP Forum and the Open Mobile Architecture Initiative, and is today the largest standardization consortium in the mobile industry domain. OMA members span the whole mobile industry value chain including operators, manufacturers, IT vendors, and content providers. This is also evident in the OMA "Memorandum and Article of Association" (OMA 2005), which distinguishes between four categories of companies: operators, wireless vendors, IT/application/ software vendors, and others (content media, financial and/or service providers, and others).

OMA typically specifies new functionality and services for mobile devices, like device management, data synchronization, messaging services (MMS, IM, PoC, mobile e-mail), location and presence services, broadcast services, and digital rights management (DRM). Most of the specifications are frameworks for creating new end-user services or better management of mobile devices. OMA provides enablers that can be used to create new end-user services. The members compete on implementing these enablers.

Membership in OMA is open for all. There are four different membership levels: sponsor, full, associate, and supporter. Sponsor, full, and associate members can provide requirements to the specification processes and negotiate the content of the specifications, while only the two highest levels, sponsor and full members, are allowed to vote in OMA and agree on the final outcome of the specification process. The last level, supporter, is only allowed to comment on specifications.

Specification in OMA goes through different stages (see Figure 3). First, a new idea is generated and agreed upon, then the requirement for the new service is specified before the technical details and the overall architecture are specified. All specifications have an architecture where the connections to other enablers are shown. This makes it possible to reuse existing enablers in new specifications. The architecture and specifications have a systemic nature. The following sample from the converged messaging specification in OMA (2008, p. 12) illustrates the reuse of components:

> The CPM Enabler is realized as enabling framework for communication services building over a client–server architecture concept. It interacts with other network elements and re-uses functions or technologies specified by other OMA Enablers and non-OMA specifications.

In OMA, the members provide their technology and intellectual property rights (IPR) as input to the specification process. All members must use reasonable endeavors to inform about essential IPR they might have related to the prepared specification. This is informed at the start of every session in a face-to-face meeting or teleconference. The OMA members must also agree to license their IPR on reasonable and nondiscriminatory terms, a RAND policy, that is quite similar to the IPR policy of the European Telecommunications Standards Institute (ETSI). RAND policies are one of the most- used IPR policies today in telecommunication (Simcoe 2006).

The OMA process is based on consensus and takes place within working groups. The participants strive to agree on the content of the requirements, architecture, and the technical specifications. In case of disagreement, it is possible to vote. OMA has a two-thirds majority rule, but this is seldom used. In the specifications, firms try to get their

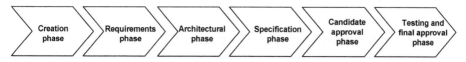

Figure 3. The OMA Standardization Process

essential IPR into the specifications or they try to make use of external components they control in the crafting of the architecture. The specifications in OMA are often high-level, making it possible to implement them in different ways. The specifications are also "bearer agnostic": they should work on top of any underlying network. The architectures and enablers are independent of operating systems and are based on open standards, protocols, and interfaces and are not locked to proprietary technologies. The specifications are modular and components are used in different settings to avoid the silo effects of many current services. For example, the charging enabler can be used by any new service that is created.

The membership and participation in OMA is large. In 2007, more than 500 individuals participated in each of the 6 face-to-face meetings that OMA held. OMA also has a large liaison activity that involves more than 30 other standardization activities. OMA tries to make their specifications available to the largest possible audience. They also use specifications from other organizations like IETF, 3GPP, and 3GPP2 as building blocks for their own specifications.

OMA has an inbound flow of IPR, technological know-how, and specifications both from the members and other standardization organizations. They use this input to create new and innovative specifications. They then disseminate the specifications as widely as possible so that anyone with the technological capability can use the specifications to implement actual technical solutions. The innovation first takes place within the working groups, where new ways of using technology are specified. The innovations are conceptualized in the specifications. Others then can create even newer innovations based on the available specifications. The firms in OMA compete on implementation but cooperate on the specification. The work in OMA is a collaborative R&D process. As one member of OMA expressed it,

> There has been a shift in standardization work. Previous standards were developed after the implementation of the product. Today standardization has become almost research and development. You come into a standardization organization with ideas. The ideas are refined in talks with others and then the standards are developed. The development of the product happens at the same time as the standard is developed.

The work in OMA is an open innovation process where the members and other standardization organizations provide technical know-how, IPR, and specifications, then there is a collective R&D process of creating architectures, frameworks, and specifications within the working groups. The output of the innovation process is specifications that the participants and others can use as a starting point for their own innovations.

The standards specified in OMA can be implemented, commercialized, and taken to market in many different ways. There are no restrictions on how the standards are used as long as the specifications are adhered to and the license fees are paid.

3.4 A Brief Comparison of the Two Cases

In the two cases, the types of firms that participate are categorized as operators, manufacturers, application vendors, or others. This can be transferred to von Hippel's

Table 1. The Distribution of Types of Firms in OMA and Android

Organization	Total Members	Operators	Chip and Handset Manufacturers	Application Vendors	Others
Android and the Open Handset Alliance (initial members)	34	7 (21%)	13 (38%)	10 (29%)	4 (12%)
The Open Mobile Alliance (voting members	118	35 (30%)	46 (39%)	31 (26%)	6 (5%)

(1988) categories of users, manufacturers, and suppliers. The operators are users, the manufacturers are (of course) manufacturers, and the application providers are suppliers. The last group, others, includes commercialization firms, finance institutions, consultants, research organizations, and content providers. If we look at the numbers, we can see that the relative numbers of operators are higher in OMA than in the Android project, but the distribution of manufacturers and application vendors is relatively similar (see Table 1).

Both use multiple sources of knowledge and IP to create their products. Both define architectures with systemic characteristics. Both let others use their end result for further innovation. These are typical traits of open innovations, so both are examples of open innovation processes. They differ in how open they are for initial participation and how further innovation can take place. OMA has more open participation and the use of IP is negotiated within the consortia. Licenses to use the IP, and thereby being able to produce products based on the specifications, are granted on reasonable and nondiscriminatory terms (RAND). Firms that are part of the process have an advantage in the development of products based on the specifications since they have better knowledge of the working of the specifications. The competition is in the provision of the different components within the architecture. The Open Handset Alliance provides their end product as open source. The idea is that third parties can innovate on top of the architecture. In Android the main innovators are third parties, while in OMA the main innovators are the participating firms (see Table 2).

Table 2. A Comparison Between OMA and the Android Project on Central Issues

Issue	OMA	Android
IPR and licensing (Outbound flow)	RAND	Open Source
Initial participation	Open participation	Participation limited to partners
End result	Technical specifications	Implemented architecture/toolkit
Inbound flow of IP	Open for all. Use of IP negotiated within consortia	Partners provide IP
Systemic character of innovation/specification	Yes	Yes
Main innovation process	Pooling of R&D	Provision of third party toolkits
Types of further innovation/competition	Innovation within the architecture	Innovation on top of architecture
Main innovators	Participating firms	Third parties
Open innovation process	Yes	Yes

4   DISCUSSION

Opening up the innovation process is about creating environments for innovation outside the boundary of the firm. These environments act as common grounds for all participating actors. One such arena can be different standardization organizations. Another arena can be different open architectures that all interested parties can use to develop new technology and services. The open Internet architecture is one such example. Such open common architectures have been called *innovation commons*. Lessig (2002) argues that such innovation commons, where all interested parties can develop new services on top of the same architecture/infrastructure, generate more innovation than closed systems, where only the IP holder can add functionality. This is the same message that the open innovation model gives. Maula et al. (2006) argue that a systemic character of innovation acts as a driver for open innovation processes. A systemic innovation is an innovation that needs specialized complementary assets before it can be brought to market. Examples of such systemic innovation systems are the Internet and 3G mobile phone systems. Because of the complexity in systemic innovations, vertical innovation is rarely an option, and the innovation process often becomes a collaborative process (Maula et al. 2006). This is the case for 3G mobile systems. Here, innovating companies become dependent on others to leverage their innovation. The systemic nature of the technology being standardized is an essential factor in both the Android project and OMA. The systemic nature of the technology and the need for cooperation leads to an open innovation process within the two cases.

Innovation in mobile telecommunication is constrained by the need for compatibility standards (West 2006). To be used, an innovation is incorporated in a formal specification/standard and these specifications are then implemented in products that are purchased by consumers and/or other producers. According to Gassmann (2006), the more the trends of globalization, technology intensity, technology fusion (industry crossover), new business models, and knowledge leveraging are present in an industry, the more appropriate the open innovation model seems to be. These traits can all be found in the mobile telecommunication industry.

With the 3G infrastructure being globalized and becoming an environment where people have to team up to leverage their inventions, standardization has become the arena where much of the collaboration is taking place. Standardization has then become an arena for open innovation in the mobile telecommunication domain.

There is a close relationship between the innovation system in mobile telecommunication and the standards making process. Lately it has been argued that the development of standards is the focal point for the changes in the mobile industry (King and Lyytinen 2002; Tilson and Lyytinen 2006; Yoo et al. 2005) and that there are three areas that shape and are shaped by the standards making process. These areas are the innovation process, the market place, and the regulatory regime. Together with standardization activities, it is argued that these three areas make up the new institutional environment for the 3G mobile infrastructure (Tilson and Lyytinen 2006). This shows the connection between standardization and the innovation process (see Figure 4).

Tilson and Lyytinen (2006) also argue that the innovation systems involves more actor groups and have become more complex and global for the 3G mobile infrastructure. The interconnection and the systemic nature of the infrastructure make it hard for any single firm to provide services and products unilaterally.

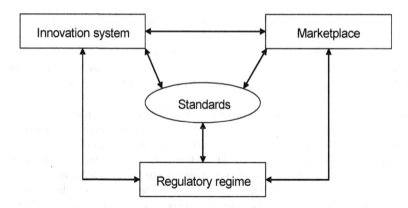

Figure 4. The Institutional Environment for the Mobile Industry (illustrating the connection between the innovation system and standards making)

As stated earlier, the cases encompass all the sources of innovation envisioned by von Hippel (1988). They have a mix of lead users, manufacturers, and suppliers. Both cases are governed by formal agreements between the participants. These are not closed but open processes, even if the OMA process was more open at the start than the Android project.

Dividing the infrastructure into three simple layers—the physical (infrastructure), code (logical infrastructure), and content layers (Benkler 1998; Lessig 2002)—one can see some differences in how additional innovation is taking place. OMA is placing their activities on the logical layer, creating standards for components that can enhance this layer. The innovation takes place on the logical layer where the participants compete to make the best implementation of the different pieces that OMA specifies for that layer. In OMA, what to build is being defined. How to implement the standards is up to the individual firms. Each component in the defined architecture (on the logical layer) can be provided by firms that have the capacity to develop it. An implementation of the architecture (the logical layer) is not provided. It is up to the individuals to realize the architecture. The Android project, on the other hand, presents a "complete" logical layer (architecture) and the innovation will take place on the content layer (architecture). This is similar to the development of new services on the Internet. The Android project provides third parties with a toolkit so they can develop new applications (new content) on top of the infrastructure. The Android model is similar to the Internet development model while OMA's approach is more in line with the telecommunication approach. As one OMA member said, "OMA creates mostly middleware while Android is higher in the stack."

In both cases, some sort of architecture/infrastructure is being specified within which the different participants can find their position. This is one of the features of open innovation (Chesbrough 2003).

Simcoe (2006) argues that changes in the nature of the innovation process, particularly an increase in the number of specialized technology developers whose business models rely heavily on intellectual property, have lead to an increasingly contentious (quarrelsome) standard setting process. He also argues that the emergence of innovation systems characterized by open innovation has pushed the participants in standards setting away from the "cooperate on standards and compete on implementation" mode that used to govern compatibility standardization toward a less cooperative standards creation environment, the main factor being that more firms are specializing and rely on the licensing of their technologies to capture value. They just provide components, not end products.

Intellectual property is an important theme in standardization. OMA and the Android project have taken on two different approaches in this regard. OMA relies on the traditional "reasonable and nondiscriminatory terms" model while the Android project relies on an open source licensing. So far, no handsets with the Android specifications have been launched so it is too early to say which licensing scheme works best. This is an interesting future research theme. In the Android project, the intellectual property issue is circumvented altogether with the use of an open source licensing. In OMA, there are some discussions on IPR but every OMA session starts with a call for IPR and there is strong internal pressure on the participants on being cooperative in licensing their technology (Grøtnes 2007). Both cases use IPR differently than the closed innovation model where the IPR is held inside the firm.

5   CONCLUSION

The key argument in this paper is that anticipatory standardization in the mobile telecommunication domain has become an arena for open innovation. This is due to the systemic character of the technology being standardized and the lack of actors that can provide all parts of the value chain. Firms must collaborate to provide a complete system.

Both the Android project and OMA innovate within a complex system where the development has a systemic nature. These systems are characterized by the interdependence between different components of the system. Innovations can typically not be promoted without the use of some other innovation provided by another actor (Maula et al. 2006). The systemic nature of the technology leads to cooperation and an open innovation process. Standardization has traditionally been the arena for cooperation in the telecommunication sector. This is also the case here and the cooperation necessary to specify the complex and global components of the 3G systems that OMA and Android provides is taking place within standardization. Anticipatory standardization has become an arena for open innovation in the mobile telecommunication domain.

Both cases have a purposely inbound flow of intellectual property rights, knowledge, and technical know-how. Together with this inbound flow they use their shared knowledge to generate new specifications in a cooperative environment. They provide their specifications to the public for use in further innovation. They also build architectures and systems within which to position their innovation. This is also the defining characteristics of the open innovation model.

The initial openness of the process and how firms position themselves in the infrastructures differs. This shows that open innovation can take on different forms in anticipatory standardization. In OMA, firms competes within the architecture and standards they specify, while in the Android project, firms compete on top of the architecture they specify. In OMA, the process of defining the architecture and the components is done in cooperation in an open environment with open participation. In Android, the architecture was defined by Google and some key partners; this is also a cooperative development but with closed participation. Both are examples of open innovation processes with inbound flow of technology and intellectual property and an outbound flow of intellectual property and technology.

Viewing anticipatory standardization as an open innovation process gives a new dimension to how we reason about standardization. It is no longer a place where firms choose technology in hindsight but an arena where innovation is taking place. To function as an arena for open innovation, the technology being standardized needs to have a systemic nature.

References

Armstrong, M. 2006. "Competition in Two-Sided Markets," *RAND Journal of Economics* (37:3), pp. 668-691.

Bekkers, R., Verspagen, B., and Smits, J. 2002. "Intellectual Property Rights and Standardization: The Case of GSM," *Telecommunications Policy* (26:3/4), pp. 171-188.

Benkler, Y. 1998. "Communications Infrastructure Regulation and the Distribution of Control Over Content," *Telecommunications Policy* (22:3), pp. 183-196.

Cargill, C. 1989. *Information Technology Standardization: Theory, Process, and Organizations*, Newton, MA: Digital Press.

Chesbrough, H. 2003. *Open Innovation: The New Imperative for Creating and Profiting from Technology*, Boston: Harvard Business School Press.

Chesbrough, H. 2006. "Open Innovation: A New Paradigm for Understanding Industrial Innovation," in *Open Innovation: Researching a New Paradigm*, H. Chesbrough, W. Vanhaverbeke, and J. West (eds.), Oxford, England: Oxford University Press, pp. 1-12.

Chesbrough, H., and Crowther, A. K. 2006. "Beyond High Tech: Early Adopters of Open Innovation in Other Industries," *R&D Management* (36:3), pp. 229-236.

Christensen, C. M., and Rosenbloom, R. S. 1995. "Explaining the Attacker's Advantage: Technological Paradigms, Organizational Dynamics, and the Value Network," *Research Policy* (24), pp. 233-257.

Creswell, J. W. 2003. *Research Design: Qualitative, Quantitative and Mixed Methods Approaches*, Thousand Oaks, CA: Sage Publications.

David, P. A., and Greenstein, S. 1990. "The Economics of Compatibility Standards: An Introduction to Resent Research," *Economic of Innovation and New Technology* (1), pp. 3-41.

Dittrich, K., and Duysters, G. 2007. "Networking as a Means to Strategy Change: The Case of Open Innovation in Mobile Telephony," *Journal of Product Innovation Management* (24:6), pp. 510-521.

Dodgson, M., Gann, D., and Salter, A. 2006. "The Role of Technology in the Shift Towards Open Innovation: The Case of Procter & Gamble," *R&D Management* (36:3), pp. 333-346.

Funk, J. L., and Methe, D. T. 2001. "Market- and Committee-Based Mechanisms in the Creation and Diffusion of Global Industry Standards: The Case of Mobile Communication," *Telecommunications Policy* (30), pp. 589-610.

Gassmann, O. 2006. "Opening Up the Innovation Process: Towards an Agenda," *R&D Management* (35:3), pp. 223-228.

Grøtnes, E. 2007. "The Creation of Standards: The Work of an International Standardization Organization," in *Proceedings of the Fifth IEEE Conference on Standardization and Innovation in Information Technology*, P. Feng, D. Meeking, and R. Hawkins (Eds.), Calgary, Alberta, Canada, October 18-19.

Hawkins, R. 1999. "The Rise of Consortia in the Information and Communication Technology
    Industries: Emerging Implications for Policy," *Telecommunications Policy* (23), pp. 159-173.
Helft, M., and Markov, J. 2007. "Google Introduces Software for New Phones," *International
    Herald Tribune*, Technology & Media Section, November 5.
Hess, M., and Coe, N. C. 2006. "Making Connections: Global Production Networks, Standards
    and Embeddedness in the Mobile-Telecommunications Industry," *Environment and Planning
    A* (38:7), pp. 1205-1227.
King, J. L. and Lyytinen, K. 2002. "Around the Cradle of the Wireless Revolution: The Emer-
    gence and Revolution of Cellular Telephony," *Telecommunications Policy* (26), pp. 97-100.
Lessig, L. 2002. The Future of Ideas, New York: Vintage Books.
Li, F., and Whalley, J. 2002. "Deconstruction of the Telecommunications Industry: From Value
    Chains to Value Networks," *Telecommunications Policy* (26:9/10), pp. 451-472.
Lyytinen, K., Keil, T., and Fromin, V. V. 2008. "A Framework to Build Process Theories of
    Anticipatory Information and Communication Standardizing," *International Journal of IT
    Standards and Standardization Research* (6:2), pp. 1-38.
Maula, M. , Keil, T., and Salmenkaita, J-P. 2006. *Open Innovation in Systemic Innovation
    Contexts* in *Open Innovation: Reserching a New Paradigm*, H. Chesbrough, W.
    Vanhaverbeke, and J. West (eds.), Oxford, England: Oxford University Press, pp. 241-257.
OHA. 2007. "Member Quotes," Open Handset Alliance (http://www.openhandsetalliance.com/
    member_quotes.html, accessed March 25, 2008).
OMA. 2005. "Memorandum and Articles of Association," Open Mobile Alliance Ltd.
    (http://www.openmobilealliance.org/document/Articles_of_Association_2006.pdf).
OMA. 2008. "Converged IP Messaging Architecture," Open Mobile Alliance, document
    OMA-AD-CPM-v1_0-20080118-D, January 18 (http://member.openmobilealliance.org/
    ftp/Public_documents/MWG/MWG-CPM/Permanent_documents/; retrieved March 1, 2008).
Piller, F. T. , and Walcher, D. 2006. "Toolkits for Idea Competitions: A Novel Method to
    Integrate Users in New Product Development," *R&D Management* (36:3), pp. 307-318.
Prugl, R., and Schreier, M. 2006. "Learning from Leading-Edge Customers at the Sims: Opening
    Up the Innovation Process Using Toolkits," *R&D Management* (36:3), pp. 237-250.
Schmidt, S. K., and Werle, R. 1998. *Coordinating Technology: Studies in the International
    Standardization of Telecommunications*, Cambridge, MA: MIT Press.
Schwandt, T. A. 1994. "Constructivist, Interpretivist Approaches to Human Inquiry," in *Hand-
    book of Qualitative Research*, N. K. Denzin and Y. S. Lincoln (eds.), London: Sage
    Publications, pp. 118-137.
Simard, C., and West, J. 2006. "Knowledge Networks and the Geographic Locus of Innovation,"
    in *Open Innovation: Researching a New Paradigm*, H. Chesbrough, W. Vanhaverbeke, and
    J. West, Oxford, UK: Oxford University Press, pp. 220-240.
Simcoe, T. S. 2006. "Open Standards and Intellectual Property Rights,"in *Open Innovation:
    Researching a New Paradigm*, H. Chesbrough, W. Vanhaverbeke, and J. West, Oxford, UK:
    Oxford University Press, pp. 161-183.
Steinbock, D. 2005. *The Mobile Revolution: The Making of Mobile Services Worldwide*,
    London: Kogan Page.
Teece, D. J. 1986. "Profiting from Technological Innovation: Implications for Integration,
    Collaboration, Licencing and Public Policy," *Research Policy* (15), pp. 285-305.
Tilson, D., and Lyytinen, K. 2006. "The 3G Transition: Changes in the US Wireless Industry,"
    Telecommunications Policy (30), pp. 569-586.
van de Vrande, V., Lemmens, C., and Vanhaverbeke, W. 2006. "Choosing Governance Modes
    for External Technology Sourcing," *R&D Management* (36:3), pp. 347-363.
Vanhaverbeke, W. 2006. "The Inter-organizational Context of Open Innovation," in *Open
    Innovation: Researching a New Paradigm*, H. Chesbrough, W. Vanhaverbeke, and J. West,
    Oxford, UK: Oxford University Press, pp. 205-219.

Vanhaverbeke, W., and Cloodt, M. 2006. "Open Innovaation in Value Networks," in *Open Innovation: Researching a New Paradigm*, H. Chesbrough, W. Vanhaverbeke, and J. West, Oxford, UK: Oxford University Press, pp. 258-281.

von Hippel, E. 1988. *The Sources of Innovation*, New York: Oxford University Press.

von Hippel, E., and von Krogh, G. 2006. "Free Revealing and the Private–Collective Model for Innovation Incentives," *R&D Management* (36:3), pp. 295-306.

Weiss, M. B. H., and Sirbu, M. 1990. "Technological Choice in Voluntary Standards Committees: An Empirical Analysis," *Economic of Innovation and New Technology* (1), pp. 111-133.

West, J. 2006. "Does Appropriability Enable or Retard Open Innovation," in *Open Innovation: Researching a New Paradigm*, H. Chesbrough, W. Vanhaverbeke, and J. West, Oxford, UK: Oxford University Press, pp. 109-133.

West, J. 2007. "Seeking Open Infrastructure: Contrasting Open Standards, Open Source and Open Innovation," *First Monday* (12:6) (http://www.firstmonday.org/issues/issue12_6/west/).

West, J., and Gallagher, S. 2006. "Challenges of Open Innovation: The Paradox of Firm Investment in Open-Source Software," *R&D Management* (36:3), pp. 319-331.

Yoo, Y., Lyytinen, K., Yang, H. 2005. "The Role of Standards in Innovation and Diffusion of Broadband Mobile Services: The Case of South Korea," *Journal of Strategic Information Systems* (14), pp. 323-353.

About the Author

Endre Grøtnes is at present a Ph.D. researcher at the University of Oslo and has a master of Informatics from that institution. Before embarking on his doctoral studies, Endre worked for many years in both the private and public sector where he developed guidelines and recommendations for the use of standards and technology within the Norwegian government. He has actively participated in standards organizations such as the Internet Engineering Task Force (IETF), World Wide Web consortium (W3C), European Telecommunications Standards Institute (ETSI), the European Committee for Standardization (CEN), the Open Group and the Open Mobile Alliance. His primary research interests are standardization, open source, and organizational innovation. Endre can be reached at endregr@ifi.uio.no.

21   CROSSING THE CHASM:
From Adoption to Diffusion
of a Telehealth Innovation

Sunyoung Cho
Virginia State University
Petersberg, Virginia U.S.A.

Lars Mathiassen
Michael Gallivan
Robinson College of Business
Georgia State University
Atlanta, Georgia   U.S.A.

Abstract   *Telehealth innovations promise to provide extensive medical benefits by increasing access to healthcare services and lowering costs at the same time. However, many telehealth initiatives fail to go beyond the status of prototype applications despite being considered technically viable and medically relevant. Based on a longitudinal investigation of a successful telehealth program, we identify a chasm between the initial adoption mode of the innovation as a prototype within a network of hospitals and the subsequent diffusion mode of the innovation as a commercialized product. Subsequently, we analyze how key actors negotiated the chasm to successfully diffuse the innovation beyond the initial hospital setting. In terms of research, the paper presents a longitudinal, empirical investigation of a successful telehealth innovation. Drawing on the metaphor of "crossing the chasm," we explain why many telehealth initiatives fail to go beyond prototype application status. In terms of practice, the paper provides lessons on how key actors can negotiate the chasm to transition from adoption mode to diffusion mode.*

Keywords   Telehealth innovations, innovation adoption, innovation diffusion, process models, chasm

Please use the following format when citing this chapter:

Cho, S., Mathiassen, L., and Gallivan, M., 2008, in IFIP International Federation for Information Processing, Volume 287, Open IT-Based Innovation: Moving Towards Cooperative IT Transfer and Knowledge Diffusion, eds. León, G., Bernardos, A., Casar, J., Kautz, K., and DeGross, J. (Boston: Springer), pp. 361-378.

1   INTRODUCTION

Telehealth innovations have great potential to enhance accessibility to healthcare, reduce cost of care, and enhance quality of care (Bangert and Doktor 2003; Institute of Medicine 1996; Office of Technology Assessment 1995). Despite such potential, many telehealth innovations are either not accepted or not successfully implemented (Bangert and Doktor 2003; Institute of Medicine 1996) due to poor technology performance, organizational issues, and legal barriers (Bashshur 2000). It is also widely acknowledged that physicians and other medical staff are notorious for their nonresponsiveness to and resistance to use of information technologies (Anderson 1997; Lapointe and Rivard 2005).

Telehealth innovations originated from the manned space-flight program by the National Aeronautics and Space Administration (NASA) and from pioneering efforts of a few physicians using off-the-shelf commercial equipment (Zundel 1996). Telehealth projects vary with respect to goals, funding, and technology, but most major projects in the 1990s were undertaken by large university hospitals with external funding from government agencies and industry (Office of Technology Assessment 1995; Zundel 1996). Although telehealth has been practiced for more than 40 years, its status was until recently evaluated as being in the early stages of development (Office of Technology Assessment 1995). However, technology advances have now contributed to increased experiments with telehealth innovations that potentially can lead to improved business and product development, commercialization, sales, and job creation, alough these impacts have not materialized yet (Jennett and Watababe 2006). In a typical life trajectory of telehealth innovations, many die out after initial funding is exhausted despite being considered medically and technically viable solutions.

In this research, we explain this paradox between the high potential of telehealth innovations, on the one hand, and the slow diffusion of telehealth innovations, on the other hand, by investigating gaps and collaboration patterns across innovation processes. The concept of an innovation gap is not new in the field of information systems. Fichman and Kemerer (1999) identify an assimilation gap between acquisition of an innovation and its actual deployment and use in an organization; and Moore (1999, 2004) uses the phrase "crossing the chasm" to denote a gap between early adopters and the early majority of innovation adopters in the marketplace. In framing this research, we rely on this notion of a gap in the process of market uptake of an innovation; however, the gap we investigate has a different focus and is framed differently than in previous studies. Specifically, we draw on Moore's concept of chasm to analyze the disrupted path to commercialization and diffusion of a telehealth innovation.

We have found few studies in the information systems literature that address the transition from adoption mode to diffusion mode of IT-enabled innovations. Moreover, in the particular context of telehealth innovations we know little about this transition. Against this backdrop, we investigate the following research questions:

- *Descriptive question:* How can we use the metaphor of *crossing the chasm* to characterize the transition of a telehealth innovation from adoption-mode to diffusion-mode?
- *Prescriptive question:* How can key stakeholders successfully cross the chasm between adoption mode and diffusion mode for a telehealth innovation?

Over a period of four years, from 2003 to 2007, we conducted a longitudinal case study in which we followed a telestroke innovation closely (Cho et al. 2007; Cho and Mathiassen 2007; Cho, Mathiassen, and Robey 2007). The innovation was initially developed and adopted by a network of hospitals and, following initial adoption, it was successfully commercialized as a new telestroke innovation. By closely examining this process, we identified a chasm between the initial adoption mode and the subsequent diffusion mode of the innovation. Moreover, we found that this chasm presented a major obstacle for the actors involved in the attempt to commercialize the innovation. As a consequence, we chose to analyze in detail how key stakeholders successfully negotiated the chasm.

The resulting analysis offers a number of contributions to research and practice. First, few studies have offered a longitudinal analysis of a telehealth innovation from initial adoption to successful diffusion in the market. Hence, we aim to contribute to telehealth innovation research by providing insights into the processes and conditions that make such innovations transcend the initial pilot stages. Second, we aim to challenge existing assumptions and boundaries of diffusion of innovation research, process-oriented approaches in particular, by identifying and characterizing the chasm that innovators face in seeking to diffuse the innovation to a broader market. Finally, we provide insights on how key actors crossed this chasm by detailing the transition process and by identifying contextual issues that facilitated or challenged it. The presentation is structured as follows. The next section reviews telehealth innovation and diffusion of innovation research. Then, we discuss the case study design and the analysis framework in the research method section. Subsequently, we present our findings in the results section. We conclude with a discussion of the contributions of the study and its implications.

2 THEORETICAL BACKGROUND

2.1 Telehealth Innovations

Healthcare has emerged as an increasingly important domain in IS research with a steadily growing body of knowledge (Chiasson and Davidson 2004). In this paper, we focus on telehealth innovations as an important subset of IT-based healthcare innovations. Advances in the form of network technologies, advanced interfaces, and mobile technology have created a renaissance of such innovations since the 1990s (Maheu et al. 2001). Increased use of IT to deliver healthcare services over distance has created new terms such as telemedicine, telehealth, and e-health (Anderson 1997; Bashshur 2000; Maheu et al. 2001). Although exact definitions and boundaries of these terms are elusive, telemedicine is broadly defined as provision of healthcare services, clinical information, and medical education over distance using telecommunications technology, whereas telehealth is seen as being a more encompassing term (Maheu et al. 2001).

Although the major contributions to telehealth innovations are often credited to the field of medical informatics (Chiasson and Davidson 2004), the IS field has begun to offer contributions in this area as well. However, within the IS literature, research questions and approaches vary a great deal. Adewale (2004) and Mbarika (2004) discuss the potential and challenges of telehealth innovations at the national level in developing countries. A study by Liang et al. (2006) focuses on development of a web-based decision support system to encourage multiple sclerosis patients to continue a specific medication. Brown et al. (2004) examine individuals' interpersonal traits and their effect on willingness to collaborate and resulting outcomes in the context of telehealth innovation. Hence, the latter studies analyze individual-level adoption of telehealth innovations. In contrast, other authors (e.g., Paul 2006; Paul and McDaniel 2004) examine how telehealth innovations (tele-radiology, distance learning, and tele-consulting) affect performance in collaborative relationships. Other organization-level studies focus on the process by which a telehealth innovation is adopted into a hospital network. For example, Constantinides and Barrett (2006) investigate implementation of a telehealth innovation in Crete with a focus on relationships among the context, the manner in which a system is used in practice, and the role of various technology artifacts; and, Chau and Hu (2004) analyze implementation of a Hong Kong-based telemedicine program using a conventional IT diffusion model (Cooper and Zmud 1990; Kwon and Zmud 1987).

We found no studies that investigate how a telehealth innovation goes beyond its context of origin, how it gains sustainability in the broader marketplace, or how it migrates from a pilot initiative to a full-blown commercial product. This paper aims to fill this gap.

2.2 Adoption and Diffusion of Innovations

Research on innovation adoption and diffusion has been established as a major research stream in the IS field (refer to summaries of this research stream by Fichman (2000) and Gallivan (2001)). Definitions of terminology vary among researchers. In his classical model of innovation diffusion, Rogers (2003) defines diffusion as the process in which an innovation is communicated through certain channels among the members of a social system over time. Fichman (2000) defines diffusion as the process by which a technology spreads across a population of organizations. We adopt this notion of diffusion with its focus on a larger population of organizations, in contrast to the notion of adoption that focuses on single innovation adopters—whether they are individuals or organizations. For example, Davis' (1989) technology acceptance model and Rogers' diffusion of innovation theory (Rogers' theory covers both individual level adoption and organizational level adoption) are among the dominant frameworks that explain individuals' adoption behavior focused on innovation characteristics and contextual factors (Fichman 2000; Gallivan 2001). Another approach to innovation adoption research at the organizational level is from a process model perspective, which we employ in this study. For organizational-level adoption and diffusion, Rogers proposed a five-stage model and Kwon and Zmud (1987) and Cooper and Zmud (1990) have suggested a similar six-stage model.

These dominant theories of innovation adoption and diffusion are often criticized for their limited explanatory power. Fichman (2000) argues that innovation research based on Rogers' classical model focuses mainly on simple innovations being adopted autonomously by individuals and it is, therefore, less relevant to technologies adopted by organizations. Gallivan (2001) argues that to explain more complex technologies and adoption scenarios we need to expand our process-oriented understanding of innovations and he suggests a hybrid framework that incorporates both processes and factors related to organizational adoption of innovations. Lyytinen and Damsgaard (2001) also recognize limitations in the assumptions underlying Rogers' diffusion of innovation theory. They argue that complex, networked technologies contain messy, complex problem-solving elements and such technologies are socially constructed as they shape and are shaped by society. For such innovations, Lyytinen and Damsgaard argue that process-oriented approaches provide greater accuracy and deeper insights into the phenomenon, as opposed to simplicity and generalizability, which are the goals of traditional innovation diffusion research.

Telehealth innovations fit well with the characteristics of complex, networked technologies suggested by Lyytinen and Damsgaard. First, they are interorganizational in nature. Second, they require considerable alignment of organizational policies and procedures by electronically linking multiple organizations and their work processes. Third, they require a sizeable critical mass of adopters in order to be effectively deployed. Finally, they unfold in complex institutional environments governed and strongly influenced by multiple regulatory and government-sponsored agencies (Bali and Naguib 2001; Bashshur et al. 1997). The process-oriented approach they advocate is, therefore, especially suitable to investigate the transition processes of a telehealth innovation from its initial pilot implementation to subsequent commercialization and throughout a broader market. Process models can explain how particular changes evolve over time (Markus and Robey 1988; Mohr 1982; Newman and Robey 1992) by investigating causal linkages and temporal relationships between key events and the context in which they unfold (Gallivan 2001). Specifically, this study adopts what Markus and Robey (1988) label an emergent perspective in which collaboration and networking among organizations emerge through dynamic interactions between diverse external forces and internal interests and motives.

Anchoring our theoretical framing on the process-oriented approach to diffusion of a complex, networked technology, we draw on, in particular, Moore's (1999, 2004) concept of chasm for the analysis of the study. Moore describes the common delay that accompanies diffusion of an innovation, following an initial period of rapid uptake. He describes this plateau in the diffusion process as a chasm that needs to be crossed—from the early adopter cohort to the much larger "early majority" in the technology adoption life cycle. His focus on identifying this chasm is to explain why many innovations fail to achieve more large-scale diffusion (i.e., the early majority), after being adopted enthusiastically by early adopters. We borrow the chasm metaphor to describe the problematic gap that can occur between the initial adoption of a telehealth innovation as a prototype within a network of hospitals and subsequent large-scale diffusion, which we regard as a commercial product generating revenues for the inventor across a broader market base.

3 RESEARCH METHOD

3.1 Case Study

Our study is based on an in-depth, longitudinal case study. Generally, a case study is a preferred mode for conducting research when *how* and *why* questions are posed (Benbasat et al. 1987; Darke et al. 1998) about a contemporary phenomenon in its context

(Yin 2003). These attributes are reflected in our process-oriented study. Moreover, a case study is also appropriate because, as researchers, we had no control over the events. Finally, a case study is appropriate because we seek to understand interactions between an IT-related innovation and the organizational contexts of various organizations in which it was developed, adopted, and subsequently diffused (Darke et al. 1998). Case studies allow researchers to investigate phenomena in depth to provide rich description and understanding (Walsham 1995).

3.2 Focal Innovation

In March 2003, the department of neurology at a large university hospital (labeled the hub hospital) in the U.S. state of Georgia launched a telestroke program named Remote Evaluation for Acute Ischemic Stroke Program, or REACH. This telestroke system allows neurologists from the hub hospital to participate in real-time stroke assessments of patients in rural hospitals. The innovation was launched and gradually expanded to a number of hospitals, with initial technical problems being detected and resolved effectively over time.

The need for the REACH system was justified by the critical lack of stroke specialist expertise in most rural areas and in many urban areas as well. This paucity of stroke specialists contributes to a higher mortality rate due to stroke in rural and underserved urban areas (Casper et al. 2003). For the case of non-bleeding, or ischemic stroke, a blood-clot dissolving agent called tPA (tissue Plasminogen Activator) greatly reduces chances of severe disabilities if it is administered within three hours from the first evidence of stroke symptoms. However, it is estimated that only a fraction of stroke patients receive the benefits of tPA, partly due to a lack of on-site stroke specialists. It is essential that a stroke specialist examine each stroke patient before tPA is administered. It is far from trivial to distinguish non-bleeding from bleeding cases, and applying tPA inappropriately (i.e., to a case of bleeding stroke) will trigger immediate and likely lethal consequences. Providing the services of stroke specialists over distance can, therefore, significantly increase the ability to diagnose whether a storke is bleeding or non-bleeeding, thus allowing tPA to be properly administered—saving many lives and reducing the risk of permanent disabilities. Between March 2003 and May 2004, doctors in the initial network of adopting hospitals used REACH to evaluate 75 patients and to qualify 12 of them for tPA treatment. By late 2006, more than 400 patients had been evaluated through REACH at 9 rural hospitals with 55 having been treated with tPA.

In January 2005, two entrepreneurs with funding from a state government research and development agency met and formed a company (labeled *BrainCare Inc.*, a pseudonym) to commercialize REACH. The first attempt at commercialization ended in failure as various stakeholders could not reach agreement on licensing and operation terms and conditions. As a result, the state's financial sponsorship of *BrainCare Inc.* ceased by the end of 2005. A few months after the first failed attempt, the REACH initiators (a team of neurologists at the hub hospital) established a second company (labeled *BrainConsult*, another pseudonym) to again attempt commercialization of REACH. Gaining some momentum from winning a state technology competition, the initiators found their first paying customers in September 2006 (a network of rural hospitals in the state of New York) and continued expanding their market nationwide.

3.3 Data Collection and Analysis

It is common for case study research to utilize multiple data sources (Miles and Huberman 1994; Yin 2003). Data sources for our study include interviews with key stakeholders, systems documentation, publicly available news articles, and observation at workshops. A total of 26 individuals in five hospitals (hub hospital and four rural hospitals) were interviewed to examine the initial pilot adoption process for REACH: nine nurses, seven doctors, six administrative staff, three IT staff, and one radiology technician. Detailed analyses of the initial adoption process of the innovation have been reported in previous studies (Cho et al. 2007; Cho and Mathiassen 2007; Cho, Mathiassen, and Robey 2007). During the commercialization process, the first two authors attended 12 workshops and follow-up meetings with the two entrepreneurs from *BrainCare Inc.* to discuss their business plans and strategy. We also interviewed five individuals from *BrainConsult* (the second firm founded to commercialize REACH) including the CEO and members of the Board of Directors. Data collection was conducted over the period from October 2004 to November 2007.

The first two authors developed customized interview protocols prior to each interview. Interview notes were recorded during and immediately following interviews and workshops and all interviews were transcribed for later analyses. In most cases, the authors held debriefing sessions in order to exchange and compare notes. This practice ensured a balanced and multifaceted understanding of data and enhanced intersubjectivity in the initial interpretation of data.

The data were later analyzed by all three authors through multiple sessions of discussion, focusing on the stages of initial adoption and subsequent commercialization and diffusion. First, events were listed to develop a chronological timeline for REACH's adoption and diffusion processes. According to Miles and Huberman (1994), such a chronology of events provides insights in terms of "what led to what and when." Such a listing provides the basis for depicting the sequence by which key events unfolded. Key actors were then identified as well as their actions and implications for further diffusion. Then, active discussions among all three authors took place to formulate a process model describing the initial pilot adoption, commercialization, and diffusion of REACH. Initially, the authors had different opinions on the number of stages and the definitions of the various stages. Disagreements among the authors were resolved through discussions that resulted in iterative refinements to the overall process model. The analysis was hence an iterative process that continued until consensus was established. The following are the results of this case analysis.

4 RESULTS

In this section, we describe the process of initial adoption and subsequent diffusion of REACH through four phases: adoption, implementation, commercialization, and diffusion (Table 1). For each phase, we identify the main actors and analyze their actions. These results provide insights in terms of how the process unfolded.

Table 1. Actors and Activities Involved in the Telestroke Innovation

Phase (When)	Actors (Who)	Actions (What)
Adoption	• Neurologists • System developer • Hub hospital	• Innovation conceptualized by hub hospital neurologists • Dedicated systems developer hired • Relationships with target rural hospitals cultivated • Innovation implemented by systems developer
Implementation	• Neurologists • Systems developer • Rural hospitals	• Innovation roll-out one rural hospital at a time • Technology issues addressed at rural hospitals • Financial issues addressed at hub and rural hospitals
Commercialization	• Firms (*BrainCare Inc.*and *BrainConsult*) • State funding agency • Hospital administration • Neurologists	• Negotiations between hub hospital and *BrainCare Inc.* • *BrainConsult* established and CEO hired • Participation in technology competition • System reengineered • Market further developed
Diffusion	• *BrainConsult* • Customers (early adopters) • Competitors • Neurologists	• Market penetrated • First customers engaged • Product expanded • Company renamed • Operation expanded and a Chief Operating Officer hired • Business models developed further

4.1 Adoption

The first phase, adoption, includes events starting with initiation of telestroke systems development in 2000 to roll-out of REACH in the first rural hospital in 2003. In terms of telemedicine systems, the hub hospital had a digitized tele-radiology system by the summer of 2004. It planned to fully migrate to the new system, which was being used in tandem with conventional film images. By the time REACH was initiated and launched, the tele-radiology system was the only telemedicine innovation in use in the hub hospital. Development of REACH was driven by a group of four neurologists, with one doctor serving as innovation champion. The physicians had long cherished the idea of a telestroke system that could link them effectively to rural hospitals. They began to implement this idea by hiring a technically savvy medical student to develop software in 2000. A year later, after the student left the area for his residency, the neurology department hired a full-time developer. During the adoption phase, the four neurologists played a key role as the primary driving force. They were simultaneously the project champions, the end-users, and the overseers the software development process. The neurologists basically controlled the process and interacted constantly with the developers by sharing their work practices and ideas and by providing necessary feedback to facilitate incremental development of the system. Also, in parallel to developing REACH, the neurologists cultivated relationships with rural hospitals in the state, visiting them and educating their medical staffs on how to leverage telehealth to collaboratively diagnose and treat ischemic strokes. During frequent visits, the neurologists gained insight into the operational conditions at the rural hospitals as well as requirements of the prospective users (ER physicians). The overall initiative was supported by top management at the hub hospital, specifically the CEO and a vice president responsible for service outreach. The neurologists actively promoted REACH and were able to secure financial support for software development and purchase of hardware for rural hospitals. The adoption phase was dominated by the activities of this small group of highly motivated neurologists. Through their leadership and close collaboration with a few other actors, they managed to develop REACH as a feasible telestroke system.

4.2 Implementation

The second phase, implementation, includes events starting with the first roll-out of REACH in March 2003, through continued expansion into a network of rural hospitals by December 2006. During this phase, REACH was gradually rolled out to a total of nine rural hospitals. The neurologists continued to play a key role by negotiating the system launch with rural hospitals in Georgia. The necessary hardware and software was provided and installed by the hub hospital without any costs incurred by the rural hospitals. As REACH expanded into more hospitals, two sets of issues emerged as critical: technical issues and financial reimbursement issues. The limited IT resources at rural hospitals surfaced as a serious problem, since most rural hospitals lacked full-time IT staff. As a result, there was no consistent process and manpower to address technical issues between the hub hospital and rural hospitals. As a result, the full-time developer at the hub hospital had to handle even minor technical problems at the rural hospitals. Later on, a second, full-time technician was hired by the hub hospital to focus on implementation problems and system trouble-shooting in the rural hospitals. Implementation of REACH in the rural hospitals often fell behind schedule due to lack of high-speed Internet connections or digital CT scanners in the rural hospitals. The knowledge base about REACH, its uses, and potential problems continued to accumulate as the system was gradually implemented in the nine hospitals. A second set of issues related to financial reimbursement. Any services provided by the hub hospital neurologists using REACH were not reimbursed by private or government insurance because the system configuration did not meet the two-way video link requirement for telemedicine to be reimbursed. Also, the rural hospitals were under-reimbursed for all REACH services because most of their patient base was covered by Medicare and Medicaid, government insurance plans that were well-known for low reimbursement rates. Despite the various problems, REACH continued to expand into more hospitals; however, there was no systematic or successful attempt to develop and negotiate sustainable business models that would effectively resolve the technical and financial issues described above.

4.3 Commercialization

Phase three, commercialization, was dominated by two entrepreneurs who established *BrainCare Inc.* to commercialize REACH. Engaged by the neurologists and funded by a government R&D agency, the entrepreneurs negotiated conditions with the hub hospital and the neurologists while creating a detailed business plan and searching for additional funding sources and customers. Unfortunately, the relationship between these entrepreneurs and the hub hospital deteriorated over issues of licensing and operation terms. The negotiations ultimately were aborted in December 2005 and *BrainCare Inc.* was dissolved right after. As the neurologists ended negotiations with *BrainCare*, they started to explore other ways to commercialize REACH, as the system had reached a local saturation point: a single hub hospital overseeing nine nearby rural hospitals. At this point, REACH's champions faced barriers to further local expansion. The neurologists increasingly sought nationwide diffusion, relying on the fact that they had proven REACH to be technically feasible within one U.S. region. The neurologists created momentum for nationwide diffusion by applying for a Small Business Innovations & Research grant and by founding a firm *(BrainConsult)* in March 2006.

At the same time, the project initiators won a state-wide technology competition, which created wider recognition of REACH and secured an award of $100,000. Winning the competition boosted the neurologists' enthusiasm and confidence. A CEO with a systems development background was hired, and the software was reengineered to increase reliability and scalability. Up to this point, these stakeholders lacked business experience and were mainly driven by their medical expertise and passion for using technology to treat ischemic stroke patients. The new CEO, who lacked healthcare industry experience, brought software experience and solid technology skills to the team. As a result, he helped formulate a new business plan and technology infrastructure, and he had generated enthusiasm among several interested hospitals by summer 2006. By late 2006, *BrainConsult* was still in a formative stage: it still lacked a physical office location and a dependable stream of revenue. On the other hand, the company had developed a solid technological infrastructure, an emerging organizational structure, and a comprehensive business plan.

4.4 Diffusion

The final phase, diffusion, began with the first commercial contract. Even before the commercialization attempts shifted to high gear, some hospitals in other regions showed interest in REACH, although their interests did not immediately lead to formal contracts and implementation. The Surgeon General of a northern state was promoting telemedicine in rural areas and he urged that REACH be considered. In September 2006, *BrainConsult* signed a contract with this state as its first paying customer. By November 2007, REACH was up and running in about 30 hospitals. Moreover, a total of 44 hospitals spread across four different states had contracted to install REACH, relying on eight hub hospitals among them. As a result, *BrainConsult* started to enjoy a steady stream of revenue, but it also faced a new set of challenges and decisions. The company defined itself as an application service provider but continued to debate the nature and scope of business. The firm eventually changed its name in late 2007 (although we continue to use the pseudonym *BrainConsult* to refer to it here). At that point, the firm still lacked any dedicated marketing plan, and its employees were entirely focused on technology and systems development. Although assured a stream of revenues, the company had limited financial resources to create a comprehensive portfolio of capabilities. Key actors debated whether to seek outside funding, although they acknowledged the potential loss of control over the company's fate that this might necessitate. As a result of this ongoing process of shaping *BrainConsult* to become a more mature business, the founding group of neurologists relinquished some control, while still maintaining their roles and positions within the original hub hospital.

5 DISCUSSION

We have presented a longitudinal case study of a telehealth innovation, describing its transition from pilot adoption within one state (Georgia) to wider commercialization and diffusion from a process-oriented research perspective. The field of IS has little understanding of such a transition process despite a large body of knowledge on the diffusion of innovation process. The overall process of the particular telehealth innovation unfolded through the four phases we described, explaining what issues the actors encountered, how those issues were resolved, and what outcomes ensued. While REACH was eventually commercialized, major challenges were faced during the transition from the early stages (the adoption and implementation phases, which were limited to an initial network of hospitals) to the later stages (commercialization of REACH and its subsequent diffusion to the broader marketplace). In this section, we characterize this *chasm* between the early stages (adoption and implementation) and later stages (commercialization and diffusion), and we discuss how REACH's champions were able to successfully cross the chasm (at least, when evaluated at this time).

5.1 Characterizing the Chasm

Our analysis reveals the existence of minor gaps at each stage of our process model. For example, new stakeholders (rural hospitals) emerged during stage two (implementation), which brought additional skills and resources—but also problems and constraints—to the original stakeholders (the neurologists and system developers). In transitioning from phase two to three, the focus shifted to resolving problems that had not previously existed—problems with technological infrastructure and financial reimbursement policies and regulations. Similarly, in transitioning from phase three (commercialization) to phase four (diffusion), we observed a realignment among many stakeholders. *Brain Consult* (the second company founded by the neurologists) became the most prominent actor while other stakeholders, including some of the REACH inventors and the original hub hospital, receded into the background to some degree. In stage four, the critical activities were focused on preparing REACH for the market and building appropriate organizational capabilities and structures. While the CEO and board members of *Brain Consult* addressed these gaps in a way that was ultimately successful, they also faced considerable challenge in progressing from the limited, initial adoption in the state of Georgia alone to a much broader pattern of diffusion in the market.

These challenges describe the problematic gap that can occur between the initial adoption of a telehealth innovation as a prototype within a network of hospitals and subsequent large-scale diffusion as a commercial product generating revenues for the inventor across a broader market base. They called for step-function changes in terms of skills, resources, and capabilities, which can be characterized in terms of four development trajectories: from a single hospital network to the marketplace; from prototype to a complete product; from government funding to market-based revenue generation; and from medical expertise to business leadership.

From a single hospital network to the marketplace: In this development trajectory, we observe that the type of target adopters changed significantly. The primary adopters in adoption mode had close ties with the hub hospital. They were all included in a restricted set of nearby rural hospitals, geographically and medically connected to the hub hospital. Each rural hospital was hand-picked by the hub hospital and the relationship between them did not involve financial transactions. The number of rural hospitals was limited by the financial resources and physician manpower available at the hub hospital. For diffusion mode, conversely, the adopting hospitals are true consumers in a marketplace. These entities have no ties of loyalty to the hub hospital, nor are they geographically close to the original hub. Hence, the relationships among the actors changed from one of collaboration within a network of hospitals to transactions involving buyers and sellers in a marketplace.

From prototype to complete product: Second, the REACH system had to undergo a transformation from a situated prototype to a commercial product. REACH was initially created to meet specific needs of the original hub hospital and associated rural hospitals. During diffusion mode, REACH had to be reengineered to meet general market requirements for a commercial product, which required enhancing reliability and scalability. Later, it was upgraded to allow two-way video streaming, hence overcoming barriers to full insurance reimbursement. As *BrainConsult* matured as an application service provider, it was essential that REACH become a complete product (Moore 1999), including the basic telestroke application and other value-added services such as training, installation, maintenance, and operational support.

From government funding to market-based revenue generation: Third, the financing mechanism for REACH completely evolved from an academic type of R&D project that relied on outside government funding to market-based revenue streams. Funding for development, implementation, and support in the initial set of rural hospitals was tied to the hub hospital's neurology department and its ability to secure research grants. With subsequent diffusion, financing options changed dramatically. As *Brain Consult* was founded and matured, the operational funds came in the form of customer revenues. By the end of our case study, the customer portfolio was large (consisting of 8 hub and 44 rural hospitals), and *BrainConsult*'s board was considering outside investors and owners. As a result, *BrainConsult* had evolved to become self-sustaining based on customer revenues.

From medical expertise to business leadership: Finally, the capabilities evolved significantly between the adoption and diffusion phases. Initially, key leadership was provided by a group of neurologists with expertise in medicine—but not business—during adoption mode. These neurologists championed the innovation, locating funding sources and seeking potential adopters. This leadership was grounded in humanitarian motives and medical expertise, and the mode of operation was focused on meeting the needs of the initial hub and set of rural hospitals. In contrast, a new firm, *BrainConsult*, oversaw most core activities during the later diffusion phase. Commercial success occurred as a result of hiring business leadership—namely, a CEO and, subsequently, a chief operating officer who were able to build the necessary structures and processes to ensure a viable business.

5.2 Crossing the Chasm

The good news is that the chasm was successfully negotiated and crossed. REACH was led by highly motivated neurologists, who played multiple roles of champions, project managers, and end-users. Their close involvement throughout the initial phases ensured that a stable technology existed and necessary relationships were established with rural hospitals, generating a solid network of initial adopters. More importantly, these champions also became a driving force in diffusion mode as well by establishing the business (*BrainConsult*) on which diffusion relied. The successful pilot stage helped to ensure that the chasm could be traversed, as it generated public awareness of REACH among a broader set of potential adopters. Another key event, REACH winning a state technology competition, helped to facilitate creation of *BrainConsult* and helped build momentum for further diffusion. Finally, the set of capabilities that ensured a successful adoption mode were also critical to diffusing REACH to the broader market.

While the chasm dividing phases two (implementation) and three (commercialization) was successfully crossed, substantial effort, resources, and ingenuity were required. Constraints associated with the rural hospitals (in the form of limited bandwidth, CT scanners, and barriers to insurance reimbursement) were not adequately considered during development. This oversight became a potential barrier to successful implementation in the rural hospitals. Misalignment of REACH's technical features with the institutional arrangements (specifically, reimbursement regulations), was a problem that had to be resolved in order to ensure successful implementation (in phase two) and the possibility of commercialization (in phase three). *BrainConsult* had to fundamentally alter REACH's technical specifications to allow for two-way video streaming, as required for insurance reimbursement. Next, there was insufficient awareness of economic issues (i.e., the capability for the first company, *BrainCare*, to negotiate contracts to which both hub and rural hospitals could agree). As a result, the REACH champions had to undergo complex negotiations with multiple potential business partners before a viable business plan and commercial entity emerged.

We summarize our learning and reflections from this study into the following recommendations in the hope that they can be of help to other entrepreneurs and managers who want to adopt telehealth innovations with the goal of subsequently diffusing them as commercial products:

*   *Develop a long-term plan for post-pilot stages*: Like many other telehealth innovations, REACH started out as a pilot system. Its inventors were motivated by their medical expertise and humanitarian goals. To facilitate subsequent diffusion of similar IT-based health innovations, we encourage champions of other innovations to develop long-term plans for what they hope to achieve post-pilot—including consideration of financial, legal, and technological issues.

• *Position innovation as win–win propositions from the start*: REACH was supported by the hub hospital, but at some point it faced difficulties gaining financial support for further expansion. The strategic alignment of REACH capabilities with the hub hospital's goals was better than that with rural hospital goals. REACH was promoted by the hub hospital, on which it relied for its funding; no attempt was made to develop a sustainable business model that explicitly considered rural hospitals' motives, capabilities, and constraints. Hence, it is critical that telehealth champions seek to position any innovation early on as win–win propositions with regard to the origination entity and other partner institutions.

• *Align with rural hospital processes*: REACH was developed by the hub hospital and then "pushed" out to the rural hospitals. Due to its origins, the processes and constraints of the rural hospitals were not actively considered when the technology was designed and created. The sooner partner institutions can be involved in design and development of a telehealth innovation, the easier it is to align the innovation with relevant partner capabilities in order to ensure subsequent adoption and diffusion.

• *Accommodate rural area technology infrastructure issues*: The project initiators encountered unexpected problems with technology infrastructure at the rural hospital sites. For example, the lack of IT staff, high-speed Internet connections, and CT scanner equipment in the rural hospitals served as barriers to adoption of REACH by these hospitals. As a result, training and trouble-shooting began to consume significant IT staff resources at the hub hospital. Recognizing partner constraints, both in terms of technology and expertise, will facilitate adoption among partner institutions, and pave the way for successful diffusion within the broader marketplace.

• *Accommodate institutional arrangements and legal issues*: The most commonly cited problems related to REACH were misalignment with institutional arrangements and legal issues. Since the neurologists failed to meet the two-way video streaming requirement by designing the flow of data one-way, the services of hub hospital physicians were not reimbursable. In addition, REACH was not an attractive proposition for the rural hospitals due to many patients having insufficient insurance coverage. Considering institutional and legal issues as key design dimensions can, therefore, greatly facilitate successful diffusion of new IT-based healthcare innovations.

• *Involve business leadership from early stages*. The evolution of REACH was driven purely based on medical leadership until the difficult transition leading to diffusion. Early involvement of business leadership can provide complementary skills needed to prepare the innovation itself and the business model for subsequent commercialization and diffusion into the market (Moore 1999). In the case of REACH, business leadership could have opted to build a useful knowledge base through experiential learning since adoption occurred incrementally (i.e., hospital by hospital). Such a knowledge base could involve developing a set of guidelines to facilitate implementation at rural hospitals related to training, maintenance, trouble-shooting, and possible system configurations. Experiences with initial development and adoption could hence be systematically managed and utilized at later diffusion stages.

6   CONCLUSION

This research makes two distinct theoretical contributions. First, it contributes to the growing body of IS research on telehealth innovations. Many studies report cases of initial adoption in a single organization or network of adopter facilities (e.g., Chau and Hu 2004; Constantinides and Barrett 2006; Davidson and Chismar 1999; Lapointe and Rivard 2005; Lau et al. 1999). There are no studies, however, that investigate the transition from initial adoption to wider diffusion into a larger population of organizations. By examining a case where the necessary transitions occurred all the way to commercialization and diffusion, this study provides important insights about why many technically viable and medically useful innovations fail to go beyond prototype applications. Observing that there is a chasm between initial adoption mode of a telehealth innovation and subsequent diffusion as a commercial product in the market, we offer lessons from our study of REACH regarding how stakeholders can successfully negotiate and cross this chasm.

Second, our case study expands the body of knowledge on diffusion of innovation research. We believe that REACH fits the definition of a complex, networked technology for which conventional innovation diffusion models are inappropriate (Lyytinen and Damsgaard 2001). Dominant theories of innovation diffusion have been criticized for their lack of explanatory power beyond the conditions in which those theories originated, that is, independent adopters evaluating a simple innovation for their own use (Fichman 2000, 2004; Gallivan 2001; Lyytinen and Damsgaard 2001). We agree with this criticism that traditional innovation diffusion models (e.g., Kwon and Zmud 1987; Rogers 2003) do not fit the context of REACH or the challenges involved in commercializing and diffusing it. This study explores this research gap of little processual understanding by providing insight into the creation of a complex, networked telehealth innovation from its initial conception to commercialization. In particular, we identified a potential barrier that was nearly fatal, in terms of obstructing progress from adoption mode to diffusion mode, and we framed it as a point of disruptive change. We presented our case study results as a process model consisting of four stages (adoption, implementation, commercialization, and diffusion) with each stage demarcated by specific actors and key activities. We framed the disruptive transition between adoption mode and diffusion as a chasm, borrowing the metaphor from Moore (1999, 2004). The study details the nature of the chasm as well as the context-specific enabling factors and challenges that the REACH champions faced in successfully negotiating the chasm. The four-phase model and our description of the events and resources required to cross this chasm constitute what Markus and Robey (1988) label an emergent perspective with regard to how IT and organizational change occurs. Theoretically identifying and framing the chasm between initial conception and commercialization in a telehealth innovation context and characterizing the attributes of the chasm are a major contribution of this study.

Although our study deals with just one telestroke innovation, our findings provide useful insights for other telehealth initiatives. However, while telehealth innovations share a set of common characteristics, it is always important to take into account the unique contexts in which they unfold. Further research is therefore needed to develop the insights we have provided, both conceptually and in terms of practical implications.

References

Adewale, O. S. 2004. "An Internet-Based Telemedicine System in Nigeria," *International Journal of Information Management* (24:3), pp. 221-234.

Anderson, J. G. 1997. "Clearing the Way for Physicians' Use of Clinical Information Systems," *Communications of the ACM* (40:8), pp. 83-90.

Bali, R. K., and Naguib, R. N. G. 2001. "Towards Gestalt Telehealth: Considering Social, Ethical and Cultural Issues," in *Canadian Conference on Electrical and Computer Engineering*, Toronto, Canada, May 13-16, pp. 1367-1371.

Bangert, D., and Doktor, R. 2003. "The Role of Organizational Culture in the Management of Clinical e-Health Systems," in *Proceedings of the 36th Annual Hawaii International Conference System Sciences*, Los Alamitos, CA: IEEE Computer Society Press, pp. 163-171.

Bashshur, R. L. 2000. "Telemedicine Nomenclature: What Does it Mean?," *Telemedicine Journal* (6:1), pp. 1-3.

Bashshur, R. L., Sanders, J. H., and Shannon, G. W. (eds.). 1997. *Telemedicine: Theory and Practice*, Springfield, IL: Charles C. Thomas.

Benbasat, I., Goldenstein, D. K., and Mead, M. 1987. "The Case Research Strategy in Studies of Information Systems," *MIS Quarterly* (11:3), pp. 369-386.

Brown, H. G., Poole, M. S., and Rodgers, T. L. 2004. "Interpersonal Traits, Complementarity, and Trust in Virtual Collaboration," *Journal of Management Information Systems* (20:4), pp. 115-137.

Casper, M. L., Barnett, E., Williams, G. I. J., Halverson, J. A., Braham, V. E., and Greenlund, K. J. 2003. *Atlas of Stroke Mortality: Racial, Ethnic, and Geographic Disparities in the United States*, National Center for Chronic Disease Preveition and Health Promotion, Centers for Disease Control and Preveition, Department of Human and Health Services, Atlanta, GA (ftp://ftp.cdc.gov/pub/Publications/stroke_atlas/).

Chau, P. Y. K., and Hu, P. J.-H. 2004. "Technology Implementation for Telemedicine Programs," *Communications of the ACM* (47:2), pp. 87-92.

Chiasson, M. W., and Davidson, E. 2004. "Pushing the Contextual Envelope: Developing and Diffusing IS Theory for Health Information Systems Research," *Information and Organization* (14:3), pp. 155-188.

Cho, S., Khasanshina, E., Mathiassen, L., Hess, D. C., Wang, S., and Stachura, M. E. 2007. "An Analysis of Business Issues in a Telestroke Project," *Journal of Telemedicine and Telecare* (13:5), pp. 257-262.

Cho, S., and Mathiassen, L. 2007. "The Role of Industry Infrastructure in Telehealth Innovations: a Multi-level Analysis of a Tele-stroke Program," *European Journal of Information Systems* (16:6), pp. 738-750.

Cho, S., Mathiassen, L., and Robey, D. 2007. "Dialectics of Resilience: A Multi-level Analysis of a Telehealth Innovation," *Journal of Information Technology* (22:1), pp. 24-35.

Constantinides, P., and Barrett, M. 2006. "Negotiating ICT Development and Use: The Case of a Telemedicine System in the Healthcare Region of Crete," *Information and Organization* (16:1), pp. 27-55.

Cooper, R. B., and Zmud, R. W. 1990. "Information Technology Implementation Research: A Technological Diffusion Approach.," *Management Science* (36:2), pp. 123-139.

Darke, P., Shanks, G., and Broadbent, M. 1998. "Successfully Completing Case Study Research: Combining Rigour, Relevance and Pragmatism," *Information Systems Journal* (8:4), pp. 273-289.

Davidson, E., and Chismar, W. G. 1999. "Planning and Managing Computerized Order Entry: A Case Study of IT-Enabled Organizational Transformation," *Top Health Information Management* (19:4), pp. 47-61.

Davis, F. D. 1989. "Perceived Usefulness, Perceived Ease-of-Use and User Acceptance of Information Technology," *MIS Quarterly* (13:3), pp. 319-339.

Fichman, R. G. 2000. "The Diffusion and Assimilation of Information Technology Innovations," in *Framing the Domains of IT Management: Projecting the Future Through the Past*, R. W. Zmud (ed.), Cincinnati, OH: Pinnaflex Educational Resources, pp. 105-127.

Fichman, R. G. 2004. "Going Beyond the Dominant Paradigm for Information Technology Innovation Research: Emerging Concepts and Methods," *Journal of the Association for Information Systems* (5:8), pp. 314-355.

Fichman, R. G., and Kemerer, C. F. 1999. "The Illusory Diffusion of Innovation: An Examination of Assimilation Gaps," *Information Systems Research* (10:3), pp. 255-275.

Gallivan, M. J. 2001. "Organizational Adoption and Assimilation of Complex Technological Innovations: Development and Application of a Network Framework," *The Database for Advances in Information Systems* (32:3), pp. 51-85.

Institute of Medicine. 1996. *Telemedicine: A Guide to Assessing Telecommunications in Health Care*, M. J. Field (ed.), Washington, DC: National Academy Press.

Jennett, P., and Watanabe, M. 2006. "Healthcare and Telemedicine: Ongoing and Evolving Challenges," *Disease Management & Health Outcomes* (14:Supplement 1), pp. 9-13.

Kwon, T. H., and Zmud, R. W. 1987. "Unifying the Fragmented Models of Information Systems Implementation," in *Critical Issues in Information Systems Research*, R. J. Boland and R. A. Hirscheim (eds.), New York: John Wiley and Sons, pp. 227-251.

Lapointe, L., and Rivard, S. 2005. "A Multilevel Model of Resistance to Information Technology Implementation," *MIS Quarterly* (29:3), pp. 461-491.

Lau, F., Doze, S., Vincent, D., Wilson, D., Noseworthy, T., Hayward, R., and Penn, A. 1999. "Patterns of improvisation for evidence-based practice in clinical settings," *Information Technology & People* (12:3), pp. 287-303.

Liang, H., Xue, Y., and Berger, B. A. 2006. "Web-Based Intervention Support System for Health Promotion," *Decision Support Systems* (42:1), pp. 435-449.

Lyytinen, K., and Damsgaard, J. 2001. "What's Wrong with the Diffusion of Innovation Theory?," in *Proceedings of the IFIP TC8 Working Group 8.6 Fourth Conference on Diffusing Software Products and Process Innovations*, M. A. Ardis and B. L. Marcolin (eds.), Deventer, The Netherlands: Kluwer B.V., pp. 173-190.

Maheu, M. M., Whitten, P., and Allen, A. 2001. *E-Health, Telehealth, and Telemedicine: A Guide to Start-Up and Success*, San Francisco: Jossey-Bass.

Markus, M. L., and Robey, D. 1988. "Information Technology and Organizational Change: Causal Structure in Theory and Research," *Management Science* (34:5), pp. 583-598.

Mbarika, V. W. A. 2004. "Is Telemedicine the Panacea for Sub-Saharan Africa's Medical Nightmare?," *Communications of the ACM* (47:7), pp 21-24.

Miles, M. B., and Huberman, A. M. 1994. *Qualitative Data Analysis* (2nd ed.), Newbury Park, CA: Sage Publications.

Mohr, L. 1982. "Approaches to Explanation: Variance Theory and Process Theory," Chapter 2 in *Explaining Organizational Behavior*, San Francisco, Jossey-Bass, pp. 35-70.

Moore, G. A. 1999. *Crossing the Chasm: Marketing and Selling High-Tech Products to Mainstream Customers*, New York: HarperBusiness.

Moore, G. A. 2004. "Darwin and the Demon: Innovating within Established Enterprises," *Harvard Business Review* (82:7/8), pp. 86-92.

Newman, M., and Robey, D. 1992. "A Social Process Model of User-Analyst Relationships," *MIS Quarterly* (16:2), pp. 249-266.

Office of Technology Assessment. 1995. *Bringing Health Care Online: The Role of Information Technologies*, Washington, DC: U.S. Government Printing Office (http://govinfo.library.unt.edu/ota/Ota_1/DATA/1995/9507.PDF).

Paul, D. L. 2006. "Collaborative Activities in Virtual Settings: A Knowledge Management Perspective of Telemedicine," *Journal of Management Information Systems* (22:4), pp. 143-176.

Paul, D. L., and McDaniel Jr., R. R. 2004. "A Field Study of the Effect of Interpersonal Trust on Virtual Collaborative Relationship Performance," *MIS Quarterly* (26:2), pp. 183-227.

Rogers, E. M. 2003. *Diffusion of Innovations* (5th ed.), New York: Free Press.

Walsham, G. 1995. "Interpretive Case Study in IS Research: Nature and Method," *European Journal of Information Systems* (4:2), pp. 74-81.

Yin, R. K. 2003. *Case Study Research Design and Methods* (3rd ed.), Thousand Oaks, CA: Sage Publications.

Zundel, K. 1996. "Telemedicine: History, Applications, and Impact on Librarianship," *Bulletin of the Medical Library Association* (84:1), pp. 71-79.

About the Authors

Sunyoung Cho received her Master's degree in computer information systems from Georgia State University in 2002 and her Ph.D. from Georgia State University under the supervision of Dr. Lars Mathiassen. She is currently an assistant professor in the Department of Computer Information Systems at Virginia State University. Her main research area is information systems in the medical domain, especially telehealth systems. Research interests cover adoption and diffusion of IT-based innovations in the healthcare domain as well as in other domains (e.g., education and the advertising industry). Her current research is oriented toward a process perspective with views from not only technological and organizational levels but also network and social levels. Her work has been published in journals including *European Journal of Information Systems, Journal of Information Technology*, and *Journal of Telemedicine and Telecare*. Sunyoung can be contacted at scho@vsu.edu.

Lars Mathiassen received his Master's degree in computer science from Aarhus University, Denmark, in 1975, his Ph.D. in informatics from Oslo University, Norway, in 1981, and his Dr. Techn. degree in software engineering from Aalborg University, 1998. He is currently a professor in the Department of Computer Information Systems and co-founder of the Center for Process Innovation at Georgia State University. His research interests are in the area of information systems and software engineering with a particular emphasis on process innovation. He is a member of IEEE, ACM, and AIS and coauthor of *Computers in Context* (Blackwell 1993), *Object Oriented Analysis & Design* (Marko Publishing, 2000), and *Improving Software Organizations* (Addison-Wesley, 2002). He currently serves as senior editor for *MIS Quarterly* and his research is published in journals such as *Information Systems Research, MIS Quarterly, IEEE Transactions on Engineering Management, Communications of the ACM, Information, Technology & People, Journal of Strategic Information Systems, Information Systems Journal, Scandinavian Journal of Information Systems, Journal of Information Technology*, and *IEEE Software*. Lars can be contacted at lmathiassen@gsu.edu.

Mike Gallivan is an associate professor in Georgia State University's Computer Information Systems Department. He holds a Ph.D. from MIT, an MBA and MHA from the University of California, Berkeley, and a B.A. from Harvard University. Mike studies how organizations adapt to technological innovations, how they develop competitive advantage through outsourcing IT, and how technical workers learn in their jobs. Prior to joining Georgia State University, he was a visiting professor at New York University. His work has been published in journals including the *Journal of Management Information Systems, European Journal of Information Systems, Information & Organization, Information Systems Journal, The Data Base for Advances in Information Systems, IEEE Transactions on Professional Communication*, and *Information & Management*. Mike can be contacted at mgallivan@gsu.edu.

Part 8

Case Studies in Software Businesses

22 EVOLUTION OF SECONDARY SOFTWARE BUSINESSES: Understanding Industry Dynamics

Pasi Tyrväinen
University of Jyväskylä
Jyväskyla, Finland

Juhani Warsta
University of Oulu
Oulu, Finland

Veikko Seppänen
University of Oulu
Oulu, Finland

Abstract   *Primary software industry originates from IBM's decision to unbundle software-related computer system development activities to external partners. This kind of outsourcing from an enterprise internal software development activity is a common means to start a new software business serving a vertical software market. It combines knowledge of the vertical market process with competence in software development. In this research, we present and analyze the key figures of the Finnish secondary software industry, in order to quantify its interaction with the primary software industry during the period of 2000–2003. On the basis of the empirical data, we present a model for evolution of a secondary software business, which makes explicit the industry dynamics. It represents the shift from internal software developed for competitive advantage to development of products supporting standard business processes on top of standardized technologies. We also discuss the implications for software business strategies in each phase.*

Keywords   Software business, industry development

Please use the following format when citing this chapter:

Tyrväinen, P., Warsta, J., and Seppänen, V., 2008, in IFIP International Federation for Information Processing, Volume 287, Open IT-Based Innovation: Moving Towards Cooperative IT Transfer and Knowledge Diffusion, eds. León, G., Bernardos, A., Casar, J., Kautz, K., and DeGross, J. (Boston: Springer), pp. 381-401.

1   INTRODUCTION

The origins of the software industry (SWI) can be tracked down to the decision by IBM to unbundle some secondary parts of its computer development to independent software companies (Campbell-Kelly 2004). Early on, computing software development was considered a secondary industry serving the core business, which was computer hardware manufacturing. Actually, this is still visible in the brand names of both the global information and communication technology (ICT) giants, such as IBM, and the major professional and scientific establishments of the field, such as ACM.

Gradually, however, the software industry has established a position as an independent industry and as a specialized focus of scientific research interests. Software business related research targeted first the core of the emerging industry, the companies developing and selling independent software products and software services. These companies are often referred to as the *primary software industry* (BMBF 2000). The term *secondary software industry* refers to software businesses being performed by companies focusing on some other industry, but using software as a part of their products or services. Simplifying, the automative industry in the 1970s, the electronics industry in the 1980s, and the telecommunications industry in the 1990s represent, globally, key host industries for secondary software businesses. At the moment, for example, the automotive and to some extent the aerospace industries are in the middle of booming secondary software businesses.

Contemporary research on software business models extensively targets the primary software market, while the business models and evolution of the secondary software market has gained only little attention, even though the importance and dependence on software applications in many fields has been growing. This is unfortunate thinking in that the emergence of new primary software companies is neither limited to new companies nor has the trend to move software businesses from the secondary to the primary industry stopped. Therefore, questions regarding the extent to which secondary software companies shift to primary software businesses, the industries from which they came, and why and how this happens are still valid.

Figure 1 represents the overall setting. The primary software companies (on the left) runs software business as their main activity, but may also include units with other business orientations. These companies are categorized mostly under category 72.2 in the NACE categorization used by OECD and EITO. Companies with other categorizations often have software-oriented business units or their operations include software development, sales, and consulting related to their products. These companies are represented on the right-hand side as the secondary software industry. The official statistics of software production include the total sales of the 72.2 category software companies including non-software sales, while software sales of the software business units in the secondary software industry are excluded.

For example, based on these numbers, according to the OECD, the sales of the Finnish primary software industry was 2,356 M€ out of the total 3,499 M€ of computer and related activities in 2000, the beginning of the observed period (Colecchia et al. 2002), while the consumption of IT products in Finland was 5,070 M€ in the same year (EITO 2004). Estimates of employer volumes have varied as well. Based on estimates

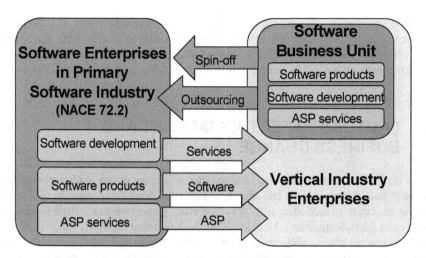

Primary Software Industry   **Secondary Software Industry**

Figure 1. Interaction between Enterprises in the Primary Software and Other Industries, Including the Secondary Software Industry

by representatives of the employees union,[1] software services companies employed about 35,000 people working in software design and implementation related activities in 2003. Of these, about 25,000 were programmers and designers, with an estimated 10,000 others working on different software-related activities. Over 80 percent of the companies employed fewer than five people, indicating that the small companies with little revenue are not visible in all estimates. According to the estimates of an annual software product business review (Kuitunen et al. 2005), the software product business portion of the primary SWI was estimated to grow from approximately 800 M€ to close to a million during the period of observation. Most of these statistics recorded sales based on the location of the headquarters and the primary industry category, regardless of the location of the software business unit and the secondary products and businesses.

According to the European Information Technology Observatory (EITO 2004), out of the 200,000 M€ worth of software products sold annually throughout the world, roughly one half are applications, one third are infrastructure software, and less than one fifth are development tools. Furthermore, out of the applications, close to one half are software meant for some vertical market and close to the second half are ERP and other horizontal software, while less than a tenth of software products were sold to private consumers (Colecchia et al. 2002).

The share of the private consumer market is also extremely small from the over 400,000 M€ software service market, while strong vertical industries drive the direction

---

[1]From interviews conducted in 2003 with J. Reinsialo, head of the association "Tietoalan toimihenkilöt," whose members are unions representing employees of professional software services in Finland.

of the development. For example, out of its over 400,000 M€ size ICT budget, the finance industry uses 160,000 M€ for software services and 20 M€ for software products, which is more than three times the volume of consumer market sales. To sum it up, the main volume of the primary software industry comes from vertical businesses.

2   FACTORS AFFECTING MARKET AND BUSINESS CHANGE

Previous research on software ventures shows that new primary software companies are born both from academic environments and technology developers, as well as from the business units of secondary software enterprises (Chesbrough and Rosenbloom 2002; Giarratana 2004; Romijn and Albaladejo 2002). Regarding the latter, which is the focus of this research, both establishment of spin-off companies and outsourcing of software development tasks move personnel and business activities to the primary software industry from vertical industries. The initial impact of vertical markets is visible in many generic and horizontal software products. For example, manufacturing resource planning systems developed initially as tailored solutions extended their scope from the first adopters to other functions of the organization and now are adopted as generic software products by other industries. In Finland, this development has been visible in extending the scope of enterprise solutions from production to other parts of the enterprise, especially in pulp and paper manufacturing industries and in the largest companies in the metal industry.

One obvious perspective of this phenomenon is diffusion and adoption of enabling technologies, with the software technology originally embedded into or at least bundled with other technologies. Previous research has approached technology diffusion and adoption from multiple viewpoints. For example, Cooper and Zmud (1990) analyze technology diffusion within an organization from the perspective of the end-user organization (i.e., the vertical industry enterprise) based on the work of Lewin (1947) and Rogers (1983). The process starts with initiation and adoption of the technology, continues with adapting it for use in the organization, and progressing to acceptance with routinization and infusion.

Moore (1995) observes the adoption of specific technologies starting from innovators and early adopters through a product creation chasm, to the early and late majority, and finally to laggards. However, in this process, vertical markets are considered from the viewpoint of the specific technology only as early markets for the technology developer. In other words, the originally generic technologies are thought to make use of vertical market segments as stepping stones toward the main horizontal market, with the role of specific vertical businesses as hosts for future generic businesses neglected. If this were the case, IBM should never have been the mother of the primary software industry, as a vertical computer hardware manufacturing company.

Along the same lines, the life-cycle and growth models proposed by Churchill and Lewis (1983), Greiner (1972), Kazanjian (1988), McHugh (1999), Nambisan (2002), and Scott and Bruce (1987), observe the life cycle of companies in general or high-technology companies in particular from the perspective of the software company, rather than

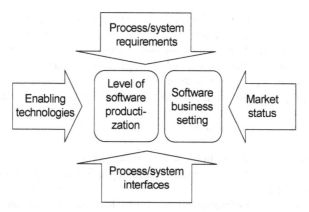

Figure 2. Factors Impacting the Success of Software Solutions in Vertical Markets

from the perspective of the status of some vertical market. However, Greiner (1972) states that the growth of a company is often related to the market environment and stage of the industry. From our perspective this is essential, since the development of software businesses servicing specific vertical markets depends both on the status of the primary software industry and the vertical market.

The key factors impacting the success of software products aimed at a vertical market can be viewed from the perspective of Figure 2. In addition to the viewpoint of the diffusion of enabling technologies (arrow from the left) and the market status (arrow from the right), these factors involve the functional requirements set forth by the processes or systems to be automated using software (arrow from above), and the interfaces through which the software interacts with these processes or systems (arrow from below). Referring to Figure 1, the level of productization and the business setting characterize the total software offering.

Considering the functional requirements, it is clear that any piece of software should be customer-oriented (McHugh 1999) in the sense of satisfying certain information processing needs. This requires expertise from the target processes or systems. Bell (1995), for example, emphasizes the importance of targeting niche markets, industry-specific conditions, and relationships with important customers in creating this expertise. In practice, the expertise may initially be realized in the form of the functionality of a unique piece of software. The level of automation of the target process or the degree of productization of the target system are often used to characterize the maturity of the solution in terms of functionality, and depend on the diffusion of the enabling technologies for which the solution has been developed.

Leaving the technology perspective aside, when an individual customer adopts a new or a modified process or system solution, a requirement to implement a new functionality emerges. When the processes or systems of a number of customers in the market settle down, it is able to productize the required solution instead of tailoring it for each individual customer. This means, however, that the software starts to depend more on the hardware and software interfaces common across the market or at least its segment. In other words, not only the required information processing functionalities and the technologies, but also system interfaces, should become standardized (Northrop 2002).

Rather than observing a vertical market from the viewpoint of particular enabling technologies or specific functional process or system requirements, we will focus on the right-hand part of Figure 2. We will, therefore, address the evolution of vertical markets as the source of software businesses, making explicit the resulting changes in business settings. In particular, our aim is to gain a better understanding of vertical market development as a basis for interaction between the secondary and primary software industries.

We need, therefore, to consider

- What is the overall change in the software markets?
- To what extent, in terms of revenues, are primary and secondary software businesses involved in the change?
- How does the change of personnel in software businesses correspond to the market change?

In this research the questions are analyzed by grounding source data to the primary and secondary software industry in Finland. The research was funded by Tekes (The National Technology Development Agency of Finland), with the aim of investigating the size and status of the national software cluster, and the potential of this cluster to expand to new markets.

3   EMPIRICAL DATA COLLECTION

Because very little empirical data has been gathered and analyzed on the secondary software industry, we will discuss in detail how the data was acquired and organized for analysis. First of all, the data collection has to take place in a relatively small country with a reasonably well-developed software industry. With this approach, data collection is feasible and the results can be generalized to some extent to represent the software industry evolution globally due to the use of global industry standards and platforms for products and services (Gawer and Cusumano 2002; Hoch et al. 2000). Previous research results related to software firms originating from Canada, Finland, Ireland, New Zealand, Norway, Malaysia, and the United States imply that software businesses are using similar strategies in their internationalization and business processes (Bell 1995; Coviello and Munro 1997). We chose Finland with its 5.2 million inhabitants as the target of our study based on relatively good access to empirical data compared to the other alternatives.

The first goal of the empirical data collection was to estimate the number of software business in Finland in terms of the annual sales volume and the number of software development professionals. For the purpose of this study, *software business* was defined as business operations based on software being developed by the organization. This includes business operations within enterprises classified as software enterprises under category 72.2, as well as similar business operations in software-oriented business units in the secondary software industry and in public administration.

Furthermore, professionals with software development competence were included also from the public sector as well, although they do not work for business organizations, while the personnel supporting the operational use of ICT systems was mostly excluded.

The rationale was that their actual software development competence could not be evaluated, thus causing problems in data collection. This definition also excluded non-software activities performed in category 72.2 companies, such as language translation and logistics consulting.

The focus was on the largest companies in Finland and on enterprises classified as software companies. The 250 largest companies measured by revenue were chosen as the target group. In addition, 71 companies ranked to positions from 251 to 500 by revenue were included in the target group, considering their potential for software business that was evaluated based on public information about their activities.

The number of employees in these 321 enterprises was about 910,000 in 2002 and the total revenue was 246,000 M€. The smallest revenue made by a company included in the data was 56 M€, and the smallest companies in terms of the personnel volume had fewer than 300 employees. Assuming these companies operate on verticals, which spend typically less than 2 percent on ICT, this would imply about 1 M€ ICT annual spending and much below 10 professionals in a single vertical enterprise. As a comparison, the employee union of software professionals has a registry of about 6,000 software service companies (with over 5,000 having some revenue), out of which 425 registered software companies had annual revenue above 1 M€ (i.e., the annual ICT budget mentioned above).

The list of 321 large companies with potential internal software business units included 16 software companies. This list was merged with a list of 348 smaller software companies, adding up to a target list of about 670 companies. Some small software companies whose basic data was not available were dropped from the target list and some individual companies with a software business were added during the data collection process.

The data was produced through two methods. We used *company-specific data* to analyze the companies, this information being available through a questionnaire, annual reports, web, or other sources. The companies were clustered according to a classification of 24 vertical markets. For each market we produced *vertical market estimates* based on the company-specific data available from the companies in that vertical market, the vertical market interviews, and other public data. These vertical market estimates include average spending on internal software development, average proportion of software professionals from the total number employees, among others. In a later phase, these vertical market estimates and the overall volume data of specific companies were used to produce estimates for companies whose data was not available. Totals were calculated by adding up the company-specific data or estimate for each of the 675 companies. Final figures include these totals, the estimated activity of companies excluded from the data collection process, as well as the software production data from the public administration.

Company-specific data was collected first by questionnaires delivered on paper and as web questionnaires. Each target company received a form for the enterprise and a form to be delivered to each business unit that produces software within the enterprise. Responses were received from 75 companies, out of which 42 were software companies. Out of the 33 responses from the vertical market enterprises, 31 were within the 250 largest companies. The percentage of the responses was considered insufficient for producing accurate estimates, and further company-specific data collection was included in the vertical market interviews. Therefore, in the second phase, the 24 vertical markets were analyzed using structured interviews.

A total of 52 interviews were conducted using phone conversations lasting from 10 minutes to an hour. The respondents were typically CIOs, CTOs, or ICT managers of the largest companies or managing directors of software companies. Typically one to two top companies from each vertical market were interviewed, with the aim of finding the person most knowledgeable about software development and utilization status at the specific vertical industry. The interviewed companies included the 10 top companies when measured with research and development spending, the largest software houses, the software trade unions, and the key public software organizations.

The interview themes included the typical spending on software development and ICT on enterprises in that vertical industry and company-specific figures for the largest players, characteristic features of software development in the verticals, size of software development organizations, existing and estimated appearance of spin-off companies, use of software services and products, outsourcing, potential for international software business based on vertical market software, and free comments. The interviews produced company-specific data for 60 software-intensive enterprises. When added to other data from 38 companies and the 75 interview results, 173 company-specific estimates were made. These results were combined with the vertical market estimates from the interviews in order to produce the final vertical market estimates. In addition, the interviews provided qualitative data.

4   CHANGES IN MARKETS AND PERSONNEL IN THE PERIOD 2000–2003

4.1   Software Competence in Finland

Based on the data gathered, an overview of the software industry in Finland is presented in Figure 3 from the viewpoint of the primary and secondary software industries (SWI) and the contemporary locations of software development professionals. The primary software industry employed about 30,000 software professionals in 2003 and somewhat less in the secondary software industry, adding up to about 60,000 employees in total. Out of these, between 11,000 and 14,000 employees worked on software products, which is defined as sales of copies of software with a license to use it. About 5,000 of the people involved in the software product business were employed in the secondary software industry, such as software business units of telecommunication and automation companies.

4.2   The Software Market

The primary software industry generated over 3,000 M€ annual revenue related to software, while the secondary software industry was estimated to produce only about

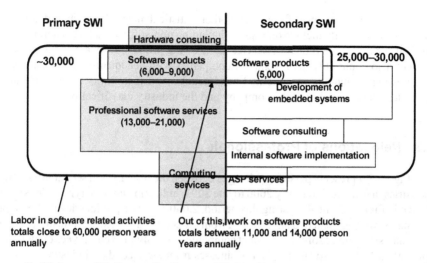

Figure 3. Volume of Software Businesses Within Units Located in Finland in 2003 (boxes with rounded corners; shadowed boxes with squared corners represent the sub-categories of enterprises, corresponding to NICE 72.2)

1,000 M€ revenue with almost the same number of employees (Figure 4). Out of the total over 4,000 M€ software revenue, roughly 1,100 M€ to 1,400 M€ was generated from software products. From this, less than one half (500+ M€) was estimated to be generated from the products of the secondary software industry. The interviews implied that this was due to the habit of vertical market enterprises to sell solutions that include software so that they are adding the software development cost to the product price, when selling embedded systems, or to the customer service price, when offering ASP services.

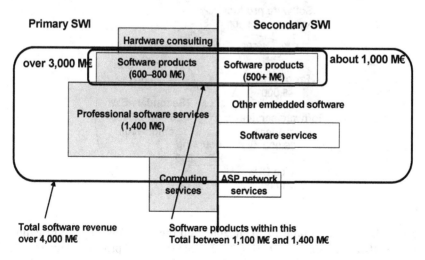

Figure 4. Total Volume of Software Business in Finland in 2003

When comparing these figures with other statistical material, one should notice that the statistics typically include only sales (including non-software sales) generated by the verticals or only the product or service sales of the primary software industry. Other sources also count only the revenue of companies with headquarters in Finland, while these estimates include revenue and head-count of business units located in Finland regardless the ownership of the company and the industry classification.

4.3 Relocations of Professionals

Figure 5 represents personnel changes between the primary and secondary software industries in Finland from early 2000 to late 2003, indicating also the types of businesses shown in Figures 3 and 4. During this period, 2,000 software product development professionals were estimated to have moved from the secondary software industry to the primary industry's small software product companies, as individual employees or along with spin-offs of entire software product businesses from the secondary industry's verticals.

Moreover, existing large software service enterprises of the primary industry acquired smaller software product companies, adding up to a total of 2,500 employees shifting from the small software ventures to the software product business units of these enterprises. Typically, this took place when the small software venture reached the size of about 20 to 30 employees, and turned profitable. In the later part of the period about 1,500 employees returned to the small software ventures from the big enterprises, for various reasons including management buy-outs. As these figures indicate, the turn-over of personnel has been rather hectic in small product ventures during the period of observation, in addition to the growing trend of personnel.

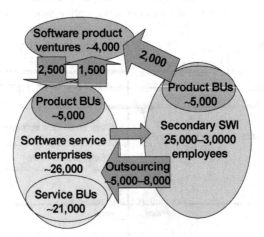

Figure 5. Employee Volumes During 2003 and the Main Employee Transitions in Finnish Software Businesses During 2003–2003 (Software product ventures refers to independent, typically small, product companies; product BUs refer to product business units within the primary [on the left] or the secondary [on the right] industry)

The number of software professionals outsourced from vertical industries to the primary software industry during this period includes between 5,000 and 8,000 employees, while little insourcing took place during the period. When the statistics of the primary software industry are checked against this data, we can see that the software service business matches well with the figures of outsourcing with little organic growth in the services business, while the software product business grew faster during the period of observation. Moreover, we also notice that, early in 2000, the secondary software business actually employed more software development professionals than the primary software business.

5   ANALYSIS OF THE INTERACTION OF SECONDARY AND PRIMARY SOFTWARE INDUSTRIES

Based on the empirical data, the interaction of the primary software and secondary software industries seems to follow a common pattern, where software development initiated within a vertical enterprise follows the life-cycle presented in Figure 6. In the first phase (the *innovation phase*), the enterprise invests increasingly in ICT, including internal software development, but cuts back the software workforce during economic downturns by relocating them to other duties. In this phase, some of the software development professionals become self-employed by establishing micro ventures to capitalize their expertise across vertical industries.

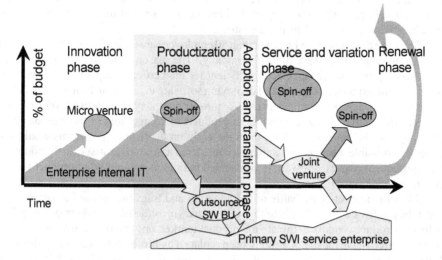

Figure 6. Life-Cycle of Software Development in a Vertical Industry Enterprise (the horizontal axis represents time and the vertical axis spending on ICT and software, which represents approximately the percentage of internal software professionals in the enterprise)

In the second phase (the *productization phase*) the percentage and volume of internal software development has risen, often as a consequence of the implementation of enterprise-specific information systems. After accomplishing such assignment, however, the whole ICT department may be outsourced during a recession, to form a separate software service business unit. Sometimes the ICT department may also spin off as a distinct software venture. During this phase, the ICT supported core processes of enterprises within the vertical market are typically being harmonized, and the operational environments and the required hardware and software interfaces are becoming standardized. The effort needed to implement a software product that stems from the evolution of a vertical market, or secondary software business, depends heavily on degree of standardization of hardware and software interfaces (Garud and Kumaraswamy 1993) as well as on the standardization of the processes. This sets the minimum for organization size sufficient for productizing the offering, leaving the majority of the small software houses out of the new market niche due to major shortcomings in their competence portfolio.

In this phase, one or some of the spin-off ventures or occasionally an existing primary software venture focusing on the emerging market has been able to create the first software products matching with the unifying functional requirements of the core processes and standardizing interfaces. In the next phase (the *adoption and transition phase*, vertical bar in Figure 6), at least some of the leading companies, if not most companies, adopt this solution. As one of the consequences, they may outsource a majority of their internal software personnel. If the number of the outsourced employees is in the range of 50 or more professionals, the enterprise can form a joint venture with a primary industry's software service house. Typically this involves a few years' agreement on maintaining the existing core operational systems of the enterprise, or an assignment to help with emerging common software solutions. During the period of observation, this was the usual approach, especially in the banking industry and in specific segments of the electronics and manufacturing industries.

Software departments with fewer than 50 employees are typically simply outsourced or asked to create a software spin-off company. The reason is that if a smaller number of software professionals have been sufficient for the vertical company to automate its main operational processes or to start deploying software in its products, it wants to focus on its core business and competences. A spin-off company or a software outsourcing partner often starts selling its services or products to competitors of the previous host company. In the innovation phase or in the early productization phase this would not have been possible, because software was considered as a strategic asset. In the adoption and subsequent phases, software is considered mainly as a commodity product (i.e., a cost to be minimized).

After the market-share battle of the adoption and transition phase has ceased, the secondary software market falls to the *service and variation phase*, where one or a few software product vendors dominate the product market, and internal software development resources have mostly or entirely been replaced by professional services purchased from the primary industry's companies. The ICT spending, which in the standardization phase was commonly over 5 percent and as much as 10 percent or more in some vertical markets (for example, retail banking and telecommunication services in our source data), falls in the service and variation phase verticals to a level of 1.5 to 2 percent (for example, in the transportation, furniture, basic metal, textile, and retail industries), relying mainly on external software and services.

The vertical markets in which companies follow this pattern of developments are defined by their major information processing needs. Automating the major process with software can be essential for reducing cost as it may account for 50 to 85 percent of all communications in an organization (Tyrväinen et al. 2005). But if the in-house software competence is outsourced when adopting an external product for the main process in the adoption phase, there is little capability to innovate new software supported business models for the enterprise. If a company that is in the middle of the service and variation phase changes its business model in such a way that it requires a new major information processing system or an innovative software solution for its product, not available in the market place, it enters a *renewal phase*. In this phase, the company has two options: either to use external partners to implement the solution or to create and keep the required knowledge in-house by developing the solution with its own personnel. In the latter case, the company creates a new vertical (sub)market and shifts back to the innovation phase, such as Merita bank establishing an Internet banking vertical in Finland in the 1990s or Wall-Mart stores in the retail industry in the United States.

6 IMPLICATIONS FOR SOFTWARE BUSINESS STRATEGIES

6.1 Drivers for Change

The drivers for change in a vertical software industry are presented in Table 1 together with the characteristic features related to the business strategies applicable in each phase. In the data we collected, the vertical industry enterprises driving the adoption of a new technology to the industry prefer using their internal processes in order to maintain their competitive advantage based on process differentiation or improved cost performance in the innovation phase. After a while, competitors are able to copy the best practices adopted in the industry and start asking for software products from the primary software industry ventures in the productization phase.

From the technology viewpoint, the innovators developing new technology try to secure it with patents and use proprietary closed interfaces for software development. The leading hardware vendors are typically reluctant to share their knowledge with software companies, creating entry barriers for competitors. They implement the software needed for operating their systems internally, creating unified hardware/software systems. In this phase, the software business is limited to company internal or external software services. Independent software houses cannot compete with a single vendor who owns the technology platform needed for operating the software. In case such software appears, the proprietary interface can be changed or the platform vendor can bundle free software with the hardware. In case the market is not large and attractive enough, the software market evolution may stop with the innovation phase. Typical examples from the Finnish software market stuck at the innovation phase include markets with globally operating strong companies, such as the elevator software market dominated by Kone Corp. and weather measurement sensor software dominated by Vaisala Group.

Table 1. Changes in Vertical Industry Processes and Available Technology Set the Pace for Vertical Software Industry Evolution

Drivers and Features	Innovation Phase	Productization Phase	Transition Phase	Service and Variation Phase
Process Drivers (Vertical Industry)	Process innovation, competitive advantage (differentiation/costs), enterprise-specific processes	SW supported processes, process harmonization, repeatability between enterprises	Process standards adopted	Process optimization, IT process cost optimization
Software Business	Customer-specific services, integrated HW/SW products, an application per enterprise	Productization, competing standards, micro ecologies, network development	Market share race, competing ecologies	New development on the dominant SW platform, open source
Technology Drivers	Technology innovation, competing with IPRs and closed interfaces, equipment vendors dominating SW market	Technology standardization within vertical market segment, multiple strong vendors	Fast technology adoption, market expansion	Technology dominance, bulk hardware with standard interface and large user base

The early console game vendors operated in the innovation phase markets with a similar strategy, competing primarily with new technology and platforms while maintaining the process of playing and game software application development in-house. However, after some years the platform was no longer the only criteria for choosing between competing game offerings, the game markets required more effort to develop software applications and forced this vertical industry to shift to the productization phase. This has enabled an increase of game software developers in independent game companies, improved offerings to customers, and the increased industry market volume. Increasing market volume also attracts more vendors, creating more competition and enabling specialization. These further lower the prices, attracting more customers.

When the productized offerings satisfy the requirements of the processes of the vertical industry companies, the market enters the transition phase. Typically, one of the competing ecologies or standards reaches a dominating position with a better offering creating a dominant design (see Murmann and Frenken 2006) in the service and variation phase while some alternative designs may be better applicable for specialized purposes, such as the Macintosh computer platform, long preferred by media processing industries. Although open source software development appears in the productization phase, it is mostly visible in the service and variation phase.

The industry evolution may also stop at the productization phase, if none of the competing technologies and interfaces gains sufficient critical mass to drive the positive cycle. For example, there has been a wide variety of field busses used by various industries, none of which has been accepted widely. Some of them have better cost structure for industries with easier requirements, while the redundant fast field busses are too expensive or less applicable for others.

6.2 Importance of Interfaces

Interfaces are commonly used as a means to modularize systems. The effort needed to implement a software system can be minimized by using existing software implemented by others through the interfaces. The existing systems act as the vessels for transferring knowledge from other organizations to the software systems developer. Thus availability of system components with easy to use interfaces greatly reduces the knowledge required from the software developers. If the interface is standardized, the software developer does not have to understand the details of the system used, while nonstandard interfaces with variations require developers to have more knowledge of the system used. The requirement to master a wide number of proprietary technologies as well as the requirements of the industry process knowledge can be too much for most software development organizations. This can limit the critical mass of organization needed for reaching the next phase in the vertical industry evolution.

Consider, for example, the software organization needed for implementing a basic retail banking system (Table 2). The system needs to interface with the customers, needs to deliver notes, needs to communicate with a teller, needs a mainframe computer, and a database management system to the server. The interfaces available for these technologies were long proprietary, as listed by configuration A in Table 2, limiting the number of vendors to a few. Instead, after evolution of the technologies, the interfaces needed were standardized, making it easy for a larger number of companies to implement the system.

From the viewpoint of the interfaces, the large IT service companies with access to a broad competence pool tend to dominate the innovation phase markets. Smaller product companies appear more often in the productization phase where emerging standards can be utilized. In the last phase, the dominating design again favors large companies. Note also that a small company adopting configuration B in the example has dropped the "note delivery" interface from the system offering, which is based on use of common Internet technologies. This means that this inexpensive offering can be used by retail banks willing to drop this functionality from their offering or able to outsource it. In other words, the development of the set of technologies needed by a vertical industry (retail banking) impacts the cost/functionality of the software offering available to the vertical industry companies, but the software offering can also impact the business model of the industry by creating a market for ATM outsourcing.

Table 2. Alternative Interfaces Used by a Retail Banking Application (The interfaces on the left are mainly from the innovation phase and require high level of competence available only in a few software enterprises or in-house; the interfaces on the right are from later date and require only knowledge available for millions of software developers)

Hardware interface	A – Early Configuration		B – Late Configuration	
User Interface	ATM hardware interface	Proprietary	Browser interface (SSH, HTML, TCP/IP)	Standard
Note Delivery	ATM message interface	Proprietary	–	–
Clark Interface	Windows workstation	Standard	Browser	Standard
Server Computer	IBM Mainframe	Proprietary	Linux / Windows	Standard
Database System	IBM DB2	Proprietary	MySQL	Standard

6.3 Shift of Software Development

One of the key findings of this research is that the focus of a vertical market shifts inevitably during the market evolution from the use of internal resources to extensive use of software products and professional software services provided by the primary software industry. Figure 7 represents this by dividing the IT spending on software related activities to internal software development, external software services, and software products (the trumpet model). In the innovation phase, a major part of the activity takes place within the enterprise while the share of software products and services increases along with development. Some verticals may remain in the early phases for years, such as several manufacturing segments where sufficient volume for software productization does not exist, while most of the verticals move forward. Thus this development is visible also in the total figures of software spending. According to EITO (2004), 52 to 59 percent of IT spending in Europe, Japan, and the United States was on internal software development in 1993, while purchased services and software packages were 14 to 32 percent and 10 to 29 percent, respectively. In our source data collected 10 years later, these three segments were roughly equal, indicating a major drop in internal spending on

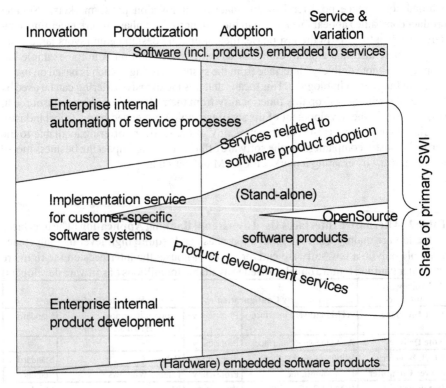

Figure 7. Share of Software Development Activity in Each Phase of the Vertical Market Change

behalf of purchased services and software products. Similar figures (33 percent, 35 percent, and 32 percent, respectively) were also produced by a commercial market study of Finnish software markets (Market-Visio 2003). There are still industries where large vertical industry enterprises want to maintain strong control over the innovative software-supported services and keep the majority of software development in-house, such as the telecom operators (see Dittberner Associates 2004).

The Finnish data indicates, in terms of the volume of software professionals, including software product developers, that the primary and secondary industries are much alike. In terms of visible revenues, the secondary software industry is considerably worse, as the added value of the software is sold along with a hardware product (e.g., a mobile phone) or in the price of a service (e.g., banking service fees). The evolution may also stop in the early phases if the market size is insufficient to attract enough competition to the segment or the dominating companies are unwilling to proceed. Some dominating players in specific market niches in the manufacturing industries are especially unwilling to open their software interfaces to open competition. Therefore, the main implication from a strategic perspective is when to initiate and how to implement responses to the market change in order to create profitable software businesses.

6.4 Software Business Opportunities in Each Phase

Because the vertical market evolution affects software business opportunities, it is useful to make an overview of the means to cope with the change during the main phases of the evolution. In the innovation phase, the software developed is customer-specific and no place exists for a profitable product business. However, software service companies can evaluate and learn new technologies and customer processes from the leading vertical market companies.

In the productization phase, the implementations made in the leading companies are used as templates or specifications for implementations in other companies. In this phase, software companies can make use of product platform strategies while standardizing their offerings to the vertical. Standardization of functionality and equipment enables division of work by hiding functionality behind proprietary or standard interfaces. As soon as all the interfaces and the application processes are standardized, the vertical market is willing to adopt a total solution serving the core business processes of the vertical. The companies involved in standardizing the key interfaces and customer processes gain the main advantage in this competition. Companies involved in standardizing a new core interface form a micro ecology, providing a strong total offering for the vertical market. This attracts new technology and software providers as well as customers willing to adopt a productized package. To get positioned well in the networks developed in the productization phase, it is important for the software houses to serve at least one of the leading customers of the vertical market and to adopt the standard interfaces or participate in their development.

For example, Digia was a small local software company until it joined the Symbian consortia, which was developing an operating system platform for intelligent mobile phones. With the aid of the micro ecology around the Symbian development, Digia was able to harness the growing use of Symbian products and grow rapidly to one of the large national software houses with a strong international customer base in the telecommunications industry. Altogether, integrating into emerging micro ecologies in the productiza-tion phase seems to be the most effective means to grow in the vertical industry software business.

In the adoption phase, the networks providing offerings for the vertical market compete with each other. A majority of the companies adopt a software package, out-source the majority of their in-house software development, and lower their IT spending. This provides an opportunity for the software service providers to extend their business. For the software product houses, this phase means competition for the critical market share. In some cases there is only a single offering, which easily dominates the market, causing a fast move to the next phase. In any case the market share battles of multiple networks or companies do not last long compared to the lengthy development in the previous phases.

In the service and variation phase, the vertical market has adopted a dominant solution. A major part of IT spending goes to software products and external services. The dominant product vendor provides little market opportunity for other software products while the service companies may deploy a customer intimacy strategy. Other software product companies may try to use disruptive innovation to evolve the vertical into a renewal phase, where the vertical market companies need to reposition themselves into a new market setting, insourcing software development or making use of external services and products to do so.

7   SUMMARY AND FURTHER WORK

This paper presented a model for evolution of the vertical software industry based on data collected from Finnish secondary and primary software industries. The model describes how industry-specific process knowledge and technology are combined with tailored software to create competitive advantage to the industry enterprise. Due to competition, the business processes tend to harmonize and technologies tend to standardize, enabling productization of the software by micro ecologies of companies. Later on, some of the solutions may become the dominant design, serving as a platform for new innovations.

The model presented here adds to the literature by taking the viewpoint of an industry with enterprises having similar dominant processes and internal software development organizations. Innovation diffusion models (e.g., Rogers 1983) tend to address the impact of single technologies on multiple industries and do not address the shift of knowledgeable software personnel from vertical industries to the primary software industry nor the changes in investments on technology development within the vertical industry. The model presented here carries some similarities with the industry life cycle theory (Gort and Klepper 1982), which predicts that the number of companies in a new product industry will grow until a shake down reduces it to a lower, stable level. Based on the data we have collected, the evolution of a secondary software industry may proceed through all of the phases presented here, producing results similar to the ones in the industry life cycle theory. However, the development may stop for a while at a phase, causing a shakeout to take place and a new take-off to appear after it. Also, neither the technology adoption model nor the industry life cycle theory addresses the shift of personnel between the secondary and the primary software industries, the inter-relationship of standardizing technology with the process of harmonization, and software market evolution as presented here.

Although the analysis presented in this paper is based on a single geographical market that represents only a small fraction on the global market, the results can be generalized with some caution to represent software industry evolution globally due to the use of global industry standards and platforms for products and services. Market statistics indicate that the vertical markets in different countries can be in different phases of development prior to reaching the final phase, usually following the development of the leading customer companies of the vertical market in the geographical area, or due to the specific technical innovations being developed.

Clearly, the software companies basing their operations in markets progressing ahead of the same vertical markets have a competitive advantage while internationalizing their business. Especially companies that establish or join new micro ecologies around new standards in the productization phase will have a clear advantage when the markets grow and they can later capitalize on their dominant design position in the mainstream market. On this basis, the Technology Agency of Finland (Tekes) initiated a further research action to analyze six chosen vertical software markets, where the potential of Finnish software companies was considered high based on their life-cycle phase. These industries were the finance, construction and real estate, forest, energy, machine manufacturing, and retail/wholesales industries. In addition, a separate project, SmarTop, was started to analyze the software market of telecom operator products (see Mazhelis et al. 2007). The results of these later studies elaborate further the phenomena, especially the role of alternative actors in the evolution as well as the impact of multiple core processes on the vertical industry company, but are beyond the scope of this paper.

Acknowledgments

The authors acknowledge gratefully the financial and other support given for the study by Tekes, especially Mr. Matti Sihto, and the other members of the steering group of the research project.

References

Bell, J. 1995. "The Internationalization of Small Computer Software Firms. A Further Challenge to 'Stage' Theories," *European Journal of Marketing* (29:8), pp. 60-75.

BMBF. 2000. *Analyze und Evaluation der Softwareentwicklung in Deutschland*, Bundesministerium für Bildung und Forschung (Federal Ministry of Education and Research), Germany.

Campbell-Kelly, M. 2004. *From Airline Reservations to Sonic the Hedgehog*, Cambridge, MA: MIT Press.

Chesbrough, H., and Rosenbloom, R. 2002. "The Role of the Business Model in Capturing Value from Innovation: Evidence from Xerox Corporation's Technology Spin-Off Companies," *Industrial and Corporate Change* (11:3), pp. 529-555.

Churchill, N. C., and Lewis, V. L. 1986. "The Five Stages of Small Business Growth," *Harvard Business Review* (61:3), pp. 30-49.

Colecchia, A., Anton-Zabalza, E., Devlin, A., and Montagnier, P. 2002. *Measuring the Information Economy*, Paris: Organisation for Economic Co-operation and Development, Directorate for Science, Technology and Industry.

Cooper, R., and Zmud, R. 1990. "Information Technology Implementation Research: A Technological Diffusion Approach," *Management Science* (36:2), pp. 123-139.

Coviello, N., and Munro, H. 1997. "Network Relationships and the Internationalization Process of Small Software Firms," *International Business Review* (6:4), pp. 361-386.

Dittberner Associates. 2004. "Dittberner's OSS/BSS KnowledgeBase™," December (http://www.dittberner.com/reports/about53.php).

EITO. 2004. *European Information Technology Observatory*, European Information Technology Observatory Portal.

Gawer, A., and Cusumano, M. A. 2002. *Platform Leadership: How Intel, Microsoft, and Cisco Drive Industry Innovation*, Boston: Harvard Business School Press.

Garud, R., and Kumaraswamy, A. 1993. "Changing Competitive Dynamics in Network Industries: an Exploration of Sun Microsystems' Open Systems Strategy," *Strategic Management Journal* (13:5), pp. 351-369.

Giarratana, M. 2004. "The Birth of a New Industry: Entry by Start-Ups and the Drivers of Firm Growth the Case of Encryption Software," *Research Policy* (33), pp. 33, 787-806.

Gort, M., and Klepper, S. 1982. "Time Paths in the Diffusion of Product Innovations," *Economic Journal* (92), pp. 630-653.

Greiner, L. E. 1972. "Evolution and Revolution as Organizations Grow," *Harvard Business Review* (50:4), pp. 37-46.

Hoch, D. J., Roeding, C. R., Purkert, G., Lindner, S. K., and Müller, R. 2000. *Secrets of Software Success*, Boston: Harvard Business School Press.

Kazanjian, R. K. 1988. "Relation of Dominant Problems to Stages of Growth in Technology-Based New Ventures," *Academy of Management Journal* (31:2), pp. 257-279.

Kuitunen, H., Maula, M., and Kontio, J. 2005. *Software Product Industry Survey 2005, Finnish Software Product Business in 2004*, Espoo, Finland: Helsinki University of Technology.

Lewin, K. 1947. "Group Decision and Social Change" in *Readings in Social Psychology*, T. M. Newcomb and E. L. Hartley (eds.), New York: Henry Holt.

Mazhelis, O., Tyrväinen, P., and Viitala, E. 2007. "Modeling Software Integration Scenarios for Telecommunications Operations Software Vendors," in *Proceedings of the IEEE International Conference on Industrial Engineering and Engineering Management*, M. Helander, M. Xie, R. Jiao, and K. C. Tan (eds.), Los Alamitos, CA: IEEE Computer Society Press, pp. 49-54.

Market-Visio. 2003. *IT-investoinnit, -kustannukset ja –hankkeet Suomessa 2003-2005*, Helsinki, Finland: Market-Visio ICT Research and Advisory Services.

McHugh, P. 1999. *Making it Big in Software*, Triverton, UK: Rubiv Publishing.

Moore, G. A. 1995. *Inside the Tornado: Marketing Strategies from Silicon Valley's Cutting Edge*, New York: HarperCollins Publishers.

Murmann, J. P., and Frenken, K. 2006. "Toward a Systematic Framework for Research on Dominant Designs, Technological Innovations, and Industrial Change," *Research Policy* (35:7), pp. 925-952.

Nambisan, S. 2002. "Software Firm Evolution and Innovation-Orientation," *Journal of Engineering and Technology Management* (19), pp. 141-165.

Northrop, L. 2002. "SEI's Software Product Line Tenets," *IEEE Software* (19:4), pp. 32-40.

Rogers, E. M. 1983. *Diffusion of Innovations* (3rd ed.), New York: The Free Press.

Romijn, H., and Albaladejo, M. 2002. "Determinants of Innovation Capability in Small Electronics and Software Firms in Southeast England," *Research Policy* (31), pp. 1053-1067.

Scott, M., and Bruce, R. 1987. "Five Stages of Growth in Small Businesses," *Long RTange Planning* (20:2), pp. 45-52.

Tyrväinen, P., Kilpeläinen, T., and Järvenpää, M. 2005. "Patterns and Measures of Digitalization in Business Unit Communication," *International Journal of Business Information Systems* (1:1/2), pp. 199-219.

About the Authors

Dr. **Pasi Tyrväinen** is Professor of Computer Science and Information Systems (Digital Media) at the University of Jyväskylä. He received his doctorate from Helsinki University of Technology in 1994. Professor Tyrväinen's research focuses on software business, digital rights management, and enterprise content management. In addition to his nine years at the University of Jyväskylä, he has twelve years of prior experience in industry as an R&D director at Honeywell Industrial Control and in the software laboratory of Nokia Research Center. He also supports the National Technology Foundation (Tekes) in directing government R&D activities related to the software industry. He has over 100 scientific and professional publications, of which about 60 appear in scientific forums. He can be reached at pasi.tyrvainen@jyu.fi.

Professor **Juhani Warsta**, Ph.D., currently works as an acting professor of software business at the Department of Information Processing Science, University of Oulu, Finland. He has several years work experience in different sectors of the software business, both from the production perspective as well as the customer perspective. He is actively involved in software business research as well as e- commerce aspects of business. He can be reached at juhani.warsta@oulu.fi.

Dr. Econ, Dr. Tech **Veikko Seppänen** is the Deputy CTO of Elektrobit Corporation Plc., a global wireless systems and automotive software company. He is also a part-time professor of software business at the Department of Information Processing Science, University of Oulu, Finland. He has defended two doctoral theses, the first on software reuse in 1990 and the second on industrial marketing in 2000. Before joining Elektrobit in 2002, he held various research and management positions at the Technical Research Centre of Finland (VTT) from 1983 to 2000 and worked as a full-time software business professor at the University of Oulu from 2000 to 2002. In 1986-1987, he was a non-degree graduate student and Asla Fulbright Scholar at the University of California at Irvine, and in 1991-1993, was a JSPS Postdoctoral Fellow at the University of Kyoto, Japan. Dr. Seppänen has authored over 100 scientific and professional publications. He can be reached atveikko.seppanen@oulu.fi.

23   A STUDY OF THE RISKS IN AN INFORMATION SYSTEM OUTSOURCING PARTNERSHIP

Shabareesh Ajitkumar
Deborah Bunker
Stephen Smith
Donald Winchester
University of New South Wales
Sydney, Australia

Abstract   *The objective of this paper is to report the findings of a case study into the risks involved in an information systems outsourcing partnership between a retail bank client and the vendor, an information technology service provider. By drawing on the case study, the paper proposes a theoretical development of shared benefits and shared risks in IT outsourcing partnerships. The paper argues that the longevity and success of the outsourcing partnership depends largely on managing shared risks and goals in the outsourcing partnership, which may gradually deteriorate over time without frequent, open interactions between partnership members. The outsourcing partnership contractual agreements alone may have limited scope in contributing to shared risk reduction in the IT outsourcing partnership if relationships deteriorate.*

This research is based on an investigation of two organizations that used a formal contract to bind each partner's benefits, risks, roles, and responsibilities in an IT outsourcing partnership. Future research should seek to explore shared outsourced partnership benefits and risks across organizations in other sectors. Findings indicate that shared outsourced partnership risks need to be actively managed in order to reap the benefits. This paper argues that success in an IT outsourcing partnership relies on managing shared risks in the outsourcing relationship.

Keywords   Information technology, IT outsourcing, partnerships, shared risk

Please use the following format when citing this chapter:

Ajitkumar, S., Bunker, D., Smith, S., and Winchester, D., 2008, in IFIP International Federation for Information Processing, Volume 287, Open IT-Based Innovation: Moving Towards Cooperative IT Transfer and Knowledge Diffusion, eds. León, G., Bernardos, A., Casar, J., Kautz, K., and DeGross, J. (Boston: Springer), pp. 403-422.

1   INTRODUCTION

Information system outsourcing has experienced remarkable growth in recent years. The rapid growth of IS outsourcing has received extensive, on-going, worldwide business and information technology attention (Walker 1996). Information systems outsourcing deals have grown in size (Currie 2000), complexity (Marchand and Jacobsen 2001), and significance (Loh and Venkatraman 1992). This has resulted in an increased concern with the actual management of the outsourcing venture, and in particular with the issues of risk and risk management (Willcocks et al. 1999). Recent high profile outsourcing failures (e.g., Myers 1994) are further indicative of the lack of understanding of risk and risk mitigation practices that appear to be perpetuating within industry.

The next section discusses the literature review. Section three outlines the methodology. The fourth section overviews the outsourcing partnership. Section five interprets the case study. Section six sets the propositions for a proposed theory for the risks of IS outsourcing partnerships, briefly summarizing the main three propositions. The final section concludes and provides implications.

2   LITERATURE REVIEW

Several risks of IS outsourcing have been revealed in the literature, with most centered on the opportunistic behavior of the vendor, financial loss, service debasement, dependency, and loss of core competencies and skills (Ang and Toh 1998; Willcocks and Lacity 1999). Despite such revelation, several authors have claimed that research into outsourcing risk is still in its infancy and that there are "all too few systematic academic studies of the types of outsourcing risks, their salience and their mitigation" (Willcocks et al. 1999, p. 286). Outsourcing risk has only been investigated within the context of traditional buyer–seller type outsourcing, with no research to date examining risks salient in outsourcing partnerships.

Information system outsourcing partnerships are working relationships between client and vendor stakeholders that reflect a long-term commitment, a sense of mutual cooperation, shared risks and benefits and the presence of shared goals (Currie and Willcocks 1998; Lee 1998; Saunders et al. 1997). In recent years, much of the literature on IS outsourcing has focused on the emergence of the outsourcing partnership. Furthermore, several researchers claim that the nature of outsourcing has changed from a contractual to a partnership based relationship (Kern and Willcocks 2002). Lee et al. (2003) attribute the recent growth of outsourcing partnerships witnessed in industry to the maturity of outsourcing over time. Today, IS outsourcing involves a much greater depth and range of services, with companies now transferring entire IT functions, and in some cases even IT personnel, to their respective IT service providers. The apparent reverse in flow of IT resources "indicates a much more proactive role by today's service providers, who assume more risk and investment than their counterparts in the past" (Lee et al. 2003, p. 87).

Despite the growing presence of IS outsourcing partnerships in both academic literature and in practice, no research to date has examined the risks pertinent to this form of outsourcing. Currie and Willcocks (1998) investigated the risks inherent in different types of outsourcing arrangements and empirically found that each type presented a set of distinct risks. Although outsourcing partnerships were not examined, the study does, however, indicate that outsourcing partnerships may potentially pose unique risks that have yet to be identified by researchers. Furthermore, IS outsourcing partnerships are distinct from other forms of outsourcing given the underlying assumption that certain risks and benefits are shared by client and vendor partners (Lee and Kim 2005; Saunders et al. 1997). Consequentially, the risks of outsourcing identified within the literature may not apply to an IS outsourcing partnership, given its unique nature. Thus, there is an unequivocal need for exploratory and empirical research of the types of risks unique to an IS outsourcing partnership, their salience, and their interrelatedness. By conducting research of this nature, this study not only addresses a significant gap in the literature, but also provides practitioners with much needed insight into a highly critical area (risk) of a growing outsourcing discipline (partnership based outsourcing). The research problem is, *what are the risks entailed within an IS outsourcing partnership for both the client and the vendor?*

3   METHODOLOGY

The following research questions are formulated:

- Question 1.   What risks are entailed within an IS outsourcing partnership for the client?
- Question 2.   What risks are entailed within an IS outsourcing partnership for the vendor?
- Question 3.   What risks are shared between the vendor and client in an IS outsourcing partnership?
- Question 4.   How do these risks interrelate during the course of an IS outsourcing partnership?

To achieve the research objectives, an independent study was conducted. The interpretive approach has been selected as the theoretical perspective of choice, because the aims and purpose of interpretivist research are most suited to answering the research questions and are most reflective of the ontological and epistemological assumptions. Informed by the interpretivist theoretical perspective and its underlying assumptions, grounded theory has been selected with the aim of generating a descriptive and explanatory theory of the multiple perspectives of risk and risk management in the case companies involved in an IS outsourcing partnership.

Grounded theory is defined as a "general methodology for developing theory that is grounded in data systematically gathered and analyzed. Theory evolves during actual research, and it does this through continuous interplay between analysis and data collection" (Strauss and Corbin 1994, p. 273). The purpose of grounded theory is to inductively derive a theory by actively coding empirical data in such a way that categories, concepts, properties, and their interrelationships may be discovered. Within the grounded theory methodology, generating theory and conducting social research are, conceptually, two parts of the same process (Glaser 1978). The Straussian approach has been employed in this study.

The data collection included semi-structured interviews with selected participants, organizational documents, and notes from direct observation. Fifteen semi-structured interviews were conducted, involving subjects from both the client and vendor organization. The number of interviews performed is within the suggested 15 to 20 interview range for qualitative research (Miles and Huberman 1984). Semi-structured interviews were used for a number of reasons. First, the nature of semi-structured interviews allowed answers evoked by initial questions to shape subsequent inquiries (Babbie 1992). Thus, the direction of the interview may be adapted according to issues and ideas raised by research participants. This allows researchers to uncover emergent issues and probe more deeply into issues of interest. This ability to uncover emergent issues is particularly appealing, given the earlier intentions of developing a substantive theory in the research area. Also, by only guiding conversation and not restricting participants in the type of information they could express, the semi-structured interview approach meets the demands of nondeterminism imposed by grounded theory (Charmaz 2000). Furthermore Rubin and Rubin (1995), also suggest that semi-structured interviews are advantageous in their ability to allow "questioning to be re-designed throughout the project" (p. 47). Thus, a greater understanding of the risks encountered during the partnership was developed, the semi-structured interview approach enabled refinement and redesign of the interview instrument to develop further insight into concepts or categories of interest. Participant subjects were interviewed face-to-face for the purposes of this study. The transcript of each participant was printed on a distinct color of paper so that they may be easily identified when placed on the "grounded theory wall." Analysis of the interview transcript followed the coding (and categorizing) procedures prescribed by Strauss and Corbin (1990), which is open, axial, and selective coding.

4   OUTSOURCING PARTNERSHIP

The joint management infrastructure (JMI) project is a partnership between two organizations, namely, a large retail bank (First Bank) and Service Co., a global IT service provider (see Figure 1). Although the outsourcing arrangement took the form of a partnership, both organizations fundamentally assumed the role of either the client or the vendor. *"Before JMI the two companies were involved in a buyer-seller type agreement"* (Project Manager, Service Co.).

First Bank, the client organization in the partnership, requested Service Co. to provision numerous services within the bank's infrastructure space, thereby subscribing Service Co. to the role of an outsourcing vendor or service provider.

Joint management infrastructure is an integrated solution of products (both hardware and software), architecture, and processes that offers a suite of delivery management technology enabling Service Co. to deliver its on-demand offering, which fulfils the promise of utility computing (i.e., the promise of "pay only for what is used") in a shareable standardized environment. The result is a significant reduction in infrastructure costs for the client and an increase in the quality of services provisioned. Joint management infrastructure also provides Service Co. with a cost-effective mechanism to deliver

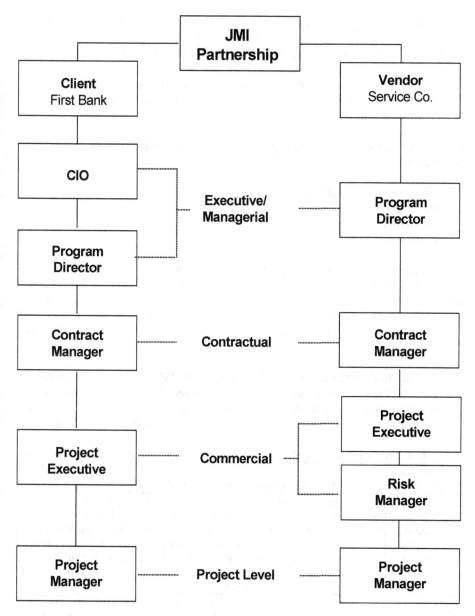

Figure 1. Overview of Interview Participants

infrastructure services for new on-demand services and new customer engagements, and to provide a platform to initiate movement of existing client accounts to an on-demand infrastructural suite. The JMI architectural model and its underlying technologies were developed by Service Co.'s technological innovation center in the United States and First Bank.

From a review of the literature (Currie and Willcocks 1998; Henderson 1990; Lee 1998; Saunders et al. 1997), a definition of the term *outsourcing partnership* was developed. A partnership, for the purpose of this study, is defined as

An interorganizational relationship involving a long-term commitment between a client and vendor where both parties collaboratively work towards shared goals, while sharing both risks and rewards.

Based on this definition, it is clear that an outsourcing partnership is characterized by the presence of

- shared benefits (rewards)
- shared risks
- long-term commitments
- shared goals

The JMI partnership embodies these defining partnership characteristics in the case study.

Table 1 shows that the JMI partnership meets the criteria outlined in the definition of an outsourcing partnership based on the literature. The JMI partnership entailed several shared benefits and risks, many of which were formally reflected in a risk and reward sharing contract. The key benefits that were shared between both organizations include:

- **Competitive advantage**. Due to the infancy of the JMI offering, the two organizations stand to gain significant competitive advantage. Joint management infrastructure offers Service Co. the opportunity to commercially test the viability of its on-demand service offering prior to its full release to the global market. The service

Table 1. Criteria for JMI to Meet the Definition of an Outsourcing Partnership

Definition Criteria	How Are These Criteria Met by the JMI Partnership?
Presence of shared risks and rewards	The JMI project entails shared risks and rewards for both First Bank (the client) and Service Co. (the vendor). Both organizations have collaborated to develop a common environment to support First Bank's financial systems. Service Co. profits from this venture by leveraging this environment into a standard platform to be sold to other banks and financial institutions. Thus, both First Bank and Service Co. have vested significant resources and capital into the venture, which consequentially will entail shared risks.
Long term commitments	The JMI venture has progressed into its fourth year (of 10). Levels of commitment from Service Co. and First Bank have been consistently high for the life of the partnership.
Shared goals	Service Co. and First Bank share a number of common goals, namely 1. To develop an on-demand Infrastructural environment, 2. To drive down long-term costs in the infrastructure space, 3. To reduce complexity within the infrastructure space by means of consolidation and standardization, and 4. To optimize efficiency in the provisioning of infrastructure services.

offering is unique and unrivaled by any competitor, thus if the implementation is a success, Service Co. gains the opportunity to exploit a niche within the infrastructure market and reap much competitive advantage. Similarly, First Bank operates in an industry where competition is heavily driven by price. Joint management infrastructure will enable the bank to significantly drive IT costs down, thus gaining a competitive advantage over competing financial institutions.

- **Financial Benefits**. Joint management infrastructure offers financial benefits for both firms. Through such measures as performance bonuses and profit sharing initiatives, both firms stand to profit equally from the venture. Furthermore, JMI enables both firms to significantly drive costs down in the infrastructure space. Prior to JMI, Service Co. was making a substantial loss on the First Bank account while the bank received poor levels of service at far too high of a cost. With the implementation of JMI, Service Co. is able to make a reasonable profit from the deal while First Bank receives significant cost reductions for provisioned infrastructure services.

- **Greater efficiency**. Joint management infrastructure promotes greater efficiency in the management and provisioning of infrastructure services. Service Co. can utilize fewer resources to build servers and board applications as the JMI architecture demands use of Service Co. specific hardware and software, all of which Service Co. technicians are experienced in using. First Bank also profits from this enhanced efficiency as the bank is able to receive a built server in only 48 hours, which is much faster than the previous provisioning process.

- **Access to and development of expertise**. By outsourcing the infrastructure function, First Bank hope to gain access to and leverage Service Co.'s global expertise. Prior to the outsourcing venture, First Bank espoused an undisciplined approach to the management of infrastructure, with servers lacking the standardization required to be effectively managed. By outsourcing the infrastructure, First Bank hoped to tap into the vendor's expertise and make its infrastructure far more manageable by means of consolidation and standardization. The partnership also presented Service Co. with the opportunity to develop expertise and experience in implementing the JMI architecture.

The partnership also required both organizations to share many risks. Contractually, a specific risk sharing model was embedded into the contract. Aside from the shared financial risks reflected in the risk sharing model, several strategic and operational risks were also shared between the two organizations.

5 CASE STUDY

This paper presents the key risks that emanated during the course of the JMI partnership. The findings revealed over 80 risk factors. Through the use of iterative coding, six substantive codes emerged:

- client strategic risks
- vendor strategic risks
- shared strategic risks
- client operational risks
- vendor operational risks
- shared operational risks

These substantive codes represent the key theoretical concepts for understanding the risks associated with IS outsourcing partnerships and address the strategic risks discussed next in this paper.

5.1 Client Strategic Risks

Client strategic risks are defined as risks whose impact pervades beyond the boundaries of the partnership, risks that have a direct, adverse impact on the client organization's long-term business strategy, competitiveness, viability, and profitability. Several studies have proposed similar definitions of strategic risk (Aron et al. 2005; Clarke and Varma 1999; Collins and Ruefli 1995; Emblemsvag and Kjolstad 2002; Smith et al. 2001; Travis and Saldanha 1999).

Dependency is another key strategic risk for First Bank. By outsourcing its entire infrastructure function to a third party vendor, First Bank inherently forms a dependency on Service Co. for the provisioning of infrastructure services. *"We need JMI to survive—so there's definitely a dependency there"* (Project Manager, First Bank). This dependency resulted from the lack of internal capabilities, which the bank retained after outsourcing its infrastructure function. One of the significant corollaries of forming a dependency on Service Co. for the provisioning of all infrastructure services was the loss of control that eventuated. Once the infrastructure function had been outsourced, a gradual loss of control over the future direction of the infrastructure was noted. This, precluded the bank's infrastructure function from serving its business needs, thus propelling a certain divide between IT and the business.

Another strategic risk that was realized by the client organization was the loss of innovative capacity within the infrastructure space. Service Co., by owning all of the infrastructure and its constituting components, assumed responsibility of all infrastructural maintenance and enhancement related activities. This presented First Bank with a significant risk as it was unable to assume immediate control of JMI's innovative and technological progression.

First Bank was also posed with significant financial risks during the course of the partnership. Such risks relate not to the loss of investments made into the partnership, although they are the wider financial repercussions of partnership failure. The costs associated with recovering from failure are quite significant for First Bank as substantial investments would be required to bring the infrastructure function back in house or to establish a new outsourcing arrangement with an alternate service provider.

5.2 Vendor Strategic Risks

Vendor strategic risks are defined as risks whose impacts go beyond the boundaries of the partnership, that is, risks that have a direct and adverse impact on the vendor organization's long-term business strategy, competitiveness, viability, and profitability.

A key strategic risk for Service Co. was the market failure of their JMI service offering. The JMI partnership presented Service Co. with the opportunity to test the commercial viability of their JMI offering. Significant investments were made to design the JMI architecture and its surrounding processes.

The JMI partnership also entailed a significant reputation risk for Service Co. *"If we don't get this implementation of JMI right, then we could lose the interest of other banks around the world"* (Risk Manager, Service Co.). Given the fact that the partnership was highly publicized, many of Service Co.'s existing and potential clients eagerly followed the progress of the partnership to gauge whether JMI could really deliver the benefits that it promised. This high degree of transparency presented Service Co. with the forbidding risk of losing potential business had the venture failed.

Dependency is a risk commonly associated with the client organization (Aubert et al. 2002; Hoecsht and Trott 2006). However, the JMI case indicates that this is a risk also experienced by the vendor. Respondents interviewed from Service Co. acknowledged that the vendor formed a dependency on the client. *"It is a big account for Service Co.; First Bank is one of our biggest clients accounting for about a fifth of our business"* (Program Director, Service Co.). The nature of this dependency was two-fold: first, a financial dependency existed as Service Co. relied on First Bank as a stable and continuous source of income, and second, a dependency of advocacy was also ingrained in the outsourcing relationship between the organizations.

By entering into the JMI partnership, Service Co. assumed a series of financial risks. Such risks do not necessarily pertain to the direct loss of capital invested into the partnership (e.g., financial risks), although they are the indirect financial implications associated with partnership failure. These include loss of future business, failing to make a return on investments in developing the JMI service offering, costs incurred in business transformation and retransformation, and the opportunity costs associated with the time and resources invested in developing and marketing the JMI service offering and on-demand business strategy.

5.3 Shared Strategic Risks

Shared strategic risks are defined as risks whose impacts go beyond the boundaries of the partnership, that is, risks that have a direct, adverse, and mutual impact on the organizations' long-term business strategy, competitiveness, viability, and profitability. Despite several studies acknowledging the presence of shared risks in outsourcing partnerships, no research to date has been able to provide any insight into the types of risks that are shared between the vendor and client. An analysis of the findings confirms that risks are indeed shared between the client and vendor and further reveals that such risks are of a strategic nature.

The JMI venture required both organizations to invest heavily into the partnership. Such investment came in the form of capital, time, and labor resources. Thus, the partnership posed a shared financial risk for both organizations. The risk–reward sharing contract also encouraged both organizations to share financial risks. Additionally, an element of profit sharing was also reflected in the contract, which aligned the two organizations financially.

Unlawful disclosure of trade secrets and confidential information was another risk to which both Service Co. and First Bank were alert. The JMI partnership demanded a high level of transparency to be established across both organizations. Thus, each organization had access to highly confidential materials belonging to their respective partner. This was indeed an alarming risk for both organizations as disclosure of such confidential materials may directly affect their respective competitive positions.

First Bank's concerns pertained more so to the disclosure of confidential customer data and the entailing legal repercussions. The design of JMI specified that all virtual servers provisioned would reside physically on Service Co.'s premises. Furthermore, several personnel from the vendor organization required access to all data managed by the infrastructure. Several cases of information leakage and disclosure have been presented in the literature (Khalfan 2004; Peltier 1996), although no studies have acknowledged that this is a risk that is also carried by the vendor.

Partner financial instability is another shared strategic risk that was noted in the case study. Given the dependencies between the two organizations, a significant risk emerges if one of the partner companies was to collapse financially, consequentially resulting in the ultimate failure of the partnership and placing the other partner further at risk. The risk of partner instability is also pertinent to Service Co., who, in the event of First Bank financially collapsing, will fail to make a return on their investment and ultimately lose a substantial source of continued income. Sullivan and Ngwenyama (2005) found that "vendor financial instability will lead to a willingness to shirk under the terms of the contract—a vendor with nothing to lose is more willing to walk away from the contract and declare bankruptcy" (p. 76).

Severance of the business relationship between First Bank and Service Co. was another shared strategic risk that emerged during the course of the JMI partnership. "We were both conscious of the fact that if JMI did not work then that would mean the end of our working relationship" (Project Manager, Service Co.). Both organizations came to the realization that JMI signified one final attempt to sustain their business relationship. The severance of the business relationship presents significant consequences for both the client and vendor.

5.4 Client Operational Risks

A client operational risk is a risk whose potential impact is contained within the boundaries of the partnership (i.e., at the project level), that is, a risk that has a direct and adverse impact on

- the client's ability to carry out its roles and responsibilities as defined in the partnership
- the client's ability to realize expected goals and benefits as defined in the partnership

Several client operational risks emerged during the course of the JMI partnership.

Perhaps the most significant client operational risk was the debasement of service that eventuated as a result of First Bank adopting the JMI service model. One of the goals that First Bank had set prior to entering into the partnership was to greatly improve the quality of infrastructural services through the implementation of JMI. This goal, however, was not entirely achieved as a result of Service Co.'s failure to meet established service levels.

The debasement of service that occurred during the JMI case clearly limited First Bank's ability to achieve its goal of enhancing the efficiency and quality of processes within the infrastructure space. Furthermore, the expected benefit of gaining a competitive advantage through the implementation of JMI was also not realized as a result of Service Co. failing to meet numerous service level targets.

First Bank's limited understanding of the JMI technology was another operational risk that precluded the client from meeting its responsibilities under the terms of the outsourcing contract. From an analysis of the findings, it is clear that personnel from the client organization did not have a sound understanding of JMI in terms of how the infrastructure set-up works, the nature of its underlying technologies, or the scope of its functionality.

The somewhat limited understanding of JMI conveyed by members of First Bank's project teams is a cause for concern. When assessing the progress of the JMI partnership, it is clear that such a lack of understanding precluded First Bank from meeting several of its assumed responsibilities. First Bank's internal project team was unable to adequately modify a significant proportion of the bank's applications and systems as part of the application refresh initiative. This may be attributed to the team's failure to achieve a satisfactory level of understanding of JMI's technical specifications.

Given the infancy of the JMI solution, it was evident during the course of the partnership that Service Co. was highly inexperienced with its delivery. Several respondents, surprisingly from both organizations, conveyed their concerns over the vendor's inexperience with the outsourced technology. It is evident from the case that the vendor's lack of experience with the outsourced technology is indeed an operational risk for the client. Service Co.'s inexperience with JMI limited First Bank's ability to achieve its goals of improving efficiency within the infrastructure space and the quality of infrastructure services.

The implementation of the JMI architecture and its surrounding processes required First Bank to undergo extensive internal changes, particularly in relation to the way in which IT teams approached system development and maintenance related projects. Prior to JMI, all server design, development, and implementation related activities were performed by system architects assigned to project teams. With the onset of JMI, all servers were now centrally provisioned and managed by Service Co. Due to large numbers of users refusing to adopt the JMI service offering, several in-house servers needed to be maintained in order to support the systems and applications of noncompliant users. The maintenance of such additional servers extends the terms of the outsourcing contract, thus presenting further costs for First Bank.

To facilitate the JMI venture, a substantial number of First Bank's system architects were permanently transferred to Service Co. Somewhat surprisingly, not all of the transferred staff were assigned to the JMI project, with many being assigned to other client engagements. Respondents interviewed from First Bank were highly critical of

Service Co.'s management of the transitional employees, conveying that the knowledge these employees had of the bank's applications, systems, and processes could not be leveraged if they weren't directly involved in the project.

A corollary of losing internal capabilities, as stated in the literature, is the gradual tendency of the client to offload complete responsibility of the outsourced function (Lacity and Willcocks 1998; Willcocks et al. 1999). This was evident in the case, with Service Co. having assumed ownership of the entire infrastructure function by the end of the implementation phase. Offloading responsibility of the management and operation of infrastructure is a prominent risk for First Bank as, in doing so, the bank had no direct control over the quality of service that it received.

5.5 Vendor Operational Risks

A vendor operational risk is a risk whose potential impact is contained within the boundaries of the partnership (i.e., at the project level), that is, a risk that has a direct and adverse impact on

- the vendor's ability to carry out its roles and responsibilities as defined in the partnership
- the vendor's ability to realize expected goals and benefits as defined in the partnership

Several vendor operational risks emerged during the course of the JMI partnership. It must be noted that the literature offers no insight into the types of risks encountered by the vendor during an outsourcing venture. Thus, this study addresses a significant gap in the literature through its identification, analysis and discussion of vendor operational risks.

This study's findings have clearly shown that the vendor's lack of experience is indeed a risk to the client at an operational level. However, an analysis of the findings further indicates that this is in fact an operational risk for the vendor as well. Service Co.'s inexperience with JMI led the partner to miss several key service level targets. This resulted in the vendor being penalized financially and further prevented the vendor from acquiring the performance bonus. It was essential for Service Co. to achieve the performance bonus in order to recover the investments made in purchasing all of the equipment required to implement JMI.

The client's lack of understanding of the outsourced technology also presented a risk for Service Co. The vendor was unable to achieve its goal of developing a truly standardized infrastructural environment due to First Bank's incessant requests to customize infrastructural components. Respondents from Service Co. attribute this to First Bank's failure to understand the nature JMI and the capabilities that it offers.

First Bank's lack of understanding of JMI also prevented the bank from adequately managing the vendor. In light of the events presented by the JMI case, it is evident that the client's lack of understanding is indeed a risk for the vendor as well. One may be inclined to classify this risk as a vendor operational risk as it clearly limited Service Co.'s ability to deliver the JMI infrastructure on time and within budget.

Another operational risk which was evident in the case was the lack of demarcation of duties between Service Co. and other subcontractors such as TelCo. TelCo. was responsible for all networking and connectivity related tasks during the course of the partnership. This included laying the network cables and installing all the network devices such as switches, routers, and hubs. The JMI infrastructure operated through the physical infrastructure implemented by TelCo. This difficulty in determining account-ability for infrastructure failures further limited Service Co.'s ability to deliver JMI within the scheduled time frame as much time was needed to uncover the source of problems.

Service Co. may have been in a better position to meet service levels and prevent many of the network failures if the vendor had direct control over TelCo. and was accountable for the subcontractor's performance. This was not the case during the partnership as the subcontractor was directly managed by First Bank. This arrangement was somewhat ineffective as First Bank had little knowledge of the network design and JMI's network requirements. Service Co. would have been in a far better position to manage TelCo. due to the corporation's thorough understanding of JMI's physical design and the infrastructure's network requirements. Thus, by limiting the vendor's ability to meet its responsibilities as defined in the partnership agreement, the risk of lack of control over subcontractors can be clearly classified as a vendor operational risk.

According to respondents from Service Co., First Bank failed to provide the vendor with adequate forecasts of expected capacity. Such forecasts were essential to Service Co.'s capacity provisioning process as the vendor needed sufficient time to scale the infrastructure to support First Bank's future capacity needs. The contract specified that First Bank was to establish a capacity pipeline that provided forecasts of capacity spanning for a period of one year. However, the bank was unable to meet this require-ment, instead providing forecasts for only a period of eight months. Thus, it is clear from the events in the case that the client's inability or unwillingness to meet commitments is indeed a vendor operational risk. The reason for this is because the risk limited Service Co.'s ability to meet certain responsibilities (i.e., deliver JMI on time, provision required levels of capacity and board the required applications) and achieve specific goals (maximize efficiency and drive down costs within the infrastructure space).

Service Co. was unfairly assessed on a number of occasions during the course of the partnership, which resulted in the company suffering financially. One such example was Service Co. enduring numerous penalties for outages experienced during the implemen-tation phase. It was established that the cause of these outages was TelCo.'s implemen-tation of an unstable network. Despite this fact, First Bank continued to penalize Service Co., even though the contract negates any liability on the part of the vendor in the event that an outage occurs due to faults in the physical network. As a result of such unfair assessments, Service Co. was unable to gain any real recoverability on investments made into the partnership.

5.6 Shared Operational Risk

A shared operational risk is a risk whose potential impact is contained within the boundaries of the partnership (i.e., at the project level), that is, a risk that has a direct and adverse impact on

- the abilities of the client and vendor to carry out their roles and responsibilities as defined in the partnership arrangement
- the abilities of the client and vendor to realize expected shared goals and benefits as defined in the partnership arrangement

Several researchers have theorized that outsourcing partnerships entail risks that mutually affect both client and vendor partners (Currie and Willcocks 1998; Lacity and Willcocks 1998; Lee and Kim 1999; McFarlan and Nolan 1995). However, no study has exposed the types of risks that are indeed shared between the client and vendor. This study addresses this gap. Six main areas of shared operational risks were identified from the events in the case and are now briefly discussed.

Relational risks refer to risks that inhibit collaboration between the vendor and client, thus preventing them from working effectively to achieve shared goals and fulfil shared responsibilities. The lack of trust between the two organizations led to several conflicts emerging during the course of the partnership. Furthermore, because the organizations did not trust each other, conflicts could not be resolved on a relational level and were often escalated to the contract managers. This greatly impeded both organizations from performing their respective responsibilities as they were constantly disputing the terms of the contract.

The requirements also posed several risks that precluded both the client and vendor from meeting their shared responsibilities. Respondents described the requirements prepared by First Bank as incomplete, unclear, and poorly specified.

The nature of the JMI technology itself posed several risks for the two organizations that potentially limited their abilities to achieve shared goals and realize planned technological benefits. One of the primary technology risks which the case revealed was the uncertainty of the technological direction taken by both organizations. It is important to note that JMI is by no means a stand-alone solution; instead it is a discipline that demands both the client and vendor to follow a specific technological direction. This direction has a diverse impact, affecting all of First Bank's operations within the infrastructure space and shaping Service Co.'s management of the bank's infrastructure.

The contextual environment in which the partnership took place also presented risks for the two organizations. Such risks had a direct and adverse impact on their ability to achieve shared goals and fulfil shared responsibilities. The Reserve Bank of Australia (RBA), a regulator within the banking industry, exerted much pressure on both organizations during the course of the JMI partnership. All infrastructure designs, business continuity plans, and disaster recovery plans were required to be submitted to the RBA for approval before the project could transition to the build and implementation phase. A comprehensive review of the literature revealed only one study (Willcocks et al. 1999) that considered environment risks.

Several risks emerged as a result of inadequate management practices. Such risks have been classified as shared operational risks as they inhibited both organizations from fulfilling their shared responsibilities of managing the outsourcing partnership. Senior management's failure to communicate the partnership presented a clear risk for both organizations. The partnership emanated from a series of negotiations between senior managers from both organizations, with personnel involved at the implementation level having no visibility of the nature of the partnership arrangement.

The use of a long-term contract posed a risk to both organizations. Traditionally, outsourcing contracts have taken the form of short term engagements. By signing a 10 year deal, Service Co. was presented with the opportunity to truly develop JMI as a global, on-demand service offering and stood to reap significant financial benefits. However, given that the partnership was driven by a risk–reward sharing contract, Service Co. was also at risk of suffering a long-term financial loss as a result of poor service provisioning or the JMI technology failing to meet expectations. Perhaps the most significant contractual risk revealed in the case was the contract's failure to represent the intent of both parties. *"We needed to communicate more... especially how we were progressing"* (Project Manager, Service Co.).

6 THE RISKS OF IS OUTSOURCING PARTNERSHIPS: A THEORY PROPOSAL

An analysis and interpretation of the JMI case study presented in section 5 suggests six substantive codes: *client strategic risks, vendor strategic risks, shared strategic risks, client operational risks, vendor operational risks,* and *shared operational risks.* It is clear that these risks are not independent, but are interrelated. At the heart of the substantive theory are the *shared operational risks.* These risks have been identified as the core risks of an outsourcing partnership. It is proposed that shared operational risks exert an influence (that is, increase the likelihood) on all of the other five types of risks. *Vendor operational risks* are also proposed to increase the likelihood of *vendor strategic risks.* Similarly, it is proposed that *client operational risks* increase the likelihood of *client strategic risks.*

Three main propositions have been put forward as part of the substantive theory and for brevity are briefly summarized as

1. Increased *shared operational risks* increase the likelihood of all *strategic risks* (*shared strategic risks, client strategic risks, and vendor strategic risks*).
2. Increased *shared operational risks* increase the likelihood of *client* and *vendor operational risks.*
3. Increased *client/vendor operational risks* increase the likelihood *client/vendor strategic risks.*

The three propositions and the directions of their interactions with the six risk categories are shown in Figure 2.

Figure 2 illustrates several minor propositions, listed below, for each main proposition (these are not discussed due to word limitations).

- Proposition 1.1: Increased shared operational risks increases the likelihood of shared strategic risks.
- Proposition 1.2: Increased shared operational risks increases the likelihood of vendor strategic risks.
- Proposition 1.3: Increased shared operational risks increases the likelihood of client strategic risks.

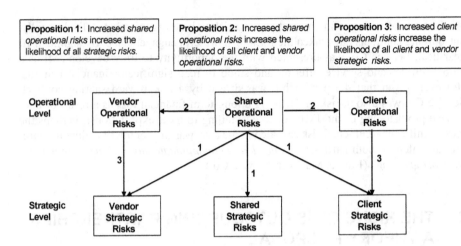

Figure 2. Three Propositions and Directional Interactions between Six Coded Risk Categories

- Proposition 2.1: Increased shared operational risks increase the likelihood of client operational risks.
- Proposition 2.2: Increased shared operational risks increase the likelihood of vendor operational risks.
- Proposition 3.1: Increased vendor operational risks increases the likelihood of vendor strategic risks.
- Proposition 3.2: Increased client operational risks increases the likelihood of client strategic risks.

6.1 Proposition 1 Summary

It is proposed that increased shared operational risks increase the likelihood of shared strategic risks, client strategic risks, and vendor strategic risks.

The likelihood is that all strategic risks increase as shared operational risks are realized by the client and vendor. The fundamental reason for this is because shared operational risks directly threaten the success of the partnership. As the case has shown, in line with the literature on outsourcing partnerships, the inability of both organizations to meet shared responsibilities and realize shared goals and benefits will ultimately drive the partnership to failure.

6.2 Proposition 2 Summary

The findings of this study revealed that increased shared operational risks increase the likelihood of client and vendor operational risks. Not meeting shared goals and shared responsibilities further limits the achievement of individual goals and the fulfill-ment of individual responsibilities. A shared goal, which the two organizations failed to meet during the course of the partnership, was to develop and implement a standardized infrastructure environment.

6.3 Proposition 3 Summary

Failure to achieve individual goals and fulfil individual responsibilities promotes risks, which directly impact the organization's strategy, viability, profitability, and competitiveness (i.e., vendor/client strategic risks).

7 CONCLUSION AND IMPLICATIONS

The theoretical framework reveals six key types of risks: vendor strategic risks, shared strategic risks, client strategic risks, vendor operational risks, shared operational risks, and client operational risks, and their interrelationships. Shared operational risks have been identified as the central risks in an IS outsourcing partnership, influencing all of the other five risk types. Additionally, it was found that client operational risks increase the likelihood of client strategic risks. Similarly, an analysis of the findings revealed that vendor operational risks increase the likelihood of vendor strategic risks.

Development of this substantive theory has contributed to the IS outsourcing research literature by addressing two key gaps within the research domain. First, a review of the literature indicated that no study of risk in the context of IS outsourcing partnerships has been conducted. Second, no research to date has examined risk from the perspective of both client and vendor stakeholders. In addressing these areas overlooked in the research field, this study presents several important implications for theory and practice. Finally, no studies of outsourcing risk have considered risk from the vendor perspective. Thus, the literature provides no insight into the types of risks experienced by the vendor during an outsourcing engagement. This study, by analyzing the empirical data gathered from the case, has uncovered several risks that are pertinent to the vendor. In doing so, this study has addressed a significant gap in the outsourcing literature.

For practitioners, the substantive theory developed in this research study offers much insight into the main areas of risk deserving management attention during an IS outsourcing partnership arrangement. In developing an awareness of the six key risk areas and their interrelatedness, practitioners will be better prepared to manage many of the risks entailed in IS outsourcing partnerships. The theoretical contribution of this research lies in its proposal of a substantive theory of risk. This theory contributes to a better understanding of the risks of IS outsourcing partnerships. A limitation of this study is the single-case study methodology employed. Further research in this area from both a theoretical and empirical nature is ongoing.

References

Ang, S., and Toh, S. K. 1998. "Failure in Software Outsourcing: A Case Analysis," in *Strategic Sourcing of Information Systems*, L. P. Willcocks and M. C. Lacity (eds.), Chichester, UK: John Wiley and Sons Ltd., pp. 351-368.

Aron, R., Clemons, E. K., and Reddi, S. 2005. "Just Right Outsourcing: Understanding and Managing Risk," *Journal of Management Information Systems* (22:2), pp. 37-56.

Aubert, B., Patry, M., Rivard, S., and Smith, H. 2001. "IT Outsourcing Risk Management at British Petroleum," in *Proceedings of the 34th Hawaii International Conference on System Sciences*, Maui, HI, January 3-6, Los Alamitos, CA: IEEE Computer Society Press.

Babbie, E. 1992. *The Practice of Social Research Methods for Social Work* (6th ed.), Belmont, CA: Wadsworth Publishing Company.

Charmaz, K. 2000. "Grounded Theory: Objectivist and Constructivist Methods," in *Handbook of Qualitative Research* (2nd ed.), N. K. Denzin and Y. S. Lincoln (eds.), Thousand Oaks, CA: Sage Publications, pp. 509-535.

Clarke C. J., and Varma S. 1999. "Strategic Risk Management: The New Competitive Edge," *Long Range Planning* (32:4), pp. 414-424.

Collins, J. M., and Ruefli, T. W. 1995. *Strategic Risk: A State-Defined Approach*, Boston: Springer.

Currie, W. 2000. "The Supply-Side of IT Outsourcing: The Trend towards Mergers, Acquisitions and Joint Ventures," *International Journal of Physical Distribution and Logistics Management* (30), pp. 238-254.

Currie, W. L., and Willcocks, L. P. 1998. "Analyzing Four Types of IT Sourcing Decisions in the Context of Scale, Client/Supplier Interdependency and Risk Mitigation," *Information Systems Journal* (8:2), pp. 119-143.

Emblemsvag, J., and Kjolstad, L. E. 2002. "Strategic Risk Analysis: A Field Version," *Management Decision* (40:9), pp. 842-852.

Glaser, B. 1978. *Theoretical Sensitivity: Advances in the Methodology of Grounded Theory*, Mill Valley, CA: Sociology Press.

Henderson J C. 1990. "Plugging into Strategic Partnerships: The Critical IS Connection," *Sloan Management Review* (31), pp. 7-18.

Khalfan, A. M. 2004. "Information Security Considerations in IS/IT Outsourcing Projects: A Descriptive Case Study of Ttwo Sectors," *International Journal of Information Management* (24:1), pp. 29-42.

Kern, T., and Willcocks, L. 2000. "Exploring Information Technology Outsourcing Relationships: Theory and Practice," *Journal of Strategic Information* Systems (9), pp. 321-350.

Lacity, M. C., Willcocks, L. P. 1998. "An Empirical Investigation of Information Technology Sourcing Practices: Lessons from Experience," *MIS Quarterly* (22:3), pp. 363-308.

Lee, J. N. 1998. "Partnership Quality in IS Outsourcing: Social Theory Perspective," paper presented at the Doctoral Consortium of the 19th International Conference on Information Systems, Helsinki, Finland.

Lee, J. N, Huynh, M. Q., Kwok, R. C-W., and Pi, S-M. 2003. "IT Outsourcing Evolution—Past, Present, and Future," *Communications of ACM* (46:5), pp. 84-89.

Lee, J. N, and Kim, Y. G. 2005. "Understanding Outsourcing Partnership: A Comparison of Three Theoretical Perspectives," *IEEE Transactions on Engineering Management* (52:1), pp. 43-58.

Loh, L., and Venkatraman, N. 1992. "Determinants of Information Technology Outsourcing: A Cross-Sectional Analysis," *Journal of Management Information Systems* (8), pp. 7-24.

Marchand, N., and Jacobsen, H. A. 2001. "An Economic Model to Study Dependencies between Independent Software Vendors and Application Service Providers," *Electronic Commerce Research* (1:3), pp. 315-334.

McFarlane, F. W., and Nolan, R. L. 1995. "How to Manage an IT Outsourcing Alliance," *Sloan Management Review* (36:2), pp. 9-23.

Miles, M. B., and Huberman, A. M. 1984. *Qualitative Data Analysis: A Sourcebook of New Methods*, London: Sage Publications.

Myers, M. D. 1994. "A Disaster for All to See: An Interpretive Analysis of a Failed IS Project," *Accounting Management and Information Technologies* (4:4), pp. 185-201.

Peltier, T. 1996. "The Risk of Allowing Outside Staff Access to Your Information Systems," *Information Security Technical Report* (1:3), pp. 18-28.

Rubin, H., and Rubin, I. 1995. *Qualitative Interviewing : The Art of Hearing Data*, Thousand Oaks, CA: Sage Publications.

Saunders, C., Gebelt, M., and Hu, Q. 1997. "Achieving Success in Information Systems Outsourcing," *California Management Review* (39:2), pp. 63-79.

Smith H. A., McKeen J. D., Staples D. S. 2001. "Risk Management in Information Systems: Problems and Potentials," *Communications of the Association for Information Systems* (7:13), pp. 1-29.

Strauss A. L., and Corbin, J. M. 1990. *Basics of Qualitative Research: Grounded Theory Procedures and Techniques*, Newbury Park, CA: Sage Publications.

Strauss, A. L., and Corbin, J. M. 1994. "Grounded Theory Methodology: An Overview," in *Handbook of Qualitative Research*, N. K. Denzin, and Y. S. Lincoln (eds.), Thousand Oaks, CA: Sage Publications, pp. 273-285.

Sullivan, W. E., and Ngwenyama, O. K. 2005. "How Are Public Sector Organizations Managing Is Outsourcing Risks? An Analysis of Outsourcing Guidelines from Three Jurisdictions," *Journal of Computer Information* (45:3), pp. 73-87.

Travis, J., and Saldanha, M. 1999. "An Investigation of IS/IT Project Risk Analysis and Management Practices in Western Australia," in *Proceedings of the 10th Australasian Conference on Information Systems*, Wellington, New Zealand, December 1-3.

Walker, C. 1996. "Giant Contracts Boost UK Outsourcing Growth," *Computer Weekly*, July 20, p. 12.

Willcocks, L. P., and Lacity, M. 1999. "IT Outsourcing in Financial Services: Risk, Creative Contracting, Business Advantage," *Information Systems Journal* (9), pp. 163-183.

Willcocks, L. P., Lacity, M., and Kern, T. 1999. "Risk Mitigation in IT Outsourcing Strategy Revisited: Longitudinal Case Research," *Journal of Strategic Information Systems* (8:2), pp. 285-314.

About the Authors

Shabareesh Ajitkumar is a management consultant with the leading Australian consultancy Portland Group. He recently completed his First Class Honours thesis on risk management in the context of IS outsourcing partnerships with the School of Information Systems, Technology and Management at the University of New South Wales. He can be contacted by e-mail at SAjitkumar@portlandgroup.com.

Stephen Smith is the Executive Officer of Emergency Management Operations in the Office of the Government Chief Information Officer, Department of Commerce, in the New South Wales State Government. He holds a Ph.D. and Master's of Commerce degree from the University of New South Wales in information systems and a Bachelor of Science in Engineering. Stephen is a casual lecturer in IS security at the School of Information Systems, Technology, and Management, University of New South Wales. His publications include articles in *Information Systems Management Journal, The International Journal of Knowledge, Culture and Change Management*, and various refereed national and international conference proceedings in IS/IT. He can be contacted by e-mail at Stephen.Smith@commerce.nsw.gov.au.

Deborah Bunker is a senior lecturer at the School of Information Systems, Technology and Management at the University of New South Wales. She holds a Ph.D. in Information Systems Management. Her research interests are in IS philosophy, IS management, IS adoption and diffusion, and e-Commerce/e-Business. She has published widely in these areas. Deborah is a founding member and the Vice-Chair of IFIP TC 8 WG 8.6 on the adoption and diffusion of IT. She can be reached at d.bunker@unsw.edu.au.

Donald Winchester is a research fellow in SEAR (Security, E-Fraud, Assurance, and Risk) within the School of Information Systems, Technology and Management, Australian School of Business, University of New South Wales. He is a Ph.D. candidate (finance) in the Australian School of Business, University of New South Wales. He holds a BCM (Lincoln University), MBA (Massey University), and MBS (Massey University), all in finance. Current research interests are in information systems security, identity crime, risks in financial institutions, outsourcing, and international financial flows. His work has been published in international journals and referred conference proceedings. Donald can be contacted by e-mail at d.winchester@unsw.edu.au or don_winchester@yahoo.com.

24   OPEN INNOVATION AND THE EROSION OF THE TRADITIONAL INFORMATION SYSTEMS PROJECT'S BOUNDARIES

Amany Elbanna
Lougborough University
Leicestershire, U.K.

Abstract   *This paper examines the notion of open innovation and its implication on information systems management. It investigates a project of an enterprise resource planning system implementation in an international organization to unravel the resemblance with the open innovation model. The study shows that the conceptualization of ERP project as an open innovation could reveal the complex architecture of today's organization from which the ERP project cannot be isolated. It argues that the traditional boundaries around IS projects are dissolving and the relationship between what used to be outside and what used to be inside the project is increasingly blurred. The study calls for a different perspective of project management that goes beyond single and multiple project management to scan the open space of innovation and actively look for partners, competitors, and collaborators.*

Keywords   Open innovation, IS project management, IS multiple projects environment, ERP

1   INTRODUCTION

Organizations are facing fierce competition and a changing global market that requires them to constantly innovate to survive and protect their market share. The innovation process within the organization attracts scholars who mainly focus on studying the process of research and development and how organizations could provide an environ-

Please use the following format when citing this chapter:

Elbanna, A., 2008, in IFIP International Federation for Information Processing, Volume 287, Open IT-Based Innovation: Moving Towards Cooperative IT Transfer and Knowledge Diffusion, eds. León, G., Bernardos, A., Casar, J., Kautz, K., and DeGross, J. (Boston: Springer), pp. 423-439.

ment that fosters innovation, detect it, and benefit from it. Recently, scholars have started to sense some changes in the innovation process. After reviewing the development of the R&D innovation process and classify it into four different generations, Rothwell (1994) concluded that we are entering a fifth generation innovation. He characterizes this fifth generation of innovation process to be "essentially lean," where "innovation is becoming more of a networking process" (p. 22). Gibbons et al. (1994) have also discussed the changing mode of knowledge in what they called "mode 2." They admit that it is unfolding and evolving and hence its characteristics and implications are far from clear at the point of writing and that their ideas are early attempts to detect the change. In mode 2, they argue, "knowledge is accumulated through the repeated configuration of human resources in flexible, essentially transient forms of organization" (p. 9). Chesbrough (2003) also detected the change in the R&D innovation process and argued that organizations are facing a new paradigm in innovation and coined it *open innovation*. Open innovation denies the closed boundaries around the innovation and the views that organizational innovation is an internal matter that needs to be isolated and protected. Chesbrough argues that innovation is distributed as knowledge and calls for the opening up of organizational boundaries to include external sources of innovation. There is also a growing body of research that links the process of innovation to network arrangements, yet focuses on R&D networks within and between organizations (Swan and Scarbrough 2005).

Despite the different names—open innovation, networked innovation, mode 2, or ffifth generation—there is a common sense of change in the R&D innovation process and different authors try to sketch the changes and their implications. The general theme underlying these studies is that organizations cannot continue to look inward in their innovation process, isolating themselves from possible collaborators, partners, and competitors. Another theme is that innovation knowledge does not necessarily entirely lie within the organization and there are other several ways to gain knowledge from the outside. A last theme is that the innovation process has to be flexible and lean to cope with changes in the business platform. In short, open innovation invites the organizations to break from its innovation silo and open up its boundaries to achieve a flexible and lean innovation.

Information systems has been long recognized as an organization innovation (Wynn and Fitzgerald 2004). Studies have explored the process of IS innovation within the organizations, the diffusion of IS innovation, and the role of IS/IT in organizational innovation (Henriksen and Kautz 2006). The process oriented studies of IS innovation tend to adopt a single project focus that looks inward into the innovation process within a certain project. This single project focus is also shared by the majority of project management literature (Payne 1995). This is despite reports that organizations are increasingly under competitive pressures to innovate and introduce change, which is usually done through projects, and therefore modern organizations are increasingly involved in several projects at the same time (Masini and Pich 2004). It is estimated that up to 90 percent of projects in general are carried out in a multiple project environment (Payne 1995, Dooley et al. 2005). However, little is known about the implications of such a busy platform on IS projects.

This paper aims to explore the notion of open innovation, its applicability and implications in the busy multiple-project platform that current IS innovations face in the software context. To this end, the study examines an enterprise resource planning implementation project in an international postage and packaging organization. It goes beyond the traditional project management view that focuses on managing budget and time to reveal the busy organizational platform through which an IS project could be run.

Following the introduction, the paper proceeds as follows. The second section discusses the project organization in software development and, in particular, packaged software. The third section presents the resemblance between actor network theory (ANT) and open innovation ideas. The fourth section presents the research methodology and the background of the case study. The fifth section presents the findings of the case. The sixth section discusses the findings and their implication.

2 PACKAGED SOFTWARE PROJECT MANAGEMENT

Packaged software development (in software houses) and implementation (in the buyer organization) usually take place in a pure project organization, a separate, largely self-contained entity that is devoted exclusively to achieving the project aims and that will be disbanded when the project is completed or abandoned (Garrety et al. 2004; Hobday 2000; Meredith and Mantel 1995). This *ad hoc* organization of projects is separated administratively from the rest of the organization, reflecting a division of labor between projects and routine operations. The management of packaged software projects has received the attention of researchers who traditionally tended to study the vendor's experience of software development and recently the implementation project in the buyer organization. In both cases, researchers tended to adopt a single project perspective in their studies of software projects. This perspective focuses solely on the single project under study and the internal dynamics of innovation. This view respects the traditional boundaries around an IS project that clearly and strictly differentiates between what is in the realm of the project and what is outside.

The single project perspective reflected in the packaged software projects literature produces valuable insight, but misses the complexity of today's organizations and their ongoing practice of having several projects running at any point of time. Overlooked in the literature, the multiple project perspective is recognized in project management methodologies adopted in IS such as PRINCE (Projects IN Closed Environment). PRINCE accommodates a multiple project management perspective while maintaining a closed innovation view that is based on bundling related IS projects under the governance of a central body, called a program, in order to allocate resources and ensure compliance with a schedule (Olson 2004). It is in this bundling that programs get separated from each other and it is for a central IS body within the organization to manage the IS portfolio of programs and allocate resources between them. It should be noted here that project management methodologies are based on the consolidation and monitoring of a project plan that is a combination of an organization plan and a project schedule. The organization plan consists of two activities: (1) a work breakdown structure (WBS) to define the tasks required and the aim of each one as well as their interdependencies, and (2) an organization breakdown structure (OBS) to allocate roles to the WBS defined tasks. Project management tools such as critical path methods or Gantt charts are then used to schedule projects (Cijsouw et al. 2007; Steyn 2002).

Studies of multiple project environments are rather scarce. Evaristo and van Fenema (1999) agree that the overwhelming number of projects presented in the literature as well as most of the practical and theoretical developments on projects are centered on single projects. They tried to reveal the complexity of current projects, presenting a classification of projects based on the number of projects and sites involved. In addition to the simple single and multiple projects categories, they introduced categories such as colocated program, multiple colocated programs, distributed projects, and multiple distributed projects in shared or discreet locations. In a different but related front, Desouza and Evaristo (2004) studied the knowledge management needs in non-colocated work environments. They applied Damm and Schindler's (2002) categorization of project knowledge: knowledge in projects, knowledge about projects, and knowledge from projects to suggest the need for a hybrid approach to project knowledge management. Knowledge in project means knowledge generated inside a project such as schedule, milestones, meeting minutes, and training manuals. Knowledge about projects refers to organizational need to keep an inventory of all projects to aid planning and controlling such as employees assignment to projects, return on investment, cost and benefit analysis, deadlines, and customer commitments and expectations. Knowledge from projects is a *post hoc* analysis and audit of key insight generated from carrying out projects. Damm and Schindler's proposed hybrid approach consists of a central repository to hold knowledge about and from projects and individual repositories available to peers. This view recognizes the different needs of project-related information yet it is limited to a traditional view of project knowledge that focuses on scheduling and allocation of resources, typically financial and human resources. Moreover, knowledge in projects is suggested to be kept individually and exchanged between individual projects upon request on a peer-to-peer basis. This proposition assumes that individual projects are aware of other projects and hence recognizes particular information needs from other projects. Currently, this proposition is not well grounded and has no evidence to support it. Desouza and Evaristo do not provide any empirical evidence to support this assumption. On the other hand, the current project and program management organization maintains strict boundaries between projects that do not support this view either. IS project organization is largely hierarchical, it encourages projects to maintain an inward view and allows program management to allocate resources and keep a schedule of their own bundle of projects. It leaves it to the organization-wide central IS organization to keep an inventory of their portfolio of projects for strategic planning purposes (Olson 2004).

The need for different types of knowledge as suggested by Desouza and Evaristo is not well aligned with the IS project management organization since the latter enforces the boundaries of projects and their governing programs. Rather, Desouza and Evaristo's model requires a flatter view of the organization that allows individual projects to look at the wider organization beyond their immediate project and even program boundaries. This study investigates whether projects follow a closed pattern that focuses on the happenings of a project and are governed by a program structure, or an open innovation pattern that is flatter and includes more elements that are typically excluded from IS project management methodologies.

3   OPEN INNOVATION AND ACTOR NETWORK THEORY

Open innovation calls for going beyond the familiar inward look of innovation to explore different possibilities. It argues that the predetermined, closed boundaries around innovation are something from the past and detects the change in the innovation process and the erosion of these boundaries. Open innovation analyzes the organization on three levels: within the firm, between firms, and within the surrounding institutional environment (Chesbrough et al. 2006). This study focuses on detecting and analyzing the open innovation model in IS project management practices in order to investigate the implication of this line of thinking on the IS organization. Therefore, a flexible framework is needed that allows phenomena to reveal itself in its empirical setting. Actor network theory is found to meet such criteria.

ANT adopts a symmetrical view of sociological dichotomies, such as those between global and local, and macro and micro phenomena. It regards the sociotechnical world as not having a fixed, unchanging scale, and understands that "it is not the observer's job to remedy this state of affairs" (Latour 1991, p. 119). The theory does not see any difference in kind between the macro-structure and the micro-structure, so treats both with the same analytical tool. Latour (1991, p. 119) emphasizes that "respecting such changes of scale, induced by the actors themselves, is just as important as respecting the displacement of translations." In that sense, ANT is largely empirical. It does not impose any *a priori* structure on actors. On the contrary, it follows actors in their construction, modification, and negotiation of their macro- and micro-structures.

ANT also treats the distinction of *inside* and *outside* as open to question and negotiation. It therefore leaves it to actors to define what is inside and what is outside and the boundary between them (Law 1992). Actors also define one another in their interaction (Callon 1991). By defining what is local and inside, actors try to create a *negotiation space*, a notion seen as having two essential characteristics: it is a private area, physical and/or metaphorical, that is relatively inaccessible to those outside; it is an area in which plans, ideas, designs, and/or possibilities with implications for control of the outside world may be generated, explored, and tested in a way that is largely invisible to those on the outside (Law 1992). The negotiation space thus represents an area of relative autonomy approved by actors in the global network in order to build a local network. The establishment of a negotiation space is one of the strategies that actors adopt in order to build stable networks of sociotechnical objects. Law and Callon (1988) explain that a negotiation space makes it possible for mistakes to occur in private; within a negotiation space, it is also possible to experiment and, if all goes well, it is possible to create relatively durable sociotechnical combinations.

Continuous work and many negotiations take place on the boundary between the global and local or the outside and inside in order to secure the existence of the inside. For example, in his book *Science in Action*, Latour identified the inside as the laboratory itself, with all its heterogeneous combinations of scientists, machines, and natural phenomena. On the other hand, the outside of the laboratory is the combination of financial institutions, governments, and others. The internal/external division becomes the provisional outcome of a relationship between the outside recruitment of interests and the inside recruitment of new allies that "each step along the path the constitution of what is 'inside' and what is 'outside' alters" (Latour 1987, p. 159).

ANT has been found useful in providing "a very good way of telling stories about 'what happens out there' that defamiliarizes what we may otherwise take for granted" (Calas and Smircich 1999, p. 663). Therefore, it is applied in this study alongside the open innovation concepts to unwrap the structural dynamic of the IS project beyond the prespecified structure of IS project and program as presented in different IS project management methodologies.

4 RESEARCH METHODOLOGY

4.1 Research Method

This study follows the interpretive tradition of research. Interpretive research does not predefine dependent and independent variables, but focuses on the complexity of human sense making as situations emerge (Kaplan and Maxwell 1994). Interpretive methods of research in IS are aimed at producing an understanding of the context of the information system, and the process whereby the information system influences and is influenced by the context (Walsham 1993, p. 4). This study examines the open innovation phenomenon in IS organization through a single case study. In doing so, it does not seek any statistical generalization but allows for insight and theoretical generalization to be drawn (Walsham 1995).

Data collection took place between February 2001 and October 2001; follow-up phone calls, e-mails, and short meetings were conducted through February 2002. Data were collected through semi-structured interviews with 34 informants. Data were also collected through participant observation, with the researcher attending most of the configuration sessions and project meetings in different organizational levels. The researcher also participated in social events, conferences, and different organization-wide events and was copied in most project e-mail correspondence.

Data was analyzed and grouped first according to the traditional structure of project management specified in methodologies into project, program, or corporate IS governance (Miles and Huberman 1994). A chart has been drawn of issues that crossed these boundaries. New charts have been drawn of each issue crossing the traditional boundaries identifying actors involved, negotiation, and resolution. Special attention has been taken to identify the negotiation space, its settling, and where it settles.

4.2 The Case of Posta

Posta is a large European postal and parcel-delivery services company. It provides national and international mail services and handles over 75 million items every day. The cost of its SAP project was around $114 million. This study focuses on examining the course of the financial project. The financial project aimed to implement SAP financial modules that include finance, material management, assets management, PS, and e-procurement in 100 different locations within the country. The total number of users reached was over 11,000.

The financial project was planned to take 30 month and be released (local implementation) in three phases. The first phase covered four business units and served around 4,000 users. This phase was initially planned to go live on May 1, 2001. However, it was rescheduled to go live three month late at the end of July 2001. The second phase covered eight business units and about 6,000 users. It was initially scheduled to go live on September 1, 2001. In order to accommodate the slippage of the first phase, however, its deadline moved to end of October 2001, then was delayed again to the end of November 2001. The third phase was planned initially to go live the first week of January 2002, and had not been formally moved to a later date, even though last contact with the organization was at the end of February 2002.

5   RESEARCH FINDINGS

The SAP finance project's management was under the umbrella of a program called Enterprise Systems. This is in line with PRINCE methodology and the wisdom of bundling related projects under the governance of a program organization. The program included four projects: a human resources project to implement the HR module of SAP, a finance project to implement finance modules of SAP, and a decision support project to implement an off-the-shelf decision support system and infrastructure project. The following sections present the interaction between the finance project and others in the organization. It follows the IS project management's predefined hierarchical structure of project and program and inside and outside to reveal the erosion of this rigid view and its traditional boundaries.

5.1   Within the Program

5.1.1 Allocating Resources or Recruiting Allies

The finance, HR, and infrastructure projects were launched at the same time and were managed under a multiproject program called enterprise systems. The finance and HR projects were colocated in the same building. The finance project, sponsored by a senior director from Finance, was problematized as "essential for the survival of Posta." The director actively convinced the organization that the "executive board [believes] that without this program we won't survive, we won't manage the group." The financial project network aligned the most powerful top management in Posta, who all had a financial background or were from the finance community. These powerful allies supported the finance project in securing a generous three floors of desk space in the building. They also backed and promoted the finance project in different departments, encouraging employees to join this powerful network and to join the finance project on a secondment basis.

The finance project succeeded to interest and enrol "sufficient internal resources" in terms of human expertise, desk space for their teams, and management support. On the other hand, the HR project found it difficult to compete with such a powerful project. It struggled to find sufficient desk space in the same building as the finance project, and 25 percent of its team did not have their own permanent personal desk space and had to "hot desk."[1] The HR project also could not recruit sufficient staff as staff preferred to be seconded to the finance project.

---

[1]Rotating and using any empty desk available that day.

The HR project complained to the enterprise systems program board that it was not able to "operate efficiently and cost effectively," particularly when some of its staff had no desk space and needed to spend hours every day trying to find suitable workspace. The board recognized the problem and commented, "indeed productivity may well suffer if the early part of the days are spent in the search for a hot desk which, when found, is unlikely to be close to the people with whom the individual needs to relate in work terms" and that "efficiency, effectiveness and costs are all likely to be adversely impacted" (from the minutes of a board meeting). Yet the board could not find a solution for the problem and gently asked the finance project to help out. The board also recognized that the HR project had a serious staff shortage and was unable to fill many of the vacancies. These problems persisted until the later termination of the HR project due to a budget reduction and prioritization exercise.

5.1.2 Negotiating Program Methodology

The enterprise systems program followed the Posta tradition of managing projects using the PRINCE methodology. It used PRINCE to manage its portfolio of projects and assumed it would be the uniform methodology for project management for all IT projects under its governance. The finance project was profoundly enrolled and recruited in the SAP network of SAP implementation methodology (ASAP) and SAP-certified consultants. Thus, the finance projects resisted the adoption of the PRINCE methodology and negotiated in favor of SAP's implementation methodology, ASAP.

The SAP system and the SAP company placed the ASAP methodology as the passage point for its implementation, drawing on the complexity of the system and the company's intense experience in developing different versions of it and implementing SAP in different contexts. In addition, the SAP-certified consultants who worked as the external consultants that comprised part of the finance project team also problematized the issue and fixed ASAP as the only way forward, commenting, "we've been there before, we saw the best and worse...this [SAP] is different, no way to implement it with PRINCE. We are here to deliver. If you use PRINCE, we cannot guarantee delivery." The program's problematization of consistency and uniformity was weaker than the SAP vendor's and external consultants' problematization of survival, ensuring delivery, and achieving the promised good results.

Furthermore, the internal teams of the SAP project, being enrolled in the SAP network, cautioned the program board against using PRINCE. They argued that it would "waste a lot of time and won't guarantee anything really." They also argued "if we use PRINCE, it would take us ten years or more to implement SAP. Do we have time?" This left the board with no way but to accept the use of the ASAP methodology despite its differences with the program methodology and Posta's tradition of using PRINCE. The program management continued to use PRINCE to govern the program.

The finance project created an unexpected boundary between itself and its governing body. This boundary, based on the use of a different methodology, deviates from the prescriptive IS project management literature.

5.2 Outside the Program

5.2.1 Negotiating Functions and Technical Components

While the finance project based on SAP was underway, there was another project in Posta called the customer relationship management project (CRM) to implement Siebel's CRM system. Both projects were taking place at the same time yet each had its own project and program management structure and hence there was no relationship between them. In February 2001, when the SAP financial system moved to the realization phase, one of the technical components that had been taken for granted—the customer database—was discovered to be held in the Siebel system. The finance project management had no idea beforehand that this database was one of the areas in the domain of the CRM project and that acquiring it would become a subject of negotiation. This jeopardized the billing functionality of the SAP system. The issue was raised first with the finance project's program board, who thought that the issue was "simple, we need it [the database] in a certain time, IS strategy will ensure this." The issue was then raised with the corporate IS strategy—the governing body of corporate IS portfolio—to "immediately resolve." IS strategy liaised between the two networks and when this did not work, they organized several negotiation meetings with the two (finance and CRM) project management teams.

The timing of the delivery of the customer database continued to be a highly debatable issue between the two projects. For the CRM team, the "push forward" of the "customer engine" (the customer database) that the SAP project asked for was not possible. The CRM actors, including technology requirements and methodology, had a different time frame for developing this database than did the SAP project network and refused to jeopardize its system.

The CRM issue that emerged started to shadow most of the configuration sessions of the finance project. Senior users kept asking questions regarding the data and where it would be held. Senior users recognized the need to establish a communication channel with the CRM. The arguments concerning what data would (and would not) be stored within the CRM system included statements such as: "there is no way that this [data] would be held there [in the CRM], it has to be in the finance system"; "we have to negotiate this with them [CRM project]"; "let's clarify what they are doing." The finance project was also concerned about how much visibility (access) would be allowed between the financial system and the CRM. In particular, the position of the billing queries part of the SAP system needed to be clarified as this required access via a SAP front to a Siebel database. The finance project raised this issue with the enterprise systems program and the business unit sponsoring the CRM was contacted. After some negotiation between the finance project, the enterprise system program, and this business unit, an agreement "allowing full visibility between the SAP billing database and the details [of customers] on the Siebel pricing database" was reached.

The enterprise systems program and the finance project initially maintained that "it is indispensable" for the customer database to meet the SAP schedule, but after a lengthy process of negotiation it realized that the CRM "won't finish for the time [they] wanted." Thus, the finance project, and enterprise system program settled with doing "many interfaces with old systems" until the CRM project delivered the pricing engine, which was due in December 2002. This meant that the finance project had to create many work-arounds until its go-live date (scheduled in February 2002) and delay work on delivering full functionality of the implemented system until after CRM delivers the pricing engine (expected in December 2002). At the time the researcher left the field work, there was speculation suggesting that a fully functional finance system would not be delivered before March 2003, causing a delay of over a year for the finance project.

Realizing the importance of recruiting the CRM network into the finance project network, a CRM representative was later invited to attend the finance project's board meetings. He was given full membership on that board in order to "bring in views about what [was] happening in the CRM" and to "ensure full integration of the finance project with the CRM."

The traditional structure of project, program, and IS corporate governing body that defines boundaries for the realm of project, program, and central management could not achieve a particular resolution for the CRM issue. It was down to both projects (finance and CRM) to negotiate functionality, components, and delivery time. When they needed to negotiate visibility, the sponsoring business unit of CRM had to be included and agree to this issue since it became a financial matter and a question of whether the finance project should financially contribute to the CRM project as one of its beneficiaries. The hierarchy of IS project's governance had to be overcome to allow direct interaction between projects that previously seemed remote and unrelated.

5.2.2 Negotiating the Organization Structure

SAP in Posta was initiated as an outcome of an organization-wide restructuring program that began in 1998. In June 2000, the government enforced something new when it published a report that stated, "Posta should urgently take forward work to maximize the...efficiency of network operation." The government allocated £270 million for Posta to implement the report's recommendations over the following three years. To achieve the necessary efficient performance, Posta identified the urgent need to change the structure of its three distribution business units. The restructuring program suggested an initiative that would involve redesigning the three distribution business units and their amalgamation into one unit.

In February 2001, rumors started to spread within Posta that the organizational structure might change again and that the Posta board was studying the creation of a new entity, known here anonymously as "distribution unit." The three distribution business units that were said to be part of further restructuring (if the rumored new distribution unit came about) constituted the majority of phase one of the finance system implementation as the latter was comprised of four business units. The finance project team was also in contact with the business units at that time in order to finalize their requirements. The finance project director heard the rumor about the distribution unit and thought to find out something more definite in discussions with the enterprise system program director. The enterprise system program board met to discuss the issue and to assess the impact of creating this new business unit on the finance project but it could not confirm what would happen and "the impact assessment [was] deferred until the situation is clarified" (minutes of an enterprise system program board meeting).

In March 2001, the finance project director arranged a general meeting to announce that "as nothing is confirmed yet, we will go on with the financial project as it is." Accordingly, in April 2001, the finance project team contacted the three distribution units and prepared sessions to sign off their business requirements, although the project team realized that their requirements were evolving and what they agreed on at that time was subject to "potential...significant rework" (interview with project manager).

In June 2001, the Posta Board announced the creation of the distribution unit as a new business unit, incorporating three of the existing distribution BUs, with the aim of having it fully operational by the end of September 2001. Since the organizational re-design wouldn't be final before September 2001, the finance project board was aware that "the window of opportunity for finalizing their optimum design is diminishing, even if it is to be included in phase three of the system build (instead of the planned phase one)." Hence, the finance project agreed with the three distribution units involved in the reengineering that they should implement a "tactical solution...to meet their current immediate requirements subject to later changes." The finance project was aware that "many changes to the current thinking [would] occur and that many things in the system built would be undone when the final organization design [is] complete" (interview with the financial project's director and comments at a project board meeting and program board update meeting).

This shows that events outside Posta, such as a government report and corporate response of restructuring has become an internal matter for the finance project, crossing traditional organizational boundaries and structure. The finance project at the start followed the traditional, closed innovation model of raising the matter to its program management but this did not pay off. The enterprise system program had no means within the closed model to seek high-level information regarding organization strategy and structure. So the finance project had to negotiate the matter directly with the business units affected to agree on a temporary solution and account for the delay and further rework on the system after going live. In effect, the finance project had to break its predetermined organizational boundary to decide on its future course of action since the whole matter was beyond its program and even corporate IS strategy unit.

6 ANALYSIS: CLOSED OR OPEN INNOVATION?

This paper started by questioning the validity of the open innovation concept in IS projects as opposed to the closed model provided by IS project management methodologies. Through a case study of an ERP implementation in an international organization, we have observed that the traditional boundaries prespecified by project management methodologies were continually crossed. The case study reveals that the project boundaries themselves are malleable and negotiable and a project should be seen in the light of other projects within the organization. An IS project cannot be seen as only a single instance within the organization, the focus taken by most IS literature. Indeed, modern organizations present a busy platform where several projects take place at any point in time. The control notion that projects should be isolated and internally managed—as echoed in project management methodologies—misses the complexity of organizational

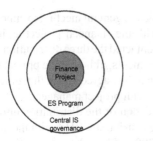
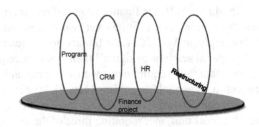

Closed Innovation View of Finance Project   Open Innovation View of Finance Project

Figure 1. Alternative Conceptualizations of the Finance Project

innovation. The reliance on integrated systems that oversee entire processes through what used to be traditionally separated functions and the complexity of these cross-functional, integrated software projects and their reliance on their particular implementation methodologies invites the inclusion of many different parties that were seen as outsiders in the closed model. Modern IS projects can no longer isolate themselves from the rest of the organization, relying on a lengthy command and control organizational structure. Projects need to overcome these barriers, to interact with each other in a horizontal manner.

The case study also shows that an IS project cannot isolate itself following a closed model for innovation where project management is defined by WBS, OBS, and a scheduling tool. The studied project extends its interaction beyond those boundaries to create its network of allies and finds ways to work collaboratively with them. The latter is in line with the open innovation model.

Figure 1 contrasts the closed innovation model, stemming from IS project management methodologies, with the open innovation model as observed in the studied case. The open innovation view of the finance project presents a network view of the project where the project seeks alliances, competes, and collaborates and in all cases negotiates with parties including (1) another project (HR) that traditionally was seen as part of the bundle of projects managed under one program (enterprise system), (2) its program management that was traditionally viewed as its governing body, (3) aother bundle of projects running under the management of a different program that was viewed in the traditional IS project management as a remote project under the governance of an IS corporate management, and (4) a corporate restructuring program that, in the traditional IS project management, was out of the realm of IS.

We have been observed in the case study that despite the existence of a traditional program management represented by the enterprise system program, colocated projects such as finance and HR continued to compete over resources. This contrasts with the stance of IS methodologies that the governance of a program ensures the fair allocation of resources between the projects involved (Cadle and Yeates 2004, pp. 52-62). The case study shows, in line with ANT propositions, that it is up to the individual project to extend its boundary and recruit powerful allies (Latour 1986, 1996). The prespecified project management structure of project and program has in effect little influence over project behavior. The finance project aligned powerful actors and created a favorable image within the organization that made potential recruits willing to join it rather than the low-key HR project. These powerful allies also helped the finance project to secure generous desk space. In effect, the HR project found itself in a weak competitive position where it had to request help from the program board. The program board could not interfere with the powerful network of corporate executives that the finance project recruited or with the image it created of itself as being "essential for the survival" of the company in the future. Therefore the enterprise system program role was limited to recognizing the problem and gently requesting that the finance project help without putting any pressure on it. The competition between HR and finance denies the view of IS project management methodologies of control over resource allocation between projects based on a command and control model that assumes projects have strict boundaries and program management will be able to exercise power over its managed projects to distribute resources. In contrast, the case study supports the ANT model of network building and negotiation (Latour 1996). It shows that each project has, in principle, the possibility to scale itself up through the creation of powerful allies. In doing so, a project bypasses the traditional, mundane organizational structure imposed by the closed model of project management. It asserts that an IS project is an open innovation that crosses traditional boundaries to recruit different actors that contribute to its success.

The assumption that program methodology presents a global context outside the project's control and that projects should only follow their governing program is also in doubt. The case study illustrated that off-the-shelf packages and, in particular, large integrated systems such as SAP come to organizations with their own methodology and support network. Implementing such a system would bring a well-established network to the organization, enhancing the negotiation power of such a project. As the case study shows, the finance project, supported by the SAP network, managed to create a negotiation space between itself and its governing program to debate its managing methodology. This process shifted the project management methodology to be an inside matter for the finance project to decide upon and not to be ruled by its governing body, the enterprise system program. This is in line with ANT proposition that the inside and outside are negotiated and it is up to actors to decide what is inside and what is outside (Law 1992). This supports the open innovation model, where a project such as ERP extends beyond the organization boundary to include partners and allies (Chesbrough 2003), then negotiates and shifts its traditional boundary.

The billing function was supposed to be a local, private matter for the finance project. It was part of the SAP technology under implementation and hence was assumed to fell within its boundary. This view was in doubt when it was discovered that the customer data base that the SAP billing functionality relied upon was held in the Siebel system of the CRM project. What once appeared to be an inside matter for the finance project to decide turned out to be a point of negotiation that required the involvement of many external parties, including CRM project management, the CRM business unit sponsor, and corporate strategy. Within an open innovation model, no boundaries are guaranteed or immune. Boundaries cannot be black boxed (Vidgen and McMaster 1996), any could be opened and negotiated and new ones created accordingly. In the studied case, the negotiation ended by agreeing that the customer data base would continue to be held in Siebel and the finance project would create work-arounds to achieve semifunctional billing until the implementation of its last phase, when it would interface the

SAP system with the Siebel system to configure a final solution for the billing function. The finance project decided afterward to collaborate with the CRM project and have a member of staff from the CRM regularly attend the finance project meetings. The need for both projects to collaborate is not supported by the methodologies. It represents a new phenomenon where participants in the field found the closed innovation model unsupportive and intuitively decided that collaborating would be more productive so they decided to exchange representatives. This finding supports the open innovation view of breaking the silos and actively seeking collaboration.

Organization structure used to be seen as a context for project implementation and part of the business requirements that need to be specified and captured in the early stages of the project. In Posta, there was another program taking place to restructuring the organization. The finance project, when faced with the rumors regarding change of organizational structure, followed the traditional project structure of raising the issue with its enterprise system program, which in turn raised it with corporate IS strategy. This route did not pay off and the finance project had to open up its boundary to treat the affected business units as partners (not clients, as in the traditional view), to discuss with them possibilities and a future course of action. This presents another instance where the open innovation model surfaced in the case study, with the project including its clients as partners and openly discussing with them the high uncertainty of the situation affecting project delivery and agreeing on a future scenario.

7   CONCLUSION

This study shows that large, integrated IS innovation follows in practice the advocated open innovation model and not the closed model that project management methodologies support. It reveals that project boundaries are flexible, changeable, and negotiable. There are no rigid, prespecified boundaries as project management assumed. In practice, IS projects are in constant negotiation of boundaries as different organizational actors emerge to renegotiate the previously set boundaries. Therefore, the inside and outside of the project are the result of negotiation rather than a preset decision of project management or program management. This negotiation and setting of boundaries tends to be a continuous activity rather than being static and imposed on IS project.

The study contributes to IS project management by uncovering the open space of innovation that an IS project sails through during its course. The perception of an IS project as an open innovation provides a dynamic, flatter view of IS project innovation and its management structure. It departs it from the silo view suggested by IS project management and the traditional organization of project and program. Accordingly, an individual IS project should actively and continuously span this open space to detect collaborators, rivals, and partners. This study provides an explanation of White and Fortune's (2002) study where 46 percent of respondents reported that their project gave rise to unexpected side effects or outputs and that nearly 70 percent of the side effects could be attributed either directly or indirectly to lack of awareness of the environment. They concluded that "this may imply that many of the tools and techniques the respondents used were poor at modeling 'real world' problems or that insufficient account was taken of project boundaries and environments" (p. 5). Indeed, this study shows that tools that focus on scheduling and cost are not enough to manage projects in the complex, open innovation space of today's organization. Mechanisms for spanning and scanning the project landscape need to be incorporated into project management practices and awareness needs to be increased that an IS project is no longer a local matter that can be treated as a closed innovation isolated from the rest of the organization. It should be noted that the inclusion of partnerships and alliances in the project does not always mean collaboration, but could bring rivalry that should be recognized and accounted for.

The study also contributes to the very thin strand of studies that consider the management of IS projects in multiple project environment. It provides a practice lens and theoretical grounding to the Desouza and Evaristo (2004) study on project knowledge management. Indeed, knowledge in and about projects should be exchanged and individual projects should actively scan the organizational open space for other projects that constitute possible collaborators, rivals, and partners. On the practice side, the study suggests the creation of a "project scout" role within each project to provide a broad view of the organization that crosses traditional boundaries and structures.

References

Cadle, J., and Yeates, D. 2004. *Project Management for Information Systems* (4th ed.), New York: Prentice Hall/Financial Times

Calas, M. B., and Smircich, L. 1999. "Past Postmodernism? Reflections and Tentative Directions," *Academy of Management Review* (24:4), pp. 649-671.

Callon, M. 1991. "Techno-Economic Networks and Irreversibility," in *A Sociology of Monsters: Essays on Power, Technology and Domination*, J. Law (ed.), London: Routledge, pp. 132-161.

Chesbrough, H. 2003. *Open Innovation: The New Imperative for Creating and Profiting from Technology*, Boston: Harvard Business School Press.

Chesbrough, H., Vanhaverbeke, W., and West, J. (eds.). 2006. *Open Innovation: Researching a New Paradigm*, New York: Oxford University Press.

Cijsouw, R. S., Jorna, R. J., Rakhorst, G., and Verkerke, G. J. 2007. "Omissions in Managing Knowledge in Innovation Processes or How to Handle Knowledge, Humans, and Tasks: A Semio-Cognitive Approach," in *Project Management and Risk Management in Complex Projects*, P.-J. Charrel and D. Galarreta (eds.), Boston: Springer, pp. 15-45.

Damm, D., and Schindler, M. 2002. "Security Issues of a Knowledge Medium for Distributed Project Work," *International Journal of Project Management* (20), pp. 37-47.

Desouza, K. C., and Evaristo, J. R. 2004. "Managing Knowledge in Distributed Projects," *Communications of the ACM* (47:4), pp. 87-91.

Dooley, L., Lupton, G., and O'Sullivan, D. 2005. "Multiple Project Management: A Modern Competitive Necessity," *Journal of Manufacturing Technology Management* (15:4), pp. 466-482.

Evaristo, R., and van Fenema, P. C. 1999. "A Typology of Project Management: Emergence and Evolution of New Forms," *International Journal of Project Management* (17:5), pp. 275-281.

Garrety, K., Robertson, P. L., and Badham, R. 2004. "Integrating Communities of Practice in Technology Development Projects," *International Journal of Project Management* (22), pp. 351-358.

Gibbons, M., Limoges, C., Nowotny, H., Schwarzman, S., Scott, P., and Trow, M. 1994. *The New Production of Knowledge*, Newbury Park, CA: Sage Publications.

Henriksen, H. Z., and Kautz, K. 2006. "An Analysis of IFIP TC8 WG 8.6: In Search of a Common Theoretical Denominator," in *The Past and Future of Information Systems: 1976-2006 and Beyond*, D. Avison, S. Elliot, J. Krogstie, and J. Pries-Heje (eds.), , Boston: Springer, pp. 143-152.

Hobday, M. 2000. "The Project-Based Organization: An Ideal Form for Managing Complex Products and Systems?," *Research Policy* (29), pp. 871-893.

Kaplan, B., and Maxwell, J. A. 1994. "Qualitative Research Methods for Evaluating Computer Information Systems," in *Evaluating Health Care Information Systems: Methods and Applications*, S. J. Jay (ed.), Thousand Oaks, CA: Sage Publications, pp. 45-68.

Latour, B. 1986. "The Powers of Association," in *Power, Action and Belief: A New Sociology of Knowledge*, J. Law (ed.), London: Routledge & Kegan Paul, pp. 264-280.

Latour, B. 1987. *Science in Action: How to Follow Scientists and Engineers Through Society*, Cambridge, MA: Harvard University Press.

Latour, B. 1991. "Technology is Society Made Durable," in *Sociology of Monsters: Essays on Power, Technology and Domination*. J. Law (ed.), London: Routledge & Kegan Paul, pp. 103-131.

Latour, B. 1996. *Aramis or the Love of Technology*, Boston: Harvard University Press.

Law, J. 1987. "Technology and Heterogeneous Engineering: The Case of the Portuguese Expansion," in *The Social Construction of Technological Systems: New Directions in the Sociology and History of Technology*, W. E. Bijker, T. P. Hughes, and T. Pinch (eds.), Cambridge, MA: MIT Press, pp. 111-134.

Law, J. 1992. "The Olympus 320 Engine: A Case Study in Design, Development, and Organizational Control," *Technology and Culture* (33:3), pp. 409-440.

Law, J., and Callon, M. 1988. "Engineering and Sociology in a Military Aircraft Project: A Network Analysis of Technological Change," *Social Problems* (35:3), pp. 284-297.

Masini, A., and Pich, M. T. 2004. "The Diffusion of Competing Technological Innovations in a Network: Exploration Versus Exploitation Revisited," working paper, London Business School WP OTM 04-021.

Meredith, J. R., and Mantel, J. S. 1995. *Project Management: A Nanagerial Approach*, New York: Wiley.

Miles, M. B., and Huberman, A. M. 1994. *Qualitative Data Analysis: An Expanded Sourcebook*, Newbury Park, CA: Sage Publications.

Olson, D. L. 2004. *Introduction to Information Systems Project Management*, New York: McGraw-Hill/Irwin.

Payne, J. H. 1995. "Management of Multiple Simultaneous Projects: A State-of-the-Art Review," *International Journal of Project Management* (13:3), pp. 163-168.

Rothwell, R. 1994. "Towards the Fifth-Generation Innovation Process," *International Marketing Review* (11:1), pp. 7-31.

Steyn, H. 2002. "Project Management Applications of the Theory of Constraints Beyond Critical Chain Scheduling," *International Journal of Project Management* (20), pp. 75-80.

Swan, J., and Scarbrough, H. 2005. "The Politics of Networked Innovation," *Human Relations* (58:7), pp. 913-943.

Vidgen, R., and McMaster, T. 1996. "Black Boxes, Non-Human Stakeholders and the Translation of IT Through Mediation," in *Information Technology and Change in Organizational Work*, W. J. Orlikowski, G. Walsham, M. R. Jones, and J. I. DeGross (eds.), London: Chapman and Hall, pp. 250-271.

Walsham, G. 1993. *Interpreting Information Systems in Organizations*, Chichester, UK: John Wiley & Sons Ltd.

Walsham, G. 1995. "Interpretive Case Studies in IS Research: Nature and Method," *European Journal of Information Systems* (4), pp. 74-81.

White, D., and Fortune, J. 2002. "Current Practice in Project Management: An Empirical Study," *International Journal of Project Management* (20),. pp. 1-11.

Wynn, E., and Fitzgerald, B. 2004. "IT Innovation for Adaptability and Competitiveness," in *IT Innovation for Adaptability and Competitiveness*, B. Fitzgerald and E. Wynn (eds.), Norwell, MA: Kluwer Academic Publishers, pp. xxv-xxxix.

About the Author

Amany Elbanna is a lecturer in information systems at the Business School at Loughborough University. Her current research is in the area of project management of large IS projects, packaged software implementation, and agile software development. Amany can be reached by e-mail at a.elbanna@lboro.ac.uk.

Part 9

Public Administration and Government

25 PUBLIC PROCUREMENT OF IS/IT SERVICES: Past Research and Future Challenges

Josep M. Marco-Simó
Joan A. Pastor
Rafael Macau
Universitat Oberta de Catalunya
Barcelona, Spain

Abstract   *In this paper we present the current state-of-the-art situation of research in public administration procurement of functions and services related to information systems and information technologies. From this review, we propose a list of open research issues according to our beliefs and practical experience. Finally we introduce a real case that we are starting to address, in which we want to consider both prior results as well as research issues. We believe that the topic of IS/IT procurement in public administration is an open area that has not received enough attention from the research community, according to the great amount of public money that is being invested.*

Keywords   Public procurement methods, IS and IT services, outsourcing in public administration

1 INTRODUCTION AND THE IMPORTANCE OF PUBLIC IS/IT PROCUREMENT

In this paper we present the current state-of-the-art of research in public administration procurement of functions and services related to information systems and information technologies. From this review we present a tentative list of open research issues

Please use the following format when citing this chapter:

Marco-Simó, M., Pastor, Joan A., and Macau, R., 2008, in IFIP International Federation for Information Processing, Volume 287, Open IT-Based Innovation: Moving Towards Cooperative IT Transfer and Knowledge Diffusion, eds. León, G., Bernardos, A., Casar, J., Kautz, K., and DeGross, J. (Boston: Springer), pp. 443-460.

and we introduce the real-life case that we are starting to address, to which we want to apply both prior results as well as open issues.

In a common trend shared with private enterprises, during the 1980s public administration organizations (PAOs) started experimenting with outsourcing as a way to acquire their IS and IT goods and services (Beyah and Gallivan 2001; Hancox and Hackney 1999). The basic purpose of outsourcing is to externalize those organizational activities that are not directly related to the core competences of the organization. The core competences of a PAO are those related to giving the citizen final services, not necessarily by *doing* these services, but *managing their acquisition and control*. Thus, the PAO needs IS and IT to develop internal functions as well as to provide citizens with external services, which could be considered a target to be outsourced (i.e., to be procured or acquired from external service companies). In general, the inherent risks and opportunities of outsourcing have been studied and rules for managing it are clearly drawn up (Lee et al. 2003), so IS/IT outsourcing is seen as a reliable option for the general case.

Currently, PAOs are investing great amounts of public money on IS and IT. According to a report by the Gartner Group (Sood 2007), the U.S. federal government spent $66 billion on IS/IT goods and services in 2006 and 11 percent of professional personal computers worldwide were purchased by government agencies. The report also mentions that the procurement of such systems and services is mainly done through market suppliers.

Given these data and from an economic point of view, at least two arguments appear in order to defend the importance of paying attention to this topic:

- Efficiency of the management of public money. Monitoring its correct use is one of the social requirements that governments must accomplish in order to address the usual citizens' concerns about PAOs.
- Leadership of PAOs as a great IS consumer. PAOs can become leaders in promoting positive changes in the way that IS outsourcing is performed. For example,
  - By including adequate references to methodologies or standards in IS calls-for-tenders (i.e., CMMI, ITIL, or COBIT), as a compulsory and valuable requirement to accepting bids from possible providers. This automatically increases the perceived importance and interest of those methodologies or standards within the IS industry.
  - By developing and following some specific methodologies for the PAO acquisition process, such as Euromethod (Helmerich 1998), ISPL (Dekker 2002), or CMMI-ACQ (Hoffman 2007).

From a scientific research point of view, it is interesting to know how IS outsourcing in PAO literature has described issues such as

- Its actual application to real cases. For example by locating, depicting, analyzing, and comparing different real experiences or case studies; by adapting existing theories (from economic ones, such as agency or transaction costs, to organizational ones, such as social exchange or power politics); by describing innovation within IS outsourcing practices (from qualifying providers to monitoring relationships), following trends (from total to selective outsourcing, from global to local out-sourcing), or studying the use of IS/IT outsourcing methodologies or relevant stan-dards (from specific ones like ISPL to general ones such as CMMI or ITIL).

• Contextual and idiosyncratic similarities and differences between the public and the private sector influence the application of IS outsourcing. For example, trying to find if accepted trends exist that work in the private sector but that cannot be applied to the public one, or that have a different level of usefulness in this specific context.

• The existence of specific recommendation frameworks for IS outsourcing in PAOs, through adapting the accepted approaches in private sectors, or by developing new ones.

A deeper knowledge on the above issues will help us to face an updated research agenda and also can give us some clues about which items could be interesting to analyze in future case studies.

The paper is organized as follows. In section 2 we present, describe, and contextua-lize all prior research that we have found directly related to PAO procurement of IS/IT services. By following the same classification of issues, in section 3 we provide, according to our conceptual point of view and our practical experience, a list of open issues to be considered for further research. In section 4 we introduce an initial explana-tion of the context of the case that we are undertaking, a case where we are considering all of the issues addressed in prior research as well as open research issues. We end by presenting some short conclusions.

2 PAST RESEARCH IN PUBLIC ADMINISTRATION PROCUREMENT OF IS/IT SERVICES

2.1 Quantitative Summarization of Past Research

In this section, we present an up-to-date review of prior research in PAO procure-ment of IS/IT services. After this rather straightforward quantitative enumeration and classification of related research, in the next section we will provide a qualitative and more commented review.

A recent paper on IS outsourcing in PAOs (Marco-Simó et al. 2007) already selected and commented in detail on those prior contributions published in scientific IS journals having to do with IS outsourcing specifically in PAOs. That study used sources given by Dibbern et al. (2004) and González et al. (2006), and used as keywords both the general term *outsourcing*, as well as its derivatives and other related names (*sourcing, insourcing, cosourcing, offshoring, nearshoring,* and *externalization*), as well as other terms more specifically related to *procurement*, as one of the first phases within out-sourcing projects (such as *acquisition, supply,* and *contract*). These keywords were used not only in title, abstract, and keyword searches, but also in the content of the entire paper.

While keeping the same search keywords and browsing carefully journal and con-ference contents, in this paper we augment the scope of our bibliographic review, both in a longitudinal and temporal way, by including papers from scientific public administration journals, international IS congresses, and some other scientific journals usually addressing issues within PA and IS, such as those related to IFIP Working Group WG8.5 (Information Systems in Public Administration).

Additionally, by following the thread of references, we have also located other papers in sources different from those originally addressed and mentioned above, that is, sources outside of our established scope and basically within the general management field. These other sources, however, have not been reviewed to find more relevant references. In order to expand our knowledge of the context, in future extensions of this work we plan to examine other sources not usually considered as research sources. Among these sources we consider publications that address professionals and publications delivered by large government bodies and organizations, for example, OECD.

As an initial quantitative description and following our review process, Tables 1 and 2 summarize the papers we found related to PAO procurement of IS/IT services.

A first and straightforward consideration is that the number of relevant references is not great, with a total of 33 research contributions from 1993 to the present. Figure 1 represents quantitatively those papers along their publication year and classified in terms of the main field (PA, IS, or management) and nature (journal or congress) of their source.

Taking into account Tables 1 and 2, Figure 1, and the specific sources, we observe that the 33 papers are quite dispersed, both in terms of source type (at the most, three papers come from a single journal or congress in the analyzed period) and time (at the most, five references were published in a single year, in 2002). IS journals have addressed the issue with more papers than PA journals (more specifically from 1996 to 2002). In fact, PA journals have included relevant papers less intensively and more sporadically, since they concentrate more on PA social, legal, and citizen service aspects, rather than on operational and technological themes.

All in all, journal publications in our addressed topic have been very few, while IS congresses have addressed it with more references, more regularly in the past years. It is significant from Table 1 that many well-known journals from PA and IS have not published yet a single contribution in PA procurement of IS/IT services. After checking all of the publications listed on the IFIP Working Group WG 8.5 website, we have to remark that none of them includes a single paper on this topic.

2.2 Qualitative Discussion of Past Research

In the previous section, we accounted for a total of 33 papers, irrespective of their relative relevance in qualitative terms such as orientation, depth, rigor or novelty of the contributions. After analyzing them along these lines, we conclude that only 10 papers can be considered as highly relevant, while another set of 7 papers are of medium relevance to our topic, with the others being of lesser interest to our research, for various reasons.

In any case, as discussed here, we detect a clear dispersion of subtopics in which the papers are focused, as well as of their respective research approaches. We attempt to group and classify in the following subsections the various contributions of the 17 most relevant papers, where subsections account for the diverse relevant classification categories that we have drawn from the study.

Table 1. References from Scientific Information Systems and Public Administration Journals

Source	Period Reviewed	Field	Author	Year
Communications of ACM	1992-2007	IS	Slaughter and Ang	1996
European Journal of Information Systems	1996-2007	IS	Currie	1996
			Willcocks and Kern	1998
			Allen et al.	2002
Information Systems Journal	1996-2007	IS	Lacity and Willcocks	1997
			Hancox and Hackney	2000
Journal of Information Technology	1988-2007	IS	De Looff	1995
			Lewis	1999
			Domberger et al.	2000
International Journal of Information Management	1998-2005	IS	No references found	
Industrial Management and Data Systems	1998-2005	IS	No references found	
Information and Management	1998-2005	IS	No references found	
Information and Organization	1998-2005	IS	No references found	
Information Systems Research	1998-2005	IS	No references found	
Journal of Management Information Systems	1998-2005	IS	No references found	
MIS Quarterly	1998-2005	IS	No references found	
Public Administration Review	2000-2007	PA	Globerman and Vining	1996
International Journal of Public Administration	1988-2007	PA	Danzinger and Andersen	2002
Public Administration	1988-2007	PA	Willcocks	1994
Information Polity(Information Infrastructure and Policy)	1996-2007	PA	Pawlowska	2004
			Peled	2000
Journal of Public Procurement	2001-2007	PA	No references found	
Journal of Public Administration Research and Theory	1991-2004	PA	No references found	
Government Information Quarterly	1996-2007	PA	No references found	
International Journal of Public Sector Management	1989-2007	PA	No references found	
British Journal of Management		Mgmt	Willcocks and Currie	1997
Decision Support Systems Journal		Mgmt	Rapcsak and Zagi	2000
Revista Venezolana de Gerencia		Mgmt	Andrade and Mandrillo	2004

Table 2. Reference from Scientific Information Systems Congresses

Source	Period Reviewed	Author	Year
International Conference on Information Systems	2001-2007	Zmud et al.	2004
		Seddon et al.	2002
Hawaii International Conference on Information Systems Science.	1999-2007	Hancox and Hackney	1999
		Beyah and Gallivan	2001
		Lindskog	2005
		Moon et al.	2007
Americas Conference on Information Systems	1995-2007	Dertz et al.	2003
		Chen	2002
		Alexander	2002
		Chen and Gant	2001
		Lawry et al.	2007
European Conference on Information Systems	1993-2007	Lewis	1998
		Davies	1993
		Willcocks and Kern	1997
		Guah and Currie	2007
European and Mediterranean Conference on Information Systems	2004-2007	No references found	
Pacific-Asian Conference on Information Systems	1993-2005	No references found	
IFIP World Conference on IT Tools		De Looff	1996

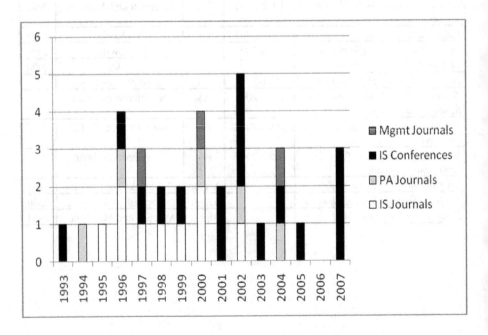

Figure 1. Amount of References, by Year, Field, and Source Type

2.2.1 Typology of Case Studies and Related Research

As usual in the research of other issues in IS, we found significant use of case studies in the contributions reviewed. Table 3 presents both the use type of these case studies and the underlying research method used for their analysis. The table also shows the geographical area of each case, as well as the administrative level of the public administration considered in the case (national/central government; state/regional government; local/municipal government).

Evident from this review is that most of the cases come from English-speaking countries, with a total of eight cases, with only three cases from other places (continental Europe, Israel, and Korea). With regard to administrative level, there are eight cases at central PA level, two at the regional level, and six at the local level. However, it should be noted that in some countries the scope and administrative responsibilities of municipalities are very extensive and can be comparable to those of regional governments in other areas or countries. Thus, in a global sense, our classification of cases in administrative levels is a rough one, more generally descriptive than clear and precise.

If we consider the research purpose of the case studies, three have a mere descriptive intention with some derived recommendations, four are used to validate a hypothesis or framework previously defined, and six bear a more complex purpose. In particular, these latter cases are used either to derive proposals for critical success or risk factors, or to derive conceptual frameworks, and the cases serve to illustrate the proposed factors or frameworks.

The research approaches used are mainly qualitative, including the in-depth case study research method, but up to four cases have been studied with quantitative methods at some points. Table 3 details research techniques for these cases.

2.2.2 Differences Between PAOs and Private Companies

One of the recurreing issues in these cases is the differences between the public and the private sectors with regard to IS/IT procurement, and if these differences are significant enough as to justify the development of different theories. It is clear that, according to this review, this is still an open issue.

This topic was directly addressed by Zmud et al. (2004) in a panel at the International Conference on Information Systems. Along a different line, we have found in Davies (1993) the first reference relevant in the topic, with the assumption of a clear difference between PAOs and private companies. Hancox and Hackney (1999, 2000) present a comparison between PAOs and the private sector from the point of view of four different conceptual frameworks. In a similar way, Moon et al. (2007) compare some conclusions about success factors with general beliefs of IT sourcing in the private sector.

The main argument for questioning the differentiation of procurement between PAOs and the private sector is the fact that many aspects that look particular to PAOs also appear in private institutions with similarities to PAOs (for instance, bureaucratic private companies or large companies). These aspects have been addressed by some of the research examined.

- A common shortage of IS management skills, specifically in procurement decisions (offer, supplier study, selection) (De Looff 1996; Lacity and Willcocks 1997)

Table 3. Case Study Typology with Research Approaches

Author	Year	Country	PA Level	Main Research Purpose	Methodological Aspects
Lacity and Willcocks	1997	USA	Central, Regional	Description, comparison and recommendation	Case-study construction, qualitative, interpretivist, short temporal span
Chen	2002	USA	Local	Hypothesis validation/ contrast (on success factors)	Survey, quantitative
Currie	1996	UK	Central Local	Description, recommendation	In-depth case analysis, qualitative, interviews and questionaires
Willcocks and Currie	1997	UK	Central	Hypothesis validation/ contrast (on success factors), description, recommendation	In-depth case analysis and construction, qualitative, interviews, interpretivist, long temporal span
Willcocks and Kern	1997, 1998	UK	Central	Hypothesis validation/ contrast (on critical dimensions), description, recommendation	In-depth case analysis, qualitative, interviews, interpretivist, long temporal span
Hancox and Hackney	1999, 2000	UK	Local	Application of conceptual frameworks, comparison, conclusions	Qualitative, interviews
Lewis	1999	Australia	Central	Proposal of method for evaluating tenders, descriptive contrast of the method	Personal application and experience with the method in two cases
Domberger et al.	2000	Australia	Regional	Proposal of method for validation/contrast of other authors' prior generalizations	Qualitative, interviews
De Looff	1995	Holland	Local	Proposal of framework, with its contrast in the case study	In-depth case analysis, qualitative, interviews, interpretivist, long temporal span
Dertz et al.	2003	Norway	Local	Description of decision criteria for acquisition	Surveys
Peled	2000	Israel	Central, Local	Proposal of models, description of cases, proposed models exemplification	Analysis of described cases
Pawlowska	2004	Poland	Central	Description of large-scale project cases, failure causes analysis	Analysis of public reports
Moon et al	2007	Korea	Central	Proposal of success factors framework	Analysis of documentation, surveys, quantitative

- Volatility and dependence of political tendencies and context (Beyah and Gallivan 2001; Looff 1996; Lacity and Willcocks 1997; Willcocks and Kern 1997, 1998)
- Long duration of development projects (mainly of bespoke software development and packaged software implementation), which implies that projects usually survive their leaders (Beyah and Gallivan 2001)
- Difficulties in the retention of specialists (PAOs usually pay less than the private sector) (Currie 1996; De Looff 1996; Lacity and Willcocks 1997)
- Lack of cooperation between departments within the same PAO with similar IS/IT procurement needs, as is often the case within private companies (De Looff, (1996)
- The fact that geographic location usually reduces the amount of providers with relevant skills for the service to be procured, which often implies that local developments become the only alternative (Dertz et al. 2003)
- Specificity and complexity of needs/solutions relevant to both situations (De Looff 1996)

On the other hand, there are aspects that are accepted as clearly exclusive in the PAO domain.

- Public control of the tasks undertaken, of their management and their results (Beyah and Gallivan 2001; Lacity and Willcocks 1997)
- Wherever happens, the mandatory nature of some outsourcing plans of some PAOs, such as the case of Compulsory Competitive Tendering in Great Britain (Currie 1996) and the National Performance Review in the United States (Hancox and Hackney 1999, 2000)

2.2.3 Services to Outsource/Procure and Reasons for Doing So

Whenever an organization confronts the possibility of undertaking the outsourcing of some of its IS/IT services, the first questions that arise are those related to the scope of such an externalization. That is, whether a wide service area should be externalized (total outsourcing) or if only some chosen functions or services should (selective sourcing), and in this case, which ones are the best candidates.

While total outsourcing was the first default option, because of pressures for reducing costs in PAOs, it can also have many drawbacks. Foremost, total outsourcing can make the organization highly dependent on providers, with the implied risks. The *de facto* monopolistic nature of this option may derive in losing control of IS/IT strategic decisions (Willcocks and Currie 1997).

In the light of the studied cases and some of the reported experiences with total outsourcing, most of them far from successful, selective sourcing appears as a more reasonable option (Beyah and Gallivan 2001). In fact, Willcocks and Kern (1997, 1998) present in their conclusions their clear belief that PAOs in the United Kingdom in the mid-1990s were only ready to successfully manage short-span contracts in the context of selective sourcing.

Regarding those IS/IT services or functions that can be outsourced, there is a clear consensus about the starting point, which are commodities, that is, those IS/IT functions that are not considered as core to the business or PA service mission (Davies 1993; Dertz et al. 2003; Willcocks 1994; Willcocks and Currie 1997). These functions, which include the procurement and operation of IT infrastructures (such as hardware, networks, and basic software) are easier to outsource because they are more tangible, they can be delimited, and they usually have wider and less specialized offerings. Under these circumstances, it becomes viable to accomplish the main advantages of outsourcing: costs advantages, access to expertise, quality of service, adaptability to changes, and core business concentration. Plus, with this option, relationships can usually be restricted to relatively short contracts, from 1 to 5 years, a period that is usual in other types of procurement contracts. More complex or longer projects, given their volume or when they imply very specific software development, are clearly inconvenient: only a few providers, usually very large, can address them (Globerman and Vining 1996; Pawlowska 2007). In these cases, we have as key factors the management of their inherent risk, the formulation of a correct contract, and the adequate management of such a contract over that long period.

Irrespective of what is outsourced, up to what level, and of the underlying motivations, from the structure of PAOs, there are basically two different situations that will condition the outsourcing politics and their adaptation:

- Given that PAOs usually have problems in hiring and keeping the best professionals (for several reasons such as public hiring constraints and salary limitations), outsourcing becomes a good alternative to obtain these competencies from a service provider (Chen 2002; De Looff 1996; Slaughter and Ang 1996). In other words, often PAOs may not spend their budgets on new personnel but can spend similar or greater amounts for contracting externally the service.
- Outsourcing becomes an alternative to overcome PAO inflexibilities and to promote change in the bureaucratic procedures, in order to introduce new management processes or tendencies, such as those under the label of e-government (Chen 2002).

2.2.4 Practices, Methods, and Methodologies

On a conceptual level, the following actions are among those considered successful behaviors, practices, and customer attitudes when facing outsourcing projects:

- To avoid running too fast toward outsourcing agreements, for example, by believing uncritically in market trends promoted by private providers when PAO investment decays or in easy cost or performance improvements, all in all ignoring experiences of failure in the private sector (Willcocks 1994; Willcocks and Currie 1997).
- The deep involvement of IS/IT executives, since their responsibility cannot also be externalized by outsourcing strategic analyses and decisions to the provider or to the technical staff (Chen 2002; Davies 1993).
- The need to adapt the CIO role to the particular characteristics of the PAO (Lawry et al. 2007), in order to align it to the specific PAO demands. This adaptation includes increasing the number of responsibilities related to the management of solutions, projects, risks, and portfolios; the promotion of standardization processes; the depicting of outsourcing agreements; or the assessment of the delivered services to the final users.

- The need to establish within the organization of a strong team with adequate management responsibilities and skills with regard to typical outsourcing processes: offer preparation, analysis of providers, provider selection, contract negotiation and preparation, project monitoring, etc. (Davies 1993; Pawlowska 2004; Willcocks 1994; Willcocks and Currie 1997).
- The need to establish and maintain within the organization a technically strong team that could eventually opt for in-sourcing some projects; in other words, that could present an internal offer in competition with the external providers and win it (Willcocks and Currie 1997).

In short, this means becoming what Willcocks and Currie (1997) call a successful *contractual organization*—changing IS/IT management within the PAO in order to end up with a less rigid organization, with less tendency to conflict and with more adaptability.

In a more detailed manner, but also along the same line, Hancox and Hackney (1999, 2000) present four conceptual frameworks (not just for PAOs) that may help to study the nature and form of outsourcing projects, to make decisions, and to manage the process.

- Core competences: In order to choose the functions and services to be outsourced, basically those that are not central to the activity of the organization and that may not report competitive advantages (Davies 1993; Dertz et al. 2003; Willcocks 1994; Willcocks and Currie 1997). Since certain uses or developments of IS and IT can eventually provide competitive advantages for some organizations, outsourcing decisions have to be taken with care and consideration to these issues.
- Transaction costs economics: In order to decide which is the best offer, not just thinking about production costs, but also about those costs for establishing and maintaining the outsourcing relationship. Among the factors that increase these coordinating costs are the specificity level of the product or service outsourced as well as the uncertainty in its development (Globerman and Vining 1996).
- Agency theory: In order to ensure maximum control in the outsourcing relationship, the contract details regarding expected behaviors and results become key to success, taking into account that the outsourcing customer and provider usually have business goals that do not always converge, with each party looking after their own interests.
- Partnership: In order to facilitate the maximum possible understanding and co-responsibility in their relationship, such a partnership must be seen as a strategic alliance by fostering the convergence and sharing of project goals among customer and provider. In other words, rather than just signing a contract (fast and too optimistically), it is much better for each party to take their time in writing the correct one, so that their relationship becomes more authentic and strategic, working toward a network organization work structure with a win–win philosophy (Davies 1993; Willcocks 1994; Willcocks and Kern 1997, 1998).

Along this same outsourcing materialization level, Lewis (1999) proposes a method based on the preventive and anticipative evaluation of those risks associated with the offer (such as uncertainty and inadequate use of requirements, technical limitations of providers, overcosts and overruns in the tender process, among others), thus also anti-cipating the appropriate redresses if any of those risks arise. Also with regard to risks,

Pawlowska (2007) presents a study of failed cases from the point of view of decision-making theory and of organizational theory.

Finally, in a more procedural and evaluative level, we find the proposal of Domberger et al. (2000), who present a quantitative method in the context of commodity outsourcing, with the aim of determining factors and relevancy measures around price and contract performance.

3   OPEN LIST OF FUTURE CHALLENGES

We believe that there is still plenty of room for more detailed research in outsourcing IS/IT services by PAOs, not just because of the relatively small volume of published research but also because there a need for more results in this particular growing trend. From the review of prior literature, and from our own experience, we present below an open list of possible research topics, classified by the same categories used in the previous section. We want to remark here that this is a tentative list, a starting point that should be validated in future work. We also make this attempt given that we have not found any similar proposal of general future challenges in our review work. We rely more directly on the third author of this paper, Rafael Macau, who held during many years the position of CEO for an IS/IT public company established by the Catalan autonomous government, and who was in charge of organizing and putting into practice a total outsourcing project for the unit. He has also held several executive posts in global IS/IT services companies. Thus, he has plenty of experience with both sides of IS/IT procurement.

3.1   Typology of Case Studies and Related Research

- Many more cases of PAO procurement of IS/IT services should be reported and studied in detail. Those cases should be compiled in wide case base.
- Both current and future cases should be analyzed and grouped by the related PA domains and, by comparing and cross-analyzing them, a first list of common and particular trends should be derived.
- Further analysis and in-depth comparison of the few existing conceptual frameworks should be pursued, eventually generating a general and more inclusive framework for future qualitative validation with reported cases.
- The few research frameworks should be extended and adapted for validating quantitatively those points in PAO IS/IT procurement that prove amenable to this type of validation.

3.2   Differences Between PA and Private Companies

- An issue that requires additional research attention is the relevancy and applicability to PAOs of those assumptions and procedures that seem to work for IS/IT procurement in private companies.

- In the reverse direction, study when some assumptions and procedures usually considered in PAOs could also be useful for private situations, as indicated by the growth of eProcurement projects also in private companies.
- To continue questioning and validating the importance of those aspects that some authors consider as differing in PAOs from private companies, so that in the future this can justify the need or not of separate theories for the two situations.

3.3 Services to Outsource/Procure and Reasons for Doing So

- To describe and report on the criteria used for deciding and managing (total or selective) outsourcing agreements, and to study the differences according to PAO levels.
- To study if there exist differences in the procurement decision depending on the final user of the procured service: civil servants (internal use) or citizens (external use, such as that of eGovernment systems).
- To define and study the perception and expectations of the outsourcing parts, and stakeholders in general, and to validate whether they are confirmed or not, and more specifically with regard to better access to professional competencies as well as avoidance of organizational inflexibilities.

3.4 Practices, Methods, and Methodologies

- To report and analyze the usage level and impact of the use by PAOs for IS/IT procurement of relevant standards and methods that have appeared in the past, such as Euromethod, ISPL, CMMI, COBIT, and ITIL. Note that we have not found any contribution to this subject in our state-of-the-art review, even though some of the methods do have a public origin (such as Euromethod, CMMI, and ITIL).
- To report and study if the general trend to so-called network organizations, virtual organizations, or contractual organizations poses specific dependency risks in outsourcing agreements in the case of IS/IT services.
- To understand what roles are put into place in IS/IT services procurement agreements, from both parties, and their usual expectations and responsibilities, as well as their evaluations.
- To do a more in-depth description and validation of critical success and risk factors in the outsourcing of complex IS/IT functions and services.
- To continue analyzing and validating the metrics for explaining successful or satisfactory situations in PAO procurement of IS/IT services.
- To study how procedures and mechanisms that are used and accepted for other types of PAO procurements may influence, be adapted, or combined for procuring IS/IT services.
- To report on, propose, and apply relationship management frameworks for improving the overall success or satisfaction levels of the outsourcing relationship, such as *ad hoc* balanced scorecards.

4   THE CASE OF GENERALITAT DE CATALUNYA

We believe it would be interesting to increase the number of explained cases.   In order to make our little contribution in this sense, here we outline one of the main cases that we have started to study, that of the *Generalitat de Catalunya,* the public administration of Catalonia's autonomous government, within Spain. Our study is now in an initial phase, so in this section we only want to describe the case and to mention the aspects we want to study.

In Spain, autonomous governments (called *autonomías*) are decentralized administrations that manage the 19 different regional territories that make up the Spanish state, each one of them with different degrees of influence and attributions in economic and political terms. Catalonia is the second most populated region and the one currently making the greatest contribution to Spain's production of goods and services (GDP: 20.8 percent in 2005).

The history of IS/IT deployment and management at the *Generalitat* has followed a typical pattern (Aibar et al. 2006). At the beginning of the 1980s, each department had its own IS group, a situation that produced unavoidable inefficiencies. In 1983, a central office in the form of a publicly owned company, CIGESA, was created, by concentrating both human and technological resources and becoming the IS/IT provider for all of the different departments of the *Generalitat.* CIGESA achieved high levels of efficiency but it also grew very fast, matching the growing needs of *Generalitat.* In order to avoid an unaffordable company size (in terms of technical teams and their skills), two possibilities were considered: selective and total outsourcing. At this point, Rafael Macau was CIGESA's CEO.

Total outsourcing was then the chosen option, pushed by the management and political trends of the moment, in spite of some of *Generalitat's* managers who considered selective outsourcing as a more appropriate decision. So, in 1998, CIGESA was finally sold to a German group, *Debis,* that some years later was taken over by *Deutsche Telekom* (Gelonch 1999). The sale included two contracts: one directly related to the CIGESA acquisition and the other related to a four-year servicing relationship. In terms of the first contract, the company had to keep the human resources inherited from CIGESA. In terms of the second one, the company also had to keep a simplified administrative process to respond to the provision for the *Generalitat* public projects. These temporary simplifications and guarantees did not produce a monopolistic situation given that, in the subsequent years, almost 50 percent of the acquisitions were made to other companies. In addition, as a way of controlling the relationships with all of the different providers, including *Debis*, CTTI was created. CTTI (IT and Telecommunications Center) is an internal entity within the *Generalitat* that also is responsible for the policy making and management of IT. Rafael Macau became the director of CTTI for IS/IT projects.

However, during the following years some criticism about this supposed-monopolistic relationship reemerged as well as some doubts about lack of price competitiveness and risky dependencies on the provider of the services. A change in the political government of *Generalitat* in 2003, prompted a reorientation toward a more explicit selective sourcing strategy. Hence, in 2004, procurement activities were addressed to create a pool of authorized providers by prequalifying them. So, after the companies passed a certification process, they were allowed to make a bid to the different *Generalitat* project proposals.

The current stage of this story is that we believe that this case needs to be studied in depth as it can be of research interest, four years after of its commencement, to understand how it has impacted IS/IT services both at the user and at the provider level, among other issues. Similar experiences of prequalification are found in the private sector but not in the public one. So, from an in-depth study of this case, we hope to shed light on the real application of selective sourcing and the prequalifying process in a large and complex situation of PAO procurement of all of its IS/IT services, the impact this has on the customer–provider relationship, and the results achieved, measured in terms of success and satisfaction indicators.

5   CONCLUSIONS

We have presented in this paper the current research status of public administration procurement of IS/IT functions and services. We believe that this is a wide-open issue that has not yet received enough attention from the research community, given the great amount of public money that is being invested without enough validated information.

In addition to the research survey, right now more useful for researchers than for practitioners, we have presented a list of open research and practical issues that we are starting to consider in an in-depth case study that we have recently undertaken. We intend to share our study with those interested in this topic, and we invite the IS and PA research communities to put this topic in an appropriate position within the research agenda.

References

Aibar, E., Urgell, F., and Web, Y. 2006. "L'organització i la gestió de la informàtica," Chapter 9 in *Project Internet Catalonia (PIC): E-governance and Citizens in the Generalitat of Catalonia*, (Catalan version) (http://www.uoc.edu/in3/pic/cat/pdf/PIC_Generalitat_2_9.pdf).

Alexander, C. 2002. "Outsourcing Information Systems: An Alternative for Local Government," in *Proceedings of the 8th Americas Conference on Information Systems*, R. Ramsower and J. Windsor (eds.), Dallas, TX, pp. 2128-2133.

Allen, D., Kern, T., and Mattison, D. 2002. "Culture, Power and Politics in ICT Outsourcing in Higher Education Institutions," *European Journal of Information Systems* (11:2), pp. 159-173.

Andrade, J. A., and Mandrillo, C. 2004. "El outsourcing de los sistemas de información en las organizaciones públicas," *Revista venezolana de gerencia* (9:28), pp. 607-622.

Beyah, G., and Gallivan, M. 2001. "Knowledge Management as a Framework for Understanding Public Sector Outsourcing," in *Proceedings of the 34th Hawaii International Conference on System Sciences*, Los Alamitos, CA: IEEE Computer Society Press.

Chen, Y. C. 2002. "Managing E-Government Outsourcing Projects: Lessons from U.S. Local Government," in *Proceedings of the 8th Americas Conference on Information Systems*, R. Ramsower and J. Windsor (eds.), Dallas, TX, pp. 558-563.

Chen, Y. C., and Gant, J. 2001. "Transforming E-Government Services: The Use of Application Service Providers in U.S. Local Governments," in *Proceedings of the 7th Americas Conference on Information Systems*, D. Strong and D. W. Straub (eds.), Boston, pp. 1605-1610.

Currie, W. L. 1996. "Outsourcing in the Private and Public Sectors: An Unpredictable IT Strategy," *European Journal of Information Systems* (4:4), pp. 226-236.

Danziger, J. N., and Andersen, K. V. 2002. "The Impacts of Information Technology on Public Administration: An Analysis of Empirical Research from the 'Golden Age' of Transformation," *International Journal of Public Administration* (25:5), pp. 591-627.

Davies, A. 1993. "The Implications of Outsourcing for Information Management in the Public Sector,"in *Proceedings of the First European Conference on Information Systems*, E. A. Whitley (ed.), Henley-on-Thames, United Kingdom, pp. 1-8.

Dekker, J., and Hendriks, L. 2002. "Best Practice in Acquisition and Procurement Management: the Information Services Procurement Library" in *The Guide to IT Services Management*, J. van Bon (ed.), London: Addison-Wesley, pp. 277-296.

De Looff, L. A. 1995. "Information Systems Outsourcing Decision Making: A Framework, Organizational Theories and Case Studies," *Journal of Information Technology* (10), pp. 281-297.

De Looff, L. A. 1996. "IS Outsourcing by Public Sector Organizations," in *Advanced IT Tools (Proceedings of the IFIP World Conference on IT Tools, 14th WCC*, N. Terashima and E. Altman (eds.), London: Chapman & Hall, pp. 89-96.

Dertz, W., Moe, C., and Hu, Q. 2003. "Influential Factors in IT Sourcing Decisions of Norwegian Public Sector: An Exploratory Study," in *Proceedings of the 9th Americas Conference on Information Systems*, J. Ross and D. Galletta (eds.), Tampa, FL, pp. 1614-1622.

Dibbern, J., Goles, T., Hirschheim, R., and Jayatilaka, B. 2004. "Information Systems Outsourcing: A Survey and Analysis of the Literature," *SIGMIS Database* (35:4), pp. 6-102.

Domberger, S., Fernandez, P., and Fiebig, D. G. 2000. "Modeling the Price, Performance and Contract Characteristics of IT Outsourcing," *Journal of Information Technology* (15:2), pp. 107-118.

González, R., Gascó, J., and Llopis, J. 2006. "Information Systems Outsourcing: A Literature Analysis," *Information and Management* (43:7), pp. 821-834.

Gelonch, A. 1999. *Incrementant l'eficàcia de l'administració i el sevei als cituadans: El procés d'externalització dels serveis informàtics de la Generalitat de Catalunya*. Barcelona: Universitat Ramon Llull.

Globerman, S., and Vining, R. 1996. "A Framework for Evaluating the Government Contracting-Out Decision with an Application to Information Technology," *Public Administration Review* (56:6), pp. 577-586.

Guah, M. W., and Currie, W. 2007. "Managing Vendor Contracts in Public Sector I.T.: A Case Study on the UK National Health Service," in *Proceedings of the 15th European Conference on Information Systems*, H. Österle, J. Schelp, and R. Winter (eds.), St. Gallen, Switzerland, pp. 2147-2160.

Hancox, M., and Hackney, R. 1999. "Information Technology Outsourcing: Conceptualizing Practice in the Public and Private Sector," in *Proceedings of the 32nd Hawaii International Conference on System Sciences*, Los Alamitos: IEEE Computer Society Press.

Hancox, M., and Hackney, R. 2000. "IT Outsourcing: Frameworks for Conceptualizing Practice and Perception," *Information Systems Journal* (10:3), pp. 217-237.

Helmerich, A. 1998. "Euromethod Contract Management," in *Handbook on Architectures of Information Systems*, P. Bernus, K. Mertins, and G. Schmidt (eds.), Boston: Springer, pp. 521-534.

Hoffman, H. F., Yedlin, D. K., Mishler, J. W., and Kushner, S. 2007. *CMMI for Outsourcing: Guidelines for Software, Systems and IT Acquisition*, Boston: Addison-Wesley.

Lacity, M., and Willcocks, L. P. 1997. "Information Systems Oourcing: Examining the Privatization Option in USA Public Administration," *Information Systems Journal* (7:2), pp. 85-108.

Lawry, R., Waddell, D., and Singh, M. 2007. "CIO's in the Public Sector: The Gap Between Theory and Reality," *Proceedings of the 12th Americas Conference on Information Systems*, L. Chidambaram and S. Ram (eds.), Keystone, CO, August 10-12.

Lee, J. N., Huynh, M. Q., Kwok, R. C. W., and Pi, S. M. 2003. "IT Outsourcing Evolution—Past, Present, and Future," *Communications of the ACM* (46:5), pp. 84-89.

Lewis, E. J. E. 1998. "The Use of the Risk-Remedy Method for Evaluating Tenders for Outsourcing Information Technology in the Australian Public Sector," in *Proceedings of the 6th European Conference on Information Systems,* W. Baets, Aix-en-Provence, France, pp. 598-611.

Lewis, E. J. E. 1999. "Using the Risk-Remedy Method to Evaluate Outsourcing Tenders," *Journal of Information Technology* (14;2), pp. 203-211.

Lindskog, H. 2005. "SOTIP as a Model for Outsourcing of Telecom Services for the Public Sector," in *Proceedings of the 38th Hawaii International Conference on System Sciences,* Los Alamitos, CA: IEEE Computer Society Press.

Marco-Simó, J. M., Macau-Nadal, R., and Pastor-Collado, J. A. 2007. "Information Systems Outsourcing in Public Administration: An Emergent Research Topic," in *Proceedings of the 4th European and Mediterranean Conference on Information Systems,* M. Rodenes and R. Hackney, Valencia, Spain, pp. 51,01-51,10.

Moon, J., Jung, G., Chung, M., and Chang, Y. 2007. "IT Outsourcing for E-Government: Lessons form IT Outsourcing Projects Initiated by Agricultural Organizations of the Korean Government," in *Proceedings of the 40th Hawaii International Conference on System Sciences,* Los Alamitos, CA: IEEE Computer Society Press.

Peled, A. 2000. "The Politics of Outsourcing: Bureaucrats, Vendors, and Public Information Technology (IT) Projects," *Information Infrastructure and Policy* (6), pp. 209-225

Pawlowska, A. 2004. "Failures in Large Systems Projects in Poland: Mission [Im]Possible?," *Information Polity* (9), pp. 167-180

Rapcsak, T., and Zagi, Z. 2000. "Evaluation of Tenders in Information Technology," *Decision Support Systems* (30:1), pp. 1-10.

Seddon, P. B., Cullen, S., and Willcocks, L. P. 2002. "Does Domberger's Theory of the Contracting Organization Explain Satisfaction with IT Outsourcing?," *Proceedings of the 23rd International Conference on Information Systems,* L. Applegate, R. D. Galliers, and J. I. DeGross (eds.), Barcelona, pp. 593-604.

Slaughter, S., and Ang, S. 1996. "Employment Outsourcing in Information Systems," *Communications of the ACM* (39:7), pp. 47-54.

Sood, R. 2007. "Report Highlight for Dataquest Insight: Partnering in the Federal Government Market," *Gartner Reports,* ID Number: G00145921.

Willcocks, L. P. 1994. "Managing Information Systems in UK Public Administration: Issues and Prospects," *Public Administration* (72), pp. 13-32.

Willcocks, L. P., and Currie, W. L. 1997. "Information Technology in Public Services: Towards the Contractual Organization?," *British Journal of Management* (8:1), pp. 107-120.

Willcocks , L. P., and Kern, T. 1997. "IT Outsourcing as Strategic Partnering: The Case of the UK Inland Revenue," in *Proceedings of the 5th European Conference on Information Systems,* R. Galliers (ed.), Cork, Ireland.

Willcocks, L. P., and Kern, T. 1998. "IT Outsourcing as Strategic Partnering: The Case of the UK Inland Revenue," *European Journal of Information Systems* (7:1), pp. 29-45.

Zmud, R., Carte, T., and Te'eni, D. 2004. "Information Systems in Nonprofits and Governments: Do We Need Different Theories?," in *Proceedings of the 25th International Conference on Information Systems* R. Agarwal, L. Kirsch, and J. I. DeGross (eds.), Washington, DC, pp. 1017-1018.

About the Authors

Josep Maria Marco-Simó holds an M.Sc. in Informatics. He is an assistant professor at Universitat Oberta de Catalunya (since 2001) and program director of Technical Engineering in

Computer Management (since 2003) at the same university. His teaching topics are related to management of information systems and software development. His research interests include information systems, ICT in the public sector, virtual organizations, and collaborative learning. Josep can be reached at jmarco@uoc.edu.

Joan Antoni Pastor holds an M.Sc. in Informatics and a Ph.D. in Software Engineering from Universitat Politècnica de Catalunya and a Global Senior Management Program from the University of Chicago Graduate School of Business and Instituto de Empresa Business School. He is an assistant professor at Universitat Oberta de Catalunya (since 2007) and a part-time lecturer at Universitat Politècnica de Catalunya. He has held several university management posts, and is starting a new research group on Information Systems and Services at UOC. His teaching and research topics are centered on information systems, IS/IT services management, software engineering, services science and curricula innovation. Joan can be reached at jpastorc@uoc.edu.

Rafael Macau holds three M.Sc. degrees, respectively, in Mathematics, Informatics, and Journalism. He is an assistant professor at Universitat Oberta de Catalunya (since 2001), and currently serves as dean of the Studies of Informatics, Multimedia and Telecommunications at that institution. He has held several executive and management posts in global IS/IT services companies and in public administration IS/IT units. His teaching and research interests are centered in information systems, IS/IT services management, services science, and people management issues in knowledge-intensive services companies. Rafael can be reached at rmacau@uoc.edu.

26 THE INVISIBLE HAND: Governmental Influences on the Field of Play During the Production and Diffusion of Mobile TV

Su-Yi Lin
Mike W. Chiasson
University of Lancaster
Lancaster, UK

Abstract   *The purpose of this paper is to examine how government agencies alter the context around the production and diffusion of technologies, and how this strengthens or weakens particular ICT trajectories. An embedded case is conducted to address this question in Taiwan, as governmental actions affected the early production and diffusion of DVB-H technology and WiMAX technology, both of which enable mobile TV services. The context around and across these two technologies are analyzed from an institutional perspective, including the framework proposed by King et al (1994). The key lesson of this paper is that government agencies are capable of influencing the diffusion of nomadic technologies through their legitimating powers, specific national policies, the allocation of radio frequency spectrum, the implementation of regulations, and the allocation of financial resources. However, the ultimate effects are determined by mixed institutional factors and sometimes contradictory governmental interventions, stemming from historical differences and conflicts across the various government agencies involved. The implications for ICT diffusion research and governmental policy makers are discussed.*

Keywords   Diffusion, institutional theory, wireless broadband technology, mobile TV

1 INTRODUCTION

Internet and mobile communication technologies have ushered in a new era of various ICT-based innovations and resulting social phenomena. For example, communi-

Please use the following format when citing this chapter:

Lin, S-Y., and Chiasson, M. W., 2008, in IFIP International Federation for Information Processing, Volume 287, Open IT-Based Innovation: Moving Towards Cooperative IT Transfer and Knowledge Diffusion, eds. León, G., Bernardos, A., Casar, J., Kautz, K., and DeGross, J. (Boston: Springer), pp. 461-481.

cation and office technologies purportedly allow telecommuters to work from anywhere, and advanced wireless broadband technologies are claimed to allow mobile TV viewers to watch digital content from any location, through wireless handsets. Lyytinen and Yoo (2002) have called this socio-technical effect the *nomadic information environment*:

> A heterogeneous assemblage of interconnected technological and organizational elements that enable the physical and social mobility of computing and communication services between organizational actors both within and across organizational borders (p. 378).

To study the development, implementation, and impact of ICT, information systems researchers have increasingly paid attention not only to ICT itself, but to the social and political context around ICT (Kling and Scacchi 1982; Markus and Robey 1988). This focus on context has lead IS researchers to study how context affects technological trajectories, including nomadic technologies, and how context is affected by the development of such technologies (Allen and Wilson 2005; Henfridsson and Lindgren 2005; Lin and Chiasson 2007; Lyytinen and Rose 2003; Tilson et al. 2006).

The complexity and pace of ICT now affects many organizations and government agencies, resulting in a shifting and complicated context around ICT-based innovation. This is particularly the case with nomadic technologies since governments generally see them as a vital means of increasing their international competitiveness, and so they have become important players and interventionists in fostering the production and diffusion of nomadic technologies. Their roles include policy makers, market accelerators, competitive environmental creators, and regime regulators (Sawyer et al. 2003). Theoretically, governments can be regarded as part of the infrastructures for the rise and continuance of nomadic technologies at the interorganizational level. The eighth theme in Lyytinen and Yoo's paper highlights such a key question in IS research: how do government agencies, policies, and actions affect the context and resulting field-of-play in developing ICT-based industries, including the effect on ICT groups and technological trajectories? In our case, we focus specifically on mobile interorganizational services.

A number of researchers have studied governmental roles and policies relating to the production and diffusion of ICT in general (Avgerou 2000; King et al. 1994; Montealegre 1999) and in nomadic computing specifically (Andersen et al. 2003; Choudrie and Lee 2004; Ishii 2004; Lee et al. 2003). However, most researchers focus on the diffusion of an innovation after it is well developed and diffusing. Little attention is paid to how governments intervene and affect the development of new ICT and the formation of new industries during the very early stages, particularly their effects on the institutional field-of-play and the trajectories of these early technical groups. Consequently, the research questions addressed in this paper are (1) how do governments intervene in the diffusion of ICT, and (2) how do the governments and their interventions affect the field-of-play and industrial setting during the initiation and early diffusion of ICT? According to Orlikowski and Barley's (2001) suggestion,

> An institutional perspective would offer IT researchers a vantage point for conceptualizing the digital economy as an emergent, evolving, embedded, fragmented, and provisional social production that is shaped as much by cultural and structural forces as by technical and economic ones (p. 154).

The remainder of this paper is structured as follows: First, institutional theory is briefly reviewed in order to identify key concepts used in this paper. We then explain our research methodology, which examines the comparative effect of the government on two emerging wireless broadband technologies in Taiwan. The next two sections present our findings and discussion using an institutional perspective. The paper concludes with suggestions for practice and further research. To our knowledge, this is the first empirical study focusing on how governments affect the initiation and early diffusion of nomadic technologies. The key lesson of this paper is that government agencies are capable of influencing ICT diffusion through their legitimating powers, specific national policies, the allocation of radio spectrum, the implementation of regulations, and the allocation of financial resources. However, the ultimate effects of varying or contradictory governmental influences, stemming from historical conflicts and separations across the various agencies involved, produce a complicated and shifting field-of-play for industrial participants, and a number of surprises due to complex institutional forces.

2 INSTITUTIONAL THEORY

In general, an *institution* is regarded as "any standing social entity that exerts influence and regulation over other social entities" (King et al. 1994, p. 148), for example, governments, universities, churches, trade and industry associations, as well as international agencies (e.g., United Nations). Institutional theorists consider *institutions* to be various contextual factors that rationalize a set of actions over time and space, through not only economic efficiency but also cultural, political, and socio-technical actions. A more precise definition of *institutions* is given by Scott (1995):

> Institutions consist of *cognitive, normative,* and *regulative* structures and activities that provide stability and meaning to social behavior. Institutions are transported by various carriers—culture, structures, and routines—and they operate at multiple levels of jurisdiction (p. 33).

Numerous studies have paid attention to the legitimacy basis for action and the mechanisms involved in the three institutional elements: regulative, normative, and cognitive. The interweaving process of the institutional elements, called *institutionalization*, can be top-down or bottom-up. While early sociologists focus on how existing cultural and structural patterns form institutions through top-down influences, late sociologists and organizational scholars observe that some institutions are driven by entrepreneurs or internal managerial participants through bottom-up creation (Scott 1995).

Extending from sociology and organizational studies, *institutional theory* has been applied to the IS field for decades, including ICT diffusion research (Avgerou 2000; King et al. 1994; Montealegre 1999; Swanson and Ramiller 1997; Teo et al. 2003). Since most IS research focuses on macro-analysis of institutions or how institutional elements are imposed upon or upheld within or across organizations, only a few studies combine the general and theoretical definitions of institutions to examine how governments, industry associations, or international agencies influence ICT diffusion (Andersen et al. 2003; Choudrie and Lee 2004; Damsgaard and Lyytinen 2001; Damsgaard and Scheepers 1999;

Table 1. Dimensions of Institutional Intervention Proposed by King et al. (Adapted with permission from J. L. King, V. Gurbaxani, K. L. Kraemer, F. W. McFarlan, K. S. Raman, and C. S. Yap, "Institutional Factors in Information Technology Innovation," *Information Systems Research* (5:2), 1994, p. 151. Copyright © 1994, The Institute for Operations Research and Management Sciences, 7240 Parkway Drive, Suite 210, Hanover, Maryland 21076.)

	Supply-Push	Demand-Pull
Influence	❶ Knowledge Building ❷ Knowledge Deployment ❸ Subsidy ❻ Innovation Directive	❷ Knowledge Deployment ❸ Subsidy ❹ Mobilization
	I	II
	III	IV
Regulation	❷ Knowledge Deployment ❸ Subsidy ❺ Standard setting ❻ Innovation Directive	❸ Subsidy ❺ Standard setting ❻ Innovation Directive

Ishii 2004; Lee et al. 2003; Miscione 2007; Silva and Figueroa 2002). An analytical framework proposed by King et al. (1994) is often used for examining how and to what extent the institutions intervene in ICT diffusion.

Table 1 shows King et al.'s framework classifying institutional interventions into four cells represented by Roman numerals I through IV, according to the strength of initiatives and the type of driving forces. Institutional forces can invoke soft persuasion as the *influence* or hard coercion as the *regulation*. Innovation can be driven by *supply-push* or *demand-pull*. Demand-pull emerges from the provision of resources to support organizational preferences while supply-push is based on providing and "pushing" services into organizations. Six complementary institutional interventions—*knowledge building, knowledge deployment, subsidy, mobilization, standard setting*, and *innovative directive*—are then put into the two-dimensional matrix.

Relating this to our study, we apply the description of each institutional intervention in the context of governmental intervention in the diffusion of nomadic technologies as follows:

- *Knowledge building*, in the influence and supply-push dimension (I), aims to support research and development activities in order to produce the basic knowledge of nomadic technologies and foster the understanding and localization of suppliers. For example, a governmental research project focused on how to maintain reliable data transmission to fast moving users would fall into this category.

- *Knowledge deployment* indicates the distribution of key concepts and techniques through education or training led or funded by governments. Interventions such as optional courses on mobile TV production at universities are classified into the influence and demand-pull dimension (II) if the main objective is to boost users' adoption. Interventions such as professional seminars or certificate tests of employees in the mobile TV industry are classified into dimension I or III if the main objective is to enrich suppliers' R&D knowledge.

- *Subsidy* describes the "institutional activities designed to produce specific innovative outcomes" (King et al. 1994, p. 154). It includes, but is not limited to, the direct or indirect governmental financial support for technical trials (I) and facility procurement (II), tax deduction (III), and governmental sponsorship (IV) for using particular types of nomadic technologies.

- *Mobilization* is an encouragement of the "best choice" favored by governments, through awareness campaigns, workshops, seminars, conferences, and other promotional activities (II) such as the announcement of national policies and related media reports.

- *Standard setting* produces boundaries that limit actors' choices. This powerful intervention could be a set of regulations for governing the suppliers (III) or a technical protocol endorsed by governments for stimulating particular innovations (IV).

- *Innovation directive* is a command for the production or adoption of specific nomadic technologies such as e- or m-government applications using particular technologies (I), an investment requirement for particular technologies (III), or an administrative order for using particular technologies (IV).

In this paper, we use an institutional view including King et al.'s framework to analyze our data in order to answer the research question. Detailed illustrations are provided in our findings and discussions.

3 RESEARCH METHODOLOGY

An *embedded single-case study design* is used in this paper to trace how the Taiwanese government affected the early diffusion of two wireless broadband technologies before the end of 2007. In Yin's (1984) research, an embedded case includes multiple units of analysis, so it is particularly applicable to multilevel analysis, which is important in institutional theoretical studies. We can simultaneously understand the effect of governmental background, policy, and intervention (at one level) on the wireless broadband technology development in two industrial clusters (another level) within the same setting. The two clusters driven by digital video broadcasting-handheld (DVB-H) technology and worldwide interoperability for microwave access (WiMAX) technology are selected because both of the technologies enable mobile TV services and have been frequently compared by every stakeholder, including government agencies, in Taiwan. As an official document states

> The research on the emerging issues, like the competition and collaboration in the spectrum demand between WiMAX technology and Digital TV (including DVB-H technology), should be increased in the future (National Science Council 2006, p. 14).

The case study data were collected from three sources. First, the first author worked in the Institute for Information Industry, a governmental think tank and management consultancy in Taiwan, for five years. She was involved in a WiMAX project authorized by the Taiwanese government from July to September 2005, including 15 interviews with ICT industrial participants and numerous meetings with the government officials as well as a consultant team. This experience assisted us in closely understanding the working logic of Taiwanese government agencies, how WiMAX technology followed the governmental plan and acquired legitimacy, and how a WiMAX cluster composed of ICT industrial actors was created over time. The second source of our data is a fieldwork for a broader mobile TV research conducted by the first author in Taiwan from January to September 2007. The forming and reshaping of DVB-H cluster was investigated through participant observation and 27 interviews with government agencies and participants in ICT and media industries. Key participants' talks and behaviors were analyzed in order to understand the context around the interplay between the government and industries in the early diffusion of mobile TV. The final data source comes from the documentary evidence, including field notes, project records, online documents, other first-hand data from interviewees or public conferences, and second-hand data from governmental publications or media reports. The documentary evidence supplied details to our case study. In summary, the data provides a rich base to compare and analyze how various Taiwanese government agencies affect the diffusion of the DVB-H and WiMAX technologies.

4   FIELD OF INSTITUTIONAL PLAY

To represent the institutional field-of-play during the initial development of mobile TV in Taiwan, we explain the concepts of the two wireless broadband technologies first. We then interpret the governmental background, including the political relations among key government agencies. Finally, King et al.'s framework is used to analyze governmental interventions in the initiation and early diffusion of DVB-H and WiMAX technologies respectively.

4.1   DVB-H and WiMAX Technologies

The technical principles and industrial strategies of DVB-H technology versus WiMAX technology are very different. DVB-H technology is a branch of digital TV technology, particularly designed for mobile TV services. One of the largest mobile handset manufacturers, Nokia, is its primary promoter. With a broadcasting format to send signals in a one-to-many manner, DVB-H technology can support digital content to be concurrently downloaded to millions of DVB-H mobile handsets as long as the handsets are within the digital signal coverage. However, it does not support two-way communication, as existing and future mobile phone systems do. Terrestrial TV stations in Taiwan, which own broadcasting networks and TV content producing teams, have included the adoption of DVB-H technology in their business plans since 2005 because the Taiwanese government declares that TV signals will be converted into digital code by 2012. Their hope is that they can enter the mobile service market and escape from their declining TV advertising market by adding DVB-H transmitters on their existing broadcasting towers, along with some technical facilities and support.

In contrast, WiMAX technology, regarded as a fourth generation (4G) technology—the next-generation of 3G—provides one-to-one, two-way, high speed, and wide broadband access. Since 2004, before the WiMAX standards were finalized by the WiMAX Forum, two WiMAX technical standards—IEEE 802.16d and 802.16e—had been promoted in Taiwan by the ICT industry giant Intel. While 802.16d supports fixed and portable wireless broadband access to laptops, 802.16e supports mobile wireless broadband access to handsets. Given Intel's lobbying of the Taiwanese government and the ambition of the Taiwanese ICT industry to take part in setting an international standard at an early stage, the majority of government agencies and industry participants in Taiwan were convinced that WiMAX technology had a great market potential, especially for Internet protocol (IP) phone and mobile video services. In contrast with the 802.16d standard, 802.16e acquired increasing attention because the other fixed or portable wireless broadband solutions (e.g., ADSL, Cable Modem, and Wi-Fi) had been widely used in homes, offices, and cafés in Taiwan. Six WiMAX commercial licenses were issued in late 2007.

From a technological perspective, DVB-H and WiMAX technologies belong to the broadcasting industry and the telecommunication industry respectively. However, their advantages and disadvantages in delivering mobile TV, like the numbers of concurrent users and the interactive functions, have resulted in their competing with each other. This highlights that the technology cannot be considered independent from its context, including the institutions produced by government agencies.

4.2 Governmental Background

Taiwan has invested heavily in the ICT infrastructure and has incubated the ICT industry since the 1970s. The fruitful result is that Taiwan has become a well-established and well-known actor in the global supply chain of ICT hardware components (Lee and Pech 1997; Mathews 1997; Saxenian 2002). In order to upgrade the local ICT industry and build a ubiquitous ICT environment in Taiwan, the Executive Yuan, the government agency that enacts executive functions of the Taiwanese government, announced the five-year, €770 million, national-level M-Taiwan Program in 2005, tied in with the preceding three-year e-Taiwan Program. One goal of the M-Taiwan Program is to build a world-class wireless broadband access environment as the foundation of mobile services, mobile learning, and even mobile life (WiMAX Forum 2007a).

Figure 1 illustrates a map developed from the central government structure in Taiwan,[1] which shows key government agencies related to the M-Taiwan Program. Two major units under the Executive Yuan are the Ministry of Economic Affairs (MOEA), the Taiwanese economic and industrial development authority, and the National Communications Commission (NCC), the communications industry regulator.

---

[1]From the Government Information Office website, http://category.www.gov.tw/Category/default.aspx?cateitem=gov1&cateab=onlineformapply (retrieved February 27, 2008).

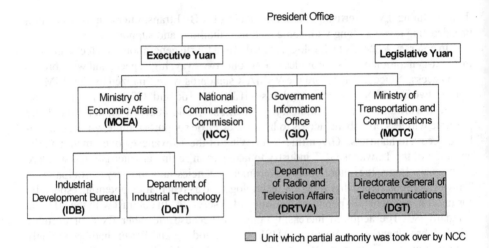

Figure 1. **Key Government Agencies Related to M-Taiwan Program**

The MOEA has been a market accelerator of Taiwanese industries for decades. It has two subunits in charge of ICT industrial affairs. One is the Industrial Development Bureau (IDB), which is responsible for promoting advanced technologies, building close interrelations among industries, and supporting the expansion of ICT industry and its markets. The other is the Department of Industrial Technology (DoIT), which coordinates national ICT research resources, including those from research institutions, universities, and firms, in order to transfer basic R&D knowledge into innovative applications. However, without good capability to develop advanced technologies through basic research, Taiwan tends to adopt the technology standards of developed countries, resulting in a high patent cost for manufacturing hardware using those standards (e.g., 3G). Moreover, the MOEA tends to pursue short-term results due to political pressure. For example, three ministers of Economic Affairs were replaced during the past four years; thus, the plans sponsored by the MOEA are generally shorter than five years and sometimes reinterpreted widely during the middle of a current plan.

The NCC became operational in February 2006, imitating the Federal Communications Commission (FCC) in the United States. To coordinate spectrum and regulatory issues derived from the competition among a variety of digital platforms across telecommunication, broadcasting, and Internet technologies, the NCC took over authority from the Directorate General of Telecommunications (DGT) and the Department of Radio and Television Affairs (DRTVA), two subunits of existing government agencies in charge of the affairs in the telecommunication and broadcasting industries respectively.

The NCC faced organizational resistance, especially from the Executive Yuan and its spokesman Government Information Office (GIO). One example is that the first set of NCC commissioners is involved in a political rivalry between the Executive Yuan and the Legislative Yuan, the congress of Taiwan, because they are dominated by the two largest political parties respectively. This occurs despite the fact that the NCC is meant to be independent from governmental or political interference, according to the spirit of the National Communications Commission Organization Act (NCC Organization Act) approved in November 2005. Yan (2007) provides evidence of this political situation by highlighting three points.

- In February 2006, the Executive Yuan argued that it should propose the list of NCC commissioners because the NCC is under the Executive Yuan. However, the Legislative Yuan argued that the FCC in the United States is an independent government agency, directly responsible to the Congress, so NCC commissioners should be appointed based on the seating percentage of political parties in the Legislative Yuan. In the end, nine commissioners were appointed using the Legislative Yuan's argument.

- In July 2006, the Justices of the Constitutional Court declared this selection violated the Constitution. The commissioners had to resign and be reselected. The commissioners then announced that their selection was legal according to the NCC Organization Act, but they would resign along with the election of Legislative members in January 2008. They also called on an amendment to the NCC Organization Act, which was not settled until December 2007.

- In April 2007, the Executive Yuan declared "Ten Crimes of NCC" based on an internal investigation, including the questioning of five NCC commissioners integrity. Subsequently, the former premier of the Executive Yuan ordered two commissioners to be suspended, leaving seven commissioners to run the system.

Another example of the organizational resistance is that the GIO has continued showing its interests in replacing the NCC. This can be evidenced by two events.

- In June 2007, the head of GIO alleged that the NCC's approval of selling a radio station once owned by the opposition party had abused its authority and benefitted both the radio station and the buyers. The NCC chief commissioner then responded by claiming there was a lack of evidence (*China Post* 2007; *United Daily News* 2007a).

- In December 2007, the chief convener of the ruling party suggested that the GIO take over the NCC if the NCC Organization Act was not amended in time. The head of GIO said that the Executive Yuan would consider this possibility (Chu 2007; *United Daily News* 2007b).

The shifting power of various conflicting institutional groups has influenced the complex and mixed governmental interventions that have affected the initiation and early diffusion of the DVB-H and WiMAX technologies. We turn to these next.

4.3 Governmental Interventions in DVB-H Technology

In this and the following section, we use the six types of governmental interventions in King et al.'s framework to analyze how government agencies intervene in the production and diffusion of wireless broadband technologies in Taiwan. The dimensions of each intervention are noted by Roman numerals I, II, III, and IV at the end of these intervention statements (see Table 1).

4.3.1 Knowledge Building

As mentioned above, the knowledge building of advanced technologies in Taiwan is usually produced through a series of localizing processes. The basic DVB-H technical knowledge was introduced by industrial associations and local firms. As Dr. C. Shih, the director general for Taiwan Digital Television Committee (DTVC) and the chief executive officer (CEO) for DAWN TV Technology Corporation, stated in our interview,

> The DTVC has organized yearly business tour groups to visit European digital [or mobile] TV companies since 2004. I'm the first leader of the group. At that moment, Nokia didn't have any mobile multimedia team in Taiwan, but we visited its Finish headquarters and met the vice president directly....Afterwards, DAWN TV began the mobile TV business in Taiwan and received significant technical support from Nokia China and then Nokia Taiwan....The government sensed the [market] potential of DVB-H technology when we did the first live trial at the Taipei TV & Film Festival 2005.

This building of localized know-how using DVB-H technology captured the government attention. Afterward, the DoIT sponsored the DVB-H Operation Platform and Business Model Research Project in 2005, the Mobile Video Interactive Application Planning Project in 2006, and the Innovative Service on Mobile TV over DVB-H Research Project in 2007 (I).[2] However, the budget of each project was less than €100,000, so the know-how was not available to the public until three to five years later.

4.3.2 Knowledge Deployment

After the industry showed interest in DVB-H technology, various government agencies started to distribute knowledge about DVB-H technology. A number of publications, conferences, and courses have been endorsed or sponsored to foster industrial development, to promote digital multimedia applications, and to train skilled technical employees (I). The main intervention was that the IDB included the issue of DVB-H technology into the last-year High Definition Video Multi-medium Industry Development Five-Year Promotion Program in 2005 and into the last two-year Broadband and Wireless Communications Industry Development Five-Year Promotion Program[3] in 2006 and 2007. Nevertheless, compared with the respective themes of each program— digital TV and WiMAX technology—DVB-H technology was a minor issue. As a result, no significant budgets or efforts were devoted to the diffusion of DVB-H technology.

---

[2]From the Department of Industrial Technology website (http://doit.moea.gov.tw; retrieved February 22, 2008.
[3]From the Government Research Bulletin website, http://www.grb.gov.tw (retrieved February 25, 2008).

4.3.3 Subsidy

Criticized by the industry, the GIO only subsidized one terrestrial TV stations, the Public Television Service Foundation (PTS), the only public TV station in Taiwan (like the BBC in the UK), for its initial DVB-H server-side systems and its interactive or made-for-mobile video content production (IV), even through the subsidization did not go smoothly. In 2005, PTS proposed a €1.35 million DVB-H subproject, which was included in a €93 million Two-Year Project of Public Broadcasting Cultural Creation and Digital Television Development (PTS 2006), but the budget was frozen by the Legislative Yuan until May 2007 (RDEC 2007). Facing this biased subsidy structure, the terrestrial TV stations applying for the scant research funding from the DoIT tended to secretly divert partial funding to the procurement of DVB-H facilities.

4.3.4 Mobilization

At the beginning, the government encouraged the decentralized actors to think of DVB-H technology in a particular way: fulfilling mobile TV services efficiently. The IDB supported establishing the Mobile TV Alliance, a community spanning the broadcasting and ICT industries, in August 2005 (II) (Lai 2005). In mid-2006, however, NCC announced the Handheld Mobile TV Trial Program and preferred to remain neutral about mobile TV technology. Five trial licenses were released not only to the consortiums using DVB-H technology but also to a consortium using *MedioFLO*, another competitive digital broadcasting technology. The awareness of DVB-H technology was unfortunately blurred.

4.3.5 Standard Setting

It is difficult to determine whether the government has set standards for the diffusion of DVB-H technology. In the Handheld Mobile TV Trial Program, the NCC not only limited the trial areas of the five consortiums (three in northern Taiwan and two in southern Taiwan) but also asked the consortiums to pass the technical examination within 6 months and to finish consumer trials in no longer than 18 months. Nonetheless, the NCC did not promise that the trial results would result in commercial licenses for mobile TV. Moreover, the spectrum allocation and the numbers of commercial licenses have not been decided yet. This confusion was recorded in our field notes, as the call made by one of the consortiums in the mid-term review seminar of the trial program on April 26, 2007:

> The vague policy has become the biggest bottleneck of our trial. Without a timetable and methods of the commercial license releasing, the members in our consortium hesitate to invest further.

4.3.6 Innovation Directive

With a long-run argument about whether the mobile TV over DVB-H should be regulated by the Radio and Television Act, which had been authorized by GIO, or the

Telecommunication ACT, which had been authorized by DGT, no clear innovation directive has been issued. As an interviewee for a terrestrial TV station said,

> We have a mother-in-law and a father-in-law [GIO and NCC], and we can't offend either of them.

Although the NCC has proposed the first draft of the Converged Communication Law in order to enhance effective competition in the digital convergence environment, the rivalry between the Executive Yuan and the Legislative Yuan is very likely to delay this act.

In summary, a notable phenomenon in the early diffusion of DVB-H technology is that industrial actions are usually ahead of governmental interventions, resulting in a bottom-up institutionalization process and an unclear governmental plan.

4.4   Governmental Interventions in WiMAX Technology

Unlike the diffusion of DVB-H technology, the government has led and even directed the diffusion of WiMAX technology. Organized institutional interventions have been deployed as a top-down strategy according to the €23 million Taiwan WiMAX Blueprint proposed by the Executive Yuan in 2005, which states

> WiMAX technology will be a focus for the future of Taiwan ICT industry and will be a preferred technology option…in the M-Taiwan Program (WiMAX Forum 2007b).

4.4.1 Knowledge Building

Supporting the Executive Yuan policy, the DoIT proposed a three-year WiMAX Speed-up Program from January 2006, with an additional and particular €5.8 million budget allocation. It subsidized some R&D projects of WiMAX chipsets, base stations, consumer premises equipment (CPEs), and application platforms (e.g., voice over IP, IP-TV broadcast, or e-Health), hoping to build a complete WiMAX supply chain in Taiwan (I) (Lin 2006). Although critical WiMAX chipset technology was still held by international companies, a few Taiwanese companies were able to provide WiMAX end-to-end solutions at the end of 2007.

4.4.2 Knowledge Deployment

To deploy WiMAX knowledge, the Executive Yuan coordinated its subunits' functions. For example, to ensure the supply of WiMAX professionals, the Executive Yuan requested the MOEA to amend the professional training and subsidization measures (I) and the Ministry of Education to review higher education courses (II) respectively (NICI 2007). Moreover, one mission of the last three-year Broadband and Wireless Communications Industry Development Five-Year Promotion Program was to bring international resources in the local ICT industry. As a result, the MOEA signed memorandums of understanding (MOU) with eight global companies (Alcatel-Lucent, Intel, Motorola, NEC, Nokia Siemens Networks, Nortel, Sprint-Nextel, and Starent) for the technical cooperation and interoperability testing of WiMAX products (I). The global fourth regulatory certification body (RCB), which can issue Taiwan WiMAX certificates, was established in January 2008 (I) (BV ADT 2008).

4.4.3 Subsidy

Under the M-Taiwan Program, a €146 million M-Taiwan Application Promotion Plan was arranged to subsidize the ICT industrial participants entering the WiMAX market. Performed by the IDB, selected ICT companies aligned with regional govern-ments were subsidized to implement the technical and business trials of "wireless broadband cities" (II) (Lin 2006). The subsidized consortiums were requested to pur-chase at least 20 percent made-in-Taiwan WiMAX base stations and 80 to 100 percent made-in-Taiwan CPEs (IV) (LANcom Express 2007). The subsidies did attract some participants that had no previous interest in WiMAX technology. As a general manager for a telecom company, which acquired a €5.8 million subsidy in 2005 and then bid a WiMAX commercial licence in 2007, stated in our interview on August 2005,

> WiMAX technology hasn't been mature yet. The price of chips and CPEs are still high.... The standard of 3G costs many years to complete global roaming.... The biggest problem is where the market [of WiMAX technology] is. The profitable high-speed data service is merely video services, but according to our previous experience, consumers pay on rare occasion.

4.4.4 Mobilization

After WiMAX technology was chosen as the focus of the national-level M-Taiwan Program, the government launched numerous awareness campaigns (e.g., Taiwan WiMAX Blueprint and WiMAX Speed-up Program) and promotional events (e.g., 2007 Taipei Summit Asia-Pacific WiMAX Conference and Exhibition and the 2007 WiMAX Forum Taipei Showcase and Conference) (II). Despite the early public confusion over which WiMAX standards were supported, the government successfully built two clearer objectives: (1) assisting local ICT manufacturers to win the overseas orders of WiMAX hardware or solutions, following either the 802.16d or the 802.16e standards; (2) supporting local mobile service providers to build Taiwan into the best test bed of the 802.16e standard in order to attract the favor of international WiMAX companies and to create innovative business models. However, the government did not persuade everyone. In late 2007, the two largest mobile service providers in Taiwan intentionally failed to win the WiMAX commercial licenses with surprising low bidding.

> "You may see our conservative attitude towards WiMAX technology from our auction price," the vice president Cliff Lai for *Taiwan Mobile Company (TMC)* said. "We don't think WiMAX will threaten the fixed network or mobile com-munication market within two years.... After two years, we will take part in the

next auction when the cost of CPEs should be already down, and TMC can wait based on the advantages of our base station coverage (because residents have protested against new base stations due to possible harmful electromagnetic wave)" (Kuang 2007).

4.4.5 Standard Setting

The auction of the six regional WiMAX commercial licenses was finalized in July 2007, after a hazy 2006, when the DGT and the NCC competed against each other for their respective plans of spectrum allocation. According to NCC's final version, WiMAX spectrum is in the 2.5 to 2.69 GHz frequency band, and the duration of the licenses is six years. Six winners are allowed to merge or invest in one another for efficient competition, and the second-run licenses are planned to be issued after two years (III). The related regulations are not ready, although the WiMAX licenses were issued. For example, the import of WiMAX facilities for the infrastructure building must pass some examinations, but the NCC has not decided how to examine facilities from abroad (Chung 2008). Such problems delay the diffusion of WiMAX technology.

4.4.6 Innovation Directive

The government used directive interventions to encourage the diffusion of WiMAX technology. In the early stage, the government directly provided practical and profitable opportunities to attract industrial participants using WiMAX technology. In the M-Taiwan Application Promotion Plan, 10 regional governments offered diverse industrial participants to implement WiMAX technology for the vision of wireless broadband cities (I). For example, the regional government of Taipei City cooperated with a personal handy phone service (PHS) provider to deploy WiMAX infrastructure and applications (e.g., the Taipei e-BUS service) (Lin 2006). After the WiMAX licenses were issued, the NCC required that license winners who did not cover any single city or county with the WiMAX infrastructure over 70 percent of the population within 18 months return their licenses (III) (Wang 2008).

In summary, governmental interventions in WiMAX technology are more comprehensive and effective than those of DVB-H technology. Nevertheless, the potential competition between WiMAX and DVB-H technologies were unveiled while the WiMAX promotion plan has shifted its focus from infrastructure to applications such as mobile TV or Karaoke over WiMAX since 2007. The key lessons we can learn from this case are discussed next.

5   KEY LESSONS

Based on the data presented above, we propose that government agencies have an important and significant influence on the diffusion of wireless broadband technologies through numerous interventions. However, the results are somewhat chaotic and unpredictable because of the constant shuffling and rebuilding of government agencies, the competing and cancelling effects of government actions across agencies, the conflict across government units and policies, and broad institutional factors.

5.1 The Width and Depth of Governmental Interventions

Table 2 summarizes Taiwanese governmental interventions in the initiation and early diffusion of DVB-H technology and WiMAX technology. Comparing the various governmental interventions and the budgets, we find that the width and depth of the governmental interventions in the diffusion of WiMAX technology are greater than those in the diffusion of DVB-H technology.

The difference has come from the top-down strategy of the WiMAX promotion plan. Supported by a national-level program, huge budgets, and efficient spectrum allocation, the government agencies have helped to speed up the early diffusion of WiMAX technology, in accordance with the common practical belief that a top-down strategy enables the integration of resources across different government agencies. However, our case also reveals how a dynamic institutional context complicates the effects of governmental interventions.

5.2 The Difficulties of Governmental Restructuring

Complexity in authorities, programs, and regulations has emerged because nomadic technologies have blurred industrial boundaries. As a result, it is time-consuming to build or to maintain consistent and mutually supporting governmental mechanisms and regulatory effects in the diffusion of complexity technologies, such as nomadic technologies. For example, mobile TV services supported by DVB-H or WiMAX technologies need cooperation among media, telecommunication, and IT industries. However, before the NCC's establishment, the media industry was governed by the GIO, the telecommunication industry was governed by the DGT, and the IT industry was governed

Table 2. Taiwanese Governmental Interventions in the Initiation and Early Diffusion of DVB-H Technology and WiMax Technology (using King et al.'s Framework)

	DVB-H		WiMAX	
	Supply-Push	**Demand-Pull**	**Supply-Push**	**Demand-Pull**
Influence	❶ Knowledge building (<€100,000) ❷ Knowledge deployment	❹ Mobilization	❶ Knowledge building (€5.8 M) ❷ Knowledge deployment	❷ Knowledge deployment ❸ Subsidy (€146 M) ❹ Mobilization
	I II		I II	
	III IV		III IV	
Regulation	(❺ Standard setting)	❸ Subsidy (€1.35 M)	❺ Standard setting ❻ Innovation directive	❸ Subsidy

by the MOEA. After NCC's establishment, the integration has encountered significant reluctance. Another example is that the government, regardless of the discontinuity of related plans and knowledge workers, allocated the DVB-H technology to be aided by the High Definition Video Multi-medium Industry Development Five-Year Promotion Program for the first year and by Broadband and Wireless Communications Industry Development Five-Year Promotion Program for the next two years because it was barely aware of the position of DVB-H technology in the early stage. Similar uncertainty existed in the copious argument of the Converged Communication Law about which part of the regulations should descend from the principle of the Broadcasting and Television Law or that of the Telecommunication Act. These situations reveal that an ambition to rebuild complete and comprehensive governmental and regulatory contexts is very difficult and adds to the complexity and lack of predictability about the form and time to market of nomadic technologies.

5.3   The Contradiction among Government Agencies

In addition to the innate difficulties of restructuring governmental agencies and policies in the face of new technology, the long-term interorganizational debate across agencies (like the Legislative Yuan and the NCC against the Executive Yuan, the GIO, and the DGT, in this case) results in an unstable political context. An obvious example in the case is the rivalry between the Legislative Yuan and the Executive Yuan, managed by the two largest opposition political parties. Another illustration is that the first mobile TV over DVB-H consortium had lobbied and convinced the GIO in 2005, but they were told to negotiate with the NCC when they attempted to do a large-scale field trial in 2006. During the first-year struggle between the NCC and the GIO, some members were uncertain whether their efforts again would be in vain and withdrew from the consortium. These contradictions among government agencies tend to frustrate industrial participants and prevent a clear path to the diffusion of technologies because of the uncertainty.

5.4   Competition between Technologies Enabling Similar Applications

Although the technical principles of the DVB-H and WiMAX technologies are apparently different, more and more stakeholders, including adopters, investors, and government officers, compare them during the decision-making stages because both of them enable the delivery of mobile TV. Thus, with WiMAX suddenly catching more attention and getting more resources through stronger governmental promotion, including the national programs and media reports, stakeholders felt increasingly confused. As the project manager of a DVB-H consortium said in the interview,

> When I invited companies from the other industries to join our group or intro-
> duced mobile TV over DVB-H in exhibitions, I was often questioned why con-
> sumers need mobile TV over DVB-H when they are having WiMAX services
> in the near future.

Moreover, in our cases, the two largest mobile service providers, which have advantages of DVB-H return channels and WiMAX base station deployment, prefer to wait and see the next-generation wireless broadband technologies instead of joining the diffusion of DVB-H and WiMAX technologies now. Such feedback reveals an important issue in government policy making: the potential competition among emerging nomadic technologies that enable similar applications. Governmental intervention in these technologies, especially the complexity of different government agencies with different and sometimes contradictory effects, has resulted in a complex environment, with numerous financial and human resources spent on producing this complexity.

5.5 ICT Diffusion Influenced by Broad Institutional Factors

In addition to the political issues, economic or socio-technical factors influence the industrial field-of-play in the diffusion of nomadic technologies. Intel's withdrawal is a clear example. In 2004, Intel announced that WiMAX chips would be integrated into laptops in 2006 and mobile handsets in 2007. At the end of 2006, however, Intel deferred its integration plan to 2007. In late 2007, Intel downgraded WiMAX modules as selective items to its cooperative hardware manufacturers (MOEA 2008). The withdrawal, due to pessimistic global market forecasts, has not only influenced the diffusion of WiMAX technology but also increased the risk of for governmental interventions.

> In 2005, Intel signed the first WiMAX MOU with the MOEA in Taiwan. Until 2008, however, Intel hasn't realized its promise to invest a local center for interoperability testing in Taiwan but invested in the Japanese telecom company KDDI, which is shameful to MOEA (Juang 2008).

Therefore, we suggest that various governmental agencies should pay attention to their own and other broad institutional factors in order to increase the comprehensiveness and the flexibility of long-term actions and plans for nomadic technologies.

6 CONCLUSION

Institutional theory provides a rich theoretical view for the study of the interplay between contexts and IT artefacts, including governmental influence on the early diffusion of nomadic technologies. Using the key concepts of institutional theory, including King et al.'s framework, we have examined how various Taiwanese government agencies affected the context around the production and diffusion of two wireless broadband technologies, DVB-H and WiMAX. Several conclusions have been drawn from the analysis.

- Governments are able to affect the diffusion of nomadic technologies through their legitimating powers, specific national policies, the allocation of radio frequency spectrum, the implementation of regulations, and the allocation of financial resources. A top-down strategy seems to be beneficial to the width and depth of governmental interventions, but the ultimate effects are uncertain because of broad institutional forces.

- Given the industrial blurring of partners involved in mobile TV, a government restructuring is time consuming and difficult, delaying the participants' development of a clear technology and standard, as well as their time to market. To speed up the communication between the agencies responsible for nomadic technologies, a more efficient mechanism is required.

- The political conflicts between government agencies have and will weaken the clear influence of any governmental unit, and increased the uncertainty involved in the production and diffusion of a nomadic technology.

- Nomadic technologies with different technical principles will compete with one another when they enable the same or similar innovative applications. Without comprehensive consideration from an application view, the effects of governmental interventions on technologies might be mutual offset, wasting governmental resources. The key actors that have irreplaceable advantages have a tendency to wait and see.

- In addition to governmental intervention, the diffusion of nomadic technologies is affected by broad institutional factors. Governments should predict and watch for these outside influences in order to respond with changes as quickly as possible.

This paper has some limitations regarding the generalizability of conditions because it discusses a single embedded case in Taiwan. However, as governmental intervention in the initiation and diffusion of ICT technologies is common in many countries, this paper is expected to raise some general insights and questions for the future. In the future, more research is needed in the diffusion of technologies, including nomadic technologies, using in an institutional view, including different institutions, other technologies, and other, different national contexts.

References

Allen, D., and Wilson, T. D. 2005. "Action, Interaction and the Role of Ambiguity in the Introduction of Mobile Information Systems in a UK Police Force," in *Mobile Information Systems*, E. Lawrence, B. Pernici, and J. Krogstie (eds.), Boston: Springer, pp. 15-36.

Andersen, K. V., Bjørn-Andersen, N., and Dedrick, J. 2003. "Governance Initiatives Creating a Demand-Driven E-Commerce Approach: The Case of Denmark," *The Information Society* (19), pp. 95-105.

Avgerou, C. 2000. "IT and Organizational Change: An Institutionalist Perspective," *Information Technology & People* (13:4), pp. 234-262.

BV ADT. 2008. "BV ADT is Authorized by NCC and Becomes the First RCB to issue WiMAX Mobile Station Certificate," Bureau Veritas Advance Data Technology, January 23 (http://www.adt.com.tw/english/news_files/2008012301.pdf).

China Post. 2007. "Cabinet Orders Probe of Approval of BCC's Sale Approval," June 28 (http://www.chinapost.com.tw/taiwan/2007/06/28/113561/Cabinet-orders.htm).

Choudrie, J., and Lee, H. 2004. "Broadband Development in South Korea: Institutional and Cultural Factors," *European Journal of Informational Systems* (13), pp. 103-114.

Chu, J. 2007. "Taking Over NCC—Wishful Thinking by the Ruling Party," National Policy Foundation, December 18 (http://www.npf.org.tw/particle-3752-1.html, in Chinese).

Chung, H. 2008. "Blank Regulation Influences the Purchase of WiMAX Facilities," *DIGITIMES.*, January 22 (in Chinese).

Damsgaard, J., and Lyytinen, K. 2001. "The Role of Intermediating Institutions in the Diffusion of Electronic Data Interchange (EDI): How Industry Associations Intervened in Denmark, Finland, and Hong Kong," *The Information Society* (17:3), pp. 195-210.

Damsgaard, J., and Scheepers, R. 1999. "Power, Influence and Intranet Implementation: A Safari of South African Organizations," *Information Technology & People* (12:4), pp. 333-358.

Henfridsson, O., and Lindgren, R. 2005. "Multi-Contextuality in Ubiquitous Computing: Investigating the Car Case through Action Research," *Information and Organization* (15), pp. 95-124.

Ishii, K. 2004. "Internet Use via Mobile Phone in Japan," *Telecommunications Policy* (28:1), pp. 43-58.

Juang, Y. 2008. "Intel Failed to Keep Its Word Despite the MOU with the Government," *DIGITIMES*, February 22 (in Chinese).

King, J. L., Gurbaxani, V., Kraemer, K. L., McFarlan, F. W., Raman, K. S., and Yap, C. S. 1994. "Institutional Factors in Information Technology Innovation," *Information Systems Research* (5:2), pp. 139-169.

Kling, R., and Scacchi, W. 1982. "The Web of Computing: Computer Technology as Social Organization," *Advances in Computers* (21), pp. 1-90.

Kuang, W. 2007. "TMC: Watch 3.5G Because WiMAX Won't be a Threat," *ZDNet*, October 25 (http://www.zdnet.com.tw/news/comm/0,2000085675,20125515,00.htm; in Chinese).

LANcom Express. 2007. "NCC Unveils Local WiMAX License, Upcoming Billions Market Forecasts," September (http://www.lancom.com.tw/Express/news/New75_03.htm).

Lai, W. H. 2005. "Report of Visiting IFA and IBC 2005—Trend of Mobile TV Technologies," December 30 (http://www.pts.org.tw/~rnd/p9/2005/IBC%209412.pdf; in Chinese).

Lee, C., and Pech, M. 1997. *The Taiwan Electronics Industry*, Boca Raton, FL: CRC Press.

Lee, H., O'Keefe, R. M., and Yun, K. 2003. "The Growth of Broadband and Electronic Commerce in South Korea: Contributing Factors," *The Information Society* (19), pp. 81-93.

Lin, B. 2006. "WiMAX Development and M-Taiwan: Blueprint, M-Taiwan, and Product Development," presentation to the 2006 Taipei Summit: Taiwan-Southeast Asia ICT Forum, June 6 (http://www.nectec.or.th/users/htk/files/20060605-WiMAXinTaiwan. pdf).

Lin, S., and Chiasson M. W. 2007. "Dynamic Approach to Context in Diffusion Research: An Actor Network Theory Study of Mobile-TV Service," in *Organizational Dynamics of Technology-Based Innovation: Diversifying the Research Agenda*, T. McMaster, D. Wastell, E. Fernely, and J. I. DeGross (eds.), Boston: Springer, 315-330.

Lyytinen K., and Rose, G. M. 2003. "Disruptive Information System Innovation: The Case of Internet Computing," *Information Systems Journal* (13:4), pp. 301-330.

Lyytinen, K., and Yoo, Y. 2002. "Research Commentary: The Next Wave of Nomadic Computing," *Information Systems Research* (13:4), pp. 377-388.

Markus, M. L., and Robey, D. 1988. "Information Technology and Organizational Change: Causal Structure in Theory and Research," *Management Science* (34:5), pp. 583-598.

Mathews, J. 1997. "Silicon Valley of the East: Creating Taiwan's Semiconductor Industry," *California Management Review* (39:4), pp. 26-54.

MOEA. 2008. "Intel Downgrade WiMAX to One of the Choices in Laptops," Ministry of Economic Affairs, January 5 (http://assist.nat.gov.tw/GIP/wSite/ct?xItem=10415&ctNode=23&mp=2; in Chinese).

Miscione, G. 2007. "Telemedicine in the Upper Amazon: Interplay with Local Health Care Practices," *MIS Quarterly* (31:2), pp. 403-425.

Montealegre, R. 1999. "Temporal Model of Institutional Interventions for Information Technology Adoption in Less-Developed Countries," *Journal of Management Information Systems* (16:1), pp. 207-232.

National Science Council. 2006. *Evaluation Results of National Telecommunication Technology Plans* (in Chinese).

NICI. 2007. "The Discussion Record of WiMAX Manpower Cultivation and Training," National Information and Communications Initiative Committee, Taiwan, July 4 (http://www.nici.nat.gov.tw/content/application/nici/meeting/guest-cnt-browse.php?cnt_id=2478; in Chinese).

Orlikowski, W. J., and Barley, S. R. 2001. "Technology and Institutions: What Can Research on Information Technology and Research on Organizations Learn from Each Other?," *MIS Quarterly* (25:2), pp. 145-165.

PTS. 2006. "Two-Year Project of Public Broadcasting Cultural Creation and Digital Television Development," Public Television Service Foundation, Taiwan (http://www.pts.org.tw/~web02/ 2years/plan1.htm; in Chinese).

RDEC. 2007. "Investigation on Two-Year Project of Public Broadcasting Cultural Creation and Digital Television Development," Research, Development and Evaluation Commission, Taiwan (http://www.rdec.gov.tw/public/Attachment/773116425371.doc; in Chinese).

Sawyer, S., Allen, J. P., and Lee, H. 2003. "Broadband and Mobile Opportunities: A Socio-technical Perspective," *Journal of Information Technology* (18), pp. 121-136.

Saxenian, A. 2002. "Transnational Communities and the Evolution of Global Production Networks: The Cases of Taiwan, China, and India," *Industry and Innovation* (37), pp. 1-35.

Scott, W. R. 1995. *Institutions and Organizations*, Thousand Oaks, CA: Sage Publications.

Silva, L., and Figueroa, E. B. 2002. "Institutional Intervention and the Expansion of ICTs in Latin America: The Case of Chile," *Information Technology & People* (15:1), pp. 8-25.

Swanson E. B., and Ramiller, N. C. 1997. "The Organizing Vision in Information Systems Innovation," *Organization Science* (8:5), pp. 458-474.

Teo H. H., Wei, K. K., and Benbasat, I. 2003. "Predicting Intention to Adopt Interorganizational Linkages: An Institutional Perspective," *MIS Quarterly* (27:1), pp. 19-49.

Tilson, D., Lyytinen, K., Sørensen, C., and Liebenau, J. 2006. "Coordination of Technology and Diverse—Organizational Actors during Service Innovation: The Case of Wireless Data Services in the United Kingdom," paper presented at the Helsinki Mobility Roundtable, Helsinki, Finland.

United Daily News. 2007a. "The Head of GIO Has No Sense of Propriety," June 28 (in Chinese).

United Daily News. 2007b. "A Whisper that the Executive Yuan Might Take Over NCC," December 16 (in Chinese).

Wang, Y. 2008. "WiMAX Implementation Deferred Because of Expensive Base Station," *The Liberty News*, March 3 (http://www.libertytimes.com.tw/2008/new/mar/3/today-e4.htm; in Chinese).

WiMAX Forum. 2007a. "M-Taiwan Program A WiMAX Ecosystem," March (http://www.wimaxforum.org/technology/downloads/M_Taiwan_Program.pdf).

WiMAX Forum. 2007b. "M-Taiwan Applications Promotion Program," Taipei Showcase & Conference website, December (http://www.wimaxforum.org/taipei/m-taiwan).

Yan, J. 2007. "The Competition Between NCC and the Executive Yuan," *ETtoday News*, April 2 (in Chinese).

Yin, R. K. 1984. *Case Study Research: Design and Methods*, Newbury Park, CA: Sage Publications.

About the Authors

Su-Yi Lin is a Ph.D. candidate in the Department of Management Science at Lancaster University. She received her MBA degree from the University of Taipei, and then worked as an industry analyst and a manager in the ICT industry for 10 years. Her research interests include the socio-technical context around Internet and mobile technologies, and the social effects of digital convergence. Su-Yi can be reached at s.lin5@lancaster.ac.uk.

Mike W. Chiasson, Ph.D., is a senior lecturer in the Department of Management Science at Lancaster University and an Advanced Institute for Management (AIM) Innovation Fellow. Mike's research examines the relationships between institutional contexts and the development and implementation of information systems. His work includes action research, user involvement, IT diffusion, privacy, outsourcing, and social foundations of IS development and use. Mike can be reached at m.chiasson@lancaster.ac.uk.

27 OPENING PUBLIC ADMINISTRATION: Exploring Open Innovation Archetypes and Business Model Impacts

Joseph Feller
Patrick Finnegan
Olof Nilsson
University College Cork
Cork, Ireland

Abstract   *This work-in-progress paper presents an exploration of a network of Swedish municipal authorities. Within this network, we have observed a move from isolated innovation to leveraging inflows and outflows of knowledge in a manner characteristic of the open innovation paradigm. This paper presents a characterization of these knowledge exchanges using an existing framework of open innovation archetypes, as well as an initial description of the business model impacts of this innovation approach on the participant municipalities, and the enabling role of information technology. The paper concludes by drawing preliminary conclusions and outlining ongoing research.*

Keywords   Open innovation, business model, public administration interorganizational network

1 INTRODUCTION

Western civilizations have tended to respect and reward individual rather than group initiatives. Such individualism extended to Western organizations, which consider their competitors, and very often their suppliers, as the enemy (Opper and Fersko-Weiss 1992; Roper and Weymes 2007). This is reflected in organizational theory as researchers

Please use the following format when citing this chapter:

Feller, J., Finnegan, P., and Nilsson, O., 2008, in IFIP International Federation for Information Processing, Volume 287, Open IT-Based Innovation: Moving Towards Cooperative IT Transfer and Knowledge Diffusion, eds. León, G., Bernardos, A., Casar, J., Kautz, K., and DeGross, J. (Boston: Springer), pp. 483-500.

traditionally view organizations as single entities characterized by bureaucratically determined hierarchical structures that operate by placing individuals in predefined functional roles (Czarniawaska-Joerges 1992). Consequently, organizational strategies have traditionally focused on neutralizing competitors to gain control over their buyers or suppliers (Porter 1985); although recognizing that some cartels did operate. In the past two decades, competitive pressures have focused greater attention on cooperative ventures with partners (Henderson 1990; Reid et al. 2007), even if some relationships are based more on power than cooperation (Webster 1995). In addition, developments in the production and use of complex product/service offerings (Davidow and Malone 1992) and the desire to focus on providing whole products (Moore 1999) have resulted in organizations with similar goals aligning themselves in IT-mediated partner networks in order to meet consumer requirements (Okamura and Vonortas 2006; Stafford 2002).

Despite the continuing importance of interorganizational cooperation in relation to servicing consumer needs for products and services (Okamura and Vonortas 2006), organizations have been slow to harness the same type of external cooperation in relation to innovation (Lane and Probert 2007). Nevertheless, innovation is the result of combining different knowledge sets (Nonaka et al. 2003; Tidd et al. 2005), and such knowledge is frequently to be found outside the organization (Chesbrough 2003; De Wit et al. 2007). However, with the exception of notable examples of collective invention (Allen 1983; von Hippel 1987), organizations have been slow to engage in open innovation (Chesbrough 2003). In addition to worries about the quality and suitability of external ideas, organizations have resisted cooperative approaches to innovation due to perceived competitive necessities and issues relating to organizational control (Chesbrough 2004). In the commercial area, adopting an open innovation process "includes various perspectives: (1) globalization of innovation, (2) outsourcing of R&D, (3) early supplier integration, (4) user innovation, and (5) external commercialization and application of technology" (Gassmann 2006, p. 224). Consequently, in order to move to an open innovation, there is a need for organizations to adopt business models (Chesbrough and Schwartz 2007) that utilize "both external and internal ideas to create value, while defining internal mechanisms to claim some portion of that value" (Chesbrough 2003, p. xxiv).

There have been numerous examples of the successful application of open innovation research and development processes in commercial settings such as consumer electronics (Blau 2007), pharmaceuticals (Lane and Probert 2007), as well as automobiles and computer hardware (Gwynne 2007). While open innovation practices are not limited to "high-tech" sectors (Chesbrough and Crowther 2006), there is a paucity of research on the application of open innovation outside the commercial environment.

This paper presents an exploration of a network of Swedish municipal authorities. Within this network, we have observed a move from isolated innovation to leveraging inflows and outflows of knowledge in a manner characteristic of the open innovation paradigm. This paper presents a characterization of these knowledge exchanges using an existing framework of open innovation archetypes, describes the impact of this innovation approach on the business models of the participant municipalities, and discusses the enabling role of IT. The remainder of the paper is structured as follows. In section 2, we present a theoretical grounding for the study in the work of Gassmann and Enkel (2004) on open innovation archetypes and Osterwalder et al. (2005) on business models. Section 3 describes the research methodology employed and section 4 presents a description of the case site. As this research is still in progress, we describe our initial findings in section 5, and discuss our preliminary conclusions and ongoing research in section 6.

2 THEORETICAL GROUNDING

This section presents the theoretical grounding for the study. We examine how extant research on business models and networks can frame our understanding of organizations seeking to form an ecosystem to exploit cooperatively developed innovation.

Interorganizational networks are critical for leveraging open innovation (Vanhaverbeke and Cloodt 2006). Participants in interorganizational networks believe that collaboration will result in adaptive efficiency, "the ability to change rapidly and at the same time provide customized services or products, and at low cost" (Alter and Hage 1993, p. 274). As shown in Figure 1, Gassmann and Enkel (2004) propose three core open innovation processes that illustrate the interconnectivity between an organization and its external network of partners:

1. The outside-in process: the sourcing of knowledge from external parties such as suppliers, customers, etc.

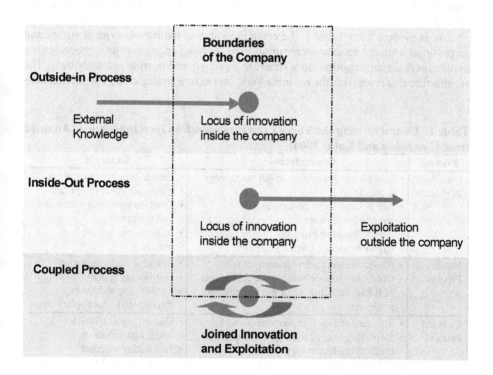

Figure 1. Three Core Processes for Open Innovation (Source: Gassmann and Enkel 2004, p. 6, used with permission of the authors)

2. The inside-out process: earning revenue by transferring ideas to the outside environment and allowing others to exploit them.
3. The coupled process: a combination of outside-in and inside-out processes by forming an alliance with external partners that can provide complementary expertise.

An interorganizational network is a social action system as it exhibits the fundamental principles of any organized form of collective behavior. These are

- Members aim to achieve collective and self-interest goals
- The division of tasks and functions among members creates interdependent processes
- The cooperative entity can act as a unit and has a separate identity from its members (Van de Ven 1976)

In order to operate, a social system imposes a structure and processes upon its members. Structure refers to administrative arrangements that establish role relationships among members. Process refers to the direction and flow of activities among members. The structural dimensions of an interorganizational relationship can be characterized by its degree of formalization, complexity, and centralization. The process dimensions of such a relationship are characterized by the direction, intensity, and variability of resource and information flows (Van de Ven 1976). Table 1 characterizes the three open innovation processes discussed above and provides examples of interorganizational interconnectivity related to each.

As is evident from Table 1, the changing locus of innovation evident within and across organizational boundaries resulting from applying open innovation processes has implications for an organization's strategic direction and operational activities. The architecture that represents the business logic connecting strategic and operational acti-

Table 1. Characterizing the Three Core Processes for Open Innovation (Adapted from Gassmann and Enkel 2004)

Process	Characteristic	Example
Outside-in Process	• Low tech industry for similar technology acquisition • Act as knowledge brokers and/or knowledge creators • Highly modular products • High knowledge intensity	• Earlier supplier integration • Customer co-development • External knowledge sourcing and integration • In-licensing and buying patents
Inside-out Process	• (Basic) Research-driven company • Objectives like decreasing the fixed costs of R&D, branding, setting standards via spillovers	• Bringing ideas to market • Out-licensing and/or selling IP • Multiplying technology through different applications
Coupled Process	• Standard setting (predominant design) • Increasing returns to industry through multiplying technology • Alliance with complementary Partners • Complementary products with critical interfaces • Relational view of the firm	• Combining outside-in and inside-out processes • Integrating external knowledge and competencies and externalizing own knowledge and competencies

vities is referred to as a business model (Osterwalder et al. 2005). Indeed, understanding the business model implications of open innovation is central to its exploitation (Chesbrough 2003; Chesbrough and Appleyard 2007; Chesbrough and Schwartz 2007).

Timmers (1999) argued that architectures for business models can be identified through the deconstruction and reconstruction of the value chain. Value chain elements are identified, as are the possible ways that information can be integrated both within the value chain and between the respective value chains of interacting parties within the interorganizational network. Furthermore, as more advanced information standards are introduced, levels of collaboration between organizations can be achieved that were previously only possible within a vertically integrated hierarchical intra-organizational structure (Evans and Wurster 2000). Indeed, it is evident from the work of Mahadevan (2000), of Osterwalder et al., and of Timmers that business models must examine both strategic and operational value-adding activities in the context of a an interorganizational network.

In developing a conceptual framework for our study, we utilize the work of Osterwalder et al., who propose a business model ontology that focuses on four aspects of the organization: product innovation, infrastructure management, customer relationship, and financials (Table 2). The application of the Osterwalder et al. framework to open innovation is not completely new. Research such as Feller et al. (2008) has applied the framework to the business model implications of companies forming a business network to leverage externally produced open source software (OSS). OSS is notable example of open innovation (West and Gallagher 2006).

Table 2. Business Model Pillars and Components (Source: Osterwalder et al., p. 18, © Association for Information Systems. Used with permission.)

Pillar	Business Model Building Block	Description
Product	Value Proposition	Gives an overall view of a company's bundle of products and services.
	Target Customer	Describes the segments of customers a company wants to offer value to.
Customer Interface	Distribution Channel	Describes the various means of the company to get in touch with its customers.
	Relationship	Explains the kind of links a company establishes between itself and its different customer segments.
	Value Configuration	Describes the arrangement of activities and resources.
Infrastructure Management	Core Competency	Outlines the competencies necessary to execute the company's infrastructure business model.
	Partner Network	Portrays the network of cooperative agreements with other companies necessary to efficiently offer and commercialize value.
Financial Aspects	Cost Structure	Sums up the monetary consequences of the means employed in the business model.
	Revenue Model	Describes the way a company makes money through a variety of revenue flows.

3   RESEARCH OBJECTIVE AND METHOD

The objective of this study is to explore a network of public administration authorities in which municipalities collaborate with each other and external parties to accelerate the creation and exploitation of internal innovations.

This type of network is in keeping with the thinking of Chesbrough and Crowther (2006) on open innovation processes. However, in order to provide a more focused consideration of the type and impact of the innovation processes, we utilize the work of Gassmann and Enkel (2004) on archetypes of open innovation processes and Osterwalder et al. (2005) on business models to formulate the following research questions:

RQ1:   *How do network participants leverage outside-in, inside-out, and coupled open innovation processes?*

RQ2:   *What is the impact of open innovation activities on the business models of the network participants?*

Given the exploratory nature of this research and the need to obtain rich data in a complex interorganizational context, a case study approach was adopted.

> A case study examines a phenomenon in its natural setting, employing multiple data collection methods to gather information from a few entities. The boundaries of the phenomenon are not clearly evident at the outset of the research and no experimental control or manipulation is used (Benbasat et al. 1987, p. 370).

Cases are most appropriate when the objective involves studying contemporary events, without the need to control variables or subject behavior (Yin 2003).

Our case study seeks to approximate reality (Guba 1990) using methods that emphasize the verification of existing knowledge and the discovery of new knowledge (Denzin and Lincoln 2000). Our method is thus consistent with the case study approach of Benbasat et al. (1987) and of Yin (2003) in that we study the phenomenon in its natural setting, employing multiple data collection methods to gather information from a few entities, without employing experimental control or manipulation. We, thus, follow in the tradition of Eisenhardt (1989) and of Madill et al. (2000) by seeking to reveal preexisting, relatively stable, and objectively extant phenomena and the relationships among them.

The case study site was chosen as a useful exemplar of the use of open innovation processes in public administration. The study began in January 2008 and is ongoing at the time of writing. The researchers first conducted an archival search of public domain material on the network and its participant municipalities. Based on this preliminary analysis, a case study protocol was prepared (Yin 2003). Having secured the cooperation of five of the six participating municipalities, interviews with key informants in the largest municipality in the network, the Municipality of Sundsvall, began in February 2008. The choice of the interviewees was based on

1.   Willingness to cooperate: In order to obtain useful material, it was necessary for a potential interviewee to be interested in the study and willing to cooperate.

2. History of network involvement: Interviewees had to be involved in the ingoing network planning and/or activity over a period of time.
3. Seniority: In order to get contextual material on strategy and experience with network activities, it was necessary to speak with senior staff within each partner firm.

The interviews, following an interview guide (Patton 1980) were of 50 to 60 minutes duration and conducted in Swedish by telephone. The interviews were transcribed and translated by one of the authors and followed up by e-mail to clarify and refine issues that emerged during the process. The respondents verified the accuracy of the transcripts. Interviews were complemented by reviews of official documents provided by the interviewees. The documents included policy statements, project reports, and official statistics published by the municipalities in the region, and by national governmental authorities. Content analysis was then carried out on both the interview and document data sets. A coding system was derived using the frameworks provided by Gassmann and Enkel and by Osterwalder et al., and a two-phase coding process was employed (Miles and Huberman 1994). During the first-level coding phase, each segment of the interview/documentation data was summarized and labeled. This was followed by a pattern coding process in which the segments of data were organized, analyzed, and synthesized within the themes/concepts embedded in the theoretical framework. While the emphasis of the first-level coding phase was on description, the pattern coding process focused on explanation. The analysis of the official documents was used primarily to supplement the data gathered through the interviews and to provide context.

4   CASE ENVIRONMENT

Traditionally, Swedish authorities have had almost a monopoly position in providing services to their citizens. *Folkhemmet* or "the people's home" (Tilton 1990, p. 125), is a concept that has played an important role during the building of the welfare state. The dominant paradigm has been that the state "takes care of you," and no one should make a profit on people's rights and needs. The welfare model is built on a taxation system which has both a broad basis of taxation, high taxation burden, and income redistribution (Andersen 2004). It is considered that a commercial or private-sector organization should put their profit interest before the public good, and is thus not suitable for running public services (e.g., schools, kindergartens, hospitals, or homes for the elderly). Swedish public authorities are organized at three levels: local, regional, and national. The Administrative Procedure Act, the principle of public access to official documents, and the Swedish Local Government Act (Government Offices of Sweden 2007a) are some of the regulations that form the framework that governs public administration activities and influences the municipalities' strategies and actions. The keywords for the Swedish authorities are *openness* and *decentralization*. In addition, the system requires that responsibility for the activities and the decision making should be located as close as possible to those concerned as such decentralization makes it possible to adjust activities to local conditions.

Municipal administration represents approximately 70 percent of the public administration in Sweden (Government Offices of Sweden 2007b). The 290 municipalities in

Sweden are all organized in a similar way: a municipality council as the highest decision-making body, a municipal executive board, and a number of boards responsible for the different areas of activity. The council consist of representatives elected in general elections every fourth year; boards are comprised of politically appointed representatives. Connected to every board is an office with civil servants charged with putting the board's decisions into practice. The municipality council takes decisions concerning the municipality's overall annual budget, as well as the level of municipality tax and fees. Each board is allocated a budget, which by law must balance (Swedish Government 2001).

This system of public administration has been subject to major overhaul in recent years. A governmental bill proposed in 2000 (Swedish Government 2000) outlined the ambition that Sweden should become "the first information society for all." This goal includes a demand upon public authorities at all levels to transform to 24/7 authorities (i.e., develop Internet-based services available day and night, year-around).

Traditionally, the municipalities have considered other municipalities as competitors in the struggle to attract visitors, migrants, and new business establishments. Escalating costs, an ageing and in many areas decreasing population, as well as increasing globalization and mobility are leading to public administration needing new ways to operate. Of particular interest, in recent years several municipalities have formed networks with the aim of sharing ideas, experiences, innovations, and software. Many of the public administration networks that have emerged can be seen as examples of open innovation processes in that they use "purposive inflows and outflows of knowledge to accelerate internal innovation, and expand the markets for external use of innovation, respectively" (Chesbrough and Crowther 2006, p. 2).

4.1 The Sundsvall Region

The Sundsvall Region (*Sundsvallsregionen*) was founded in 2004 as a cooperative network of six Swedish municipalities, situated geographically in the middle of Sweden (Figure 2). The idea behind the Sundsvall Region is that, through cooperation, synergetic effects will strengthen both the individual municipalities' and the region's ability to provide services to citizens as well as the prerequisites for sustainability and growth.

The six municipalities, Härnösand, Timrå, Sundsvall, Ånge, Nordanstig, and Hudiksvall, vary in character. The variety of labor markets, attractive shopping centers, good communications infrastructure, the county hospital, the university and the large population (94,044) all contribute to the centrality of the municipality of Sundsvall, which must be considered as the hub in the Region. The municipality of Härnösand (25,227 inhabitants) is characterized by small towns, but is the administrative center for the County of Västernorrland, and also has a university campus (which is the largest employer in the public sector). The municipality of Timrå (17,747 inhabitants) is a small coastal municipality dominated by the forest industry. The municipality of Ånge (10,692 inhabitants) is the only inland municipality within the network. It is a sparsely populated (3 persons/km^2) rural area and has lost almost half of its population since 1960. The municipality of Nordanstig is the smallest municipality in the Sundsvall Region, both in terms of area and population (9,847). Like Ånge, the municipality is a sparsely populated rural area. Finally, the municipality of Hudiksvall (37,004), situated along the coast com-

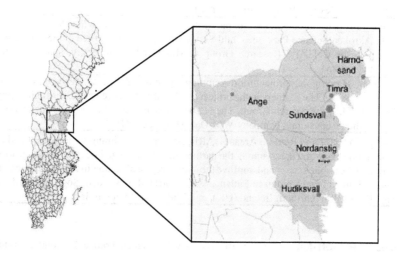

Figure 2. Geography of Sundsvall Region

prises small towns. The private economic life is dominated by the forest and engineering industries, and the public sector employs almost 38 percent.

The vision for the Sundsvall region has been expressed as follows:

> *In a region with 200,000 inhabitants we can through cooperation create better conditions for individuals and companies, create strong and sustainable growth, and increase our competitiveness. Härnösand, Timrå, Sundsvall, Ånge, Nordanstig and Hudiksvall; we are all unique and independent municipalities. Together we are now building a strong joint identity for our region, while putting every municipality's uniqueness forward. It will give us the strength to become a successful part, not only of Sweden but also of Europe. (Kortfattat om Sundsvallsregionen)[1]*

5 FINDINGS

Our study revealed that the three open innovation process archetypes described by Gassmann and Enkel (2004) were evident in both the municipal and network level activities in the Sundsvall Region. Our initial research focused on three specific projects (see Table 3). Figure 3 depicts the inside-out, outside-in, and coupled innovation processes at work, using the development and subsequent deployment of the ECHOES software project (described later in this section) to illustrate the inflows and outflows of knowledge and exploitation.

---

[1]Http://www.sundsvall.se/download/18.2980dd9910f81b06233800039/kortfattat_36sidor_061211.pdf, 2006.

Table 3. Examples of Open Innovation Projects

ECHOES – an open source web tool for parent-teacher communication developed in cooperation with Åkroken Science Park, the Child Service and Education Office at the Municipality of Sundsvall, the CITIZYS Research Group at Mid Sweden University, and a private IT consultant company.
Pensiostorm – an on-going project for developing a web portal for the elderly, based on open source components. The partners in the project are Åkroken Science Park, the Municipality of Sundsvall, CITIZYS Research Group, The National Government Employee Pensions Board (SPV), and the IT consultant company WM-Data (LogicaCMG).
Digital Age in Rural and Remote Areas (DARRA) – a project aiming to decrease the digital divide in remote and rural areas among the partner regions, through boosting the usage of ICT by SMEs and the public sector, and improve the overall regional competitiveness. Participating regions are Lapland and Kainuu in Finland, Västernorrland in Sweden, Sogn og Fjordane in Norway, Donegal in Northern Ireland (UK), and Mid West Region in Ireland.

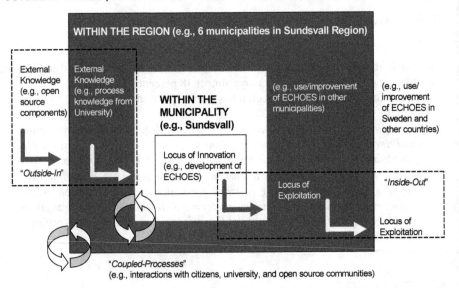

Figure 3. Open Innovation Flows in the Network

5.1 The Open Innovation Process Archetypes

The *outside-in process*: Individual municipalities have traditionally been more receptive to the concept of outside knowledge flowing in than to that of internal knowledge flowing out, as organizational controls around such knowledge are still quite "closed" in character. External knowledge has been welcomed and used in the development of systems and the performance of operational activities, but the willingness to share innovations or experiences was been limited; traditionally, other municipalities were considered as competitors. That situation is now undergoing a change toward openness and cooperation, although many in the public administration have a wait-and-see attitude about open source solutions. For example, the CEO of one municipality describes their engagement with a national collaborative software repository as

> *When we look at eGovforge.org[2] there are not so much activity around the applications that have been uploaded, but I think that it is because this area (Open Source) is still pretty new in the public sector here in Sweden. I believe that we soon would see a rapid development in this area.*

The outside-in process also includes an enhanced cooperation with academic institutions, neighboring municipalities, and the commercial sector. Indeed, in keeping with the increasing pace of globalization, innovation processes increasingly involve cooperation with organizations outside the country. By leveraging external knowledge, municipality's not only avoid "reinventing the wheel" by investing resources in innovation challenges that have already been addressed by others, but are also able to fill the gaps within their own internal set of competencies.

The strategic investigator at the Mnicipality Executive Board's Executive Office state,

> *There is a more open attitude nowadays in which we share ideas, and a number of networks to facilitate this sharing have been launched. In some areas, such as efforts to attract companies to the municipality, it has been difficult to be open or to cooperate since we compete with other municipalities for business establishments and job opportunities. But we have started discussions to also become more open and cooperative in this area as well. If, for example, we have discussions with a company and find it to be unsuitable for us, it is better for us if one of our neighbors gets it than if it goes somewhere outside the region....We also work developing models for how to run and steer the municipality, and in that area we are very open and share experiences and ideas with others. If we put questions to other municipalities regarding this, it is very rare that they don't share their experiences with us.*

The *inside-out process*: The municipality's main task to-date has been to serve the citizens and companies within the municipality, and the exploitation of innovation has been secondary to the operational concerns of organizing and delivering services within budget constraints. However, perceptions of how services should be organized and provided are changing, influenced by factors such as an ageing population, an increased mobility among people and companies, globalization and computerization. Public administration is a nonprofit endeavor; nevertheless, the external exploitation of ideas is seen as potentially contributing to an increase in the municipality's revenues by a strengthened attractiveness for migration and new establishment. As expressed by the CEO,

---

[2]eGOVForge.org is a Swedish national repository of open source software designed to "meet the demand for increased cooperation both between and inside…government bodies" and provides mechanisms for the "conversion of software developed within the public sector into open software," increasing the deployment of this software and stimulating collaborative development and open formats and standards" (see http://eGOVForge.org).

I don't see us [the municipality] as just consumers of free software, or that we use the open source community without giving anything back. I, myself, have been active for many years in introducing open software in schools also at a national level. For example, we were a group that was given the task to start and handle a site called "Utbytet" [the exchange], which was the first Swedish site [2003] for exchange of open software and experience in the school area in Sweden. Our contribution to the OS community has been an active use and promotion which have contributed to "break the ice", but also source code like Parent-Teacher Meeting.

The *coupled process*: The open innovation processes in the public administration context examined can be best understood in terms of the interactivity characterizing the coupled process archetype. The municipalities in the network work together in an alliance, but are not locked-in by this cooperation. One example of this cooperation is the development of the software to support Parent-Teacher communication (the ECHOES project), a web-based application for connecting homes and schools. The project was a joint project with Åkroken Science Park, the Child Service and Education Office at the Municipality of Sundsvall, the CITIZYS Research Group at Mid Sweden University, and a private IT consultant company as partners. Open source components were used during the whole process, and after test and evaluation the application was released in the software pool eGovforge.org (an initiative for collaboration through open software development for the public sector in Sweden) under an open source license. The successful project has lead to initiation of a new project, *Pensiostorm*, a web portal for the elderly, which now is under development. Like ECHOES, this new project seeks to build on open source components. The partners are Åkroken Science Park, Municipality of Sundsvall, CITIZYS Research Group, The National Government Employee Pensions Board (SPV), and the IT consultant company WM-Data (LogicaCMG).

The Municipality of Sundsvall is also a member in a common foundation for e-service development called *Sambruk*, which includes both cooperation around a selection of e-services as well as cooperation around the knowledge and technical components required for developing and running e-services. The initiative is in line with the Swedish government's ambitions to move to a coordinated public sector with integrated e-services. Finally, the municipality is a member of *e-Ringen*, a network for sharing ideas and experiences regarding e-administration in the public sector. According to the CEO,

I can see a future where more municipalities jointly contract suppliers and developers, and then give a more mature and developed product back to the OS community. For example, our municipality together with five other municipalities is developing an invoice module in open source that later should be uploaded at eGovforge.org for public use.

5.2   The Impact on Business Models

We have a preliminary understanding of the impact of openness on the business models of the participating municipalities in the Sundsvall Region, summarized in Table 4.

Table 4. Effects of the Sundsvall Region Network on Participating Municipalities' Business Models

Business Model Pillar		Effect of Sundsvall Region member's Business Models
Product	Value Proposition	Innovation has resulted in an extended geographic coverage, a wider range of services, an extended offer of living, education, work and leisure, raised attractiveness for migration, start-ups, tourism and a strengthened bargaining position.
Customer Interface	Target Customer	Shift from existing residents to a collaborative approach to attracting inwards-migration, company establishments, and visitors.
	Distribution Channel	Collaborative implementation of multiple IT enabled channels for the delivery of citizen services.
	Relationship	Deeper engagement with a wider range of customers.
Infrastructure Management	Value Configuration	Value shop configuration. The network strengthens the possibilities to fulfill customer needs.
	Core Competency	An extended base of core competencies, possibility to share specialist competencies.
	Partner Network	The network increases the partners' ability to find solutions inside the network, and strengthen bargaining position. Cooperation instead of competition.
Financial Aspects	Cost Structure	Enables cost-sharing among the municipalities (e.g., emergency services, education, water and sewer, public trustee office).
	Revenue Model	A raised attractiveness increases the incomes, and sharing resources reduces costs.

The Sundsvall Region network strengthens the partner municipalities' ability to offer present and potential customers an enhanced value *(value proposition)* by providing the different municipalities' unique features as one "product." The region covers a geographical area that includes a wide choice of living conditions, from coast to inland, and from big and small towns to countryside. The municipalities' different characteristics regarding commercial and industrial life and education constitute a single labor and educational market with many possibilities. The cooperation increases the attractiveness for migration while a broad labor market often is a crucial factor for couples. The fact that the network brings synergetic effects means that the smaller municipalities within the network can compete with bigger ones outside in striving for growth and sustainability. Acting as one "brand" also enhances the possibilities for state-funded infrastructure investments (such as roads and railways), which in turn raises the attractiveness of the region. According to a recent report,

The Sundsvall Region, northern Sweden's biggest labor market with its own university, is in many ways the best alternative to the metropolises. (Kortfattat om Sundsvallsregionen)

While current inhabitants and companies located within the region remain the primary **target customers**, branding the Region also raises the opportunity to successfully market the member municipalities to a broader customer base, for example, attracting tourists, day visitors, potential migrants and companies from both national and international locations.

In pace with the computerization of the society and the raised demands for e-services, the **distribution channels** have been extended. Today the Internet plays one of the leading roles in communication with existing and potential customers. It is believed that one joint web site that acts like a "one-stop-shop" or gateway to the region will gain more attention than six separate ones.

The **relationship** with the citizens is important in order to keep them as customers. By building a region, it is believed that citizenship identity and incentives for staying in the area are strengthened.

By acting as one region instead of six rival municipalities the necessary **core competency** is enhanced. A number of the municipalities' tasks and services require specialist competences, which could be costly for a small municipality. By sharing these types of competences, the service level can be kept at a desired level, without turning to actors outside the network.

The **partner network** facilitates the municipalities' ability to find solutions inside the region. It also strengthens the bargaining position to act as a region (rather than as a single municipality) while dealing with potential contractors. In contrast to the historical model in which each county council delivers transportation services in isolation, recent innovations in public transportation (as an example of the coupled-process archetype) demonstrate greater cooperation between municipalities, county councils, etc.; other coupled-process innovations (e.g., labor market innovations) also involve the county administrative board, the universities, and other public and private partners.

A key aspect of the network is the effect on the financial affairs to members. **Revenues**, which mainly are based on the municipalities' taxes and state grants, are directly dependent on the size of the population and the labor market. Due to current laws, these revenues cannot be transferred or shared between the members of the network, but accrue to the municipality where it is generated. Despite this, the region's increased attractiveness for companies, visitors, and tourists is likely to increase mobility within the region, and consequently bring benefits to all of the municipalities. As the strategic investigator reveals,

> The municipality's revenues are more or less fixed and hard to influence. Today 73 percent of the municipality's revenues comes from the municipality tax, 5 percent from general state grants, 10 percent from fees and 12 percent from other sources [e.g., directed state grants, dividends from the municipality's own companies]. The way for us to increase our revenues is to make the municipality attractive so people settle here, but also to facilitate the establishment of companies within the municipality.

Cooperation enables cost-sharing among the municipalities, which affects the **cost structure**. There are a number of basic services (e.g., water and sewer services, emergency services, and education) where cooperation has reduced costs. The strategic investigator continues,

> In other areas where we act, like elderly care, waste management, water supply and sewer management, private companies are not allowed to establish busi-

ness unless the municipality gives permission. But, even if permission is given, it is the municipality that still has the overall responsibility, which implies that if the private company decides to withdraw their business, the municipality must be prepared to fill the gap. In all sectors where we are responsible by law we must have an overcapacity, or at least some kind of plan, to be able to handle these kinds of situations.

Additionally, IT costs have been growing in pace with computerization of systems and the development of e-services. One way to tackle these costs is a strategy for using open source solutions. The CEO argues,

For us as organization, another important reason for the use of open source tools in this project is that now we can sign a contract for operation, maintenance, and development with one supplier, and after the contract period we are free to contract another supplier without loosing control over the application when it is open source. We are also free to contract different suppliers—one for the further development and another for the operation and maintenance.

6 PRELIMINARY CONCLUSIONS AND ONGOING WORK

While this research is still at an early stage, we have been able to draw some preliminary conclusions from the analysis of data gathered to date. The case study reveals that the growing movement toward more open innovation processes in Swedish public administration is being driven by two factors: (1) the changes in the national objectives regarding the delivery of public services and (2) the resource constraints (both in terms of limited budget and the internal availability of relevant capabilities) under which the municipal authorities must operate. In embracing "open innovation," we have seen evidence of all three open innovation process archetypes described by Gassmann and Enkel (2004). It is evident that in the early stages of moving toward this process, the management control activities within the authorities make these organizations most receptive to the outside-in approach. However, as the region studied has been engaged in this process for four years, we do see an increasing use of both inside-out and coupled processes, some with significant success (e.g., the ECHOES project).

However, effective participation in open innovation processes (particularly coupled processes) creates significant process, structural, and business model challenges in coordinating intermunicipality and interorganizational activities. While our work to date has focused on characterizing the collaborative processes emerging in this context, we have also found some evidence suggesting that there are significant business model changes associated with the effective exploitation of open innovation processes. The work to date represents an initial analysis of the implications of open processes for the product, customer interface, infrastructure management, and financial aspects of the public administration business model. Additionally, we found some evidence that collaborative IT platforms such as those used by open source communities (and deployed in the eGOVForge repository) have the potential to address these coordination challenges. It is noteworthy, however, that the municipalities have demonstrated a reluctance to embrace open source solutions for their operational systems; this reluctance appears to be driven by fear of the risks introduced by changing from their established (proprietary) platforms.

Our on-going work in this study comprises a closer examination of both the ways in which network participants engage in open innovation processes and the business model impacts of these activities. Future data gathering includes engagement with the remaining municipalities within the region, as well as a greater number and diversity of informants within each municipality.

Acknowledgments

This work has been funded by the Irish Research Council for the Humanities and Social Sciences (IRCHSS) through the O3C Business Models Project.

References

Allen, R. C. 1983. "Collective Invention," *Journal of Economic Behavior and Organization* (4), pp. 1-24.

Alter, C., and Hage, J. 1993. *Organisations Working Together*, London: Sage Publications.

Andersen, T. M. 2004. "Challenges to the Scandinavian Welfare Model," *European Journal of Political Economy* (20:3), pp. 743-754.

Benbasat, I., Goldstein, D. K., and Mead, M. 1987. "The Case Research Strategy in Studies of Information Systems," *MIS Quarterly* (11:3), pp. 369-386.

Blau, J. 2007. "Philips Tears Down Eindhoven R&D Fence," *Research Technology Management*. (50:6), pp. 9-10.

Chesbrough, H. 2003. *Open Innovation: The New Imperative for Creating and Profiting from Technology*, Boston: Harvard Business School Press.

Chesbrough, H. 2004. "Managing Open Innovation," *Research & Technology Management* (47:1), pp. 23-26.

Chesbrough, H., and Appleyard, M. 2007. "Open Innovation and Strategy," *California Management Review* (50:1), pp. 57-76.

Chesbrough, H., and Crowther, A. K. 2006. "Beyond High Tech: Early Adopters of Open Innovation in Other Industries," *R&D Management* (36:3), pp. 229-236.

Chesbrough, H., and Schwartz, K. 1007. "Innovating Business Models with Co-Development Partnerships," *Research Technology Management* (50:1), pp. 55-59.

Czarniawaska-Joerges, B. 1992. *Exploring Complex Organisations: A Cultural Perspective*, London: Sage Publications.

Dawidow, W. H., and Malone, M. S. 1992. *The Virtual Corporation*, New York: HarperCollins.

Denzin, N. K., and Lincoln, Y. S. 2000. "The Discipline and Practice of Qualitative Research," in *Handbook of Qualitative Research*, N. K. Denzin and Y. S. Lincoln (eds.), Thousand Oaks, CA: Sage Publications.

De Wit, J., Dankbaar, B., and Vissers, G. 2007. "Open Innovation: the New Way of Knowledge Transfer?," *Journal of Business Chemistry* (4:1), pp. 11-19.

Eisenhart, K. M. 1989. "Building Theories from Case Study Research," *Academy of Management Review* (14:4), pp. 532-550.

Evans, P., and Wurster, T S. 2000. *Blown to Bits: How the New Economics of Information Transforms Strategy*, Boston: Harvard Business School Press.

Feller, J., Finnegan, P., and Hayes, J. 20008. "Delivering the 'Whole Product': Business Model Impacts and Agility Challenges in a Network of Open Source Firms," *Journal of Database Management* (12:2), pp. 95-108.

Gassmann, O. 2006. "Opening up the Innovation Process: Towards an Agenda," *R&D Management* (36:3), pp. 223-228.

Gassmann, O., and Enkel, E. 2004. "Towards a Theory of Open Innovation: Three Core Process Archetypes," in *Proceedings of the R&D Management Conference* (RADMA), Sesimbra, Portugal, July 7-9 (http://www.alexandria.unisg.ch/EXPORT/DL/20417.pdf).

Government Offices of Sweden. 2007a. *How Sweden Is Governed*, IR 2007:010, Information Rosenbad, Stockholm, Sweden.

Government Offices of Sweden. 2007b. *Handlingsplan för eFörvaltning – Nya grunder för IT-baserad versamhetsutveckling i offentlig förvaltning*, Dnr: Fi2007/1981/SF, The Ministry of Finance, Stockholm, Sweden.

Guba, E. G. 1990. "The Alternative Paradigm Dialog," in *The Paradigm Dialog*, E. G. Guba (ed.), Newbury Park, CA: Sage Publications.

Gwynne, P. 2007. "Open Innovation's Promise and Perils," *Research Technology Management* (50:6), pp. 8-9.

Henderson, J. C. 1990. "Plugging into Strategic Partnerships: The Critical IS Connection," *Sloan Management Review*, Spring, pp. 7-18.

Lane, C., and Probert, J. 2007. "The External Sourcing of Technological Knowledge by US Pharmaceutical Companies: Strategic Goals and Inter-organizational Relationships," *Industry & Innovation* (14:1), pp. 5-25.

Madill, A., Jordan, A., and Shirley, C. 2000. "Objectivity and Reliability in Qualitative Analysis: Realist, Contextualist and Radical Constructionist Epistemologies," *British Journal of Psychology* (91:1), pp. 1-20.

Mahadevan, B. 2000. "Business Models for Internet Based E-Commerce: An Anatomy," *California Management Review* (42:4), pp. 55-69.

Miles, M. B., and Huberman, A. M. 1994. *Qualitative Data Analysis* (2nd ed.), Thousand Oaks, CA: Sage Publications.

Moore, G. 1999. *Crossing the Chasm*, New York: Harper-Perennial.

Nonaka, I., Keigo, S., and Ahmed, M. 2003. "Continuous Innovation: The Power of Tacit Knowledge," in *International Handbook of Innovation*, K. Shavinina (ed.), New York: Elsevier.

Okamura, K., and Vonortas, N. 2006. "European Alliance and Knowledge Networks," *Technology Analysis & Strategic Management* (18:5), pp. 535-560.

Opper, S., and Fresko-Weiss, H. 1992. *Technology for Teams: Enhancing Productivity in Networked Organizations*, New York: Van Nostrand Reinhold.

Osterwalder, A., Pigneur, Y., and Tucci, C. 2005. "Clarifying Business Models: Origins, Present, and Future of the Concept," *Communications of the AIS* (15), pp. 1-43.

Patton, M. Q. 1980. *Qualitative Evaluation and Research Methods*, Newbury Park, CA: Sage Publications.

Porter, M. E. 1985. *Competitive Advantage: Creating and Sustaining Superior Performance*, New York: Free Press.

Reid, N., Carroll, M., and Smith, B. 2007. "Critical Steps in the Cluster Building Process," *Economic Development Journal* (6:4), pp. 44-52.

Roper, J., and Weymes, E. 2007. "Reinstating the Collective," *Journal of Corporate Citizenship* (26), pp. 135-144.

Stafford, T. 2002. "Trust, Transactions, and Relational Exchange: Virtual Integration and Agile Supply Chain Management," in *Proceedings of the 8th Americas Conference on Information Systems*, R. Ramsower and J. Windsor (eds.), Dallas, TX, pp. 2365-2371.

Swedish Government. 2000. "Ett informationssamhälle för alla," *Governmental bill 1999/2000: 86*, Stockholm, Sweden.

Swedish Government. 2001. "God ekonomisk hushållning i kommuner och landsting," *SOU 2001:76*, The Ministry of Finance, Stockholm, Sweden.

Tidd, J., Bessant, J., and Pavitt, K. 2005. *Managing Innovation: Integrating Technological, Market and Organisational Change*, Chichester, UK: Wiley & Sons.

Tilton, T. 1990. *The Political Theory of Swedish Social Democracy: Through the Welfare State to Socialism*, Oxford, UK: Clarendon Press.

Timmers, P. 1999. *Electronic Commerce: Strategies and Models for Business-to-Business Trading*, Chichester, UK: Wiley & Sons.

Van de Ven, A. H. 1976. "On the Nature, Formation and Maintenance of Relations among Organizations," *Academy of Management Review* (1), pp. 24-36.

Vanhaverbeke, W., and Cloodt, M. 2006. "Open Innovation in Value Networks," in *Open Innovation: Researching a New Paradigm*, H. Chesbrough, W. Vanhaverbeke, and J. West (eds.), Oxford, UK: Oxford University Press.

von Hippel, E. 1987. "Cooperation Between Rivals: Informal Know-How Trading," *Research Policy* (16:6), pp. 291-302.

Webster, J. 1995. "Networks of Collaboration or Conflict? Electronic Data Interchange and Power in the Supply Chain," *Journal of Strategic Information Systems* (4:1), pp. 31-42.

West, J., and Gallagher, S. 2006. "Challenges of Open Innovation: The Paradox of Firm Investment in Open-Source Software," *R&D Management* (36:3), pp. 319-331.

Yin, R. K. 2003. *Case Study Research, Design and Methods* (3rd ed.), Newbury Park, CA: Sage Publications.

About the Authors

Joseph Feller, Ph.D., is a senior lecturer in Business Information Systems at University College Cork, Ireland. His research focuses on open source software and other forms of collaborative production. He has published four books and his work has appeared in leading international journals and conferences including *Information Systems Research, Information Systems Journal, Journal of Strategic Information Systems, Journal of Database Management,* the International Conference on Information Systems, the European Conference on Information Systems, and working conferences of IFIP. He has also published widely in practitioner-oriented publications and is a frequent contributor to the *Cutter Consortium*. He was program chair for the IEEE/ACM workshop series on open source software engineering (2001–2005) and the 3rd International Conference on Open Source Systems (IFIP 2.13) and has edited several journal special issues on the subject of open source. He can be reached at jfeller@afis.ucc.ie.

Patrick Finnegan received his Ph.D. from the University of Warwick, England, and is currently a senior lecturer in information systems at University College Cork, Ireland. His research on interorganizational systems and electronic business has been published in a number of international journals and conferences, including *Information Systems Research, Information Systems Journal, Information Technology and People, DATABASE, Journal of Information Technology, International Journal of Electronic Commerce, Electronic Markets,* the International Conference on Information Systems, the European Conference on Information Systems, and working conferences of IFIP. He is currently an associate editor of *Information Systems Journal* and president of the Irish Association for Information Systems. He can be reached at p.finnegan@ucc.ie.

Olof Nilsson is a senior lecturer in Social Informatics at Mid Sweden University and, during 2008, a Post-Doctoral Research Fellow at University College Cork, Ireland. His research has been focused on access to public information systems, and he has taken an active part in two "triple helix" projects developing open source applications for public authorities. His research on access has been published in *International Journal of Public Information Systems,* in a forthcoming edition of *International Journal for Humanistic and Social Computing,* and also in a number of international conference proceedings. He is currently researching how open source and open innovation facilitates changes to the traditional approach to public service and government in Sweden. He can be reached at o.nilsson@ucc.ie.

Part 10

On-Going Research

Part 10

On-Going Research

28 COMMUNITY FOR INNOVATIONS: Developing an Integrated Concept for Open Innovation

Ulrich Bretschneider
Michael Huber
Jan Marco Leimeister
Helmut Krcmar
Technische Universität München
Munich, Germany

Abstract   *This paper presents a research project called GENIE. It aims at developing a concept for integrating external stakeholders into a company's innovation management through a virtual community. This novel instrument for opening up a company's innovation process to external stakeholders enables collaborative creation and implementation of innovations along the entire innovation process. We focus on software companies and aim at developing and testing this approach in several real-world settings.*

Keywords   Open innovation, wisdom of crowds, virtual communities for innovations

1 INTRODUCTION

1.1 Innovation Problem for Software Companies

Innovative strength in Germany compared to other countries can be found in the domain of engineering and industrial commodities. A prominent example is the German automobile industry (Holl et al. 2006). However, this cannot be said of German software producers, who are only average when compared to other countries such as the United

Please use the following format when citing this chapter:

Bretschneider, U., Huber, M., Leimeister, J. M., and Krcmar, H., 2008, in IFIP International Federation for Information Processing, Volume 287, Open IT-Based Innovation: Moving Towards Cooperative IT Transfer and Knowledge Diffusion, eds. León, G., Bernardos, A., Casar, J., Kautz, K., and DeGross, J. (Boston: Springer), pp. 503-510.

States or other leading European countries. A survey conducted by the German Federal Ministry of Education and Research found that German software producers lack a business culture fostering systematic innovation activities. There is no systematic brainstorming in order to generate ideas for innovations. Idea generation takes place informally without sustainability and is often driven by coincidence (Holl et al. 2006, p. 118). Furthermore, the management of innovation by software producers does not use the innovative potential of customers. Customers' demands, wishes, and requirements often are not used systematically for new product development. Usually, customers are merely treated as recipients of products, not as a source of innovations.

As a consequence, German software producers generate fewer "real" innovations compared to software producers from other countries. Usually, software companies, which are often organized as a one-man as well as one-product business, generate incremental innovations. They "just" improve their existing software products over a long period of time without generating disruptive or radical innovations. However, this situation will endanger the future prospects of software producers in the highly competitive software market.

1.2 Potential of Open Innovation

The chance for software companies to overcome these problems depends on opening up innovation activities to other resources (e.g., employees or other stakeholders), but especially to customers and software users. Customers and other stakeholders should take part in innovative value creating activities, making their integration into innovation activities an important competitive strategy, especially for small and medium sized software producers.

This approach, often referred to as *open innovation* (Chesbrough 2003; von Hippel 2005; von Hippel and Katz, 2002), increases in importance in product development. The literature describes the integration of customers as one of the biggest resources for innovations (Tidd et al. 2005; Wagner and Prasarnphanich 2007). The underlying idea is that the integration of stakeholders will open up the company's innovation funnel, with more potential perspectives or ideas for creating innovations entering the innovation process. In other words, the amount of innovation potential that can be poured into the innovation funnel is rising because more actors are actively involved. Therefore, the company gains more ideas for innovation. Thus, the principle of *collective intelligence* or *wisdom of crowds* is the underlying assumption of open innovation (Libert and Spector 2008; Surowiecki 2005).

1.3 Existing Methods and Practices for Integrating Customers in Innovation Activities

Open innovation systems require communication and interaction between all parties involved, namely the company's internal actors as well as its external stakeholders. In practice, a couple of methods and instruments are in use, allowing stakeholder integration into the early stages of the innovation process. The literature describes three core methods: the lead user method, Internet toolkits, and idea competitions. The lead user method implies systematic identification of single innovative customers (so called lead users) and their integration into workshops in order to generate ideas and concepts for new products or services together with the company's employees (von Hippel 1988). With the help of toolkits, customers are asked to design concepts for new products via the Internet or a software application (von Hippel and Katz 2002). By conducting idea competitions, companies attempt to collect innovative ideas from customers (Walcher 2007).

The problem with existing methods and practices is that none of them fosters collaboration among involved parties, especially customers. In idea competitions, competitive situations are induced, preventing collaboration among idea contributors. Collaboration has been identified a s a great potential of stakeholder integration (Gasco-Hernandez and Torres-Coronas 2004). Research shows that most innovations are not the result of a single inventor but rather of collaboration processes where many individuals contribute their individual knowledge, experiences, and strengths (Franke and Shah 2003; Gasco-Hernandez and Torres-Coronas 2004; Nemiro 2001; Sawhney et al. 2005). Furthermore, established methods and practices solely serve the early stages of the innovation process where ideas for innovation are generated. There are no practices or methods available that allow involved parties to enhance or elaborate collected ideas into innovation concepts or even prototypes.

2   COMMUNITIES FOR INNOVATION

2.1   The Concept of Communities for Innovations

Opening up the innovation funnel to external stakeholders depends heavily on their willingness to interact and share ideas with each other. This willingness to share and collaborate can often be found in virtual communities, for example, in the context of open source software (von Hippel and von Krogh 2003). Therefore, we introduce the concept of a company-induced virtual community for innovations consisting of the stakeholders of a software company, especially customers and company members. Previous work on community building in other domains has shown that, to a certain extent, it is possible to influence building and establishing virtual communities according to specified goals (Leimeister and Krcmar 2005, 2006).

The proposed community for innovation aims at supporting software companies at every stage of their innovation process. Acting via an Internet platform, community members can generate ideas and collaborate with each other. Each member of the community can submit ideas, connect with idea contributors who submitted similar or complementary ideas, and elaborate ideas in collaboration with matched members. Thus, the community enables forming various networks/teams that will collaboratively elaborate better, more meaningful, and relevant ideas compared to those initially submitted. Using this mechanism will help select the best ideas and will increase the benefit for the company significantly.

Furthermore, we assume that ideas generated in this manner will likely carry *solution information*, representing not only the customer's needs and wishes but also customer suggestions describing how to transfer these ideas into marketable products (von Hippel

1994). On the basis of the ideas elaborated, the networks/teams can start to develop innovative software prototypes collaboratively.

2.2 Requirements for Communities for Innovations

Building communities for innovations has both organizational and technical requirements. From an organizational perspective, the concept has to account for motivational aspects. The underlying question is: why should software users participate in the community for innovation? Research into open source communities may give insight for answering this question, as our concept is comparable to an open source community. Several research projects analyzed the motivations of participants in open source projects (Hars and Ou 2002; Hertel et al. 2003; Lakhani and Wolf 2003; Lerner and Tirole 2000). Open source project participants' motivation falls into two broad categories: internal factors (e.g., intrinsic motivation, altruism) and external reward (e.g., expected future returns, personal needs) (Hars and Ou 2002). Understanding the motivational reasons of potential participants is essential for developing adequate incentives.

Every virtual community has its own social framework, which is embedded in the daily life of every participant and is represented in its underlying Internet platform (Kelly and Jones 2001), so another organizational requirement for building communities for innovation is to design a social framework. When designing a community for innovations from scratch, one has to develop norms, rituals, and policies about how members get to know each other, start debates, collaborate, and perform other activities. Other questions that arise in this context are: What kind of governance should be established? Which rules should be included and how should they be enforced? Research in the field of virtual communities has acknowledged the importance of social settings in communities (Preece and Maloney-Krichmar 2003) that can give insights for our research.

From a technical perspective, the community for innovations requires an adequate IT-based platform. This platform needs to offer a mutable and freely composeable set of IT tools. Needed IT tools can be categorized as follows: (1) tools for communicating (chat, bulletin board, usenet etc.), (2) tools for visualizing and presenting ideas, and (3) tools for collaborating. The design of IT tools for the community has to be adjusted according to interaction practices of the community for innovation members, otherwise the tools will not be used (Orlikowski et al. 1995). For example, computer-supported cooperative work media have different effects in specific settings (Olson and Olson 1997). Furthermore, research on virtual communities shows different impacts of technologies on different kinds of communities as there are significant differences between the various technologies available for supporting online communities (Preece and Maloney-Krichmar 2003). So, the right set of technologies out of each category has to be identified for the technical design of the community for innovations.

3 RESEARCH APPROACH AND METHODOLOGY

As the concept of *community for innovations* is new and hardly investigated, general theories about this novel approach do not yet exist. Stating and validating hypotheses that are purely deduced from theory—common in empirical–analytical research designs—cannot be applied here. We need to develop the concept in a real-world setting and continuously improve it as we learn.

For designing novel, socio-technical innovations such as communities for innovations, explorative methods are often most fruitful. We therefore design this research as an action research project. According to Baskerville's (1999) action research cycle, the project is structured in circular phases.

Diagnosing: In this phase, aspects of the community for innovations—namely, the domain of customer integration into innovation processes, motivation, collaboration, etc.—will be analyzed from a theoretical as well as from a practical perspective. We will develop requirements for community building and management. For example, we will employ the *inducements–contributions theory* in order to account for motivational incentives of the community members. The requirements identified will give guidance for the further research process.

Action Planning: Based on the results of phase one, we will plan the concept of communities for innovations in detail. We will design an organisational concept as well as an IT platform that will offer adequate IT support for the different tasks of the community. Thus, we will give answers to the following questions: (1) What are adequate incentives for the community members to submit ideas as well as to link to other members and to collaborate with them? (2) How does the community have to be organized, and what will these organizational structures look like, so that the concept will work? (3) What will be the interaction and communication needs of the community members? (4) Which existing or not-yet-developed IT tools are needed to support the activities and tasks occurring in communities for innovations? (5) How can these IT tools be integrated and orchestrated on a single IT-based platform?

Action Taking: In this phase, the concept planned in phase two will be tested. As a main goal of the field test, we will analyze if, how, and why the concept works or not. We will run the test in cooperation with a large ERP software company in order to access to its customer base. The customers will be potential members of our pilot community.

Evaluating: After implementing the concept, the observed results will be evaluated according to a pre-defined evaluation scheme. We aim to find out if the following questions can be answered: (1) Will the community breed ideas for innovations? (2) Will the community members elaborate ideas collaboratively? (3) Will the elaborated ideas arising from collaboration processes be more useful compared to those arising from other methods and practices of stakeholder integration? (How can the quality of ideas be measured?) (4) Will the elaborated ideas arising from communities for innovations contain solution information? (If yes, to which degree?) (5) Will the IT tools provided to support creative activities be accepted by the community?

4 CONCLUSION

The concept of community for innovations seems to be a promising approach. Two main aspects make us believe that this concept will work: (1) From an organizational perspective, the open source phenomenon shows that collaborative software development via the Internet can work. (2) From a motivational perspective, several research results confirm that customers will actively involve themselves in manufacturers' innovation processes without asking for monetary reward (Franke and Shah 2003; Harhoff et al.

2003; Henkel and von Hippel 2003). This phenomenon is discussed in the literature as *free revealing* (Harhoff et al. 2003).

As our concept of community for innovations is new, it has to be tested and verified in practice. The results of our field tests will answer to the question, are communities for innovations an alternative or even a better method for integrating customers and stakeholders into manufacturers' innovation process compared to user toolkits or idea competitions? At the end of our research project, the following open research questions should be addressed: What are the implications for open innovation theory applying the concept of communities for innovations? What are the key lessons learned after testing the concept in the field?

References

Baskerville, R. 1999. "Investigating Information Systems with Action Research," *Communications of the Association of Information Systems* (2:19) (http://cais.aisnet.org/articles/2-19/default.asp?View=html&x=47&y=11).

Chesbrough, H. W. 2003. *Open Innovation: The New Imperative for Creating and Profiting from Technology*, Boston: Harvard Business School Press.

Franke, N., and Shah, S. 2003. "How Communities Support Innovative Activities: An Exploration of Assistance and Sharing among End-Users," *Research Policy* (32:1), pp. 157-178.

Gasco-Hernandez, M., and Torres-Coronas, T. 2004. "Virtual Teams and Their Search for Creativity," in *Virtual and Collaborative Teams*, S. H. Godar and S. P. Ferris (eds.), Hershey, PA: Idea Group Publishing, pp. 213-231.

Harhoff, D., Henkel, J., and von Hippel, E. 2003. "Profiting from Voluntary Information Spillovers: How Users Benefit by Freely Revealing Their Innovations," Research Policy (32:10), pp. 1753-1769.

Hars, A., and Ou, S. 2002. "Working for Free? Motivations for Participating in Open-Source Projects," *International Journal of Electronic Commerce* (6:3), pp. 25-39.

Henkel, J., and von Hippel, E. 2003. "Welfare Implications of User Innovations," working paper, Sloan School of Management, Massachusetts Institute of Technology.

Hertel, G., Niedner, S., and Herrmann, S. 2003. "Motivation of Software Developers in Open Source Projects: An Internet-Based Survey of Contributors to the Linus Kernel," *Research Policy* (32:1), pp. 1159-1177.

Holl, F. L., Menzel, K., Morcinek, P., Mühlberg, J. T., Schäfer, I., and Schüngel, H. 2006. *Studie zum Innovationsverhalten deutscher Software-Entwicklungsunternehmen*, Berlin: Eigenverlag.

Kelly, K., and Jones, M. 2001. "Groupware and the Social Infrastructure of Communication," *Communications of the ACM* (44:12), pp. 77-79.

Lakhani, K. R., and Wolf, R. 2003. "Why Hackers Do What They Do: Understanding Motivation Effort in Free/Open Source Software Projects," MIT Sloan School of Management Working Paper No. 4425-03 (http://papers.ssrn.com/sol3/papers.cfm?abstract_id=443040).

Leimeister, J. M., and Krcmar, H. 2005. "Evaluation of a Systematic Design for a Virtual Patient Community," *Journal of Computer-Mediated Communication* (10:4) (http://jcmc.indiana.edu/vol10/issue4/leimeister.html).

Leimeister, J. M., and Krcmar, H. 2006. "ommunity-Engineering: Systematischer Aufbau und Betrieb Virtueller Communitys im Gesundheitswesen," *Wirtschaftsinformatik* (48:6), pp. 418-429.

Lerner, J., and Tirole, J. 2000. "The Simple Economics of Open Source," working paper, Harvard Business School (available online at http://www.hbs.edu/research/facpubs/workingpapers/papers2/9900/00-059.pdf).

Libert, B., and Spector, J. 2008. *We Are Smarter Than Me: How to Unleash the Power of Crowds in Your Business*, Upper Saddle River, NJ: Wharton School Publishing.

Nemiro, J. E. 2001. "Connection in Creative Virtual Teams," *Journal of Behavioral and Applied Management* (3:2), pp. 92-112.

Olson, G. M., and Olson, J. S. 1997. "Research on Computer Supported Cooperative Work," in *Handbook of Human Computer Interaction* (2nd ed.), M. Helander, T. K. Landauer, and P. Prabhu (eds.), Amsterdam: Elsevier, pp. 1433-1456.

Orlikowski, W., Yates, J., Okamura, K., and Fujimoto, M. 1995. "Shaping Electronic Communication: The Metastructuring of Technology in Use," *Organization Science* (6:4), pp. 423-444.

Preece, J., and Maloney-Krichmar, D. 2003. "Online Communities," in *Handbook of Human-Computer Interaction*, J. Jacko and A. Sears (eds.), Mahwah, NJ: Lawrence Erlbaum Associates, pp. 596-620.

Rapaport, R. N. 1970. "Three Dilemmas in Aaction Research," *Human Relations* (23:4), pp. 499-513.

Sawhney, M., Verona, G., and Prandelli, E. 2005. "Collaborating to Create: The Internet as a Platform for Customer Engagement in Product Innovation," *Journal of Interactive Marketing* (19:4), pp. 4-17.

Surowiecki, J. 2005. *The Wisdom of Crowds: Why the Many Are Smarter Than the Few*, New York: Anchor Books.

Tidd, J., and Bessant, J. R., and Pavitt, K. 2005. *Managing Innovation: Integrating Technological, Market and Organizational Change* (2nd ed.), Chichester: John Wiley & Sons.

von Hippel, E. 1988. *The Source of Innovation*, New York: Oxford University Press.

von Hippel, E. 1994. "Sticky Information and the Locus of Problem Solving," *Management Science* (14:4), pp. 429-439.

von Hippel, E. 2005. *Democratizing Innovation*, Cambridge, MA: The MIT Press.

von Hippel, E., and Katz, R. 2002. "Shifting Innovation to Users via Toolkits," *Management Science* (48:7), pp. 821-833.

von Hippel, E., and von Krogh, G. 2003. "Open Source Software and the 'Private-Collective' Innovation Model: Issues for Organization Science," *Organization Science* (14:2), pp. 209-223.

Wagner, C., and Prasarnphanich, G. 2007. "Innovating Collaborative Content Creation: The Role of Altruism and Wiki Technology," in *Proceedings of the 40th Hawaii International Conference on System Sciences*, Big Island, Hawaii, January 3-6.

Walcher, D. 2007. *Der Ideenwettbewerb als Methode der aktiven Kundenintegration: Theorie, Analyze und Implikationen für den Innovationsprozess*, Wiesbaden, Germany: Gabler.

About the Authors

Ulrich Bretschneider graduated from University of Paderborn, Germany, with a diploma in business administration (Dipl. Kfm.) in 2003. From 2003 until 2005, he was research associate at the Cooperative Computing & Communication Laboratory (C-LAB), Paderborn, where he worked in several research projects on open source communities. From 2005 until 2006, he was a research associate at the University of Witten/Herdecke, Witten, Germany. In Witten, he researched in the field of online health communities. In 2007, he changed to Technische Universität München, Germany, where he works as research associate. Ulrich's current research experiences and interests include virtual communities as well as open innovation, especially idea competitions. He can be reached at ulrich.bretschneider@in.tum.de.

Michael Huber graduated from Technische Universität München, Germany, with a Master's in Computer Science in 2007. Since 2007, he has worked as a research associate at Technische

Universität München. His research interests include community engineering, virtual communities, communities for innovations, IT support of collaborative activities, and human-computer interaction. He is engaged in the GENIE project supporting customer-driven development of innovations for software companies. Michael can be reached at hubermic@in.tum.de.

Jan Marco Leimeister holds the Chair for Information Systems at the University of Kassel, Germany. He also runs research groups on mobile/ubiquitous computing, IT innovation management, and eHealth at Technische Universität München. He is active in the Munich Competence Center on eHealth. Dr. Leimeister's research interests include the design, introduction, and management of IT-supported organizations and innovations, strategic Information management, collaboration and service engineering, as well as virtual communities. His work has been published in journals such as *Journal of Management Information Systems*, *IT & People*, *Communications of the AIS*, *Journal of Organizational Computing & Electronic Commerce*, and *WIRTSCHAFTSINFORMATIK*. He can be reached at leimeister@in.tum.de.

Helmut Krcmar is a professor of Information Systems and holds the Chair for Information Systems at the Department of Informatics, Technische Universität München, Germany. He worked as Post Doctoral Fellow at the IBM Los Angeles Scientific Center, as assistant professor of Information Systems at New York University's Leonard Stern School of Business, and at Baruch College, City University of New York. From 1987 to 2002, he was Chair for Information Systems, Hohenheim University, Stuttgart, Germany. His research interests include information and knowledge management, IT-enabled value webs, service management, computer-supported cooperative work, and information systems in health care and eGovernment. Dr. Krcmar can be reached at krcmar@in.tum.de.

29

GOVERNANCE STRUCTURES FOR OPEN INNOVATION: A Preliminary Framework

Joseph Feller
Patrick Finnegan
Jeremy Hayes
Philip O'Reilly
University College, Cork
Cork, Ireland

Abstract   *This research-in-progress paper presents a preliminary framework of four open innovation governance structures. The study seeks to describe four distinct ways in which firms utilize hierarchical relationships, organizational intermediaries, and the market system to supply and acquire intellectual property and/or innovation capabilities from sources external to the firm. This paper reports on phase one of the study, which involved an analysis of six open innovation exemplars based on public data. This phase of the study reveals that governance structures for open innovation can be categorized based on whether they (1) are mediated or direct or (2) seek to acquire intellectual property or innovation capability. We analyze the differences in four governance structures along seven dimensions, and reveal the importance of knowledge dispersion and uncertainty to the use of open innovation hierarchies, brokerages, and markets. The paper concludes by examining the implications of the findings and outlining the next phase of the study.*

Keywords   Open innovation, governance structures, hierarchies, markets, brokerages

Please use the following format when citing this chapter:

Feller, J., Finnegan, P., Hayes, J., and O'Reilly, P., 2008, in IFIP International Federation for Information Processing, Volume 287, Open IT-Based Innovation: Moving Towards Cooperative IT Transfer and Knowledge Diffusion, eds. León, G., Bernardos, A., Casar, J., Kautz, K., and DeGross, J. (Boston: Springer), pp. 511-525.

1   INTRODUCTION

Research has confirmed that firms that innovate their processes, products, and/or services outperform their competitors (Tidd 2000). However, the management of such innovation is both difficult and risky (Tidd et al. 2005) and many managers are dissatisfied with their firm's approach to managing this challenge (Arthur D. Little 2005). At its core, innovation is about knowledge and emerges as a result of combining different knowledge sets (Nonaka, et al. 2003; Tidd et al. 2005). However, such knowledge is frequently to be found outside the firm, and over the last few years increasing attention has been given to the concept of *open innovation*, namely,

> The use of purposive inflows and outflows of knowledge to accelerate internal innovation, and expand the markets for external use of innovation, respectively. Open innovation is a paradigm that assumes that firms can and should use external ideas as well as internal ideas, and internal and external paths to market, as they look to advance their technology....This approach places external ideas and external paths to market on the same level of importance as that reserved for internal ideas and paths to market in the earlier era. (Chesbrough 2005, p. 1)

In the open innovation paradigm, firms supplement, or even supplant, internal research and development efforts by leveraging a variety of sources for knowledge *inflows* including suppliers, partners, customers, competitors, academic researchers, etc. Firms also supplement existing models and markets by exploiting intellectual property (IP) in a variety of ways such as licensing IP to those outside of the firm and spinning off ventures that can tackle new markets in ways the originating firm cannot (*outflows*) (Chesbrough 2003). To date, research on open innovation has focused primarily on the internal business model aspects of the concept (Chesbrough 2003, 2006; West et al. 2006). However, less attention has been devoted to interorganizational and business network aspects (Vanhaverbeke 2006; Vanhaverbeke and Cloodt 2006). Because firms seeking to implement open innovation practices are embedded within sectors, industries, and networks, future research on open innovation must consider the economic structures, institutions, and regulatory environments in which these firms operate (West et al. 2006).

This paper presents the initial findings from phase one of a study examining governance structures for open innovation. The concept of governance, adopted from the economics literature, refers to the contractual frameworks that govern interfirm relationships for supplying and acquiring resources, thus leading to mutual gains (Hayek 1945). The paper begins by drawing on extant research to examine the conditions that give rise to hierarchies, markets, and intermediaries as governance structures for interfirm relationships. We argue that firms may seek to acquire innovation resources (skills and solutions) outside the firm due to factors such as resource scarcity, cost, economies of scale, resource utilization, and relative advantage. We illustrate that while traditional interfirm licensing agreements are characterized by hierarchical arrangements, the dispersed nature of knowledge outside firm boundaries will lead to the use of other governance structures such as mediated and direct market structures. This is followed by an overview of the methodology used for the study. Our analysis reveals four governance structures for open innovation. We characterize these structures to reveal the importance of knowledge dispersion and uncertainty to the use of open innovation hierarchies, brokerages, and markets. Finally, we conclude by outlining the future stages of the study.

2   THEORETICAL GROUNDING

Researchers such as Coase (1937) envisaged that all resource production would take place within a firm unless the cost of doing so exceeded the cost of acquiring the resource externally. Building on the cost view, other researchers acknowledge the importance of factors such as economies of scale, increased resource utilization, and utilizing relative advantage such as productive capacity, managerial capacity, and technological know-how in determining what is produced within a firm and what is acquired externally (Clemons and Row 1992; Kumar and van Dissel 1996). In particular, resource dependency theory proposes that actors lacking in essential resources will seek to establish cooperative relationships with other organizations in order to obtain resources and reduce uncertainty (Pfeffer and Salancik 1978; Tilquist et al. 2002). Drawing upon Benson's (1975) work on political economy and social exchange mechanisms (see Emerson 1962, 1972), Pfeffer and Salancik (1978) identify three factors that determine the dependence of one organization on another:

- The importance of the resource (the extent to which an organization requires it for continued operation and survival).
- The extent of the discretion over the allocation and use of a resource possessed by the organization.
- The extent to which there are few alternatives, or concentration, of resource control.

Transactions with external parties to acquire resources entail uncertainty about their outcome due to bounded rationality and opportunism of agents. To overcome this uncertainty, and as a means of reducing transaction costs, agents implement a governance structure (Williamson 1991). A governance structure is "the explicit or implicit contractual framework within which a transaction is located" (Williamson 1981, p. 1544). Therefore, governance is viewed as a mechanism that instils order in an interorganizational relationship where potential conflict threatens to undo or upset opportunities to realize mutual gains (Williamson 1999).

Governance structures are generally regarded as being either hierarchical or market structures (Hess and Kemerer 1994; Schmid 199). A hierarchy is defined as a structure that spans two separate entities; it both represents a long-term relationship between organizations, and also governs that relationship by managerial decisions (Schmid 1993). Consequently, predefined standards and rules are used to coordinate activities between organizations (Robey and Sales 1994). In determining why organizations choose hierarchies, rather than the market mechanism, Coase (1937, p. 337) stated that

> It may be desired to make a long-term contract for the supply of some article or service. This may be due to the fact that if one contract is made for a longer period, instead of several shorter ones, then certain costs of making contracts

will be avoided. Or owing to the risk attitude of the people concerned they may prefer to make a longer rather than a short term contract.

Firms acquiring IP from outside of the firm is not a new concept. For many years, firms have sought to acquire externally developed IP, perceiving that it is more efficient and effective to purchase or license existing IP, rather than reinvent the IP internally. The traditional approach by which firms acquire external IP can be characterized as being primarily hierarchical in nature (Oxley 1999).

The second structure by which extra-organizational activities may be coordinated is a market; representing arm's-length and short-term relationships between participants (Malone et al. 1987). Traditionally, the price mechanism has been used to coordinate the activities of firms operating in a particular market (Hayek 1945). However, other factors (such as quantity, design, and delivery target schedule) may also be utilized to coordinate activities in the market (Hess and Kemerer 1994; Malone et al. 1987).

Revealing the importance of knowledge to the choice of governance structure, Hayek (1945) argued that knowledge does not exist in a concentrated or integrated form but as "dispersed bits of incomplete and frequently contradictory knowledge which all separate individuals possess" (p. 77). He argued that the main problem for individual firms is how to secure the best use of resources given the dispersed nature of knowledge. He believed that one of the key considerations in what he defines as the *knowledge economy* is the process by which individuals obtain such knowledge in order to make their decisions. In addition to markets and hierarchies, Hayek saw the emergence of intermediaries to aggregate disparate information and knowledge. Researchers (e.g., Clemons and Weber 1990; Lee and Clarke 1996) have adopted the concept of market intermediaries to distinguish between decentralized (direct search) and centralized (mediated) markets. The characteristics of decentralized and centralized market relationships together with hierarchies are summarized in Table 1.

A decentralized market refers to a market without an intermediary while a centralized market refers to a market with intermediaries. In a decentralized market, all participants are in contact with all possible trading partners and they each make their own decisions about which transactions to accept. Thus, there are high search costs due to the fact

Table 1. Characteristics of Hierarchical, Decentralized, and Centralized Market Relationships

Type of Relationship	Characteristics
Hierarchy	• Structure that spans two separate firms • Long-term relationship between firms • Relationship governed by managerial decisions
Decentralized Market	• Parties search each other out directly • No intermediary involved • High search costs • Typically arm's length and short term in nature
Centralized Market	• Intermediaries assist in search process • Intermediaries possess market knowledge • Improved search capabilities possibly offset by higher uncertainty • Typically arm's length and short term in nature

that each party must directly discover each possible partner (Palmer and Lindemann 2003). In a centralized market, by contrast, participants do not need to contact all potential trading counterparts because an intermediary is already in contact with them (Lee and Clarke 1996). Such markets are commonly referred to as broker markets (or brokerages). In brokerages, the role of the broker is to provide additional processes to the market and lower search costs. This is commonly achieved through the additional information available to the broker about the market. In such markets, participants utilize the brokers to conduct the research for them, and to provide specialized knowledge of assets traded in a particular market (Bodie et al. 2004). However, higher uncertainty, time delays, suboptimal prices, participation fees, etc. may offset the value of improved search capabilities and external market knowledge in a broker market (Palmer and Lindemann 2003).

3   RESEARCH METHOD

The objective of our study is to explore governance structures for open innovation. Our research method follows in the tradition of Eisenhardt (1989) and Madill et al. (2000); it is designed to reveal preexisting, relatively stable, and objectively extant phenomena and the relationships among them in a manner that is not limited to examining only pre-identified constructs.

In the current phase of the study, we began with extant theories of governance to frame our exploration of the use of hierarchical, decentralized, and centralized market relationships for open innovation. This is in line with Lee and Baskerville (2003) who, in addressing the issue of generalization, document the process of generalizing from theory to empirical description (research seeks to apply theoretical findings confirmed in one setting to another setting). This phase of the study was concerned with achieving an increased understanding of the open innovation phenomenon. In particular, we sought to develop a rich description (based on secondary data analysis and publicly available primary data) of six exemplars of open innovation: InnoCentive, Yet2, YourEncore, Threadless, NineSigma, and Proctor and Gamble's Connect + Develop Initiative (see Table 2). Several researchers (e.g., Huston and Sakkab 2006; Motzek 2007) have identified these sites as being among the leading systems in terms of open innovation.

Data for the study was gathered over a three-month period. Data was gathered from (1) published content from the companies, (2) analysis of the web-based systems utilized by the companies (where applicable), and (3) academic and industry publications related to the companies.

Content analysis was undertaken using grounded theory coding techniques as proposed by Strauss and Corbin (1990) and exemplified by the research of Orlikowski, (1993) and Urquhart (1997). This approach necessitates the researchers to be immersed in the data (Glaser and Strauss 1967) and to draw on existing theoretical knowledge without imposing a theory (Corbin and Strauss 1990; Urquhart 1997). It thus encourages the researcher to be flexible and creative (Sarker et al. 2000) while imposing systematic coding procedures (Strauss and Corbin 1990).

The first step (open coding) involved the data being examined line by line to ascertain the main ideas. These were then grouped by meaningful headings to reveal categories and subcategories/properties. The next step (axial coding) was the process of determining hypotheses about the relationships between a category and its subcategories (e.g., conditions, context, action/interaction strategies, and consequences). The focus then turned to the data to assess the validity of these hypothesized relationships. Relational and variational sampling (see Strauss and Corbin 1990) was used to select data for this analysis. This process continued in an iterative manner and resulted in the modification of categories and relationships. Finally, selective coding was undertaken to identify the relationships between categories (constructs) using hypothesized conditions, context, strategies, and consequences. Discriminate sampling (Strauss and Corbin 1990) was used to select data to examine strong and weak connections between categories.

Table 2. Open Innovation Exemplars Examined in this Study

Company	Overview
InnoCentive	Established in 2001, InnoCentive (www.innocentive.com) provides a web site where firms (called "seekers") can post problems to be solved (called "challenges") in over 40 industry disciplines in the areas of physical, life and computer sciences, chemistry, engineering and design, and business and entrepreneurship. A community of over 125,000 experts (called "solvers") review the posted challenges, and possibly propose solutions. Seekers evaluate the solutions, and possibly purchase one or more that meet their needs.
NineSigma	Established in 2000, NineSigma (www.ninesigma.com) work on behalf of clients to source ideas, technologies, products and services from innovators outside the client's organization. NineSigma possess a multinational, multi-disciplinary proprietary network of scientists, university researchers, and technology incubators (referred to as "solution providers") that have signed up to NineSigma through their website. NineSigma works closely with clients throughout the due diligence, request for proposal, response management, and solution evaluation processes.
Yet 2	Established in 1999, Yet2 (www.yet2.com) provides a web site through which companies can list existing technology solutions they wish to sell/license or list technology needs they wish to fulfill. Yet2 assist buyers in locating appropriate technology solutions for their problems, and facilitates sellers in generating revenue through the sale/licensing of IP. Yet2 has over 100,000 registered users and thousands of listings of technologies and technology needs.
YourEncore	Established in 2003, YourEncore (www.yourencore.com) maintains a network of retired/veteran scientists, engineers, and other experts, and offer companies (in the United States only) the ability to utilize these experts to solve problems on a short-term assignment basis, either remotely or on-site.
Threadless	Established in 2000, Threadless (www.threadless.com) is an online t-shirt retailer that derives all of its t-shirt designs from members of its online community through a weekly competition. Members of the community create all designs, and the community votes on contributed designs to determine what shirts are actually manufactured and sold. In 2006, Threadless sold $16 million worth of t-shirts (Weingarten 2007).
Proctor and Gamble	Established in 1999, Proctor and Gamble's Connect + Develop initiative (www.pgconnectdevelop.com) has a dual purpose. First, it provides a mechanism for solution providers to either address specific P&G needs, or to propose innovations that may be of interest to the firm. Second, it provides a mechanism for P&G to make potential buyers aware of existing IP that is available for licensing.

In the next phase of the study, we will continue our investigation of the organizations examined in the current phase using interviews and a survey. That phase is outlined at the end of this paper.

4 FINDINGS

In this section, we describe the findings from the first phase of our study, which has revealed four potential open innovation governance structures, differentiated along two axes (see Figure 1):

- Configuration: whether the structure is direct (e.g., a hierarchy or decentralized market) or mediated (e.g., a brokerage)
- Focus: whether the structure enables the sale/purchase of existing intellectual property or of innovation capability (access to experts capable of creating new IP)

4.1 Solution Hierarchy

The Connect + Develop initiative is part of Proctor and Gamble's commitment to having 50 percent of the company's ideas and innovations come from external sources (Chesbrough 2003). The initiative facilitates P&G's effort to supplement the innovation capabilities of approximately 8,600 internal researchers with the capabilities of an esti-

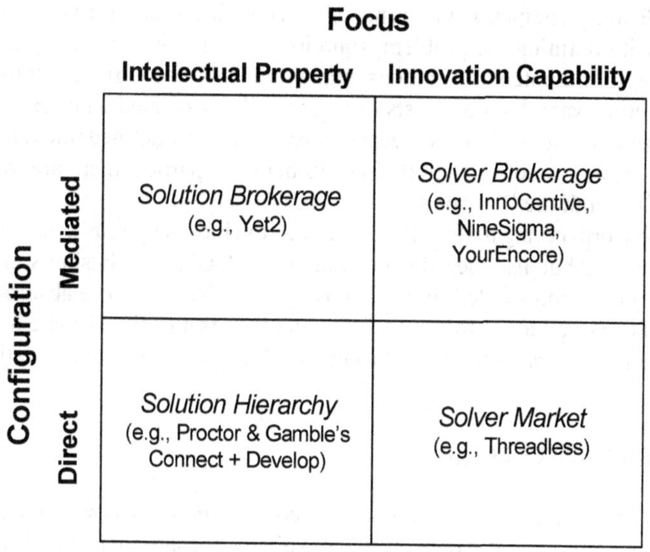

Focus

		Intellectual Property	Innovation Capability
Configuration	**Mediated**	*Solution Brokerage* (e.g., Yet2)	*Solver Brokerage* (e.g., InnoCentive, NineSigma, YourEncore)
	Direct	*Solution Hierarchy* (e.g., Proctor & Gamble's Connect + Develop)	*Solver Market* (e.g., Threadless)

Figure 1. Open Innovation Governance Structures

mated 1.5 million external innovators with relevant skills (Chesbrough 2003). In order to access and manage the large number of potential external researchers, Connect + Develop utilizes a dedicated website to facilitate parties proposing new innovations. Additionally, the firm monitors a wide variety of innovation sources including professional and academic events, publications, and research labs in an ongoing commitment to identifying external innovation capabilities. Finally, P&G utilizes the Connect + Develop website as a mechanism for marketing their own IP which is available for sale/licensing.

We characterize the Connect + Develop initiative as a *solution hierarchy* (as noted in the literature review section, the traditional approach to sourcing external IP can also be characterized in this way). P&G utilizes the Connect + Develop website to discover and directly acquire externally developed IP to create new products or significantly improve existing products. For example, P&G's blockbuster product, Olay Regenerist, was initially developed by a small cosmetics company in France. After P&G's skin-care researchers became aware of the product, they purchased the IP for the product. The French company now continues to collaborate with P&G to develop new products for P&G. The Olay Regenerist example illustrates some of the key characteristics of the solution hierarchy structure.

First, the primary activity is on the direct acquisition of existing IP. Second, the solution was acquired from a well-known provider, the identification of which was facilitated by the use of IT (the web site) to coordinate discovery activities. Third, the subsequent engagement with the seller was direct and involved strong ties between the parties and the establishment of a long-term relationship with a large amount of interaction taking place between personnel from both firms. Fourth, although the transaction has led to ongoing collaboration between the two firms, the actual acquisition of the existing IP by P&G is characterized by low levels of interdependency between the buyer and seller. Fifth, participation in this model involves high costs for P&G (or any buyer) associated with defining the problem, sourcing the solution, evaluating both potential trading partners and potential solutions, managing legal and logistic details, etc. In the Olay Regenerist example, these costs were primarily associated with search, evaluation and negotiation for the IP. Finally, because there are clearly defined rules and procedures (legal agreements) to define the relationship between parties, there are lows levels of uncertainty for both the licensor and licensee.

It is also worth noting that for P&G, the solution hierarchy is used not only to enable the purchase of IP but also the sale. For example, P&G's prior business in producing a line of fruit juice products led to the discovery of Calsura, a more absorbable form of calcium that can be added to food or drink to increase its nutritional content. Calsura has been licensed to several companies through the Connect + Develop initiative.

4.2 Solution Brokerage

Yet2 is an example of what we have labeled a *solution brokerage*, in which an intermediary company aggregates both products available for sale (IP available for licensing) and demand (a large and diverse population of potential buyers). Yet2 operates an electronic brokerage at Yet2.com, and also provides related professional services to both sellers (IP portfolio assessment and licensing services) and buyers (need specification and discovery services).

In doing so, the company seeks to

- enable sellers to realize a higher return on their IP investments
- enable buyers to acquire IP and access technology solutions rapidly and economically

From the seller's point of view, Yet2 provides the ability to reach a much wider and more diverse market than they could through direct sales. John Donofrio, Chief Patent Counsel at Honeywell, stated that "listing our technologies on Yet2.com enables our technology to benefit applications in industries where we would not normally participate, which provides us with new revenue growth opportunities that lead to added shareowner value" (Malik 2000).

From the buyer's perspective, the company reduces search costs through economies of scale and the prefiltering of false positives (all IP listed at Yet2.com is definitely available for purchase). Shunichi Samejima, of the Asahi Glass Company, notes that Yet2 provides their firm with "access to previously undisclosed technologies from companies in the forefront of global technology development."[1] Additionally, Yet2 provides services to help innovation seekers clearly define their technology needs and manage the acquisition process.

In this governance structure, the broker works with solution providers to classify existing assets, devise opportunities for licensing, and provide access to buyers. For solution seekers, the broker applies its market knowledge to refine requirements specifications and locate prevalidated solutions. In doing so, the solution brokerage can mitigate the limitations of the solution hierarchy by lowering search costs and reducing uncertainty *vis-à-vis* problem definition and solution availability. In this structure, the intermediary owns the customer relationship, and all parties are governed by the rules and regulations set by the intermediary. Thus, ties between seekers and solvers are weak and low levels of interdependence exist between them.

4.3 Solver Market

Threadless is an example of the *solver market* structure, in which an organization goes directly to the market seeking to leverage the innovation capabilities of market participants in order to create new innovations to address organizational needs.

Threadless is an online t-shirt manufacturer/retailer that has shifted all new product development activity to the market. Members of its online community submit all of its t-shirt designs, and this same community votes on a weekly basis to determine what designs are actually manufactured. Thus the market is both the source of innovation capability and the mechanism for evaluating potential innovations. On average, over 700 designs will compete to be selected in any given week. The firm provides financial incentives to innovators (each creator of a selected design receives $2,000 in cash as well as either an additional $200 in cash or $500 in store credit).

---

[1] Retrieved from http://www.yet2.com/app/about/about/quotes.

In a solver market, the solution or innovation being sought does not already exist; it is created as an output of market participation. While the buyer may be confident that the innovation capabilities sought are present in the market, a high level of uncertainty remains regarding whether or not a solution to a specific problem can be found. Thus, while firms could seek to acquire innovation capability to address either specific or general problems, the structure would appear to work particularly well in scenarios where organizations are seeking capabilities to address a loosely defined problem space. For example, Threadless defines two broad categories for submissions—designs and slogans—rather than soliciting specific t-shirt designs.

In this governance structure, it is up to the seeker organization to deal with all financial and legal issues in relation to acquiring the desired capabilities, thus transaction costs remain high. Ties and interdependencies between seekers and solvers in such a structure may be either very weak or very strong depending on the mechanics of how the capability is eventually leveraged by the firm. For example, on Threadless, some innovators submit a single design that may or may not go into production. However, it also appears that some t-shirt designers have had multiple designs produced by Threadless and play a key ongoing role in the Threadless community.

4.4 Solver Brokerage

InnoCentive, NineSigma, and YourEncore are examples of our final governance structure, the *solver brokerage*. In this structure, an intermediary company aggregates both demand for capabilities (firms seeking innovators capable of meeting specific challenges) and supply (a large and diverse population of innovators). These companies all implement the structure in slightly different ways. InnoCentive emphasizes the demand side (potential innovators search catalogues of problems) while NineSigma and YourEncore emphasize the supply side (matchmaking firms with needs with potential solvers). In all instances, the broker creates additional value by helping firms define problems and evaluate potential solvers and their proposed solutions.

In this structure, the broker has the knowledge of the most likely solvers for a specific problem, thus lowering uncertainty for the seeker. However, it remains uncertain whether a solution can be developed for a specific problem; this is illustrated by the fact that not all problems published on InnoCentive, NineSigma, and YourEncore are actually solved.

As noted, the broker also acts to assist the seeker in defining the problem. For example, the exemplars examined all provide expertise to organizations to facilitate problem definition, bounding, and communication. The ways in which solvers are matched to problems varies from site to site. For example, YourEncore recommends specific problem solvers for specific tasks while InnoCentive allows solvers to self-select and then compete on the quality of their innovations; with either mechanism, there is a reduction of uncertainty for the seekers.

As with the solution brokerage, in this structure, the broker owns the customer relationship, and all parties are governed by the rules and regulations set by the broker. Thus, ties between seekers and solvers are weak. However, since the focus of this structure is on capabilities rather than products, interdependence between parties is high (as they must work together to achieve the actual solution). Costs for solution seekers and solvers are mitigated by the economies of scale of the intermediary.

5   CONCLUSIONS AND FUTURE RESEARCH

The first phase of our study, as detailed in this research-in-progress paper, has delineated four governance structures for open innovation and illustrated differences between these structures in relation to seven characteristics (Table 3). Our analysis has illustrated the importance of knowledge/uncertainty in relation to open innovation. Of particular note is the uncertainty caused by the information asymmetry evident in the various exemplars of open innovation studied. This uncertainty manifests itself in relation to

* the existence and availability of potential solutions and solvers
* the suitability of potential innovation partners (solution providers and solvers)
* the acquisition process for external innovations (including problem specification, solution evaluation, transfer, etc)

As predicted by extant research, such uncertainty leads to high transactions costs (Williamson 1981, 1991) and the use of intermediaries (Hayek 1945). It is evident that intermediaries (solver/solution brokerages) allay uncertainty by (1) integrating the knowledge of seekers and solvers and (2) providing value-added services. In addition, the economies of scale created by brokers reduce transaction costs.

Building on transaction cost economics, organization theory, and political economy, the information processing perspective examines how uncertainty in interorganizational relations may be reduced using structures, processes, and technology (Bensaou and Venkatraman 1995). Moving forward, we seek to expand our treatment of the four governance structures discussed above by examining the interorganizational relationships within each of the governance structures, and how the structures and related processes and technology can be used to manage the knowledge dispersion and uncertainty evident in open innovation processes.

The next phase of the study thus involves an empirical investigation of the exemplars examined in phase one, together with other firms involved in open innovation. Data is being gathered using both (1) interviews and (2) a survey of seekers and solvers. This will enable us to

* more richly characterize the seeker–solver relationships prevalent within each governance structure
* examine how information processing capabilities (structure, process, and technology) may allay the environmental, partner and task uncertainty arising within each of these configurations

Acknowledgments

This work has been supported by the Irish Research Council for the Humanities and Social Sciences (IRCHSS) through the O3C Business Models Project.

Table 3. Characteristics of Open Innovation Governance Structures

Characteristic	Solution Hierarchy	Solution Brokerage	Solver Brokerage	Solver Market
Knowledge of solution/ solver availability: Which party knows where a solution (or the expertise to develop a solution) can be found?	The seeker has knowledge of (or a mechanism for discovering) the availability of potential solutions within a narrow range of firm alliances.	Intermediary has knowledge of the availability of potential solutions.	Intermediary has knowledge of the availability of potential solvers.	The seeker has knowledge of the availability of potential solvers within a broad setting.
Problem specification: Who specifies the problem together with the process of bounding and communicating the problem?	Seeker specifies the problem.	Intermediary helps solution seekers specify the problem.	Intermediary helps solution seekers specify the problem.	Seeker specifies the problem in broad terms.
Knowledge of acquiring innovation: Who has expertise in solution evaluation, financial and legal issues for the transfer of IP, etc.?	Seeker and solution provider.	Intermediary provides the value-added services for both parties.	Intermediary provides the value-added services for both parties.	For financial and legal issues, the seeker. However, the community of solution providers can potentially be used for evaluation and related issues.
Seeker Uncertainty: What is the degree of uncertainty for seekers in relation to potential partners (solver/solution provider) and product availability?	Low – solution and provider known in advance.	Low – solution can be evaluated before investment is made. Intermediary vets solution provider.	Medium – no guarantee of solution. Intermediary vets solver.	High – no guarantee of solution. No advance vetting of solver.
Seeker – solver ties: What is the strength of the relationship between seekers and solvers?	Strong – usually a medium to long-term relationship.	Weak - usually a short-term relationship.	Weak - usually a short-term relationship.	Varies from solver to solver.
Interdependency between seeker and solver: How dependent is one party on the other?	Low – seeker licenses the existing solution.	Low – seeker licenses the existing solution.	High – seeker and solver work together to develop the solution.	High – seeker and solver work together to develop the solution.
Transaction Cost: Who is responsible for the cost of finding a solution/solver?	Seekers must absorb all costs of locating, evaluating, and acquiring all solutions.	Costs for seekers and providers are mitigated by the economies of scale of the intermediary.	Costs for seekers and providers are mitigated by the economies of scale of the intermediary.	Seekers must absorb all costs of locating, evaluating and acquiring all solutions.

References

Arthur D. Little. 2005. *Global Innovation Excellence Study 2005*, April (http://www.vno-ncw.nl/web/servlet/nl.gx.vno.client.http.StreamDbContent?code=1244).

Bensaou, M., and Venkatraman, N. 1995. "Configurations of Interorganizational Relationships: A Comparison Between U.S. and Japanese Automakers," *Management Science* (41:9), pp. 1471-1492.

Benson, J. K. 1975. "The Interorganizational Network as a Political Economy," *Administrative Science Quarterly* (20), pp. 229-249.

Bodie, Z., Kane, A., and Marcus, A. 2004. *Essentials of Investment* (5th ed.), New York: McGraw-Hill.

Charmaz, K. 2000. "Grounded Theory: Objectivist and Constructivist Methods," in *Handbook of Qualitative Research*, N. K. Denzin and Y. S. Lincoln (eds.), Thousand Oaks, CA: Sage Publications.

Chesbrough, H. 2003. *Open Innovation: The New Imperative for Creating and Profiting from Technology*, Boston: Harvard Business School Press.

Chesbrough, H. 2005. "Open Innovation: A New Paradigm for Understanding Industrial Innovation," in *Open Innovation: Researching a New Paradigm*, H. Chesbrough, W. Vanhaverbeke, and J. West (eds.),Oxford, UK: Oxford University Press, pp. 1-14.

Chesbrough, H. 2006. *Open Business Models: How to Thrive in the New Innovation Landscape*, Boston: Harvard Business School Press.

Clemons, E. K., and Row, M. C. 1992. "Information Technology and Industrial Cooperation: The Role of Changing Transaction Costs," *Journal of Management Information Systems* (9:2), pp. 9-28.

Clemons, E. K., and Weber, B. W. 1990. "London's Big Bang: A Case Study of Information Technology, Competitive Impact and Organizational Change," *Journal of Management Information Systems* (6:4), pp. 41-60.

Coase, R. 1937. "The Nature of the Firm," *Economica* (4:16), pp. 386-405.

Corbin, J., and Strauss, A. 1990. "Grounded Theory Research: Procedures, Canons, and Evaluative Criteria," *Qualitative Sociology* (13:1), pp. 3-21.

Eisendardt, K. M. 1989. "Building Theories from Case Study Research," *Academy of Management Review* (14:4), pp. 532-550.

Emerson, R. 1962. "Power-Dependence Relations," *American Sociological Review* (27), pp. 31-41.

Emerson, R 1972. "Exchange Theory, Part II: Exchange Relations and Networks," in *Sociological Theories in Progress*, J. Berger, M. Zelditch Jr., and B. Anderson (eds.), Boston: Houghton Mifflin, pp. 58-87.

Glaser, B., and Strauss, A. 1967. *The Discovery of Grounded Theory: Strategies for Qualitative Research*, Chicago: Aldine Publishing Company.

Hayek, F. A. 1945. "The Use of Knowledge in Society," *American Economic Review* (35), pp. 519-530.

Hess, C. M., and Kemerer, C. F. 1994. "Computerized Loan Origination Systems: An Industry Case Study of the Electronic Market Hypothesis," *MIS Quarterly* (18:3), pp. 251-275.

Huston, L., and Sakkab, N. 2006. "Connect and Develop—Inside Procter & Gamble's New Model for Innovation," *Harvard Business Review*, March, pp. 63-64.

Kumar, K., and van Dissel, H. G. 1996. "Sustainable Collaboration: Managing Conflict and Cooperation in Interorganizational Systems," *MIS Quarterly* (20:3), pp. 279-300.

Lee, A. S., and Baskerville, R. L. 2003. "Generalizing Generalizability in Information Systems Research," *Information Systems Research* (14:3), pp. 221-243.

Lee, H. G., and Clark, T. H. 1996. "Impacts of Electronic Marketplace on Transaction Cost and Market Structure, *International Journal of Electronic Commerce* (1:1), pp. 127-149.

Madill, A., Jordan, A., and Shirley, C. 2000. "Objectivity and Reliability in Qualitative Analysis: Realist, Contextualist and Radical Constructionist Epistemologies," *British Journal of Psychology* (91:1), pp. 1-20.

Malone, T., Yates, J., and Benjamin, R. 1987. "Electronic Markets and Electronic Hierarchies," *Communications of the ACM* (30:6), pp. 484-497.

Malik, O. 2000. "Technology's Clearinghouse: Yet2.com," *Forbes.com*, February 7 (http://www.forbes.com/2000/02/07/mu3.html).

Motzek, R 2007. *Motivation in Open Innovation*, Saarbrücken, Germany: VDM Verlag Dr. Mueller e.K.

Nonaka, I., Keigo, S., and Ahmed, M. 2003. "Continuous Innovation: The Power of Tacit Knowledge," in *International Handbook of Innovation*, K. Shavinina (ed.), New York: Elsevier.

Orlikowski, W. J. 1993. "CASE Tools as Organizational Change: Investigating Incremental and Radical Changes in Systems Development," *MIS Quarterly* (17:3), pp. 309-340.

Oxley, J. E. 1999. "Institutional Environment and the Mechanisms of Governance: The Impact of Intellectual Property Protection on the Structure of Interfirm Alliances," *Journal of Economic Behavior and Organization* (38:3), pp. 283-309.

Palmer, J., and Lindemann, M. 2003. "Business Models and Market Mechanisms: Evaluating Efficiencies in Consumer Electronic Markets," *ACM SIGMIS Database* (34:2), pp. 23-38.

Pfeffer, J., and Salancik, G. R. 1978. *The External Control of Organizations: A Resource Dependence Perspective*, New York: Harper and Row.

Robey, D., and Sales, C. 1994. *Designing Organizations*, Burr Ridge, IL: Richard D. Irwin.

Sarker, S., Lau, F., and Sahay, S. 2000. "Building an Inductive Theory of Collaboration in Virtual Teams: An Adapted Grounded Theory Approach," in *Proceedings of the 33rd Hawaii International Conference on System Sciences*, Los Alamitos, CA: IEEE Computer Society Press.

Schmid, B. 1993. "Electronic Markets," *International Journal of Electronic Markets* (3:9/10), pp. 3-4.

Strauss, A., and Corbin, J. 1990. *Basics of Qualitative Research: Grounded Theory Procedures and Techniques*, Newbury Park, CA: Sage Publications.

Tidd, J. 2000. *From Knowledge Management to Strategic Competence: Measuring Technological, Market and Organizational Innovation*, London: Imperial College Press.

Tidd, J., Bessant, J., and Pavitt, K. 2005. *Managing Innovation: Integrating Technological, Market and Organizational Change*, Chichester, UK: Wiley & Sons.

Tilquist, J., King, J., and Woo, C. 2002. "A Representational Scheme for Analyzing Information Technology and Organization Dependency," *MIS Quarterly* (26:2), pp. 91-118.

Urquhart, C. 1997. "Exploring Analyst-Client Communication: Using Grounded Theory Techniques to Investigate Interaction in Informal Requirements Gathering," in *Information Systems and Qualitative Research*, A. S. Lee, J. Liebenau, and J. I. DeGross (eds.), London: Chapman and Hall.

Vanhaverbeke, W. 2006. "The Interorganizational Context of Open Innovation," in *Open Innovation: Researching a New Paradigm*, H. Chesbrough, W. Vanhaverbeke, and J. West (eds.), Oxford, UK: Oxford University Press, pp. 205-219.

Vanhaverbeke, W., and Cloodt, M. 2006. "Open Innovation in Value Networks," in *Open Innovation: Researching a New Paradigm*, H. Chesbrough, W. Vanhaverbeke, and J. West (eds.), Oxford, UK: Oxford University Press, pp. 258-281.

Weingarten, M. 2007. "'Project Runway' for the T-Shirt Crowd," *Business 2.0 Magazine*, June 18(retrieved from http://money.cnn.com/magazines/business2/business2_archive/2007/06/01/100050978/index.htm).

West, J., Vanhaverbeke, W., and Chesbrough, H. 2006. "Open Innovation: A Research Agenda," *Open Innovation: Researching a New Paradigm*, H. Chesbrough, W. Vanhaverbeke, and J. West (eds.), Oxford, UK: Oxford University Press, pp. 285-307

Williamson, O. E 1981. "The Modern Corporation: Origins, Evolution, Attributes," *Journal of Economic Literature* (19:4), pp. 1537-1568.
Williamson, O. E. 1991. "Comparative Economic Organization: The Analysis of Discrete Structural Alternatives," *Administrative Science Quarterly* (36:2), pp. 269-296.
Williamson, O. E. 1999. "Strategy Research: Governance and Competence Perspectives," *Strategic Management Journal* (20), pp. 1087-1108.

About the Authors

Joseph Feller, Ph.D., is a senior lecturer in Business Information Systems at University College Cork, Ireland. His research focuses on open source software and other forms of collaborative production. He has published four books and his work has appeared in leading international journals and conferences including *Information Systems Research, Information Systems Journal, Journal of Strategic Information Systems, Journal of Database Management,* the International Conference on Information Systems, the European Conference on Information Systems, and working conferences of IFIP. He has also published widely in practitioner-oriented publications and is a frequent contributor to the *Cutter Consortium*. He was program chair for the IEEE/ACM workshop series on open source software engineering (2001–2005) and the 3rd International Conference on Open Source Systems (IFIP 2.13) and has edited several journal special issues on the subject of open source. He can be reached at jfeller@afis.ucc.ie.

Patrick Finnegan received his Ph.D. from the University of Warwick, England, and is currently a senior lecturer in information systems at University College Cork, Ireland. His research on interorganizational systems and electronic business has been published in a number of international journals and conferences, including *Information Systems Research, Information Systems Journal, Information Technology and People, DATABASE, Journal of Information Technology, International Journal of Electronic Commerce, Electronic Markets,* the International Conference on Information Systems, the European Conference on Information Systems, and working conferences of IFIP. He is currently an associate editor of *Information Systems Journal* and president of the Irish Association for Information Systems. He can be reached at p.finnegan@ucc.ie.

Jeremy Hayes is a lecturer in Business Information Systems at University College Cork, Ireland. His research interests are in the area of electronic business models, interorganizational systems, open source software, and business agility. His research is published in leading international journals and conferences, including *Information Systems Research, European Journal of Operational Research, Journal of Database Management,* the European Conference on Information Systems, and working conferences of IFIP. He can be reached at j.hayes@ucc.ie.

Philip O'Reilly holds a Ph.D. from the National University of Ireland and is a tenured lecturer in Business Information Systems at University College Cork. He is presently involved in research projects focusing on new business forms, open innovation, open source software, and virtual worlds. He has published his research findings at international conferences and journals including the European Conference on Information Systems, the Americas Conference on Information Systems, IIFP Working Group 8.3, *Electronic Markets, Journal of Enterprise Information Management,* and *The Journal of Systems and Information Technology.* He can be reached at philip.oreilly@ucc.ie.

30 REASSEMBLING THE INFORMATION TECHNOLOGY INNOVATION PROCESS: An Actor Network Theory Method for Managing the Initiation, Production, and Diffusion of Innovations

Gerardo Zendejas
Mike Chiasson
University of Lancaster
Lancaster, UK

Abstract   *This paper will propose and explore a method to enhance focal actors' abilities to enroll and control the many social and technical components interacting during the initiation, production, and diffusion of innovations. The reassembling and stabilizing of such components is the challenging goal of the focal actors involved in these processes. To address this possibility, a healthcare project involving the initiation, production, and diffusion of an IT-based innovation will be influenced by the researcher, using concepts from actor network theory (ANT), within an action research methodology (ARM). The experiences using this method, and the nature of enrolment and translation during its use, will highlight if and how ANT can provide a problem-solving method to help assemble the social and technical actants involved in the diffusion of an innovation. Finally, the paper will discuss the challenges and benefits of implementing such methods to attain widespread diffusion.*

Keywords   Innovation, diffusion, enrolment, translation

Please use the following format when citing this chapter:

Zendejas, G., and Chiasson, M., 2008, in IFIP International Federation for Information Processing, Volume 287, Open IT-Based Innovation: Moving Towards Cooperative IT Transfer and Knowledge Diffusion, eds. León, G., Bernardos, A., Casar, J., Kautz, K., and DeGross, J. (Boston: Springer), pp. 527-539.

1   THEORETICAL FOUNDATIONS

1.1   Innovation Diffusion Theory (IDT)

Roger's definitions of innovation and diffusion are by now generally accepted as the starting point for most IDT research. Innovation is understood as an idea, practice, or object that is perceived as new by an individual or other unit of adoption. Diffusion is defined as the process by which an innovation is communicated through certain channels over time among the members of a social system (Rogers 1962).

Although Roger's IDT has vastly influenced subsequent diffusion research, one of its main limitations in its practical and research applications is an assumption that innovations are largely unchanged during the diffusion process, thus restricting its relevance to many aspects of information systems and information technology in which the innovations continue to change and adapt during diffusion.

Slappendel (1996) performed a comprehensive literature review of research on innovations in organizations and provided a framework to classify the existing research work in three categories based on innovation causality: the *individualist*, the *structuralist*, and the *interactive* process perspectives.

The individualist perspective assumes that individuals are the main source of change in organizations. In contrast, the structuralist perspective assumes that existing organizational characteristics enable innovation. Both perspectives consider innovations as relatively static objects and the innovation process as a linear continuum of design, development, and adoption phases.

The interactive perspective assumes that innovation is a dynamic and continuous phenomenon of change over time in which various factors dialectically influence each other. Since the actions of innovative individuals cannot be divorced from the activities of other individuals or from the organizational structures within which they operate, innovation is the result of the continuous interaction of the actions of individuals, structural influences, and the innovation itself (Kautz and Nielsen 2004).

On the other hand, the increasing decentralization of IT innovation processes, characterized by the rapid formation and dissolution of innovation networks composed of heterogeneous and complex actors must be taken into account. To do so, we believe that a method, based on *actor network theory* (ANT), is required. The *interactive* perspective provides the best starting point for the analysis. We will show that a socio-technical theoretical approach is needed to reassemble the IT innovation process and to facilitate a problem-solving method for managing it.

1.2   Actor Network Theory (ANT)

There are many definitions of ANT, but probably the best one is also the shortest: ANT is the science of associations. It provides an epistemological basis upon which human and nonhuman actors can be enrolled and associated within networks, engaging in collective action by translating the various actors' interests into a common force that will help transform claims into facts or innovations (Latour 1999). So the context, using

ANT, is the set of human and nonhuman actors fused together into networks, mobilized actors engaged in collective action to realize collective and individual interests (Latou 2005).

Therefore, we believe that ANT can be instrumental in selecting, understanding, and influencing the collective of social and technical factors interacting during the innovation process. First of all, ANT would be effective in recasting the IT innovation context as a dynamic, distributed interplay of human and nonhuman actors pursuing the establishment of irreversible and maintainable innovations by enrolling providers and receivers, and by searching these various translations in establishing agreements for moving collectively through the different phases of the innovation process: initiation, production, and diffusion.

Secondly, if considered as a method for facilitating enrolment and translation, an ANT approach could be viewed as a distributed project management method, focused on the generation and stabilization of networks. To develop and assess a particular method informed by ANT, we would need to follow and observe the language and actions of actors during all phases of the innovation process. Such a method would be consistent with ANT's ontology, which is primarily based on the fact that reality is a linguistic and political outcome of a stabilized and negotiated interplay among actors. ANT approaches to reflection and action would focus on understanding the network stabilization process and its irreversibility, that is, the specific interplay among actors in a network that results in "black boxes" (Cordella and Shailch 2006).

A research and problem-solving approach based on this, however, would differ from traditional "opening the black-box" studies of ANT, which primarily focus on the retrospective processes that made a network stable, and would turn to the "tracks the process before the blackbox gets closed" (Lanzara 1999). This would move beyond the traditional use of ANT in IS as an interpretative lens. For tracking the stabilization process, an active and longitudinal research approach is required.

Further to ANT's theoretical, epistemological, and ontological insight in reassembling the IT innovation process, ANT can also inform the nature and processes involved in the uptake of innovations. ANT theorists would thus consider traditional approaches to IDT as incomplete at best, flawed at worst, in their implicit assumptions that society is the medium through which innovations diffuse more successfully or not depending upon the level of resistance of particular groups. These groups might eventually change their mind one way or the other in supporting or not the innovation based primarily on their psychological profiling. These assumptions suggest that the diffusion of innovations arises in a society that is initially disengaged and ignorant of an innovation, but through heroic innovators, is eventually able to overcome degrees of social resistance in adopting innovations.

In contrast, an ANT view on innovation uptake, from translation, would claim that uptake dynamics are linguistic, political, and social, involving the convincing heterogeneous actors by means of translating their interests through bridging dialogues, which tenuously enrol them into a socio-technical ensemble. The implications of such a view on innovation uptake suggest that diffusers have a different and initially more difficult task of reassembling and stabilizing a socio-technical set of relations across technology and participants, which often span long times and large distances. This paper will explore an ANT-based notion of innovation uptake.

1.3 Action Research Methodology (ARM)

In accord with ANT's ontology, the goal of the researcher is to understand the associations that stabilize the network and make the innovation maintainable and irreversible, implying that the researcher's role can include an active part in the production of networks, participating and observing how actors create reality. Therefore, an action research methodology (ARM) could use ANT's ontology to lay the groundwork for both documenting and participating in the construction of a collective reality.

Furthermore, Chiasson et al. (forthcoming) suggest that action research lends itself to pluralist approaches that facilitate the production of both problem-solving and theoretical knowledge in an iterative and cyclical process.

1.4 Innovation Management Techniques (IMTs)

Since this paper is arguing that an ANT-based method is required to reassemble and stabilize the IT distributed innovation network and ultimately promote widespread diffusion of innovations, it is relevant to study the application and effects of innovation management techniques (IMTs) used in the production and diffusion of innovations. Theoretical and practical outcomes from these studies are likely to contribute to the construction of such methods.

Terré i Ohme (2002) conducted a comprehensive review of existing IMTs within the European Community. His examination indicated that despite the fact that numerous IMTs have been developed and made available to European organizations involved with innovation, its diffusion in time and space is rather limited. He developed a comprehensive guide for managing innovation based on Chiesa et al. (1996) and Brown (1997). The guide was aimed at small and medium-sized enterprises to help them assess their capacity for innovation. The guide facilitates the process for identifying the basic issues at the organization level for improving its capacity for innovation, and it is currently used as an audit and consulting tool. We believe that such a tool will also assist the process of identifying social and technical components affecting innovation and the construction of the ANT-based method.

Hidalgo and Albors (2008) created a comprehensive study of the many social and technological components involved in the development and use of methods to manage innovation in a knowledge-driven economy. Their review identifies the main IMTs currently in use for improving competitiveness by means of implementing a knowledge management approach. Therefore, it concentrates on those IMTs that focus on knowledge as a relevant component of the innovation process. The review concluded that a knowledge-driven economy affects the innovation process and approach and, therefore, traditional IDT is challenged. A more comprehensive review of Hidalgo and Albors' work is pending for determining potential contributions based on knowledge-driven IMTs for constructing the required ANT-based method.

On the other hand, Hidalgo and Albors' work promotes awareness with regard to recent developing trends of methodologies and tools for supporting business innovation management. Both public and private sector organizations are involved in this effort. However, the proliferation of such methodologies together with the lack of national and international guidelines and standards would likely create an important challenge for standardization and uptake of such methodologies and tools in the long term. Therefore, the efforts of initiating, producing, and diffusing the required ANT-based method will carefully follow ANT's prescription for creating the proper socio-technical ensemble for the widespread uptake of innovations.

2   RESEARCH PLAN

2.1   Research Design

The data for producing and assessing the ANT-based method will flow from a healthcare project involving the initiation, production, and diffusion of an Electronic Synoptic Report (ESR) system across the entire province of Alberta, Canada, with an initial target audience of 250 health providers dispersed across seven health regions. ESR is an innovation because it would replace the traditional procedural dictated report, which has been used for documenting scope-driven procedures ever since the scopes were introduced into medical diagnostic practices. Manually produced dictated reports are today the status quo for most reporting purposes within the medical industry, despite numerous but rather uncoordinated efforts in diffusing automatic forms of reporting.

The ESR project will be influenced and documented using an IMT based on ANT's epistemology and ontology. The project manager will also act as a researcher and spokesperson for ESR, employing an ARM. The interventions will focus on the various arguments and reactions of actors to the discussions of various spokespersons about the IT innovation process. Theoretically, such interventions might then serve as the basis for designing a general problem-solving method to facilitate enrolment and translation in the initiation, production, and diffusion of innovations. Following Chiasson et al.'s (forthcoming) views on ARM, the successful implementation of such a problem-solving method will explore the applicability of ANT's theoretical knowledge to a practical problem setting, and in the process, contribute to ANT and IT-based versions of ANT.

2.2   Research Methodology

To explore how the ESR project is mobilized using ANT as an approach, the researcher will facilitate, observe, and document the early stages of the initiation phase that will consist of a handful of expert panel gatherings aimed at reaching consensus as to what the innovation shall be, which organizational functions shall have the required IT solution, and which vendor might be best suited to facilitate the solution. During these gatherings, an empirical grasp of which techniques promote (or not) the enrolment and translation of heterogeneous groups' interests will be gained and used for designing a preliminary problem-solving method.

The researcher will be involved in the production phase, using ANT both as a theoretical perspective and as a problem-solving method, for promoting enrolment of healthcare providers to the ESR's network and facilitating the required translations to convert the individual interests into a collective force. During this time, the researcher will employ semi-structured interviews to capture arguments and reactions of actors to the ANT-influenced production phase discussion. The data will be analyzed and the outcomes (both planned and unplanned) will be used to evaluate and explore various problem-solving methods. During this phase we expect to identify, select, understand, and influence the collective of social and technical factors that later will be used for designing the required ANT-based method and reassembling the IT innovation processes.

Finally, the outcomes of the diffusion phase will be measured and analyzed in terms of the improvements gained by implementing the ANT-based method in this project as it compares with a parallel project not benefiting from it. The "control" project has been identified and will also comprise the initiation, production, and diffusion of another ESR technology. The ESR project team has been isolated from the control project team to ensure valid measurement and comparison of variables. The timing of these projects is very similar, at least from the planning perspective. Their budgets are also comparable. Based on the projects' similarities and the independence between projects, we expect to obtain reliable data in terms of diffusion improvements or setbacks.

2.3 Preliminary Research Outcomes of the Initiation Phase

Due to the fact that the initiation phase of this project started roughly a year before the research and intervention activities, a retrospective collection of events will be used to understand early enrolment and translation practices for this project. As no research-lead influence was exerted at the time of the initial events, the outcomes of this analysis might be used to compare and contrast the ones obtained before and after the researcher interventions were introduced.

The innovation initiation phase of the Electronic Synoptic Report (ESR) project started on 2006 and it consisted of individual efforts from the Alberta Colorectal Cancer Screening Program (ACRCSP) management team members to enrol others into the idea of using synoptic reporting to facilitate standardized collection of data on colonoscopy procedures. Its purpose was to implement an ongoing quality improvement process of colonoscopy practices at a provincial level.

Synoptic reporting is a synopsis or summary of data that uses standardized nomenclature and data as well as a consistent report structure. Colonoscopy is a procedure in which a long flexible viewing tube known as the colonoscope is threaded up through the rectum for the purpose of inspecting the entire colon and rectum. If there is an abnormality, the colonoscope allows for taking a biopsy of it and/or removing it.

By April of 2007, the ACRCSP published the first hard proof of the innovation's existence, a document titled "Enhanced Delivery of Colorectal Cancer Screening through Information Management: The Development of an Automated Synoptic Colonoscopy Reporting System." This document was distributed among many potential actors and their reactions generated an initial set of controversies to be settled.

The content of the document denoted a moderate degree of technical determinism; the technological role on enhancing the delivery of colorectal cancer screening was overemphasized, with most of the social components involved in the IT innovation process ignored. It is noted that many of the missing social components could be brought to light by means of including a change management methodology.

A primitive network composed of a handful of leading colonoscopy practitioners and the ACRCSP medical lead for the colorectal program emerged in the form of an expert panel. The panel's initial work on settling the above mentioned controversies was primarily an evolutionary decision-making process characterized by the debate arising from opposing views in terms of personal versus regional and regional versus provincial goals. A second set of controversies arose from the first set, providing a list of contrasting views regarding the required functionality and the potential ways to supply it.

The ACRCSP assumed the lead role in facilitating, documenting, and analyzing the outcomes of this entire phase, which was mainly composed of three face-to-face expert panel meetings, plus a handful of video and phone conferences occurring within a year's time. It is the intention of the researcher to strengthen the lead role assumed by the ACRCSP up to the extent of transforming it, along with its innovation artefact, into an *obligatory passage point* (OPP), using ANT terms; the researcher's goal is that anyone in the province needing to implement a synoptic reporting artefact would consult with the ACRCSP experts. Next, the outcomes from these expert panel meetings were analyzed and used to produce an initial set of problem-solving scenarios for managing the initiation phase.

2.3.1 First Expert Panel Meeting (August 21, 2007)

The conversation focused on understanding discrepancies in the production and distribution of colonoscopy related data and reports across the province. Many of these differences were related to personal preferences, regional constraints, and lack of provincial guidelines on the matter. These differences were perceived as a barrier to establishing a provincial quality improvement process. Empirically, then, future enrolment techniques would have to consider the influence of personal preferences, regional constraints, and the upcoming availability of provincial guidelines.

Actors made important progress in defining the data elements required regionally to establish an effective ESR project. One of the outcomes of this stage—a standardized data set—would later indicate the existence of a regional versus provincial controversy, mainly characterized by the different uses and amount of data required at the regional versus the provincial level. While the regions were interested in collecting large amounts of procedural and clinical data, the province was learning that the actual data requirements to establish an ongoing quality improvement process were rather limited, consisting of approximately 20 data fields.

Flowing from the data elements conversation, an empirical grasp as to which techniques promoted enrolment at the regional level was gained. Such techniques would have to provide means for translating numerous well established interests such as clinical sufficiency of the data, adequacy of the resulting procedural report for legal and record purposes, restricted regional report accessibility, and the ability of managing digital images. It is expected that the ANT-based problem-solving method would include careful displacements of regional interests by avoiding or dissolving geographical boundaries.

Translating the above mentioned regional interests into the provincial ones of the ACRCSP was achieved by its medical lead by implementing the following strategy: "The success of a province wide program is largely a by-product of supporting the needs of regional programs first." Such a strategy matches very closely Latour's (1987) first translation strategy, consisting of catering to others' interest. Due to the known limitations of the first strategy, the researcher will focus on applying the appropriate tactics to understand and enrol the interests and goals of actors, aiming to achieve a translation strategy comparable to Latour's fifth strategy: *becoming indispensable.*

Reviewing the ACRCSP's managerial context is relevant in terms of understanding currently established practices and its effect on the ESR project. The ACRCSP does not follow a project management methodology (PMM) for implementing its projects, however this situation is changing as a result of increased project complexity and the need to manage multiple projects in parallel. It is believed that the lack of a PMM has also had a positive influence on developing actors' negotiation skills above and beyond what is traditionally offered by PMM. As a result, holding all other things equal, it is suspected that implementing effective translation strategies may be easier than with well established practitioners of PMM or similar methodologies.

Therefore, the incipient status of PMM at the ACRCSP might positively influence the implementation of the ANT-based method as the implementer would face significantly less resistance than otherwise. By the same token, implementing supplementary ITMs might be easier too. It must be noted that ITMs might benefit organizations differently and so selecting the right ITMs becomes a highly contextual exercise. The virtual lack of PMM is an unexpected situation that might serve further research purposes in terms of comparing the effects of ANT's interventions in organizations with and without PMMs.

2.3.2 Second Expert Panel Meeting (October 15, 2007)

For the most part, the conversation gravitated around the different ways in which the ESR project could be implemented, considering existing off-the-shell solutions and one in-house option. This was likely the case due to the sufficient level of comfort achieved by actors with regard to the first controversy's settlement, facilitated by the translation strategy outlined during the first meeting. Implementation options and their related uptake factors were introduced into the conversation, indicating actor's willingness to move forward into the production phase of the project.

The language of the actors at this stage indicated that the once primitive network was evolving into a stronger one, searching for preliminary ways to achieve stabilization, with all the regional and provincial goals clarified, a translation to amalgamate them, and, for the most part, personal goals properly translated into network ones. Their approach is mostly consistent with the four-stage model of group development produced by Tuckman (1965). The model identifies the forming, storming, norming, and performing stages. The fact that the network was seeking stabilization can be interpreted as a motion to depart from storming into norming.

Comparing stabilization with norming is relevant due to the fact that the network, at that point in time, had not been directly influenced by the researcher using ANT concepts, and the only known approach to the group for measuring the network/team success was Tuckman's model. Other indications of network development at the time included the establishment of clear leadership, and the willingness to expand the network with more colonoscopy experts, IT experts, healthcare consultants and a "nucleus group," as defined by the ESR network chair, for starting the production phase of the project by producing the first synoptic report prototype. Given this level of network maturity, we will call it the ESR network from this point forward.

As per the technology conversation, the ESR network created three options for producing the ESR artefact: bare bones, add on, and complete package. These tags strongly related to scope extent; however, their descriptions were based on the advantages or disadvantages that each would likely produce if chosen. These descriptions were very comparable in form and content with traditional SWOT analysis, with the exception that the actors merged strengths and opportunities under the advantage section, weaknesses and threats under the disadvantages section.

The innovation uptake factors were also included as part of the advantages and disadvantages. Assumptions were made in terms of which option might produce a particular uptake level; however, they were not based on any particular uptake forecast model or theory. Uptake expectations mainly rely on previous experiences and observations from actors and, therefore, they are quite possibly out of context. More concerning, the assumptions used by the ESR network only partially considered the fact that diffusing an innovation is fundamentally different than diffusing a well known and already accepted technology.

During the ANT intervention time, the researcher will develop different activities to promote the understanding and application of ANT's views on technology uptake. Contrasting and comparing ANT's views with traditional IDT views will be done to aid the learning process due to the fact that most uptake assumptions recorded during this meeting were somehow related to Roger's views on uptake.

One of the most challenging tasks during this learning process will consist of raising awareness within the ESR network about the dangers of oversimplifying the effect of uptake strategies as it is often during this last phase when most projects fall apart. Furthermore, convincing the actors with regard to the positive implications of adopting ANT's uptake model, including the claim that it would avoid and productively work with the resistance of particular groups during the diffusion phase, will enhance the overall acceptance of problem-solving methods based on ANT as a preferred approach for dealing with IT innovation projects.

2.3.3 ANT Intervention Begins (February 11, 2008)

As a result of the ESR network's willingness to expand, the next logical step for the network consisted of creating and staffing the ESR production team by hiring a program manager, a project coordinator, and a project manager. Up until this point in time, the medical lead acted as project manager. The transition was characterized by a soft learning curve and some essential interaction with the other network members. The project manager (the lead author) was initially asked to produce a comprehensive set of project management documents and a technology assessment among three different IT vendors, and to reach consensus among network members.

The first ANT intervention consisted of supporting a learning process to improve the ESR network awareness of the many social and technical components that support the initiation, production, and diffusion of innovations. Previous to this intervention, a great majority of the actors considered stakeholders, both internal and external, as the primary force resisting or preventing the free flow of innovations. This is mainly consistent with traditional IDT views on innovation uptake. As it is the purpose of this paper to support ANT's views on uptake, the researcher started to spread the notion of enrolment and translation, as well as the implications of using the translation theory instead of the diffusion theory for explaining uptake dynamics.

The researcher used an oversimplification to convey the concepts of both enrolment and translation; by enrolling all internal and external stakeholders since the initiation phase and during the entire production phase of the project, minimal or not resisting force would act against the collective efforts in achieving wide diffusion, since the enrolled stakeholders will support the process. Enrolling stakeholders can be done by translating their explicit interest into the ones pursued by the innovator. The negotiation efforts will include subtle and incremental displacements of explicit personal or subgroup interests into the larger ones of the collective.

The results of this dialect and oversimplified version of ANT are showing some promising initial results. Later conversations with actors denoted an increased awareness of technical and social components affecting the innovation process. Furthermore, the network notion of collaboration evolved a step or two as the network is now considering not only its obvious short term benefits—improved quality and efficiency—but also the possibility of working with what were considered the resisting forces of dissenters during the diffusion phase.

2.3.4 Third Expert Panel Meeting (April 25, 2008)

The language of the actors at this stage clearly indicated the preliminary effects of the ANT interventions. However, these effects were showed unevenly among the ESR network members as a result of the recent network expansion and the challenges of propagating the influence across geographically disperse actors. This is perhaps the most important challenge identified by the researcher at this point in time: exerting ANT influences beyond geographical borders.

The researcher called this meeting to facilitate a decision-making process with regard to selecting an IT vendor as the basis for building the ESR artefact. After due deliberation, the ESR network's chairman came to the conclusion that the ESR network didn't have enough knowledge of all social and technical components affecting innovation practices on every single regional health authority (RHA) in Alberta and, therefore, it was not prepared to produce a top-down policy to enforce adoption of a particular solution. Instead, it was prepared to influence the decision process on every region by chairing informational gatherings, producing environmental assessments, and elaborating a regional recommendation once all social and technical components have been identified, analyzed, and ranked according to the regional priorities and strategies.

The effects of such a decision are expected to be very relevant for the matters of expanding the network first, which now include a critical mass of actors to move forward the innovation artefact, and by further positioning the ACRCSP as the OPP, making sure that essential components of the overall program would be included during the initiation phase of each region, and that those components could be made operational at the provincial level at a later time.

Indeed, at this point in time the ESR network was in need of including many more actors. For example, selecting at least two pilot regions to implement the yet-to-be-produced ESR innovation was required. It is prudent by now to characterize and differentiate a number of new potential actors. Alberta is broken into nine health regions, two of which are significantly larger than the others as they are both located at the two main metropolitan areas of the province. Both the Calgary Health Region and Capital Health Region in Edmonton account for almost 80 percent of the patients in the province.

As a logical rule of thumb, the larger the region, the more stakeholders and the more complex it is. Both metropolitan regions already moved unilaterally toward creating their own ESR artefact. In fact, the Calgary Health Region has already completed both the initiation and production phases of their project. The diffusion phase is on the go and it achieved some success thanks to their centralization strategy, which concentrates the delivery of colonoscopy services in a single location that is fully equipped with the ESR artefact and staffed by mostly ESR supporters.

The ACRCSP expectations on the pilot sites mainly consist of gaining experience over the complete implementation process of the ESR artefact. Therefore, neither metropolitan area is adequate for fulfilling this purpose. On the other hand, the expert panel was poorly represented in terms of all other regions, having originally only one representative from the non-metropolitan regions, the Chinook region. An unexpected representative from the Peace Country region showed up the meeting. As part of the efforts toward stabilizing the network, the researcher will focus on expanding the ESR network with representatives of all regions.

It must be noted that it was not possible to exert significant ANT influence during this third meeting, as the time was mainly used by presenters from the potential IT technology providers. The closing remarks emphasized as much as possible the importance of working in collaboration with the ACRCSP and, therefore, promoted the mobilization of turning the ACRCSP and its innovation artefact into an OPP, however, significantly more work is required in this direction. The ACRCSP team remains optimistic with regard to securing at least the two pilot projects before the end of 2008.

3 EXPECTED RESULTS AND CONTRIBUTIONS

3.1 Expected Results

The successful implementation of ANT-based problem-solving methods will determine the applicability of our specific implementation of ANT concepts as a practical problem-solving method within a particular setting. This confirmation will provide, in-turn, important insights for IT implementation theory and practice as well as into the project management discipline, through an ANT-based demonstration of the case and the problem-solving method.

3.2 Expected Contributions

Producing a workable method based on ANT would contribute to a widespread diffusion of numerous IT innovations by providing a specialized and highly efficient alternative to the traditional PMMs and IMTs currently used. Therefore, the ANT-based method for managing the initiation, production, and diffusion of innovations would strongly contribute to the advancement and specialization of the project management discipline.

Chiasson et al. (forthcoming) suggest that further work is required to determine the specific research epistemologies and their methodologies that are consistent with ARM. Demonstrating ANT's compatibility with ARM would promote further research work based on this research paradigm, producing an abundance of problem-solving methods for a number of practical settings.

References

Brown, D. 1997. *Innovation Management Tools: A Review of Selected Methodologies*, Luxembourg: European Commission.

Chiasson, M., Germonprez, M., and Mathiassen, L. Forthcoming. "Pluralist Action Research: A Review of the Information Systems Literature," *Information Systems Journal*.

Chiesa, V., Coughlan, P., and Voss, C. A. 1996. "Development of a Technical Innovation Audit," *Journal of Product Innovation Management* (13:2), pp. 105-136.

Cordella, A., and Shaikh, M. 2006. "From Epistemology to Ontology: Challenging the Constructed 'Truth' of ANT," working paper, Department of Information Systems, London School of Economics.

Hidalgo, A., and Albors J. 2008. "Innovation Management Techniques and Tools: A Review from Theory and Practice," *R&D Management* (38:2), pp. 113-127.

Kautz, K., and. Nielsen, P. A. 2004. "Understanding the Implementation of Software Process Improvement Innovations in Software Organisations," *Information Systems Journal* (14:1), pp. 3-22.

Lanzara, G. 1999. "Designing Systems In-Action: Between Transient Constructs and Permanent Structures," keynote presentation, European Conference on Information Systems, Copenhagen, June 23-25.

Latour, B. 1987. *Science in Action: How to Follow Scientists and Engineers through Society*, Cambridge, MA: Harvard University Press.

Latour, B. 1999. "On Recalling ANT," in *Actor Network Theory and After*, J. Law and J. Hassard (eds.), Oxford, UK: Blackwell, pp. 15-25.

Latour, B. 2005. *Reassembling the Social: An Introduction to Actor-Network-Theory*, Oxford, UK: Oxford University Press.

Rogers, E, M. 1962. *Diffusion of Innovation*, New York: Free Press.

Slappendel, C. 1996. "Perspectives on Innovation in Organizations," *Organization Studies* (17), pp. 107-129.

Terré i Ohme, E. 2002. "Guide for Managing Innovation," Centre for Innovation and Business Development, Barcelona, Spain

Tuckman, B. 1965. "Developmental Sequence in Small Groups," *Psychological Bulletin* (63), pp. 384-399

About the Authors

Gerardo Zendejas is currently a Ph.D. student at the Department of Management Science, Management School, Lancaster University. Before joining Lancaster University, he held various managerial and consultant positions in both the health care and energy sectors. He also completed his Master of Business Administration with specialization in Management of Information Systems in the Haskayne School of Business, University of Calgary, in 2006, and a Bachelor's of Cybernetic Engineering and Computer Science at the La Salle University in 1995. His research examines and proposes methods to enhance focal actors' abilities to enroll and control the many social and technical components interacting during the initiation, production, and diffusion of innovations. By extension, his research focuses on understanding the reassembling and stabilizing of such components into the overall innovation process. His initial work has been qualitative in nature, using actor network theory extensively. Gerardo can be reached at gerardoz@lancaster.ac.uk.

Mike Chiasson is currently an AIM (Advanced Institute of Management) Innovation Fellow and a Senior Lecturer at Lancaster University''s Management School, in the Department of Management Science. Before joining Lancaster University, he was an associate professor in the Haskayne School of Business, University of Calgary, and a postdoctoral fellow at the Institute for Health Promotion Research at the University of British Columbia. His research examines how social context affects IS development and implementation, using a range of social theories (actor network theory, structuration theory, critical social theory, ethnomethodology, communicative action, power knowledge, deconstruction, and institutional theory). In studying these questions, he has examined various development and implementation issues (privacy, user involvement, diffusion, outsourcing, cyber-crime, and system development conflict) within medical, legal, engineering, entrepreneurial, and governmental settings. Most of his work has been qualitative in nature, with a strong emphasis on participant observation. Mike can be reached at m.chiasson@lancaster.ac.uk.

Part 11

Panels

31 OPEN INNOVATION IN MOBILE AND CONVERGENT COMMUNICATIONS

Organizer: José Jiménez
Telefónica I+D
Spain
jimenez@tid.es

The concept of open innovation seems to be very well suited to information and communication technologies. In the first place, as in any other field, the complexity of the new technology makes it necessary for companies to use ideas, processes and inventions from other players. As in any other field, we need the collaboration of the university, of SMEs, of inventors, and of the general public.

But open innovation is particularly applicable to ICT.

First of all, telecommunications imply talking and transmitting information to others. This requires using a common language and a communication protocol. This has to be agreed beforehand and it has to be standardized. Agreeing in a common standard requires the effort and collaboration of many and the suggestions cannot come only from one side. This is further complicated when we talk about convergence between mobile and fixed. Ideas from both worlds have to be taken together and combined.

In the second place, ICT is not just telecoms but the result of the collaboration between transmission engineers, radio experts, and information technology scientists. The most known result, the Internet, is not just a telecommunications protocol, but a suite of solutions adapted to the computers and networks.

But this already complex scenario has evolved. The Internet is becoming much more than a protocol, turning into a place where new services and ideas in the areas of information services, communications, and electronic commerce are developing; it is becoming, more a more, a space (the cyberspace) where people meet and interact.

We cannot do things alone.

Unfortunately, the complex nature of the open innovation process does not contribute to making things simple: There are many entry points and not less exit possibilities. The process is complicated for all: telecommunicationes companies, universities, opera-

Please use the following format when citing this chapter:

Jiménez, J., 2008, in IFIP International Federation for Information Processing, Volume 287, Open IT-Based Innovation: Moving Towards Cooperative IT Transfer and Knowledge Diffusion, eds. León, G., Bernardos, A., Casar, J., Kautz, K., and DeGross, J. (Boston: Springer), pp. 543-544.

tors, government agencies. There is significant controversy about the final outcome and the use of the results. Who will benefit? How can we assure everybody gets their share of the results?

In the end, this open innovation process implies reinventing the company, finding a new business model. The information will not, as in the past, flow only in the top–down direction; it is necessary to learn how firms can utilize communities as complementary assets without having ownership or hierarchical control over them.

But this change is not limited to the company and the technological systems that need to change. The more external innovation is sourced by the firm, the more systems, processes, value, and culture also needs to be transformed. There is an internal resistance to open innovation. Company people are trained to think internally, and this tendency is strengthened by concepts such as core competences and Six Sigma, already entrenched in our organizations. How can we overcome those difficulties? Learning to broaden our views, align with the ecosystem, adapt our company tolerance for risk, and put the focus on learning and not just results, are some of the difficulties we are facing.

As usual, the devil is in the details: What is the degree of customer and supplier integration? How do we set up the innovation clusters? How are we going to handle IPRs and patents? What is the policy toward spin-offs and spin-in? How can we stimulate the people to give their ideas for others to use? The well known poker metaphor introduced by Chesbrough is a good image of the difficulties of playing the game: We have to judge and decide with limited information.

In this session we are very lucky to count on three experts who are going to describe their experiences, from the point of view of an operator, a manufacturer and a university professor who is very much involved with telecommunications research. The three different roles of innovation, as suggested by Chesbrough, *funding, generating,* and *bring innovation to the market,* are present.

The first presentation, from Telefónica, describes the new process that will transform Telefónica from a telecommunications provider into a service provider, using talent and ideas both from its internal workforce and from the outside world: The "open Telefónica."

The second will consider how a leading telecom manufacturer, Ericsson, is facing this transformation and how they collaborate in European funded and internal projects with universities and other players.

We close our session with the participation of some other partners from industry who will describe their experiences.

32 CORPORATE EXPERIENCES IN OPEN INNOVATION

Organizer: Juan Mulet

Fundación Cotec para la Innovación Tecnológica
Spain
juan.mulet@cotec.es

In the 21st century, companies are facing new challenges in a rapidly changing environment. Global competition and technological progress, in particular of information and communication technologies, have shortened life cycle products, opened up new markets, and lowered barriers to firm entry. These changes are compelling firms to find new and more rapid ways to innovate.

In this context, we observe a growing trend toward more open innovation models. Firms reformulate their innovation strategies, giving a prominent place to R&D and technology available from external sources in the public and private sectors. Knowledge in universities, research organizations, customers, suppliers, and competitors is seen as a highly valuable resource, needed to bring new, innovative products quickly to the global market.

At the same time, in open business models, business R&D units exploit two ways to create value from generated knowledge and to demonstrate financial returns on R&D investments: commercializing new innovative products and spinning out technologies and intellectual property rights developed internally.

This is bringing about changes in the value chain, which is increasingly fragmented across countries, especially in high tech sectors. New players are entering not only production activities, but also research and technology development areas, which favors the development of a global technology market.

In this session, four organizations will share their experiences and strategies in the new ecosystem. Ericsson, Everis, and ATOS Origin representatives will give their views on how their businesses handle and profit from open innovation, explaining their new sources of knowledge and technology and their collaboration models with external entities. The fourth member, an academic, will discuss how universities can be integrated in these open collaboration models to extend the R&D capabilities of companies.

Please use the following format when citing this chapter:

Mulet, J., 2008, in IFIP International Federation for Information Processing, Volume 287, Open IT-Based Innovation: Moving Towards Cooperative IT Transfer and Knowledge Diffusion, eds. León, G., Bernardos, A., Casar, J., Kautz, K., and DeGross, J. (Boston: Springer), pp. 545.

Part 12

Notes from Industry Experience

33   OPEN, COLLABORATIVE INNOVATION IN THE 21ST CENTURY

Irving Wladawsky-Berger
Chairman Emeritus
IBM Academy of Technology

There have been many turning points in history. One of the most prominent in my mind is the Industrial Revolution, characterized by new technologies that enabled us to reorganize the production of goods and services. It is pretty clear that we are in the early stages of a similar historical turning point. While no one knows for sure what future generations of historians will call this new period we are entering—perhaps the Knowledge Economy—we can certainly identify the forces at work around us.

I believe that there are three interrelated and very profound such forces. First is the digital revolution, led by continuing advances in information technologies. Second is a business revolution, which is a product of those advances in IT. And third is a societal revolution, born of the Internet and other open standards that are enabling collaborative innovation on a global scale. Each of these revolutions is very powerful in its own right, but they are converging like weather fronts and creating the conditions for a "perfect storm" of innovation.

IT is to our era what steam power was to the industrial revolution: a huge catalyst for change at many, many levels. We see it all around us. The environment is going digital all over the world, in emerging economies as well as advanced ones. Think of iPODs, DVDs, and digital TVs in entertainment and voice-over-IP in communication. Mobile devices and cell phones have become extensions of ourselves. Software is almost as important to planes and automobiles as gasoline. IT is being embedded in everything, giving our physical world, in effect, a fourth dimension—a digital dimension.

Simultaneously, these inexpensive digital technologies are being aggregated into tremendously powerful supercomputers like Roadrunner, the first petaflops supercomputer developed by IBM for the U.S. Department of Energy and installed at Los Alamos National Laboratory earlier this year. A petaflop is a 1 followed by 15 zeros. That is how many calculations per second Roadrunner can perform. When talking about peta-

Please use the following format when citing this chapter:

Wladawsky-Berger, I., 2008, in IFIP International Federation for Information Processing, Volume 287, Open IT-Based Innovation: Moving Towards Cooperative IT Transfer and Knowledge Diffusion, eds. León, G., Bernardos, A., Casar, J., Kautz, K., and DeGross, J. (Boston: Springer), pp.549-552.

flops, the numbers are so large that it is hard to comprehend what they mean. We are almost into numbers of astronomical dimensions.

The advent of petaflop supercomputing will enable major advances in applications of all sorts, in medicine, science, engineering, and business. It will help us explore the major challenges associated with climate change, making it possible for scientists to test global climate models with far higher accuracy than has been possible so far. We can expect advances in a wide range of application of critical importance to society, such as the development of biofuels, the design of more fuel efficient cars, personalized genomics-based medicine, and the ability to better understand and manage the behavior of our global, integrated—and increasingly unpredictable—digital economy.

Los Alamos researchers have already started to use Roadrunner in a project called Petavision that simulates extremely complex neurological processes. Such applications are critical to help us better understand the structure of the brain, which hopefully will lead to breakthroughs in treating major disabilities like Alzheimer's, autism, and schizophrenia.

Since the beginning of the industrial era, business and other institutions have constantly adapted processes to take advantage of new methodologies and technologies. But today's process adaptations are taking advantage of sophisticated architectures and computing infrastructures, resulting in the wholesale integration and refashioning of business processes across the enterprise and beyond. Perhaps more profound, companies are beginning to use rigorous, engineering-like methodologies to identify the processes in which they have unique expertise and efficiencies of scale, so they can determine which are strategic and give the firm, in a phrase, "economies of expertise."

Business operations and processes can be viewed more as components, and each function—be it finance, manufacturing, or human resources—can be treated as a separate service. At the same time, open standards are making the underlying IT applications so flexible that a company can take apart and recombine those services more quickly to address changing needs. That flexibility frees a company to focus on what it does best and to pursue its comparative advantage.

In a historic departure from conventional one-to-one relationships between businesses, this new-found flexibility and focus herald the emergence of collaborative, interconnected industry ecosystems composed of diverse centers of expertise around the world. What holds true for business processes is just as true for all processes across industry ecosystems.

This business process revolution, combined with the rapid growth of services in the economic mix, is giving rise to a much more disciplined, more scientific approach to business. Historically most scientific research has been geared to manufacturing, once the dominant force in the world's economy. Now, industrial and academic research facilities are beginning to apply more scientific rigor and engineering discipline to the practices of services in order to train people in business and information technology, and also the human factors that go into a successful services operation.

Many leading universities have begun exploring and investing in this area, working in tandem with thought leaders in the business world to establish Services Sciences, Management and Engineering as a new discipline. The University of California at Berkeley, for example, has implemented a Services Science curriculum with help from IBM Research—much the way the first Computer Science department was founded at Columbia University over 30 years ago, also with help from IBM. Quite a number of other universities around the world have already embraced Services Sciences or are considering doing so.

The dynamism propelling this business revolution is collaboration on a global scale—between businesses, between industries, and between economies; between companies and all their stakeholders; and between governments and their constituents. It is giving rise to a truly societal revolution.

I believe that when those historians I mentioned try to assess this societal revolution—this new, as yet unnamed era—they will be compelled to focus on the mid-1990s, when the Internet burst upon the larger society. That is when open standards really began to come into their own, and offer the promise of near-universal connectivity, a promise that is being fulfilled year by year.

Around a billion people are already connected to the Internet via personal computers. Billions more will do so over inexpensive mobile devices in a few years. Trillions of sensors will be connected to the Internet in the not too distant future. Online commerce keeps growing and is now counted in the trillions of dollars.

The need to support these billions of mobile devices and trillions of sensors is giving rise to "cloud computing." I think of clouds basically as Internet-based networks made up of a very large number of servers and storage components. They contain vast amounts of information, and provide a variety of services to large numbers of people—to their mobile devices as well as their PCs. The users of clouds only care about the services and information they have access to, not about the underlying details of how the cloud works.

In my opinion, two key factors take cloud computing into a qualitatively different dimension. One is massive scalability. I believe that the kinds of advances that we have become used to in the world of supercomputing are now coming to the more general purpose computing world. A number of new applications are emerging that will likely grow by two to three orders of magnitude over the next decade.

The other factor is the much higher quality of experience that cloud applications provide to their users. Cloud applications are very different from classic IT applications, whose intrinsic complexities are barely hidden from their users. You truly want users of cloud applications to just be able to access them in the most natural and simplest way possible. Cloud applications should be able to provide a really high quality of experience to massive numbers of users without missing a beat. They should significantly improve the way people deal with the many tasks and devices that surround them in their everyday life—at work, at home, on-the-go, and wherever they happen to be.

What are some of the workloads in the horizon that will likely grow at prodigious rates and require a human-like quality of experience? Quite a few, I believe: real-time information access and analysis, such as RFID-based supply chains, transportation management and security systems; myriads of new consumer applications in entertainment, healthcare, payments and financial services; social networks and virtual worlds involving large numbers of people interacting with each other; support of billions and billions of new mobile devices and sensors; and so on.

Ever since the advent of the Internet, open standards have been increasingly finding their way into all aspects of IT, integrating systems, information, and people on a truly historic scale. And it's not over yet. Information technology is becoming increasingly pervasive and generating prodigious amounts of information, and colossal amounts of processing power to turn that information into useful knowledge in real-time. Couple that with the open-standards-based Internet that facilitates communication worldwide and it's no wonder that a global, infrastructure—the very nature of which is collaborative—is emerging and moving society into a new era.

Already we are seeing the emergence of open, collaborative innovation as a serious mode of economic production that has arisen because large numbers of individuals can now organize themselves for productive work. This challenges the long-held notion of the "firm" as the only way to organize work that creates value. Indeed, social networks are creating all kinds of new communities, and all that information out there is very likely to transform the way companies deal with each other and with individuals—employees, customers, partners, shareholders, and others.

We don't know how this new marketplace will evolve—any more than people in the 18th century could foresee the full impact of industrialization on business, economies, and nations. But I think we have enough evidence to say with some confidence that open, collaborative approaches are not transient, as we see an increasing number of open communities working together in areas like Linux, Grids, cloud computing, and application development tools. What is different today is that for the first time, in large part because of the Internet, we have the capacity to "self-organize" into groups fluidly and globally. And that promises a much more diverse, exciting—and very innovative—marketplace.

Collaborative innovation must be at the heart of all the policies that shape the direction of a nation's economy and be at the center of the national agenda. Designing and implementing the right mix of policies to spark innovation will no doubt be a challenge, but it's a challenge no one can ignore with impunity. Technology and open standards have us at the brink of a new era. We are connecting all of society's institutions—governmental, educational, commercial—across a global IT infrastructure.

The name of this new era will be devised decades from now by historians with the perspective of time. But we can say this with some certainty: Those future historians will be investigating an era when we experienced, not merely a new round of innovation, but a new style of innovation—one that pools the most fertile minds in the world, and frees them to create the 21st century.

34 APPLYING OPEN INNOVATION PRINCIPLES FOR TRIGGERING AND ACCELERATING INNOVATIONS: The Experience of Ericsson Spain, 2004 Through 2007

M. Lorenzo
Ericsson España
Madrid, Spain

Abstract   *Ericsson Spain is an important subsidiary of the Ericsson Group. It hosts one principal research and development center and counts on a strong local marketing, sales, and delivey force to address a vibrant market of telecommunications. A landscape of abundant knowledge including leading universities in Madrid and a growing number of local technology and business partners complete the scene for a company that puts in practice open innovation approaches as introduced by Chesbrough (2003).*

The experiences of Ericsson Spain with its recent successful application of open innovation approaches will be described. The resulting improvements to the innovation effectiveness and the lessons learned from these experiences are also outlined.

Keywords   Open innovation, innovation ecosystems, R&D

1 INCREASING THE FLOWS OF NEW TECHNOLOGIES AND KNOWLEDGE

As many other technology-intensive companies with decentralized research and development and a global market presence, Ericsson creates subsidiary companies, as is the case of Ericsson Spain, with strong local R&D organizations, reporting to corporate

Please use the following format when citing this chapter:

Lorenzo, M., 2008, in IFIP International Federation for Information Processing, Volume 287, Open IT-Based Innovation: Moving Towards Cooperative IT Transfer and Knowledge Diffusion, eds. León, G., Bernardos, A., Casar, J., Kautz, K., and DeGross, J. (Boston: Springer), pp. 553-560.

R&D functions and business units, and a highly specialized local sales force to address the local market.

Ericsson's product development and delivery processes enable products developed in the Madrid R&D center to be shipped to all Ericsson markets, Market Unit Iberia (serving Spanish and Portuguese markets) being one of them. The general model is for a technology-push supply chain, where R&D creates new products for the strategic business units (BUs) and then local market units (MUs) ultimately broker them to the actual end-customers, the local telecom operators and other enterprise customers.

Although working perfectly fine, this model does not exploit all of the synergies that may arise between the R&D and MU sides of Ericsson Spain, and in the context of a highly demanding local market, it is absolutely key that additional processes for cross-border cooperation are in place in order to really make the difference for both improving success in the local market and enhancing the global portfolio of products.

We will shortly introduce, out of the number of processes to serve this purpose, the processes that genuinely follow open innovation approaches in the sense that the R&D becomes an open system to MU and local customers, exposing and accessing new knowledge and technologies rather than simply delivering standard products in the standard way.

One of the most successful experiences is a collaboration program for architecting brand-new customer solutions based on emerging technologies. Some technologies have been created in our labs in Madrid and are in the early development stages; others were still at the conceptualization stages, being worked on with other R&D centers; a few have been created by partners and competitors; most are actually pending business modeling and therefore desperately looking for the input that only market reality can bring. The cooperation between R&D and MU is articulated in three ways:

- Business (and technology) consulting projects ordered by our local customers. Most times, these projects are actually promoted proactively to our customers as a consequence of the previous exchange of ideas and identification of opportunities based on new R&D concepts and technologies. Mixed R&D–MU–customer teams are created and daily and jointly evaluate new alternatives to new or old problems, starting with the architecture and going down to the supporting technologies.
- Prospective customers' RFIs, and RFQs, on new architectures and solutions not available from either our portfolio of products and services or those of other technology providers. For such cooperative efforts, R&D engineers took the solution architect role inside the team preparing the response. Evaluation of potential partners that could complement our portfolio to satisfy the required needs was essential.
- Early phases of complex integration projects, where R&D staff directly assisted the customer in creating the best architectural solutions, normally involving products of several providers, onto customers' environments with Ericsson and non-Ericsson technologies in place.

In all cases, the essential exchange was on knowledge and new technologies, either third parties' or exposed pre-commercial technologies under development in Ericsson. The knowledge horizons of both Ericsson and its customers were significantly expanded and a first cooperation usually led to further and broader cooperation.

The direct benefits of this approach have proven enormous.

- In a number of the new solutions created in this way, several providers could create and capture in return a portion of the value delivered to the customer. Most valuable new partners were identified and now their products are part of the global extended portfolio of Ericsson.
- Quite a few technologies at the lab, some even waiting on the shelf for quite a while, reached an end customer and got the standard product label, therefore becoming innovations actually creating new businesses.
- The positioning of Ericsson as primary integrator of new solutions was significantly strengthened and an increased footprint in new business areas achieved.
- Local customers integrated locally developed and brokered technologies meeting their needs in a timely and accurate manner.
- As a result of the success in this way of working, a few similarly successful projects were also run internationally with other market units.

We judge that such achievements over a period of time, mainly from 2001 to today, confirm that deliberate openness in the innovation process involving internal and external customers as co-innovators, avoiding vertically integrated solutions, and instead creating room for new suppliers of valuable emerging technology, yields better-quality and faster results than other traditional approaches and, even more importantly, enables expansion to adjacent or even radically new business areas and models more easily. Similar experiences in other companies with technology incubation stages in a discovery–incubation–acceleration process can be found in Chesbrough (2005).

2   IDENTIFYING AND PROMOTING EXTERNAL INNOVATION

Three initiatives will be introduced in this section: Ericsson Mobility World, the IMS Program, and the Application Expert Center.

2.1   Ericsson Mobility World (Ericsson Partnership Program)

Content providers rely on Ericsson's competence and channels to reach the mobile market, and we assist application developers in creating and selling innovative and marketable applications. Ericsson Mobility World is a global Ericsson initiative launched in 2001 that helps operators increase traffic on their networks and grow their business. We provide expert assistance, from strategy to market launch, in analyzing the business potential of new mobile services. Before new services are launched, Ericsson Mobility World tests, verifies, and optimizes them for operators' networks and continues to monitor them afterward.

The Ericsson Mobility World Developer Program helps developers' successfully plan, develop, verify, and get applications to operators and their customers. The program offers the technical, business, and sales support that developers need to transform ideas into reality. By exposing new technologies to our customers new open business models are identified where Ericsson, the operator, and the partner companies in Mobility world add value and capture return on their investment.

Through the program, developers' applications and content can be included in the Ericsson Mobility World application portfolio and presented to our customers around the world.

The impact of Ericsson Mobility World in the Spanish innovation ecosystem is two-fold. Our customers reach an extended portfolio of hundreds of applications and other innovating local companies in the mobility services field can adhere to the program and internationalize their offerings backed by Ericsson's local support and global market presence. In Spain, as well as in many other Ericsson market units, the Mobility World program is a huge success with both indirect and direct returns for Ericsson.

2.2   IMS Program

In 2005, Ericsson Spain kicked off a cross-border task force involving business unit network infrastructure, business unit multimedia solutions, and local R&D staff with the purpose of stimulating the adoption of IMS technology in the local market. As a fore-runner in this new technology, it is essential for Ericsson to promote well-coordinated internal teams as well as open external ecosystems of partners, third parties, and institutions contributing with innovations. An important strategy in this task force was to create a critical mass of awareness on the technology in third parties that allowed starting and sustaining open value chains and value networks where Ericsson would try to position them before our customer in at least three roles: preferred IMS infrastructure supplier, preferred IMS services integrator, and preferred supplier/partner of key enabling services such as Presence, Push-to Talk, etc.

This ambition *necessarily* leaves a lot of room for third parties to contribute and capitalize added value.

We will refer here only to a side branch of actions inspired in open innovation principles that was triggered from this initiative and that mainly had to do with promoting innovation in this field by a local university, UPM (Universidad Politécnica de Madrid).

It would have been an easy temptation to take the closed innovator hat and have thought that Ericsson, as non-disputed leader in the IMS market, was the one to train the UPM researchers and provide them with our ideas, guidance, and funding so that they could develop research-stage prototypes, potentially adding some technical or marketing value. But we were lucky to try other approaches based on open innovation principles.

We certainly did train the UPM researchers on Ericsson IMS systems and also provided them with our tools devised for creation of IMS-based services—and of all this was actually an important part of extending awareness on the technology and helping develop new skills required for creating new services. However, we did not specify or order the research work to be done. Instead we gave them the freedom to create from scratch new services on top of IMS and we obtained amazing results. Based on the core competency and knowledge of one of the UPM teams engaged in this initiative, they came up with a proposal combining other (Web2.0) technologies that they mastered and pioneered with IMS in order to create new technology proposals compatible with a variety of target business models they were not aware of or even concerned with.

The investment in UPM, therefore, paid off. The technology developed has been showcased ever since to a number of prospective customers and is one of the best IMS openers, showing the potential and advantages of combining IMS with other widespread new technologies. Several further research and innovation projects have evolved the ideas and there is on-going internal evaluation for product development in a new area for Ericsson.

Beyond the IMS program scope, this was but one successful innovation cell project with UPM following the open model. The power of combining deep expertise in new technologies developed in the research groups at UPM with open basic technologies created by industry was demonstrated. The superiority of this open collaboration model, where both parties (industry and university) openly contribute and complement each other from their core competencies and knowledge over closed models where the university merely would have played an on-demand, externally directed contract research role, is also clear.

2.3 IMS Application Expert Center

As part of the Ericsson Mobility World Development Program, an on-going program in Ericsson's Market Unit Iberia since May 2006, is the IMS Application Expert Center, which further develops the partnering-for-innovation approach and builds on similar strategic principles to those introduced above for the IMS program.

Content and applications providers will have the opportunity to propose new ideas to Ericsson and to develop new services in specific areas. They will also get assistance in realizing these ideas and taking them to market as products that can be sold to operators all over the world. Operators will get a unique channel for close contact with the developer community, enabling faster conceptualizing and development of future services. The model allows operators to get a glimpse of technologies, services, and concepts launched all over the world, leveraging on the Ericsson Mobility World network that is present in 35 countries.

An Expert Center is also a way for operators to connect with new services, differentiating them from competitors. In Italy, the Expert Center provides operators with a live environment where they can prototype and test new applications and concepts from developers in order to have a concrete basis for making decisions.

This initiative, therefore, activates a development community and creates an IMS services ecosystem that is beneficial for our customers, for third parties joining in, and ultimately for Ericsson in the roles it is strategically seeking to play in the long and open value chain of SIP services. The IMS Application Expert Center actively showcases IMS-based applications created by local third parties as well as internally or in open cooperation with new partners and research institutions, as is the case for the local collaboration with UPM. Most of the open innovation principles inspire and motivate this initiative, which is also in place in other Ericsson market units.

3   SHARED R&D WITH CUSTOMER PARTNERS: OPENING OUR RESEARCH TO CUSTOMERS

Another far-reaching initiative in innovation management at Ericsson Spain is a program of alliances with key customers for engaging in innovation from early research stages to commercialization. This is a rich type of cooperation protected by mutual non-disclosure agreements, where both Ericsson and the customer contribute with new concepts, technologies, and R&D effort.

Our R&D becomes an open system to the customer. In particular, our local and global research outcomes are exposed and become a piece to play with in joint innovation projects that seek to test those technologies in business contexts that are yet to be identified. Business models are worked together for the solutions researched and it is up to each party to further define their contribution or the involvement of other parties.

With the set-up model, both parties retain rights over the R&D artifacts they share and it is the exposure of technology research and business opportunities to each other that helps the other party to tune and steer their internal innovation.

Of course, some ideas are created jointly as a result of the dialog, and some enter the patent process, separately or jointly, but it is not exclusion but inclusion principles what motivates deeper and further collaboration.

After the three first projects with one customer engaged in this model, we have verified the trend to share and jointly identify more and more opportunities for collaboration and more and more partners, which creates a positive domino effect in the speed of innovation implementation and adoption. We have also verified that joint projects mutate at some point in time from shared R&D prospective projects to business unit supported projects at both ends of the collaboration and therefore the innovation time-to-market is significantly improved.

4   PROMOTING AND LEVERAGING UNIVERSITY RESEARCH FOR CREATING AND SPEEDING INTERNAL INNOVATIONS

We can also report two relevant local cases where university-initiated research on apparently noncore businesses for Ericsson is followed by a technology transfer and spin-in.

One is kept aside for confidentiality issues. The other one is the case of the knowledge transfer into Ericsson Research of methods, practices, and technology for advanced data mining developed by Universidad Carlos III de Madrid (UCIIIM). Over 10 years of continued research has taken UCIIIM to their leadership position in this field. Ericsson Spain, as result of technology surveillance and networking activities, knew of this technology potential and devised new applications. A match with potential new Ericsson business models was found and acknowledged by our corporate strategic research organization (Ericsson Research). As a result, an intensive and extensive technology transfer process was initiated in order to spin in their technology and base new products on it. In one year, a go-ahead decision for a product in the field has been granted in Ericsson and it is UCIIM, not Ericsson, that has spent long years in growing this technology to its current state and potential. Of course, the potential applications and interactions with other systems envisioned by Ericsson were not guessed by UCIIM and this again proves the power of open innovation.

5 CREATING ALTERNATIVE PATHS FOR DEVELOPMENT AND COMERCIALIZATION

We have finally identified the need to strengthen efforts in finding alternative paths for ideas we are unsure how to exploit. We are practicing an approach for virtually spinning out high-risk/high-potential innovations with several potential business models. Since several business models are possible, they might actually compete with each other and in principle Ericsson could more easily support and implement only one of them, so the uncertainty may have a big effect that is not easy—probably not even possible—to anticipate. Such uncertainty is better cared for with a extrovert approach that would be difficult to secure should the project be kept internal.

One of our largest technology innovation projects on-going today follows this approach, which guarantees independence and autonomy for the team to explore and validate the idea and develop a new core technology without concerns on the funding that is guaranteed by Ericsson after a complex decision process involving a number of stake-holders. Rounds of verification, where internal sponsors play the internal venture capital role and the project team shows progress à la startups, secure alignment with the high expectations set on these projects and provides the basis for further rounds of funding.

6 CONCLUSIONS

The application of open innovation approaches is not per se a guarantee of success but allows Ericsson to promote and try out innovations that otherwise would be parked forever or not even generated at all. A number of open innovation approaches have been illustrated in the previous experiences. Such approaches seem to mix well with the dynamics of the market and the industry of information technology and communications in Spain.

We have reviewed how new business opportunities based on R&D knowledge and technologies at early stages can be generated, accelerating the pace of the innovation process with near-market research.

We have seen how nonintrusive funding of university research may create higher value than large research contracts, an investment that sustains the base of the open innovation paradigm, which is the promotion of external complementary creativity in the environment. Return on investment may, however, not be guaranteed unless a critical mass of companies fund this type of research with an open approach.

The efforts to create ecosystems for new technology diffusion where several players can create value and have business chances deserve special attention. These players (third parties, business partners, and even competitors) will play a critical role as innovators and the environment (institutions, universities, consultancy companies, etc.) need to become aware and stimulated as well in order to provide a solid background for their success.

References

Chesbrough, H. 2003. *Open Innovation: The New Imperative for Creating and Profiting from Technology*, Boston: Harvard Business School Press.
Chesbrough, H. 2005. *Open Innovation: Researching a New Paradigm*, New York: Oxford University Press.

About the Author

Manuel Lorenzo is head of the Technology & Innovation Unit of Ericsson Spain. His unit performs IPR Management and Strategic Research integrated in Ericsson's Corporate Technology function, as well as business innovation projects performed in coordination with the local Market Unit (Spain and Portugal), as well as with national and European institutions and technology and busienss partners. Manuel holds a B.Eng. degree in Telecommunications from Universidad Politécnica de Madrid with a specialization in Computer Networks. Since 1994, he has developed his professional career in Ericsson (Spain, Sweden, and Ireland) in several technology and business fields, including Telecom Management, Mobile Internet Infrastructure and Applications, Network Databases and Digital Identities. He is a member of Ericsson-wide communities and initiatives, including the Ericsson Global Innovation Forum, and actively promotes networking among companies as well as between the industrial and academic worlds with the aim of exchanging, extending, and applying knowledge and best practices in management of technology and innovation. Manuel can be reached at manuel.lorenzo@ericsson.com.

Part 13

Annex

35 INFORMATION TECHNOLOGY DIFFUSION IN ACADEMIC TEACHING: An Institutional Perspective[1]

Gali Naveh
Dorit Tubin
Nava Pliskin
Ben Gurion University of the Negev
Beer-Sheva, Israel

Abstract   *Even though diffusion of information and communication technology (ICT) in academic teaching has been fast, the expected benefits in pedagogy and structure have yet to materialize. Rogers' diffusion theory, which focuses on adoption and rejection of innovation, can explain the proliferation of ICT usage in academia, but the lack of ICT-based pedagogical and structural changes are beyond the scope of diffusion theory. The objective of this paper is to broaden the theoretical base for explaining the state of ICT in academia via the alternative conceptual lens of institutional theory, which focuses on the relationship between the organization and its environment. With the institutional theory perspective in mind, we suggest that further pedagogical and structural changes in academic courses should not be expected as a result of ICT implementation in academic teaching.*

Keywords   Institutional theory, academic teaching, ICT diffusion

---

[1]This paper was inadvertently omitted from *Organizational Dynamics of Technology-Based Innovation: Diversifying the Research Agenda* (T. McMaster, D. Wastell, E. Ferneley, and J. I. DeGross, eds.), the proceedings of the IFIP 8.6 conference in Manchester, England, June 14–16, 2007 (Volume 235).

Please use the following format when citing this chapter:

Naveh, G., Tubin, D., and Pliskin, N., 2008, in IFIP International Federation for Information Processing, Volume 287, Open IT-Based Innovation: Moving Towards Cooperative IT Transfer and Knowledge Diffusion, eds. León, G., Bernardos, A., Casar, J., Kautz, K., and DeGross, J. (Boston: Springer), pp. 563-567.

1   BACKGROUND

A large investment has been made in integrating information and communication technology (ICT) into academic courses (see Bennett and Bennett 2003; Collis and Moonen 2001; Harasim 2000; Macchiusi and Trinidad 2001; Mason 2000; Noble 2001; Rafaeli et al. 2003). Surveys show massive ICT usage in academic courses (Green 2002, 2003, 2004), but only sparse anecdotal evidence of fundamental instructional change is found in the literature (Chiang and Fung 2004; Ellis et al. 2005; Thompson and MacDonald 2005). In fact, massive diffusion did not bring about much change either in the pedagogic way professors teach (Burgess 2003; Frank and Barzilai 2004; OECD 2005), or in the basic ways that universities structure their study programs (Guri-Rosenblit 2005; OECD 2005). This situation raises the question of whether expectations that ICT implementation will bring about change in the pedagogy and structure of academic teaching will ever materialize.

According to diffusion theory (Rogers 1995), the relative advantage of ICT-based courses, compared to traditional courses, explains diffusion but does not discern between different users of the same innovation. Thus, this theory cannot explain why successful cases, in which students and professors report fundamental instructional change, remain anecdotal in nature.

In the next section, a polemical perspective of diffusion theory and its explanation for the current status of ICT in academia are presented, followed in the third section by the alternative perspective of institutional theory (Meyer and Rowan 1992; Rowan and Miskel 1999). Some conclusions are presented in the closing section of this paper.

2   ICT ADOPTION IN ACADEMIA

Rogers' diffusion-of-innovation theory (1995), which treats adoption of innovation dichotomously, might not be sufficient for explaining a situation where the innovation is being used without fulfilling its potential, as in the case of ICT-based academic courses. Rogers ascribes innovation success to its use but does not consider consequences of use as relevant to determining the success of the adoption process. Thus, the current status of massive ICT usage in academic courses would be considered successful according to diffusion theory, leaving the question of missing pedagogical and structural change unexplained. Part of the answer rests on the definition and measurement of success in the complex context of ICT innovation, as evident in research by DeLone and McLean (1992, 2003) and Seddon et al. (1999).

DeLone and McLean thoroughly examined the definition and measurement of success in implementing ICT and found dozens of definitions, techniques, and tools. One of the implications of their work is that ICT success in implementation may be defined and measured in more than one way. Seddon et al. emphasize that the criteria for success may differ from one stakeholder to another, even in the same situation.

The relevant stakeholders according to the diffusion-of-innovation model are the users of the innovation. The users in the academic context could be the students, professors, university officials, or different entities in the academic organizational field. Rogers' theory does not discern among stakeholders, and thus success for one entity could be perceived completely different by another entity. Better explanation could perhaps be obtained by institutional theory (Meyer and Rowan 1992; Rowan and Miskel 1999), which suggests that agents in the academic environment are relevant to defining ICT-based use as success.

3   INSTITUTIONAL THEORY PERSPECTIVE

Every organization belongs to an organizational field or sector. According to institutional theory, many organizational processes and changes, with which an organization allegedly intends to promote efficiency, are actually performed in order to achieve environmental legitimacy by meeting regulations, norms, and ideology of its organizational field (Rowan and Miskel, 1999). Thus, to enhance its survival prospects in its competitive environment, sometimes an organization seeks to increase environmental support and resources flow at the expense of organizational efficiency (Meyer and Rowan 1992; Scott 2003).

Universities are expected by their stakeholders (students, potential students, regulators, and funding agencies) to be in a leading position in the process of adopting technological innovations. Since higher education has become more competitive in recent years, the pressure to become more efficient and offer better service to student customers is increasing.

Once perceived as adopting technological innovation (ICT, in this case) as a means for improving the service provided to students, the university, as an institute acting according to institutional theory, has achieved its goal of maintaining environmental legitimacy. This may be accomplished without the need to perform meaningful, significant, resource-consuming pedagogical and structural changes in academic courses and programs. Organizational field expectations, therefore, might be met even with superficial and symbolic ICT adoption. Thus, with the institutional theory perspective in mind, one should not expect in-depth changes as a result of ICT implementation in academic teaching. Rather, the ICT adoption process could be considered successful as long as, while adopting ICT, universities are able to sustain environmental legitimacy by being perceived in their organizational field as adopters of technological innovations. Indeed, while massive adoption of ICT in academic teaching has occurred, lack of further impact on the technical core (i.e., the set of activities required in order to achieve the organizational goals) of the university may indicate that the goal of maintaining environmental legitimacy has been accomplished.

4   CONCLUSIONS

ICT, while used widely, has yet to meet its pedagogic and structural potential. This suggests that the mere adoption of a technological innovation may not be perceived as successful by some stakeholders and presents a more complex picture than diffusion theory. DeLone and McLean suggest that ICT success may be measured in various ways in different situations and according to different stakeholders, in line with institutional theory. With an institutional theory perspective in mind, the university as an institution strives to maintain environmental legitimacy by being perceived as using ICT in academic teaching, without making significant changes in its technical core. This perspective suggests that further pedagogical and structural changes resulting from ICT integration in academic courses should not be expected.

References

Bennett, J., and Bennett, L. 2003. "A Review of Factors that Influence the Diffusion of Innovation When Structuring a Faculty Training Program," *The Internet and Higher Education* (6), pp. 53-63.

Burgess, L. A. 2003. "WebCT as an e-Learning Tool: A Study of Technology Students' Perceptions," *Journal of Technology Education* (15), pp. 6-15.

Chiang, A. C., and Fung, I. P. 2004. "Redesigning Chat Forum for Critical Thinking in a Problem-Based Learning Environment," *The Internet and Higher Education* (7), pp. 311-328.

Collis, B., and Moonen, J. 2001. *Flexible Learning in a Digital World: Experiences and Expectations*, London: Kogan Page.

DeLone, W. H., and McLean, E. R. 1992. "Information Systems Success: The Quest for the Dependent Variable," *Information Systems Research* (3), pp. 60-95.

DeLone, W. H., and McLean, E. R. 2003. "The DeLone and McLean Model of Information System Success: A Ten-Year Update," *Journal of Management Information Systems* (19), pp. 9-30.

Ellis, R. A., Marcus, G., and Taylor, R. 2005. "Learning through Inquiry: Student Difficulties with Online Course-Based Materials," *Journal of Computer Assisted Learning* (21), pp. 239-252.

Frank, M., and Barzilai, A. 2004. "Designing Course Web Sites for Supporting Lecture-Based Courses in Higher Education—Some Pedagogical Aspects," *International Journal of Instructional Technology and Distance Learning* (1:12).

Green K. C. 2002. *The 2002 National Survey of Information Technology in U.S. Higher Education*, Encino, CA: The Campus Computing Project.

Green K. C. 2003. *The 2003 National Survey of Information Technology in U.S. Higher Education*, Encino, CA: The Campus Computing Project.

Green K. C. 2004. *The 2004 National Survey of Information Technology in U.S. Higher Education*, Encino, CA: The Campus Computing Project.

Guri-Rosenblit, S. 2005. "Eight Paradoxes in the Implementation Process of E-Learning in Higher Education," *Higher Education Policy* (18), pp. 5-29.

Harasim, L. 2000. "Shift Happens: Online Education as a New Paradigm in Learning," *The Internet and Higher Education* (3), pp. 41-61.

Macchiusi, L., and Trinidad, S. 2001. "Information and Communication Technologies: The Adoption by an Australian University," in *Expanding Horizons in Teaching and Learning: Proceedings of the 10th Annual Teaching Learning Forum*, A. Herrmann and M. M. Kulski (eds.), February 7-9, Curtin University of Technology, Perth, Australia (http://cleo.murdoch.edu.au/confs/tlf/tlf2001/macchiusi.html; retrieved March 9, 2003).

Mason, R. 2000. "From Distance Education to Online Education," *The Internet and Higher Education* (3), pp. 63-74.

Meyer, J. W., and Rowan, B. 1992. "The Structure of Educational Organizations," in *Organizational Environments: Ritual and Rationality*, J. W. Meyer and W. R. Scott (eds.), Thousand Oaks, CA: Sage Publications, Inc.

Noble, D. F. 2001. *Digital Diploma Mills*, New York: Monthly Review Press.

OECD. 2005. "E-Learning in Tertiary Education," *Policy Brief*, Organisation for Economic Co-operation and Development, December (http://www.oecd.org/dataoecd/55/25/35961132.pdf; retrieved July 14, 2006).

Rafaeli, S., Barak, M., Dan-Gur, Y., and Toch, E. 2003. "QSIA—A Web-Based Environment for Learning, Assessing and Knowledge Sharing in Communities," *Computers and Education* (43), pp. 273-289.

Rogers, E. M. 1995. *Diffusion of Innovation* (4th ed.), New York: Free Press.

Rowan, B., and Miskel, C. G. 1999. "Institutional Theory and the Study of Educational Organizations," in *Handbook of Research on Educational Administration*, J. Murphy and K. S. Louis (eds.), San Francisco: Jossey-Bass Inc.

Scott, W. R. 2003. *Organizations: Rational, Natural, and Open System* (5th ed.), Upper Saddle River, NJ: Prentice Hall.

Seddon, P. B, Staples, D. S., Patnayakuni, R., and Bowtell, M. J. 1999. "The Dimensions of Information Systems Success," *Communications of the Association for Information Systems* (2:20) (http://cais.isworld.org/articles/2-20/article.pdf; retrieved July 31, 2006).

Thompson, T. L., MacDonald, C. J. 2005. "Community Building, Emergent Design and Expecting the Unexpected: Creating a Quality eLearning Experience," *The Internet and Higher Education* (8), pp. 233-249.

About the Authors

Gali Naveh is a Ph.D. candidate in the Department of Industrial Engineering and Management, Ben-Gurion University in Israel. Gali's research is focused on organizational aspects of ICT integration in academic teaching. Gali can be reached at galin@bgu.ac.il.

Dorit Tubin, Educational Sociologist, is a faculty member in the Department of Education, Ben-Gurion University, Israel. Dr. Tubin's main interests are organizational aspects of educational innovation and higher education. Dr. Tubin can be reached at dorittu@bgu.ac.il

Nava Pliskin is in charge of the Information Systems programs at the Department of Industrial Engineering and Management, Ben-Gurion University in Israel. Previously she was a Thomas Henry Carroll Ford Foundation Visiting Associate Professor at the Harvard Business School. She acquired her Ph.D. and S.M. degrees from Harvard University. Her research, focused on longitudinal analysis of IS impacts at the global, national, organizational, and individual levels, has been published in such journals as *IEEE Transactions on Engineering Management, ACM Transactions on Information Systems, The Information Society, Communications of the ACM, Decision Support Systems, Information & Management,* and *Database*. Professor Pliskin can be reached at pliskinn@bgu.ac.il.

Index of Contributors